1986
SEASON

THE COMPLETE HANDBOOK OF BASEBALL

1986
SEASON

THE COMPLETE HANDBOOK OF
BASEBALL

EDITED BY ZANDER HOLLANDER

A SIGNET BOOK
NEW AMERICAN LIBRARY

ACKNOWLEDGMENTS

As history tells us, baseball skippers have no job security. But what is certain is that 1986 marks the major-league managerial debuts of Toronto's Jimy Williams, the Yankees' Lou Piniella, Pittsburgh's Jim Leyland and Houston's Hal Lanier. The new season also heralds the 16th edition of *The Complete Handbook of Baseball*. We acknowledge with appreciation the team that made it happen: contributing editor Howard Blatt, the various writers listed on the contents page, Lee Stowbridge, Dot Gordineer of Libra Graphics, Richard Rossiter, Steve Wisniewski, Eric Compton, Fred Cantey, Seymour Siwoff, Bob Rosen, Rick Cerrone, Phyllis Merhige, Blake Cullen, Katy Feeney, Phyllis Hollander, the publicity directors of the major-league teams and the staff at Westchester Book Composition.

Zander Hollander

PHOTO CREDITS: Cover—Paul Bereswill; back cover—Rich Pilling. Inside photos—Ira Golden, George Gojkovich, Steve Jenner, Vic Milton, Rich Pilling, Kevin Reece, Mitchell Reibel/Fotosport, AP/Wide World, UPI and the team photographers.

SIGNET TRADEMARK REG. U.S. PAT. OFF. AND FOREIGN COUNTRIES
REGISTERED TRADEMARK—MARCA REGISTRADA
HECHO EN CHICAGO, U.S.A.

SIGNET, SIGNET CLASSICS, MENTOR, PLUME, MERIDIAN AND NAL BOOKS are published by New American Library, 1633 Broadway
New York, New York 10019

First Printing, March 1986

1 2 3 4 5 6 7 8 9

PRINTED IN THE UNITED STATES OF AMERICA

CONTENTS

Editor's Note: The material herein includes trades and rosters up to final printing deadline.

HOW TO HIT DWIGHT GOODEN

By MARTY NOBLE

The points of reference already have been revised. They have been updated, streamlined and, in several instances, inverted. And all this after only two seasons. In 1984, when the commotion began, the references were to Bob Gibson, Sandy Koufax, Tom Seaver, Herb Score, Grover Alexander, etc. Dwight Gooden was compared with each of them. And now that Gooden has produced a second remarkable season—24-4, 1.53 ERA and 268 strikeouts—others are being compared with him. In two seasons, after only 66 starts, Gooden has become a standard by which others are measured.

As a point of reference, Gooden is set apart from others. Hitters will speak generally about pitchers and then qualify their remarks with "...except for Gooden." Pitchers will generalize about the demands of their craft and then quickly add "...unless you're a Gooden." Managers usually will decline to compare contemporaries, claiming it serves no purpose other than to offend one of the players. But not in Gooden's case. "Who are you going to offend," said Cards' manager Whitey Herzog, "if you say he's not as good as Gooden?"

And so on. Gooden is different from all others. As Mets' vice-president Joe McIlvaine says, "Dwight breaks all the rules." As Tim McCarver, the Mets' broadcaster, says, "Dwight doesn't make you forget Gibson, Koufax and Seaver. He makes you think of them."

Gooden rarely suffers in comparison with such luminaries; not even when he is compared with Cy Young. And he always is favorably compared with his contemporaries. But, on Aug. 20 of last season, Chili Davis offered an implied comparison in which Gooden emerged a distant second.

Marty Noble takes his turn at bat as a free-swinging baseball writer for Newsday.

Only a precious few have solved the deliveries of Dr. K.

"He ain't God, man," the Giants' center fielder said.

Davis made that assertion in the aftermath of Gooden's 16-strikeout, seven-hit shutout of the Giants. So his remark did not go unchallenged by some teammates, who considered it heresy. Gooden had been so dominant that the Giants had batted with a modest primary intention—to not strike out.

It was that way for each of them, save Davis. Having discounted Gooden as a deity, Davis then denied Gooden the respect given to most mortal pitchers. Not only did Davis refuse to strike out—he was the only Giants starter with that distinction—he also accumulated three hits in four at-bats. Such utter disrespect for the Doctor.

That performance afforded Davis a place among a select group of National League hitters, the ones who have looked up the barrel of Gooden's gun and not flinched, those who have legitimate reason to boast, "I own Dwight Gooden."

With those three hits, Davis improved his career batting average against Gooden to .583, some 382 points higher than the National League's two-year average against Gooden. It hardly mattered that in a sequel confrontation 11 days later, Davis was hitless with two strikeouts in two at-bats against Gooden. He still ended the season with a .500 career average—on 7-for-14—against the best pitcher in the world.

That average places Davis atop what should be known as the Kryptonite List, those batters who treat the unanimous 1985 National League Cy Young Award winner the way Lois Lane treats Clark Kent. Here is how they have fared against Gooden.

		AB	H	Avg.
1.	**Chili Davis, Giants**	**14**	**7**	**.500**
2.	**Willie McGee, Cards**	**23**	**11**	**.478**
3.	**Bill Doran, Astros**	**21**	**9**	**.429**
4.	**Steve Garvey, Padres**	**17**	**7**	**.412**
5.	**Wayne Krenchicki, Reds**	**13**	**5**	**.385**
6.	**Andy Van Slyke, Cards**	**26**	**9**	**.349**
7.	**Dennis Walling, Astros**	**12**	**4**	**.333**
8.	**Pete Rose, Reds**	**20**	**6**	**.300**
9.	**Dan Driessen, Giants**	**24**	**7**	**.292**
10.	**Ryne Sandberg, Cubs**	**36**	**10**	**.278**

And that list doesn't include Jack Clark, who has only four hits—including two home runs—in 17 career at-bats against Gooden, but who is regarded by Gooden as the one batter he doesn't want to face with the game on the line in the late innings.

The list does include batters of all sorts: Rose, who has the most singles in history, and Garvey, the lone slugger among the 10; a journeyman such as Krenchicki; four switch-hitters (Rose, McGee, Davis and Doran); two right-handed hitters in Garvey and Sandberg and four left-handed hitters. About all they have in common is their ability to hit Gooden.

And though they share that distinction, they share no secret of success. Each applies what batters usually apply against any pitcher—they try to be patient, concentrate on making contact. But these 10 are dramatically more successful than most when they employ the standard theories against Gooden.

Says Davis: "As great as he is, once in a while he makes a mistake. You have to wait for the mistake and then take advantage

Giant Chili Davis has the best average against Gooden.

of it. His stuff is so good that sometimes it's tough just to hit his mistakes.

"I try not to overswing against him. I see a lot of guys taking real big cuts. They don't have a chance. I figure he's throwing so hard in the first place, just let him do most of the work . . . Maybe it's because I concentrate so much more when Gooden is pitching. I wish I had that concentration against every pitcher in the league. I'd have a much higher average."

Rose has employed the same philosophy in his 20 at-bats against Gooden as he applies to all his at-bats. "Look for the fastball and adjust to the others. You can't look for a breaking ball and then adjust when he throws the fastball. It's by you.

"Dwight Gooden has exceptional pitches and exceptional control. The control helps the batters because they know (his pitches) are going to be around the plate. It's tough to face their (the Mets') left-hander (Sid Fernandez). His pitches are all over the place. With Gooden, you have an idea. It helps, but it doesn't make it easy."

Davis keys on Gooden's fastball, too. "I just hope he doesn't get his curveball over too much. If he does . . ."

But Gooden respects Davis' ability to adjust to his curve. "I can tease him with it if he has two strikes, but he adjusts to it real well," he says. "I've made a lot of good pitches to Chili and he's hit them. I don't like to jam him because he'll hit it. I've got to have something on it to come inside on him."

Davis may have the highest batting average vs. Gooden, but McGee, the 1985 NL Most Valuable Player, has had more hits (11) than any other player against the pitcher who placed fourth in the MVP voting last year. It is not surprising Gooden identifies McGee as "my toughest out," and considering McGee, Van Slyke and Clark are on Gooden's expanded Kryptonite List, it is small wonder the Cardinals rank as the team that most troubles Gooden.

"They're not a strikeout team," Gooden says, a contention that is supported by his record against them. Gooden has averaged 6.4 strikeouts per nine innings against the Cardinals in two seasons. His average against the rest of the league is 10.4 strikeouts per nine. McGee is one of the primary reasons.

"His bat is so quick," Gooden says. "He adjusts to the curve and slaps at the fastball. He can reach anything outside and, if I come inside, he has a great inside-out swing."

McGee's philosophy is simple. "I try to keep a short swing against him and not chase the high pitches. He tries to get me to chase upstairs, but I don't. I just look for the fastball in the strike zone. If he throws me 3-2 curves, I'll tip my hat to him every time and take a seat on the bench."

McGee also has created a secret mind game that he plays to full advantage. "It's weird," he says. "But I feel like I'm Dwight's big brother. I'm older than he is, and I use that. It makes me relax. He's a great pitcher, but I tell myself, 'He's only human.'"

Of course, Gooden, who turned 21 in November, has been younger than almost every batter he has faced in his two seasons and each of them recognized him as human. It didn't seem to help the others as much as it helped McGee.

Doran is six years older than Gooden and Garvey had a junior high school named in his honor while Gooden still was in junior high school in Tampa. But neither hitter feels superior to the Mets' ace. In fact, Doran says his success against Gooden can be partly attributed to the inordinate number of mistakes Gooden has made

Gooden has good reason to respect the Astros' Bill Doran.

against him.

"To hit him, you have to be the beneficiary of his mistakes," Doran says. "If he does what he wants, he'll blow you away. But it seems like Dwight makes a lot of mistakes when he pitches against me. I'm ahead in the count a lot—a lot of 2-0 and 3-1. When I'm ahead like that, I feel pretty safe in looking for the fastball."

Not that Gooden's fastball is easy to hit when it's expected. "They say it's physically impossible to make a pitch rise," Doran says. "But anything he throws me above the waist just takes off in the last few feet. It looks real good and then, all of a sudden, it's right up there around your neck. I try to be selective and hope he falls behind. I don't chase too many of his curves . . . maybe

Padre Steve Garvey makes the most of Gooden's fastball.

because I'm usually fooled by them."

Whatever the reason for Doran's success, it has impressed Gooden, who regards the Astros' second baseman as "the most improved hitter in the National League."

"Last year, I could get him up and away all the time. Now he just goes with the pitch. He's a good fastball hitter and he stays back on my curveball, maybe better than anyone," said Gooden.

The Astros, as a team, haven't been particularly successful against Gooden—he has beaten them five times in six starts and his first major-league victory came against them. But they did administer the most lopsided defeat of Gooden's career—scoring eight runs in 2⅓ innings against him May 6, 1984. The Astros also hold the distinction of having limited Gooden to one strikeout in 6⅓ innings May 15 of last season.

Garvey has been the most successful of the power hitters against Gooden. Though he has not hit a home run against Gooden—Gooden has allowed 20 home runs in two seasons and only Clark and Pedro Guerrero have hit as many as two—Garvey does have three doubles among his seven hits.

Says Gooden: "Until I have two strikes on him, Garvey's guess-hitting all the time. If he's looking curve and he gets it, he can take me deep. He's a better hitter when he has two strikes on him, believe it or not. When I'm ahead, I'll throw curveballs in the dirt. Once in a while, he'll chase one, but not too much. He hits my fastball away better than anyone in the league."

Garvey agrees almost point by point. "I look for patterns in the way Dwight pitches me, although (because he throws) only two pitches, there can't be many patterns. When I get a fastball I like I try to go the other way. I try to pull his curveballs. I stay away from his high fastball and his low curve. That's much easier said than done. But if it makes him throw a fastball at the thighs, you've got a chance.

"But even if he does, it's not easy. His motion is so fluid and the ball comes at you in such a hurry, you don't even have time to blink."

The majority of the hitters in the National League and the ones who have seen Gooden in spring training and All-Star competition have had far less success against him. The league certainly hasn't caught up with Gooden. Witness the NL's .201 batting average against Gooden last season, one point lower than the NL's average against him in 1984.

And, while Chili Davis and Willie McGee may "have papers" on Gooden, there are other hitters who are owned by The Good Doctor. This is a list of the doctor's favorite patients.

		AB	H	Avg.
1.	Marvel Wynne, Pirates	15	0	.000
2.	Eddie Milner, Reds	12	0	.000
3.	Mariano Duncan, Dodgers	9	0	.000
4.	*Tim Wallach, Expos	15	1	.053
5.	Tony Pena, Pirates	13	1	.077
6.	Garry Templeton, Padres	13	1	.077
7.	Terry Whitfield, Dodgers	13	1	.077
8.	Johnny Ray, Pirates	17	2	.118
9.	Bob Dernier, Cubs	23	3	.130
10.	Tommy Herr, Cards	27	4	.148

*Wallach struck out 11 times.

"There are some guys who had no chance against him when he came up," teammate Ron Darling says. "Now he's even better and those same hitters have it in their heads that they can't hit him. It's not a very positive way to go up to the plate. Some guys may catch up with him a little. I think that happens to every pitcher. But most of them don't have a prayer of ever being consistently successful against him."

Met catcher Gary Carter wonders, "How do you catch up with Dwight? He can be unhittable and then, if you get a guy on base, somehow he gets better. If you get two hits off him in a game, he takes that as an insult. And the next time you face him, he's going to show you something you won't believe.

"But overall, Dwight doesn't have to improve to be the best in the game and stay the best. Unless someone else comes along who's just like him—and that's hard to believe. There's only one like him in every generation and we've got ours already . . . I'm just glad I don't have to face him anymore. Catching him is a lot more fun than trying to hit what he throws. I've caught him, and I'm not sure that I've figured out what to do (to hit him)."

The league doesn't even have a clue. After Gooden had disposed of the Cubs in a 2-1 victory, July 27, 1984, Cubs catcher Jody Davis said he never had seen the league "so geared up to beat one pitcher." But since then, the league barely has been able to touch Gooden.

Gooden lost his next two starts, but in his subsequent 44 starts, Gooden has compiled a 32-5 record and a 1.43 ERA, to say nothing of his 373 strikeouts in 352⅔ innings—an average of 9.52 per nine innings.

"You might find a way to beat him early in the season," Mets manager Davey Johnson says. "But once he gets his rhythm and his body gets accustomed to working every fifth day, you're not going to find many times late in the season when he isn't sharp. And one of the things that was so impressive about him this year was that even when he didn't have his best stuff, he was able to hold them off. He gave us a good chance to win almost every time he pitched.

"That's what a pitcher's job is. Dwight just redefines it a little. But really, all you're usually looking for is seven or eight innings of two- or three-run ball. Dwight just goes a little overboard once in a while and gives you nine innings with no runs . . . It's a nice excess."

The compliments continue for Gooden, but his manager and teammates now find themselves consulting dictionaries to find new adjectives. It was Keith Hernandez, a man with perspective and a more than adequate vocabulary, who may have put Gooden in

Pete Rose's lifetime BA is .304; he's .300 vs. Gooden.

his rightful place last season following the Aug. 20 defeat of the Giants, when he said Gooden "just may be the best pitcher who ever was."

When he was told of Davis' remark, Hernandez replied, "Dwight may not be God, but as a pitcher, he's close."

Willie McGee worked his way to the top in NL batting.

BOGGS & McGEE: TWO WAYS TO WIN A BATTING CROWN

By PETER GAMMONS

Wade Boggs has averaged .351 in four years in the bigs.

Sometimes people forget about the roads Wade Boggs and Willie McGee have traveled to get to .368 and .353 respectively. When one hears Bobby Cox say that watching Boggs hit "is watch-

---

Peter Gammons is the Boston Globe's *nationally syndicated baseball columnist.*

ing magic performed" or hears Whitey Herzog say that McGee "is such a great natural talent that a hitting coach might have messed him up," it's easy to forget that Boggs once sat unprotected in Triple-A and that McGee struggled in the Yankee farm system, batting .236, .251 and .243.

According to Boggs, "The key to success is overcoming adversity" and so it has been with both of baseball's 1985 batting champions.

They were born five months apart in 1958, Boggs the son of a career military officer, McGee the son of a deacon in the pentacostal church. Boggs is articulate and outgoing and admits he "loves to talk about hitting." McGee is soft-spoken and shy and admits, "I really feel extremely uneasy talking about myself." Boggs is a throwback to a Rogers Hornsby or a Pete Rose—a pure hitter. McGee is the prototype of the modern turf player. Boggs batted .332, .311, .325, .306 and .335 in the minor leagues. McGee hit .300 once in five minor-league seasons and was traded by the Yankees to the Cardinals' organization for someone named Bob Sykes.

But the two men share a bond: the work ethic. Boggs has a coach hit grounders to him for 20 minutes every afternoon. When McGee was called up to St. Louis from the minors in 1982, the Cardinals were playing in Pittsburgh. Since McGee had never played in that park, Herzog, his manager, suggested that the rookie take a few outfield flies during batting practice to get accustomed to the park. McGee has followed the same routine every day since then. "Herzog never told me to stop doing it," McGee explained last summer.

The intriguing thing to consider now that Boggs is making millions and McGee is the 1985 NL MVP is how both men had to struggle to overcome adversity to get the chance to prove that they belonged in the big leagues and how they immediately proved their worth once they got there.

Boggs was drafted by the Red Sox in 1976, out of Plant High School in Tampa, and scout George Digby, one of the best who ever lived, told the Boston farm people the kid was destined to be a great hitter. "I'd been watching him for three years," Digby recalled, "and not only was he a superb hitter, he had the desire to be great."

The only time in Boggs' career that he didn't hit .300 came that first summer at Elmira, when he batted .263 in 179 at-bats. The next four years he finished second in batting races in three different leagues, but, after the 1980 season, when he lost out to Toledo's Dave Engle by .0007, he still wasn't put on Boston's roster. That meant any team could have taken him in the minor-league draft for $25,000.

"We felt he had a way to go defensively," said Red Sox player personnel director Ed Kenney at the time, "and he has to show us a little more power."

To that point, Boggs had hit four homers and never had as many as 23 extra-base hits in a season. So, after being passed up by every club that winter, Boggs practiced driving the ball for power 30 minutes every day of the next season with Pawtucket. The result? He led the International League in batting at .335 and had 41 doubles and five homers. The next season he batted .349 for the Red Sox.

"McGee really could do only one thing exceptionally well when he signed—run," said scout Wayne Morgan, who suggested that the Yankees draft him in January 1977, out of Diablo Valley Junior College. "He had raw skills, but, like a lot of high school kids, he was a project. Yet I knew he was worth the investment, because he is such a fine person."

Just when McGee finally put it together—in 1981, the same year as Boggs—and batted .322 for the Yankees' Nashville club in the Double-A Southern League, George Steinbrenner shipped him off to the Cardinals for Sykes, who never won another major-league game.

"Our reports on McGee were excellent," Herzog recalled. "Sure enough, one look in spring training and we knew we really had something. We brought him up in late April and after two weeks I told someone, 'This Willie McGee is one of the damnedest players I've ever seen.'"

McGee batted .296 as a rookie, then had one of the most memorable World Series games of the last decade when he slugged two homers and made two homer-saving catches in Game 3.

Now Boggs and McGee are at the top of the list of the game's stars. "I don't think I've ever seen anyone make consistent contact like Boggs," claims Boston's renowned batting coach Walter Hriniak. "He comes as close as anyone in my lifetime to hitting the ball hard every time at bat." To back Hriniak's contention, consider this: over the entire 1985 season, Boggs popped up to the infield twice. He did it six times in 1984. "That," says Boggs, "is why I had such a bad season." Boggs considers a .325 year a "bad season."

To get some historic perspective on Boggs' accomplishments, consider that only six players in baseball history have had averages higher than Boggs' .351 through their first four full major-league seasons (or after 2,000 at-bats). They are Joe Jackson (.378), Chuck Klein (.360), Lefty O'Doul (.359), Paul Waner (.356), Ted Williams (.356) and Al Simmons (.355)—and not one of them broke in after 1940.

All you may have heard about Boggs' eccentricities is probably true, although he'd prefer to refer to them as "consistencies." Boggs believes "that one has to try to eliminate all the happenstances that upset routine and interrupt concentration."

So, after he eats his daily meal of chicken at 2 P.M. at home with his wife Debbie and their children—for a two-week homestand, he'll usually go for the 14-day, 13-recipe chicken rotation, preferring lemon chicken once a week because he hits better with it—he gets to the park between 3 and 3:05. He undresses at a specific time, puts in his dip of chewing tobacco at a specific time, rubs his bats—he uses one vs. left-handed pitchers and another vs. right-handers and never tucks his gamers in the racks with other bats for fear they'll pick up bad habits—at a specific time, then finally goes out to field the ground balls coach Joe Morgan hits to him at a specific time. After batting practice, he runs at 7:17. When he hits, he draws an Hebraic "7" before every at-bat and he follows the same path back to the dugout after every inning. By August, his well-worn path is visible to the Fenway Park audience.

Some consider Boggs' hitting habits unusual. "Sometimes I think you're the most screwed-up hitter I've ever seen," teammate Bill Buckner once told him. "Then I notice you're on base three or four times a game in front of me." What drives some crazy is Boggs' patience at the plate, his propensity for taking two strikes nearly every other time. "What's so amazing about him is that as he takes pitches, he seems to set pitchers up," said Cox. "Then the pitcher throws what he thinks is a good two-strike pitch and Boggs is looking for it."

Exactly 124 of Boggs' 240 hits came with two strikes and he batted .404 after letting the count start at 0-2. Throw in 96 walks and one finds that only Babe Ruth and Ted Williams reached base via a hit or walk more times in a single season than did Boggs in 1985. Boggs reached 336 times, eclipsed thrice by Ruth (375 in '23, 348 in '21, 342 in '24) and twice by Williams (356 in '49, 343 in '47).

However, because of the one-dimensional style of the Red Sox offense, Boggs also set a record for the most times reaching base and not scoring. Since he scored only 107 runs, he reached base without scoring 229 times, breaking Ruth's record of 224 in 1923.

Those who would detract from Boggs' accomplishments claim that he simply doesn't hit for enough power, that he is this generation's Rod Carew, the master of the meaningless 2-for-5. But don't think that Boggs can't hit a ball a long way, because he can. During his rookie year, he picked out a home-run landmark in

Boggs' patience pays off with walks, hits and a crown.

every park in the American League—the Tiger Stadium generator that Reggie Jackson cleared in the 1971 All-Star Game, the second-row, third-deck seat at Yankee Stadium that became the final resting place for George Brett's drive off Goose Gossage that won the 1980 pennant, for instance—and hit every one in batting practice, including the waterfall in Royals Stadium.

"I've worked hard for the time when I have to pull the ball more and try to contribute power," said Boggs. "I work 10 minutes every day pulling the ball inside. I take time in batting practice where I envision myself in first-pitch fastball situations and drive the ball for power. But, at least for now, my job is to try to get on base as many times as possible for Jim Rice, Bill Buckner, Tony Armas, Mike Easler and Rich Gedman."

"With the money they're paying him, someday soon they'll ask him to hit for more power," said Boggs' idol and close friend, George Brett. "He'll find that he has to sacrifice his average to some degree and that sometimes he can't be as patient, that he'll have to swing at pitches he now disdains. But he's such a great hitter that I wouldn't be surprised if he turned out to be someone who consistently can bat .330 and hit 25-to-30 homers. Remember, he is so strong that he can hit the ball up that net in Fenway. He can use the park as well as Freddie Lynn did."

Just as Brett, who finally earned a Gold Glove in 1985 after years of defensive proficiency at third, has begun to be recognized for his all-around play, so will Boggs. When he reached the major leagues, Boggs was expected to wind up as a first baseman or a designated hitter. When Boston third baseman Carney Lansford got hurt in June 1982, Boggs replaced him. He missed the first two balls hit to him and soon teammates kidded him by calling him "Captain Clank." That didn't last long, however, and the Red Sox dealt Lansford for Armas at the end of that season so Boggs could have the third-base position.

However, as recently as 1984, Boggs was still taking abuse for his glove. Red Sox pitcher Bob Stanley suggested that the reason Glenn Hoffman's range at shortstop was criticized was that Hoffman was shading the hole to compensate for Boggs' lack of range. "That just spurred me on to work all the harder," Boggs said. And by the end of last season Boggs ranked with Brett, Doug DeCinces and Mike Pagliarulo as the AL's finest defensive third basemen.

Of course, McGee's game has always been defense first and hitting second. Someone asked John Tudor what he felt was the biggest factor in his astounding 23-2 streak between June 1 and Game Seven of the World Series. Tudor simply looked over his shoulder towards center field. "I don't know how many times I had balls hit off me that I knew were uncatchable, then I'd turn around and there was Willie, waiting as if the bus were coming," said Tudor. "I've never seen anything like it."

"We were second in baseball in team earned-run average and allowed fewer runs than anyone, including the Dodgers," said Herzog. "Defense is a big part of it. It's practically impossible to hit the ball through the left side of our team, what with Terry Pendleton, Ozzie Smith, Vince Coleman and McGee. Then, given that confidence, the pitchers get far more aggressive in throwing strikes, which in turn makes the defense that much better, because they're always playing up on their toes. I don't see now where there's much question about McGee being the best defensive center fielder in the game right now."

Part of McGee's hitting style involves his speed. During the last two years, nearly 20 percent of his hits have been in the infield. "He's the prototype turf star," said Pittsburgh scout Howie Haak. "He's got the speed to bunt. He can hit the ball weakly and beat it out. That, in turn, brings the infield in, and he has developed the strength hit the ball hard enough to skip it past the infielders."

"I think I've probably gotten about 50 percent stronger in the last five years," said McGee. "I never used to be able to do anything but tap the ball and run as fast as I could. But every year the ball has jumped off my bat just a little bit more. I'm no Punch-and-Judy hitter."

Last season, for instance, among his 216 hits were 26 doubles, 18 triples and 10 homers. He used his tremendous speed in the spot behind Coleman and stole 56 bases, including two when he and Coleman pulled off their famous double-double steal. The addition of Coleman, the NL's top base thief, obviously helped McGee as a hitter. When Coleman was missing from the leadoff spot in the World Series, McGee was fed a constant diet of off-speed pitches and he was not the same hitter.

However, it is also fair to say that while McGee was winning his batting championship, he had to make unselfish adjustments to accommodate Coleman's ability to steal. "I'm the type who walks up to the plate, sees a pitch I like and hacks away," said McGee. "Never before have I been in the position of having to think about taking pitches, but I realize that I have to, so Vince can steal. I tried to be patient and take pitches to allow him to run, which meant that I was hitting behind on the count more than I have ever been before."

By the end of the season, teams were trying to neutralize Coleman's base-stealing with so many pitchouts that McGee ended up ahead on the count more often than not. Every scout in the National League will tell you that McGee will hit the ball for power when he's ahead 2-0 or 3-1. "He's just in the learning stage," said Herzog. "Just wait until he stops scratching the surface of his ability."

Both Boggs and McGee have worked hard to overcome adversity and become stars.

"I think you'll find in most cases that personal discipline and background are the keys to any individual's achievement of goals others never thought possible," said Ozzie Smith.

In the cases of these two batting champions, Smith is right on the money. Boggs and McGee owe their success to their backgrounds, Boggs to his military father's discipline—to this day, his father will call him to tell him that he saw a game on television and noticed his falling into a bad habit with his knee—and McGee to his minister father's values. Every spring before he leaves for Florida, McGee's feet are anointed in oil by his father for good luck.

No, Wade Boggs and Willie McGee didn't hit .368 and .353 by accident.

Mickey & Billy: From *The Mick*

By MICKEY MANTLE
with HERB GLUCK

From outward appearances, they would have to be ranked among baseball's oddest couples. The taciturn, All-American boy from Oklahoma with the magnificent physique that embodied power and speed was an epic hero with 536 home runs and a .298 lifetime average in an 18-year, Hall-of-Fame career spent entirely in Yankee pinstripes. The tough-as-nails Italian street fighter from the other side of the Berkeley, Cal., tracks with the scarecrow frame and the world's shortest fuse was a battler with limited physical gifts who wound up an 11-year career as a journeyman with 64 homers and a .257 lifetime average. But, during the six-plus seasons that Mickey Charles Mantle and Alfred Manuel Pesano were teammates, they combined their talents to win four world championships on the field and raise considerable hell together off it. Mantle and Martin were close friends, roommates and partners in partying and they remain tight now, 28 years after the day in June 1957 that the Yankees traded Martin to the Kansas City Athletics. Mantle named his third son after his former teammate who shared his appetite for a rollicking good time. In the following excerpts from his best-selling book, The Mick, *Mantle fondly recalls the carousing, the brawling and the belly laughs of the days of Wine and Billy.*

BATTLING BILLY

Billy Martin was back at second base, his ankle mended, when all of a sudden his big nose attracted the attention of Jimmy Piersall. It happened before a game in Fenway Park. Piersall, a rookie shortstop then, waltzed up and started agitating Billy. "Hey,

Billy Martin (l.) and Mickey Mantle examine the ball that Mickey clouted 565 feet at Washington's Griffith Stadium in 1953.

Pinocchio, what's with the schnozz?" That did it. They squared off under the grandstand. According to Billy, he whipped two short rights to Piersall's face and knocked him flat—and if Bill Dickey hadn't jumped in as a peacemaker, he would've beaten the living daylights out of Piersall. "Nobody screws with my nose," he said. And weird, shortly after the fight, Piersall ended up in a mental institution. When we got the news, Billy said, "You think I can't punch. Hell, I knocked that guy crazy."

Casey Stengel loved this kind of combative spirit. At a clubhouse meeting after the fight, he said in plain English, "If we're gonna win this thing, you better move your asses like Billy here. Of course, I want your enthusiasm directed to the finer points of baseball, which is a wonderful sport for young gentlemen, I would say."

I guess I should mention a brawl at Sportsman's Park, one of those baseball fights that started when Browns' catcher Clint

---

Courtney singled and deliberately spiked Phil Rizzuto, who was covering second base. He cut Phil's leg in two places. The Yankees immediately reacted. Billy led the charge. I also saw Whitey Ford, Gil McDougald, Allie Reynolds, Joe Collins, Hank Bauer, and a few other guys jump in to pound the shit out of Courtney. If Casey weren't so old, I think he would've joined the fight. Me? I'm not a fighter. Most of the time I used to run in to be a peacemaker. Billy Martin and Clint Courtney liked to fight. When this one was over, one of the umpires had a dislocated collarbone. Gene Woodling narrowly missed getting skulled by a bottle thrown from the stands and Courtney's glasses were ground into smithereens. Whitey claims that particular contribution.

"Look at all the money Rocky Marciano gets for knocking guys out," said Billy. "I didn't make nothing and put on a better fight. On top of which, I got fined!"

Me and Whitey planned a birthday party for Billy in 1957, May 16, an open date on our schedule. We invited Yogi, Hank Bauer, Johnny Kucks, and their wives and made all the arrangements. Everything was set, right down to the baby-sitters.

Then the commissioner's office rescheduled a rain-out game for the sixteenth. However, the fifteenth was still open, so we did some last-minute phoning and the party was booked for that night.

We met at Danny's Hideaway, had dinner, and then somebody suggested that it would be a swell idea to catch Sammy Davis, Jr., at the Copacabana. We arrived a few minutes before he went on. The maître d' set up a special table. We ordered a round of drinks and the show began. Sammy came out singing and dancing. He was fabulous. Meanwhile, sitting at a table next to us was a group of guys who were members of a bowling team. Most of them were three sheets to the wind.

Before long the bowlers got kinda crude. They started to heckle the singer. We were embarrassed—in fact, they were ruining the show for us.

There was some unfriendly banter back and forth. We told them to shut up and they told us to shut up. It got worse and worse. We were recognized—loudly—when one of the bowlers stood up and said, "Well, the Yankees are here. Big deal!"

Some birthday party. People from all sides were straining their necks and buzzing about the *real* show going on in the back. Finally Billy says to one of the bowlers, "Listen, we're trying to have a nice time. Why don't you give us a break and be quiet, huh?" The guy staggers to his feet, leans against his chair with one hand, holds a shot glass in the other, and stares at Billy. "Why don't we talk about it outside?" Billy says, "Sure, pal, let's go."

Bauer came off his seat. "Where are you going, Billy?" "I'm gonna talk to him, that's all." I looked at Merlyn [Mantle's wife]. "I think I better see what Billy's doing." At that moment I heard a loud crash. The next moment one of the drunks was lying in a heap over by the cloakroom, knocked cold. I thought it was Billy. I turned around and saw a couple of other bowlers near the kitchen, spitting curses at Hank. Whitey had a lock on his arms.

I know this. Bauer never laid a hand on anybody. Neither did Billy. And the only thing I touched during the entire uproar was a scotch and soda. The way I saw it, in the midst of everything, several Copa bouncers with zap probably grabbed the ringleader and clobbered him. Whatever, we were hustled through the kitchen, down a narrow passageway, out a side exit which led to the lobby of the Hotel Fourteen, and into the street for a quick disappearing act.

While we waited for cabs to whisk us away, Billy's saying to me, "Please, from now on don't throw me any more birthday parties." And Yogi's going "Ho, ho, ho" through clenched teeth. Then a cab arrived. Hank opened the rear door, bowed his wife Charlene in, and jumped in after her as if he had just been airlifted off Guadalcanal.

The next morning I read it in the papers: YANKEES BRAWL AT THE COPA.

Whitey called me from his Long Island home. "The shit has really hit the fan. George Weiss is going to fine the whole bunch of us. Not only that, we have to appear before the Manhattan Grand Jury."

"Why? We didn't do anything."

"Exactly what I told Weiss, but he says one of us hit the guy and we're all in trouble."

We testified at the Criminal Court Building. Johnny Kucks was so nervous his legs quaked. After they finished with him, Billy took the stand and told his story. Then Whitey, Yogi, and Hank told theirs. By midafternoon I was getting tired of waiting to be called and worked up a real bitch of a headache. Finally an attendant motioned me into the chamber.

I sat in the witness chair. About fifty grand jurors were solemnly peering down. Remember the Nuremberg trails? Same atmosphere.

The judge's first question:

"Mr. Mantle, are you chewing gum?"

"Yes, sir."

"Well, get rid of it."

Then the district attorney started in:

"Now, Mickey, were you at the Copa the night of May fifteenth?"

"Yes, sir."

"Did you see a fight take place while you were there?"

"No, sir, I didn't."

"Well, did you see a gentleman lying unconscious on the floor near the Copa entrance?"

"Yes, I did."

"All right. Do you have an opinion as to how this could have happened?"

I thought about it and said, "I think Roy Rogers rode through the Copa on his horse and Trigger kicked that man in the head."

The grand jury was still laughing when the judge dismissed the case for insufficient evidence.

The same day I came to the ballpark and found Billy packing his stuff. I said, "What the hell are you doing?" He said, "I'm gone, Mick. Guaranteed, I'm out of here . . ." I said, "You're not going anywhere." I felt he was just too valuable to the team, that there was no way he would be traded in spite of [GM George] Weiss' animosity. I honestly felt that Weiss was too shrewd, too much of a perfectionist when it came to winning with good players. He would overlook whatever reason he had to suspect Billy of doing crazy things, as long as it didn't affect his skills on the field. No matter what either of us did privately, when it got down to playing, we knew it was our bread and butter. We played sober, full blast every game.

He gazed around the clubhouse and spoke quietly. "This is just the excuse Weiss needs to ship my ass to another club. I'm telling you, it's gonna happen any moment now."

CURFEW BUSTERS

Billy and I were roommates that year [1952]. In fact, we roomed together from then until he was traded in 1957. And let me tell you, we had some fun. The team put us up in swanky hotels around the league, places like the Shoreham, the Kenmore, the Book Sheraton, the Chase, the Del Padro on Lake Michigan in Chicago, the Wade Park Manor in Cleveland.

Between road trips Billy and I and our wives would sit around in our New York apartment, taking strolls, sitting in air-conditioned movies, but mostly sitting around at home in our bathing suits—no cross ventilation and all that heat—just watching to see if the cord hanging from the window shade would move. Sometimes a whole day would pass with no breeze, the cord straight and still.

We had some funny nights in the apartment. I remember once, it must have been one in the morning. Billy came creeping on his hands and knees down the hallway to peek into our bedroom. I was creeping along to peek into his and we bumped heads in the dark, "*Shhhhh!*" he whispered, then we both cracked up.

Terrific times. If I tasted the high life in 1951, I got a bellyful starting in 1952—especially on the road. Parties, flashy people, hard liquor, staying out really late. Billy and I were often the life of the party. We wouldn't go upstairs to our old room until we were just about ready to drop.

Whitey and Billy were a lot alike. And I'm not so sure they would have been as close if I hadn't been there. They were both leaders, strong-willed and stubborn. I was more of the follower; I went along with their ideas. Who knows what might have happened if I hadn't provided a softer edge. The point is, we always enjoyed each other's company. Usually we were all together. There were cartoons that came out in the New York papers in those days that showed the three of us as the Dead End Kids. Casey would be the principal up on the platform and we would be like three truant schoolboys awaiting our punishment—but we'd be hiding slingshots and BB guns behind our backs, ready to cut loose again.

Billy and Whitey have heard me joke often enough that if it weren't for them, I could've played ball till I was forty years old.

On April 10, 1953, I hit a home run over the 100-foot-high grandstand at Forbes Field. Until then only Babe Ruth and Ted Beard had done it. Of course I'm proud of that. But let's be honest. The greater accomplishment was getting to Forbes Field in the first place.

On April 9, we were winding our way back from Florida to open the season, living on the train and playing exhibition games along the way. It's bitter cold when we arrive in Cincinnati. So we play the game, and then Whitey, Billy and I make a beeline across the river, to Covington, Kentucky, a live-wire place, to have some fun before catching the train to Pittsburgh. We had to be back at the station at ten o'clock for the all-night ride, which would get us in the next morning in plenty of time for batting practice.

Okay.

At nine-thirty I started looking for the others. We finally found each other at eleven, too late for the train. We said, "The hell with it. We'll catch a plane in the morning and get to Forbes Field with time to spare." We said, "Yeah, Casey will never know. We'll act like we were on the train." Billy: "That sounds okay."

I get up at dawn, unglue my eyes, and stare through the window. A frigging blizzard. An hour later we're at the airport. It's socked in, snow up to your ass and all of the flights are canceled. Holy shit, what do we do now? Whitey says, "No problem. Follow me." So we grab a cab. I slide into the front seat and tell the driver, "Take us to Pittsburgh." He goes, "C'mon, buddy, I hear that crap all the time." He thinks we're either off our rockers, wise guys, or eccentric millionaires out on a lark. Finally I convince him that we're serious. He gets on the horn and calls his router. "Listen, I got three monkeys here who say they want to go to Pittsburgh. What's the charge?" It comes to $500. And somehow we get there. But the team is already taking batting practice. All Whitey has to do is run with the pitchers. Who'd ever notice? The batting cage is another story altogether. You show up or else. Well, me and Billy are in the locker room, pulling our socks on as fast as we can, praying Casey hasn't missed us yet. We're hunched over, tying our shoes. I'm whispering to Billy, at the same time concentrating on getting dressed. Finally I give him a sidelong glance and see that I'm actually talking to myself. Billy's gone. He's in the toilet. And there's a hand on my shoulder. Casey's voice: "I don't know where you assholes have been. I don't know what you've done, but I wanta know . . . Where's the other little bastard?"

He storms out, saying me and Billy are going to play the whole ball game, every inning. Believe me, after that long drive from Cincinnati, slugging through the snow while dozing in fits and starts along the way, besides being nearly $200 short because of the cab fare, I'm not looking forward to playing tiddlywinks, let alone baseball.

And here's Billy, sneaking out of the toilet, laughing like hell. We go out, no batting practice, just a couple of minutes left to play catch and limber up. My first time at bat I hit that long home run over the grandstand.

Casey has a pasty smile waiting. "Nice hit, Mickey. Take the rest of the day off."

I walk right past Billy, who's sitting at the far end of the dugout, his eyes upturned, and he's whining, "Teacher's pet . . . teacher's pet . . ."

We were boys then.

One time in Boston Casey did impose a curfew after we blew a couple of games. He got hotter than a pistol. The veins in his neck bulged like Dizzy Gillespie's as he went on about how lousy we were going. "Yes siree, until I see more improvement I'm placing you all on a twelve o'clock midnight curfew!"

So that very evening Billy Martin and I get dressed in our best suits and go out to a classy chop house across town. We're sitting there talking and joking and the hours slip by. Billy glances at his watch. "Christ! It's half past eleven!"

We rushed into the street and hailed a cab. Ten minutes later we fly up the front steps of our hotel, swing through the door, and there's Casey standing in the lobby, giving a long-winded oration before a group of writers.

We made a U-turn and got the hell out of there. No way in the world to reach the elevator without walking past him. However, they had a back door to the Kenmore that you could use by going through an alley. It was a shortcut. The team often went in and out of there when we wanted to avoid the fans. This time Billy and I came from the other end and grabbed ahold of the back door. The damn thing was locked.

But he sees a little window above the door. Now he's perched on my back and I'm boosting him up to the window. Finally he clutches the ledge, pulls himself off my shoulders and head, and squeezes through. I'm waiting in the alley and I'm saying to myself, "What luck. He'll open the door and we'll be safe and sound in our room."

I hear Billy calling me. I look up. His eyes are sticking out the window. He says, "I can't open the door from the inside. It's locked. I'll see you tomorrow." It dawns on me that the only chance I have to get into the hotel undetected is to follow the same route he took. Well, there's a stack of trash cans piled in the alley. Must've been sitting there a week because they were spilling over with the garbage. I push a few against the door, lift two more on top, and climb up on them. My shoes sink into the goop. I smell worse than a toilet from all the rotten vegetables. But the greasy stains on my suit help me to slide right through the window. I finally get in and there I am, sneaking up the stairs to my room.

I throw open the door. Billy is acting like he's snoring in his bed.

"Wake up!"

"Wha . . . Wha . . ."

"Look at all this crap over me! You coulda reached down and got me, you son of a bitch!"

Billy only laughed, turned over, and went to sleep.

THOSE WERE THE DAYS

And that winter I was on the *go*. Kinda made it tough for Merlyn, though it sure was good for me and Billy Martin. He had come down from Berkeley to visit us and he will tell you it was one of the best times he ever had, especially when we went out hunting quail.

There's an old saying in Oklahoma: "You can't eat a quail a day seven days in a row." But Billy could eat four of them every morning for breakfast. Gained twenty pounds over the winter. When he wasn't eating at our house, he would be at my mother's. She'd fix him biscuits and gravy, a half-dozen eggs, pork chops. Once his plate was loaded, he'd wolf it all down and come up for more. We were like family to him.

Billy more or less accepted the world as he saw it. You are what you are and don't bother me beyond that point. His nature overrode everything else. Still, there were moments when he'd start thinking about Lois and he'd get down. He couldn't accept the reality of a divorce. During the 1953 season I'd see him on the phone, begging her to take him back. Nothing worked. She'd hang up and he'd get so distraught. One particular day, when he realized there was no longer any hope for a reconciliation, he wrecked our hotel room. I mean, he literally tore it apart.

After the season Billy went on a Far East tour with the Eddie Lopat All-Stars. Before he left, we agreed that he would winter with us in Commerce. We'd do some hunting and fishing. He didn't have to ask. I knew he had nothing left in Berkeley.

So there he was, in front of our house, squeezing out of a brand-new Cadillac convertible, all weighed down with a bunch of Japanese cameras, field binoculars, silk dressing robes, little statues, a samurai sword, jewelry cases, probably $5,000 worth of stuff. He stood there, wrapped in a sheepskin coat, grinning from ear to ear. "Hi, pard, let's have a drink."

Merlyn was wondering what the hell we were getting into next. We took off in his car. The state was dry, no liquor served at bars or restaurants. I said, "We can get served at a place called the Stables. It's a private club over in Miami." Before going in, he removed his coat, placed it lovingly on the front seat, and went around to lock the doors. I said, "Don't bother." He said, "Are you nuts? I've got valuable merchandise with me." I said, "Billy, this is Oklahoma. You don't have to lock your doors." So we went in and had a couple of drinks apiece, rushing it because Merlyn was waiting on us to have dinner. Then we came out and found his car totally emptied. No cameras, nothing. He said, "You idiot, if we stayed in there for another drink, I wouldn't have had any wheels left either." Fortunately, he had locked the trunk, or they might have stolen his clothes, too. As we drove and drove around Commerce, he was half out the window, gawking at passing cars. He kept saying, "Man, oh man, if I see a guy wearing my sheepskin coat, I'll kill him." It was his introduction to Oklahoma. We never did find the coat.

In the dead of winter, it gets colder than hell around Commerce, Oklahoma—just perfect weather for duck hunting. So we put on all the clothes we could find—long johns, galoshes over our shoes, sweaters, coats—you name it. Billy weighed about 165 pounds, but by the time we got him dressed, he probably weighed closer to 200.

We'd get into the car, Billy and me, along with my twin brothers Roy and Ray, and drive around the countryside. Some of the farmers welcomed hunters, others didn't, but sitting real close to about every farm there would be a tank (our term for a pond to water animals) and the tank would be dammed up at one end. Now, the trick in duck hunting is to sneak up on the dam side of the tank, then check to see if there were any wild ducks on the surface of the water. Technically, you couldn't shoot at tame ducks, but that rule—like many others—wouldn't stop us. The best way around the problem was to get the ducks to fly and then shoot because the tame ducks won't fly and the wild ducks will. Anyway, it's all poaching if you don't get the farmer's permission, which we never did. You've got to know what you're doing and this was Billy's first time.

That morning we found two or three tanks and got a few birds. Our third stop was at a pond located 50 to 100 yards from the road. We parked, inched up to the dam, and opened fire.

Then I looked over my shoulder and saw a white pickup truck parking next to our car. On the side was a painted sign: OKLAHOMA GAME COMMISSION.

The first thing you do, of course, is run, even though what you really have to do is get back to your car, which in this case was parked on the other side of the game warden's truck.

We started running and those heavy clothes really weighed us down—especially Billy, who began to fall behind. Next thing I knew, Billy stopped.

"You guys go ahead. I'm going to shoot it out with him."

The game warden must have heard him because he turned tail and started back for his truck. He must have thought we were just plain crazy 'cause nobody had probably ever threatened to shoot at him before. The moment he was safely in the truck, he took off. We jumped in our car and went off in the other direction.

That's the last we heard of it.

Harold [Mantle's friend Harold Youngman] and Billy and I were on Waikiki beach: Harold with a coat and tie and straw hat under an umbrella, Billy and me in trunks sprawled on a mat. Billy must have been watching the surfers because he suddenly tapped my arm.

"Let's rent a couple of surfboards." He knows I can't swim, yet a few minutes later I'm stroking away on a board in crystal clear water. I look back and the beach seems to be shrinking. Billy's close by and I yell, "Hey, we're getting too far out! Let's turn around!" He says, "You're only twenty-feet from the beach. You can still see the bottom. Don't worry. Nothin's gonna happen."

So I keep stroking and look back again. The beach is gone, the waves are getting higher and higher, and the surfboard and me are riding up and down like mad. "Hey, Billy, these waves are scaring the shit out of me!" He laughs. "What are you talking about? You can still see the bottom."

The hell with that. I see a ten-story wave coming directly at me. As I start turning back, it flips me off the board. I go straight down, hit bottom, and shoot up like a Polaris missile.

Billy tries to grab the board, misses it, and swims over. I'm losing my strength: I think I'm a goner. I imagine the headlines: YANKEE STAR DROWNS! And Billy is yelling, "I got you, pard! Take it easy! Relax!"

As he tries to pull me up, I put a headlock on him and pull him under. And suddenly we rise to the surface again. Billy flops me over his board and a gentle wave carries us in. I'm flat on my back on the sand, limp as a rag.

"You okay, Mick?"

"Yeah . . ."

"Good. I shoulda hit you. You almost ended my career."

He had saved my life.

BILLY BALL

During our Yankee years Billy wasn't the most graceful infielder you ever saw. Certainly Jerry Coleman was a lot smoother at second base. No, Billy wasn't pretty to watch, but he would always find a way to beat you. Which is why he became a great manager.

Mickey visits Billy's western wear shop in New York in 1978.

There was a guy named Harry Byrd. He pitched for a while for the Philadelphia Athletics. A tall right-hander from South Carolina. Great big guy. Threw real hard. Sometimes he'd run our right-handed hitters right out of the box with sidearm fastballs inside, shaving them closer than the family barber. So one time before starting a series against the A's, Casey calls a clubhouse meeting and says, "Listen, we gotta do something about this guy Byrd. I'll give anybody a hundred dollars for getting hit tonight."

Sure enough, Billy got hit three times. He stood a hair away from the plate, practically over it, taking three shots in the ribs. After the game he walked over to Casey and said, "Skip, you owe me three hundred bucks."

BRET & BRETT: THE ROYALS' BEST BETS

By GIB TWYMAN

Bret Saberhagen was about to let fly with the last pitch of the 1985 baseball season when George Brett trotted over to the mound from third base. "When you get the last out, don't run away from me," said Brett. "I want to be next to you."

"Don't worry," said the Royals' right-hander. "I'm comin' right for you."

The St. Louis Cardinals' Andy Van Slyke lifted a fly to right field and Darryl Motley squeezed it. Bret and Brett raced into each other's arms and danced a wild Mexican hatless dance around third base before being buried by an avalanche of Kansas City teammates.

"By the time the ball hit Darryl's glove, we were an inch apart," said Saberhagen. "We just screamed at each other, 'We did it. We're world champions.'"

The two men were entitled to celebrate because the Kansas City Royals had completed one of the most improbable comebacks in baseball history. Coming out of the grave more often than Bela Lugosi, the Royals had rebounded from three-games-to-one post-season deficits to defeat Toronto and St. Louis. And the Royals accomplished this despite an incredible shrinking offense that ranked 13th in the league in run production (687); a starting shortstop whose weak hitting made him the object of comic ridicule on late-night television (Buddy Biancalana) and a left fielder who should do U.S. Steel commercials after winning another Iron Glove as one of the AL's worst-fielding outfielders (Lonnie Smith).

Essentially, the 1985 Royals were to baseball what the bumblebee is to aerodynamics. There was no way they could fly.

Gib Twyman is a feature sportswriter for the Kansas City Star *and the author of* Born to Hit: The George Brett Story.

Bret & Brett celebrate Royals winning World Series.

But fly, somehow, they did.

Basically, the Royals kept on flying for two major reasons: Bret and Brett, bosom buddies and co-stars in Kansas City's championship season.

Saberhagen was the cornerstone of a young pitching staff that could rival any in recent memory. His 20-6 record and 2.87 ERA brought him the AL Cy Young Award. He allowed a league-leading ratio of 9.4 runners per nine innings, gave up more than four runs only twice in 32 starts and posted a 158-38 strikeout-to-walk ratio, stamping him as a power pitcher with excellent control.

Meanwhile, Brett, rejuvenated by a rigid offseason conditioning program, enjoyed perhaps the best overall season of his 12-year career, hitting .335 with 30 homers and 112 RBI. As usual, he was at his best when the games were most crucial, going 9-for-20 with five home runs and 11 RBI in the Royals' final five victories, which included Kansas City's AL West title-clinching showdown series against California.

As outstanding as those regular-season numbers were for Bret and Brett, they merely set the stage for an even more memorable postseason.

Brett continued to establish himself as a clutch hitter for the ages as Kansas City stormed back to overcome the Blue Jays in the AL Championship Series. During the ALCS, Brett led all hitters in average (.348), home runs (3), runs (6), total bases (19), walks (7), slugging percentage (.826), extra-base hits (5) and on-base percentage (.500), earning recognition as the playoff MVP. He now holds AL career playoff records for homers (9), RBI (19), runs (22), hits (35), total bases (75) and slugging percentage (.728).

The third baseman singlehandedly brought Kansas City back from the doorstep to extinction when, with the Royals trailing the Blue Jays two games to none, he belted two huge home runs and a double as part of a 4-for-4 performance that paved the way to a 6-5 victory in Game 3. Then, in the World Series, Brett hit .370 with five runs scored, winding up his season with another four-hit night in Game 7.

However, the World Series belonged to the other Bret. The Royals' pulse was barely detectable after St. Louis grabbed a two-games-to-none advantage, but Saberhagen administered CPR with a 6-1, six-hit, complete-game victory in Game 3.

Then, when it came down to ace against ace—Saberhagen vs. the Cards' John Tudor in the finale—Saberhagen registered an 11-0, five-hit, complete-game victory to earn World Series MVP honors.

There has always been something special about the relationship between the 21-year-old Saberhagen and the 32-year-old Brett.

There is a kinship, a commonality of spirit, despite the difference in their ages.

Brett took Saberhagen under his roof when the pitcher first came to the majors and the two men have adjoining lockers. The rapport really isn't all that surprising considering that when Brett looks at Saberhagen, he must be able to see himself through the filter of a decade of growth.

Both hail from Southern California; Brett from El Segundo and Saberhagen from Reseda. Both were talented youngsters who saw their first major-league action at a very young age; Brett at 20 and Saberhagen at 19. Both possess profound beliefs in their abilities, a refreshing awareness of their powers that falls just short of cockiness. But perhaps the most significant quality the two men share is the sense of playfulness they bring to their work.

For instance, there was the weekend series in Toronto when Saberhagen was spotted chasing butterflies in the outfield during batting practice. And Saberhagen's bullpen buddies still haven't forgotten his distinctive, eye-rolling, head-twisting style in the tobacco-spitting championships during his rookie year. "It was messy, but creative," said Dan Quisenberry. And then there was the wall-climbing catch Saberhagen made on a batting-practice blast off the bat of Hal McRae.

"I kind of like to have a good time," said Saberhagen. "When I go out on the mound, I'm probably the most serious guy in the ballpark. But you still have to have a good time out there. You can't be really stiff and tense. You have to be able to relax. I think that's one reason I've thrown a lot of strikes."

Saberhagen's antics prompted teammate Mark Gubicza to tag him with the nickname "Geisha," a reference to the goofy character played by Jerry Lewis in the film "The Geisha Boy."

Saberhagen's free spirit recalls the image of a young George Brett, whom hitting instructor Charlie Lau called "Mullet," a reference to a crazy-acting fish from the Gulf of Mexico. The nickname stuck when Brett did things like hiding in a trash can after striking out and rollerskating down a runway and into the Stadium parking lot to commemorate the birth of a new line of roller skates by one of the shoe companies for which he did endorsements.

Free-spiritedness is characteristic of both players, both of whom are distinguished by their self-confidence and their ability to respond under pressure.

"I'm sure the adrenalin will be flowing," Saberhagen said before facing Toronto in Game 3 of the playoffs. "And there will be some butterflies. But I'm going to enjoy it. I'm going to be psyched. I think the team feels confident with me out there. They know I'm going to throw strikes. They seem to play the best

Saberhagen became the fifth-youngest to win 20 games.

games with me out there."

That sounded a lot like Brett after his 4-for-4 night against Toronto. "I don't go up there telling anybody I'm going to do anything," he said. "I just try to perform to the best level George Brett can. But I know I feel very confident in those situations."

Saberhagen's knack of not blinking in the face of pressure can be traced to his boyhood, according to his father Bob.

He could see it way back when Bret used to come to the flying school where his dad worked. Brett was 11 or 12 at the time and he helped out after school, checking fuel levels and washing planes. Every now and then Herb Levy, Bob's partner, would take Bret up in a plane and let him take the controls, but Bret's father discouraged his son from continuing with flying. "I worried for him, because he just had no fear of flying," his father said. "He has no fear. Never had any."

Maybe that explains why Saberhagen didn't panic when his career almost ended during his senior year at Cleveland High.

He developed shoulder problems and his fastball fell from the 88-mile-an-hour range to the high 70s. One doctor diagnosed it as a rotator cuff injury and when the scouts got wind of that, they practically collided in midair while jumping off the Saberhagen bandwagon.

The Saberhagens sought a second opinion from a chiropractor, who straightened Bret out after a couple of treatments. Soon after, he pitched in a high-school game witnessed by Royals' scout Gary Hansen.

"About the third inning of the game, we started hearing a 'pop, pop' into the catcher's glove," said Bob Saberhagen. "Gary looked at me and I looked at him and we smiled. Bret walked in off the mound and said, 'I'm back.'"

"The scout asked me if I'd mind if he got the radar gun out," Bret said. "He took it out in the fourth. I was throwing about 86-87 miles an hour. In the last inning I was still right there."

But the Royals didn't take him until the 19th round of the June 1982 draft. Saberhagen had a 9-0 record and 0.83 ERA as a senior, leading his team to the Los Angeles city championship. In the title game, he pitched a no-hitter.

In 1983, Saberhagen began his pro career with Ft. Myers (A) in the Florida State League, where he posted a 10-5 record and 2.30 ERA. Later that summer, he moved up to Jacksonville in the Southern Association (AA), where he went 6-2 with a 2.91 ERA.

The next stop was Kansas City in 1984. He struggled in the spring as a starter, then worked his way back into the rotation and was a factor as the Royals won the AL West title. He became the youngest starter ever in an AL Championship Series game, losing a six-hit performance to Detroit. His season record was 10-11 with a 3.48 ERA.

Off to a 2-3 start in 1985, Bret went on an 18-3 binge and became the fifth-youngest pitcher in major-league history to win 20 games. The four younger than Saberhagen were Bob Feller, Christy Mathewson, Dwight Gooden and Al Mamaux.

Usually the hallmark of a Saberhagen performance is his control. Veteran catcher Jim Sundberg said, "I've caught 12 years and the only other guys I caught that had his kind of control were Ferguson Jenkins and Gaylord Perry."

In his first year in the big leagues, Saberhagen relied almost exclusively on his fastball. Last season, he added a mix of curves and sliders. But the bad news for hitters is that his fastball is getting faster. It has been regularly clocked in the low 90s.

"As he gets older, he seems to be getting stronger," said his manager, Dick Howser. "The fastball is really the pitch that sets him apart."

While Saberhagen's career is dawning, his buddy George is experiencing a rebirth that began with the sleeker, streamlined model that he rolled out during spring training in 1985. Brett

Brett twice had four-hit games in postseason play.

showed up weighing 193 pounds, instead of the 214 he had carried in 1984, which he called "undoubtedly my worst year in the majors."

He missed one-third of the 1984 season due to injuries and ended up with a .284 batting average, his lowest since he hit .282 during his rookie year in 1974.

"After the season I had the worst feeling about myself I ever had," he said. "I wanted to beat the Tigers in the AL playoffs, but once it was over I was never so glad to be at home and not at the ballpark."

Ringing in his ears was some advice Reggie Jackson had given him after Brett suffered a torn hamstring. "Reggie told me I was going to have to work on getting into shape, that I was getting up in age," Brett said.

Also ringing in his ears was the sound of the cash register, to the tune of the $1.78 million he is reportedly averaging on a "lifetime" contract that runs through 1991.

The 1985 season was the first year on that huge contract and the third baseman was repelled by the thought that fans would think he was feeling complacent. "I felt with the money the Royals are paying me and my pride, I wanted to play in 162 games," he said.

So, he underwent an offseason conditioning program for the first time in his career. He stopped drinking alcohol and went for a month without eating any red meat, fried foods, bread or butter. He hired Bobby Lowe, a friend from his El Segundo High School days and an avid marathoner, to supervise his workouts. They played racquetball, worked on the Nautilus machine, jogged and lifted weights.

Brett's fervor for going to the ballpark re-emerged and he reported early to spring training, able to wear size-34 pants instead of the usual size 38.

Brett's earnest efforts were rewarded as he played in 155 games, finished second to Boston's Wade Boggs in the AL batting race, second in total bases (322), on-base percentage (.436) and extra-base hits (73) and led the league in slugging percentage (.585). He wound up as runnerup to the Yankees' Don Mattingly in AL MVP balloting.

For the 10th straight year, he was a starter in the All-Star Game and he posted a .967 fielding percentage at third base last season.

"I think it was the best all-around year I've ever had," Brett said.

Contemplating the drudgery of winter workouts this year, Brett said: "I have great recall. When the workout program starts to drag, I can press a button in my mind and play back any part of the past season."

Saberhagen can press his own button. Or maybe he'll just pinch himself to see if it all was a dream. Twenty victories, a world championship, a World Series MVP trophy, a visit to the White House, a first child born two days before the Series clincher.

What will he do for an encore?

"Win 21 games, take the Series in six and have twins," he said with a grin.

Young Bret sure sounds like the old Brett.

INSIDE THE NATIONAL LEAGUE

By NICK PETERS
Oakland Tribune

PREDICTED ORDER OF FINISH

East	*West*
New York Mets	Los Angeles Dodgers
Montreal Expos	Cincinnati Reds
St. Louis Cardinals	Atlanta Braves
Chicago Cubs	San Diego Padres
Philadelphia Phillies	Houston Astros
Pittsburgh Pirates	San Francisco Giants

Playoff winner: **New York**

EAST DIVISION

	Team	Owner	1985	Morning Line Manager
1	**METS** Orange, white & blue Gooden-ough to win	N. Doubleday/F. Wilpon	W 98 L 64	**3-2** Dave Johnson
2	**EXPOS** Scarlet, white & royal blue A force from the north	Charles Bronfman	W 84 L 77	**2-1** Buck Rodgers
3	**CARDS** Red & white Will fade at the finish	August A. Busch Jr.	W 101 L 61	**3-1** Whitey Herzog
4	**CUBS** Royal blue & white Cey it isn't so	Tribune Company	W 77 L 84	**5-1** Jim Frey
5	**PHILLIES** Crimson & white Ain't what they used to be	Bill Giles	W 75 L 87	**25-1** John Felske
6	**PIRATES** Old gold, white & black New owners, same horses	Malcolm Prine	W 57 L 104	**50-1** Jim Leyland

Strong arms to crack whip for **METS**, who get stiffest challenge from healthy **EXPOS**. Defending champ **CARDINALS** rest on laurels and run out of gas while aging **CUBS** falter following strong getaway. **PHILLIES** fall even farther back in the race, but still outlast **PIRATES**, who simply don't have the horses.

NEW YORK STAKES

110th Running. National League Race. Distance: 162 games plus playoff. Payoff (based on '85): $76, 341 per winning player, World Series: $54,921 per losing player, World Series. A field of 12 entered in two divisions.

Track Record: 116 wins—Chicago, 1906

WEST DIVISION		Owner		Morning Line Manager
1	**DODGERS** Class of the field	Peter O'Malley Royal blue & white	1985 W 95 L 67	3-2 Tommy Lasorda
2	**REDS** A run for the Rose	Marge Schott Red & white	1985 W 89 L 72	3-1 Pete Rose
3	**BRAVES** New jockey makes a difference	Ted Turner Royal blue & white	1985 W 66 L 96	10-1 Chuck Tanner
4	**PADRES** A stable in disarray	Joan Kroc Brown, gold & white	1985 W 83 L 79	12-1 Dick Williams
5	**ASTROS** More power not the answer	John McMullen Orange & white	1985 W 83 L 79	15-1 Hal Lanier
6	**GIANTS** Looking for a new stable	Bob Lurie White, orange & black	1985 W 62 L 100	50-1 Roger Craig

DODGERS, surprise 1985 winner, confident from the start while winning two-team race from frisky **REDS**. Rest of field slow, with refurbished **BRAVES** best of a bad lot. Constant tugging of reins hurts **PADRES**, but they edge speedier **ASTROS** while sluggish **GIANTS** head for the glue factory.

CHICAGO CUBS

TEAM DIRECTORY: Pres.-GM: Dallas Green; Dir. Minor Leagues/ Scouting: Gordon Goldsberry; VP-Adm.: E.R. Saltwell; Dir. Med. Rel.: Ned Colletti; Trav. Sec.: Peter Durso; Mgr.: Jim Frey. Home: Wrigley Field (38,040). Field distances: 335, l.f. line; 400, c.f.; 353, r.f. line. Spring training: Mesa, Ariz.

SCOUTING REPORT

HITTING: Despite an horrendous team slump last year, the Cubs were dangerous at the plate, smacking a league-leading 150 homers and getting solid performances from 1984 NL MVP Ryne Sandberg (.305, 26 homers, 83 RBI) and Keith Moreland (.307, 14 homers, 106 RBI). Offense will not be a problem, especially if Bob Dernier snaps back and Shawon Dunston fulfills his promise as a potentially great all-around shortstop.

Leon Durham (21 homers, 75 RBI) is another solid bat in the order, but there is concern about the ravages of time on the production of third baseman Ron Cey and left fielder Gary Matthews. Cey needed a fast finish to bring his 1985 power totals to a respectable 22 homers and 63 RBI, but it seems likely he will be playing less. Ditto for Matthews, who almost had his Sarge stripes removed after a pitiful .235 season. Perhaps Jerry Mumphrey, acquired from Houston, will win an outfield job and Manny Trillo, acquired from San Francisco, will usurp some of Cey's time at third.

The Cubs found the right combination in 1984, with Dernier and Sandberg forming a one-two punch at the top of the order. That magic was gone last year and Cey definitely is in the twilight of an outstanding career. However, Chicago doesn't have offensive problems that a pitching comeback couldn't overcome.

PITCHING: A once-promising staff was demolished by injuries last year. Nobody in the rotation was able to make more than 25 starts and the staff's ace was 11-game winner Dennis Eckersley. Rick Sutcliffe, coming off a Cy Young Award campaign, contributed only 20 starts due to hamstring problems. The prospect of his presence in Chicago for an entire season made the Cubs the 1985 title pick of many observers.

Now, there's skepticism because it is not known how well Sutcliffe (8-8, 3.18), Eckersley (11-7, 3.08), Scott Sanderson (5-6, 3.12) and Steve Trout (9-7, 3.39) will bounce back from their physical ills. What was a solid staff one year ago is now

Ryne Sandberg, a Cub who runneth over foes, had 54 steals.

riddled with question marks. Fortunately, there is room for error because the bullpen is headed by Lee Smith, who had a hand in 40 of the Cubs' 77 victories last year. Only the Expos' Jeff Reardon did better out of the pen than Smith (3.04, 33 saves).

FIELDING: Sandberg won a Gold Glove at second and Durham is a good athlete at first base, but the rest of the Cubs' defense is shaky. Moreland has worked hard to improve his fielding in right, but he's no gazelle. Matthews, always aggressive, is mistake-prone in left. Maybe the reason Dernier committed nine errors in center last year was that his tongue was hanging out from all the running he had to do. Cey is statuesque at third and Dunston is making a lot of errors while developing at short. This is an average defensive team.

OUTLOOK: The Cubs don't look nearly as good as they did one year ago. Jim Frey's 1985 club seemed to have enough going to sustain its 1984 success, but a rash of injuries and advancing age took their toll. Now, it seems like it'll be a struggle for the Cubs to crack the top three spots in the NL East. Any team that is barely better than .500 at home (41-39) is in trouble.

Unless the pitchers stage a dramatic turnaround, the Cubs are more likely to finish around .500 than to contend in 1986. All of a sudden, all that talk about lights for Wrigley Field—a necessity for postseason play—may be moot. You need more than just decent pitching to win in the friendly confines.

CHICAGO CUBS 1986 ROSTER

MANAGER Jim Frey
Coaches—Ruben Amaro, Billy Connors, Johnny Oates, John Vukovich, Don Zimmer

PITCHERS

No.	Name	1985 Club	W-L	IP	SO	ERA	B-T	Ht.	Wt.	Born
32	Abrego, John	Pittsfield	6-6	156	92	2.76	R-R	6-1	185	7/4/62 Corpus Christi, TX
		Chicago (NL)	1-1	24	13	6.38				
48	Baller, Jay	Iowa	8-9	149	119	4.23	R-R	6-6	215	10/6/60 Stayton, OR
		Chicago (NL)	2-3	52	31	3.46				
47	Botelho, Derek	Iowa	11-7	125	94	4.30	R-R	6-2	180	8/2/56 Long Beach, CA
		Chicago (NL)	1-3	44	23	5.32				
41	Brusstar, Warren	Chicago (NL)	4-3	74	34	6.05	R-R	6-3	200	2/2/52 Oakland, CA
43	Eckersley, Dennis	Chicago (NL)	11-7	169	117	3.08	R-R	6-2	195	10/3/54 Oakland, CA
49	Engel, Steve	Pittsfield	3-6	76	52	3.89	R-L	6-0	180	12/31/61 Springdale, OH
		Iowa	4-2	62	53	3.18				
		Chicago (NL)	1-5	51	29	5.57				
31	Fontenot, Ray	Chicago (NL)	6-10	155	70	4.36	L-L	6-0	175	8/8/57 Lake Charles, LA
39	Frazier, George	Chicago (NL)	7-8	76	46	6.39	R-R	6-5	200	10/13/54 Oklahoma City, OK
45	Gumpert, Dave	Iowa	3-4	63	32	4.39	R-R	6-1	190	5/5/58 South Haven, MI
		Chicago (NL)	1-0	10	4	3.48				
51	Hamilton, Carlton	Winston-Salem	11-10	155	152	2.72	L-L	6-2	175	11/4/64 Gary, IN
38	Meridith, Ron	Iowa	4-1	41	28	1.32	L-L	6-0	174	11/26/55 San Pedro, CA
		Chicago (NL)	3-2	46	23	4.47				
35	Parmenter, Gary	Pittsfield	6-5	121	62	2.44	R-R	6-2	190	6/24/62 Bennington, VT
52	Patterson, Reggie	Iowa	8-10	132	78	4.77	L-R	6-4	180	11/7/58 Birmingham, AL
		Chicago (NL)	3-0	39	17	3.00				
44	Ruthven, Dick	Chicago (NL)	4-7	87	26	4.53	R-R	6-3	190	3/27/51 Sacramento, CA
21	Sanderson, Scott	Chicago (NL)	5-6	121	80	3.12	R-R	6-5	200	7/22/56 Dearborn, MI
46	Smith, Lee	Chicago (NL)	7-4	98	112	3.04	R-R	6-6	225	12/4/57 Jamestown, LA
42	Sorensen, Lary	Chicago (NL)	3-7	82	34	4.26	R-R	6-2	205	10/4/55 Detroit, MI
40	Sutcliffe, Rick	Chicago (NL)	8-8	130	102	3.18	L-R	6-7	215	6/21/56 Independence, MO
34	Trout, Steve	Chicago (NL)	9-7	141	44	3.39	L-L	6-4	190	7/30/57 Detroit, MI

CATCHERS

No.	Name	1985 Club	H	HR	RBI	Pct.	B-T	Ht.	Wt.	Born
7	Davis, Jody	Chicago (NL)	112	17	58	.232	R-R	6-3	210	11/12/56 Gainesville, GA
16	Lake, Steve	Chicago (NL)	18	1	11	.151	R-R	6-1	190	3/14/57 Inglewood, CA

INFIELDERS

17	Brumley, Mike	Pittsfield	127	3	58	.276	B-R	5-10	165	4/9/63 Oklahoma City, OK
11	Cey, Ron	Chicago (NL)	116	22	63	.232	R-R	5-9	185	2/15/48 Tacoma, WA
12	Dunston, Shawon	Iowa	73	2	28	.268	R-R	6-1	175	3/21/63 Brooklyn, NY
		Chicago (NL)	65	4	18	.260				
10	Durham, Leon	Chicago (NL)	153	21	75	.282	L-L	6-2	210	7/31/57 Cincinnati, OH
18	Hebner, Richie	Chicago (NL)	26	3	22	.217	L-R	6-1	200	11/26/47 Norwood, MA
23	Sandberg, Ryne	Chicago (NL)	186	26	83	.305	R-R	6-2	180	9/18/59 Spokane, WA
28	Speier, Chris	Chicago (NL)	53	4	24	.243	R-R	6-1	180	6/28/50 Alameda, CA
—	Trillo, Manny	San Francisco	101	3	25	.224	R-R	6-1	165	12/25/50 Venezuela
26	Woods, Tony	Pittsfield	60	2	29	.248	R-R	6-2	185	1/6/62 Merced, CA
		Iowa	17	1	4	.230				

OUTFIELDERS

29	Bernstine, Nehames	Pittsfield	63	1	17	.312	B-R	5-10	175	11/26/60 Las Vegas, NV
27	Bosley, Thad	Chicago (NL)	59	7	27	.328	L-L	6-3	175	9/17/56 Oceanside, CA
24	Dayett, Brian	Iowa	14	1	11	.378	R-R	5-10	180	1/22/57 New London, CT
		Chicago (NL)	6	1	4	.231				
20	Dernier, Bob	Chicago (NL)	119	1	21	.254	R-R	6-0	165	1/5/57 Kansas City, MO
30	Jackson, Darrin	Pittsfield	82	3	30	.252	R-R	6-1	170	8/22/63 Los Angeles, CA
		Chicago (NL)	1	0	0	.091				
		Iowa	7	0	1	.175				
15	Lopes, Davey	Chicago (NL)	78	11	44	.284	R-R	5-9	170	5/3/46 E. Providence, RI
1	Martinez, Dave	Winston-Salem	132	5	54	.342	L-L	5-10	150	9/26/64 New York, NY
36	Matthews, Gary	Chicago (NL)	70	13	40	.235	R-R	6-3	205	7/5/50 San Fernando, CA
6	Moreland, Keith	Chicago (NL)	180	14	106	.307	R-R	6-0	200	5/2/54 Dallas, TX
—	Mumphrey, Jerry	Houston	123	8	61	.277	B-R	6-2	200	9/9/52 Tyler, TX
25	Woods, Gary	Chicago (NL)	20	0	4	.244	R-R	6-2	190	7/20/53 Santa Barbara, CA

CUB PROFILES

RYNE SANDBERG 26 6-2 180 Bats R Throws R

His 1985 season paled in comparison to his NL MVP campaign of 1984, but that was to be expected . . . "Ryno" overcame a terrible start (0-for-13, 1-for-20 and 16-for-81) to rank among league leaders in batting, runs, steals, hits, homers and slugging percentage last year . . . Turned around his season with a .311 May . . . Got up to .291 by All-Star break . . . Erupted in July, hitting .355 with six homers, 20 RBI and 10 steals, then continued his blazing batting down the stretch . . . Batted .308 with 20 RBI in August and .347 with 20 RBI and 13 steals in September . . . Best offensive second baseman in baseball and an outstanding defensive player, too . . . Born Sept. 18, 1959, in Spokane, Wash. . . . A find by Phillies in 20th round of June 1978 draft . . . But Phils didn't know what they had, stupidly swapping him to Cubs along with Larry Bowa for Ivan DeJesus prior to 1982 season . . . Chicago GM Dallas Green's biggest coup.

Year	Club	Pos.	G	AB	R	H	2B	3B	HR	RBI	SB	Avg.
1981	Philadelphia	SS-2B	13	6	2	1	0	0	0	0	0	.167
1982	Chicago (NL)	3B-2B	156	635	103	172	33	5	7	54	32	.271
1983	Chicago (NL)	2B-SS	158	633	94	165	25	4	8	48	37	.261
1984	Chicago (NL)	2B	156	636	114	200	36	19	19	84	32	.314
1985	Chicago (NL)	2B	153	609	113	186	31	6	26	83	54	.305
	Totals		636	2519	426	724	125	34	60	269	155	.287

LEON DURHAM 28 6-2 210 Bats L Throws L

Like Ron Cey, "Bull" was rapped for his failures in the clutch, but his final stats were respectable enough . . . Batted .327 in June . . . Hasn't met high expectations of Cubs' fans since local favorite Bill Buckner was traded to open up first base for him . . . But he has been a solid, productive player when healthy . . . Born July 31, 1957, in Cincinnati . . . Drafted in first round by Cardinals in June 1976 . . . Tabbed as future superstar while in St. Louis system . . . Named American Association Rookie of the Year after hitting .310 with 23 homers for Springfield (AA) in 1979 . . . Was most important of three players acquired by Cubs in deal that sent Bruce Sutter to Cardinals prior to 1981 season

... Switched from outfield to first base, where he appears to be more comfortable.

Year	Club	Pos.	G	AB	R	H	2B	3B	HR	RBI	SB	Avg.
1980	St. Louis	OF-1B	96	303	42	82	15	4	8	42	8	.271
1981	Chicago (NL)	OF-1B	87	328	42	95	14	6	10	35	25	.290
1982	Chicago (NL)	OF-1B	148	539	84	168	33	7	22	90	28	.312
1983	Chicago (NL)	OF-1B	100	337	58	87	18	8	12	55	12	.258
1984	Chicago (NL)	1B	137	473	86	132	30	4	23	96	16	.279
1985	Chicago (NL)	1B	153	542	58	153	32	2	21	75	7	.282
	Totals		721	2522	370	717	142	31	96	393	96	.284

KEITH MORELAND 31 6-0 200 Bats R Throws R

One of the few Cubs to avoid a collapse last year, he responded to adversity with his finest season ... Ranked among NL leaders in four categories, including RBI ... Batted .315 in May and .311 in June to enter All-Star break with .301 average ... Did even better in second half, sparked by .354 September that included four homers and a remarkable 32 RBI ... Born May 2, 1954, in Dallas ... Attended Texas, where he was a starting defensive back as a sophomore and an All-American third baseman ... Selected by Phillies in seventh round of June 1975 draft ... Began catching in minors in 1976 ... Traded to Cubs along with Dickie Noles and Dan Larson for Mike Krukow prior to 1982 season ... Lack of speed hurts his fielding in right, but he has worked hard to become adequate defensively ... Led club in game-winning RBI with 12 last season.

Year	Club	Pos.	G	AB	R	H	2B	3B	HR	RBI	SB	Avg.
1978	Philadelphia	C	1	2	0	0	0	0	0	0	0	.000
1979	Philadelphia	C	14	48	3	18	3	2	0	8	0	.375
1980	Philadelphia	C-3B-OF	62	159	13	50	8	0	4	29	3	.314
1981	Philadelphia	C-3B-1B-OF	61	196	16	50	7	0	6	37	1	.255
1982	Chicago (NL)	C-OF-3B	138	476	50	124	17	2	15	68	0	.261
1983	Chicago (NL)	OF-C	154	533	76	161	30	3	16	70	0	.302
1984	Chicago (NL)	OF-1B-3B-C	140	495	59	138	17	3	16	80	1	.279
1985	Chicago (NL)	OF-1B-3B	161	587	74	180	30	3	14	106	12	.307
	Totals		731	2496	291	721	112	13	71	398	17	.289

BOB DERNIER 29 6-0 165 Bats R Throws R

His work as a leadoff man made Cubs click in 1984, but June foot surgery slowed him and the Cubs down last season ... Another steal from the Phillies ... Helped Ryne Sandberg to become NL MVP by consistently getting on base in front of him as Cubs won NL East title in 1984 ... Born Jan. 5, 1957, in Kansas City, Mo. ... Signed as free agent by Phillies in 1977 ... Stole more than 70 bases in three different minor-league seasons . . . Acquired by Cubs along with Gary Matthews and Porfi Altamirano for Bill Campbell and Mike Diaz prior to 1984 season . . . As a first-year pro for Helena (A) in 1978, he was a third baseman playing alongside a shortstop named Sandberg . . . Became Phillies' best base-stealer in more than 70 years, but didn't bloom as a hitter until he became Cubs' center fielder.

Year	Club	Pos.	G	AB	R	H	2B	3B	HR	RBI	SB	Avg.
1980	Philadelphia	OF	10	7	5	4	0	0	0	1	3	.571
1981	Philadelphia	OF	10	4	0	3	0	0	0	0	2	.750
1982	Philadelphia	OF	122	370	56	92	10	2	4	21	42	.249
1983	Philadelphia	OF	122	221	41	51	10	0	1	15	35	.231
1984	Chicago (NL)	OF	143	536	94	149	26	5	3	32	45	.278
1985	Chicago (NL)	OF	121	469	63	119	20	3	1	21	31	.254
	Totals		528	1607	259	418	66	10	9	90	158	.260

JODY DAVIS 29 6-3 210 **Bats R Throws R**

Internal disorder struck him in June and led to horrible second half . . . His RBI production fell off sharply, but, when he's healthy, he ranks with the best-hitting catchers in baseball . . . Injuries and illness retarded his progress in minors, but were not a factor in his major-league career until 1985 . . . Born Nov. 12, 1956, in Gainesville, Ga. . . . Mets' third-round draft choice in January 1976 draft . . . Plucked from Cardinals' system by Cubs in December 1980 draft of minor leaguers . . . Tied Ron Cey for club home-run lead with 24 in 1983, the most by a Cubs' catcher since 1930 . . . Lost more than 50 pounds following ulcer surgery early in 1980 . . . Offensive ability always has surpassed his defensive skills, but he has made marked improvement behind the dish, improving his release to keep opposition base-stealers honest.

Year	Club	Pos.	G	AB	R	H	2B	3B	HR	RBI	SB	Avg.
1981	Chicago (NL)	C	56	180	14	46	5	1	4	21	0	.256
1982	Chicago (NL)	C	130	418	41	109	20	2	12	52	0	.261
1983	Chicago (NL)	C	151	510	56	138	31	2	24	84	0	.271
1984	Chicago (NL)	C	150	523	55	134	24	2	19	94	5	.256
1985	Chicago (NL)	C	142	482	47	112	30	0	17	58	1	.232
	Totals		629	2113	213	539	110	7	76	309	6	.256

RON CEY 38 5-9 185 **Bats R Throws R**

Appeared to be washed up during miserable start, but rallied to finish with respectable power figures . . . Was hitting .211 with 12 homers and 27 RBI at All-Star break, but a .340 August got him going . . . Criticized for failures in clutch and immobility at third base . . . But "The Penguin" has been a tough out most of his career . . . Was a driving force behind Cubs' pennant push in 1984 . . . Born Feb. 15, 1948, in Tacoma, Wash. . . . Attended Washington State . . . Dodgers' third-round draft pick in June 1968 . . . Reached majors to stay after amassing total of 226 RBI in two Triple-A seasons . . . Besides providing solid long-ball production, he also played well at third base . . . In 1979, he tied NL record by making only nine errors, the fewest by a third baseman . . . Named to NL All-Star team from 1974-79.

Year	Club	Pos.	G	AB	R	H	2B	3B	HR	RBI	SB	Avg.
1971	Los Angeles	PH	2	2	0	0	0	0	0	0	0	.000
1972	Los Angeles	3B	11	37	3	10	1	0	1	3	0	.270
1973	Los Angeles	3B	152	507	60	124	18	4	15	80	1	.245
1974	Los Angeles	3B	159	577	88	151	20	2	18	97	1	.262
1975	Los Angeles	3B	158	566	72	160	29	2	25	101	5	.283
1976	Los Angeles	3B	145	502	69	139	18	3	23	80	0	.277
1977	Los Angeles	3B	153	564	77	136	22	3	30	110	3	.241
1978	Los Angeles	3B	159	555	84	150	32	0	23	84	2	.270
1979	Los Angeles	3B	150	487	77	137	20	1	28	81	3	.281
1980	Los Angeles	3B	157	551	81	140	25	0	28	77	2	.254
1981	Los Angeles	3B	85	312	42	90	15	2	13	50	0	.288
1982	Los Angeles	3B	150	556	62	141	23	1	24	79	3	.254
1983	Chicago (NL)	3B	159	581	73	160	33	1	24	90	0	.275
1984	Chicago (NL)	3B	146	505	71	121	27	0	25	97	3	.240
1985	Chicago (NL)	3B	145	500	64	116	18	2	22	63	1	.232
	Totals		1931	6802	923	1775	301	21	299	1092	24	.261

JERRY MUMPHREY 33 6-2 200 Bats S Throws R

Departed Houston in December in outfielder exchange for Billy Hatcher and a player to be named . . . Posted his lowest average since 1978, but remained a productive hitter in 1985 . . . Earned first All-Star Game berth in 1984 . . . Career was rejuvenated when he was traded to Astros by Yankees for Omar Moreno, Aug. 10, 1983 . . . Was batting .262 with New York and jumped to .336 with Astros . . . Born Sept. 9, 1952, in Tyler, Tex. . . . Selected by Cardinals in fourth round of June 1971 draft . . . Speed was his top asset in early years . . . Had a career-high 52 steals for Padres in 1980.

Year	Club	Pos.	G	AB	R	H	2B	3B	HR	RBI	SB	Avg.
1974	St. Louis	OF	5	2	2	0	0	0	0	0	0	.000
1975	St. Louis	OF	11	16	2	6	2	0	0	1	0	.375
1976	St. Louis	OF	112	384	51	99	15	5	1	26	22	.258
1977	St. Louis	OF	145	463	73	133	20	10	2	38	22	.287
1978	St. Louis	OF	125	367	41	96	13	4	2	37	14	.262
1979	St. Louis	OF	124	339	53	100	10	3	3	32	8	.295
1980	San Diego	OF	160	564	61	168	24	3	4	59	52	.298
1981	New York (AL)	OF	80	319	44	98	11	5	6	32	13	.307
1982	New York (AL)	OF	123	477	76	143	24	10	9	68	11	.300
1983	New York (AL)	OF	83	267	41	70	11	4	7	36	2	.262
1983	Houston	OF	44	143	17	48	10	2	1	17	5	.336
1984	Houston	OF	151	524	66	152	20	3	9	83	15	.290
1985	Houston	OF	130	444	52	123	25	2	8	61	6	.277
	Totals		1293	4309	579	1236	185	51	52	490	170	.287

STEVE TROUT 28 6-4 190 — Bats L Throws L

Another injury victim, following a great start . . . Was 4-1 with a 1.51 ERA in April, but he barely equalled that win total the rest of the way . . . Like Rick Sutcliffe, he signed a hefty contract to remain with Cubs after testing free-agent market following excellent 1984 campaign . . . Capped his finest season with victory in NLCS two years ago . . . Born July 30, 1957, in Detroit . . . Father Dizzy was a major-league pitcher . . . Nicknamed "Rainbow" in high school . . . First-round pick of White Sox in June 1976 draft . . . Joined crosstown Cubs with Warren Brusstar in deal for Dick Tidrow, Randy Martz, Pat Tabler and Scott Fletcher prior to 1983 season . . . Had been 1-5 in NL debut season before winning half of his last 18 decisions.

Year	Club	G	IP	W	L	Pct.	SO	BB	H	ERA
1978	Chicago (AL)	4	22	3	0	1.000	11	11	19	4.09
1979	Chicago (AL)	34	155	11	8	.579	76	59	165	3.89
1980	Chicago (AL)	32	200	9	16	.360	89	49	229	3.69
1981	Chicago (AL)	20	125	8	7	.533	54	38	122	3.46
1982	Chicago (AL)	25	120⅓	6	9	.400	62	50	130	4.26
1983	Chicago (NL)	34	180	10	14	.417	80	59	217	4.65
1984	Chicago (NL)	32	190	13	7	.650	81	59	205	3.41
1985	Chicago (NL)	24	140⅔	9	7	.563	44	63	142	3.39
	Totals	205	1133	69	68	.504	497	388	1229	3.83

LEE SMITH 28 6-6 225 — Bats R Throws R

NL's second-best reliever last year, behind Expos' Jeff Reardon . . . Allowed only one run in 10⅔ innings in April, striking out 18, walking one and saving five games . . . Slipped to 2.49 ERA in May, but was 3-0 with seven saves . . . Had seven saves in July and five in August en route to 33 for season . . . Finished a close second to Reardon in Rolaids relief competition with 76 points, two behind leader . . . Born Dec. 4, 1957, in Jamestown, La. . . . Outstanding high-school basketball player who went 15-1 in his last two years as a prep pitcher, striking out 124 in 53 innings as a senior . . . Cubs' second round selection in June 1975 draft . . . His blazing fastball and his size make him an intimidating guy to face . . . Has 113 career saves after notching 66 in last two seasons.

Year	Club	G	IP	W	L	Pct.	SO	BB	H	ERA
1980	Chicago (NL)	18	22	2	0	1.000	17	14	21	2.86
1981	Chicago (NL)	40	67	3	6	.333	50	31	57	3.49
1982	Chicago (NL)	72	117	2	5	.286	99	37	105	2.69
1983	Chicago (NL)	66	103⅓	4	10	.286	91	41	70	1.65
1984	Chicago (NL)	69	101	9	7	.563	86	35	98	3.65
1985	Chicago (NL)	65	97⅔	7	4	.636	112	32	87	3.04
	Totals	330	508	27	32	.458	455	190	438	2.85

DENNIS ECKERSLEY 31 6-2 195 Bats R Throws R

Supplanted Rick Sutcliffe as ace following hot start, but also succumbed to injury bug, missing 11 starts with midseason elbow problems... Posted 3-1 record and 1.85 ERA in April, continuing work that made him an outstanding acquisition for 1984 stretch run... Acquired from Boston for Bill Buckner, May 25, 1984... Made trade look bad with 1-5 start in NL, but rallied with 9-3 mark and 2.06 ERA in final three months of 1984... Born Oct. 3, 1954, in Oakland... Indians' third-round pick in June 1972 draft... Made jump from Double-A to majors after posting 14-3 record for San Antonio in 1974... In 1978, he became first Red Sox hurler to win 20 games in seven years... Fired a no-hitter vs. California for Cleveland in 1977.

Year	Club	G	IP	W	L	Pct.	SO	BB	H	ERA
1975	Cleveland	34	187	13	7	.650	152	90	147	2.60
1976	Cleveland	36	199	13	12	.520	200	78	155	3.44
1977	Cleveland	33	247	14	13	.519	191	54	214	3.53
1978	Boston	35	268	20	8	.714	162	71	258	2.99
1979	Boston	33	247	17	10	.630	150	59	234	2.99
1980	Boston	30	198	12	14	.462	121	44	188	4.27
1981	Boston	23	154	9	8	.529	79	35	160	4.27
1982	Boston	33	224⅓	13	13	.500	127	43	228	3.73
1983	Boston	28	176⅓	9	13	.409	77	39	223	5.61
1984	Boston	9	64⅔	4	4	.500	33	13	71	5.01
1984	Chicago (NL)	24	160⅓	10	8	.556	81	36	152	3.03
1985	Chicago (NL)	25	169⅓	11	7	.611	117	19	145	3.08
	Totals	343	2295	145	117	.553	1490	581	2175	3.59

RICK SUTCLIFFE 29 6-7 215 Bats L Throws R

Never regained Cy Young magic of 1984 in injury-filled season, but still topped Cubs' starters with three shutouts and had an excellent ERA... Missed three starts early, but came back with 2-2 mark and 1.62 ERA in June before missing most of the second half with severe hamstring pull... Unquestionably the reason the Cubs won NL East title in 1984 after being acquired from Cleveland in June deal that sent Joe Carter and Mel Hall to Indians... Lost only once in 20 games after trade and became third Cubs' pitcher ever to win Cy Young honors... Won 14 straight games to end season and was 1-1 in NLCS... Born June 21, 1956, in Independence, Mo.... Prep All-American in football and basketball... Dodgers' first-round pick in June 1974 draft . . . Named NL Rookie of the Year in 1979 . . . Re-signed with Cubs as a free agent following 1984 campaign.

Year	Club	G	IP	W	L	Pct.	SO	BB	H	ERA
1976	Los Angeles.	1	5	0	0	.000	3	1	2	0.00
1978	Los Angeles.	2	2	0	0	.000	0	1	2	0.00
1979	Los Angeles.	39	242	17	10	.630	117	97	217	3.46
1980	Los Angeles.	42	110	3	9	.250	59	55	122	5.56
1981	Los Angeles.	14	47	2	2	.500	16	20	41	4.02
1982	Cleveland	34	216	14	8	.636	142	98	174	2.96
1983	Cleveland	36	243⅓	17	11	.607	160	102	251	4.29
1984	Cleveland	15	94⅓	4	5	.444	58	46	111	5.15
1984	Chicago (NL)	20	150⅓	16	1	.941	155	39	123	2.69
1985	Chicago (NL)	20	130	8	8	.500	102	44	119	3.18
	Totals	223	1240	81	54	.600	812	503	1162	3.73

TOP PROSPECT

JAY BALLER 25 6-6 215 **Bats R Throws R**

Because young shortstop Shawon Dunston is now more of a fixture than a prospect, the Cubs' best young comer appears to be this late-season pitching surprise who was acquired from the Indians . . . Last season constituted a major comeback after he had struggled to combined 5-14 mark for Charleston (AAA) and Buffalo (AA) in 1983 . . . Born Oct. 6, 1960, in Stayton, Ore. . . . Phillies' third-round pick in June 1979 draft . . . Led Eastern League with 2.68 ERA for Reading (AA) in 1982 before being swapped to Indians with four others for Von Hayes after that season . . . Went 8-9 with 4.23 ERA for Iowa (AAA) in 1985, then went 2-3 with one save and 3.46 ERA for Cubs.

MANAGER JIM FREY: Last year was quite a comedown following startling success of 1984, but the reason for the Cubs' collapse was a rash of injuries to pitching staff, not his managing . . . His 1984 squad was franchise's biggest winner since 1945 as Cubs ended 39-year title drought by winning NL East . . . Was named 1984 NL Manager of the Year . . . Named Cubs' skipper following fifth-place finish in 1983 and brought a Midas touch to club . . . Managed the Royals to AL pennant in 1980, but was fired Aug. 31, 1981, although club was only one-half game out of first place during second half of strike-shortened season . . .

He's in good company, considering Whitey Herzog also was bounced by Kansas City . . . Born May 26, 1931, in Cleveland . . . Schoolboy chum of Don Zimmer at Western High in Cincinnati, which is also Pete Rose's alma mater . . . Attended Ohio State before embarking on successful minor-league career that included two batting titles and saw him post a lifetime .302 average . . . Texas League MVP for Tulsa in 1957 . . . Never played in majors . . . Spent 15 years in Orioles' organization . . . Has 300-254 record as major-league manager after 77-84 finish last year.

GREATEST SHORTSTOP

Unlike the Pirates' legendary Honus Wagner, the Cubs' greatest shortstop was a man who fielded his position well and was a slugger, too. Ernie Banks did it all for Chicago. His home-run accomplishments disguised the fact he won three fielding titles at shortstop prior to his permanent shift to first base in 1962.

Banks brought a new dimension to the position with his MVP performances of the late '50s. No other shortstop had a year like the one Ernie did in 1958, when he led the league with 47 home runs, 129 RBI and a .614 slugging percentage. One year later, he had a league-leading 143 RBI and, for good measure, topped National League shortstops with a .985 fielding percentage, making only 12 errors.

"Mr. Cub" was moved to first base to lengthen his career, but was at his best as a lethal blend of power and quickness during his early shortstop days. Banks had an exuberance for the game unmatched by most players and it added to his luster as a performer.

ALL-TIME CUB SEASON RECORDS

BATTING: Rogers Hornsby, .380, 1929
HRs: Hack Wilson, 56, 1930
RBIs: Hack Wilson, 190, 1930
STEALS: Frank Chance, 67, 1903
WINS: Mordecai Brown, 29, 1908
STRIKEOUTS: Ferguson Jenkins, 274, 1970

MONTREAL EXPOS

TEAM DIRECTORY: Chairman: Charles Bronfman; Pres.-Chief Exec. Off.: John McHale; VP-Play. Dev.: Jim Fanning; VP-GM: Murray Cook; VP-Baseball Adm.: Bill Stoneman; Group VP: Pierre Gauvreau; Dirs. Pub. Rel.: Monique Giroux, Richard Griffin; Mgr.: Bob (Buck) Rodgers. Home: Olympic Stadium (59,149). Field distances: 325, l.f. line; 375, l.c.; 404, c.f.; 375, r.c.; 325, r.f. line. Spring training: West Palm Beach, Fla.

SCOUTING REPORT

HITTING: Andre Dawson's late-season surge gives hope that the Montreal offense will be formidable once again in 1986. If "The Hawk" can put it together for an entire season, Terry Francona can stay healthy and Mitch Webster and Hubie Brooks show their 1985 punch was no fluke, the Expos should be flying high come October.

Only a few years ago, Dawson (23 homers, 91 RBI) was regarded as the finest player in the league. Knee problems have

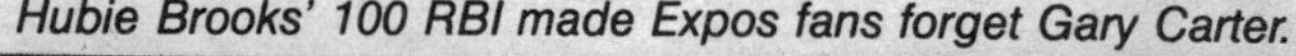

Hubie Brooks' 100 RBI made Expos fans forget Gary Carter.

reduced his effectiveness, but he still has a star quality that this club desperately needs to complement the all-around excellence of Tim Raines (.320, 70 steals).

Brooks surprised with 100 RBI in his Montreal debut and if he, Dawson, Raines and Tim Wallach (22 homers, 81 RBI) all click, this club will be operating on all cylinders. The Expos seem to have a nice balance of power and speed and, if all the components fit, their attack could be vastly improved this season.

PITCHING: The Expos enjoyed success last year despite injuries to two of their best pitchers, Charlie Lea and Joe Hesketh. If they bounce back, Montreal has what it takes to challenge the Mets. Lea, a potential 20-game winner, did not throw an inning in 1985 and Hesketh was sidelined following a 10-5 start.

Still, there was sufficient depth to overcome the injuries. Bryn Smith (18-5, 2.91) developed into a big winner, Tim Burke (9-4, 8 saves) was a rookie relief sensation and Jeff Reardon was the most prolific stopper in the league with his club-record 41 saves. With the addition of promising Jay Tibbs (10-16, 3.92) from the Reds in the Bill Gullickson trade, this is a potentially outstanding staff.

FIELDING: The Expos placed just behind the Cardinals and the Mets in the NL defensive rankings last year and should improve once second baseman Vance Law and shortstop Brooks become more comfortable as a double-play combination. Law committed only 10 errors in his NL debut last year and Brooks . . . well, he's in the lineup for his bat. Gold Gloves went to third baseman Wallach and to Dawson. The catching spot remains a problem, even with the acquisition of former Red Dann Bilardello.

OUTLOOK: This is the sleeper team of the NL East this season because the Expos' pitching staff could be awesome if healthy. The Mets' staff is more spectacular because of its prodigious strikeout total and Gooden, but if Lea and Hesketh can bounce back, nobody will be able to match the quality depth of the Expos. They can form a rotation of Lea, Hesketh, Smith, Tibbs and David Palmer, who may be ready to fulfill his promise.

There's not a weak link among them and they're backed by a stout bullpen. With that kind of pitching and a formidable attack, Buck Rodgers' Expos can't help but finish better than last year's 84-77. To have a shot at a division title, however, they're going to have to improve their road performance (40-40), do better against the West (36-36) and find a way to win one-run (23-24) and extra-inning (11-10) games.

MONTREAL EXPOS 1986 ROSTER

MANAGER Buck Rodgers
Coaches—Larry Bearnarth, Ron Hansen, Joe Kerrigan, Rick Renick, Bobby Winkles

PITCHERS

No.	Name	1985 Club	W-L	IP	SO	ERA	B-T	Ht.	Wt.	Born
44	Burke, Tim	Montreal	9-4	120	87	2.39	R-R	6-3	205	2/19/59 Omaha, NE
54	Dopson, John	Jacksonville	3-0	32	20	1.11	L-R	6-4	220	7/14/63 Baltimore, MD
		Indianapolis	4-7	95	48	3.78				
		Montreal	0-2	13	4	11.08				
38	Hesketh, Joe	Montreal	10-5	155	113	2.49	L-L	6-2	170	2/15/59 Lackawanna, NY
59	Holman, Brian	W. Palm Beach	9-9	143	103	3.96	R-R	6-4	185	1/25/65 Denver, CO
53	Lea, Charlie	Montreal	Disabled list				R-R	6-4	205	12/25/56 France
37	McGaffigan, Andy	Denver	11-5	107	91	2.95	R-R	6-3	195	10/25/56 W. Palm Beach, FL
		Cincinnati	3-3	94	83	3.72				
32	O'Connor, Jack	Indianapolis	3-4	69	63	4.72	L-L	6-3	210	6/2/58 Yucca Valley, CA
		Montreal	0-2	24	16	4.94				
46	*Palmer, David	Montreal	7-10	136	106	3.71	R-R	6-1	205	10/19/57 Glens Falls, NY
—	Parrett, Jeff	Stockton	7-4	127	120	2.75	R-R	6-3	185	8/26/61 Indianapolis, IN
41	Reardon, Jeff	Montreal	2-8	88	67	3.18	R-R	6-1	195	10/1/55 Dalton, MA
40	Riley, George	Phoenix	6-7	89	64	4.84	L-L	6-4	200	10/6/56 Philadelphia, PA
42	Roberge, Bert	Indianapolis	0-0	2	2	4.50	R-R	6-3	195	10/3/54 Lewiston, ME
—	Sanchez, Luis	California	2-0	61	34	5.72	R-R	6-2	215	8/24/53 Venezuela
		Edmonton	0-0	5	4	10.13				
51	St. Claire, Randy	Indianapolis	0-1	20	11	1.83	R-R	6-2	195	8/23/60 Glens Falls, NY
		Montreal	5-3	69	25	3.93				
43	Schatzeder, Dan	Indianapolis	0-0	3	3	0.00	L-L	5-11	204	12/1/54 Elmhurst, IL
		Montreal	3-5	104	64	3.80				
48	Sebra, Bob	Oklahoma City	10-6	140	84	3.80	R-R	6-2	195	12/11/61 Ridgewood, NJ
		Texas	0-2	20	13	7.52				
28	Smith, Bryn	Montreal	18-5	222	127	2.91	R-R	6-2	205	8/11/55 Marietta, GA
58	Stoll, Rich	Indianapolis	9-9	146	57	4.08	R-R	5-11	180	9/23/62 Williamsport, IN
—	Stuper, John	Cincinnati	8-5	99	38	4.55	R-R	6-2	200	5/9/57 Butler, PA
—	Tibbs, Jay	Denver	1-2	32	15	2.27	R-R	6-1	180	1/4/62 Birmingham, AL
		Cincinnati	10-16	218	98	3.92				
33	Youmans, Floyd	Jacksonville	7-3	86	86	3.36	R-R	6-0	190	5/11/64 Tampa, FL
		Indianapolis	3-2	38	38	3.11				
		Montreal	4-3	77	54	2.45				

CATCHERS

No.	Name	1985 Club	H	HR	RBI	Pct.	B-T	Ht.	Wt.	Born
11	Bilardello, Dann	Denver	57	10	37	.242	R-R	6-0	190	5/26/59 Santa Cruz, CA
		Cincinnati	17	1	9	.167				
20	Fitzgerald, Mike	Montreal	61	5	34	.207	R-R	6-0	198	7/13/60 Long Beach, CA
14	Yost, Ned	Indianapolis	70	2	24	.263	R-R	6-1	185	8/19/55 Eureka, CA
		Montreal	2	0	0	.182				

INFIELDERS

No.	Name	1985 Club	H	HR	RBI	Pct.	B-T	Ht.	Wt.	Born
17	Barnes, Skeeter	Den.-Ind.	95	8	63	.279	R-R	5-10	180	3/7/57 Cincinnati, OH
		Montreal	4	0	0	.154				
7	Brooks, Hubie	Montreal	163	13	100	.269	R-R	6-0	188	9/24/56 Los Angeles, CA
16	Francona, Terry	Montreal	75	2	31	.267	L-L	6-0	175	4/22/59 Aberdeen, SD
12	Galarraga, Andres	Indianapolis	118	25	87	.269	R-R	6-3	230	6/18/61 Venezuela
		Montreal	14	2	4	.187				
19	Gonzales, Rene	Indianapolis	78	0	25	.230	R-R	6-2	180	9/3/61 Austin, TX
56	Hocutt, Mike	Jacksonville	129	28	92	.261	L-R	6-2	198	9/11/61 Laporte, IN
2	Law, Vance	Montreal	138	10	52	.266	R-R	6-2	190	10/1/56 Boise, ID
6	Manrique, Fred	Indianapolis	98	8	37	.239	R-R	6-1	175	11/5/61 Venezuela
		Montreal	4	1	1	.308				
4	Newman, Al	Indianapolis	85	0	23	.282	B-R	5-8	175	6/30/60 Kansas City, MO
		Montreal	5	0	1	.172				
57	Rivera, Luis	Jacksonville	129	16	72	.240	R-R	5-9	165	3/1/64 Puerto Rico
24	Thompson, Scot	SF-Mon.	32	0	10	.224	L-L	6-2	200	12/7/55 Grove City, PA
29	Wallach, Tim	Montreal	140	22	81	.260	R-R	6-3	200	9/14/57 Huntington Park, CA
1	*Washington, U. L.	Montreal	46	1	17	.249	B-R	5-11	175	10/27/60 Stringtown, OK

OUTFIELDERS

No.	Name	1985 Club	H	HR	RBI	Pct.	B-T	Ht.	Wt.	Born
10	Dawson, Andre	Montreal	135	23	91	.255	R-R	6-3	195	7/10/54 Miami, FL
22	Frobel, Doug	Indianapolis	21	2	11	.284	L-R	6-3	191	6/6/59 Canada
		Pit.-Mon.	25	1	11	.189				
56	Moore, Bill	Jacksonville	132	33	104	.259	R-L	6-1	185	10/6/60 Los Angeles, CA
30	Raines, Tim	Montreal	184	11	41	.320	B-R	5-8	178	9/16/59 Sanford, FL
23	Webster, Mitch	Toronto	0	0	0	.000	B-L	6-1	185	5/16/59 Larned, KS
		Syracuse	52	3	23	.280				
		Montreal	58	11	30	.274				
3	Winningham, Herm	Indianapolis	6	0	2	.167	L-R	5-11	175	12/1/61 Orangeburg, SC
		Montreal	74	3	21	.237				
5	Wohlford, Jim	Montreal	24	1	15	.192	R-R	5-10	180	2/28/51 Visalia, CA

*Free agent unsigned at press time

EXPO PROFILES

HUBIE BROOKS 29 6-0 188 **Bats R Throws R**

Achieved a rarity for a shortstop with 100-RBI season in his Montreal debut, softening loss of Gary Carter's potent bat . . . Started fast with new club, batting .310 in April . . . Had 21 RBI and .313 average in August . . . Deal that sent Carter to Mets following 1984 season also brought Floyd Youmans, Mike Fitzgerald and Herm Winningham to Expos, but this guy alone matched Carter's RBI production in 1985 . . . Led Expos in game-winning RBI with 13 last season . . . A two-time All-American as outfielder and shortstop at Arizona State, he set school record with .396 career average . . . Born Sept. 24, 1956, in Los Angeles . . . Drafted six times—including by Expos—before signing with Mets as their first-round pick in June 1978 . . . Enjoyed sensational start in majors, batting above .300 in his first two seasons with Mets . . . Reluctantly agreed to shift to shortstop from third base late in 1984 season, a move that dramatically increased his market value . . . Has proven adequate defensively at shortstop, silencing critics.

Year	Club	Pos.	G	AB	R	H	2B	3B	HR	RBI	SB	Avg.
1980	New York (NL)	3B	24	81	8	25	2	1	1	10	1	.309
1981	New York (NL)	3B-OF-SS	98	358	34	110	21	2	4	38	9	.307
1982	New York (NL)	3B	126	457	40	114	21	2	2	40	6	.249
1983	New York (NL)	3B-2B	150	586	53	147	18	4	5	58	6	.251
1984	New York (NL)	3B-SS	153	561	61	159	23	2	16	73	6	.283
1985	Montreal	SS	156	605	67	163	34	7	13	100	6	.269
	Totals		707	2648	263	718	119	18	41	319	34	.271

ANDRE DAWSON 31 6-3 195 **Bats R Throws R**

Right fielder used a fast finish to salvage what would have been a terrible year . . . His late spree prompted some re-evaluation of his future . . . Knee injuries have kept "The Hawk" from superstardom, but when he's hot, look out . . . Closing in on Gary Carter for top spot on Expos' all-time home-run list . . . Batted .329 in April before midseason slump . . . Recovered with .288 average and 23 RBI in August . . . On Sept. 24 in Chicago, he homered for the fourth straight game and had six RBI in the fifth inning, tying a major-league record . . . Finished that game with three homers and eight RBI . . . Born July 10, 1954, in

Miami . . . Attended Florida A&M and was an 11th-round pick of Expos in June 1976 draft . . . Had 12 game-winning RBI last season.

Year	Club	Pos.	G	AB	R	H	2B	3B	HR	RBI	SB	Avg.
1976	Montreal	OF	24	85	9	20	4	1	0	7	1	.235
1977	Montreal	OF	139	525	64	148	26	9	19	65	21	.282
1978	Montreal	OF	157	609	84	154	24	8	25	72	28	.253
1979	Montreal	OF	155	639	90	176	24	12	25	92	35	.275
1980	Montreal	OF	151	577	96	178	41	7	17	87	34	.308
1981	Montreal	OF	103	394	71	119	21	3	24	64	26	.302
1982	Montreal	OF	148	608	107	183	37	7	23	83	39	.301
1983	Montreal	OF	159	633	104	189	36	10	32	113	25	.299
1984	Montreal	OF	138	533	73	132	23	6	17	86	13	.248
1985	Montreal	OF	139	529	65	135	27	2	23	91	13	.255
	Totals		1313	5132	763	1434	263	65	205	760	235	.279

TIM RAINES 26 5-8 178 — Bats S Throws R

Left fielder reinforced status as one of the premier all-around players in the game last year, ranking among NL leaders in seven offensive categories . . . Finished second in stolen bases with 70, but theft percentage was all-time high . . . Had an awesome finish after taking .295 mark into All-Star break . . . Hottest hitter in NL during second half, batting .346 in June, .390 in August and .319 in September . . . Born Sept. 16, 1959, in Sanford, Fla. . . . Expos' fifth-round choice in June 1977 draft . . . Minor League Player of the Year for Denver (AAA) in 1980 with .354 average and 77 steals . . . He and winner Fernando Valenzuela dominated NL Rookie-of-the-Year balloting in strike-shortened 1981, when this speedster stole 71 bases in only 88 games.

Year	Club	Pos.	G	AB	R	H	2B	3B	HR	RBI	SB	Avg.
1979	Montreal	PR	6	0	3	0	0	0	0	0	2	.000
1980	Montreal	2B-OF	15	20	5	1	0	0	0	0	5	.050
1981	Montreal	OF-2B	88	313	61	95	13	7	5	37	71	.304
1982	Montreal	OF-2B	156	647	90	179	32	8	4	43	78	.277
1983	Montreal	OF-2B	156	615	133	183	32	8	11	71	90	.298
1984	Montreal	OF-2B	160	622	106	192	38	9	8	60	75	.309
1985	Montreal	OF	150	575	115	184	30	13	11	41	70	320
	Totals		731	2702	513	834	145	45	39	252	391	299

TIM WALLACH 28 6-3 200 — Bats R Throws R

A consistent power hitter and run producer, he also fields with the best at third base . . . Finished fast and attained career high in doubles . . . Batted .315 in April, but was even better down the stretch, belting 10 homers and driving in 18 runs in September . . . Born Sept. 14, 1957, in Huntington Park, Cal. . . . Attended Fullerton State and led school to national title in 1979

... Named College Player of the Year and best amateur in nation ... Expos' first-round pick in June 1979 draft ... Had only 209 games of minor-league seasoning before he reached bigs, but he produced 54 homers and 175 RBI during brief stay in bushes ... Accumulated an outrageous 39 RBI for Denver (AAA) in June 1980 ... Expos dealt Larry Parrish to Texas to make room for him at third and they haven't regretted it.

Year	Club	Pos.	G	AB	R	H	2B	3B	HR	RBI	SB	Avg.
1980	Montreal	OF-1B	5	11	1	2	0	0	1	2	0	.182
1981	Montreal	OF-1B-3B	71	212	19	50	9	1	4	13	0	.236
1982	Montreal	3B-OF-1B	158	596	89	160	31	3	28	97	6	.268
1983	Montreal	3B	156	581	54	156	33	3	19	70	0	.269
1984	Montreal	3B-SS	160	582	55	143	25	4	18	72	3	.246
1985	Montreal	3B	155	569	70	148	36	3	22	81	9	.260
	Totals		705	2551	288	659	134	14	92	335	18	.258

VANCE LAW 29 6-2 190 **Bats R Throws R**

This acquisition from White Sox wasn't greeted with fanfare attendant to arrival of Hubie Brooks, but this versatile infielder was a solid performer in his NL debut ... Showed some pop as Expos' second baseman ... Obtained by Expos in deal for Bob James prior to 1985 season ... Combined with Brooks to greatly improve offensive production of Montreal infield ... Born Oct. 1, 1956, in Boise, Idaho, just before father Vern gained pitching prominence with the Pirates ... Attended Brigham Young and was 39th-round pick of Pirates in June 1978 draft ... Batted above .300 for his first three minor-league clubs and reached majors in 1980 ... Got a break when an injury to Phil Garner enabled him to start with Bucs in 1981.

Year	Club	Pos.	G	AB	R	H	2B	3B	HR	RBI	SB	Avg.
1980	Pittsburgh	2B-SS-3B	25	74	11	17	2	2	0	3	2	.230
1981	Pittsburgh	2B-SS-3B	30	67	1	9	0	1	0	3	1	.134
1982	Chicago (AL)	SS-3B-2B-OF	114	359	40	101	20	1	5	54	4	.281
1983	Chicago (AL)	3B-2B-SS-OF	145	408	55	99	21	5	4	42	3	.243
1984	Chicago (AL)	3B-2B-SS-OF	151	481	60	121	18	2	17	59	4	.252
1985	Montreal	2B-SS-3B	147	519	75	138	30	6	10	52	6	.266
	Totals		612	1908	242	485	91	17	36	213	20	.254

BRYN SMITH 30 6-2 205 **Bats R Throws R**

A late bloomer, he became Expos' ace last year in his 11th pro season ... Went 13-3 from June 2 to end of season ... Posted 4-2 mark in June ... Was 3-1 with 1.74 ERA in July, 3-0 in August and 3-1 in September and October ... Unlike some teammates, he was blessed with solid offensive support—nearly five runs per game ... Born Aug. 11, 1955, in Marietta, Ga.

... After attending junior college in California, he signed with Orioles as free agent in 1974 ... Acquired from Baltimore with Rudy May and Randy Miller for Gary Roenicke, Don Stanhouse and Joe Kerrigan prior to 1978 season ... Came to Expos as relief pitcher, but worked his way into rotation during 1984 ... American Association Pitcher of the Year in 1981, when he posted 15-5 record for Denver (AAA) ... Throws effective palm ball, changes speeds very well and has excellent control.

Year	Club	G	IP	W	L	Pct.	SO	BB	H	ERA
1981	Montreal	7	13	1	0	1.000	9	3	14	2.77
1982	Montreal	47	79⅓	2	4	.333	50	23	81	4.20
1983	Montreal	49	155⅓	6	11	.353	101	43	142	2.49
1984	Montreal	28	179	12	13	.480	101	51	178	3.32
1985	Montreal	32	222⅓	18	5	.783	127	41	193	2.91
	Totals	163	649	39	33	.542	388	161	608	3.08

JOE HESKETH 27 6-2 170 **Bats L Throws L**

Was heading for an outstanding rookie season when he landed on disabled list with fractured shin Aug. 24 ... Got chance to enter rotation because of injuries to others and made the most of it ... Posted 3-1 record with 1.26 ERA in May and also went 3-1 in July ... Born Feb. 15, 1959, in Lackawanna, N.Y. ... Attended Buffalo, where he went 18-3 over three seasons ... Expos' second-round pick in June 1980 draft ... Posted 7-0 mark in first eight pro games for West Palm Beach (A) in 1980 ... Missed entire 1981 season following elbow surgery ... American Association Pitcher of the Year in 1984, when he went 12-3 for Indianapolis (AAA) before promotion to Expos ... Should enjoy bright future—if he stays healthy.

Year	Club	G	IP	W	L	Pct.	SO	BB	H	ERA
1984	Montreal	11	45	2	2	.500	32	15	38	1.80
1985	Montreal	25	155⅓	10	5	.667	113	45	125	2.49
	Totals	36	200⅓	12	7	.632	145	60	163	2.34

JEFF REARDON 30 6-1 195 **Bats R Throws R**

Somewhat paradoxical season for NL Rolaids Award winner ... Amassed career-high 41 saves, but lost six more games than he won ... Quick getaway included 1-0 record, 1.26 ERA and five saves in April ... Had nine saves in May, yielding two runs in 19⅓ innings ... Saved eight games in August ... Shattered Mike Marshall's previous club record of 31 saves and boosted career total to 127 . . . Born Oct. 1, 1955, in Dalton, Maine . . . Fired a 21-strikeout no-hitter as prep and struck out 240 in 240 innings for the University of Massachusetts . . . Signed with Mets as free agent in 1977 . . . Joined Expos in one-sided swap for Ellis Valentine, May 29, 1981 . . . Has averaged 27.8 saves the last four years . . . Suffers from chronic back problems, but he stayed healthy last season.

Year	Club	G	IP	W	L	Pct.	SO	BB	H	ERA
1979	New York (NL)	18	21	1	2	.333	10	9	12	1.71
1980	New York (NL)	61	110	8	7	.533	101	47	96	2.62
1981	N.Y. (NL)-Mont.	43	70	3	0	1.000	49	21	48	2.19
1982	Montreal	75	109	7	4	.636	86	36	87	2.06
1983	Montreal	66	92	7	9	.438	78	44	87	3.03
1984	Montreal	68	87	7	7	.500	79	37	70	2.90
1985	Montreal	63	87⅔	2	8	.200	67	26	68	3.18
	Totals	394	576⅔	35	37	.486	470	220	468	2.62

TIM BURKE 27 6-3 205 **Bats R Throws R**

A non-roster player in spring training last year, he blossomed into a rookie relief sensation . . . Jeff Reardon earned the headlines and the saves, but this guy led NL with 78 appearances and had excellent hits-to-innings-pitched ratio . . . Set club record with eight straight victories from start of season . . . Was 3-0 with 0.96 ERA in June . . . Born Feb. 19, 1959, in Omaha, Neb. . . . Attended Nebraska . . . Selected by Pittsburgh in second round of June 1980 draft . . . Traded by Pirates to Yankees in Lee Mazzilli deal prior to 1983 season . . . Acquired by Expos for Pat Rooney in a minor-league deal that was a steal, one year later . . . Enjoyed best minor-league season for Nashville (AA) in 1983, when he went 12-4 . . . Was second on Expos with eight saves last season.

Year	Club	G	IP	W	L	Pct.	SO	BB	H	ERA
1985	Montreal	78	120⅓	9	4	.692	87	44	86	2.39

JAY TIBBS 24 6-1 180 **Bats R Throws R**

Was expected to be an important starter with the Reds this year, but they traded him to the Expos in a six-player deal that brought Bill Gullickson . . . Endured losing record and brief demotion to minors in 1985, but his fast finish encouraged Reds . . . Was 3-0 in September . . . Born Jan. 4, 1962, in Birmingham, Ala. . . . High-school teammate of pitcher Britt Burns . . . MVP of Alabama prep baseball in 1980 . . . Drafted in second round by Mets in June 1980 . . . Struggled in minors until he and Dwight Gooden pitched Lynchburg (A) to Carolina League title in 1983 . . . Was 14-8 with 2.92 ERA that year . . . Next season was a topsy-turvy experience because he pitched with four different teams . . . Was swapped by Mets to Reds as part of package for Bruce Berenyi, June 15, 1984 . . . Did his best work with Cincinnati late in the season, including a three-hit shutout of Giants.

Year	Club	G	IP	W	L	Pct.	SO	BB	H	ERA
1984	Cincinnati	14	100⅔	6	2	.750	40	33	87	2.86
1985	Cincinnati	35	218	10	16	.385	98	83	216	3.92
	Totals	49	318⅔	16	18	.471	138	116	303	3.59

TOP PROSPECT

ANDRES GALARRAGA 24 6-3 230 Bats R Throws R
Latin slugger struggled in trial with parent club last year, hitting .187 with two homers and four RBI in 75 at-bats, but his minor-league credentials suggest he'll be in majors soon . . . Won Southern League MVP award for Jacksonville (AA) with .289 average, 27 homers and 87 RBI in 1984 . . . Had .269 average, 25 homers and 87 RBI for Indianapolis (AAA) prior to 1985 promotion . . . First baseman was born June 18, 1961, in Caracas, Venezuela . . . Was signed as a 17-year-old free agent in 1979, on Felipe Alou's recommendation.

MANAGER BUCK RODGERS: Despite injuries to key pitchers, he kept the club competitive most of the year and finished with a winning record (84-77) in first year with Expos . . . Earned Montreal job by being named Minor League Manager of the Year in 1984, when he guided Indianapolis (AAA) to a 91-63 record and American Association pennant . . . Received nickname "Buck" from Bill Rigney, his manager with the Angels . . . Real name is Bob . . . Born Aug. 16, 1938, in Delaware, Ohio . . . Attended Ohio Wesleyan and Ohio Northern . . . Came up through Tigers' system and was selected by Angels in expansion draft . . . Set rookie record for catchers by playing 150 games in 1962 . . . Played entire major-league career with Angels, batting .232 in

932 games . . . First managing job was with Salinas (A) in 1975 . . . Prior to that, he served as Twins' pitching coach . . . Took El Paso (AA) to Texas League title in 1977 . . . Replaced ailing George Bamberger as Brewers' manager in 1980 and took club to second-half title in 1981 . . . Has 208-179 record as major-league manager.

GREATEST SHORTSTOP

It's difficult to determine the finest Expos' shortstop because Montreal has had seven different Opening Day shortstops in its 17-year history. Hubie Brooks deserves a mention after his 100-RBI campaign of 1985, but Tim Foli and Chris Speier are more worthy of consideration because they had longer stays in Montreal.

Foli and Speier were Expos' regulars for at least six years each. In fact, Foli was traded to the Giants for Speier early in 1977. Each player was more steady than spectacular, though Speier did equal Bobby Wine's club record with a .982 fielding percentage in 1982.

Speier topped Foli in games played at shortstop for the Expos (863-701) and was at his best when he made only 13 errors in a full season in 1982. Speier was helpful at the plate, but was a more dangerous hitter in his early San Francisco days. Foli was similar in his style, aggressive in the field and respectable at the plate. Let's call it a tie.

ALL-TIME EXPO SEASON RECORDS

BATTING: Al Oliver, .331, 1982
HRs: Andre Dawson, 32, 1983
RBIs: Andre Dawson, 113, 1983
STEALS: Ron LeFlore, 97, 1980
WINS: Ross Grimsley, 20, 1978
STRIKEOUTS: Bill Stoneman, 251, 1971

NEW YORK METS

TEAM DIRECTORY: Chairman: Nelson Doubleday; Pres.: Fred Wilpon; Exec. VP-GM: Frank Cashen; VP-Baseball Oper.: Joe McIlvaine; Sr. VP-Adm.: Al Harazin; Dir. Scouting: Roland Johnson; Dir. Minor Leagues: Steve Schryver; Dir. Pub. Rel.: Jay Horwitz; Asst. GM-Trav. Sec.: Arthur Richman; Mgr.: Davey Johnson. Home: Shea Stadium (55,300). Field distances: 338, l.f. line; 371, l.c.; 410, c.f.; 371, r.c.; 338, r.f. line. Spring training: St. Petersburg, Fla.

SCOUTING REPORT

HITTING: A healthy Darryl Strawberry and Mookie Wilson should make the Mets an even better offensive club than the one that ranked fourth in the NL in hitting (.257), third in homers (134) and third in runs scored (695) last year. Strawberry was limited to 111 games by a broken thumb, but he still belted 29 homers and drove in 79 runs. It's scary to think of what he's capable of doing once he gets into a groove for an entire season.

Wilson used to be the sparkplug of the offense. If Mookie's post-operative shoulder allows him to play more than the 93 games

Gritty Gary is turning the Big Apple into Carter Country.

he managed last year, he could be to the Mets what Vince Coleman is to the Cardinals—a catalyst. The Mets have plenty of pop, but they need the little guys to get on base for the big boppers.

Among the big boys, Strawberry, Gary Carter (32 homers, 100 RBI), Keith Hernandez (.309, 91 RBI) and George Foster (21 homers, 77 RBI) form a dangerous Murderers' Row, though it's apparent Foster has seen better days. As his skills diminish, younger players will earn more playing time, but the heart of the Mets' batting order should still rank with the best in the league.

PITCHING: Let us count the ways the Mets can mesmerize opponents. As if they didn't have enough heat, the club added Bob Ojeda (9-11, 4.00) from the Red Sox over the winter, which just might be the straw that breaks the Cardinals' backs. There isn't a younger, deeper or more imposing staff in the National League.

Dwight Gooden (24-4, 1.53) is the epitome of a stopper and he has lots of help. Sid Fernandez (9-9, 2.80), another strikeout specialist, appears ready to make a contribution over a full season, joining Gooden, Ojeda, Ron Darling (16-6, 2.90) and possibly a mended Bruce Berenyi in a rotation that commands respect and suggests success for a number of years.

The bullpen should be stronger, with Roger McDowell (17 saves) having added experience as the right-handed complement to Jesse Orosco (17 saves).

FIELDING: This is another area in which the Mets excel. Only the Cardinals made fewer errors than the Mets' 115 last year. That total could shrink if shortstop Rafael Santana continues to improve and if the third-base situation is solidified. Gold Glover Hernandez is as good as they come at first base, Carter is a standout behind the plate and Wally Backman's .989 percentage topped all second basemen last year.

OUTLOOK: A deeper rotation and an improved performance by the bullpen should reward the Mets with a pennant. The club has all the parts for success and manager Davey Johnson seems quite capable of putting all the pieces together. It doesn't hurt when the main man is Gooden, a pitcher of extraordinary skill who is able to keep the Mets out of a prolonged slump.

The Mets must get more production from their bullpen. Despite winning 98 games last year, the club was merely average in one-run games (33-31) and in extra innings (12-10), suggesting weakness at the end of games. If the relievers come through, Ojeda makes an impact and Foster can produce one more year, the Cardinals shouldn't be able to hold off this potential powerhouse.

NEW YORK METS 1986 ROSTER

MANAGER Davey Johnson
Coaches—Bud Harrelson, Vern Hoscheit, Greg Pavlick, Bill Robinson, Mel Stottlemyre

PITCHERS

No.	Name	1985 Club	W-L	IP	SO	ERA	B-T	Ht.	Wt.	Born
38	Aguilera, Rick	Tidewater	6-4	79	55	2.51	R-R	6-5	193	12/31/61 San Gabriel, CA
		New York (NL)	10-7	122	74	3.24				
67	Bautista, Jose	Lynchburg	15-8	169	109	2.34	R-R	6-1	177	7/25/64 Dominican Republic
31	Berenyi, Bruce	New York (NL)	1-0	14	10	2.63	R-R	6-3	215	8/21/54 Bryan, OH
		Tidewater	0-0	1	1	9.00				
12	Darling, Ron	New York (NL)	16-6	248	167	2.90	R-R	6-3	195	8/19/60 Honolulu, HI
64	Dobie, Reggie	Lynchburg	12-5	168	144	2.63	R-R	6-1	174	8/17/64 Rosedale, MS
50	Fernandez, Sid	Tidewater	4-1	35	42	2.04	L-L	6-1	220	10/12/62 Honolulu, HI
		New York (NL)	9-9	170	180	2.80				
16	Gooden, Dwight	New York (NL)	24-4	277	268	1.53	R-R	6-3	198	11/16/64 Tampa, FL
29	Gorman, Tom	New York (NL)	4-4	53	32	5.13	L-L	6-4	200	12/16/57 Portland, OR
63	Hartshorn, Kyle	Lynchburg	17-4	171	98	1.69	L-R	6-2	185	10/3/64 Trenton, NJ
		Jackson	0-2	16	6	6.80				
44	Latham, Bill	Tidewater	13-8	158	66	2.68	L-L	6-2	190	8/29/60 Birmingham, AL
		New York (NL)	1-3	23	10	3.97				
36	Lynch, Ed	New York (NL)	10-8	191	65	3.44	R-R	6-5	207	2/25/56 Brooklyn, NY
34	McCarthy, Tom	Pawtucket	5-6	91	68	3.76	R-R	6-0	180	6/18/61 West Germany
		Boston	0-0	5	2	10.80				
42	McDowell, Roger	New York (NL)	6-5	127	70	2.83	R-R	6-1	175	12/21/60 Cincinnati, OH
66	Mitchell, John	New Britain	12-8	190	108	2.70	R-R	6-2	165	8/11/65 Dickinson, TN
48	Myers, Randy	Jackson	4-8	120	116	3.96	L-L	6-1	190	9/19/62 Vancouver, WA
		Tidewater	1-1	44	25	1.84				
		New York (NL)	0-0	2	2	0.00				
27	Ojeda, Bob	Boston	9-11	158	102	4.00	L-L	6-1	190	12/17/57 Los Angeles, CA
47	Orosco, Jesse	New York (NL)	8-6	79	68	2.73	R-L	6-2	185	4/21/57 Santa Barbara, CA
39	Sisk, Doug	Tidewater	0-2	15	4	7.20	R-R	6-2	210	9/26/57 Renton, WA
		New York (NL)	4-5	73	26	5.30				
46	West, Dave	Columbia	10-9	150	194	4.56	L-L	6-6	207	9/1/64 Memphis, TN

CATCHERS

No.	Name	1985 Club	H	HR	RBI	Pct.	B-T	Ht.	Wt.	Born
8	Carter, Gary	New York (NL)	156	32	100	.281	R-R	6-2	210	4/8/54 Culver City, CA
7	Gibbons, John	Tidewater	96	9	30	.259	R-R	5-11	187	6/8/62 Great Falls, MT
33	Lyons, Barry	Jackson	149	11	106	.307	R-R	6-1	205	6/3/60 Biloxi, MS
9	Reynolds, Ronn	Tidewater	3	0	2	.300	R-R	6-0	200	9/28/58 Wichita, KS
		New York (NL)	9	0	1	.209				

INFIELDERS

No.	Name	1985 Club	H	HR	RBI	Pct.	B-T	Ht.	Wt.	Born
6	Backman, Wally	New York (NL)	142	1	38	.273	B-R	5-9	160	9/22/59 Hillsboro, OR
19	Gardenhire, Ron	Tidewater	15	1	10	.211	R-R	6-0	174	10/24/57 West Germany
		New York (NL)	7	0	2	.179				
17	Hernandez, Keith	New York (NL)	183	10	91	.309	L-L	6-0	185	10/20/53 San Francisco, CA
20	Johnson, Howard	New York (NL)	94	11	46	.242	B-R	5-10	175	11/29/60 Clearwater, FL
22	Knight, Ray	New York (NL)	59	6	36	.218	R-R	6-2	190	12/28/52 Albany, GA
65	Magadan, Dave	Jackson	144	0	76	.309	L-R	6-3	190	9/30/62 Tampa, FL
35	Mitchell, Kevin	Tidewater	101	9	43	.291	R-R	5-11	210	1/13/62 San Diego, CA
3	Santana, Rafael	New York (NL)	136	1	29	.257	R-R	6-1	160	1/31/58 Dominican Republic

OUTFIELDERS

No.	Name	1985 Club	H	HR	RBI	Pct.	B-T	Ht.	Wt.	Born
11	Beane, Billy	Tidewater	143	19	77	.284	R-R	6-4	195	3/29/62 Orlando, FL
		New York (NL)	2	0	1	.260				
21	Blocker, Terry	Tidewater	82	5	38	.307	L-L	6-2	195	8/18/59 Columbia, SC
		New York (NL)	1	0	0	.067				
4	Dykstra, Len	Tidewater	71	1	25	.310	L-L	5-10	160	2/10/63 Santa Ana, CA
		New York (NL)	60	1	19	.254				
15	Foster, George	New York (NL)	119	21	77	.263	R-R	6-1	198	12/1/48 Tuscaloosa, AL
25	Heep, Danny	New York (NL)	76	7	42	.280	L-L	5-11	185	7/3/57 San Antonio, TX
32	Jefferson, Stan	Jackson	145	8	30	.277	B-R	5-11	175	12/4/62 New York NY
62	Lawton, Marcus	Columbia	126	1	53	.268	B-R	6-1	159	8/18/65 Gulfport, MS
18	Strawberry, Darryl	New York (NL)	109	29	79	.277	L-L	6-6	190	3/12/62 Los Angeles, CA
1	Wilson, Mookie	New York (NL)	93	6	26	.276	B-R	5-10	160	2/9/56 Bamberg, SC

MET PROFILES

GARY CARTER 31 6-2 210 Bats R Throws R

An impressive start and an awesome finish made it a great year for the best catcher in Expos' and Mets' history . . . Won his debut as a Met with 10th-inning homer Opening Day and had three game-winning RBI in opening week . . . Batted .343 in September with 13 homers and 34 RBI . . . Had eight game-winning RBI in September, enabling him to tie Reds' Dave Parker for second in NL with 18 . . . NL Player of the Month in September . . . "The Kid" destroyed Padres' pitching with five home runs in two games, Sept. 3-4, tying major-league mark . . . Limped through season with torn cartilage in right knee and he underwent postseason surgery on joint for second straight year . . . Born April 8, 1954, in Culver City, Cal. . . . Was headed for a football ride at UCLA when Expos drafted him in third round in June 1972 . . . After tremendous stretch with Montreal, he was traded to Mets for four players, including Hubie Brooks, following 1984 season . . . Some of his ex-teammates blamed him for causing friction on dissension-torn Expos by courting media attention . . . Credited with hastening development of Mets' young pitchers last season with his pitch-calling and leadership.

Year	Club	Pos.	G	AB	R	H	2B	3B	HR	RBI	SB	Avg.
1974	Montreal	C-OF	9	27	5	11	0	1	1	6	2	.407
1975	Montreal	OF-C-3B	144	503	58	136	20	1	17	68	5	.270
1976	Montreal	C-OF	91	311	31	68	8	1	6	38	0	.219
1977	Montreal	C-OF	154	522	86	148	29	2	31	84	5	.284
1978	Montreal	C-1B	157	533	76	136	27	1	20	72	10	.255
1979	Montreal	C	141	505	74	143	26	5	22	75	3	.283
1980	Montreal	C	154	549	76	145	25	5	29	101	3	.264
1981	Montreal	C-1B	100	374	48	94	20	2	16	68	1	.251
1982	Montreal	C	154	557	91	163	32	1	29	97	2	.293
1983	Montreal	C-1B	145	541	63	146	37	3	17	79	1	.270
1984	Montreal	C-1B	159	596	75	175	32	1	27	106	2	.294
1985	New York (NL)	C-1B	149	555	83	156	17	1	32	100	1	.281
	Totals		1557	5573	766	1521	273	24	247	894	35	.273

KEITH HERNANDEZ 32 6-0 185 Bats L Throws L

A pressure performer despite distraction of drug trial . . . Set major-league record with 24 game-winning RBI, breaking mark of 21 he shared with Jack Clark in NL and Harold Baines' major-league standard of 22 . . . NL batting champ in 1979 posted his fifth .300 season and his second in a row with Mets . . . NL Player of the Month in July with a .392 average and 29 RBI

... Hot finish included a .373 September ... Hit for cycle July 4 and had two five-hit games last season ... Born Oct. 20, 1953, in San Francisco ... Cardinals' 40th-round draft choice in July 1971 ... Father John and brother Gary played in Cards' minor-league system ... An avid Civil War buff ... Regarded as the best defensive first baseman of his era ... NL's co-MVP with Pirates' Willie Stargell in 1979.

Year	Club	Pos.	G	AB	R	H	2B	3B	HR	RBI	SB	Avg.
1974	St. Louis	1B	14	34	3	10	1	2	0	2	0	.294
1975	St. Louis	1B	64	188	20	47	8	2	3	20	0	.250
1976	St. Louis	1B	129	374	54	108	21	5	7	46	4	.289
1977	St. Louis	1B	161	560	90	163	41	4	15	91	7	.291
1978	St. Louis	1B	159	542	90	138	32	4	11	64	13	.255
1979	St. Louis	1B	161	610	116	210	48	11	11	105	11	.344
1980	St. Louis	1B	159	595	111	191	39	8	16	99	14	.321
1981	St. Louis	1B-OF	103	376	65	115	27	4	8	48	12	.306
1982	St. Louis	1B-OF	160	579	79	173	33	6	7	94	19	.299
1983	St.L.-NY (NL).....	1B	150	538	77	160	23	7	12	63	9	.297
1984	New York (NL)	1B	154	550	83	171	31	0	15	94	2	.311
1985	New York (NL)	1B	158	593	87	183	34	4	10	91	3	.309
	Totals		1572	5539	875	1669	338	57	115	817	94	.301

MOOKIE WILSON 30 5-10 168 **Bats S Throws R**

Rotator-cuff tear in throwing shoulder kept him out for most of the season, but center fielder returned and excelled for Mets in September ... Batted .306 with 11 stolen bases in May ... Shoulder regarded as good as new following additional postseason surgery ... Had led club in stolen bases four straight years prior to 1985 ... Mets' all-time stolen-base king ... Born Feb. 9, 1956, in Bamberg, S.C. ... Starred at South Carolina, guiding Gamecocks to runnerup honors at College World Series in 1977 ... Mets' second choice in June 1977 draft ... Enjoys baking, using recipes handed down by grandmother ... International League Rookie of the Year with Tidewater (AAA) in 1979 ... One of six major leaguers who reached double figures in doubles, triples and homers in 1984 ... Will battle young Len Dykstra for job as Mets' offensive catalyst.

Year	Club	Pos.	G	AB	R	H	2B	3B	HR	RBI	SB	Avg.
1980	New York (NL)	OF	27	105	16	26	5	3	0	4	7	.248
1981	New York (NL)	OF	92	328	49	89	8	8	3	14	24	.271
1982	New York (NL)	OF	159	639	90	178	25	9	5	55	58	.279
1983	New York (NL)	OF	152	638	91	176	25	6	7	51	54	.276
1984	New York (NL)	OF	154	587	88	162	28	10	10	54	46	.276
1985	New York (NL)	OF	93	337	56	93	16	8	6	26	24	.276
	Totals		677	2634	390	724	107	44	31	204	213	.275

DARRYL STRAWBERRY 24 6-6 190 Bats L Throws L

After missing seven weeks with broken thumb, this right fielder rallied to enjoy a solid second half . . . Belted three home runs at Chicago Aug. 5 . . . Batted .303 in July and .313 in August, amassing 15 homers and 45 RBI in those months . . . This tantalizing combination of speed and power may have only scratched the surface of his potential . . . Resisted temptation to brood and sulk as he had done in 1984 . . . Born March 12, 1962, in Los Angeles . . . Article in national mag tabbed him can't-miss superstar as a prep and compared him to Ted Williams . . . Predictions of greatness created extra pressure for No. 1 pick in nation in June 1980 draft . . . Struggled with average in low minors, but became Texas League MVP for Jackson (AA) in 1982 and was promoted to majors in May 1983 . . . "The Straw" that stirs the Mets.

Year	Club	Pos.	G	AB	R	H	2B	3B	HR	RBI	SB	Avg.
1983	New York (NL)	OF	122	420	63	108	15	7	26	74	19	.257
1984	New York (NL)	OF	147	522	75	131	27	4	26	97	27	.251
1985	New York (NL)	OF	111	393	78	109	15	4	29	79	26	.277
	Totals		380	1335	216	348	57	15	81	250	72	.261

WALLY BACKMAN 26 5-9 160 Bats S Throws R

Mets' unsung hero during pennant race, enjoying solid season while stars reaped the glory . . . Second baseman was leading base-stealer on club . . . Batted .340 with nine stolen bases in June . . . Born Sept. 22, 1959, in Hillsboro, Ore. . . . Mets' first pick in June 1977 draft . . . Enjoyed solid minor-league career, capped by banner 1983 at Tidewater (AAA), where he batted .316 during season and .391 in playoffs . . . Overcame broken collarbone suffered in freak bicycle accident in 1982 . . . Very consistent performer the last two seasons, but has struggled against left-handed pitching and could find himself back in a platoon situation in 1986 . . . Has shown big improvement defensively and has become very adept at bunting for hits.

Year	Club	Pos.	G	AB	R	H	2B	3B	HR	RBI	SB	Avg.
1980	New York (NL)	2B-SS	27	93	12	30	1	1	0	9	2	.323
1981	New York (NL)	2B-3B	26	36	5	10	2	0	0	0	1	.278
1982	New York (NL)	2B-3B-SS	96	261	37	71	13	2	3	22	8	.272
1983	New York (NL)	2B-3B	26	42	6	7	0	1	0	3	0	.167
1984	New York (NL)	2B-SS	128	436	68	122	19	2	1	26	32	.280
1985	New York (NL)	2B	145	520	77	142	24	5	1	38	30	.273
	Totals		448	1388	205	382	59	11	5	98	73	.275

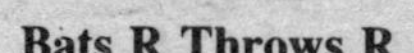

GEORGE FOSTER 37 6-1 198 **Bats R Throws R**

No longer ominous at the plate, but still plenty tough . . . No sensational surges in 1985, but a steady year to complement other stars on club . . . Has suffered from comparisons to his halcyon days with Reds, when he went on an RBI orgy partly attributable to the ability of his superstar teammates to get on base in front of him . . . Replaced Bobby Bonds in 40th spot on all-time homer list . . . Born Dec. 1, 1948, in Tuscaloosa, Ala. . . . Giants' third choice in January 1968 draft . . . Giants didn't appreciate what they had, giving him to Reds for Frank Duffy and Vern Geishert, May 29, 1971 . . . NL MVP in 1977 . . . Totaled 390 RBI and 121 homers from 1976-78 . . . Has a .326 World Series average . . . Drove in 90 runs in 108 games during strike-shortened 1981 before joining Mets in deal for Alex Trevino, Jim Kern and Greg Harris prior to 1982 . . . Left fielder is gradually being phased out of Mets' plans.

Year	Club	Pos.	G	AB	R	H	2B	3B	HR	RBI	SB	Avg.
1969	San Francisco. . .	OF	9	5	1	2	0	0	0	1	0	.400
1970	San Francisco. . .	OF	9	19	2	6	1	1	1	4	0	.316
1971	S.F.-Cin.	OF	140	473	50	114	23	4	13	58	7	.241
1972	Cincinnati	OF	59	145	15	29	4	1	2	12	2	.200
1973	Cincinnati	OF	17	39	6	11	3	0	4	9	0	.282
1974	Cincinnati	OF	106	276	31	73	18	0	7	41	3	.264
1975	Cincinnati	OF-1B	134	463	71	139	24	4	23	78	2	.300
1976	Cincinnati	OF-1B	144	562	86	172	21	9	29	121	17	.306
1977	Cincinnati	OF	158	615	124	197	31	2	52	149	6	.320
1978	Cincinnati	OF	158	604	97	170	26	7	40	120	4	.281
1979	Cincinnati	OF	121	440	68	133	18	3	30	98	0	.302
1980	Cincinnati	OF	144	528	79	144	21	5	25	93	1	.273
1981	Cincinnati	OF	108	414	64	122	23	2	22	90	4	.295
1982	New York (NL) . .	OF	151	550	64	136	23	2	13	70	1	.247
1983	New York (NL) . .	OF	157	601	74	145	19	2	28	90	1	.241
1984	New York (NL) . .	OF	146	553	67	149	22	1	24	86	2	.269
1985	New York (NL) . .	OF	129	452	57	119	24	1	21	77	0	.263
	Totals		1890	6739	956	1861	301	44	334	1197	50	.276

DWIGHT GOODEN 21 6-3 198 **Bats R Throws R**

Oh, Doctor! . . . People wondered what he would do for an encore and he showed them . . . An absolutely phenomenal sophomore season . . . The jinx was on his opponents . . . Topped NL in four major pitching categories and was major-league leader in wins, ERA and strikeouts . . . Hard to imagine he can get any better after winning 41 of 54 decisions in first two years, but he's working on slider and changeup . . . Youngest 20-game winner in history and first to strike out 200-plus in each of his first two years in NL . . . Set club record with 14 straight victories

... Has gone 32-5 since Aug. 11, 1984 ... Born Nov. 16, 1964, in Tampa ... Remarkably consistent in 1985: 3-1, 1.38 ERA in April; 4-2, 2.14 ERA in May; 4-0, 1.41 ERA in June; 5-0, 1.66 ERA in July; 4-1, 2.45 ERA in August and 3-0 in September, when he didn't allow an earned run and won NL Pitcher-of-the-Month honors ... NL Cy Young Award winner last year after earning Rookie-of-the-Year honors in 1984 ... Set rookie record for strikeouts and set major-league mark with 33 Ks in two straight games in 1984 ... Showed greatly improved pickoff move last season.

Year	Club	G	IP	W	L	Pct.	SO	BB	H	ERA
1984	New York (NL)	31	218	17	9	.654	276	73	161	2.60
1985	New York (NL)	35	276⅔	24	4	.857	268	69	198	1.53
	Total	66	494⅔	41	13	.759	544	142	359	2.00

RON DARLING 25 6-3 195 Bats R Throws R

Toiled in Dwight Gooden's shadow, but enjoyed excellent year as club's No. 2 starter ... Was 9-2 with a 2.52 ERA at All-Star break and won next start before going winless for more than a month ... Snapped slump with four-hit, 1-0 shutout at Montreal Aug. 19 ... Got off to good start, combining with Jesse Orosco on one-hitter April 16 at Pittsburgh ... Posted 3-1 mark with 1.66 ERA in August ... Born Aug. 19, 1960, in Honolulu ... As Yale standout, he set NCAA Tournament mark with 11 innings of no-hit ball against St. John's before losing in 12th ... Also played defensive back for Ivy Leaguers ... Rangers' first-round pick in June 1981 draft ... Traded to Mets with Walt Terrell for Lee Mazzilli just prior to start of 1982 season.

Year	Club	G	IP	W	L	Pct.	SO	BB	H	ERA
1983	New York (NL)	5	35⅓	1	3	.250	23	17	31	2.80
1984	New York (NL)	33	205⅔	12	9	.571	136	104	179	3.81
1985	New York (NL)	36	248	16	6	.727	167	114	214	2.90
	Totals	74	489	29	18	.617	326	235	424	3.28

SID FERNANDEZ 23 6-1 220 Bats L Throws L

"El Sid" became solid third starter after returning from Tidewater (AAA), where he worked out spring control problems ... Had best strikeouts-per-innings-pitched ratio of any starter in majors with 180 in 170⅓ innings in 1985 ... Changes speeds well, with moving fastball and big, slow curve the key pitches in his repertoire ... Hard luck left him with .500 record despite 2.80 ERA after 6-6 showing for Mets in 1984 ... Born

Oct. 12, 1962, in Honolulu . . . Chosen by Dodgers in third round of June 1981 draft . . . Posted 13-4 record with 2.82 ERA and 209 strikeouts in 153 innings for San Antonio (AA) in 1983, but was dealt to Mets for Carlos Diaz and Bob Bailor following that season . . . Sometimes struggles to keep composure . . . Allowed only 108 hits last season, but walked 80 . . . Along with Dwight Gooden and Ron Darling, he gives Mets three young starters to anchor rotation for years to come . . . Continues to fight battle of the bulge.

Year	Club	G	IP	W	L	Pct.	SO	BB	H	ERA
1983	Los Angeles.	2	6	0	1	.000	9	7	7	6.00
1984	New York (NL)	15	90	6	6	.500	62	34	74	3.50
1985	New York (NL)	26	170⅓	9	9	.500	180	80	108	2.80
	Totals	43	266⅓	15	16	.484	251	121	189	3.11

JESSE OROSCO 28 6-2 185 **Bats R Throws L**

Tender elbow made manager Davey Johnson exercise caution in using bullpen ace . . . Saved 14 fewer games last year than he did when he set club record with 31 in 1984 . . . Did some of his best pitching after All-Star break . . . In a span of 16 appearances, he posted 3-0 record with eight saves and a 0.81 ERA . . . Born April 21, 1957, in Santa Barbara, Cal. . . . Following successful junior-college career, he was Twins' second choice in January 1978 draft . . . Traded to Mets for Jerry Koosman prior to 1979 season . . . Blossomed in 1983 and 1984, when he had a hand in 71 victories with 48 saves and 23 wins . . . Gave up several costly homers last season, prompting concern about his future and leading to speculation that he might lose stopper's job to Roger McDowell.

Year	Club	G	IP	W	L	Pct.	SO	BB	H	ERA
1979	New York (NL)	18	35	1	2	.333	22	22	33	4.89
1981	New York (NL)	8	17	0	1	.000	18	6	13	1.59
1982	New York (NL)	54	109⅓	4	10	.286	89	40	92	2.72
1983	New York (NL)	62	110	13	7	.650	84	38	76	1.47
1984	New York (NL)	60	87	10	6	.625	85	34	58	2.59
1985	New York (NL)	54	70	0	0	.571	08	34	66	2.73
	Totals	256	437⅓	36	32	.529	366	174	338	2.51

TOP PROSPECTS

TERRY BLOCKER 25 6-2 195 **Bats L Throws L**

The Mets don't have a pitching superstar on the horizon for a change, but this speedy outfielder seems about to fulfill his promise after three years of Triple-A seasoning . . . Looked great in first year at Tidewater in 1983, batting .305, but fell to .220 in 1984 before rallying to .307 last year . . . Born Aug. 18, 1959, in Columbia, S.C. . . . Earned degree from Tennessee State and was Mets' first-round draft choice in June 1981 . . . Looms as potential base-stealing whiz, but doesn't have much power . . . Had five homers and 38 RBI with Tides in 1985 . . . Hit .067 in 15 at-bats during early-season stint with Mets.

BARRY LYONS 25 6-1 205 **Bats R Throws R**

This 15th-round pick in June 1982 draft has turned into a bonus as a catcher and first baseman . . . Probably still a year away, but progressing rapidly through the system . . . Born June 3, 1960, in Biloxi, Miss. . . . Attended Delta State . . . Has demonstrated a penchant for clutch hitting, knocking in 46 runs in 45 games as a first-year pro with Shelby (A) in 1982 and becoming Carolina League MVP for Lynchburg (A) in 1984, when he amassed 87 RBI in 115 games . . . Hit .307 with 11 homers and 106 RBI for Jackson (AA) in 1985 . . . Appears to be heir apparent to Gary Carter as Mets' catcher.

MANAGER DAVE JOHNSON: Added to gaudy reputation by keeping club in contention most of the way . . . Mets came within one game of tying Cardinals before suffering key loss at St. Louis Oct. 3 . . . Mets finished at 98-64, an improvement of eight games from 1984 mark, and registered second runnerup finish in his two seasons at the helm . . . Mets' fortunes turned around as soon as he was given major-league job following 1983 season . . . Of course, Dwight Gooden's arrival helped, too . . . Born Jan. 30, 1943, in Orlando, Fla. . . . Played baseball and basketball at Texas A&M . . . A computer whiz, he earned math degree from Trinity . . . Signed with Orioles and was their second baseman in glory years of 1966-72 . . . Played in four World Series . . . Showed unexpected power after being swapped to Atlanta, blasting 43 homers in 1973 . . . Played in Japan and has distinction of being ex-teammate of both Hank Aaron and Sadaharu Oh . . . Three-time Gold Glove winner . . . Managed two years in Mets' organization before landing present job, winning Triple-A World Series with Tidewater in 1983 . . . Overall major-league managerial record is 188-136, but this season the pressure will be on him to win divisional crown.

GREATEST SHORTSTOP

Bud Harrelson, who played with the Mets from 1965-77 and became their third-base coach last year, really has no competition for the title of the best shortstop in club history. His successors simply have not shown the consistency that marked Harrelson's play.

He'll long be remembered for his NLCS altercation with Pete Rose, but Harrelson earned his greatest distinction as the infield leader of the 1969 world champions and the 1973 pennant winners. He was a National League All-Star in 1970 and 1971 and earned his only Gold Glove in 1971.

Because of his longevity with the club, Harrelson ranks among the Mets' leaders in many offensive categories. But he made his mark with solid play afield, taking an active role in transforming thc franchisc from a rag-tag expansion club into a champion with his physical skills and leadership.

ALL-TIME MET SEASON RECORDS

BATTING: Cleon Jones, .340, 1969
HRs: Dave Kingman, 37, 1976, 1982
RBIs: Rusty Staub, 105, 1975
STEALS: Mookie Wilson, 58, 1982
WINS: Tom Seaver, 25, 1969
STRIKEOUTS: Tom Seaver, 289, 1971

PHILADELPHIA PHILLIES

TEAM DIRECTORY: Pres.: William Y. Giles; Exec. VP: David Montgomery; VP: Paul Owens; VP-Baseball: Tony Siegle; VP-Pub. Rel.: Larry Shenk; VP-Dir. Play. Dev./Scouting: Jim Baumer; Trav. Sec.: Eddie Ferenz; Mgr.: John Felske. Home: Veterans Stadium (65,454). Field Distances: 330, l.f. line; 408, c.f.; 330, r.f. line. Spring training: Clearwater, Fla.

SCOUTING REPORT

HITTING: One wouldn't think a lineup that includes Mike Schmidt, Juan Samuel, Von Hayes and Glenn Wilson would have trouble offensively, yet the Phillies batted a collective .245, the second-worst average in the NL last season. It doesn't figure and a repeat performance could prove fatal, because the pitching definitely is shaky.

Schmidt (33 homers, 93 RBI) didn't take off with the bat until he was switched to first base. That experiment apparently has ended. The 1986 plan is to move him back to third to make room at first for Hayes (13 homers, 70 RBI). These shifts are designed to add punch to the lineup by opening up a spot in the outfield for one or two newcomers.

Wilson (14 homers, 102 RBI) is a fixture, but former Red Gary Redus and former Brave Milt Thompson will battle for playing time. Redus, who never reached his potential in Cincinnati, has the inside track, because his speed (48 steals) makes him an ideal complement to Samuel (53 steals) and Hayes (21 steals) and he has more power than Thompson. Thompson led the league with a .433 average as a pinch-hitter and may be best suited to that role. Ozzie Virgil's power will be missed behind the plate, putting young Darren Daulton on the spot.

PITCHING: Unless Steve Carlton (1-8, 3.33) performs a miracle and reverts to previous form, the Phils' staff is hurting. John Denny was dealt to Cincinnati, so it'll be up to youngsters to fill the gaps around Shane Rawley (13-8, 3.31), Kevin Gross (15-13, 3.41) and Charles Hudson (8-13, 3.78). With manager John Felske likely to be going to the bullpen often, the Phils spent the winter stockpiling relievers.

Former Brave Steve Bedrosian and former Red Tom Hume are two of the newcomers who'll augment holdovers like Kent Tekulve and the surprise of the 1985 staff, Don Carman (9-4, 2.08, 7 saves). There is some depth in this bullpen and it's likely to be needed because the starting rotation is lacking.

Mike Schmidt crushed whispers that he was finished.

FIELDING: The Phillies were not a good defensive club last year and they could be even worse in 1986. They have unsettled situations at shortstop and catcher, a new first baseman and Schmidt returning to third. Schmidt once was a Gold Glover at the position, but his fielding percentage was a poor .927 when he made the switch to first last year.

None of the club's shortstops performed with distinction afield last year and the catching could suffer without Virgil, whose .994 percentage was tops in the NL. On the positive side, Samuel cut down his errors at second base and Redus is an excellent outfielder.

OUTLOOK: It looks grim for this club in transition. The Phils made a commitment to go with youth two years ago, but many of the newcomers simply weren't as talented as the people they replaced. There is alleged dissension among the veterans who question Felske's managing, so this is a team that could have serious problems if things go badly.

Adversity is likely because of so-so starting pitching and some holes in the batting order. What if this is the year the aging Schmidt proves unable to salvage his season with a fast finish? On the positive side, the club bolstered its bullpen, hoping to win some of those one-run decisions (23-35) that got away last year en route to a 75-87 finish.

PHILADELPHIA PHILLIES 1986 ROSTER

MANAGER John Felske
Coaches—Jim Davenport, Lee Elia, Claude Osteen, Mike Ryan, Del Unser

PITCHERS

No.	Name	1985 Club	W-L	IP	SO	ERA	B-T	Ht.	Wt.	Born
47	Andersen, Larry	Philadelphia	3-3	73	50	4.32	R-R	6-3	205	5/6/53 Portland, OR
—	Bedrosian, Steve	Atlanta	7-15	207	134	3.83	R-R	6-3	195	12/6/57 Methuen, MA
41	Caraballo, Ramon	Reading	0-0	4	3	6.23	R-R	6-4	200	8/20/62 Dominican Republic
32	Carlton, Steve	Philadelphia	1-8	92	48	3.33	L-L	6-5	210	12/22/44 Miami, FL
42	Carman, Don	Philadelphia	9-4	86	87	2.08	L-L	6-3	190	8/14/59 Oklahoma City, OK
50	Childress, Rocky	Portland	5-2	57	30	1.27	R-R	6-2	195	2/18/62 Santa Rosa, CA
		Philadelphia	0-1	33	14	6.21				
52	Gonzalez, Arturo	Portland	10-10	165	85	3.22	R-R	6-3	185	10/29/55 Mexico
46	Gross, Kevin	Philadelphia	15-13	206	151	3.41	R-R	6-5	203	6/8/61 Downey, CA
49	Hudson, Charles	Philadelphia	8-13	193	122	3.78	R-R	6-3	185	3/16/59 Ennis, TX
—	Hume, Tom	Cincinnati	3-5	80	50	3.26	R-R	6-1	185	3/29/53 Cincinnati, OH
44	Maddox, Mike	Portland	9-12	166	96	5.41	R-R	6-2	180	8/27/61 Dayton, OH
48	Rawley, Shane	Philadelphia	13-8	199	106	3.31	R-L	6-0	180	7/27/55 Racine, WI
39	Rucker, Dave	Portland	1-0	16	17	4.50	L-L	6-1	190	9/1/57 San Bernardino, CA
		Philadelphia	3-2	79	41	4.31				
33	Shipanoff, Dave	Portland	8-5	92	115	2.65	R-R	6-2	185	11/13/59 Canada
		Philadelphia	1-2	36	26	3.22				
48	Stewart, Dave	Texas	0-6	81	64	5.42	R-R	6-2	200	2/19/57 Oakland, CA
		Philadelphia	0-0	4	2	6.23				
27	Tekulve, Kent	Pit.-Phi.	4-10	76	40	3.57	R-R	6-4	185	3/5/47 Cincinnati, OH
43	Toliver, Fred	Denver	11-3	122	84	3.24	R-R	6-1	170	2/3/61 Natchez, MS
		Philadelphia	0-4	25	23	4.68				

CATCHERS

No.	Name	1985 Club	H	HR	RBI	Pct.	B-T	Ht.	Wt.	Born
—	Cipolloni, Joe	Reading	70	4	34	.244	R-R	5-8	180	8/12/60 Philadelphia, PA
10	Daulton, Darren	Portland	19	2	10	.297	L-R	6-2	190	1/3/62 Arkansas City, KS
		Philadelphia	21	4	11	.204				
6	Knicely, Alan	Denver	45	7	29	.413	R-R	6-0	195	5/19/55 Harrisonburg, VA
		Portland	22	3	11	.286				
		Cin.-Phi.	40	5	26	.242				
29	Russell, John	Portland	15	4	11	.306	R-R	6-0	200	1/5/61 Oklahoma City, OK
		Philadelphia	47	9	23	.218				

INFIELDERS

16	Aguayo, Luis	Philadelphia	46	6	21	.279	R-R	5-9	185	3/13/59 Puerto Rico
—	Day, Randy	Reading	53	9	34	.228	R-R	6-2	185	12/30/60 Fullerton, CA
—	Escobar, Jose	Reading	31	1	8	.254	R-R	6-0	160	8/24/66 Venezuela
		Portland	35	1	8	.321				
11	Foley, Tom	Cin.-Phi.	60	3	23	.240	L-R	6-1	175	9/9/59 Columbus, GA
30	Jeltz, Steve	Portland	21	1	9	.296	R-R	5-11	170	5/28/59 France
		Philadelphia	37	0	12	.189				
—	Jordan, Ricky	Clearwater	146	7	62	.277	R-R	6-3	185	5/26/65 Richmond, CA
28	Melendez, Francisco	Portland	111	2	54	.280	L-L	6-0	170	1/25/64 Puerto Rico
8	Samuel, Juan	Philadelphia	175	19	74	.264	R-R	5-11	170	12/9/60 Dominican Republic
20	Schmidt, Mike	Philadelphia	152	33	93	.277	R-R	6-2	203	9/27/49 Dayton, OH
15	Schu, Rick	Portland	42	4	22	.280	R-R	6-0	170	1/26/62 Philadelphia, PA
		Philadelphia	105	7	24	.252				

OUTFIELDERS

21	Gross, Greg	Philadelphia	44	0	14	.260	L-L	5-11	175	8/1/52 York, PA
9	Hayes, Von	Philadelphia	150	13	70	.263	L-R	6-5	180	8/31/58 Stockton, CA
34	James, Chris	Portland	160	11	73	.316	R-R	6-1	190	10/4/62 Rusk, TX
23	Lefebvre, Joe	Philadelphia		Disabled list			L-R	5-10	180	2/22/56 Concord, NH
21	Maddox, Garry	Philadelphia	52	4	23	.239	R-R	6-3	190	9/1/49 Cincinnati, OH
2	Redus, Gary	Cincinnati	62	6	28	.252	R-R	6-1	185	11/1/56 Limestone Cty, AL
26	Stone, Jeff	Portland	83	2	28	.329	L-R	6-0	175	12/26/60 Kennett, MO
		Philadelphia	70	3	11	.265				
18	*Thomas, Derrel	Philadelphia	19	4	12	.207	B-R	6-0	160	1/14/51 Los Angeles, CA
—	Thompson, Milt	Richmond	98	2	22	.314	L-R	5-11	165	1/5/59 Washington, DC
		Atlanta	55	0	6	.302				
—	Ward, Kevin	Reading	40	1	21	.303	R-R	6-1	195	9/28/61 Lansdale, PA
12	Wilson, Glenn	Philadelphia	167	14	102	.275	R-R	6-1	190	12/22/58 Baytown, TX

*Free agent unsigned at press time

PHILLIE PROFILES

MIKE SCHMIDT 36 6-2 203 Bats R Throws R

Last year began as sub-par season, but veteran slugger was rejuvenated by May 29 switch to first base . . . Seven-time NL home-run champ had only 11 at All-Star break, but finished among leaders with 22 in second half . . . Enjoyed a torrid final two months, batting .323 in August and September with 17 homers and 44 RBI . . . Won back-to-back NL MVP honors in 1980 and 1981 . . . Selected greatest Phillies player ever in 1983 by the same fans who have booed him during slumps over the years . . . Born Sept. 27, 1949, in Dayton, Ohio . . . Earned business degree from Ohio University . . . Phillies' second-round pick in June 1971 draft . . . Endured horrible pro debut for Reading in 1971, batting .211, but he was in majors for good one year later . . . His 403 homers in the last 11 years is the most in majors—73 more than Dave Kingman and Jim Rice . . . Named 1980 World Series MVP after batting .381 . . . Perennial Gold Glove winner at third base.

Year	Club	Pos.	G	AB	R	H	2B	3B	HR	RBI	SB	Avg.
1972	Philadelphia	3B-2B	13	34	2	7	0	0	1	3	0	.206
1973	Philadelphia	3B-2B-1B-SS	132	367	43	72	11	0	18	52	8	.196
1974	Philadelphia	3B	162	568	108	160	28	7	36	116	23	.282
1975	Philadelphia	3B-SS	158	562	93	140	34	3	38	95	29	.249
1976	Philadelphia	3B	160	584	112	153	31	4	38	107	14	.262
1977	Philadelphia	3B-SS-2B	154	544	114	149	27	11	38	101	15	.274
1978	Philadelphia	3B-SS	145	513	93	129	27	2	21	78	19	.251
1979	Philadelphia	3B-SS	160	541	109	137	25	4	45	114	9	.253
1980	Philadelphia	3B	150	548	104	157	25	8	48	121	12	.286
1981	Philadelphia	3B	102	354	78	112	19	2	31	91	12	.316
1982	Philadelphia	3B	148	514	108	144	26	3	35	87	14	.280
1983	Philadelphia	3B-SS	154	534	104	136	16	4	40	109	7	.255
1984	Philadelphia	3B-1B-SS	151	528	93	146	23	3	36	106	5	.277
1985	Philadelphia	1B-3B	158	549	89	152	31	5	33	93	1	.277
	Totals		1947	6740	1250	1794	323	56	458	1273	168	.266

JUAN SAMUEL 25 5-11 170 Bats R Throws R

Tailed off somewhat following sensational rookie year, but still ranked among league leaders in several categories . . . Became the first major leaguer to reach double figures in doubles, triples, homers and stolen bases in first two years of career . . . Best month was August, when he batted .301 with seven homers and 21 RBI . . . Born Dec. 9, 1960, in San Pedro de Macoris, Dominican Republic . . . Purchased from Escogido of the

Dominican Winter League in 1980 at age 19 . . . Earned many rookie honors in 1984 after ousting Joe Morgan from second-base job . . . Set NL mark with 701 at-bats and set major-league stolen-base mark for a rookie with 72.

Year	Club	Pos.	G	AB	R	H	2B	3B	HR	RBI	SB	Avg.
1983	Philadelphia	2B	18	65	14	18	1	2	2	5	3	.277
1984	Philadelphia	2B	160	701	105	191	36	19	15	69	72	.272
1985	Philadelphia	2B	161	663	101	175	31	13	19	74	53	.264
	Totals		339	1429	220	384	68	34	36	148	128	.269

VON HAYES 27 6-5 180 Bats L Throws R

Center fielder slipped down the stretch following a hot start . . . Batted .366 in April . . . Became only major leaguer to hit two homers in first inning when he connected against the Mets June 11. One of the homers was a grand slam . . . With all his extra-base power, he should be driving in more runs . . . Born Aug. 31, 1958, in Stockton, Cal. . . . Attended St. Mary's College and was teammate of Mike Young, now an Orioles' outfielder . . . Star of USA-Japan College World Series in 1979 . . . Seventh-round draft pick of Indians in June 1979 obviously caught Phillies' eye with 82 RBI in first full major-league season . . . Philadelphia traded five players, including Manny Trillo and Julio Franco, to get him after the 1982 season . . . Has yet to prove he was worth it, but the potential for stardom is there.

Year	Club	Pos.	G	AB	R	H	2B	3B	HR	RBI	SB	Avg.
1981	Cleveland.	OF-3B	43	109	21	28	8	2	1	17	8	.257
1982	Cleveland.	OF-3B-1B	150	527	65	132	25	3	14	82	32	.250
1983	Philadelphia	OF	124	351	45	93	9	5	6	32	20	.265
1984	Philadelphia	OF	152	561	85	164	27	6	16	67	48	.292
1985	Philadelphia	OF	152	570	76	150	30	4	13	70	21	.263
	Totals		621	2118	292	567	99	20	50	268	129	.268

GLENN WILSON 27 6-1 190 Bats R Throws R

Came cheaper than Von Hayes and is proving a better investment . . . Right fielder had team-leading 102 RBI last season . . . Had 24 RBI in June and notched 61 RBI by All-Star break . . . Attained career highs in most offensive departments . . . Didn't have even half as many homers as Mike Schmidt, yet topped club in RBI, attesting to his ability in the clutch . . . Born Dec. 22, 1958, in Baytown, Tex. . . . Two-time All-American at Sam Houston State, where he also played football

. . . Detroit's first-round selection in June 1980 . . . A regular for Tigers in 1983, he was traded to Phillies just prior to start of 1984 season with John Wockenfuss for Dave Bergman and Willie Hernandez, a nondescript reliever in NL who won AL Cy Young Award and AL MVP in 1984.

Year	Club	Pos.	G	AB	R	H	2B	3B	HR	RBI	SB	Avg.
1982	Detroit	OF	84	322	39	94	15	1	12	34	2	.292
1983	Detroit	OF	144	503	55	135	25	6	11	65	1	.268
1984	Philadelphia	OF-3B	132	341	28	82	21	3	6	31	7	.240
1985	Philadelphia	OF	161	608	73	167	39	5	14	102	7	.275
	Totals		521	1774	195	478	100	15	43	232	17	.269

STEVE CARLTON 41 6-5 210 — Bats L Throws L

Some question if "Lefty" has a future after a year in which it appeared he might be washed up, but his 1985 record is not an accurate barometer . . . Besides being disabled for the first time in his career, June 22, with a rotator-cuff strain, he was a victim of non-support, as his decent ERA suggests . . . Entered final month at 1-7, yet ERA was flashy 2.43 . . . In his first 13 starts, Phils scored only 16 runs while he was pitching . . . Born Dec. 22, 1944, in Miami . . . Set major-league record with 500th consecutive start, April 23 . . . NL leader with six career one-hitters . . . Last year was first time in 19 seasons he didn't win in double figures . . . Second behind Nolan Ryan on career strikeout chart . . . Six-time 20-game winner has collected four Cy Young Awards . . . Signed by St. Louis as a free agent in 1963 . . . Traded by Cardinals to Phillies for Rick Wise prior to 1972 season.

Year	Club	G	IP	W	L	Pct.	SO	BB	H	ERA
1965	St. Louis.	15	25	0	0	.000	21	8	27	2.52
1966	St. Louis.	9	52	3	3	.500	25	18	56	3.12
1967	St. Louis.	30	193	14	9	.609	168	62	173	2.98
1968	St. Louis.	34	232	13	11	.542	162	61	214	2.99
1969	St. Louis.	31	236	17	11	.607	210	93	185	2.17
1970	St. Louis.	34	254	10	19	.345	193	109	239	3.72
1971	St. Louis.	37	273	20	9	.600	172	98	275	3.56
1972	Philadelphia.	41	346	27	10	.730	310	87	257	1.98
1973	Philadelphia.	40	293	13	20	.394	223	113	293	3.90
1974	Philadelphia.	39	291	16	13	.552	240	136	249	3.22
1975	Philadelphia.	37	225	15	14	.517	102	104	217	3.56
1076	Philadelphia	35	253	20	7	.741	195	72	224	3.13
1977	Philadelphia.	36	283	23	10	.697	198	89	220	2.64
1978	Philadelphia.	34	247	16	13	.552	161	63	228	2.84
1979	Philadelphia.	35	251	18	11	.621	213	89	202	3.62
1980	Philadelphia.	38	304	24	9	.727	286	90	243	2.34
1981	Philadelphia.	24	190	13	4	.765	179	62	152	2.42
1982	Philadelphia.	38	295⅔	23	11	.676	286	86	253	3.10
1983	Philadelphia.	37	283⅔	15	16	.483	275	84	277	3.11
1984	Philadelphia.	33	229	13	7	.650	163	79	214	3.58
1985	Philadelphia.	16	92	1	8	.111	48	53	84	3.33
	Totals.	673	4878⅓	314	215	.594	3920	1656	4291	3.04

STEVE BEDROSIAN 28 6-3 195 **Bats R Throws R**

A tough-luck pitcher in 1985, he received three or fewer runs of support in 24 of 37 starts with the Braves . . . They traded him and minor leaguer Milt Thompson to the Phils for Ozzie Virgil and Pete Smith at the winter meetings . . . Winless in April, July, August and October in a strange season for former reliever . . . Was exclusively a starter for first time since 1980 . . . "Bedrock" still throws heat, but his walk total almost matches his strikeout total . . . May be better suited for bullpen . . . Born Dec. 6, 1957, in Methuen, Mass . . . Attended New Haven . . . Picked in third round of June 1975 draft . . . Fastball has been clocked at 95 mph . . . Appeared in relief only once as minor leaguer, but he had only nine starts in 189 appearances with Braves prior to 1985 . . . Totaled 41 saves from 1982-84, but Bruce Sutter's presence dramatically altered his role.

Year	Club	G	IP	W	L	Pct.	SO	BB	H	ERA
1981	Atlanta	15	24	1	2	.333	9	15	15	4.50
1982	Atlanta	64	137⅔	8	6	.571	123	57	102	2.42
1983	Atlanta	70	120	9	10	.474	114	51	100	3.60
1984	Atlanta	40	83⅔	9	6	.600	81	33	65	2.37
1985	Atlanta	37	206⅔	7	15	.318	134	111	198	3.83
	Totals	226	572	34	39	.466	461	267	480	3.26

KEVIN GROSS 24 6-5 203 **Bats R Throws R**

A pleasant surprise . . . Blossomed into club's big winner in his first full year as a starter . . . Allowed two runs or fewer in 18 of his first 24 starts . . . Was at his best in July, posting 4-1 record and 2.59 ERA . . . Replaced injured John Denny in rotation in 1984, but was more effective in relief, going 4-0 in that capacity . . . Born June 8, 1961, in Downey, Cal. . . . Attended Cal Lutheran and was selected by Orioles in 32nd round of June 1979 draft . . . Turned down Baltimore and was picked by Phils in secondary phase of January 1981 draft . . . An accomplished artist who has sold many of his paintings.

Year	Club	G	IP	W	L	Pct.	SO	BB	H	ERA
1983	Philadelphia	17	96	4	6	.400	66	35	100	3.56
1984	Philadelphia	44	129	8	5	.615	84	44	140	4.12
1985	Philadelphia	38	205⅔	15	13	.536	151	81	194	3.41
	Totals	99	430⅔	27	24	.529	301	160	434	3.66

DON CARMAN 26 6-3 190 **Bats L Throws L**

Developed into club's top reliever last year after brief stints with Phils in 1983 and 1984 . . . Had fourth-lowest ERA in NL, thanks to a sizzling September in which he was 2-0 with a 0.64 ERA, yielding one run in 14 innings and striking out 21 . . . Wound up with seven saves . . . His ability to throw heat from the left side made former bullpen ace Al Holland expendable . . . Born Aug. 14, 1959, in Oklahoma City, Okla. . . . Attended Oklahoma and was signed as a free agent by Philadelphia in 1978 . . . As a starter, he went 14-5 in second pro season for Peninsula (A) in 1980, striking out 141 in 150 innings . . . Converted to reliever in 1983 and posted 23 saves for Reading.

Year	Club	G	IP	W	L	Pct.	SO	BB	H	ERA
1983	Philadelphia	1	1	0	0	.000	0	0	0	0.00
1984	Philadelphia	11	13⅓	0	1	.000	16	6	14	5.40
1985	Philadelphia	71	86⅓	9	4	.692	87	38	52	2.08
	Totals	83	100⅔	9	5	.643	103	44	66	2.50

SHANE RAWLEY 30 6-0 180 **Bats R Throws L**

Blossomed as ace of rotation, picking up where he left off in 1984 . . . Established himself with 3-0 record and 1.82 ERA in April and was NL Pitcher of the Month in August with a 4-0 record and a 1.72 ERA . . . Primarily a reliever until he entered Yankees' rotation in middle of 1982 . . . Born July 27, 1955, in Racine, Wis. . . . After turning down Dodgers, he was selected in secondary phase of June 1974 draft by Montreal . . . Traded by Yankees to Philadelphia for Marty Bystrom and Keith Hughes, June 30, 1984 . . . Won five straight between Aug. 2 and Sept. 2 in 1984 and became fixture in rotation . . . Has been with five different major-league organizations, but appears to have found a home . . . Has a pilot's license and enjoys flying and golf.

Year	Club	G	IP	W	L	Pct.	SO	BB	H	ERA
1978	Seattle	52	111	4	9	.308	66	51	114	4.14
1979	Seattle	48	84	5	9	357	48	40	88	3.86
1980	Seattle	59	114	7	7	.500	68	63	103	3.32
1981	Seattle	46	68	4	6	.400	35	38	64	3.97
1982	New York (AL)	47	164	11	10	524	111	54	165	4.06
1983	New York (AL)	34	238⅓	14	14	.500	124	79	246	3.78
1984	New York (AL)	11	42	2	3	.400	2	227	46	6.21
1984	Philadelphia	18	120⅓	10	6	.625	58	27	117	3.81
1985	Philadelphia	36	198⅔	13	8	.619	106	81	188	3.31
	Totals	351	1140⅓	70	72	.493	640	460	1131	3.84

Shane Rawley's 3.31 ERA was lowest of Phils' starters.

TOP PROSPECTS

FRED TOLIVER 25 6-1 170 **Bats R Throws R**
Acquired by Phillies in August in deal that sent Bo Diaz to Reds ... Was regarded as an outstanding prospect in the Cincinnati system, going 11-3 with a 3.24 ERA for Denver (AAA) before joining Philadelphia ... Born Feb. 3, 1961, in Natchez, Miss. ... Drafted on third round by Yankees in June 1979, he went 10-2 for Oneonta as first-year pro ... Traded to Reds in 1981 deal involving Ken Griffey and pitched two-hit shutout for Indianapolis (AAA) in 1982 playoffs ... After going 11-6 for Wichita (AAA) in 1984, he pitched 10 innings for Reds, yielding only one earned run ... Was 0-4 with 4.68 ERA and one save for Phillies last season, but had 23 strikeouts in 25 innings.

DAVE SHIPANOFF 26 6-2 185 **Bats R Throws R**
Posted 1-2 record, three saves and 3.22 ERA after being recalled from minors by Phillies ... Regarded as a prime pitching prospect, along with Fred Toliver ... Born Nov. 13, 1959, in Edmonton, Alb. ... Attended Wabash Valley College in Illinois and was signed as a free agent by Toronto in 1980 ... Groomed as a reliever from the start, he saved 30 games in the Carolina League in 1982 and added 18 in Double-A the next year ... Traded by Blue Jays to Phillies in Len Matuszek deal last spring ... Was 8-5 with 13 saves, a 2.65 ERA and 115 strikeouts in 92 innings for Portland (AAA) last season.

MANAGER JOHN FELSKE: A tough rookie season for the man who was being groomed to succeed Paul Owens as the Phils' skipper as early as 1983 ... Phils' slide in September 1984 accelerated the process and Owens returned to the front office after that season ... Was almost same age as two of his pitchers last year, Steve Carlton and Jerry Koosman ... Club was 17-28 after two months, but played almost .500 ball the rest of the way to finish at 75-87 ... Born May 30, 1942, in Chicago ... Attended Illinois before beginning pro career in 1962 ... Played from 1962-73, getting a taste of big-league ball as a catcher with the Cubs and Brewers ... Became a manager in Brew-

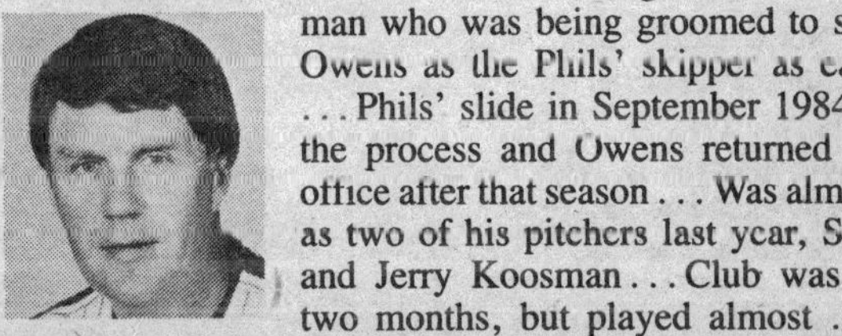

ers' system in 1974 and gained respect for his handling of pitchers . . . Won Pacific Coast League playoffs with Vancouver (AAA) in 1979 . . . Joined Phillies' system in 1982 and guided Portland (AAA) to PCL pennant in 1983 . . . Joined Owens as a coach in 1984 and replaced him when Phils disappointed with 81-81 season following trip to World Series in 1983.

GREATEST SHORTSTOP

Dick Bartell and Davey Bancroft had short, successful flings and Granny Hamner did a good job with the Whiz Kids, but the Phillies haven't had a shortstop who matched Larry Bowa's contributions from 1970-81. The fact he has played more games at shortstop than any other player in National League history attests to his proficiency with a glove.

Bowa won the Gold Glove in 1972, after setting NL records for fewest errors (9) and best fielding percentage (.9874) by a shortstop. In 1979, Larry led the league in fielding a fifth straight year, surpassing his previous marks by making only six errors and recording a .991 fielding percentage—a major-league record.

Bowa, who won two Gold Gloves and deserved many more, was a productive shortstop into his 40s, a remarkable achievement considering the demands of the position. He also contributed with the bat, hitting as high as .305 in 1975, perennially ranking among the league leaders in stolen bases and triples and batting .375 in the 1980 World Series.

ALL-TIME PHILLIE SEASON RECORDS

BATTING: Frank O'Doul, .398, 1929
HRs: Mike Schmidt, 48, 1980
RBIs: Chuck Klein, 170, 1930
STEALS: Juan Samuel, 72, 1984
WINS: Grover Alexander, 33, 1916
STRIKEOUTS: Steve Carlton, 310, 1972

PITTSBURGH PIRATES

TEAM DIRECTORY: President: Malcolm Prine; Treas.: Doug McCormick; VP-GM Baseball Oper.: Syd Thrift; Trav. Sec.: Charles Muse; Mgr.: Jim Leyland. Home: Three Rivers Stadium (58,438). Field distances: 335, l.f. line; 375, l.c.; 400, c.f.; 375, r.c.; 335, r.f. line. Spring training: Bradenton, Fla.

SCOUTING REPORT

HITTING: Unless imports Mike Brown (.332, 5 homers, 33 RBI as a Pirate) and R.J. Reynolds (.282, 3 homers, 42 RBI) pick up where they left off last year and Joe Orsulak (.300) continues to improve as a hitter, the Bucs could be feeble offensively once again this summer. They hit the fewest home runs in the league in 1985 with 80 and only the Giants scored fewer runs than the Pirates' 568. The days of The Lumber Company are long gone.

Jason Thompson (12 homers, 61 RBI) has become a liability

Cat-quick Tony Pena ranks among NL's best two-way catchers.

now that he is no longer a consistent power threat and has given way to young Sid Bream at first. Even reliable Tony Pena got caught up in the club's demise, sinking to .249 last year. Among the veterans, only Johnny Ray (.274, 70 RBI) finished with respectable figures, so new manager Jim Leyland has a good opportunity to reshape the offense to his thinking. He plans to go to a running game in an effort to boost the Pirates' dwindling status.

PITCHING: The Bucs topped the NL in team ERA in 1984, but it got them nowhere. Consequently, they sacrificed pitching to obtain hitting last year and it didn't work. Pittsburgh had the worst record in the league and the pitching declined without John Tudor, who went on to fame with the Cardinals.

Fortunately, the Pirates had the wisdom to sign the discarded Rick Reuschel (14-8, 2.27), who promptly became their ace. His presence and the development of Cecilio Guante (2.72, 5 saves) as a dependable reliever were highlights of an otherwise bleak season that was epitomized by Jose DeLeon's baffling 2-19 record.

DeLeon, who allowed only 138 hits in 162⅔ innings, obviously isn't as bad as his record suggests. A turnaround by him and improvement by Rick Rhoden (10-15, 4.47), Lee Tunnell (4-10, 4.01) and Larry McWilliams (7-9, 4.70) would be a step in the right direction. The bullpen needs a boost from lefty Pat Clements (5-0 as Angel, 0-2 as Pirate) and perhaps young Bob Kipper can win a spot in the rotation.

FIELDING: Reuschel and Pena, the NL's top catcher, earned Gold Gloves and shortstop Sammy Khalifa showed promise, but there are fielding problems at third and first. Even Ray, a dependable second baseman, fell off defensively last year, so a top priority is shoring up the inner defense. The outfield isn't much better, as Brown and Reynolds made too many errors last season considering their limited playing time.

OUTLOOK: When you lose 104 games and virtually stand pat over the winter, it's difficult to be optimistic. The Bucs have the look of a last-place team again unless they can find a way to reverse their numerous close losses (20-38 in one-run games) and give a decent pitching staff reasonable support.

New ownership means new hope for success, but what the Pirates really need is better players. Even Chuck Tanner, a respected motivator, couldn't light the fire under this rag-tag collection, so it could be another long season unless Brown, Reynolds and Orsulak continue to make strides and Ray and Pena play at peak efficiency.

PITTSBURGH PIRATES 1986 ROSTER

MANAGER Jim Leyland

Coaches—Mick Kelleher, Gene Lamont, Ron Schueler, Bill Virdon, Rich Donnelly

PITCHERS

No.	Name	1985 Club	W-L	IP	SO	ERA	B-T	Ht.	Wt.	Born
34	Bielecki, Mike	Pittsburgh	2-3	46	22	4.53	R-R	6-3	200	7/31/59 Baltimore, MD
		Hawaii	8-6	129	111	3.83				
15	Clements, Pat	California	5-0	62	19	3.34	R-L	6-0	180	2/2/62 McCloud, CA
		Pittsburgh	0-2	34	17	3.67				
25	DeLeon, Jose	Hawaii	4-0	41	45	0.88	R-R	6-3	219	12/20/60 Dom. Republic
		Pittsburgh	2-19	163	149	4.70				
59	Fansler, Stan	Nashua	9-7	159	74	3.01	R-R	5-11	185	2/12/65 Elkins, WV
		Hawaii	1-0	12	8	2.31				
35	Green, Chris	Hawaii	3-6	98	91	4.24	L-L	6-4	210	9/5/60 Los Angeles, CA
47	Guante, Cecilio	Pittsburgh	4-6	109	92	2.72	R-R	6-3	200	2/2/60 Dominican Republic
51	Kipper, Bob	California	0-1	3	0	21.60	R-L	6-2	182	7/8/64 Aurora, IL
		Midland	3-3	50	31	3.08				
		Edm.-Haw.	3-0	50	42	1.99				
		Pittsburgh	1-2	25	13	5.11				
46	Krawczyk, Ray	Hawaii	5-3	56	54	2.26	R-R	6-1	186	10/9/59 Sewickley, PA
		Pittsburgh	0-2	8	9	14.04				
55	Lind, Orlando	Prince Williim	11-7	148	149	1.82	R-R	6-1	201	1/30/65 Puerto Rico
49	McWilliams, Larry	Pittsburgh	7-9	126	52	4.70	L-L	6-5	176	2/10/54 Wichita, KS
48	Reuschel, Rick	Hawaii	6-2	54	46	2.50	R-R	6-3	230	5/16/49 Quincy, IL
		Pittsburgh	14-8	194	138	2.27				
29	Rhoden, Rick	Pittsburgh	10-15	213	128	4.47	R-R	6-4	203	5/16/53 Boynton Beach, FL
43	Robinson, Don	Pittsburgh	5-11	95	65	3.87	R-R	6-4	235	6/8/57 Ashland, KY
22	Tunnell, Lee	Hawaii	4-1	47	29	2.31	R-R	6-1	178	10/30/60 Tyler, TX
		Pittsburgh	4-10	132	74	4.01				
18	Walk, Bob	Hawaii	16-5	173	124	2.65	R-R	6-4	212	11/26/56 Van Nuys, CA
		Pittsburgh	2-3	59	40	3.68				
41	Winn, Jim	Hawaii	5-2	43	33	3.38	R-R	6-3	219	9/23/59 Stockton, CA
		Pittsburgh	3-6	76	22	5.23				
44	Zaske, Jeff	Hawaii	2-7	69	75	3.41	R-R	6-5	188	10/6/60 Seattle, WA

CATCHERS

No.	Name	1985 Club	H	HR	RBI	Pct.	B-T	Ht.	Wt.	Born
59	Diaz, Mike	Por.-Haw.	139	22	85	.312	R-R	6-2	205	4/15/60 San Francisco, CA
26	Ortiz, Junior	Pittsburgh	21	1	5	.292	R-R	5-11	176	10/24/59 Puerto Rico
6	Pena, Tony	Pittsburgh	136	10	59	.249	R-R	6-0	181	6/4/57 Dominican Republic
57	Rodriguez, Ruben	Nashua	73	3	40	.214	R-R	6-0	170	8/4/64 Dominican Republic
		Hawaii	1	0	0	.250				

INFIELDERS

No.	Name	1985 Club	H	HR	RBI	Pct.	B-T	Ht.	Wt.	Born
12	Almon, Bill	Pittsburgh	66	6	29	.270	R-R	6-3	191	11/21/52 Providence, RI
37	Belliard, Rafael	Pittsburgh	4	0	1	.200	R-R	5-6	152	10/24/61 Dom. Republic
		Hawaii	84	1	18	.246				
5	Bream, Sid	Albuquerque	110	17	57	.370	L-L	6-4	215	8/3/60 Carlisle, PA
		LA-Pit.	34	6	21	.230				
14	Distefano, Benny	Hawaii	114	14	67	.238	L-L	6-1	195	1/23/62 Brooklyn, NY
24	Gonzalez, Denny	Hawaii	105	12	57	.288	R-R	5-11	185	7/22/63 Dominican Republic
		Pittsburgh	28	4	12	.226				
27	Khalifa, Sammy	Hawaii	61	1	22	.281	R-R	5-11	180	12/5/63 Fontana, CA
		Pittsburgh	76	2	31	.238				
10	LeMaster, Johnnie	Cleveland	3	0	2	.150	R-R	6-2	175	6/19/54 Portsmouth, OH
		SF-Pit.	9	1	6	.122				
54	Miscik, Bobby	Hawaii	115	10	48	.274	R-R	6-0	190	5/16/58 Calumet, PA
2	Morrison, Jim	Pittsburgh	62	4	22	.254	R-R	5-11	186	9/23/52 Pensacola, FL
3	Ray, Johnny	Pittsburgh	163	7	70	.274	B-R	5-11	185	3/1/57 Chouteau, OK
56	Renteria, Rich	Mex. City Tigers	169	19	125	.349	R-R	5-9	172	12/25/61 Harbor City, CA
		Hawaii	6	0	2	.104				
30	Thompson, Jason	Pittsburgh	97	12	61	.241	L-L	6-3	218	7/6/54 Hollywood, CA

OUTFIELDERS

No.	Name	1985 Club	H	HR	RBI	Pct.	B-T	Ht.	Wt.	Born
4	Brown, Mike	California	41	4	20	.268	R-R	6-2	195	12/29/59 San Francisco, CA
		Pittsburgh	68	5	33	.332				
13	Kemp, Steve	Pittsburgh	59	2	21	.250	L-L	6-0	190	8/7/54 San Angelo, TX
28	Lezcano, Sixto	Pittsburgh	24	3	9	.207	R-R	5-10	192	11/28/53 Puerto Rico
16	Mazzilli, Lee	Pittsburgh	33	1	9	.282	B-R	6-1	180	3/25/55 New York, NY
11	Orsulak, Joe	Pittsburgh	119	0	21	.300	L-L	6-1	185	5/31/62 Glen Ridge, NJ
39	Reynolds, R. J.	LA-Pit.	95	3	42	.282	B-R	6-0	190	4/19/60 Sacramento, CA
36	Wynne, Marvell	Pittsburgh	60	2	10	.205	L-L	5-11	170	12/17/59 Chicago, IL

PIRATE PROFILES

TONY PENA 28 6-0 181 Bats R Throws R

An off year for one of the premier catchers in the game . . . Carried lifetime .296 mark into 1985, when he posted a career-low .249 average . . . Enjoyed only one good streak, batting .359 in June . . . Was close to .200 the rest of the time . . . A streak hitter who has always lacked discipline at the plate, but there were too many valleys and not enough peaks last season . . . Born June 4, 1957, in Montecristi, Dominican Republic . . . Signed by Bucs as a free agent in 1975 and gradually improved as a hitter in minors . . . Won second straight Gold Glove in 1984, when he caught staff with best ERA in majors . . . Was top Triple-A catcher in nation in 1980, when he hit .329 for Portland . . . Speed gives him added dimension for a catcher . . . Has 12 stolen bases in each of the past two seasons.

Year	Club	Pos.	G	AB	R	H	2B	3B	HR	RBI	SB	Avg.
1980	Pittsburgh	C	8	21	1	9	1	1	0	1	0	.429
1981	Pittsburgh	C	66	210	16	63	9	1	2	17	1	.300
1982	Pittsburgh	C	138	497	53	147	28	4	11	63	2	.296
1983	Pittsburgh	C	151	542	51	163	22	3	15	70	6	.301
1984	Pittsburgh	C	147	546	77	156	27	2	15	78	12	.286
1985	Pittsburgh	C-1B	147	546	53	136	27	2	10	59	12	.249
	Totals		657	2362	251	674	114	13	53	288	33	.285

JOHNNY RAY 29 5-11 185 Bats S Throws R

One of the best second basemen in the game, he would receive more attention on a contender . . . His average dipped last year, but he did collect career-high 70 RBI . . . Batted .320 in May and finished season on a high note, earning NL Player-of-the-Week distinction for final week with .406 average and 13 RBI . . . Born March 1, 1957, in Chouteau, Okla. . . . Selected by Houston in 12th round of June 1979 draft . . . Acquired from Astros as key player in three-for-one deal that sent Phil Garner to Houston, Aug. 31, 1981 . . . One of toughest batters to strike out in majors . . . Accounted for game-winning RBI in four consecutive games in 1984, an NL record . . . Attended Arkansas . . . Compiled lifetime .327 minor-league average.

Year	Club	Pos.	G	AB	R	H	2B	3B	HR	RBI	SB	Avg.
1981	Pittsburgh	2B	31	102	10	25	11	0	0	6	0	.245
1982	Pittsburgh	2B	162	647	79	182	30	7	7	63	16	.281
1983	Pittsburgh	2B	151	576	68	163	38	7	5	53	18	.283
1984	Pittsburgh	2B	155	555	75	173	38	6	6	67	11	.312
1985	Pittsburgh	2B	154	594	67	163	33	3	7	70	13	.274
	Totals		653	2474	299	706	150	23	25	259	58	.285

JASON THOMPSON 31 6-3 218 — Bats L Throws L

After averaging nearly 22 homers per season in first nine seasons, this slugging first baseman dipped to a team-leading 12 last year . . . Slump created speculation Pirates would try to move him, but his contract is prohibitive . . . His best month was July, when he hit one homer and batted .272 . . . Lack of aggressiveness at plate is blamed for his decline as power hitter . . . Born July 6, 1954, in Hollywood, Cal. . . . Selected by Tigers in fourth round of June 1975 draft . . . Among the few players to hit 30 home runs in each league . . . Acquired from Angels for Ed Ott and Mickey Mahler prior to 1981 season . . . Has gradually slipped every season since 1982 . . . Has become a one-dimensional player and didn't even provide his specialty—home runs—last year . . . A liability on the bases, he strikes out too much and has poor range afield.

Year	Club	Pos.	G	AB	R	H	2B	3B	HR	RBI	SB	Avg.
1976	Detroit	1B	123	412	45	90	12	1	17	54	2	.218
1977	Detroit	1B	158	585	87	158	24	5	31	105	0	.270
1978	Detroit	1B	153	589	79	169	25	3	26	96	0	.287
1979	Detroit	1B	145	492	58	121	16	1	20	79	2	.246
1980	Det.-Cal.	1B	138	438	69	126	19	0	21	90	2	.288
1981	Pittsburgh	1B	86	223	36	54	13	0	15	42	0	.242
1982	Pittsburgh	1B	156	550	87	156	32	0	31	101	1	.284
1983	Pittsburgh	1B	152	517	70	134	20	1	18	76	1	.259
1984	Pittsburgh	1B	154	543	61	138	22	0	17	74	0	.254
1985	Pittsburgh	1B	123	402	42	97	17	1	12	61	0	.241
	Totals		1388	4751	634	1243	200	12	208	778	8	.262

JOE ORSULAK 23 6-1 185 — Bats L Throws L

Enjoyed an excellent rookie season . . . Gave an indication of what was to come with a .375 April . . . Born May 31, 1962, in Glen Rock, N.J. . . . Selected in sixth round of June 1980 draft, following three-sport stardom as a prep that included all-state honors as a soccer goalie . . . Batted .315 as a first-year pro for Greenwood in 1981 . . . Had 13 triples and 38 steals for Hawaii (AAA) in 1983, prior to reaching parent club . . . Hit safely in 11 straight games late in the 1984 season . . . Injury to center fielder Marvell Wynne gave him big chance and he made most of it.

Year	Club	Pos.	G	AB	R	H	2B	3B	HR	RBI	SB	Avg.
1983	Pittsburgh	OF	7	11	0	2	0	0	0	1	0	.182
1984	Pittsburgh	OF	32	67	12	17	1	2	0	3	3	.254
1985	Pittsburgh	OF	121	397	54	119	14	6	0	21	24	.300
	Totals		160	475	66	138	15	8	0	25	27	.291

MIKE BROWN 26 6-2 195 **Bats R Throws R**

Key player for Pirates in deal that sent John Candelaria to Angels . . . Though he had only 205 NL at-bats, he topped Pirates in hitting at .332 and has a bright future . . . Joined Bucs in August and was an immediate sensation, batting .341 for the month . . . Born Dec. 29, 1959, in San Francisco . . . Attended San Jose State and was picked by Angels in seventh round of June 1980 draft . . . Developed into outstanding Triple-A hitter at Edmonton in 1983, batting .354 with 22 homers and 106 RBI . . . Was promoted to bigs following .343 start in 1984 . . . Had a pair of two-homer games in one week for Angels in 1984 . . . Began career as catcher and outfielder, but he's strictly a fly-chaser now.

Year	Club	Pos.	G	AB	R	H	2B	3B	HR	RBI	SB	Avg.
1983	California	OF	31	104	12	24	5	1	3	9	1	.231
1984	California	OF	62	148	19	42	8	3	7	22	0	.284
1985	California	OF	60	153	23	41	9	1	4	20	0	.268
1985	Pittsburgh	OF	57	205	29	68	18	2	5	33	2	.332
	Totals		210	610	83	175	40	7	19	84	3	.287

R.J. REYNOLDS 25 6-0 190 **Bats S Throws R**

Outfielder got a new lease on life when he joined Bucs as part of Bill Madlock swap in August and made the best of the opportunity . . . Batted .314 with nine stolen bases in September . . . A minor-league standout in the Dodgers' system, he got caught in numbers trap and his progress was retarded by groin injury . . . Born April 19, 1960, in Sacramento, Cal. . . . Dodgers' second pick in January 1980 draft . . . Batted .337 with 18 homers, 89 RBI and 43 stolen bases for San Antonio (AA) in 1983 and improved to .347 for Albuquerque (AAA) in 1984 . . . Became a switch-hitter in 1982 . . . First major-league hit was a three-run homer off Ed Whitson in 1983 . . . Concentrated on basketball in junior college, but returned to baseball after a three-year absence.

Year	Club	Pos.	G	AB	R	H	2B	3B	HR	RBI	SB	Avg.
1983	Los Angeles	OF	24	55	5	13	0	0	2	11	5	.236
1984	Los Angeles	OF	73	240	24	62	12	2	2	24	7	.258
1985	L.A.-Pitt.	OF	104	337	44	95	15	7	3	42	18	.282
	Totals		201	632	73	170	27	9	7	77	30	.269

RICK REUSCHEL 36 6-3 230 Bats R Throws R

Comeback Pitcher of the Year . . . Recorded most wins since 1979 and his lowest ERA ever . . . What made it more surprising is that this veteran had to beg for work in spring training . . . Was turned down by Giants . . . Started 1985 in minors at Hawaii (AAA) . . . Earned job in Bucs' rotation with solid June, posting 4-1 mark with 2.79 ERA during that month . . . Born May 16, 1949, in Quincy, Ill. . . . Cubs' third-round draft choice in June 1970 . . . Succeeded Fergie Jenkins as ace of Chicago staff and has enjoyed distinguished career . . . After stint with Yankees and trips to minors, he returned to Cubs in 1983, but was granted free agency after 1984 season . . . Fooled 'em all by bouncing back to rank among NL ERA and complete-game leaders, despite late start . . . Went 4-0 with 1.29 ERA in September.

Year	Club	G	IP	W	L	Pct.	SO	BB	H	ERA
1972	Chicago (NL)	21	129	10	8	.556	87	29	127	2.93
1973	Chicago (NL)	36	237	14	15	483	168	62	244	3.00
1974	Chicago (NL)	41	241	13	12	.520	160	83	262	4.29
1975	Chicago (NL)	38	234	11	17	.393	155	67	244	3.73
1976	Chicago (NL)	38	260	14	12	.538	146	64	260	3.46
1977	Chicago (NL)	39	252	20	10	.667	166	74	233	2.33
1978	Chicago (NL)	35	243	14	15	.483	115	54	235	3.41
1979	Chicago (NL)	36	239	18	12	.600	125	75	251	3.62
1980	Chicago (NL)	38	257	11	13	.458	140	76	281	3.40
1981	Chicago (NL)	13	86	4	7	.364	53	23	87	3.45
1981	New York (AL)	12	71	4	4	.500	22	10	75	2.66
1982	New York (AL)					Did Not Play				
1983	Chicago (NL)	4	20⅔	1	1	.500	9	10	18	3.92
1984	Chicago (NL)	19	92⅓	5	5	.500	43	23	123	5.17
1985	Pittsburgh	31	194	14	8	.600	138	52	153	2.27
	Totals	401	2556	153	139	.524	1527	702	2593	3.38

RICK RHODEN 32 6-4 203 Bats R Throws R

Endured worst season of major-league career, going 3-2 in May, 3-1 in August and a putrid 4-12 rest of the time . . . Entered 1985 with lifetime 3.45 ERA, but his 1985 mark was more than one run higher than that . . . Overcame disease that left him with withered leg as a youngster and became solid major-league pitcher through hard work . . . Helps himself with the bat and is a good fielder . . . A tough competitor who couldn't overcome poor support last year the way he did in 1984 . . . Born May 16, 1953, in Boynton Beach, Fla. . . . Selected by Dodgers in first round of June 1971 draft . . . Reached majors in 1974 and was on NL All-Star squad by 1976 . . . Had great season with LA one year later, but was traded to Bucs for Jerry Reuss prior to

1979 . . . Shoulder injury in 1979 required surgery . . . During rehabilitation, he pitched a no-hitter for Portland (AAA) in 1980.

Year	Club	G	IP	W	L	Pct.	SO	BB	H	ERA
1974	Los Angeles.	4	9	1	0	1.000	7	4	5	2.00
1975	Los Angeles.	26	99	3	3	.500	40	32	94	3.09
1976	Los Angeles.	27	181	12	3	*.800	77	53	165	2.98
1977	Los Angeles.	31	216	16	10	.615	122	63	223	3.75
1978	Los Angeles.	30	165	10	8	.556	79	51	160	3.65
1979	Pittsburgh	1	5	0	1	.000	2	2	5	7.20
1980	Pittsburgh	20	127	7	5	.583	70	40	133	3.83
1981	Pittsburgh	21	136	9	4	.692	76	53	147	3.90
1982	Pittsburgh	35	230⅓	11	14	.440	128	70	239	4.14
1983	Pittsburgh	36	244⅓	13	13	.500	153	68	256	3.09
1984	Pittsburgh	33	238⅓	14	9	.609	136	62	216	2.72
1985	Pittsburgh	35	213⅓	10	15	.400	128	69	254	4.47
	Totals	299	1864⅓	106	85	.555	1018	567	1897	3.56

JOSE DeLEON 25 6-3 219 — Bats R Throws R

If he ever learns to become a pitcher instead of a thrower, NL hitters will be in trouble . . . A lot of teams would love to have him because of his stuff, but a combined record of 9-32 the last two years suggests he's not a thinking man's pitcher . . . Included among the Bucs' top hurlers because he has the potential to blossom . . . As the saying goes, you have to be good to be allowed to lose 19 games . . . Born Dec. 20, 1960, in Rancho Viejo LaVega, Dominican Republic . . . Signed as third-round pick in June 1979 draft . . . Gave an indication of his promise in 1983, combining for 18-9 mark at Hawaii (AAA) and Pittsburgh, including near no-hitters against Padres, Mets and Reds . . . A specialist in strikeouts and losses last two years, but too good to give up on.

Year	Club	G	IP	W	L	Pct.	SO	BB	H	ERA
1983	Pittsburgh	15	108	7	3	.700	118	47	75	2.83
1984	Pittsburgh	30	192⅓	7	13	.350	153	92	147	3.74
1985	Pittsburgh	31	162⅔	2	19	.095	149	89	138	4.70
	Totals	76	463	16	35	.314	420	228	360	3.87

CECILIO GUANTE 26 6-3 200 — Bats R Throws R

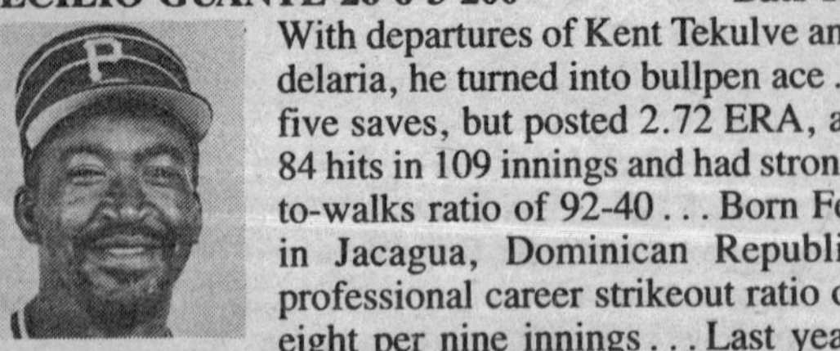

With departures of Kent Tekulve and John Candelaria, he turned into bullpen ace . . . Had only five saves, but posted 2.72 ERA, allowed only 84 hits in 109 innings and had strong strikeouts-to-walks ratio of 92-40 . . . Born Feb. 2, 1960, in Jacagua, Dominican Republic . . . Has a professional career strikeout ratio of more than eight per nine innings . . . Last year, he developed the control to accompany his blazer, so stardom may be in the offing . . . Signed by the Bucs as a free agent in 1979 . . . Has been a reliever in all but one appearance since 1981 season... Posted a career-high 19 saves and 114 strikeouts in 90 innings as a pro rookie for Shelby in 1980... Injuries marred his 1984 season, but he proved his worth as one of Bucs' few bright spots during dismal 1985.

Year	Club	G	IP	W	L	Pct.	SO	BB	H	ERA
1982	Pittsburgh	10	27	0	0	.000	26	5	28	3.33
1983	Pittsburgh	49	100⅓	2	6	.250	82	46	90	3.32
1984	Pittsburgh	27	41⅓	2	3	.400	30	16	32	2.61
1985	Pittsburgh	63	109	4	6	.400	92	40	84	2.72
	Totals	149	277⅔	8	15	.348	230	107	234	2.98

TOP PROSPECT

SID BREAM 25 6-4 215 Bats L Throws L

R.J. Reynolds and Mike Brown have played too many games in the majors to qualify as prospects, but this fellow newcomer to Pirates organization fills the bill... Will be the Bucs' first baseman when Jason Thompson and his fat contract are unloaded... He's ready following a successful minor-league career with the Dodgers ... Born Aug. 3, 1960, in Carlisle, Pa.... Dodgers' second pick in June 1981 draft... Attended Liberty Baptist College and once hit four homers in a college game... Topped PCL with 118 RBI for Albuquerque (AAA) in 1983, when he blasted 32 homers... Joined Pirates in Bill Madlock deal... Hit .230 with six homers and 21 RBI in 148 major-league at-bats in 1985... Hit .370 with 17 homers and 57 RBI for Albuquerque (AAA) last season.

MANAGER JIM LEYLAND: Filled last major-league managerial vacancy when the Bucs hired him on Nov. 19... Gained a reputation as an astute baseball man in Tigers' system and served the White Sox as third-base coach the last four years... Reportedly was nosed out by Hal Lanier for the Houston job before Bucs beckoned ... Predicts that second-guessers will have fun in 1986 because he doesn't regard himself as a conventional manager... Born Dec. 15, 1944, in Toledo, Ohio ... Was a minor-league catcher in Tigers' organization, but never reached bigs... Became minor-league manager at age 26 with Bristol of Appalachian League in 1971... Managed 11 seasons

in Detroit farm system and made playoffs six times, winning three pennants . . . Three-time Manager of the Year, with Lakeland of Florida State League in 1977 and 1978 and with Evansville of American Association in 1981 . . . Joined White Sox in 1982 and became touted as major-league managerial timber.

GREATEST SHORTSTOP

Sure, the Bucs have had smoother fielders at shortstop and oldtimers Glenn Wright and Arky Vaughan were good enough to rank as the best on many clubs, but it would be heresy to choose anyone but Hall of Famer Honus Wagner as the best at that position for Pittsburgh. With apologies to Roberto Clemente and Willie Stargell, Wagner still ranks as the greatest Pirate of them all.

"The Flying Dutchman" would make 50 errors in a season, but the shortstops of his day had little leather on their hands and infields were rocky. And Honus compensated for his fielding by being the most prolific offensive shortstop in the history of the game, as evidenced by his .327 lifetime average over 21 years.

Wagner won eight batting titles, never hitting less than .320 from 1899-1912. He added four stolen-base crowns, had five RBI titles and led the league in doubles seven times. Frankly, we don't know how good Wagner was in the field, but anyone who can do that much damage with the bat can play anywhere he wants.

ALL-TIME PIRATE SEASON RECORDS

BATTING: Arky Vaughan, .385, 1935
HRs: Ralph Kiner, 54, 1949
RBIs: Paul Waner, 131, 1927
STEALS: Omar Moreno, 96, 1980
WINS: Jack Chesbro, 28, 1902
STRIKEOUTS: Bob Veale, 276, 1965

ST. LOUIS CARDINALS

TEAM DIRECTORY: Chariman-Pres.: August A. Busch, Jr.; GM: Dal Maxvill; Senior VP: Stan Musial; Dir. Play. Pers.: Lee Thomas; Dir. Pub. Rel.: Jim Toomey; Trav. Sec.: C.J. Cherre; Mgr.: Whitey Herzog. Home: Busch Stadium (50,122). Field distances: 330, l.f. line; 414, c.f.; 330, r.f. line. Spring training: St. Petersburg, Fla.

SCOUTING REPORT

HITTING: The pennant winners were woefully deficient in power (87 homers) last year, but that didn't deter them from leading the league in runs scored (747) and compiling one of history's highest stolen-base figures (314). Those same ingredients will be evident this season, as the Running Redbirds attempt to steal another pennant with the same formula.

A healthy Jack Clark (22 homers, 87 RBI) could mean 30 homers, so the lineup isn't devoid of power, yet the success of the club hinges on the table-setters at the top of the order, Vince Coleman (.267, 107 runs, 110 steals) and NL MVP Willie McGee (.353, 114 runs, 56 steals). Coleman's absence in the World Series, along with parsimonious Royals' pitching, underscored how important the running game is to the St. Louis attack.

The Cardinals don't need power because they are tailored to

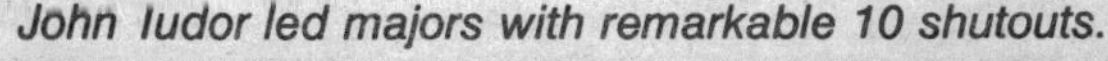

John Tudor led majors with remarkable 10 shutouts.

spacious Busch Stadium, where their speed produced a 54-27 record, the best home mark in the league in 1985. McGee and Tom Herr (.302, 110 RBI) will be hard-pressed to duplicate the best seasons of their careers, but it's not unrealistic to expect improvement from youngsters like Coleman and Terry Pendleton plus an offensive boost from former A's catcher Mike Heath.

PITCHING: It was much better than anyone could have expected minus the services of Bruce Sutter last year. Whitey Herzog's "bullpen by committee" more than picked up the slack, going until Game 6 of the World Series before blowing a ninth-inning lead. Sutter's absence enabled the club to develop Jeff Lahti (1.84, 19 saves), Ken Dayley (2.76, 11 saves) and future star Todd Worrell (2.91, 5 saves).

Among the starters, the Cardinals must find a replacement for exiled 21-game winner Joaquin Andujar and Bob Forsch isn't getting any younger. John Tudor (21-8, 1.93) and Danny Cox (18-9, 2.88), however, are real solid, so the club should be above-average on the hill with a deeper and more experienced bullpen. However, it's difficult to imagine Tudor enjoying a better season than he did in 1985, Game 7 of the World Series notwithstanding.

FIELDING: This is the Cardinals' forte. Defense often is overlooked in judging baseball teams, but the Redbirds have no peers afield. It all starts with Ozzie Smith's wizardry at shortstop and McGee's skill in center, which make the club magnificent up the middle. Herr is no slouch at second base, either, and Pendleton came on strong at the end of the year to prove his value at third base. Heath has a gun behind the plate. The NL champs made a league-low 108 errors last year and there's no reason to expect a change.

OVERALL: The Cardinals will have difficulty repeating simply because it doesn't happen very often. They got by without Sutter last year, but it remains to be seen whether the Andujar void can be filled. Despite criticism of his temperament and erratic performance, he was a proven winner. Now, it all falls on the shoulders of Tudor and Cox, who may not be capable of pitching better than they did in 1985.

Offense will not be a problem unless a key player or two are injured. In fact, the Cardinals' attack may be even more potent than the one that produced 101 victories last season. But pitching could be a thorn. Everything went right for the bullpen last year and the Cards had better quality and depth in the rotation. It will be interesting to see if St. Louis is hungry enough to deny the Mets again.

ST. LOUIS CARDINALS 1986 ROSTER

MANAGER Whitey Herzog
Coaches—Rich Hacker, Johnny Lewis, Nick Leyva, Dave Ricketts, Mike Roarke, Red Schoendienst

PITCHERS

No.	Name	1985 Club	W-L	IP	SO	ERA	B-T	Ht.	Wt.	Born
40	*Bair, Doug	Detroit	2-0	49	39	6.24	R-R	6-0	180	8/22/49 Defiance, OH
		St. Louis	0-0	2	0	0.00				
36	Boever, Joe	Arkansas	2-1	38	45	1.19	R-R	6-1	200	10/4/60 St. Louis, MO
		Louisville	3-2	35	37	2.04				
		St. Louis	0-0	16	20	4.41				
44	Buonantony, Rich	Arkansas	10-11	147	121	4.64	R-R	6-4	205	11/28/62 Hoboken, NJ
—	Conroy, Tim	Tacoma	11-3	129	167	3.27	L-L	6-1	185	4/3/60 Monroeville, PA
		Oakland	0-1	25	8	4.26				
34	Cox, Danny	St. Louis	18-9	241	131	2.88	R-R	6-4	230	9/21/59 England
46	Dayley, Ken	St. Louis	4-4	65	62	2.76	L-L	6-0	178	2/25/59 Jerome, IN
42	Dunn, Greg	Springfield	4-9	80	114	2.48	R-R	6-0	180	1/7/62 Atwater, CA
31	Forsch, Bob	St. Louis	9-6	136	48	3.90	R-R	6-4	200	1/13/50 Sacramento, CA
25	Hagen, Kevin	Louisville	10-9	170	63	3.28	R-R	6-2	185	3/8/60 Renton, WA
49	Horton, Rick	St. Louis	3-2	90	59	2.91	L-L	6-2	195	7/30/59 Poughkeepsie, NY
33	*Keough, Matt	St. Louis	0-1	10	10	4.50	R-R	6-3	185	7/3/55 Pomona, CA
50	Kepshire, Kurt	St. Louis	10-9	153	67	4.75	L-R	6-2	195	7/3/59 Bridgeport, CT
32	Lahti, Jeff	St. Louis	5-2	68	41	1.84	R-R	6-0	180	10/8/56 Oregon City, OR
40	Ownbey, Rick	Louisville	10-9	166	121	3.41	R-R	6-3	185	10/20/57 Corona, CA
37	Perry, Pat	Louisville	4-3	91	62	2.37	L-L	6-1	170	2/4/59 Taylorville, IL
		St. Louis	1-0	12	6	0.00				
—	Ross, Mark	Tucson	8-5	77	31	3.62	R-R	6-0	195	8/8/57 Galveston, TX
		Houston	0-2	13	3	4.85				
41	Shade, Mike	Louisville	0-2	31	31	5.74	R-R	6-2	205	3/7/61 Pottsville, PA
		Arkansas	0-7	41	36	4.39				
30	Tudor, John	St. Louis	21-8	275	169	1.93	L-L	6-0	185	2/2/54 Schenectady, NY
38	Worrell, Todd	Louisville	8-6	128	126	3.60	R-R	6-5	200	9/28/59 Arcadia, CA
		St. Louis	3-0	22	17	2.91				

CATCHERS

No.	Name	1985 Club	H	HR	RBI	Pct.	B-T	Ht.	Wt.	Born
2	Heath, Mike	Oakland	109	13	55	.250	R-R	5-11	180	2/5/55 Tampa, FL
10	Hunt, Randy	Louisville	25	1	8	.278	R-R	6-0	185	1/3/60 Montgomery, AL
		Oklahoma City	24	0	15	.240				
		St. Louis	3	0	1	.158				
—	Hurdle, Clint	New York (NL)	16	3	7	.195	L-R	6-3	195	7/30/57 Big Rapids, MI
11	Lavalliere, Mike	Louisville	47	4	26	.203	L-R	5-10	200	8/18/60 Charlotte, NC
		St. Louis	5	0	6	.147				
23	Nieto, Tom	St. Louis	67	0	34	.225	R-R	6-1	205	10/27/60 Downey, CA
19	Pagnozzi, Tom	Arkansas	43	4	29	.309	R-R	6-1	190	7/30/62 Tucson, AZ
		Louisville	72	5	40	.269				

INFIELDERS

No.	Name	1985 Club	H	HR	RBI	Pct.	B-T	Ht.	Wt.	Born
22	Clark, Jack	St. Louis	124	22	87	.281	R-R	6-3	205	11/10/55 New Brighton, PA
11	*DeJesus, Ivan	St. Louis	16	0	7	.222	R-R	5-11	182	1/9/53 Puerto Rico
28	Herr, Tom	St. Louis	180	8	110	.302	B-R	6-0	185	4/4/56 Lancaster, PA
19	*Jorgensen, Mike	St. Louis	22	0	11	.196	L-L	6-0	187	8/16/48 Passaic, NJ
12	Lawless, Tom	Louisville	36	1	12	.290	R-R	5-9	165	12/19/56 Erie, PA
		St. Louis	12	0	8	.207				
13	Lindeman, Jim	Arkansas	127	10	63	.282	R-R	6-1	200	1/10/62 Evanston, IL
5	Oquendo, Jose	Louisville	81	1	28	.211	R-R	5-10	160	7/4/63 Puerto Rico
9	Pendleton, Terry	St. Louis	134	5	69	.240	B-R	5-9	180	7/16/60 Los Angeles, CA
1	Smith, Ozzie	St. Louis	140	6	54	.276	B-R	5-10	150	12/26/54 Mobile, AL

OUTFIELDERS

No.	Name	1985 Club	H	HR	RBI	Pct.	B-T	Ht.	Wt.	Born
26	Braun, Steve	St. Louis	16	1	6	.239	L-R	5-10	180	5/8/48 Trenton, NJ
7	*Cedeno, Cesar	Cin.-St. L.	86	9	49	.291	R-R	6-2	195	2/25/51 Dominican Republic
29	Coleman, Vince	Louisville	3	0	0	.143	B-R	6-0	170	9/22/61 Jacksonville, FL
		St. Louis	170	1	40	.267				
27	Ford, Curt	Louisville	121	7	45	.255	L-R	5-10	150	10/11/60 Jackson, MS
		St. Louis	6	0	3	.500				
25	Harper, Brian	St. Louis	13	0	8	.250	R-R	6-2	195	10/16/59 Los Angeles, CA
21	Landrum, Tito	St. Louis	45	4	21	.280	R-R	5-11	175	10/25/54 Joplin, MO
51	McGee, Willie	St. Louis	216	10	82	.353	B-R	6-1	175	11/2/58 San Francisco, CA
33	Morris, John	Oma.-Lou.	117	5	50	.251	L-L	6-1	185	2/23/61 Freeport, NY
18	Van Slyke, Andy	St. Louis	110	13	55	.259	L-R	6-1	190	12/21/60 Utica, NY

*Free agent unsigned at press time

CARDINAL PROFILES

JACK CLARK 30 6-3 205 **Bats R Throws R**

Cardinals said they acquired him to lead them to a pennant and he took their words literally . . . His three-run, two-out, ninth-inning homer in Game 6 of NLCS gave Cards a flag and broke Dodgers' hearts . . . It was only his second homer since being shelved by strained muscles along rib cage Aug. 23 . . . Topped club in World Series RBI with four . . . Ranked among NL leaders in power categories at time of injury . . . Born Nov. 10, 1955, in New Brighton, Pa. . . . Giants' 13th-round pick in June 1973 draft . . . Blossomed in second full season as a regular in 1978, setting all-time Giant marks with 46 doubles and a 26-game hitting streak . . . Fell out of favor in San Francisco because of constant complaints about losing atmosphere . . . Cards liberated him by sending Dave LaPoint, David Green, Jose Uribe and Gary Rajsich to Giants prior to 1985 season . . . A great clutch hitter with a quick bat . . . Made smooth conversion from outfield to first base last year.

Year	Club	Pos.	G	AB	R	H	2B	3B	HR	RBI	SB	Avg.
1975	San Francisco.	OF-3B	8	17	3	4	0	0	0	2	1	.235
1976	San Francisco.	OF	26	102	14	23	6	2	2	10	6	.225
1977	San Francisco.	OF	136	413	64	104	17	4	13	51	12	.252
1978	San Francisco.	OF	156	592	90	181	46	8	25	98	15	.306
1979	San Francisco.	OF-3B	143	527	84	144	25	2	26	86	11	.273
1980	San Francisco.	OF	127	437	77	124	20	8	22	82	2	.284
1981	San Francisco.	OF	99	385	60	103	19	2	17	53	1	.268
1982	San Francisco.	OF	157	563	90	154	30	3	27	103	6	.274
1983	San Francisco.	OF-1B	135	492	82	132	25	0	20	66	5	.268
1984	San Francisco.	OF-1B	57	203	33	65	9	1	11	44	1	.320
1985	St. Louis	1B-OF	126	442	71	124	26	3	22	87	1	.281
	Totals		1170	4173	668	1158	223	33	185	682	61	.277

TOM HERR 29 6-0 185 **Bats S Throws R**

Joined Rogers Hornsby and Frankie Frisch as only Cardinals' second basemen to notch 100 RBI in a season . . . Enjoyed fantastic year, battling teammate Willie McGee for NL batting lead during first half . . . A .391 April was followed by a .358 May . . . Batted .333 with team-leading six RBI in NLCS . . . Born April 4, 1956, in Lancaster, Pa. . . . A force in September pennant dash with a 10-game hitting streak . . . Signed with St. Louis as a free agent in 1974 . . . Became regular in 1981, when manager Whitey Herzog shifted Ken Oberkfell to third . . . Got off to great start in 1983 before a knee injury limited him to 89 games . . . A solid fielder whose defense was overlooked because of his offense last season . . . Thrived in No. 3 spot, hitting behind speedy Vince Coleman and McGee . . . Had 14 game-winning RBI last season.

Year	Club	Pos.	G	AB	R	H	2B	3B	HR	RBI	SB	Avg.
1979	St. Louis	2B	14	10	4	2	0	0	0	1	1	.200
1980	St. Louis	2B-SS	76	222	29	55	12	5	0	15	9	.248
1981	St. Louis	2B	103	411	50	110	14	9	0	46	23	.268
1982	St. Louis	2B	135	493	83	131	19	4	0	36	25	.266
1983	St. Louis	2B	89	313	43	101	14	4	2	31	6	.323
1984	St. Louis	2B	145	558	67	154	23	2	4	49	13	.276
1985	St. Louis	2B	159	596	97	180	38	3	8	110	31	.302
	Totals		721	2603	373	733	120	27	14	288	108	.282

WILLIE McGEE 27 6-1 175 **Bats S Throws R**

Topped NL in batting, hits and triples . . . Joined Pete Rose as only switch-hitters to win an NL batting title. . . . Recorded highest average ever by NL switch-hitter, surpassing .348 posted by Rose and Frankie Frisch . . . His 216 hits were most in league in 12 years . . . NL Player of the Month in August with a .436 average and 19 RBI . . . Batted .349 in May with 16 steals . . . Batted .346 in June and .355 in July . . . Remarkably consistent season left him weary in postseason . . . Born Nov. 2, 1958, in San Francisco . . . Yankees' top choice in secondary phase of January 1977 draft . . . Emerged as star at Nashville (AA) in 1981, where he teamed with Don Mattingly . . . Traded to Cardinals for Bob Sykes following 1981 season . . . Nice going, George . . . A defensive standout who covers lots of ground in Busch Stadium's spacious center field . . . Led Cards with 17 game-winning RBI last season . . . Named NL MVP.

Year	Club	Pos.	G	AB	R	H	2B	3B	HR	RBI	SB	Avg.
1982	St. Louis	OF	123	422	43	125	12	8	4	56	24	.296
1983	St. Louis	OF	147	601	75	172	22	8	5	75	39	.286
1984	St. Louis	OF	145	571	82	166	19	11	6	50	43	.291
1985	St. Louis	OF	152	612	114	216	26	18	10	82	56	.353
	Totals		567	2206	314	679	79	45	25	263	162	.308

OZZIE SMITH 31 5-10 150 **Bats S Throws R**

"The Wizard" did it again last year, earning sixth straight Gold Glove for his excellence at shortstop . . . Added a power dimension as MVP of NLCS . . . His game-winning homer off Dodgers' Tom Niedenfuer in Game 6 of playoffs was his first career homer from the left side and he wound up with .435 average in series . . . Slumped along with teammates in World Series . . . Best month of season was May, when he hit .308 . . . Posted a career-high batting average after signing lucrative four-year contract extension . . . Cards had been ridiculed for creating the first million-dollar-per-year glove man, but he showed critics

...Born Dec. 26, 1954, in Mobile, Ala.... Attended Cal Poly San Luis Obispo... Drafted by Padres in fourth round in June 1977, he was their regular shortstop one year later... A dazzling, acrobatic fielder from the start, but now he also holds his own offensively... Set major-league mark for assists in 1980... A solid, all-around player whose other accomplishments pale in comparison to his spectacular fielding.

Year	Club	Pos.	G	AB	R	H	2B	3B	HR	RBI	SB	Avg.
1978	San Diego	SS	159	590	69	152	17	6	1	46	40	.258
1979	San Diego	SS	156	587	77	124	18	6	0	27	28	.211
1980	San Diego	SS	158	609	67	140	18	5	0	35	57	.230
1981	San Diego	SS	110	450	53	100	11	2	0	21	22	.222
1982	St. Louis........	SS	140	488	58	121	24	1	2	43	25	.248
1983	St. Louis........	SS	159	552	69	134	30	6	3	50	34	.243
1984	St. Louis........	SS	124	412	53	106	20	5	1	44	35	.257
1985	St. Louis........	SS	158	537	70	148	22	3	6	54	31	.276
	Totals..........		1164	4225	516	1025	160	34	13	320	272	.243

VINCE COLEMAN 24 6-0 170 Bats S Throws R

Batted .286 in first three games of NLCS before killer automatic tarp in St. Louis caused knee injury that shelved him for remainder of postseason... Originally called up to replace injured Willie McGee, he became regular in eighth game of season and went on to shatter rookie record with 110 steals... Left fielder had more steals than five NL teams... Started with .300 average and dozen steals in April... Stole 20 bases in July... His 73rd steal erased Juan Samuel's rookie record Aug. 1... Born Sept. 22, 1961, in Jacksonville, Fla.... Attended Florida A&M and had dreams of becoming an NFL punter... Cardinals' 10th-round pick in June 1982 draft... Set all-time pro record with 145 steals for Mason (A) in 1983... Named NL Rookie of the Year.

Year	Club	Pos.	G	AB	R	H	2B	3B	HR	RBI	SB	Avg.
1985	St. Louis........	OF	151	636	107	170	20	10	1	40	110	.267

TITO LANDRUM 31 5-11 175 Bats R Throws R

A postseason surprise for Cardinals, he hit .429 in NLCS and .360 in World Series as sub for injured Vince Coleman in left... Club's top pinch-hitter during season with .333 mark... Has a Midas touch for landing on pennant winners, playing on three in last four years... Played only 26 games in AL, but posted .310 average for 1983 Orioles... Put Baltimore in World Series with clutch ALCS homer off White Sox' Britt Burns... Reacquired from O's for Jose Brito prior to 1984 season... Born Oct. 25, 1954, in Joplin, Mo.... Never played high-school ball... Models men's clothing... Originally signed by Cardinals as free agent in 1973 . . . Has made only three errors during his six years in majors . . . Wonders why he doesn't play more, but doesn't make waves.

Year	Club	Pos.	G	AB	R	H	2B	3B	HR	RBI	SB	Avg.
1980	St. Louis	OF	35	77	6	19	2	2	0	7	3	.247
1981	St. Louis	OF	81	119	13	31	5	4	0	10	4	.261
1982	St. Louis	OF	79	72	12	20	3	0	2	14	0	.278
1983	St. Louis	OF	6	5	0	1	0	1	0	0	1	.200
1983	Baltimore	OF	26	42	8	13	2	0	1	4	0	.310
1984	St. Louis	OF	105	173	21	47	9	1	3	26	3	.272
1985	St. Louis	OF	85	161	21	45	8	2	4	21	1	.280
	Totals		417	649	81	176	29	10	10	82	12	.271

DANNY COX 26 6-4 230 — Bats R Throws R

An even more pleasant surprise than John Tudor . . . In his first full season in majors, he won nine of his first 11 decisions and was 11-4 at All-Star break . . . As No. 3 starter on staff, he ranked among NL leaders in several pitching departments . . . Only Dwight Gooden and Tudor made more quality starts . . . Won his only NLCS start and posted 1.29 ERA in two World Series no-decisions . . . Season took off during a 5-0 May . . . Born Sept. 21, 1959, in Northhampton, England . . . Reared in Alabama and attended Troy State, where he was an All-American . . . Cards' 12th-round choice in June 1981 draft . . . Played with three minor-league clubs in 1983 before reaching St. Louis.

Year	Club	G	IP	W	L	Pct.	SO	BB	H	ERA
1983	St. Louis	12	83	3	6	.333	36	23	92	3.25
1984	St. Louis	29	156⅓	9	11	.450	70	54	171	4.03
1985	St. Louis	35	241	18	9	.667	131	64	226	2.88
	Totals	76	480⅓	30	26	.536	237	141	489	3.32

JOHN TUDOR 32 6-0 185 — Bats L Throws L

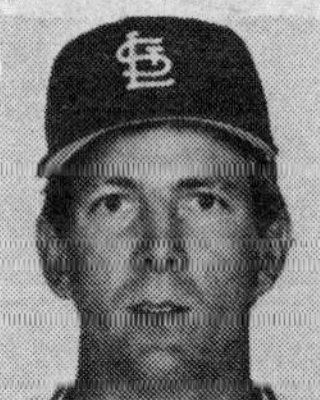

A spectacular season ended on a sour note in Game 7 of World Series . . . Going to the well once too often on three days' rest, he had nothing and was battered by Royals in 11-0 defeat . . . Took frustration out on metal fan in dugout and required stitches to close gash on index finger of pitching hand . . . Entered Game 7 with 23 victories in previous 25 decisions, following 1-7 start . . . Topped majors with incredible 10 shutouts and added another in World Series . . . NL Cy Young Award shoo-in were it not for Dwight Gooden . . . NL Player of the Month in June with a 6-0 record and 1.34 ERA . . . Went 5-1 in July and 5-0 in September . . . Born Feb. 2, 1954, in Schenectady, N.Y. . . . Attended Georgia Southern . . . Signed with Red Sox and was traded to Pirates prior to 1984 season . . . Joined Cardinals with Brian Harper in deal for George Hendrick and Steve Barnard prior to last season . . . Fired one-hitter vs. Cubs in 1985 . . . Tip from his former high-school catcher helped him correct mechanical flaw in his delivery and turn his season around last year.

Year	Club	G	IP	W	L	Pct.	SO	BB	H	ERA
1979	Boston	6	28	1	2	.333	11	9	39	6.43
1980	Boston	16	92	8	5	.615	45	31	81	3.03
1981	Boston	18	79	4	3	.571	44	28	74	4.56
1982	Boston	32	195⅔	13	10	.565	146	59	215	3.63
1983	Boston	34	242	13	12	.520	136	81	236	4.09
1984	Pittsburgh	32	212	12	11	.522	117	56	200	3.27
1985	St. Louis	36	275	21	8	.724	169	49	209	1.93
	Totals	174	1123⅔	72	51	.585	668	313	1054	3.33

JEFF LAHTI 29 6-0 180 **Bats R Throws R**

Chairman of "bullpen committee" that made Cards forget loss of Bruce Sutter . . . Entered last season with one career save . . . Wound up with 19 saves and 1.84 ERA in 1985 . . . Was 1-0 in NLCS with two scoreless innings, but got roughed up by Royals in World Series . . . Todd Worrell is pushing him for right-handed relief ace role . . . Tough down the stretch . . . Didn't allow an earned run in July, when he saved six games . . . Was 3-0 with two saves and 0.57 ERA during September pennant push . . . Born Oct. 8, 1956, in Oregon City, Ore. . . . Attended Portland State . . . Originally signed by Reds as fifth-round pick in June 1978 draft . . . Swapped to St. Louis for Bob Shirley prior to 1982 season . . . Overcame shoulder problems to pitch well down the stretch in 1983 and reached majors to stay in 1984.

Year	Club	G	IP	W	L	Pct.	SO	BB	H	ERA
1982	St. Louis	33	56⅔	5	4	.556	22	21	53	3.81
1983	St. Louis	53	74	3	3	.500	26	29	64	3.16
1984	St. Louis	63	84⅔	4	2	.667	45	34	69	3.72
1985	St. Louis	52	68⅓	5	2	.714	41	26	63	1.84
	Totals	201	283⅔	17	11	.607	134	110	249	3.14

TOP PROSPECT

TODD WORRELL 26 6-5 200 **Bats R Throws R**

Made an immediate impact on Cardinals by winning three games, saving five and posting 2.91 ERA in 18 major-league appearances late last season . . . Tendency to get in trouble in late innings as a starter prompted shift to relief role in minors last season . . . Born Sept. 28, 1959, in Arcadia, Cal. . . . After moving to bullpen with Louisville (AAA) last season, he went 3-0 with 11 saves and 1.19 ERA in 17 games . . . His overall record for Louisville was 8-6 with 3.60 ERA and 126 strikeouts in 128 innings . . . Drafted in first round of June 1982 talent pool . . . His 94-mph fastball and hard slider made him good bet for stardom . . . Sparkled in post-season with 1-0 mark in NLCS and a record-tying six straight strikeouts over two innings of World Series Game 5 . . . Wound up as hard-luck loser in Game 6, when Royals rallied for two runs off him in ninth.

MANAGER WHITEY HERZOG: Cardinals just missed going all the way in 1985, but their total of 108 victories were the most in the majors . . . Was testy during World Series after a few critical calls went against his club and was ejected from Game 7 . . . Bemoaned the absence of injured catalyst Vince Coleman from Series, citing it as a factor for his club's .185 team batting average and scoring drought . . . "The Clydesdales have been on second base more than our players have," Herzog said while observing team owner August Busch and his famous team of horses on the infield in Series pregame ceremonies . . . Has 912-767 record as major-league manager after last season's 101-61 finish . . . Born Nov. 9, 1931, in New Athens, Ill. and makes home five minutes from Royals Stadium . . . Originally signed with Yankees and played eight years in majors as an outfielder-first baseman . . . Retired as a player in 1963 and started major-league managing career with Texas in 1973 . . . Won three straight division titles with Royals from 1976-78 . . . Took Cardinals all the way in 1982, building team to suit Busch Stadium during brief stint as general manager . . . Nicknamed "The White Rat." . . . Named NL Manager of the Year

GREATEST SHORTSTOP

Ozzie Smith is featured in the Padres' section and it wouldn't be fair to make "The Wizard" big-headed. Consequently, Marty

Marion is the current choice as the greatest shortstop in Cardinals' history. "Slats" wasn't as flashy as Ozzie—who is?—but, at 6-2 and 170 pounds, he brought the same grace to his position that Fred Astaire brought to the stage and screen.

Marion led National League shortstops in fielding percentage four times during his reign as the glue of the Cardinals' infield from 1940-50 and, if Gold Gloves had been awarded during his career, he would have earned his share. Moreover, Marion was a better-than-average hitter for a shortstop.

He belted a league-leading 38 doubles in 1942 and batted .357 in the 1943 World Series, one of four in which he participated. Slats hit a career-high .280 in 1943 and his lifetime average was .263, which was more than respectable considering his value in the field. In 1941, he played all 155 games at shortstop and, in 1947, he made only 15 errors and posted an extraordinary .981 percentage.

ALL-TIME CARDINAL SEASON RECORDS

BATTING: Rogers Hornsby, .424, 1924
HRs: Johnny Mize, 43, 1940
RBIs: Joe Medwick, 154, 1937
STEALS: Lou Brock, 118, 1974
WINS: Dizzy Dean, 30, 1934
STRIKEOUTS: Bob Gibson, 274, 1970

ATLANTA BRAVES

TEAM DIRECTORY: Chairman: Bill Bartholomay; Pres.: R.E. (Ted) Turner III; Exec. VP: Al Thornwell, Jr.; GM: Bobby Cox; Exec. Asst.: John Mullen; VP-Dir. Play. Dev.: Hank Aaron; Dir. Scouting: Paul Snyder; Dir. Pub. Rel.: Wayne Minshew; Trav. Sec.: Bill Acree; Mgr.: Chuck Tanner. Home: Atlanta Stadium (53,046). Field distances: 330, l.f. line; 402, c.f.; 330, r.f. line. Spring training: West Palm Beach, Fla.

SCOUTING REPORT

HITTING: Even a reasonably healthy Bob Horner (27 homers, 89 RBI) couldn't keep the Braves' offense from disappointing last season, when many experts had predicted a division crown for Atlanta. This is a mystifying team, one that always looks better on paper than between the lines.

A lineup with Horns, perennial MVP candidate Dale Murphy (.300, 37 homers, 111 RBI), Claudell Washington (15 homers, 43 RBI) and improving Terry Harper (17 homers, 72 RBI) should do lots of damage, but the Braves' .246 average ranked 10th in

Dale Murphy, brawniest of Braves, led NL with 37 homers.

the NL in 1985.

The presence of Murphy and Horner and the addition of catcher Ozzie Virgil (19 homers, 55 RBI) from the Phillies give Atlanta a lethal heart of the order. Harper has some pop in his bat, too. Rafael Ramirez tailed off to .248 last season after being the league's best offensive shortstop in previous years. The potential for an offensive explosion is there.

PITCHING: The offense has hope, but the starting pitching is putrid for a team that ranked dead last in the NL with a 4.19 ERA last year. Pascual Perez (1-13, 6.14), Len Barker (2-9, 6.35) and Craig McMurtry (0-3, 6.60) remain question marks, so the best bets for success are workhorse Rick Mahler (17-15, 3.48) and Zane Smith (9-10, 3.80).

The bullpen is deep and strong. A healthy Bruce Sutter (4.48, 23 saves) can be the league's best, but he fell into a rut last year when he was expected to carry the club to a title. Gene Garber, Terry Forster, Rick Camp and Jeff Dedmon are a capable supporting cast in an overworked bullpen.

FIELDING: Only the Dodgers made more errors than the Braves' 159 last season. But Atlanta has a Gold Glover in center fielder Murphy and, in Virgil, the Braves have added the catcher who was tops in fielding percentage last season. Horner didn't make an error in 87 games as the new first baseman and third baseman Ken Oberkfell and second baseman Glenn Hubbard are regarded as sound fielders. But Ramirez must commit fewer errors at shortstop.

OUTLOOK: The Braves have an excellent chance of being the division sleeper this season. They can't go anywhere but up under new manager Chuck Tanner after being dreadfully mismanaged by Eddie Haas en route to a 66-96 finish in 1985. Tanner's enthusiasm should spread throughout the team and the addition of Virgil could really spark an offense that is being asked to give merely average starting pitching plenty of support.

But the Braves are not what they pretend to be. The trend in recent years has been to expect a lot of zip from the batting order, especially at cozy Fulton County Stadium. Unfortunately, the players haven't gotten the message and were less successful at home (32-49) than on the road (34-47) last year.

Except for 1982, when they won a division title, the Braves have been a disappointment. But Tanner's presence, Virgil's arrival and a comeback by Sutter should at least make the Braves a contender for one of the top three spots in the NL West.

ATLANTA BRAVES 1986 ROSTER

MANAGER Chuck Tanner
Coaches—Tony Bartirome, Al Monchak, Russ Nixon, Johnny Sain, Bob Skinner, Willie Stargell

PITCHERS

No.	Name	1985 Club	W-L	IP	SO	ERA	B-T	Ht.	Wt.	Born
59	Assenmacher, Paul	Durham	3-2	38	36	3.29	L-L	6-3	200	12/10/60 Detroit, MI
		Greenville	6-0	53	56	2.56				
39	Barker, Len	Greenville	1-0	5	7	1.80	R-R	6-5	225	7/7/55 Ft. Knox, KY
		Atlanta	2-9	74	47	6.35				
37	Camp, Rick	Atlanta	4-6	128	49	3.95	R-R	6-1	200	6/10/53 Trion, GA
65	Clary, Marty	Richmond	8-12	157	76	4.19	R-R	6-4	195	4/3/62 Detroit, MI
49	Dedmon, Jeff	Richmond	1-1	12	7	1.50	L-R	6-2	200	3/4/60 Torrance, CA
		Atlanta	6-3	86	41	4.08				
51	Forster, Terry	Atlanta	2-3	59	37	2.28	L-L	6-4	250	1/14/52 Sioux Falls, SD
26	Garber, Gene	Atlanta	6-6	97	66	3.61	R-R	5-10	172	11/13/47 Lancaster, PA
38	Johnson, Joe	Greenville	6-3	60	29	4.07	R-R	6-2	195	10/30/61 Brookline, MA
		Richmond	7-1	72	50	2.13				
		Atlanta	4-4	86	34	4.10				
42	Mahler, Rick	Atlanta	17-15	267	107	3.48	R-R	6-1	202	8/5/53 Austin, TX
29	McMurtry, Craig	Richmond	7-5	107	74	3.27	R-R	6-5	192	11/5/59 Temple, TX
		Atlanta	0-3	45	28	6.60				
47	Payne, Mike	Greenville	0-1	8	4	5.87	R-R	5-11	181	11/15/61 Woonsocket, RI
		Richmond	5-4	60	18	5.10				
27	Perez, Pascual	Atlanta	1-13	95	57	6.14	R-R	6-3	162	5/17/59 Dominican Republic
57	Puleo, Charlie	Denver	1-5	61	40	4.57	R-R	6-3	200	2/7/55 Glen Ridge, NJ
		Richmond	5-4	71	63	2.79				
43	Shields, Steve	Richmond	6-7	133	88	2.64	R-R	6-5	230	11/30/58 Gadsden, AL
		Atlanta	1-2	68	29	5.16				
34	Smith, Zane	Atlanta	9-10	147	85	3.80	L-L	6-2	195	12/28/60 Madison, WI
40	Sutter, Bruce	Atlanta	7-7	88	52	4.48	R-R	6-2	190	1/8/53 Lancaster, PA
56	Ward, Duane	Greenville	11-10	150	100	4.20	R-R	6-4	205	5/28/64 Farmington, NM
		Richmond	0-1	5	3	11.81				
45	West, Matt	Richmond	8-9	133	73	3.71	B-R	6-4	195	1/13/60 Santa Monica, CA

CATCHERS

No.	Name	1985 Club	H	HR	RBI	Pct.	B-T	Ht.	Wt.	Born
20	Benedict, Bruce	Atlanta	42	0	20	.202	R-R	6-2	195	8/18/55 Birmingham, AL
5	Cerone, Rick	Atlanta	61	3	25	.216	R-R	5-11	195	5/19/54 Newark, NJ
25	Owen, Larry	Richmond	57	5	32	.231	R-R	5-10	190	5/31/55 Cleveland, OH
—	Virgil, Ozzie	Philadelphia	105	19	55	.246	R-R	6-1	205	12/7/56 Puerto Rico

INFIELDERS

No.	Name	1985 Club	H	HR	RBI	Pct.	B-T	Ht.	Wt.	Born
10	Chambliss, Chris	Atlanta	40	3	21	.235	L-R	6-1	225	12/26/48 Dayton, OH
60	Guerrero, Inocencio	Greenville	117	16	68	.279	R-R	6-0	200	12/28/60 Dom. Republic
		Richmond	6	0	3	.400				
11	Horner, Bob	Atlanta	129	27	89	.267	R-R	6-1	215	8/6/57 Junction City, KS
17	Hubbard, Glenn	Atlanta	102	5	39	.232	R-R	5-7	170	9/25/57 Germany
24	Oberkfell, Ken	Atlanta	112	3	35	.272	L-R	6-1	210	5/4/56 Highland, IL
28	Perry, Gerald	Atlanta	51	3	13	.214	L-R	6-0	190	10/30/60 Savannah, GA
16	Ramirez, Rafael	Atlanta	141	5	58	.248	R-R	6-0	185	2/18/59 Dominican Republic
12	Runge, Paul	Atlanta	19	1	5	.218	R-R	6-0	175	5/21/58 Kingston, NY
14	Thomas, Andres	Greenville	114	9	59	.249	R-R	6-1	185	11/10/63 Dom. Republic
		Richmond	5	1	5	.179				
		Atlanta	5	0	2	.278				
18	Zuvella, Paul	Richmond	7	1	3	.219	R-R	6-0	178	10/31/58 San Mateo, CA
		Atlanta	48	0	4	.253				

OUTFIELDERS

No.	Name	1985 Club	H	HR	RBI	Pct.	B-T	Ht.	Wt.	Born
2	Hall, Albert	Richmond	22	0	5	.224	B-R	5-11	158	3/7/59 Birmingham, AL
		Atlanta	7	0	3	.149				
19	Harper, Terry	Atlanta	130	17	72	.264	R-R	6-1	202	8/19/55 Douglasville, GA
36	Komminsk, Brad	Atlanta	68	4	21	.227	R-R	6-2	205	4/4/61 Lima, OH
3	Murphy, Dale	Atlanta	185	37	111	.300	R-R	6-5	215	3/12/56 Portland, OR
31	Rabb, Johnny	Phoenix	7	0	0	.318	R-R	6-1	180	6/23/60 Los Angeles, CA
		Richmond	93	21	62	.252				
		Atlanta	0	0	0	.000				
—	Sample, Billy	New York (AL)	40	1	15	.288	R-R	5-9	175	4/2/55 Roanoke, VA
15	Washington, Claudell	Atlanta	110	15	43	.276	L-L	6-0	215	8/31/54 Los Angeles, CA

BRAVE PROFILES

DALE MURPHY 30 6-5 215 Bats R Throws R

Braves faltered, but their center fielder enjoyed another superstar season with a .300 average, a career-high 37 homers and a fourth straight 100-RBI season . . . Topped NL in homers, walks (90) and runs (118) . . . Virtually a wire-to-wire homer leader after torrid April in which he batted .380 with nine homers and 29 RBI . . . The 29 RBI tied Ron Cey's major-league mark for opening month . . . Batted .332 in final 51 games . . . NL Player of the Month in April . . . Didn't miss a game in 1985, extending his streak to 657 straight, ranking him 15th on all-time iron-man list . . . Had 14 game-winning RBI . . . Born March 12, 1956, in Portland, Ore. . . . Selected in first round of June 1974 draft . . . Was groomed as a catcher when he first entered majors . . . Exceptionally well-liked and lives up to All-American image . . . One of the few players who can do it all, but he has kept his success in perspective . . . Two-time NL MVP, in 1982 and 1983 . . . A franchise player.

Year	Club	Pos.	G	AB	R	H	2B	3B	HR	RBI	SB	Avg.
1976	Atlanta	C	19	65	3	17	6	0	0	9	0	.262
1977	Atlanta	C	18	76	5	24	8	1	2	14	0	.316
1978	Atlanta	C-1B	151	530	66	120	14	3	23	79	11	.226
1979	Atlanta	1B-C	104	384	53	106	7	2	21	57	6	.276
1980	Atlanta	OF-1B	156	569	98	160	27	2	33	89	9	.281
1981	Atlanta	OF-1B	104	369	43	91	12	1	13	50	14	.247
1982	Atlanta	OF	162	598	113	168	23	2	36	109	23	.281
1983	Atlanta	OF	162	589	131	178	24	4	36	121	30	.302
1984	Atlanta	OF	162	607	94	176	32	8	36	100	19	.290
1985	Atlanta	OF	162	616	118	185	32	2	37	111	10	.300
	Totals		1200	4403	724	1225	185	25	237	739	122	.278

BOB HORNER 28 6-1 215 Bats R Throws R

Braves finally found a way to keep "Horns" healthy—they shifted him from third to first . . . Played 130 games, his second-highest total, exceeded only by his 140 in 1982 . . . Had only four homers and 15 RBI before being switched June 10, then amassed 23 homers and 74 RBI and didn't make an error the rest of the way . . . Celebrated move with .293 June and went on a .378 spree in July, notching nine homers and 27 RBI . . . Bounced back thanks to operation on twice-injured wrist following washout 1984 season . . . Born Aug. 6, 1957, in Junction City, Kan. . . . Has averaged more than 23 homers per season despite numerous injuries . . . No. 1 draft pick in nation in June 1978, following remarkable career at Arizona State . . . Set NCAA record with 25-homer season and was College Player of the Year in 1978 . . . Hit 14 homers and had 33 RBI in July 1980 . . . Injuries have kept him from superstardom, but he's close.

Year	Club	Pos.	G	AB	R	H	2B	3B	HR	RBI	SB	Avg.
1978	Atlanta	3B	89	323	50	86	17	1	23	63	0	.266
1979	Atlanta	3B-1B	121	487	66	153	15	1	33	98	0	.314
1980	Atlanta	3B-1B	124	463	81	124	14	1	35	89	3	.268
1981	Atlanta	3B	79	300	42	83	10	0	15	42	2	.277
1982	Atlanta	3B	140	499	85	130	24	0	32	97	3	.261
1983	Atlanta	3B-1B	104	386	75	117	25	1	20	68	4	.303
1984	Atlanta	3B	32	113	15	31	8	0	3	19	0	.274
1985	Atlanta	1B-3B	130	483	61	129	25	3	27	89	1	.267
	Totals		819	3054	475	853	138	7	188	565	13	.279

RAFAEL RAMIREZ 27 6-0 185 **Bats R Throws R**

An ailing elbow contributed to a late-season slump that dropped his average far below the levels he had reached the previous three years . . . Has been replaced by Padres' Garry Templeton as the best offensive shortstop in the league, so his job may be in jeopardy because his fielding is still below par . . . Batted .136 in the final 37 games after going on a 14-game hitting streak . . . Born Feb. 18, 1959, in San Pedro de Macoris, Dominican Republic . . . Signed by Braves as a free agent in 1976 . . . Started career as an outfielder, but he was switched to infield as a first-year pro . . . Had undistinguished minor-league hitting career, but blossomed with Braves in 1982, his first year as a major-league regular . . . More spectacular than consistent at the plate and in the field.

Year	Club	Pos.	G	AB	R	H	2B	3B	HR	RBI	SB	Avg.
1980	Atlanta	SS	50	165	17	44	6	1	2	11	2	.267
1981	Atlanta	SS	95	307	30	67	16	2	2	20	7	.218
1982	Atlanta	SS	157	609	74	169	24	4	10	52	27	.278
1983	Atlanta	SS	152	622	82	185	13	5	7	58	16	.297
1984	Atlanta	SS	145	591	51	157	22	4	2	48	14	.266
1985	Atlanta	SS	138	568	54	141	25	4	5	58	2	.248
	Totals		737	2802	308	763	106	20	28	247	68	.267

KEN OBERKFELL 29 6-1 210 **Bats L Throws R**

Club ended speculation it would swap "Obie" by making him regular third baseman and shifting Bob Horner to first in June . . . Batted .188 in April, but was close to .300 rest of the year, batting .333 in August . . . Greatly improved Braves' defense . . . Took over at third June 10 and made only 10 errors thereafter . . . Born May 4, 1956, in Highland, Ill. . . . Junior-college All-

American at Belleville (Ill.) . . . Signed as a free agent by Cardinals in 1975 . . . Became .300 hitter for St. Louis and topped NL third basemen in fielding in 1982 and 1983 . . . Obtained by Atlanta for Ken Dayley and Mike Jorgensen, June 15, 1984, after Horner was injured . . . Originally a second baseman, he was moved to third in 1981 to accommodate Tom Herr . . . Batted .292 in 1982 World Series and had the game-winning RBI against the Braves in an NLCS game.

Year	Club	Pos.	G	AB	R	H	2B	3B	HR	RBI	SB	Avg.
1977	St. Louis	2B	9	9	0	1	0	0	0	1	0	.111
1978	St. Louis	2B-3B	24	50	7	6	1	0	0	0	0	.120
1979	St. Louis	2B-3B-SS	135	369	53	111	19	5	1	35	4	.301
1980	St. Louis	2B-3B	116	422	58	128	27	6	3	46	4	.303
1981	St. Louis	3B-SS	102	376	43	110	12	6	2	45	4	.293
1982	St. Louis	3B-2B	137	470	55	136	22	5	2	34	11	.289
1983	St. Louis	3B-2B-SS	151	488	62	143	26	5	3	38	12	.293
1984	St.L.-Atl.	3B-2B-SS	100	324	38	87	19	2	1	21	2	.269
1985	Atlanta	3B-2B	134	412	30	112	19	4	3	35	1	.272
	Totals		908	2920	346	834	145	33	15	255	38	.286

CLAUDELL WASHINGTON 31 6-0 215 Bats L Throws L

Limited to 122 games by injuries, but this right fielder still enjoyed a consistent season . . . Had only one poor month, batting .257 in August . . . Batted .294 against right-handers . . . Has the distinction of being one of three men with three-homer games in each league, joining Babe Ruth and Johnny Mize . . . Born Aug. 31, 1954, in Los Angeles . . . Didn't play prep baseball, but was discovered on sandlots and signed as a free agent by A's in 1972 . . . Reached majors to stay in third year as a pro and batted .308 for Oakland in first full season . . . Batted .571 in 1974 World Series as a rookie . . . Has two hits in three All-Star Game trips . . . Signed with Braves as a free agent in 1981 and batted .333 for Atlanta in 1982 NLCS.

Year	Club	Pos.	G	AB	R	H	2B	3B	HR	RBI	SB	Avg.
1974	Oakland.	OF	73	221	16	63	10	5	0	19	6	.285
1975	Oakland.	OF	148	590	86	182	24	7	10	77	40	.308
1976	Oakland.	OF	134	490	65	126	20	6	5	53	37	.257
1977	Texas	OF	129	521	63	148	31	2	12	68	21	.284
1978	Texas-Chi (AL)	OF	98	356	34	90	16	5	6	33	5	.253
1979	Chicago (AL)	OF	131	471	79	132	33	5	13	66	19	.280
1980	Chicago (AL)	OF	32	90	15	26	4	2	1	12	4	.289
1980	New York (NL)	OF	79	284	38	78	16	4	10	42	17	.275
1981	Atlanta	OF	85	320	37	93	22	3	5	37	12	.291
1982	Atlanta	OF	150	563	94	150	24	6	16	80	33	.266
1983	Atlanta	OF	134	496	75	138	24	8	9	44	31	.278
1984	Atlanta	OF	120	416	62	119	21	2	17	61	21	.286
1985	Atlanta	OF	122	398	62	110	14	6	15	43	14	.276
	Totals		1435	5216	726	1455	259	61	119	635	260	.279

OZZIE VIRGIL 29 6-1 205 **Bats R Throws R**

Chased Bo Diaz to Cincinnati and firmly established himself as one of the best power-hitting catchers around with career-high 19 homers for the Phils . . . And now he's a Brave, traded at the winter meetings with minor leaguer Pete Smith for Steve Bedrosian and minor leaguer Milt Thompson . . . Still has trouble hitting breaking pitches, but is much more patient at the plate and has become a tougher out . . . Improved defense drastically, making fewest errors among regular catchers . . . Born Dec. 7, 1956, in Mayaguez, Puerto Rico . . . Selected in sixth round of June 1976 draft . . . Career took off in 1978, when he was Carolina League MVP for Peninsula (A), batting .303 with league-leading 29 homers . . . Two years later, he hit 28 homers and led Eastern League with 104 RBI for Reading (AA) . . . Played only 83 Triple-A games before reaching majors to stay.

Year	Club	Pos.	G	AB	R	H	2B	3B	HR	RBI	SB	Avg.
1980	Philadelphia	C	1	5	1	1	1	0	0	0	0	.200
1981	Philadelphia	C	6	6	0	0	0	0	0	0	0	.000
1982	Philadelphia	C	49	101	11	24	6	0	3	8	0	.238
1983	Philadelphia	C	55	140	11	30	7	0	6	23	0	.214
1984	Philadelphia	C	141	456	61	119	21	2	18	68	1	.261
1985	Philadelphia	C	131	426	47	105	16	3	19	55	0	.246
	Totals		383	1134	131	279	51	5	46	154	1	.246

TERRY HARPER 30 6-1 202 **Bats R Throws R**

Wasn't highly regarded at the start of the season, but capitalized on Claudell Washington's injury and Brad Komminsk's ineffectiveness to earn more playing time . . . Responded with his best big-league season, ranking third on club in power departments . . . Flourished in July with .301 average, seven homers and 22 RBI . . . Hit .338 in September . . . Born Aug. 19, 1955, in Douglasville, Ga. . . . A 16th-round draft pick in June 1973 . . . Took him awhile to become a major-league regular, because his progress was retarded by shoulder problems . . . Originally signed as a pitcher, he was converted into outfielder in 1976 . . . A solid Triple-A hitter before emerging as a major leaguer last year . . . Better late than never.

Year	Club	Pos.	G	AB	R	H	2B	3B	HR	RBI	SB	Avg.
1980	Atlanta	OF	21	54	3	10	2	1	0	3	2	.185
1981	Atlanta	OF	40	73	9	19	1	0	2	8	5	.260
1982	Atlanta	OF	48	150	16	43	3	0	2	10	7	.207
1983	Atlanta	OF	80	201	19	53	13	1	3	26	6	.264
1984	Atlanta	OF	40	102	4	16	3	1	0	8	4	.157
1985	Atlanta	OF	138	492	58	130	15	2	17	72	9	.264
	Totals		367	1072	109	271	37	5	24	133	33	.253

BRUCE SUTTER 33 6-2 190 **Bats R Throws R**

Perennial bullpen superstar didn't deliver a division title, as expected, in his Atlanta debut, but 23 saves isn't too shabby for most relievers . . . Ted Turner's mistake when he signed this split-fingered fastballer to that multi-million-dollar contract as a re-entry free agent prior to 1985 was that he didn't get Cardinals' pitching coach Mike Roarke, too . . . When there was a flaw in his delivery, as evidenced by his high ERA and hits total, old friend Roarke wasn't around to pull him out of it . . . Looked good for awhile, though, because he was 1-0 with 1.42 ERA and four saves in April . . . Born Jan. 8, 1953, in Lancaster, Pa. . . . Drafted by Senators in 21st round in June 1970 and signed as free agent by Cubs in 1971 . . . NL's all-time leader with 283 saves . . . Led league in saves five times in six years, capped by record-setting total of 45 in 1984.

Year	Club	G	IP	W	L	Pct.	SO	BB	H	ERA
1976	Chicago (NL)	52	83	6	3	.667	73	26	63	2.71
1977	Chicago (NL)	62	107	7	3	.700	129	23	69	1.35
1978	Chicago (NL)	64	99	8	10	.444	106	34	82	3.18
1979	Chicago (NL)	62	101	6	6	.500	110	32	67	2.23
1980	Chicago (NL)	60	102	5	8	.385	76	34	90	2.65
1981	St. Louis.	48	82	3	5	.375	57	24	64	2.63
1982	St. Louis.	70	102⅓	9	8	.529	61	34	88	2.90
1983	St. Louis.	60	89⅓	9	10	.474	64	30	90	4.23
1984	St. Louis.	71	122⅔	5	7	.417	77	23	109	1.54
1985	Atlanta	58	88⅓	7	7	.500	52	29	91	4.48
	Totals.	607	976⅔	65	67	.492	805	289	813	2.72

ZANE SMITH 25 6-2 195 **Bats L Throws L**

Meteoric rise through Braves' farm system culminated in respectable rookie year in 1985 . . . Topped staff with two shutouts in only 18 starts . . . Not counted on heavily at season's start, but turned into pleasant surprise while others faltered . . . Born Dec. 28, 1960, in Madison, Wis. . . . Didn't play prep baseball, but he was a football and basketball standout . . . Posted 9-3 pitching record as a junior at Indiana State and was selected in third round of June 1982 draft . . . Had spotty success his first two years, but blossomed with a 7-0 start at Greenville (AA) in 1984 . . . Earned promotion to Atlanta by September of that year and won his major-league debut . . . A decent hitter, he has lifetime .239 major-league average.

Year	Club	G	IP	W	L	Pct.	SO	BB	H	ERA
1984	Atlanta	3	20	1	0	1.000	16	13	16	2.25
1985	Atlanta	42	147	9	10	.474	85	80	135	3.80
	Totals.	45	167	10	10	.500	101	93	151	3.61

RICK MAHLER 32 6-1 202 **Bats R Throws R**

Posted a career-high 17 victories, yet his season was somewhat disappointing, considering his fantastic start . . . Was 5-0 in April and won seven straight decisions before losing five of seven . . . Rallied with a 4-1 July, but was winless from Sept. 6 on, partially because of a finger injury . . . Born Aug. 5, 1953, in Austin, Tex. . . . Signed as a free agent by Braves in 1975 . . . Didn't reach bigs for good until age 30, but he has worked hard to become a better-than-average pitcher . . . Helps himself with hitting ability, batting .296 in 1984 and notching eight RBI, including three game-winners, last year . . . A true stopper, he halted a pair of five-game losing streaks in 1985.

Year	Club	G	IP	W	L	Pct.	SO	BB	H	ERA
1979	Atlanta	15	22	0	0	.000	12	11	28	6.14
1980	Atlanta	2	4	0	0	.000	1	0	2	2.25
1981	Atlanta	34	112	8	6	.571	54	43	109	2.81
1982	Atlanta	39	205⅓	9	10	.474	105	62	213	4.21
1983	Atlanta	10	14⅓	0	0	.000	7	9	16	5.02
1984	Atlanta	38	222	13	10	.565	106	62	209	3.12
1985	Atlanta	39	266⅔	17	15	.531	107	79	272	3.48
	Totals	177	846⅓	47	41	.534	392	266	849	3.56

TOP PROSPECTS

JOE JOHNSON 24 6-2 195 **Bats R Throws R**

Joined Braves as an injury replacement last year, went 4-4 with 4.10 ERA and impressed enough to warrant a longer look . . . Decline of Len Barker, Pascual Perez and Craig McMurtry could open spot in rotation . . . Born Oct. 30, 1961, in Brookline, Mass. . . . Braves' second-round pick in June 1982 draft . . . Brilliant career at Maine, blanking champion Cal-State Fullerton in College World Series.

ANDRES THOMAS 22 6-1 170 **Bats R Throws R**

Young middle infielder may be a year away, but is regarded as fine prospect by Braves, who signed him as a free agent in December 1981 . . . Another in a long line of swift shortstops from the Dominican Republic . . . Born Nov. 10, 1963, in Boca Chica . . . In only second pro season, at age 19, he batted .315 for Anderson (A) of South Atlantic League . . . Displayed his speed by scoring four times as Atlanta pinch-runner down the stretch . . . Hit .249 with nine homers and 59 RBI for Greenville (AA) and .278 in 18 at-bats with Braves in 1985.

MANAGER CHUCK TANNER: The toughest season in his career produced a 57-104 record and the end of a long relationship with the Pirates . . . But his reputation preceded him and, less than one week later, he signed a lucrative, five-year contract to manage Braves . . . Prior to 1985, the most games one of his teams had lost was 87, by the 1984 Bucs . . . Woes were compounded last year by Pittsburgh drug case, which created turmoil and tension on Pirates . . . Career major-league record is 1,199-1,173 . . . Born July 4, 1929, in New Carlisle, Pa. . . . Was an outfielder as a player, batting above .300 on nine occasions before reaching the bigs with the Braves in 1955 . . . Homered on the first pitch he saw in majors . . . This season is a homecoming in more ways than one, because he played with an Atlanta farm team from 1951-54, never batting below .318 . . . Posted .261 lifetime average in majors and began managing in 1963 . . . White Sox were his first major-league assignment, in 1970 . . . As A's manager in 1976, he was swapped to Pittsburgh, where 1979 World Series crown was his highlight.

GREATEST SHORTSTOP

This one's tough. Johnny Logan was the unsung hero of the powerful Braves of the late '50s and Davey Bancroft had four solid years at the position from 1924-27. However, the greatest shortstop in the history of the franchise probably was Hall of Famer Rabbit Maranville, a colorful character with staying power.

Maranville, only 5-5 and 155 pounds, played with the Braves for 16 years in two different eras. He was their shortstop from 1912-20, saw service with four other clubs, returned to Boston in 1929 and then served as the regular shortstop four more years.

Only Luke Appling had played more games at shortstop than Maranville's 2,154 until Larry Bowa became the National League record holder last summer. But Rabbit was more active than anyone else and his 5,139 putouts are a record that still stands. Only Bill Dahlen, with 13,325, accepted more chances than Maranville's 13,124. Rabbit twice topped the league in fielding percentage and had a lifetime average of .258 with 177 triples and 291 stolen bases.

ALL-TIME BRAVE SEASON RECORDS

BATTING: Rogers Hornsby, .387, 1928
HRs: Eddie Mathews, 47, 1953
Hank Aaron, 47, 1971
RBIs: Eddie Mathews, 135, 1953
STEALS: Ralph Myers, 57, 1913
WINS: Vic Willis, 27, 1902
Charles Pittinger, 27, 1902
Dick Rudolph, 27, 1914
STRIKEOUTS: Phil Niekro, 262, 1977

Bruce Sutter has fingers split, hoping for return to form.

CINCINNATI REDS

TEAM DIRECTORY: Principal Owner-Pres.: Marge Schott; GM: Bill Bergesch; Scouting Dir.: Larry Doughty; VP-Play. Pers.: Sheldon Bender; VP-Publ.: Jim Ferguson; Trav. Sec.: Steve Cobb; Mgr.: Pete Rose. Home: Riverfront Stadium (52,392). Field Distances: 330, l.f. line; 404, c.f.; 330, r.f. line. Spring training: Tampa, Fla.

SCOUTING REPORT

HITTING: The Reds' offense got a lot of mileage out of player-manager Pete Rose's pursuit of Ty Cobb's record last year, rising to unexpected heights on a crest of emotion. Normalcy will return this season, so it remains to be seen whether regulars Dave Parker (.312) and Ron Oester (.295) and part-timers Tony Perez (.328) and Rose (.264) can match their outstanding performances of last year.

Parker, a legitimate NL MVP choice, virtually carried the attack while Rose was commanding most of the attention. It's difficult to imagine Parker improving on his 1985 totals of 34 homers and 125 RBI, but that may not be necessary. Nick Esasky (21 homers, 66 RBI) should step up his production with a full year of regular duty under his belt and Eric Davis may be ready to blossom after struggling in 1985.

Potential problem areas involve aging veterans like Dave Concepcion, Buddy Bell, Perez and Rose, so it remains to be seen how much impact they'll have on the offense. On the plus side, a healthy Bo Diaz should give the Reds their most pop from a catcher since the days of Johnny Bench and Davis has the power and the speed to suddenly emerge as a superstar.

PITCHING: Only the Dodgers will have a better rotation among NL West teams if ex-Phil John Denny (11-14, 3.82) shakes off the injury jinx and becomes a solid complement to Mario Soto (12-15, 3.58), Tom Browning (20-9, 3.55) and former Expo Bill Gullickson (14-12, 3.52). Denny and Gullickson can make a good rotation great and Soto has the ability to turn his 1985 record around.

It may be asking too much of Browning to repeat his rookie success, but the Reds have a formidable one-two punch in the bullpen in Ted Power (8-6, 2.70, 27 saves) and John Franco (12-3, 2.18, 12 saves), so this is a staff that appears to be a cinch to improve on its 1985 team ERA of 3.71.

Dave Parker located stroke and became Red menace.

FIELDING: Defense was a strength of the Cincinnati clubs of the '70s and the Reds remain respectable in this area. Concepcion has lost a step at shortstop, but he and Oester are a solid double-play combo and Parker's arm in right ranks with the strongest in the game. Eddie Milner and Davis can fly, so the outfield defense will remain strong, even without Gary Redus.

OUTLOOK: The Reds won't sneak up on anyone as they did when they finished second at 89-72 last year, so they could slip a notch unless their gamble on Denny pays off. Quality starters are hard to find, so it was a risk worth taking. Consequently, much of the club's success hinges on the contributions of Denny and Gullickson and on Soto reverting to his 1984 form.

Offensively, the club needs someone to help Parker carry the load. It could be Esasky, who produced when he got a chance last season. More than likely, it will be Davis, who will become a star once he reduces his strikeout total. Look for Rose to do more managing and less playing now that Cobb has been passed. If Pete feels managing isn't enough involvement for him, it could hurt the club.

CINCINNATI REDS 1986 ROSTER

MANAGER Pete Rose
Coaches—Scott Breeden, Billy DeMars, Tommy Helms, Bruce Kimm, George Scherger

PITCHERS

No.	Name	1985 Club	W-L	IP	SO	ERA	B-T	Ht.	Wt.	Born
32	Browning, Tom	Cincinnati	20-9	261	155	3.55	L-L	6-1	190	4/28/60 Casper, WY
40	Denny, John	Philadelphia	11-14	231	123	3.82	R-R	6-3	190	11/8/52 Prescott, AZ
31	Franco, John	Cincinnati	12-3	99	61	2.18	L-L	5-10	175	9/17/60 Brooklyn, NY
—	Gullickson, Bill	Montreal	14-12	181	68	3.52	R-R	6-3	220	2/20/59 Marshall, MN
58	Hawley, Billy	Vermont	7-8	101	52	4.63	L-R	6-3	195	3/12/64 Lexington, SC
53	Kemp, Hugh	Tampa	5-1	69	54	1.56	L-R	6-3	185	12/13/60 Nashville, TN
		Vermont	5-3	78	67	3.33				
		Denver	2-3	40	33	3.12				
51	Konderla, Mike	Vermont	10-5	92	96	2.55	R-R	6-3	225	7/9/61 Austin, TX
46	Murphy, Rob	Denver	5-5	84	66	4.61	L-L	6-2	200	5/26/60 Miami, FL
		Cincinnati	0-0	3	1	6.00				
35	Pastore, Frank	Cincinnati	2-1	54	29	3.83	R-R	6-3	215	8/21/57 Alhambra, CA
48	Power, Ted	Cincinnati	8-6	80	42	2.70	R-R	6-4	225	1/31/51 Guthrie, OK
49	Price, Joe	Cincinnati	2-2	65	52	3.90	R-L	6-4	215	11/29/56 Inglewood, CA
33	Robinson, Ron	Denver	2-1	40	24	2.72	R-R	6-4	215	3/24/62 Woodlake, CA
		Cincinnati	7-7	108	76	3.99				
34	Smith, Mike	Denver	5-4	69	67	4.85	R-R	6-1	195	2/23/61 Jackson, MS
		Cincinnati	0-0	3	2	5.40				
36	Soto, Mario	Cincinnati	12-15	257	214	3.58	R-R	6-0	190	7/12/56 Dominican Republic
59	Terry, Scott	Denver	11-12	179	101	4.43	R-R	5-11	195	11/21/59 Hobbs, NM
38	Tibbs, Jay	Denver	1-2	32	15	2.27	R-R	6-1	180	1/4/62 Birmingham, AL
		Cincinnati	10-16	218	98	3.92				

CATCHERS

No.	Name	1985 Club	H	HR	RBI	Pct.	B-T	Ht.	Wt.	Born
11	Butera, Sal	Indianapolis	4	1	4	.222	R-R	6-0	185	9/25/52 Richmond Hill, NY
8	Diaz, Bo	Phi.-Cin.	58	5	31	.245	R-R	5-11	190	3/23/53 Venezuela
52	McGriff, Terry	Vermont	92	13	60	.253	R-R	6-2	180	9/23/63 Ft. Pierce, FL
55	Oliver, Joe	Tampa	104	7	62	.269	R-R	6-3	205	7/24/65 Memphis, TN
23	Van Gorder, Dave	Cincinnati	36	2	24	.238	R-R	6-2	205	3/27/57 Los Angeles, CA

INFIELDERS

No.	Name	1985 Club	H	HR	RBI	Pct.	B-T	Ht.	Wt.	Born
25	Bell, Buddy	Texas	74	4	32	.236	R-R	6-2	185	8/27/51 Pittsburgh, PA
		Cincinnati	54	6	36	.219				
13	Concepcion, Dave	Cincinnati	141	7	48	.252	R-R	6-1	190	6/17/48 Venezuela
56	Harris, Lenny	Tampa	129	3	51	.259	L-R	5-11	180	10/28/64 Miami, FL
15	Krenchicki, Wayne	Cincinnati	47	4	25	.272	L-R	6-1	180	9/17/54 Trenton, NJ
54	Lee, Terry	Vermont	118	12	62	.289	R-R	6-5	200	3/13/62 San Francisco, CA
16	Oester, Ron	Cincinnati	155	1	34	.295	B-R	6-2	190	5/5/56 Cincinnati, OH
24	Perez, Tony	Cincinnati	60	6	33	.328	R-R	6-2	205	5/14/42 Cuba
14	Rose, Pete	Cincinnati	107	2	46	.264	B-R	5-11	200	4/14/41 Cincinnati, OH
17	Rowdon, Wade	Denver	132	19	78	.289	R-R	6-2	170	9/7/60 Riverhead, NY
		Cincinnati	2	0	2	.222				
22	Stillwell, Kurt	Denver	48	1	22	.264	B-R	5-11	165	6/4/65 Thousand Oaks, CA

OUTFIELDERS

No.	Name	1985 Club	H	HR	RBI	Pct.	B-T	Ht.	Wt.	Born
28	Daniels, Kal	Denver	86	15	43	.302	L-R	5-11	185	8/20/63 Vienna, GA
44	Davis, Eric	Denver	57	15	38	.277	R-R	6-2	175	5/29/62 Los Angeles, CA
		Cincinnati	30	8	18	.246				
12	Esasky, Nick	Cincinnati	108	21	66	.262	R-R	6-3	205	2/24/60 Hialeah, FL
57	Jones, Tracy	Vermont	90	4	31	.317	R-R	6-3	180	3/31/61 Inglewood, CA
		Denver	69	10	31	.337				
20	Milner, Eddie	Cincinnati	115	3	33	.254	L-L	5-11	170	5/21/55 Columbus, OH
21	O'Neill, Paul	Denver	155	7	74	.305	L-L	6-4	205	2/25/63 Columbus, OH
		Cincinnati	4	0	1	.333				
39	Parker, Dave	Cincinnati	198	34	125	.312	L-R	6-5	230	6/9/51 Jackson, MS
9	Venable, Max	Ind.-Den.	42	4	19	.244	L-R	5-10	185	6/6/57 Phoenix, AZ
		Cincinnati	39	0	10	.289				

RED PROFILES

DAVE PARKER 34 6-5 230 — Bats L Throws R

Enjoyed superstar season, his best since he won back-to-back NL batting titles for Pittsburgh in 1977 and 1978 . . . "The Cobra" reached career highs in homers and RBI, leading the league in latter category and in doubles . . . Ranked high on some MVP ballots . . . NL Player of the Month in May with .366 average, eight homers and 28 RBI . . . Batted .320 with six homers and 22 RBI in June . . . Had 62 RBI before All-Star break and 63 during second half . . . Finished strong, batting .386 with seven homers and 33 RBI in September . . . Tied Mets' Gary Carter for second-highest number of game-winning RBI in NL with 18 . . . Born June 9, 1951, in Jackson, Miss. . . . Reared in Cincinnati, he signed with Reds as a re-entry free agent prior to 1984 season . . . Pirates' 14th-round pick in June 1970 draft . . . A .300-plus hitter in each of four years in minors . . . NL MVP in 1978 and All-Star Game MVP in 1979 before he fell out of favor in Steel City . . . Knee surgery in 1980 and other injuries in 1981 and 1982 hindered his progress . . . Critics also blamed weight problems for right fielder's decline with Pirates.

Year	Club	Pos.	G	AB	R	H	2B	3B	HR	RBI	SB	Avg.
1973	Pittsburgh	OF	54	139	17	40	9	1	4	14	1	.288
1974	Pittsburgh	OF-1B	73	220	27	62	10	3	4	29	3	.282
1975	Pittsburgh	OF	148	558	75	172	35	10	25	101	8	.308
1976	Pittsburgh	OF	138	537	82	168	28	10	13	90	19	.313
1977	Pittsburgh	OF-2B	160	637	107	216	44	8	21	88	17	.338
1978	Pittsburgh	OF	148	581	102	194	32	12	30	117	20	.334
1979	Pittsburgh	OF	158	622	109	193	45	7	25	94	20	.310
1980	Pittsburgh	OF	139	518	71	153	31	1	17	79	10	.295
1981	Pittsburgh	OF	67	240	29	62	14	3	9	48	6	.258
1982	Pittsburgh	OF	73	244	41	66	19	3	6	29	7	.270
1983	Pittsburgh	OF	144	552	68	154	29	4	12	69	12	.279
1984	Cincinnati	OF	156	607	73	173	28	0	16	94	11	.285
1985	Cincinnati	OF	160	635	88	198	42	4	34	125	5	.312
	Totals		1617	6090	889	1850	366	66	216	977	139	.304

BO DIAZ 33 5-11 190 — Bats R Throws R

Catcher was given a new lease on life by mid-season swap that brought him to Reds . . . Had been languishing on Phillies' bench behind Ozzie Virgil . . . Should add some pop to Reds . . . Finished fast with new club, batting .318 in a 34-game stint through end of September . . . Born March 23, 1953, in Cua, Venezuela . . . Signed as a free agent with Red Sox in 1970 . . . Traded to Indians, but career didn't take off until he joined Philadelphia in three-team deal that sent Lonnie Smith to Cards prior to 1982 season . . . Enjoyed big year in first full season as a regular in 1982 . . . Lost regular job to Virgil during injury-marred 1984, when he missed 135 games . . . Batted .333 in 1983 World Series and was rehabilitating knee in minors one year later.

Year	Club	Pos.	G	AB	R	H	2B	3B	HR	RBI	SB	Avg.
1977	Boston	C	2	1	0	0	0	0	0	0	0	.000
1978	Cleveland.	C	44	127	12	30	4	0	2	11	0	.236
1979	Cleveland.	C	15	32	0	5	2	0	0	1	0	.156
1980	Cleveland.	C	76	207	15	47	11	2	3	32	1	.227
1981	Cleveland.	C	63	182	25	57	19	0	7	38	2	.313
1982	Philadelphia	C	144	525	69	151	29	1	18	85	3	.288
1983	Philadelphia	C	136	471	49	111	17	0	15	64	1	.236
1984	Philadelphia	C	27	75	5	16	4	0	1	9	0	.213
1985	Phil.-Cin..	C	77	237	21	58	13	1	5	31	0	.245
	Totals		584	1857	196	475	99	4	51	271	7	.256

DAVE CONCEPCION 37 6-1 190 — Bats R Throws R

Collected 2,000th career hit May 11 . . . Batted .301 in June, but less than .250 in the other months . . . Skills are fading for one of the remaining stars of Big Red Machine . . . No longer regarded as best all-around shortstop in game, but he is durable and can do more at plate than many at his position . . . Graceful fielder who developed bounce throw to first base to get ball to bag quicker on artificial surfaces . . . Born June 17, 1948, in Aragua, Venezuela . . . Signed as free agent by Reds in 1968 and was a major leaguer two years later . . . Five-time Gold Glove winner . . . After Reds had gotten rid of big hitters of '70s, he played a more prominent role on offense . . . Earned club MVP honors in 1981, when he became first Cincinnati shortstop to hit .300 since 1913 . . . Won 1977 Roberto Clemente Award as top Latin player in majors . . . MVP of 1982 All-Star Game . . . A .351 hitter in 15 NLCS games.

Year	Club	Pos.	G	AB	R	H	2B	3B	HR	RBI	SB	Avg.
1970	Cincinnati	SS-2B	101	265	38	69	6	3	1	19	10	.260
1971	Cincinnati	SS-2B-3B-OF	130	327	24	67	4	4	1	20	9	.205
1972	Cincinnati	SS	119	378	40	79	13	2	2	29	13	.209
1973	Cincinnati	SS-OF	89	328	39	94	18	3	8	46	22	.287
1974	Cincinnati	SS-OF	160	594	70	167	25	1	14	82	41	.281
1975	Cincinnati	SS-3B	140	507	62	139	23	1	5	49	33	.274
1976	Cincinnati	SS	152	576	74	162	28	7	9	69	21	.281
1977	Cincinnati	SS	156	572	59	155	26	3	8	64	29	.271
1978	Cincinnati	SS	153	565	75	170	33	4	6	67	23	.301
1979	Cincinnati	SS	149	590	91	166	25	3	16	84	19	.281
1980	Cincinnati	SS-2B	156	622	72	162	31	8	5	77	12	.260
1981	Cincinnati	SS	106	421	57	129	28	0	5	67	4	.306
1982	Cincinnati	SS-1B-3B	147	572	48	164	25	4	5	53	13	.287
1983	Cincinnati	SS-3B-1B	143	528	54	123	22	0	1	47	14	.233
1984	Cincinnati	SS-3B-1B	154	531	46	130	26	1	4	58	22	.245
1985	Cincinnati	SS-3B	155	560	59	141	19	2	7	48	16	.252
	Totals		2210	7936	908	2117	352	46	97	879	301	.267

NICK ESASKY 26 6-3 200 Bats R Throws R

Emerged as solid power hitter when he got the chance in 1985 . . . Only Dave Parker had more pop among Reds . . . Best month was August, when he batted .287 with seven homers and 15 RBI . . . Finished strong with 16 RBI in 16 games during last two weeks of September . . . Third baseman was Reds' No. 1 choice in June 1978 draft . . . Belted 30 homers as Eastern League MVP for Waterbury (AA) in 1980 and hit 30 more for Indianapolis (AAA) in 1982, including three in playoffs . . . First major-league homer was an inside-the-park blow off Braves' Phil Niekro in 1983 . . . Batted poorly enough in 1984 to lose a job, but manager Pete Rose gave him a chance last season and he took advantage of it . . . Born Feb. 24, 1960, in Hialeah, Fla.

Year	Club	Pos.	G	AB	R	H	2B	3B	HR	RBI	SB	Avg.
1983	Cincinnati	3B	85	302	41	80	10	5	12	46	6	.265
1984	Cincinnati	3B-1B	113	322	30	62	10	5	10	45	1	.193
1985	Cincinnati	OF-3B-1B	125	413	61	108	21	0	21	66	3	.262
	Totals		323	1037	132	250	41	10	43	157	10	.241

RON OESTER 29 6-2 190 Bats S Throws R

Unsung hero of Reds' turnaround season, he just missed hitting .300 because of final-week slump . . . Batted .315 from All-Star break until beginning of October . . . Got best season going with a .373 May . . . Batted .323 in July . . . Superb season afield at second base . . . Born May 5, 1956, in Cincinnati . . . Pete Rose was his boyhood hero . . . Reds' ninth selection in June 1974 draft . . . If he ever hits well in both halves of a season, he could be a superstar . . . Played shortstop most of minor-league career . . . Slow start in 1984 was forgotten when he had 21-game hitting streak, longest on club since Rose's 44 in 1978 . . . Started fast in 1982 and 1983 before fading at the finish.

Year	Club	Pos.	G	AB	R	H	2B	3B	HR	RBI	SB	Avg.
1978	Cincinnati	SS	6	8	1	3	0	0	0	1	0	.375
1979	Cincinnati	SS	6	3	0	0	0	0	0	0	0	.000
1980	Cincinnati	2B-SS-3B	100	303	40	84	16	2	2	20	0	.277
1981	Cincinnati	2B-SS	105	354	45	96	16	7	5	42	2	.271
1982	Cincinnati	2B-SS-3B	151	549	63	143	19	4	9	47	5	.260
1983	Cincinnati	2B	157	549	63	145	23	5	11	58	2	.264
1984	Cincinnati	2B-SS	150	553	54	134	26	3	3	38	7	.242
1985	Cincinnati	2B	152	526	59	155	26	3	1	34	5	.295
	Totals		827	2845	325	760	126	24	31	240	27	.267

TOM BROWNING 25 6-1 190 **Bats L Throws L**

Just another young pitcher at start of season, he earned rookie honors with 20-victory debut . . . Totally unexpected success story got off ground with 2-0 April, when he yielded one run in 24 innings . . . Enjoyed tremendous final two months, going 5-1 with 2.49 ERA in August and 6-0 in September . . . Became first rookie to win 20 in 31 years . . . Born April 28, 1960, in Casper, Wyo. . . . Reds' ninth-round choice in June 1982 draft . . . Fired no-hitter for Wichita (AAA) and was American Association strikeout king in 1984 . . . Earned September promotion to Reds, looked sharp and proved it was no fluke in 1985.

Year	Club	G	IP	W	L	Pct.	SO	BB	H	ERA
1984	Cincinnati	3	23⅓	1	0	1.000	14	5	27	1.54
1985	Cincinnati	38	261⅓	20	9	.690	155	73	242	3.55
	Totals	41	284⅔	21	9	.700	169	78	269	3.38

JOHN FRANCO 25 5-10 175 **Bats L Throws L**

Like Tom Browning, "Generalissimo" blossomed into star in his first full big-league season after impressing in 1984 . . . Has a penchant for winning in relief, doing it 18 times in two years . . . Was 5-0 with 2.00 ERA in July . . . Had 2-0 mark with four saves in August, relinquishing only one earned run in 30⅓ innings . . . Posted 11th straight victory Aug. 23 . . . Born Sept. 17, 1960, in Brooklyn, N.Y. . . . Played at St. John's, then Dodgers made him fifth-round choice in June 1981 draft . . . Joined Reds in deal for Rafael Landestoy, May 9, 1983 . . . Had high ERA as minor-league starter, but has been exclusively a reliever with Reds and a very successful one . . . Had 12 saves last season.

Year	Club	G	IP	W	L	Pct.	SO	BB	H	ERA
1984	Cincinnati	54	79⅓	6	2	.750	55	36	74	2.61
1985	Cincinnati	67	99	12	3	.800	61	40	83	2.18
	Totals	121	178⅓	18	5	.783	116	76	157	2.37

BILL GULLICKSON 27 6-3 220 **Bats R Throws R**

Expos traded him and Sal Butera in December for Jay Tibbs, Andy McGaffigan, John Stuper and Dann Bilardello . . . Consistent '85 season was marred by groin injury that disabled him for almost five weeks . . . Also was a victim of tough luck as the Expos scored total of eight runs in his first nine losses . . . Born Feb. 20, 1959, in Marshall, Minn. . . . Expos made him second pick in the nation, behind White Sox' Harold Baines, in June 1977 draft . . . Discovered diabetic condition in spring of 1980, but reached Expos to stay that year . . . Set major-league rookie mark with 18 strikeouts against Cubs, Sept. 10, 1980 . . . Has been known to throw an occasional brushback pitch.

Year	Club	G	IP	W	L	Pct.	SO	BB	H	ERA
1979	Montreal	1	1	0	0	.000	0	0	2	0.00
1980	Montreal	24	141	10	5	.667	120	50	127	3.00
1981	Montreal	22	157	7	9	.438	115	34	142	2.81
1982	Montreal	34	236⅔	12	14	.462	155	61	231	3.57
1983	Montreal	34	242⅓	17	12	.586	120	59	230	3.75
1984	Montreal	32	226⅔	12	9	.571	100	37	230	3.61
1985	Montreal	29	181⅓	14	12	.538	68	47	187	3.52
	Totals	176	1186	72	61	.541	678	288	1149	3.44

MARIO SOTO 29 6-0 190 **Bats R Throws R**

An enigma . . . A loser on a team 17 games above .500 . . . Obviously pitched better than his record suggests . . . A victim of tough losses, he wound up on wrong end of five shutouts . . . Started strong with 4-1 April . . . Struck out more than 200 batters for third time in four years . . . Closing in on Jim Maloney's club career strikeout mark . . . Born July 12, 1956, in Bani, Dominican Republic . . . Signed as a free agent by Reds in 1973 . . . Struck out 274 in 1982 to break Maloney's single-season club mark . . . Strikeout figure was highest ever by a Latin pitcher.

Year	Club	G	IP	W	L	Pct.	SO	BB	H	ERA
1977	Cincinnati	12	61	2	6	.250	44	26	60	5.31
1978	Cincinnati	5	18	1	0	1.000	13	13	13	2.50
1979	Cincinnati	25	37	3	2	.600	32	30	33	5.35
1980	Cincinnati	53	190	10	8	.556	182	84	126	3.08
1981	Cincinnati	25	175	12	9	.571	151	61	142	3.29
1982	Cincinnati	35	257⅔	14	13	.519	274	71	202	2.79
1983	Cincinnati	34	273⅔	17	13	.567	242	95	207	2.70
1984	Cincinnati	33	237⅓	18	7	.720	185	87	181	3.53
1985	Cincinnati	36	256⅔	12	15	.444	214	104	196	3.58
	Totals	258	1506⅓	89	73	.549	1337	571	1160	3.28

JOHN DENNY 33 6-3 190 **Bats R Throws R**

Traded from the Phils in December with minor leaguer Jeff Gray for Gary Redus and Tom Hume . . . This veteran right-hander was healthy for a change in '85, when he notched the third-highest total of innings pitched in his career and posted a respectable ERA . . . Hit stride in June, going 3-0 with a 3.03 ERA . . . Won NL Cy Young Award in 1983 and was off to a great start in 1984 before injury jinx struck . . . Had a league-leading 1.55 ERA when he was placed on disabled list with inflamed nerve in elbow, May 31, and he missed two months . . . Finished 1984 season with 2.45 ERA to top NL, but fell eight innings shy of qualifying for title . . . Born Nov. 8, 1952, in Prescott, Ariz. . . . Attended Southern Illinois and was selected by Cardinals in 29th round of June 1970 draft.

Year	Club	G	IP	W	L	Pct.	SO	BB	H	ERA
1974	St. Louis.	2	2	0	0	.000	1	0	3	0.00
1975	St. Louis.	25	136	10	7	.588	72	51	149	3.97
1976	St. Louis.	30	207	11	9	.550	74	74	189	2.52
1977	St. Louis.	26	150	8	8	.500	60	62	165	4.50
1978	St. Louis.	33	234	14	11	.560	103	74	200	2.96
1979	St. Louis.	31	206	8	11	.421	99	100	206	4.85
1980	Cleveland	16	109	8	6	.571	59	47	116	4.38
1981	Cleveland	19	146	10	6	.625	94	66	139	3.14
1982	Cleveland	21	138⅓	6	11	.353	94	73	126	5.01
1982	Philadelphia.	4	22⅓	0	2	.000	19	10	18	4.03
1983	Philadelphia.	36	242⅔	19	6	.760	139	53	229	2.37
1984	Philadelphia.	22	154⅓	7	7	.500	94	29	122	2.45
1985	Philadelphia.	33	230⅔	11	14	.440	123	83	252	3.82
	Totals.	298	1978⅓	112	98	.533	1031	722	1914	3.53

TOP PROSPECTS

ERIC DAVIS 23 6-2 170 **Bats R Throws R**

A disappointment after being handed center-field job last spring . . . His inability to make consistent contact led to trip to Denver (AAA) . . . Hit 15 homers and stole 35 bases in 40 attempts in 64 games for Denver before rejoining Reds . . . Born May 29, 1962, in Los Angeles . . . Topped Northwest Rookie League with 40 stolen bases for Eugene in 1981 . . . Late-season power surge saw him hit 10 homers for Reds in 1984 and he hit three in final week of 1985 season . . . This speedy slugger looks like a young Bobby Bonds, including the strikeouts . . . Wound up hitting .246 with eight homers, 18 RBI and 16 stolen bases in 122 at-bats for Reds in 1985.

WADE ROWDON 25 6-2 170 **Bats R Throws R**

Groomed as Reds' third baseman of the future after being acquired from White Sox in swap for Jim Kern, Aug. 23, 1982 . . . Exhibited excellent power with 19 homers and 31 doubles for Denver (AAA) last year, when he hit .289 and had 78 RBI . . . Born Sept. 7, 1960, in Riverhead, N.Y. . . . Attended Stetson and was drafted by White Sox in eighth round in June 1981 . . . Shifted to shortstop in 1984, after leading Eastern League third basemen in fielding percentage for Waterbury (AA) in 1983 . . . Good power for a middle infielder . . . High-school teammate of Phillies' infielder Tom Foley.

MANAGER PETE ROSE 44 5-11 200 Bats S Throws R

What else is there to say about Charlie Hustle? . . . His pursuit of Ty Cobb's record overshadowed job he did as a manager, but he worked wonders instilling pride and enthusiasm in what had been a dead horse in 1984 . . . Kept club competitive down to last week and Reds surprised everyone by finishing 89-72 . . . Belted a single against San Diego's Eric Show in the first inning Sept. 11 to break Ty Cobb's all-time record for career hits with No. 4,192 . . . Having fulfilled an obsession to be No. 1, he wants to keep playing . . . Can't blame him following a year in which he showed he still can get on base . . . Drew 86 walks in 1985 . . . Scored NL-record 2,108th run May 22 . . . Set another major-league mark by posting his 23rd consecutive season with 100 or more hits . . . Born April 14, 1941, in Cincinnati . . . Signed with Reds in 1960 and the rest is history . . . Started at five different positions in All-Star Games . . . Switch-hitter who platooned himself with old pal Tony Perez at first base in 1985 . . . A paragon of longevity, consistency, hustle and excellence . . . Only man in history to play more than 500 games at five different positions . . . Three-time NL batting champ . . . Not known for power, but hit three homers in a 1978 game vs. Mets . . . Went to Phillies as re-entry free agent and helped them win 1983 World Series . . . Acquired from Montreal for Tom Lawless, he became Reds' manager Aug. 16, 1984 and led club to 19-22 record the rest of the way . . . Credits coaches for his managerial success . . . Holds modern NL mark with 44-game hitting streak in 1978.

Year	Club	Pos.	G	AB	R	H	2B	3B	HR	RBI	SB	Avg.
1963	Cincinnati	2B-OF	157	623	101	170	25	9	6	41	13	.273
1964	Cincinnati	2B	136	516	64	139	13	2	4	34	4	.269
1965	Cincinnati	2B	162	670	117	209	35	11	11	81	8	.312
1966	Cincinnati	2B-3B	156	654	97	205	38	5	16	70	4	.313
1967	Cincinnati	OF-2B	148	585	86	176	32	8	12	76	11	.301
1968	Cincinnati	OF-2B-1B	149	626	94	210	42	6	10	49	3	.335
1969	Cincinnati	OF-2B	156	627	120	218	33	11	16	82	7	.348
1970	Cincinnati	OF	159	649	120	205	37	9	15	52	12	.316
1971	Cincinnati	OF	160	632	86	192	27	4	13	44	13	.304
1972	Cincinnati	OF	154	645	107	198	31	11	6	57	10	.307
1973	Cincinnati	OF	160	680	115	230	36	8	5	64	10	.338
1974	Cincinnati	OF	163	652	110	185	45	7	3	51	2	.284
1975	Cincinnati	3B-OF	162	662	112	210	47	4	7	74	0	.317
1976	Cincinnati	3B-OF	162	665	130	215	42	6	10	63	9	.323
1977	Cincinnati	3B	162	655	95	204	38	7	9	64	16	.311
1978	Cincinnati	3B-OF-1B	159	655	103	198	51	3	7	52	13	302
1979	Philadelphia . .	1B-3B-2B	163	628	90	208	40	5	4	59	20	.331
1980	Philadelphia . .	1B	162	655	95	185	42	1	1	64	12	.282
1981	Philadelphia . .	1B	107	431	73	140	18	5	0	33	4	.325
1982	Philadelphia . .	1B	162	634	80	172	25	4	3	54	8	.271
1983	Philadelphia . .	1B-OF	151	493	52	121	14	3	0	45	7	.245
1984	Mont.-Cin. . . .	1B-OF	121	374	43	107	15	2	0	34	1	.286
1985	Cincinnati	1B	119	405	60	107	12	2	2	46	8	.264
	Totals		3490	13,816	2150	4204	738	133	160	1289	195	.304

GREATEST SHORTSTOP

Roy McMillan won three straight fielding titles from 1956-58 and added another with the Braves, so he may have been the greatest defensive shortstop in Cincinnati history. However, all-around honors belong exclusively to rangy Venezuelan Dave Concepcion, who has manned the position from 1970 to the present.

During the heyday of the Big Red Machine, Concepcion was best known for his fielding prowess. But, when the superstars of that powerhouse began to fade, Davey emerged as an offensive threat, too. When he batted .301 in 1978, he became the first Cincinnati shortstop to hit that high since Joe Tinker in 1913 and Concepcion improved to a career-high .306 in 1981.

But fielding remained his forte. Displaying great range and a rifle arm, Davey won four straight Gold Gloves from 1974-77 and added a fifth in 1979. Concepcion developed a unique style, making one-hop throws to first base from deep in the hole that are designed to capitalize on the fast, artificial surface.

ALL-TIME RED SEASON RECORDS

BATTING: Cy Seymour, .377, 1905
HRs: George Foster, 52, 1977
RBIs: George Foster, 149, 1977
STEALS: Bob Bescher, 81, 1911
WINS: Adolfo Luque, 27, 1923
Bucky Walters, 27, 1939
STRIKEOUTS: Mario Soto, 274, 1982

HOUSTON ASTROS

TEAM DIRECTORY: Chairman: Dr. John J. McMullen; Pres.-GM: Dick Wagner; VP-Baseball Oper.: Fred Stanley; Special Asst.: Donald Davidson; Dir. Minor League Oper.: Bud Nelson; Dir. Pub. Rel.: Rob Matwick; Trav. Sec.: John Davis; Mgr.: Hal Lanier. Home: Astrodome (45,000). Field distances: 330, l.f. line; 380, l.c.; 400, c.f.; 380, r.c.; 330, r.f. line. Spring training: Kissimmee, Fla.

SCOUTING REPORT

HITTING: It's hard to believe, but the Astros had one of the best offenses in the league last year. Only the Cardinals hit for a higher average than Houston's .261 and scored more runs than the Astros' 706. Moreover, Houston hit more home runs (121) than six NL clubs, so that powder-puff image is unwarranted.

The man most responsible for giving the club a new look in 1985 is power-hitting first baseman Glenn Davis, who socked

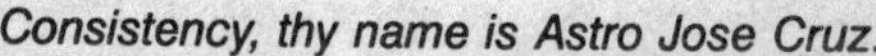

Consistency, thy name is Astro Jose Cruz.

20 homers in only 100 games. Outfielder Kevin Bass (16 homers, 68 RBI), catcher Mark Bailey (10 homers, 45 RBI) and second baseman Bill Doran (14 homers, 59 RBI) also can hit them out of the park, so the Astros no longer rely solely on Jose Cruz (.300, 9 homers, 79 RBI) to supply the pop. A healthy Terry Puhl is no slouch at the dish, either, and it surely would be a bonus if Dickie Thon regains his pre-beaning form. Don't sell this offense short.

PITCHING: Now that the Astros have perked up their offense, their traditionally tough pitching staff seems to be on the decline. Joe Niekro is gone and Nolan Ryan (10-12, 3.80) is aging, so the rotation has taken a new look behind instant ace Mike Scott (18-8, 3.29), veteran Bob Knepper (15-13, 3.55) and promising youngster Charlie Kerfeld (4-2, 4.06).

Scott's development into a big winner placed the Astros over the hump last year and made Niekro expendable. But it remains to be seen if the erratic Knepper can continue to win or whether youngsters like Kerfeld and Jeff Heathcock can blossom into winners. Ryan can still throw heat, but he found it more difficult to win last year, so "The Express" may be running out of steam.

FIELDING: Only the Dodgers had a worse fielding percentage than the Astros' .976 last year, so this area isn't a strength. The least of the concerns, however, is the play of second baseman Doran and shortstops Thon and Craig Reynolds. That strength up the middle makes the Astros look better defensively than they are.

Bass adds to that strength with his outstanding fielding in the outfield. The problem areas are the corners, where Davis made too many errors at first base and Phil Garner and Dennis Walling did likewise at third. The decline of the Astros' defense is not unrelated to the demise of a pitching staff that once was among the league's finest.

OUTLOOK: The Astros are an enigma. They are not what they seem. The stereotype casts Houston as a pitching-rich club well-suited to the Astrodome, but the fact of the matter is that the Astros have evolved into more of an offensive club. Their image definitely has changed and now new manager Hal Lanier plans to install a go-go attack patterned after the Cardinals, for whom he served as a coach last season.

The Astros played well at home (44-37) last year, but were deficient on the road (39-42), against the NL East (33-39) and against right-handers (44-50). Consequently, they were fortunate to have a winning record at 83-79. Another winning season is questionable in an improved division in 1986.

HOUSTON ASTROS 1986 ROSTER

MANAGER Hal Lanier
Coaches—Yogi Berra, Matt Galante, Denis Menke, Les Moss, Gene Tenace

PITCHERS

No.	Name	1985 Club	W-L	IP	SO	ERA	B-T	Ht.	Wt.	Born
49	Calhoun, Jeff	Houston	2-5	64	47	2.54	L-L	6-2	190	4/11/58 LaGrange, GA
46	Dawley, Bill	Houston	5-3	81	48	3.56	R-R	6-4	240	2/6/58 Norwich, CT
43	DeShaies, Jim	Columbus	8-6	132	106	4.31	L-L	6-4	222	6/23/60 Massena, NY
		Houston	0-0	3	2	0.00				
11	DiPino, Frank	Houston	3-7	76	49	4.03	L-L	6-0	180	10/22/56 Syracuse, NY
54	Friederich, Mike	Osceola	8-9	142	125	3.29	B-R	6-5	225	2/26/65 Windfield, IL
31	Heathcock, Jeff	Tucson	7-10	142	59	5.08	R-R	6-4	195	11/18/59 Covina, CA
		Houston	3-1	56	25	3.36				
38	Hernandez, Manny	Tucson	1-1	38	25	3.58	R-R	6-0	150	5/7/61 Dominican Republic
37	Kerfeld, Charlie	Tucson	10-11	163	123	4.46	R-R	6-6	257	9/28/63 Knobnoster, MO
		Houston	4-2	44	30	4.06				
39	Knepper, Bob	Houston	15-13	241	131	3.55	L-L	6-2	210	5/25/54 Akron, OH
41	Knudson, Mark	Tucson	8-5	146	68	4.01	R-R	6-5	215	10/28/60 Denver, CO
		Houston	0-2	11	4	9.00				
53	Madden, Mike	Tucson	2-0	23	14	3.52	L-L	6-1	190	1/13/58 Denver, CO
		Houston	0-0	19	16	4.26				
51	Montalvo, Rafael	Alb.-Tuc.	2-7	75	42	4.20	R-R	6-0	185	3/31/65 Puerto Rico
34	Ryan, Nolan	Houston	10-12	232	209	3.80	R-R	6-2	210	1/31/47 Refugio, TX
33	Scott, Mike	Houston	18-8	222	137	3.29	R-R	6-3	215	4/26/55 Santa Monica, CA
45	Smith, Dave	Houston	9-5	79	40	2.27	R-R	6-1	195	1/21/55 San Francisco, CA
52	Solano, Julio	Tucson	2-3	32	23	3.98	R-R	6-1	160	1/8/60 Dominican Republic
		Houston	2-2	34	17	3.48				
56	Vargas, Jose	Ashville	13-7	161	136	3.19	R-R	6-2	160	7/14/65 Dominican Republic

CATCHERS

No.	Name	1985 Club	H	HR	RBI	Pct.	B-T	Ht.	Wt.	Born
16	Afenir, Troy	Osceola	80	6	41	.248	R-R	6-4	185	9/21/63 Meadville, PA
14	Ashby, Alan	Houston	53	8	25	.280	B-R	6-2	195	7/8/51 Long Beach, CA
6	Bailey, Mark	Houston	88	10	45	.265	B-R	6-5	195	11/4/61 Springfield, MO
4	Mizerock, John	Tucson	47	1	19	.211	L-R	5-11	190	12/8/60 Punxsutawney, PA
		Houston	9	0	6	.237				
7	Wine, Robbie	Columbus	73	21	55	.191	R-R	6-2	200	7/13/62 Norristown, PA

INFIELDERS

No.	Name	1985 Club	H	HR	RBI	Pct.	B-T	Ht.	Wt.	Born
27	Davis, Glenn	Tucson	67	5	35	.305	R-R	6-3	208	3/28/61 Jacksonville, FL
		Houston	95	20	64	.271				
10	Doran, Bill	Houston	166	14	59	.287	B-R	6-0	175	5/28/58 Hamilton, OH
3	Garner, Phil	Houston	124	6	51	.268	R-R	5-10	175	4/30/49 Jefferson City, TN
20	Pankovits, Jim	Houston	42	4	14	.244	R-R	5-10	174	8/6/55 Pennington Gap, VA
1	Pena, Bert	Tucson	53	1	19	.260	R-R	5-11	165	7/11/59 Puerto Rico
		Houston	8	0	4	.276				
12	Reynolds, Craig	Houston	103	4	32	.272	L-R	6-1	175	12/27/52 Houston, TX
23	Rivera, German	Alb.-Tuc.	108	8	44	.281	R-R	6-2	195	7/6/59 Puerto Rico
		Houston	7	0	2	.194				
2	Rood, Nelson	Columbus	59	1	17	.262	R-R	5-10	172	6/15/60 West Palm Beach, FL
		Tucson	66	0	16	.245				
—	*Spilman, Harry	Houston	9	1	4	.136	L-R	6-1	190	7/18/54 Albany, GA
10	Thon, Dickie	Houston	63	6	28	.251	R-R	5-11	175	6/20/58 South Bend, IN
20	Walling, Denny	Houston	92	7	45	.270	L-R	6-1	185	4/17/54 Neptune, NJ

OUTFIELDERS

No.	Name	1985 Club	H	HR	RBI	Pct.	B-T	Ht.	Wt.	Born
17	Bass, Kevin	Houston	145	16	68	.269	B-R	6-0	180	5/12/59 Redwood City, CA
9	Bullock, Eric	Tucson	149	4	57	.319	L-L	5-11	185	2/16/60 Los Angeles, CA
		Houston	7	0	2	.280				
25	Cruz, Jose	Houston	163	9	79	.300	L-L	6-0	185	8/8/47 Puerto Rico
24	Gainey, Ty	Tucson	78	5	46	.336	R-L	6-1	190	12/25/60 Cheraw, SC
		Houston	6	0	0	.162				
22	Hatcher, Billy	Iowa	78	4	19	.280	R-R	5-9	175	10/4/60 Williams, AZ
26	Meadows, Louie	Columbus	111	14	67	.233	L-L	5-11	189	4/29/61 Onslow County, NC
21	Puhl, Terry	Houston	55	2	23	.284	L-R	6-2	200	7/8/56 Canada
30	Walker, Tony	Columbus	156	12	65	.294	R-R	6-2	204	7/1/59 San Diego, CA

*Free agent unsigned at press time

ASTRO PROFILES

JOSE CRUZ 38 6-0 185 **Bats L Throws L**

Durable left fielder enjoyed his sixth .300 season last year and retained position as club's offensive leader . . . Became Houston's all-time hits leader with his 1,660th Aug. 4, passing Cesar Cedeno . . . Showed remarkable consistency, batting .299 at All-Star break and .300 thereafter . . . Off to a great start with a .321 April and a .341 May . . . Fell back at midseason, but regained pop with a .366 August that included 11 doubles and 19 RBI . . . Born Aug. 8, 1947, in Arroyo, Puerto Rico . . . Brother of former major-leaguers Hector and Tommy Cruz . . . Four-time Astros' MVP . . . Named Puerto Rico's Pro Athlete of the Year in 1981 . . . Signed as free agent by Cardinals in 1966 . . . Purchased by Astros from St. Louis following the 1974 season and career took off with .303 season in 1976 . . . Tied Phil Garner for club lead in game-winning RBI with nine last season.

Year	Club	Pos.	G	AB	R	H	2B	3B	HR	RBI	SB	Avg.
1970	St. Louis	OF	6	17	2	6	1	0	0	1	0	.353
1971	St. Louis	OF	83	292	46	80	13	2	9	27	6	.274
1972	St. Louis	OF	117	332	33	78	14	4	2	23	9	.235
1973	St. Louis	OF	132	406	51	92	22	5	10	57	10	.227
1974	St. Louis	OF-1B	107	161	24	42	4	3	5	20	4	.261
1975	Houston	OF	120	315	44	81	15	2	9	49	6	.257
1976	Houston	OF	133	439	49	133	21	5	4	61	28	.303
1977	Houston	OF	157	579	87	173	31	10	17	87	44	.299
1978	Houston	OF-1B	153	565	79	178	34	9	10	83	37	.315
1979	Houston	OF	157	558	73	161	33	7	9	72	36	.289
1980	Houston	OF	160	612	79	185	29	7	11	91	36	.302
1981	Houston	OF	107	409	53	109	16	5	13	55	5	.267
1982	Houston	OF	155	570	62	157	27	2	9	68	21	.275
1983	Houston	OF	160	594	85	189	28	8	14	92	30	.318
1984	Houston	OF	160	600	96	187	28	13	12	95	22	.312
1985	Houston	OF	141	544	69	163	34	4	9	79	16	.300
	Totals		2048	6993	932	2014	350	86	143	960	310	.288

GLENN DAVIS 25 6-3 208 **Bats R Throws R**

Enjoyed exceptional rookie season, providing Astros with much-needed long-ball threat . . . Accumulated 20 homers and 64 RBI in only 350 at-bats in 1985 . . . Demonstrated his punch with seven homers and 21 RBI in July . . . Finished strong with .303 average, eight homers and 23 RBI in September . . . First baseman's development made Enos Cabell expendable . . . Looks like a regular for many years to come . . . Born March 28,

1961, in Jacksonville, Fla. . . . Attended Georgia and was Astros' first-round pick in secondary phase of January 1981 draft . . . Solid power figures in minors prompted his promotion to Astros in September 1984 . . . In his last three minor-league seasons, he produced 65 homers and 274 RBI in 393 games.

Year	Club	Pos.	G	AB	R	H	2B	3B	HR	RBI	SB	Avg.
1984	Houston	1B	18	61	6	13	5	0	2	8	0	.213
1985	Houston	1B-OF	100	350	51	95	11	0	20	64	0	.271
	Totals		118	411	57	108	16	0	22	72	0	.263

MARK BAILEY 24 6-5 195 **Bats S Throws R**

Saw more playing time and looms as eventual successor to No. 1 catcher Alan Ashby . . . His 19 homers in two years as part-time player attest to his power, considering spaciousness of Astrodome . . . Was at his peak in midseason last year, batting .400 with four home runs in June . . . Born Nov. 4, 1961, in Springfield, Mo. . . . Attended Southwest Missouri State and was selected in sixth round of June 1982 draft . . . Signed as a first baseman and third baseman, he was moved behind the plate at the suggestion of VP Bob Kennedy . . . Didn't play Triple-A ball . . . Was promoted from Columbus (AA) when Ashby was injured in 1984 and showed enough pop to stick on his own merits last year . . . Switch-hitting is an asset, as are his power and strong throwing arm.

Year	Club	Pos.	G	AB	R	H	2B	3B	HR	RBI	SB	Avg.
1984	Houston	C	108	344	38	73	16	1	9	34	0	.212
1985	Houston	C	114	332	47	88	14	0	10	45	0	.265
	Totals		222	676	85	161	30	1	19	79	0	.238

BILL DORAN 27 6-0 175 **Bats S Throws R**

His third year as a regular was his most productive in all phases . . . Solid finish made him second-best hitter on club, behind Jose Cruz . . . Showed consistency, batting .341 in May, .314 in July and .314 with 18 RBI in August . . . Born May 28, 1958, in Hamilton, Ohio . . . Earned All-American distinction at Ohio University before Astros drafted him in sixth round of June 1979 lottery . . . Improved every year in minors, posting .302 average and stealing 48 bases for Tucson (AAA) in 1982 . . . Joined Houston late in 1982 and went hitless in debut before embarking on 10-game hitting streak . . . Traditionally a slow starter in past, he cured that habit with his hot May . . . A solid fielder at second base, though he is more steady than spectacular.

Year	Club	Pos.	G	AB	R	H	2B	3B	HR	RBI	SB	Avg.
1982	Houston	2B	26	97	11	27	3	0	0	6	5	.278
1983	Houston	2B	154	535	70	145	12	7	8	39	12	.271
1984	Houston	2B-SS	147	548	92	143	18	11	4	41	21	.261
1985	Houston	2B	148	578	84	166	31	6	14	59	23	.287
	Totals		475	1758	257	481	64	24	26	145	61	.274

KEVIN BASS 26 6-0 180 **Bats S Throws R**

Blossomed as a regular, providing deft outfield defense and turning in a solid performance at the plate . . . Got better as season progressed, batting .333 in September . . . Only Jose Cruz had more RBI among Astros . . . Was Astros' top pinch-hitter in 1983 and 1984 before becoming a starter last year . . . Born May 12, 1959, in Redwood City, Cal . . . Brewers' second-round pick in June 1977 draft came to Houston as one of three prospects in Don Sutton deal, Aug. 30, 1982 . . . Batted .315 for Vancouver (AAA) that year and came up to stay with Astros in September . . . Struggled in 1983, but made vast strides toward more playing time in 1984, when he belted three doubles in one game and put together a 12-game hitting streak.

Year	Club	Pos.	G	AB	R	H	2B	3B	HR	RBI	SB	Avg.
1982	Milwaukee	OF	18	9	4	0	0	0	0	0	0	.000
1982	Houston	OF	12	24	2	1	0	0	0	0	0	.042
1983	Houston	OF	88	195	25	46	7	3	2	18	2	.236
1984	Houston	OF	121	331	33	86	17	5	2	29	5	.260
1985	Houston	OF	150	539	72	145	27	5	16	68	19	.269
	Totals		389	1098	136	278	51	13	20	116	26	.253

NOLAN RYAN 39 6-2 210 **Bats R Throws R**

"The Express" keeps rolling along . . . Registered 10th 200-strikeout season of career last year and his first since 1982 . . . Notched 4,000th career strikeout against Mets' Danny Heep July 11 and finished season with 4,083, the most in major-league history . . . Best month was May, when he went 3-1 with 2.56 ERA and 48 strikeouts in 45⅔ innings . . . Lost seven in a row after 8-3 start as he was a victim of poor support . . . Born

K King Nolan Ryan can still turn up the heater at 39.

Jan. 31, 1947, in Refugio, Tex. . . . Mets' eighth-round selection in June 1965 draft, but pitching-rich club gave up on him after 1971 season . . . Blossomed with Angels, striking out a remarkable total of 1,079 batters in 1972, 1973 and 1974, including a major-league record 383 in '73 . . . Besides strikeout standards, he holds major-league mark with five no-hitters . . . Also has nine one-hitters . . . Signed with Astros as a re-entry free agent following 1979 season.

Year	Club	G	IP	W	L	Pct.	SO	BB	H	ERA
1966	New York (NL)	2	3	0	1	.000	6	3	5	15.00
1968	New York (NL)	21	134	6	9	.400	133	75	93	3.09
1969	New York (NL)	25	89	6	3	.667	92	53	60	3.54
1970	New York (NL)	27	132	7	11	.389	125	97	86	3.41
1971	New York (NL)	30	152	10	14	.417	137	116	125	3.97
1972	California	39	284	19	16	.543	329	157	166	2.28
1973	California	41	326	21	16	.568	383	162	238	2.87
1974	California	42	333	22	16	.578	367	202	221	2.89
1975	California	28	198	14	12	.538	186	132	152	3.45
1976	California	39	284	17	18	.486	327	183	193	3.36
1977	California	37	299	19	16	.543	341	204	198	2.77
1978	California	31	235	10	13	.435	260	148	183	3.71
1979	California	34	223	16	14	.533	223	114	169	3.59
1980	Houston	35	234	11	10	.524	200	98	205	3.35
1981	Houston	21	149	11	5	.688	140	68	99	1.69
1982	Houston	35	250⅓	16	12	.571	245	109	196	3.16
1983	Houston	29	196⅓	14	9	.609	183	101	134	2.98
1984	Houston	30	183⅔	12	11	.522	197	69	143	3.04
1985	Houston	35	232	10	12	.455	209	95	205	3.80
	Totals	581	3937⅓	241	218	.525	4083	2186	2871	3.14

DAVE SMITH 31 6-1 195 **Bats R Throws R**

Only Expos' Jeff Reardon and Cubs' Lee Smith had better years than this relief ace in 1985 . . . Amassed 27 saves, the most ever by a Houston right-hander and only two shy of Fred Gladding's club mark . . . Went 3-1 with 0.59 ERA and three saves in April . . . Added five saves in August and capped season with a 2-0 record, 0.68 ERA and five more saves in September . . . Mixes fastballs and forkballs and is very proficient in avoiding home runs . . . Born Jan. 21, 1955, in San Francisco . . . Attended San Diego State and was Astros' eighth-round choice in June 1976 draft . . . Took awhile to attain stardom, but showed flashes as a rookie in 1980 with 1.92 ERA, 10 saves and an NLCS victory.

Year	Club	G	IP	W	L	Pct.	SO	BB	H	ERA
1980	Houston	57	103	7	5	.583	85	32	90	1.92
1981	Houston	42	75	5	3	.625	52	23	54	2.76
1982	Houston	49	63⅓	5	4	.556	28	31	69	3.84
1983	Houston	42	72⅔	3	1	.750	41	36	72	3.10
1984	Houston	53	77⅓	5	4	.556	45	20	60	2.21
1985	Houston	64	79⅓	9	5	.643	40	17	69	2.27
	Totals	307	470⅔	34	22	.607	291	159	414	2.60

MIKE SCOTT 30 6-3 215 **Bats R Throws R**

Unquestionably the new ace of the Astros, after improving from 5-11 in 1984 to 18-8 in 1985 thanks to addition of split-finger fastball . . . Went 7-2 from Aug. 15 through end of season and had a chance at 20 wins before losing in final week . . . Did bulk of his damage with a great midseason, going 4-2 with 2.47 ERA in June, 4-1 with 2.06 ERA in July and 4-2 with 2.72 ERA in August . . . Born April 26, 1955, in Santa Monica, Cal. . . . Attended Pepperdine . . . Mets' second pick in June 1976 draft . . . Got lost amid all the Mets' outstanding pitching prospects and was traded to Astros for Danny Heep following 1982 season . . . Had his finest season last year as he finally learned how to pitch . . . Was accused of doctoring baseball by Cubs, who insisted they found piece of sandpaper on mound during one of his starts last season.

Year	Club	G	IP	W	L	Pct.	SO	BB	H	ERA
1979	New York (NL)	18	52	1	3	250	21	20	59	5.37
1980	New York (NL)	6	29	1	1	.500	13	8	40	4.34
1981	New York (NL)	23	136	5	10	.333	54	34	130	3.90
1982	New York (NL)	37	147	7	13	.350	63	60	185	5.14
1983	Houston	24	145	10	6	.625	73	46	143	3.72
1984	Houston	31	154	5	11	.313	83	43	179	4.68
1985	Houston	36	221⅔	18	8	.692	137	80	194	3.29
	Totals	175	884⅔	47	52	.475	444	291	930	4.16

BOB KNEPPER 31 6-2 210 **Bats L Throws L**

Finished fast to salvage season after going winless in July . . . Enjoyed a 4-0 May, then slumped until he went 7-4 in final two months to finish with winning record . . . Has 30 victories in last two seasons after going a combined 11-28 in 1982 and 1983 . . . Very strange career . . . At times, he has looked like one of the top southpaws in the game. Other times, he has impersonated a batting tee . . . Born May 25, 1954, in Akron, Ohio . . . Second-round pick of Giants in June 1972 draft . . . Had sensational season in 1974, going 20-5 with 247 strikeouts for Fresno (A) . . . Reached majors to stay with Giants in 1977 and had a great first full year in 1978 . . . Traded to Houston for Enos Cabell following

1980 season . . . Enjoys opera and listens to it to relax before pitching.

Year	Club	G	IP	W	L	Pct.	SO	BB	H	ERA
1976	San Francisco	4	25	1	2	.333	11	7	26	3.24
1977	San Francisco	27	166	11	9	.550	100	72	151	3.36
1978	San Francisco	36	260	17	11	.607	147	85	218	2.63
1979	San Francisco	34	207	9	12	.429	123	77	241	4.65
1980	San Francisco	35	215	9	16	.360	103	61	242	4.10
1981	Houston	22	157	9	5	.643	75	38	128	2.18
1982	Houston	33	180	5	15	.250	108	60	193	4.45
1983	Houston	35	203	6	13	.316	125	71	202	3.19
1984	Houston	35	233⅔	15	10	.600	140	55	223	3.20
1985	Houston	37	241	15	13	.536	131	54	253	3.55
	Totals	298	1887⅔	97	106	.478	1063	580	1877	3.48

TOP PROSPECT

CHARLIE KERFELD 22 6-6 225 Bats R Throws R

A pleasant surprise down the stretch . . . Hulking right-hander didn't allow a run in his last two starts for Houston, yielding only seven hits in 14⅓ innings . . . Born Sept. 28, 1963, in Knobnoster, Mo. . . . Attended Yavapai College in Arizona . . . Turned down offers from Phillies and Mariners, then signed with Astros, who selected him in secondary phase of June 1982 draft . . . As a first-year pro in 1983, he was South Atlantic League Pitcher of the Year with 16-10 record and 2.91 ERA for Asheville (A) . . . Went 14-9 with 2.99 ERA for Columbus (AA) in 1984 . . . Was 10-11 with 4.46 ERA for Tucson (AAA) last season before joining Astros . . . Posted 4-2 record and 4.06 ERA for Houston.

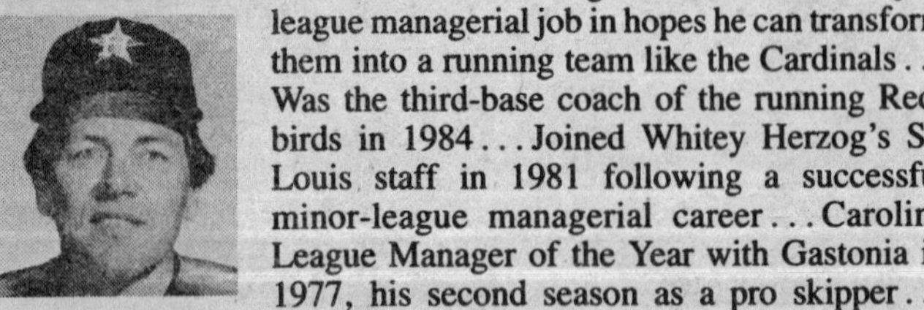

MANAGER HAL LANIER: Astros gave Lanier first major-league managerial job in hopes he can transform them into a running team like the Cardinals . . . Was the third-base coach of the running Redbirds in 1984 . . . Joined Whitey Herzog's St. Louis staff in 1981 following a successful minor-league managerial career . . . Carolina League Manager of the Year with Gastonia in 1977, his second season as a pro skipper . . . Named 1980 Minor League Manager of the Year by *The Sporting News* after guiding Springfield (Ill.) to the American Association crown . . . Born July 4, 1942, in Denton, N.C. . . . Son of Max Lanier, former major-league pitcher . . . Signed a bonus contract with the Giants in 1961 and became their regular second baseman in 1964 . . . Switched to shortstop in 1967 and was a regular four more years, topping NL in fielding percentage in 1968 . . . Concluded major-league career with Yankees in 1973, compiling .228 lifetime average in 1,196 games.

GREATEST SHORTSTOP

It would be unfair to award Dickie Thon the distinction of being Houston's greatest shortstop on the basis of one great year, so the honor goes to slender Roger Metzger, a regular from 1971-78. Metzger wasn't a sensational player, but he was a sure-handed fielder and his speed enabled him to lead the National League in triples two times.

Metzger was the Astros' MVP in 1973, when he won his only Gold Glove. His 14 triples that year remain a club record and his 62 three-baggers as an Astro have been exceeded only by Joe Morgan and Jose Cruz. In 1976, Metzger established a phenomenal club record, posting a .986 fielding percentage.

Thon deserves mention because of his tremendous 1983 campaign, which stamped him as the Astros' shortstop of the future until a serious eye injury cast doubt on that claim. Craig Reynolds also has played the position well for Houston, as did the club's first shortstop, 1962 team MVP Bob Lillis.

ALL-TIME ASTRO SEASON RECORDS

BATTING: Rusty Staub, .333, 1967
HRs: Jimmy Wynn, 37, 1967
RBIs: Bob Watson, 110, 1977
STEALS: Cesar Cedeno, 61, 1977
WINS: Joe Niekro, 21, 1979
STRIKEOUTS: J. R. Richard, 313, 1979

LOS ANGELES DODGERS

TEAM DIRECTORY: Pres.: Peter O'Malley; Exec. VP: Fred Claire; VP-Play. Pers.: Al Campanis; VP-Minor Leagues; Bill Schweppe; Dir. Publ.: Steve Brener; Trav. Sec.: Bill DeLury; Mgr.: Tom Lasorda. Home: Dodger Stadium (56,000). Field distances: 330, l.f. line; 370, l.c.; 395, c.f.; 370, r.c.; 330, r.f. line. Spring training: Vero Beach, Fla.

SCOUTING REPORT

HITTING: Only the Cardinals had a higher average than the Dodgers' .261 last season, so offense is not a concern for a team which should dramatically improve its attack following a confidence-building 1985. After all, the Dodgers weren't supposed to contend last year and they won the NL West.

Los Angeles' hopes for an even better 1986 are based on almost certain improvement by young Mariano Duncan and the availability of veteran RBI man Bill Madlock for an entire season.

Pedro Guerrero (.320, 33 homers, 87 RBI) and Mike Marshall (.293, 28 homers, 95 RBI) are established slugging stars and, now that Greg Brock (21 homers, 66 RBI) shows signs of joining them, the club no longer has a first-base problem. Ditto behind the plate, where Mike Scioscia (.296) has bounced back from injury to become one of the league's best. Steve Sax and Ken Landreaux are less spectacular than some of their teammates, but they complement the others with solid offensive contributions.

PITCHING: With this much quality pitching, it doesn't take much hitting for the Dodgers to be successful. Most staffs would love to have one or two pitchers with earned-run averages below 3.00. On this club, it's the rule, as a major-league-leading 2.96 team ERA would suggest. And that was achieved without injured Alejandro Pena, who was the NL's ERA champ in 1984.

In Pena's absence, the Dodgers developed yet another pitching superstar in Orel Hershiser (19-3, 2.03), whose credentials cried out for Cy Young recognition. Add Fernando Valenzuela (17-10, 2.45), Bob Welch (14-4, 2.31), Jerry Reuss (14-10, 2.92) and Rick Honeycutt (8-12, 3.42) and you have the NL's best five.

If that isn't enough, the club has improved its bullpen with the addition of former Mariner lefty Ed Vande Berg, who should find Dodger Stadium more comfortable than the Kingdome. Tom Niedenfuer (2.71, 19 saves), his nightmarish postseason notwithstanding, also is a quality reliever.

Hershiser performs Orel surgery on NL hitters.

FIELDING: Defense never has been a Dodgers' strong suit and 1985 was no exception. The club won its division despite making the most errors in the NL with 166. The club's fielding is bound to improve when Duncan settles in at shortstop and second baseman Sax (22 errors) gets over his throwing woes. There are no Gold Glove candidates, but nobody blocks the plate better than Scioscia.

OUTLOOK: The Dodgers get enough pitching and offense to overcome their defensive shortcomings, just as they did when they won flags in the '70s. This club proves pitching is 80 percent of the game. Success on the mound has become a Dodger tradition and it invariably disguises other problems.

Pitching once again will carry the Dodgers to the top. If they could win 95 games and a division title last year while rebuilding, there's no telling what will happen in 1986 with a more settled lineup and an even deeper pitching staff. Los Angeles is a team that seemingly can't miss, barring a plague of injuries.

Guerrero should be even more productive with Madlock in the lineup and Marshall and Brock also are capable of big power numbers. If Duncan raises his average above the .244 mark and ignites the offense, Tom Lasorda's team will probably win 100 games.

LOS ANGELES DODGERS 1986 ROSTER

MANAGER Tom Lasorda
Coaches—Joe Amalfitano, Monty Basgall, Mark Cresse, Manny Mota, Ron Perranoski

PITCHERS

No.	Name	1985 Club	W-L	IP	SO	ERA	B-T	Ht.	Wt.	Born
37	Castillo, Bobby	Los Angeles	2-2	68	57	5.43	R-R	5-10	186	4/18/55 Los Angeles, CA
27	Diaz, Carlos	Los Angeles	6-3	79	73	2.61	R-L	6-0	170	1/7/58 Honolulu, HI
52	Galvez, Balvino	San Antonio	10-9	171	111	4.54	R-R	6-0	180	3/31/64 Dominican Republic
59	Heredia, Hector	San Antonio	1-0	5	2	1.93	R-R	6-2	190	5/20/60 Mexico
55	Hershiser, Orel	Los Angeles	19-3	240	157	2.03	R-R	6-3	190	9/16/58 Buffalo, NY
40	Honeycutt, Rick	Los Angeles	8-12	142	67	3.42	L-L	6-1	193	6/29/54 Chattanooga, TN
43	Howell, Ken	Los Angeles	4-7	86	85	3.77	R-R	6-3	216	11/28/60 Detroit, MI
31	May, Scott	San Antonio	10-6	192	125	3.47	R-R	6-1	185	11/11/61 West Bend, WI
49	Niedenfuer, Tom	Los Angeles	7-9	106	102	2.71	R-R	6-5	225	8/13/59 St. Louis Park, MN
26	Pena, Alejandro	Los Angeles	0-1	4	2	8.31	R-R	6-1	205	6/25/59 Dominican Republic
48	Powell, Dennis	Albuquerque	9-0	112	55	2.74	L-L	6-3	200	8/13/63 Detroit, MI
		Los Angeles	1-1	29	19	5.22				
41	Reuss, Jerry	Los Angeles	14-10	213	84	2.92	L-L	6-5	225	6/19/49 St. Louis, MO
56	Tejeda, Felix	Bakersfield	1-0	23	18	2.70	B-L	6-1	172	2/28/63 Mexico
		Albuquerque	2-0	16	14	7.71				
34	Valenzuela, Fernando	Los Angeles	17-10	272	208	2.45	L-L	5-11	195	11/1/60 Mexico
—	Vande Berg, Ed	Seattle	2-1	68	34	3.72	R-L	6-2	180	10/26/58 Redlands, CA
35	Welch, Bob	Vero Beach	0-0	17	9	2.12	R-R	6-3	190	11/3/56 Detroit, MI
		Los Angeles	14-4	167	96	2.31				

CATCHERS

No.	Name	1985 Club	H	HR	RBI	Pct.	B-T	Ht.	Wt.	Born
15	Reyes, Gilberto	Albuquerque	97	6	54	.265	R-R	6-2	205	12/10/63 Dom. Republic
		Los Angeles	0	0	0	.000				
14	Scioscia, Mike	Los Angeles	127	7	53	.296	L-R	6-2	220	11/27/58 Upper Darby, PA
—	Trevino, Alex	San Francisco	34	6	19	.217	R-R	5-11	170	8/26/57 Mexico

INFIELDERS

No.	Name	1985 Club	H	HR	RBI	Pct.	B-T	Ht.	Wt.	Born
10	Anderson, Dave	Albuquerque	28	3	16	.289	R-R	6-2	185	8/1/60 Louisville, KY
		Los Angeles	44	4	18	.199				
21	Bailor, Bob	Los Angeles	29	0	7	.246	R-R	5-10	165	7/10/51 Connellsville, PA
9	Brock, Greg	Los Angeles	110	21	66	.251	L-R	6-3	205	6/14/57 McMinnville, OR
23	Cabell, Enos	Hou.-LA	91	2	36	.272	R-R	6-5	190	10/8/49 Fort Riley, KS
25	Duncan, Mariano	Los Angeles	137	6	39	.244	B-R	6-0	160	3/3/63 Dominican Republic
33	Hamilton, Jeff	San Antonio	125	13	59	.332	R-R	6-3	205	3/19/64 Flint, MI
12	Madlock, Bill	Pit.-LA	141	12	56	.275	R-R	5-11	206	1/12/51 Memphis, TN
17	Matuszek, Len	Toronto	32	2	15	.212	L-R	6-2	205	9/27/54 Toledo, OH
		Los Angeles	14	3	13	.222				
18	Russell, Bill	Los Angeles	44	0	13	.260	R-R	6-0	187	10/21/48 Pittsburgh, KS
3	Sax, Steve	Los Angeles	136	1	42	.279	R-R	5-11	185	1/29/60 West Sacramento, CA
22	Stubbs, Franklin	Albuquerque	118	32	93	.280	L-L	6-2	215	10/21/60 Laurinburg, NC
		Los Angeles	2	0	2	.222				

OUTFIELDERS

No.	Name	1985 Club	H	HR	RBI	Pct.	B-T	Ht.	Wt.	Born
29	Amelung, Ed	Albuquerque	163	8	61	.291	L-L	6-0	185	4/13/59 Fullerton, CA
46	Bryant, Ralph	Albuquerque	107	15	64	.268	L-R	6-2	205	5/20/61 Ft. Gaines, GA
		Los Angeles	2	0	1	.333				
36	Gonzalez, Jose	San Antonio	137	13	62	.306	R-R	6-2	190	11/23/64 Dom. Republic
		Los Angeles	3	0	0	.273				
28	Guerrero, Pedro	Los Angeles	156	33	87	.320	R-R	6-0	195	6/29/56 Dominican Republic
44	Landreaux, Ken	Los Angeles	129	12	50	.268	L-R	5-11	179	12/22/54 Los Angeles, CA
5	Marshall, Mike	Los Angeles	152	28	95	.293	R-R	6-5	220	1/12/60 Libertyville, IL
57	Pederson, Stu	Albuquerque	94	8	54	.328	L-L	6-0	189	1/28/60 Palo Alto, CA
		Los Angeles	0	0	1	.000				
38	Ramsey, Mike	San Antonio	87	1	23	.238	R-L	6-0	170	7/8/60 Harlem, GA
45	Whitfield, Terry	Los Angeles	27	3	16	.260	L-R	6-1	200	1/12/53 Blythe, CA
51	Williams, Reggie	San Antonio	127	10	53	.291	R-R	5-10	180	8/29/60 Memphis, TN
		Los Angeles	3	0	0	.333				

DODGER PROFILES

PEDRO GUERRERO 29 6-0 195 Bats R Throws R

Finished high in voting for NL MVP after turning club around with astonishing June . . . Took off after being switched from third base to left field June 1 . . . Was NL Player of the Month in June with .344 average, 15 homers and 26 RBI . . . Had five homers in four-game stretch in June, tying a Los Angeles record . . . Reached base in 14 straight trips during blazing stretch in July . . . Hit .348 with 29 homers and 69 RBI after shift to outfield . . . Born June 29, 1956, in San Pedro de Macoris, Dominican Republic . . . Signed as free agent by Indians, he was traded to Dodgers for pitcher Bruce Ellingsen prior to 1974 season . . . First Los Angeles player to post back-to-back 30-homer seasons . . . Shared World Series MVP honors in 1981 . . . Back spasms kept him from playing in 1985 All-Star Game, but he batted .460 in July . . . Led club with 16 game-winning RBI last season.

Year	Club	Pos.	G	AB	R	H	2B	3B	HR	RBI	SB	Avg.
1978	Los Angeles	1B	5	8	3	5	0	1	0	1	0	.625
1979	Los Angeles	OF-1B-3B	25	62	7	15	2	0	2	9	2	.242
1980	Los Angeles	OF-INF	75	183	27	59	9	1	7	31	2	.322
1981	Los Angeles	OF-3B-1B	98	347	46	104	17	2	12	48	5	.300
1982	Los Angeles	OF-3B	150	575	87	175	27	5	32	100	22	.304
1983	Los Angeles	3B-1B	160	584	87	174	28	6	32	103	23	.298
1984	Los Angeles	OF-3B-1B	144	535	85	162	29	4	16	72	9	.303
1985	Los Angeles	OF-3B-1B	137	487	99	156	22	2	33	87	12	.320
	Totals		794	2781	441	850	134	21	134	451	75	.306

BILL MADLOCK 35 5-11 206 Bats R Throws R

"Mad Dog" learned some new tricks, reviving his career after coming to Dodgers August 31 . . . Traded by Pittsburgh for three prospects, he immediately snapped out of doldrums, batting .348 with new club . . . Had three hits in first start with Dodgers . . . Third baseman enjoyed a 17-game hitting streak in September, matching his previous pro high . . . Batted .340 in September . . . Crashed three home runs in NLCS . . . Hit .409 with four homers for Bucs from Aug. 12-18 . . . Born Jan. 12, 1951, in Memphis . . . An avid antique collector who especially likes clocks . . . Signed with Senators after being drafted 99th in January 1970 . . . Traded to Cubs, for whom he won NL batting titles in 1975 and 1976 . . . His average dipped as a Giant, but he won two more batting crowns with Pittsburgh . . . Joined Pirates in 1979, helped them to flag and batted .375 in World Series.

Year	Club	Pos.	G	AB	R	H	2B	3B	HR	RBI	SB	Avg.
1973	Texas	3B	21	77	16	27	5	3	1	5	3	.351
1974	Chicago (NL)	3B	128	453	65	142	21	5	9	54	11	.313
1975	Chicago (NL)	3B	130	514	77	182	29	7	7	64	9	.354
1976	Chicago (NL)	3B	142	514	68	174	36	1	15	84	15	.339
1977	San Francisco	3B-2B	140	533	70	161	28	1	12	46	13	.302
1978	San Francisco	2B-1B	122	447	76	138	26	3	15	44	16	.309
1979	S.F.-Pitt.	3B-2B-1B	154	560	85	167	26	5	14	85	32	.298
1980	Pittsburgh	3B-1B	137	494	62	137	22	4	10	53	16	.277
1981	Pittsburgh	3B	82	279	35	95	23	1	6	45	18	.341
1982	Pittsburgh	3B-1B	154	568	92	181	33	3	19	95	18	.319
1983	Pittsburgh	3B	130	473	68	153	21	0	12	68	3	.323
1984	Pittsburgh	3B-1B	103	403	38	102	16	0	4	44	3	.253
1985	Pitt.-L.A.	3B-1B	144	513	69	141	27	1	12	56	10	.275
	Totals		1587	5828	821	1800	313	34	136	743	167	.309

MIKE SCIOSCIA 27 6-2 220 — Bats L Throws R

Made most of the first full season as a regular . . . Just missed becoming first Dodgers catcher to hit .300 since Roy Campanella did it in 1955 . . . Finished second in NL with .407 on-base percentage . . . Batted .322 in June . . . Outstanding defensively and especially adroit at blocking the plate . . . Shook off concussion suffered in collision with Cards' Jack Clark on play at plate July 21 . . . Born Nov. 27, 1958, in Upper Darby, Pa. . . . Dodgers' first-round selection in June 1976 draft . . . Solid Triple-A performances got him to Dodgers in 1980 . . . Limited to 12 games in 1983 following shoulder injury, he made a stirring comeback in 1984.

Year	Club	Pos.	G	AB	R	H	2B	3B	HR	RBI	SB	Avg.
1980	Los Angeles	C	54	134	8	34	5	1	1	8	1	.254
1981	Los Angeles	C	93	290	27	80	10	0	2	29	0	.276
1982	Los Angeles	C	129	365	31	80	11	1	5	38	2	.219
1983	Los Angeles	C	12	35	3	11	3	0	1	7	0	.314
1984	Los Angeles	C	114	341	29	93	18	0	5	38	2	.273
1985	Los Angeles	C	141	429	47	127	26	3	7	53	3	.296
	Totals		543	1594	145	425	73	5	21	173	8	.267

MARIANO DUNCAN 23 6-0 160 — Bats S Throws R

Regarded as one of the keys to club's success story in 1985 after making leap from San Antonio (AA) to majors . . . After making club as temporary replacement for injured second baseman Steve Sax, he flashed enough ability to win starting shortstop job . . . Topped Dodgers with 38 steals . . . Much stronger as right-handed hitter, posting .286 mark as opposed to .224 average from left side . . . Shift to shortstop coincided with

Dodgers' rise . . . Born March 13, 1963, in San Pedro de Macoris, Dominican Republic . . . Boyhood chum of Phils' Juan Samuel and Blue Jays' Tony Fernandez . . . Cesar Cedeno was his idol . . . Signed by Dodgers as free agent in 1982 . . . In second pro season, he led Florida State League with 56 stolen bases for Vero Beach (A) . . . Invites comparisons with Ozzie Smith because of his flamboyance in the field.

Year	Club	Pos.	G	AB	R	H	2B	3B	HR	RBI	SB	Avg.
1985	Los Angeles	SS-2B	142	562	74	137	24	6	6	39	38	.244

MIKE MARSHALL 26 6-5 220 Bats R Throws R

Right fielder missed 27 games with injuries, yet attained career highs in several categories . . . Finished strong during flag drive, batting .323 with nine homers and 30 RBI in September . . . Has four grand slams, one shy of Los Angeles record . . . Born Jan. 12, 1960, in Libertyville, Ill. . . . Dodgers' sixth-round pick in June 1978 draft . . . Nicknamed "Big Foot" because of size-14 shoe . . . An awesome minor-league slugger . . . Batted .354 with 116 RBI for Lodi (A) in 1979 and .373 with 34 homers and 137 RBI for Albuquerque (AAA) in 1981 . . . Named Minor League Player of the Year in 1981 . . . Had 12 game-winning RBI in 1985.

Year	Club	Pos.	G	AB	R	H	2B	3B	HR	RBI	SB	Avg.
1981	Los Angeles	1B-OF	14	25	2	5	3	0	0	1	0	.200
1982	Los Angeles	OF-1B	49	95	10	23	3	0	5	9	2	.242
1983	Los Angeles	OF-1B	140	465	47	132	17	1	17	65	7	.284
1984	Los Angeles	1B-OF	134	495	69	127	27	0	21	65	4	.257
1985	Los Angeles	OF-1B	135	518	72	152	27	2	28	95	3	.293
	Totals		472	1598	200	439	77	3	71	235	16	.275

OREL HERSHISER 27 6-3 190 Bats R Throws R

Had season worthy of Cy Young Award, were it not for Mets' Dwight Gooden and Cards' John Tudor . . . Won last 11 regular-season decisions and his victory in NLCS was his 20th of year . . . Looks anemic, but is deceptively strong . . . Only person in Los Angeles without a tan . . . Posted 11-0 record and 1.08 ERA at home . . . Fired one-hitters against Padres and Pirates . . . Went 3-0 with 1.86 ERA in April . . . Went 4-1 with 2.16 ERA in July . . . Finished with a 5-0 record and 1.24 ERA in September . . . Born Sept. 16, 1958, in Buffalo . . . Attended Bowling Green and became a standout junior hockey player . . . Selected in 17th round by Dodgers in June 1979 draft . . . Had mixed results as minor-league reliever before he caught fire as starter in second half of 1984 for Dodgers . . . Finished third in NL ERA race for two straight years.

Year	Club	G	IP	W	L	Pct.	SO	BB	H	ERA
1983	Los Angeles.	8	8	0	0	.000	5	6	7	3.38
1984	Los Angeles.	45	189⅔	11	8	.579	150	50	160	2.66
1985	Los Angeles.	36	239⅔	19	3	.864	157	68	179	2.03
	Totals.	89	437⅓	30	11	.732	312	124	346	2.33

FERNANDO VALENZUELA 25 5-11 195 Bats L Throws L

Has been more consistent than spectacular since his extraordinary arrival in majors in 1981 . . . His tough luck in 1985 was reflected in bizarre April, when he was NL Pitcher of the Month despite 2-3 record. He had incredible 0.21 ERA . . . Didn't allow an earned run in his first 41 innings last season, the best season-opening streak since ERA became a statistic in 1912 . . . Repeated as NL Pitcher of the Month in July with 5-0 record and 1.24 ERA . . . Went 4-1 in August . . . Won 12 of last 15 decisions . . . Born Nov. 1, 1960, in Navajoa, Sonora, Mexico . . . Came out of sandlots to attain professional stardom . . . Enjoyed absolutely sensational rookie season in strike-shortened 1981, when he became first pitcher to capture Cy Young and Rookie of the Year awards in the same season . . . Poor support the last two years explains his so-so 29-27 record . . . Helps himself with the bat and is a good fielder . . . Has great control and baffling screwball.

Year	Club	G	IP	W	L	Pct.	SO	BB	H	ERA
1980	Los Angeles.	10	18	2	0	1.000	16	5	8	0.00
1981	Los Angeles.	25	192	13	7	.650	180	61	140	2.48
1982	Los Angeles.	37	285	19	13	.594	199	83	247	2.87
1983	Los Angeles.	35	257	15	10	.600	189	99	245	3.75
1984	Los Angeles.	34	261	12	17	.414	240	106	218	3.03
1985	Los Angeles.	35	272⅓	17	10	.630	208	101	211	2.45
	Totals.	176	1285⅓	78	57	.578	1032	455	1069	2.89

BOB WELCH 29 6-3 190 Bats R Throws R

Enjoyed finest season of his career last year . . . Posted 5-0 record and 1.56 ERA in July . . . Was 4-1 with 2.62 ERA in September . . . Won well-publicized bout with booze to become one of baseball's most dependable pitchers . . . Elbow injury prevented him from having an even greater 1985 . . . Pitched only once prior to June 5 and underwent rehabilitation in minors . . . Born Nov. 3, 1956, in Detroit . . . Attended Eastern Michigan, where he was an All-American as a sophomore . . . Dodgers' first-round selection in June 1977 draft . . . Made only 25 starts in minors before promotion to majors . . . Gained attention with strikeout of Reggie Jackson in 1978 World Series . . . Has two career one-hitters.

Year	Club	G	IP	W	L	Pct.	SO	BB	H	ERA
1978	Los Angeles.	23	111	7	4	.636	66	26	92	2.03
1979	Los Angeles.	25	81	5	6	.455	64	32	82	4.00
1980	Los Angeles.	32	214	14	9	.609	141	79	190	3.28
1981	Los Angeles.	23	141	9	5	.643	88	41	141	3.45
1982	Los Angeles.	36	235⅔	16	11	.593	176	81	199	3.36
1983	Los Angeles.	31	204	15	12	.556	156	72	164	2.65
1984	Los Angeles.	31	178⅔	13	13	.500	126	58	191	3.78
1985	Los Angeles.	23	167⅓	14	4	.778	96	35	141	2.31
	Totals.	224	1332⅔	93	64	.592	913	424	1200	3.10

TOM NIEDENFUER 26 6-5 225 Bats R Throws R

Horrid finish marred an otherwise excellent season . . . Relinquished game-winning homers to Cards' Ozzie Smith and Jack Clark in final two games of NLCS . . . Posted six saves and a 0.48 ERA in August . . . His 19 saves were most on club since 1978 . . . Born Aug. 13, 1959, in St. Louis Park, Minn. . . . Attended Washington State and was signed by Dodgers as free agent in 1980 . . . Went 13-3 for San Antonio (AA) and 3-1 for Dodgers as first-year pro in 1981 . . . Strictly a reliever throughout his pro career . . . Nicknamed "Buffalo" because of his bulk, he is compared to Goose Gossage because of his size and heat . . . Injuries marred solid 1984, when he saved 11 games as Steve Howe's replacement.

Year	Club	G	IP	W	L	Pct.	SO	BB	H	ERA
1981	Los Angeles.	17	26	3	1	.750	12	6	25	3.81
1982	Los Angeles.	55	69⅔	3	4	.429	60	25	71	2.71
1983	Los Angeles.	66	94⅔	8	3	.727	66	29	55	1.90
1984	Los Angeles.	33	47⅓	2	5	.286	45	23	39	2.47
1985	Los Angeles.	64	106⅓	7	9	.438	102	24	86	2.71
	Totals.	235	344	23	22	.511	285	107	276	2.54

JERRY REUSS 36 6-5 225 Bats L Throws L

Formerly a power pitcher, he relied on finesse and overcame a slow start to figure prominently in Dodgers' 1985 success . . . Personable lefty was 3-1 in June and 4-1 with 1.17 ERA in August . . . Over last six years, his 2.87 ERA is tops in majors . . . Had three shutouts to lift his career total to 37 . . . Made a great comeback from injury-plagued 1984 . . . Born June 19, 1949, in St. Louis . . . Attended Southern Illinois, Central Missouri State and UC-Santa Barbara . . . Selected by St. Louis in second round of June 1967 draft . . . Reached majors with Cardinals and played with Astros and Pirates before being swapped to Dodgers for Rick Rhoden prior to 1979 season . . . Topped NL with six shutouts in 1980, including no-hitter against the Giants . . . A noted clubhouse comedian who has made more than one comeback from injuries.

Year	Club	G	IP	W	L	Pct.	SO	BB	H	ERA
1969	St. Louis	1	7	1	0	1.000	3	3	2	0.00
1970	St. Louis	20	127	7	8	.467	74	49	132	4.11
1971	St. Louis	36	211	14	14	.500	131	109	228	4.78
1972	Houston	33	192	9	13	.409	174	83	177	4.17
1973	Houston	41	279	16	13	.552	177	117	271	3.74
1974	Pittsburgh	35	260	16	11	.593	105	101	259	3.50
1975	Pittsburgh	32	237	18	11	.621	131	78	224	2.54
1976	Pittsburgh	31	209	14	9	.609	108	51	209	3.53
1977	Pittsburgh	33	208	10	13	.435	116	71	225	4.11
1978	Pittsburgh	23	83	3	2	.600	42	23	97	4.88
1979	Los Angeles	39	160	7	14	.333	83	60	178	3.54
1980	Los Angeles	37	229	18	6	.750	111	40	193	2.52
1981	Los Angeles	22	153	10	4	.714	51	27	138	2.29
1982	Los Angeles	39	254⅔	18	11	.621	138	50	232	3.11
1983	Los Angeles	32	223⅓	12	11	.522	143	50	233	2.94
1984	Los Angeles	30	99	5	7	.417	44	31	102	3.82
1985	Los Angeles	34	212⅔	14	10	.583	84	58	210	2.92
	Totals	518	3144⅔	192	157	.550	1715	1001	3110	3.44

TOP PROSPECT

FRANKLIN STUBBS 25 6-2 215 **Bats L Throws L**

Hopes to follow in footsteps of Albuquerque sluggers who have moved up to the parent club in recent years, but there's no room for this first baseman unless incumbent Greg Brock is traded . . . Got a good look in 1984, but didn't help himself with .194 average, eight homers and 17 RBI in 217 at-bats . . . Born Oct. 21, 1960, in Laurinburg, N.C. . . . Attended Virginia Tech and was selected by Dodgers in first round of June 1982 draft . . . Totaled 22 homers and 82 RBI in only 105 games for Albuquerque (AAA) in 1983 and 1984 . . . Used sparingly by Dodgers last year, when he hit .222 in nine at-bats for LA, but seems ready to play somewhere after hitting .280 with 32 homers and 93 RBI for Albuquerque.

MANAGER TOM LASORDA: Will be remembered for pitching to Jack Clark with first base open in disastrous ninth inning of Cards' pennant clincher, but that shouldn't detract from the outstanding job of managing he did in 1985 . . . Dodgers showed little promise in spring, but the human cannelloni did a masterful juggling act . . . Guiding Dodgers to 95-67 record and NL West crown is probably his finest achievement, because he had less to work with than in past . . . Only Walt Alston and Wilbert Robinson have managed longer for this franchise . . . With Chuck

Tanner changing uniforms, this guy tops current skippers in longevity with one club . . . In his nine years, Dodgers have won five NL West titles, three pennants and one World Series (1981) . . . Born Sept. 22, 1927, in Norristown, Pa. . . . Has a 780-627 record with Dodgers and has been a part of their organization 36 years . . . Known for his voracious appetite . . . Loves his wife, food, baseball and Frank Sinatra—not necessarily in that order . . . Pitched many years in minors, including long stay with Montreal . . . Posted 18-6 record in that Canadian city during 1948 season . . . Struck out 25 in 15 innings of a minor-league game . . . Posted 0-4 lifetime record as pitcher with Dodgers . . . Began managing in 1965, at Pocatello, Idaho.

GREATEST SHORTSTOP

Harold Henry Reese, best known as "Pee Wee," was a 5-10, 160-pound dynamo who anchored the Brooklyn infield from 1940-57. No Dodger shortstop did it better for a longer period, though Maury Wills' base-stealing exploits for Los Angeles had him in the headlines more often.

Reese, who led National League shortstops with a .977 fielding percentage in 1949, was known less for his glove than for his aggressive play, which typified the Dodgers of his day. He was no slouch with the bat, either, hitting as high as .309 in 1954 and going above .300 in three of the seven World Series in which he participated, topped by a .345 mark in 1952. Pee Wee scored more than 90 runs eight straight years as a vital cog for The Boys of Summer, including 116 in 1949 and a league-leading 104 in 1947. He also topped the league with 30 steals in 1952.

Wills, who was not much bigger than Reese at 5-11, 170 pounds, took over the job in 1959 and gave the Dodgers many of the same leadership qualities that Pee Wee had displayed in Brooklyn. But Wills was best known for being the man who broke Ty Cobb's record for stolen bases in a season with a remarkable 104 in 1962, when Wills played an amazing 165 games at shortstop.

ALL-TIME DODGER SEASON RECORDS

BATTING: Babe Herman, .393, 1930
HRs: Duke Snider, 43, 1956
RBIs: Tommy Davis, 153, 1962
STEALS: Maury Wills, 104, 1962
WINS: Joe McGinnity, 29, 1900
STRIKEOUTS: Sandy Koufax, 382, 1965

SAN DIEGO PADRES

TEAM DIRECTORY: Owner: Joan Kroc; Pres.: Ballard Smith; VP-Baseball Oper.: Jack McKeon; Senior VP: Elten Schiller; Adm. Minor Leagues/Scouting: Tom Romenesko; Dir. Pub. Rel.: Bill Beck; Trav. Sec.: John Mattei; Mgr.: Dick Williams. Home: San Diego Jack Murphy Stadium (58,580). Field Distances: 327, l.f. line; 405, c.f.; 327, r.f. line. Spring training: Yuma, Ariz.

SCOUTING REPORT

HITTING: Any team with Tony Gwynn (.317) and Steve Garvey (17 homers, 81 RBI) in the lineup can't be bad offensively, yet the Padres' run production dipped to a mediocre 650 last season because of trouble at the top of the order. The Padres kept pointing out that Tim Flannery and Jerry Royster had solid stats as the platoon second basemen, but they didn't bring to the club what Alan Wiggins did in 1984.

It's an oversimplification to blame the Padres' woes on Wiggins' problems and eventual exile because there were other factors. However, his absence was glaring on a club which suddenly lacked the element of speed. In just a few years, the Padres have gone from the runningest team in the NL to one that stole a league-low 60 bases in 1985.

Wiggins' absence made it more difficult for No. 2 hitter Gwynn to be as effective as he was while winning the batting title in 1984. Kevin McReynolds (.234, 15 homers, 75 RBI) and Terry Kennedy (.261, 10 homers, 74 RBI) also tailed off. On the plus side, Garry Templeton (.282) had his best season in San Diego, Carmelo Martinez (21 homers, 72 RBI) posted some solid numbers and aging Graig Nettles (15 homers, 61 RBI) is still productive.

PITCHING: The Padres lost more one-run games (30) than any winning team in the NL, indicating a bullpen problem. Rich Gossage (1.82, 26 saves) did his job when he was healthy, but the flaw was in long relief. If the Padres had been more efficient in this area, Goose would have had many more saves. It's up to pitchers like Craig Lefferts and Lance McCullers to do their part.

The rotation certainly is respectable. LaMarr Hoyt (16-8, 3.47) was everything the Padres expected in his NL debut. He combined with a formidable threesome of Eric Show (12-11, 3.09), Dave Dravecky (13-11, 2.93) and Andy Hawkins (18-8, 3.15) to make the fans forget Ed Whitson and Tim Lollar. This pitching staff has all the components of a winner if the Padres can get their offense and defense clicking again.

Tony Gwynn, 1984 NL batting champ, "slumped" to .317.

FIELDING: San Diego is merely average defensively. The Padres' fielding strength is in outfielders Gwynn and McReynolds. The infield defense is shaky because Nettles and Garvey aren't what they used to be at the corners. Templeton had a good season at shortstop and the Flannery-Royster combination at second was so-so. Martinez is a liability in left and Kennedy is no better than average behind the plate.

OUTLOOK: The future isn't as bright as it should be because of the intangibles. The Padres were an unhappy team last year en route to an 83-79 finish. And, when the club fell out of contention, lots of grumbling was directed toward Dick Williams, who survived a front-office coup to return as manager. We haven't heard the end of that story yet, and a disappointing start by San Diego in 1986 could mean an early exit for the demanding skipper.

The Padres may have peaked in 1984, when everything broke right for a team nobody expected to post a runaway victory. The Padres can't surprise people nowadays, and they're just not as effective without Wiggins. This is a club as likely to crumble as to recapture its winning ways.

SAN DIEGO PADRES 1986 ROSTER

MANAGER Dick Williams
Coaches—Galen Cisco, Harry Dunlop, Deacon Jones, Jack Krol

PITCHERS

No.	Name	1985 Club	W-L	IP	SO	ERA	B-T	Ht.	Wt.	Born
51	Booker, Greg	Las Vegas	1-1	45	16	5.40	R-R	6-6	233	6/22/60 Lynchburg, VA
		San Diego	0-1	22	7	6.85				
35	DeLeon, Luis	Las Vegas	2-1	23	19	5.40	R-R	6-1	159	8/19/58 Puerto Rico
		San Diego	0-3	39	31	4.19				
43	Dravecky, Dave	San Diego	13-11	215	105	2.93	R-L	6-1	193	2/14/56 Youngstown, OH
54	Gossage, Rich	San Diego	5-3	79	52	1.82	R-R	6-3	220	7/5/51 Colorado Springs, CO
40	Hawkins, Andy	San Diego	18-8	229	69	3.15	R-R	6-3	205	1/21/60 Waco, TX
58	Hayward, Ray	Las Vegas	11-10	191	150	4.00	L-L	6-1	190	4/27/61 Enid, OK
31	Hoyt, LaMarr	San Diego	16-8	210	83	3.47	R-R	6-2	244	1/1/55 Columbia, SC
39	Jackson, Roy Lee	Rochester	1-1	27	25	3.00	R-R	6-2	205	5/1/54 Opelika, AL
		Las Vegas	1-0	6	3	1.59				
		San Diego	2-3	40	28	2.70				
45	Jones, Jimmy	Beaumont	7-5	85	57	4.66	R-R	6-2	175	4/20/64 Dallas, TX
37	Lefferts, Craig	San Diego	7-6	83	48	3.35	L-L	6-1	196	9/29/57 West Germany
41	McCullers, Lance	Las Vegas	11-8	149	148	3.98	R-R	6-1	185	3/8/64 Tampa, FL
		San Diego	0-2	35	27	2.31				
46	Patterson, Bob	Las Vegas	10-11	186	146	3.14	R-L	6-2	185	5/16/59 Jacksonville, FL
		San Diego	0-0	4	1	24.75				
30	Show, Eric	San Diego	12-11	233	141	3.09	R-R	6-1	175	5/19/56 Riverside, CA
53	Sierra, Candy	Beaumont	3-6	104	93	4.74	R-R	6-2	190	3/27/67 Puerto Rico
49	Stoddard, Tim	San Diego	1-6	60	42	4.65	R-R	6-7	250	1/24/53 East Chicago, IN
38	Thurmond, Mark	San Diego	7-11	138	57	3.97	L-L	6-0	193	9/12/56 Houston, TX
50	Vosberg, Ed	Beaumont	9-11	175	124	3.91	L-L	6-1	190	9/28/61 Tucson, AZ
48	Walter, Gene	Las Vegas	7-5	95	107	2.75	L-L	6-4	200	11/22/60 Chicago, IL
		San Diego	0-2	22	18	2.05				
26	Wojna, Ed	Las Vegas	5-8	111	66	4.45	R-R	6-1	185	8/20/60 Bridgeport, CT
		San Diego	2-4	42	18	5.79				

CATCHERS

No.	Name	1985 Club	H	HR	RBI	Pct.	B-T	Ht.	Wt.	Born
15	Bochy, Bruce	San Diego	30	6	13	.268	R-R	6-4	229	4/16/55 France
16	Kennedy, Terry	San Diego	139	10	74	.261	L-R	6-4	224	6/4/56 Euclid, OH
27	Parent, Mark	Las Vegas	87	7	45	.241	R-R	6-5	215	9/16/61 Ashford, OR
10	Santiago, Benito	Beaumont	111	5	51	.298	R-R	6-1	180	9/3/65 Puerto Rico

INFIELDERS

No.	Name	1985 Club	H	HR	RBI	Pct.	B-T	Ht.	Wt.	Born
7	*Bevacqua, Kurt	San Diego	33	3	25	.239	R-R	6-2	194	1/23/47 Miami, FL
11	Flannery, Tim	San Diego	108	1	40	.281	L-R	5-11	175	9/29/57 Tulsa, OK
6	Garvey, Steve	San Diego	184	17	81	.281	R-R	5-10	190	12/22/48 Tampa, FL
9	Nettles, Graig	San Diego	115	51	61	.261	L-R	6-0	189	8/20/44 San Diego, CA
12	Ramirez, Mario	Las Vegas	13	0	6	.277	R-R	5-9	173	9/12/57 Puerto Rico
		San Diego	17	2	5	.283				
—	Roberts, Leon	Nashua	109	1	23	.272	B-R	5-7	160	10/27/63 Berkeley, CA
3	Royster, Jerry	San Diego	70	5	31	.281	R-R	6-0	165	10/18/52 Sacramento, CA
1	Templeton, Garry	San Diego	154	6	55	.282	B-R	5-11	192	3/24/56 Lockey, TX

OUTFIELDERS

No.	Name	1985 Club	H	HR	RBI	Pct.	B-T	Ht.	Wt.	Born
20	Brown, Bobby	San Diego	13	0	6	.155	B-R	6-1	231	5/24/54 Turbeville, VA
4	*Bumbry, Al	San Diego	19	1	10	.200	L-R	5-8	175	4/21/47 Fredericksburg, VA
28	Davis, Jerry	Las Vegas	18	0	9	.286	R-R	6-0	185	12/25/58 Trenton, NJ
		San Diego	17	0	2	.293				
17	*Dilone, Miguel	Mon.-SD	26	0	7	.200	B-R	6-0	160	11/1/54 Dominican Republic
19	Gwynn, Tony	San Diego	197	6	46	.317	L-L	5-11	206	5/9/59 Los Angeles, CA
44	Kruk, John	Las Vegas	148	7	59	.351	L-L	5-10	170	2/9/61 Charleston, WV
14	Martinez, Carmelo	San Diego	130	21	72	.253	R-R	6-2	210	7/28/60 Puerto Rico
18	McReynolds, Kevin	San Diego	132	15	75	.234	R-R	6-1	207	10/16/59 Little Rock, AK
52	Steels, James	Las Vegas	103	5	46	.261	L-L	5-10	180	5/30/61 Jackson, MI
47	Tillman, Rusty	Las Vegas	139	12	75	.337	R-R	6-0	175	8/29/60 Jacksonville, FL

*Free agent unsigned at press time

PADRE PROFILES

STEVE GARVEY 37 5-10 190 **Bats R Throws R**

Last year wasn't a typical season for this guy . . . Age may be taking its toll on one of game's most consistent players . . . Hit .304 in April and .321 in May before slump struck . . . Rallied with .317 August, but his statistics didn't measure up to his numbers in previous years . . . Committed error April 15, snapping streak of 193 games without one, a major-league mark for a first baseman . . . Started 162 games in 1985 . . . Hit .447 in last nine games to bring average up to respectable level . . . Born Dec. 22, 1948, in Tampa . . . Played baseball and football at Michigan State . . . First-round choice of Dodgers in June 1978 draft . . . There was strong reaction by Dodger fans when Mr. Nice Guy was not re-signed by Los Angeles following 1982 season . . . Enjoyed last laugh by helping Padres to first World Series in 1984 . . . Brought club back from 2-0 NLCS deficit and was named playoff MVP, duplicating honor he won as Dodger in 1978 . . . NL MVP in 1974 . . . Known for clutch hitting, he has .356 career mark in NLCS play and .319 average in 28 World Series games . . . National League's "Mr. October."

Year	Club	Pos.	G	AB	R	H	2B	3B	HR	RBI	SB	Avg.
1969	Los Angeles.	3B	3	3	0	1	0	0	0	0	0	.333
1970	Los Angeles.	3B-2B	34	93	8	25	5	0	1	6	1	.269
1971	Los Angeles.	3B	81	225	27	51	12	1	7	26	1	.227
1972	Los Angeles.	3B-1B	96	294	36	79	14	2	9	30	4	.269
1973	Los Angeles.	1B-OF	114	349	37	106	17	3	8	50	0	.304
1974	Los Angeles.	1B	156	642	95	200	32	3	21	111	5	.312
1975	Los Angeles.	1B	160	659	85	210	38	6	18	95	11	.319
1976	Los Angeles.	1B	162	631	85	200	37	4	13	80	19	.317
1977	Los Angeles.	1B	162	646	91	192	25	3	33	115	9	.297
1978	Los Angeles.	1B	162	639	89	202	36	9	21	113	10	.316
1979	Los Angeles.	1B	162	648	92	204	32	1	28	110	3	.315
1980	Los Angeles.	1B	163	658	78	200	27	1	26	106	6	.304
1981	Los Angeles.	1B	110	431	63	122	23	1	10	64	3	.283
1982	Los Angeles.	1B	162	625	66	176	35	1	16	86	5	.282
1983	San Diego	1B	100	388	76	114	22	0	14	59	4	.294
1984	San Diego	1B	161	617	72	175	27	2	8	86	1	.284
1985	San Diego	1B	162	654	80	184	34	6	17	81	0	.281
	Totals		2150	8202	1080	2441	416	43	250	1218	82	.298

GARRY TEMPLETON 30 5-11 192 Bats S Throws R

Shortstop bounced back with best season since his early days in St. Louis . . . Batted .420 in his last 12 games and was voted club's MVP . . . Was at his best during .356 June . . . Had a tough act to follow after being obtained for Ozzie Smith prior to 1982 season . . . Born March 24, 1956, in Lockey, Tex. . . . Cardinals' first-round pick in June 1974 draft . . . Sensational at Double-A level, batting .401 for Arkansas in 42 games in 1975 . . . Became first switch-hitter in history to collect 100 hits from each side in 1979 . . . Also led NL in triples a third straight year, tying a record . . . Slowed by injuries after being regarded as one of top talents in the game, but still a productive, all-around player . . . Doesn't have Ozzie's glove, but is a tougher out.

Year	Club	Pos.	G	AB	R	H	2B	3B	HR	RBI	SB	Avg.
1976	St. Louis	SS	53	213	32	62	8	2	1	17	11	.291
1977	St. Louis	SS	153	621	94	200	19	18	8	79	28	.322
1978	St. Louis	SS	155	647	82	181	31	13	2	47	34	.280
1979	St. Louis	SS	154	672	105	211	32	19	9	62	26	.314
1980	St. Louis	SS	118	504	83	161	19	9	4	43	31	.319
1981	St. Louis	SS	80	333	47	96	16	8	1	33	8	.288
1982	San Diego	SS	141	563	76	139	25	8	6	64	27	.247
1983	San Diego	SS	126	460	39	121	20	2	3	40	16	.263
1984	San Diego	SS	148	493	40	127	19	3	2	35	8	.258
1985	San Diego	SS	148	546	63	154	30	2	6	55	16	.282
	Totals		1276	5052	661	1452	219	84	42	475	205	.287

CARMELO MARTINEZ 25 6-2 210 Bats R Throws R

Left fielder supplanted Kevin McReynolds as Padres' best power-hitting prospect when latter slipped in second half . . . Opened eyes with fast finish . . . Batted .320 in final 23 games and was on base 44 times in last 87 plate appearances . . . Despite late start because of injury, he was team home-run leader . . . Born July 28, 1960, in Dorado, Puerto Rico . . . Signed by Cubs as free agent in 1978 . . . Averaged nearly 23 homers per year in four minor-league seasons before joining Cubs in 1983 . . . Traded to Padres along with Craig Lefferts for Scott Sanderson prior to 1984 season . . . Led club with 13 game-winning RBI in 1985.

Year	Club	Pos.	G	AB	R	H	2B	3B	HR	RBI	SB	Avg.
1983	Chicago (NL)	1B-3B-OF	29	89	8	23	3	0	6	16	0	.258
1984	San Diego	OF-1B	149	488	64	122	28	2	13	66	1	.250
1985	San Diego	OF	150	514	64	130	28	1	21	72	0	.253
	Totals		328	1091	136	275	59	3	40	154	1	.252

TERRY KENNEDY 29 6-4 224 **Bats L Throws R**

His home-run total dipped in 1985, but he had 17 more RBI than in 1984 . . . Caught more than 140 games a fourth straight season . . . Did his best hitting in May with .369 average and 22 RBI . . . Has improved work behind the plate after getting reputation as poor defensive catcher at start of career . . . Reportedly wants out of San Diego because of his disenchantment with manager Dick Williams, but he's not the only one . . . Born June 4, 1956, in Euclid, Ohio . . . Son of former major-leaguer Bob Kennedy . . . Starred at Florida State and was Cardinals' top pick in June 1977 draft . . . Traded to Padres in 10-player deal involving Rollie Fingers prior to 1981 season . . . Superstardom has been predicted for him, but he's not quite there yet.

Year	Club	Pos.	G	AB	R	H	2B	3B	HR	RBI	SB	Avg.
1978	St. Louis	C	10	29	0	5	0	0	0	2	0	.172
1979	St. Louis	C	33	109	11	31	7	0	2	17	0	.284
1980	St. Louis	C-OF	84	248	28	63	12	3	4	34	0	.254
1981	San Diego	C	101	382	32	115	24	1	2	41	0	.301
1982	San Diego	C-1B	153	562	75	166	42	1	21	97	1	.295
1983	San Diego	C-1B	149	549	47	156	27	2	17	98	1	.284
1984	San Diego	C	148	530	54	127	16	1	14	57	1	.240
1985	San Diego	C	143	532	54	139	27	1	10	74	0	.261
	Totals		821	2941	301	802	155	9	70	420	3	.273

TONY GWYNN 25 5-11 206 **Bats L Throws L**

NL batting champ of 1984 didn't come close to matching awesome .351 figure, but right fielder finished fast to rank fourth in NL last year . . . Lifetime average is the best of any NL player . . . Used .336 June to take a .302 mark into All-Star Game . . . Picked up pace down the stretch, batting .330 in August and .337 in September . . . Concluded season with 12-game hitting streak during which he hit .417 . . . Batted .364 in final 29 games . . . Topped NL with 63 multiple-hit games . . . Born May 9, 1959, in Los Angeles . . . Played point guard on San Diego State basketball squad and was good enough to be drafted by NBA's Clippers . . . Opted for baseball when Padres grabbed him in third round of June 1981 draft . . . Never batted below .328 for four minor-league clubs . . . Played second half of 1983 season with Padres and set club mark with 25-game hitting streak.

Year	Club	Pos.	G	AB	R	H	2B	3B	HR	RBI	SB	Avg.
1982	San Diego	OF	54	190	33	55	12	2	1	17	8	.289
1983	San Diego	OF	86	304	34	94	12	2	1	37	7	.309
1984	San Diego	OF	158	606	88	213	21	10	5	71	33	.351
1985	San Diego	OF	154	622	90	197	29	5	6	46	14	.317
	Totals		452	1722	245	559	74	19	13	171	62	.325

RICH GOSSAGE 34 6-3 220 Bats R Throws R

Goose's solid season was obscured because of Padres' collapse . . . Had one more save than in 1984 with 26, despite missing more than one month following August knee surgery . . . Had five saves and 1.98 ERA in April . . . Relievers tend to be erratic, but this guy has had ERAs of 2.90 or lower for nine straight years since being made a full-time bullpen resident in 1977 . . . Born July 5, 1951, in Colorado Springs, Colo. . . . Attended Southern Colorado State . . . Ninth-round choice of White Sox in June 1970 draft . . . Began career as starter . . . Was an amazing 18-2 for Appleton (A) in 1971, leaping to majors next year . . . Gained notoriety in Yankees' bullpen and signed with Padres as a re-entry free agent in 1984 . . . Has career total of 257 saves plus eight more in postseason play.

Year	Club	G	IP	W	L	Pct.	SO	BB	H	ERA
1972	Chicago (AL)	36	80	7	1	.875	57	44	72	4.28
1973	Chicago (AL)	20	50	0	4	.000	33	37	57	7.38
1974	Chicago (AL)	39	89	4	6	.400	64	47	92	4.15
1975	Chicago (AL)	62	142	9	8	.529	130	70	99	1.84
1976	Chicago (AL)	31	224	9	17	.346	135	90	214	3.94
1977	Pittsburgh	72	133	11	9	.550	151	49	78	1.62
1978	New York (AL)	63	134	10	11	.476	122	59	87	2.01
1979	New York (AL)	36	58	5	3	.625	41	19	48	2.64
1980	New York (AL)	64	99	6	2	.750	103	37	74	2.27
1981	New York (AL)	32	47	3	2	.600	48	14	22	0.77
1982	New York (AL)	56	93	4	5	.444	102	28	63	2.23
1983	New York (AL)	57	87⅓	13	5	.722	90	25	82	2.27
1984	San Diego	62	102⅓	10	6	.625	84	36	75	2.90
1985	San Diego	50	79	5	3	.625	52	17	64	1.82
	Totals	680	1417⅔	96	82	.539	1212	572	1127	2.80

LaMARR HOYT 31 6-2 244 Bats R Throws R

Adjusting to NL was no problem for this hefty hurler . . . Tied Andy Hawkins' club record with 11 wins in a row in midseason . . . Has averaged 18 victories over last four years . . . Posted 5-0 record and 2.05 ERA in June . . . Notched 3-1 record and won MVP honors at All-Star Game in July . . . Finished strong, going 3-0 with 2.03 ERA in September . . . Rarely walks batters . . . Denied shot at 20-win season when he missed four starts with shoulder problem . . . Born Jan. 1, 1955, in Columbia, S.C. . . . Yankees' fifth-round choice in June 1973 draft . . . An 18-4 season at Appleton (A) in 1978 was his ticket to majors . . . Earned AL Cy Young Award with White Sox in 1983 and has compiled most victories in majors over the last four seasons . . . Acquired prior to 1985 season in seven-player deal that sent Ozzie Guillen to White Sox.

Year	Club	G	IP	W	L	Pct.	SO	BB	H	ERA
1979	Chicago (AL)	2	3	0	0	.000	0	0	2	0.00
1980	Chicago (AL)	24	112	9	3	.750	55	41	123	4.58
1981	Chicago (AL)	43	91	9	3	.750	60	28	80	3.56
1982	Chicago (AL)	39	239⅔	19	15	.559	124	48	248	3.53
1983	Chicago (AL)	36	260⅔	24	10	.706	148	31	236	3.66
1984	Chicago (AL)	34	235⅔	13	18	.419	126	43	244	4.47
1985	San Diego	31	210⅓	16	8	.667	83	20	210	3.47
	Totals	209	1152⅓	90	57	.612	596	211	1143	3.83

DAVE DRAVECKY 30 6-1 193 **Bats R Throws L**

Enjoyed fine season, topping Padres' starters in ERA . . . Ranked among NL ERA leaders during first half, posting 1.99 mark and 8-4 record by early July . . . Was toughest in May with 4-0 mark and 2.19 ERA . . . Followed with 4-2 mark and 1.40 ERA in June . . . Stumbled down the stretch and was a victim of poor support . . . Born Feb. 14, 1956, in Youngstown, Ohio . . . Attended Youngstown State and was picked by Pirates in 21st round of June 1978 draft . . . Career took off after Padres acquired him from Bucs for Bobby Mitchell prior to 1981 season . . . Posted 15-5 record for Amarillo (AA) that year and reached majors in 1982 . . . Didn't allow a run in 10⅔ postseason innings in 1984.

Year	Club	G	IP	W	L	Pct.	SO	BB	H	ERA
1982	San Diego	31	105	5	3	.625	59	33	86	2.57
1983	San Diego	28	183⅔	14	10	.583	74	44	181	3.58
1984	San Diego	50	156⅔	9	8	.529	71	51	125	2.93
1985	San Diego	34	214⅔	13	11	.542	105	57	200	2.93
1985	San Diego	34	214⅔	13	11	.542	105	57	200	2.93
	Totals	143	660	41	32	.562	309	185	592	3.05

ERIC SHOW 29 6-1 175 **Bats R Throws R**

Much better than his 1985 record suggests . . . Won fewer games than Andy Hawkins and LaMarr Hoyt, yet topped Padres in innings pitched and strikeouts . . . Avoided losing record by going 3-1 in September, when he posted 1.37 ERA . . . Born May 19, 1956, in Riverside, Cal. . . . A physics major at UC-Riverside . . . Plays jazz guitar professionally . . . A bonus considering he was chosen by Padres in 18th round of June 1978 draft . . . Posted 37-20 mark in minors before joining Padres in 1981 . . . Already Padres' No. 2 all-time winner, behind Randy Jones . . . Primarily a reliever until he entered rotation in 1983, he has been a reliable starter ever since . . . Had temper tantrum after surrendering Pete Rose's record-breaking hit last season.

Year	Club	G	IP	W	L	Pct.	SO	BB	H	ERA
1981	San Diego	15	23	1	3	.250	22	9	17	3.13
1982	San Diego	47	150	10	6	.625	88	48	117	2.64
1983	San Diego	35	200⅔	15	12	.556	120	74	201	4.17
1984	San Diego	32	206⅔	15	9	.625	104	88	175	3.40
1985	Los Angeles	35	233	12	11	.522	141	87	212	3.09
	Totals	164	813⅓	53	41	.564	475	306	722	3.35

ANDY HAWKINS 26 6-3 205 **Bats R Throws R**

Opened season with club-record 11 straight victories and then came back to Earth . . . Was 4-0 with 2.70 ERA in April and NL Pitcher of the Month in May with 6-0 mark and 2.72 ERA . . . Entered season with 15 career wins and won club-high 18 in only 33 appearances in 1985 . . . Posted 11-2 mark before All-Star break . . . Went 3-1 with 2.72 ERA in August . . . Born Jan. 21, 1960, in Waco, Tex. . . . First-round selection of Padres in June 1978 draft . . . Had mixed results in minors until he reached Hawaii (AAA) in 1982, when he produced six shutouts and 2.17 ERA in 18 starts . . . Last season was by far his best at any level.

Year	Club	G	IP	W	L	Pct.	SO	BB	H	ERA
1982	San Diego	15	63⅔	2	5	.286	25	27	66	4.10
1983	San Diego	21	119⅔	5	7	.417	59	48	106	2.93
1984	San Diego	36	146	8	9	.471	77	72	143	4.68
1985	San Diego	33	228⅔	18	8	.692	69	65	229	3.15
	Totals	105	558	33	29	.532	230	212	544	3.61

TOP PROSPECT

LANCE McCULLERS 22 6-1 185 **Bats S Throws R**

Raised eyebrows by pitching extremely well for Padres down the stretch . . . During one six-game span, this reliever yielded only one hit in 11 innings . . . Wound up 0-2 with 2.31 ERA and five saves for Padres . . . Born March 8, 1964, in Tampa . . . Phillies' second-round draft pick in June 1982 came to Padres in complex deal involving Sixto Lezcano, Aug. 31, 1983 . . . Demonstrated consistency as minor-league hurler, posting 25-15 combined record for four clubs from 1982-84 . . . Was 11-8 with 3.98 ERA as starter for Las Vegas (AAA) in 1985 . . . Has a knack for not yielding home runs that impresses Padres' management.

LaMarr Hoyt found NL to his liking, posting 16-8 mark.

MANAGER DICK WILLIAMS: Defending NL champs finished with disappointing 83-79 record and his job was in jeopardy at season's end . . . However, quashing rumors he would be moving on, he signed one year contract with Padres, who have never won big without him . . . Has a Billy Martin-like pattern of doing well in new surroundings until his abrasive personality rubs people the wrong way . . . Regarded as a whiz in game tactics, but gets low marks for way he deals with people . . . He's tolerated longer than most because he's a proven winner . . . Has taken Red Sox, A's, Expos and Padres to postseason play, including four trips to World Series . . . Born May 7, 1929, in St. Louis . . . Signed with the Dodgers' organization in 1947 and played

18 years . . . Had lifetime .260 average in 1,023 major-league games . . . Began managing in minors in 1965 . . . Two years later, he guided Miracle Red Sox to 1967 flag . . . Won three straight AL West titles with Oakland from 1971-73 . . . Led Padres to best record ever in 1984 . . . Has overall managerial mark of 1,412-1,259.

GREATEST SHORTSTOP

Although Ozzie Smith won most of his Gold Gloves as a member of the Cardinals, his early play with the Padres was equally impressive. In fact, "The Wizard" set the standard for all San Diego shortstops in his four years with the Padres. Smith had a sensational rookie season in 1978 and earned two of his seven consecutive Gold Gloves with the expansion club.

Ozzie has become a much better hitter with age, but his defensive work was phenomenal from the start. As a rookie, he played in 159 games, led the league with 28 sacrifice hits and stole 40 bases. Two years later, he won his first Gold Glove after topping a record that was in the books 56 years. Smith amassed 621 assists in 1980, shattering Glenn Wright's mark of 601.

In 1981, his final season with San Diego, Smith led National League shortstops with a .976 fielding percentage. Garry Templeton, for whom Ozzie was traded, has played a fine, all-around game for the Padres, but he's no wizard.

ALL-TIME PADRE SEASON RECORDS

BATTING: Tony Gwynn, .351, 1984
HRs: Nate Colbert, 38, 1970
RBIs: Dave Winfield, 118, 1979
STEALS: Alan Wiggins, 70, 1984
WINS: Randy Jones, 22, 1976
STRIKEOUTS: Clay Kirby, 231, 1971

SAN FRANCISCO GIANTS

TEAM DIRECTORY: Owner: Bob Lurie; Pres.-GM: Al Rosen; Exec. VP-Adm.: Corey Busch; VP-Baseball Oper.: Bob Kennedy; VP-Business Oper.: Pat Gallagher; Asst. GM: Ralph Nelson; Dir. Scouting: Bob Fontaine; Dir. Publ.: Duffy Jennings; Dir. Community and Pub. Rel.: Stu Smith; Trav. Sec.: Dirk Smith; Mgr.: Roger Craig. Home: Candlestick Park (58,000). Field distances: 335, l.f. line; 365, l.c.; 400, c.f.; 365, l.c.; 335, r.f. line. Spring training: Scottsdale, Ariz.

SCOUTING REPORT

HITTING: The failure of the Giants to hit the ball last season was one of the most baffling developments in the NL. The Giants plunged from second in hitting during 1984 to dead last in the majors at .233 in 1985. It's disappointing because players like Chili Davis, Jeff Leonard, Bob Brenly and Dan Gladden had already proven they could hit in previous years.

Gladden's dip from .351 in 1984 to .243 was the most damaging because it deprived the Giants of a leadoff hitter who could reach base consistently. If Gladden can perform as expected in that role

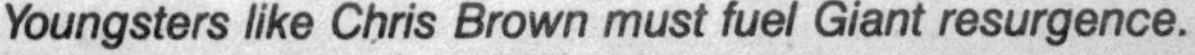

Youngsters like Chris Brown must fuel Giant resurgence.

this season, everything could fall into place. Leonard (.241, 17 homers, 62 RBI), Brenly (.220, 19 homers, 56 RBI) and Davis (.270, 13 homers, 56 RBI) are capable of much more.

The 1985 bright spot was rookie third baseman Chris Brown (.271, 16 homers, 61 RBI), a surprise leader in hitting on a team that didn't have much. When Al Rosen took over as general manager, he promised a housecleaning. Players like Manny Trillo, David Green and Joel Youngblood were scratched from the plans for this season and Dan Driessen was likely to follow suit, so the Giants will have a new-look offense in 1986. It can't be any worse.

PITCHING: For one-half of the season, the Giants' pitching topped the NL in earned-run average, but a second-half collapse and the appointment of Roger Craig as manager assures a revamped rotation. Dave LaPoint was dealt to Detroit and other starters were being shopped at the winter meetings.

Newcomer Roger Mason could be the big surprise on a staff hoping for help from a healthy Atlee Hammaker (5-12, 3.74), Jim Gott (7-10, 3.88) and Mike Krukow (8-11, 3.38). The strength entering this season is a bullpen of 1985 sensation Scott Garrelts (9-6, 2.30, 13 saves), Mark Davis and Greg Minton. Davis might start this year, as might Vida Blue. The 1986 rotation is anybody's guess.

FIELDING: The Giants' fielding, ranked last in 1984, improved to ninth last year and it could get even better with ex-Tiger farmhand Bob Melvin behind the plate and slick Jose Uribe entering his second season at shortstop. Brown was a whiz at third last year and the outfield of Leonard, Gladden and Davis is solid, especially at the corners. It's still anyone's guess as to whom will play second base, which could be a defensive thorn.

OUTLOOK: The picture isn't pretty unless Craig can work the same magic with the Giants' pitching staff that he did with Detroit as the pitching coach of the 1984 Tigers. The Giants are a team without an identity because they did nothing well last season under laughable management. The new regime is more professional in its approach, suggesting improved results.

Last year's Giants were the biggest losers in club history with a 62-100 finish, so there's nowhere to go but up. If the pitching holds up and the hitters prove 1985 was a fluke, the Giants could move up a notch or two. It also would help if the players stop using Candlestick Park as a crutch. As much as they moan about the home park, the Giants play better there (38-43) than on the road (24-57), so where's the beef?

SAN FRANCISCO GIANTS 1986 ROSTER

MANAGER Roger Craig
Coaches—Bill Fahey, Bob Lillis, Norm Sherry, Gordon MacKenzie

PITCHERS

No.	Name	1985 Club	W-L	IP	SO	ERA	B-T	Ht.	Wt.	Born
—	Berenguer, Juan	Detroit	5-6	95	82	5.59	R-R	5-11	215	11/30/54 Panama
14	Blue, Vida	San Francisco	8-8	131	103	4.47	B-L	6-0	200	7/28/49 Mansfield, LA
—	Buchanan, Bob	Denver	4-3	41	36	2.18	L-L	6-1	185	5/3/61 Sharon Hill, PA
		Cincinnati	1-0	16	3	8.44				
13	Davis, Mark	San Francisco	5-12	114	131	3.54	L-L	6-4	195	10/19/60 Livermore, CA
—	Downs, Kelly	Phoenix	9-10	137	109	4.01	R-R	6-4	200	10/25/60 Ogden, UT
50	Garrelts, Scott	San Francisco	9-6	106	106	2.30	R-R	6-4	195	10/30/61 Urbana, IL
51	Gott, Jim	San Francisco	7-10	148	78	3.88	R-R	6-4	210	8/3/59 Hollywood, CA
—	Grant, Mark	Phoenix	8-15	183	133	4.52	R-R	6-2	195	10/24/63 Aurora, IL
7	Hammaker, Atlee	San Francisco	5-12	171	100	3.74	L-L	6-2	195	1/24/58 Carmel, CA
39	Krukow, Mike	San Francisco	8-11	195	150	3.38	R-R	6-4	205	1/21/52 Long Beach, CA
45	Laskey, Bill	SF-Mon.	5-16	148	60	4.91	R-R	6-5	190	12/20/57 Toledo, OH
19	Mason, Roger	Phoenix	12-1	167	120	3.33	R-R	6-6	225	9/18/58 Bellaire, MI
		San Francisco	1-3	30	26	2.12				
—	McKnight, Jack	Shreveport	2-1	38	40	1.66	R-R	6-2	180	6/7/61 Alvin, TX
		Phoenix	8-4	99	55	3.44				
38	Minton, Greg	San Francisco	5-4	97	37	3.54	B-R	6-2	190	7/29/51 Lubbock, TX
—	Moore, Bobby	Phoenix	6-2	90	60	3.50	R-R	6-4	200	11/8/58 Sweetwater, LA
		San Francisco	0-0	17	10	3.24				
49	Robinson, Jeff	Phoenix	9-9	161	80	5.14	R-R	6-4	200	12/13/60 Santa Ana, CA
		San Francisco	0-0	12	8	5.11				
47	Williams, Frank	Phoenix	1-1	14	10	3.95	R-R	6-1	180	2/13/58 Seattle, WA
		San Francisco	2-4	73	54	4.19				

CATCHERS

No.	Name	1985 Club	H	HR	RBI	Pct.	B-T	Ht.	Wt.	Born
15	Brenly, Bob	San Francisco	97	19	56	.220	R-R	6-2	210	2/25/54 Coshocton, OH
18	Melvin, Bob	Nashville	48	9	24	.271	R-R	6-4	205	10/28/61 Palo Alto, CA
		Detroit	18	0	4	.220				

INFIELDERS

No.	Name	1985 Club	H	HR	RBI	Pct.	B-T	Ht.	Wt.	Born
—	Aldrete, Mike	Shreveport	147	15	77	.333	L-L	5-11	180	1/29/61 Carmel, CA
		Phoenix	1	0	1	.125				
35	Brown, Chris	San Francisco	117	16	61	.271	R-R	6-0	185	8/15/61 Jackson, MS
25	Driessen, Dan	Mon.-SF	120	9	47	.243	L-R	5-11	200	7/29/51 Hilton Head, SC
—	Escobar, Angel	Fresno	97	1	34	.251	B-R	6-1	160	5/12/65 Venezuela
—	Hayes, Charlie	Fresno	132	4	68	.283	R-R	6-0	195	5/29/65 Hattiesburg, MS
—	Owen, Dave	Iowa	73	11	40	.227	B-R	6-1	175	4/25/58 Cleburne, TX
		Chicago (NL)	7	0	4	.368				
—	Quinones, Luis	Maine	8	1	2	.178	B-R	6-0	165	4/28/62 Puerto Rico
		Phoenix	78	8	47	.257				
—	Thompson, Rob	Shreveport	117	9	40	.261	R-R	5-11	160	5/10/62 West Palm Beach, FL
23	Uribe, Jose	San Francisco	113	3	26	.237	B-R	5-10	165	1/21/60 Dominican Republic
36	Wellman, Brad	San Francisco	41	0	16	.236	R-R	6-0	170	8/17/59 Lodi, CA
41	Woodard, Mike	Phoenix	181	3	63	.316	L-R	5-9	160	3/2/60 Melrose Park, IL
		San Francisco	20	0	9	.244				

OUTFIELDERS

No.	Name	1985 Club	H	HR	RBI	Pct.	B-T	Ht.	Wt.	Born
30	Davis, Chili	San Francisco	130	13	56	.270	B-R	6-3	195	1/17/60 Jamaica
32	Gladden, Dan	San Francisco	122	7	41	.243	R-R	5-11	180	7/7/57 San Jose, CA
20	Leonard, Jeff	San Francisco	122	17	62	.241	R-R	6-4	200	9/22/55 Philadelphia, PA
—	Maldonado, Candy	Los Angeles	48	5	19	.225	R-R	5-11	197	9/5/60 Puerto Rico
—	Reid, Jessie	Fresno	82	8	55	.323	L-L	6-1	200	6/1/62 Honolulu, HI
		Phoenix	47	7	32	.263				
10	Roenicke, Ron	Phoenix	66	5	48	.308	B-L	6-0	180	8/19/56 Covina, CA
		San Francisco	34	3	13	.256				

GIANT PROFILES

CHILI DAVIS 26 6-3 195 Bats S Throws R

Led Giants in batting, but his 1985 season was nothing to brag about . . . Right fielder was most consistent player on a consistently bad team until shoulder problem shelved him down the stretch . . . Club's most dangerous hitter in April at .266, which tells you what type of a year it was for Giants . . . Batted .309 in May . . . Born Jan. 17, 1960, in Kingston, Jamaica . . . Was a catcher when he signed as Giants' 11th-round selection in June 1978 draft . . . Batted .350 with 40 steals in 88 games at Phoenix (AAA) in 1981 after making major-league squad in spring training . . . Endured disappointing sophomore season in majors in 1983 before making NL All-Star squad one year later . . . A nemesis of Mets' Dwight Gooden.

Year	Club	Pos.	G	AB	R	H	2B	3B	HR	RBI	SB	Avg.
1981	San Francisco.	OF	8	15	1	2	0	0	0	0	0	.133
1982	San Francisco.	OF	154	641	86	167	27	6	19	76	24	.261
1983	San Francisco.	OF	137	486	54	113	21	2	11	59	10	.233
1984	San Francisco.	OF	137	499	87	157	21	6	21	81	12	.315
1985	San Francisco.	OF	136	481	53	130	25	2	13	56	15	.270
	Totals		572	2122	281	569	94	16	64	272	61	.268

CHRIS BROWN 24 6-0 185 Bats R Throws R

Posted decent stats during controversial rookie season, but was unpopular with back-stabbing teammates . . . Criticized for missing too many games with injuries, but was club's most productive hitter by wide margin . . . Also sparkled at third base, easing spring-training concerns about his defense . . . Has been hounded about alleged lack of intensity throughout career . . . Enjoyed best month with .322 July . . . Belted more homers in 1985 than he had previously managed at any level as a pro . . . Born Aug. 15, 1961, in Jackson, Miss. . . . Grew up in Los Angeles and was a prep teammate of Mets' Darryl Strawberry . . . Drafted in second round by Giants in June 1979 . . . Especially tough in clutch situations, he led club with 10 game-winning RBI last season . . . Shows very little emotion.

Year	Club	Pos.	G	AB	R	H	2B	3B	HR	RBI	SB	Avg.
1984	San Francisco.	3B	23	84	6	24	7	0	1	11	2	.286
1985	San Francisco.	3B	131	432	50	117	20	3	16	61	2	.271
	Totals		154	516	56	141	27	3	17	72	4	.273

DAN GLADDEN 28 5-11 180 **Bats R Throws R**

Had disappointing 1985 season after enjoying sensational rookie year . . . Center fielder snapped back to reality after amassing 213 hits and 63 steals for Phoenix (AAA) and San Francisco in 1984 . . . Batted .301 last April, but slumped until September, when hot finish removed him from doghouse . . . Planned to work on switch-hitting in offseason and there were plans to shift him to second base in 1986 . . . Born July 7, 1957, in San Jose, Cal. . . . Attended Fresno State . . . Signed with club as free agent in 1979 . . . Impressed on minor-league level, never batting below .295 . . . His phenomenal 1984, which included a .397 start in 59 games with Phoenix and a .351 mark in 86 games with Giants, stamped him as a potential star.

Year	Club	Pos.	G	AB	R	H	2B	3B	HR	RBI	SB	Avg.
1983	San Francisco	OF	18	63	6	14	2	0	1	9	4	.222
1984	San Francisco	OF	86	342	71	120	17	2	4	31	31	.351
1985	San Francisco	OF	142	502	64	122	15	8	7	41	32	.243
	Totals		246	907	141	256	34	10	12	81	67	.282

JEFF LEONARD 30 6-4 200 **Bats R Throws R**

Another of many Giant disappointments last year . . . Besides suffering from hitting woes, "Hack Man" was involved in Pittsburgh drug trial, an embarrassing experience for Giants' captain . . . Only decent month for this free swinger was June, when he batted .282 with seven homers . . . Hit for the cycle at Cincinnati June 27, becoming first Giant to do it since Dave Kingman in 1972 . . . Left fielder marches to a different drummer and is not quite understood by teammates . . . Born Sept. 22, 1955, in Philadelphia . . . Signed as free agent by Dodgers in 1973 . . . Batted .365 for Albuquerque (AAA) in 1978 and was traded to Houston, where he was named NL Rookie of the Year in 1979 . . . Acquired by Giants for Mike Ivic, April 20, 1981 . . . Batted .401 for Phoenix (AAA) to earn promotion in 1981 . . . Blossomed in 1983 and 1984, but withered a little last year.

Year	Club	Pos.	G	AB	R	H	2B	3B	HR	RBI	SB	Avg.
1977	Los Angeles	OF	11	10	1	3	0	1	0	2	0	.300
1978	Houston	OF	8	26	2	10	2	0	0	4	0	.385
1979	Houston	OF	134	411	47	119	15	5	0	47	23	.290
1980	Houston	OF	88	216	29	46	7	5	3	20	4	.213
1981	Hou.-S.F.	OF-1B	44	145	21	42	12	4	4	29	5	.290
1982	San Francisco	OF-1B	80	278	32	72	16	1	9	49	18	.259
1983	San Francisco	OF	139	516	74	144	17	7	21	87	26	.279
1984	San Francisco	OF	136	514	76	155	27	2	21	86	17	.302
1985	San Francisco	OF	133	507	49	122	20	3	17	62	11	.241
	Totals		773	2623	331	713	116	28	75	386	104	.272

BOB BRENLY 32 6-2 210 **Bats R Throws R**

Like most of his teammates, he fell on his face last year . . . Never shook slump, but did become first catcher to lead Giants in homers since Buck Ewing in 1885 . . . A versatile athlete who also can play third, first and the outfield . . . Took over Giants' postgame radio show when Duane Kuiper retired . . . Born Feb. 25, 1954, in Coshocton, Ohio . . . All-American at Ohio University, where stats were comparable to fellow alumnus Mike Schmidt . . . Earned degree in health education . . . Signed with club as free agent in 1976 . . . Started pro career as a third baseman . . . Blossomed as a major leaguer in 1984, earning NL All-Star distinction, before taking a step backward last year.

Year	Club	Pos.	G	AB	R	H	2B	3B	HR	RBI	SB	Avg.
1981	San Francisco	C-3B-OF	19	45	5	15	2	1	1	4	0	.333
1982	San Francisco	C	65	180	26	51	4	1	4	15	6	.283
1983	San Francisco	C-1B-OF	104	281	36	63	12	2	7	34	10	.224
1984	San Francisco	C-1B-OF	145	506	74	147	28	0	20	80	6	.291
1985	San Francisco	C-1B-3B	133	440	41	97	16	1	19	56	1	.220
	Totals		466	1452	182	373	62	5	51	189	23	.257

DAN DRIESSEN 34 5-11 200 **Bats L Throws R**

Acquired by Giants from Montreal for Bill Laskey during last season because of San Francisco's shortage of left-handed pop, but really didn't provide much . . . A consistent, unspectacular player throughout career . . . Probably will be platooned at first base if Giants elect to keep him . . . Born July 29, 1951, in Hilton Head, S.C. . . . Uncle of Braves' Gerald Perry . . . Signed by Reds as free agent in 1969 . . . Hit .409 for Indianapolis (AAA) in 1973 and finished the season swinging a hot bat for the Big Red Machine . . . Averaged 16 homers and 71 RBI as successor to Tony Perez in Cincinnati . . . First DH used by NL team in World Series, batting .357 in 1976.

Year	Club	Pos.	G	AB	R	H	2B	3B	HR	RBI	SB	Avg.
1973	Cincinnati	3B-1B	102	366	49	110	15	2	4	47	8	.301
1974	Cincinnati	3B-1B-OF	150	470	63	132	23	6	7	56	10	.281
1975	Cincinnati	1B-OF	88	210	38	59	8	1	7	38	10	.281
1976	Cincinnati	1B-OF	98	219	32	54	11	1	7	44	14	.247
1977	Cincinnati	1B	151	536	75	161	31	4	17	91	31	.300
1978	Cincinnati	1B	153	524	68	131	23	3	16	70	28	.250
1979	Cincinnati	1B	150	515	72	129	24	3	18	75	11	.250
1980	Cincinnati	1B	154	524	81	139	36	1	14	74	19	.265
1981	Cincinnati	1B	82	233	35	55	14	0	7	33	2	.236
1982	Cincinnati	1B	149	516	64	139	25	1	17	57	11	.269
1983	Cincinnati	1B	122	386	57	107	17	1	12	57	6	.277
1984	Cin.-Mont.	1B-OF	132	387	47	104	24	0	16	60	2	.269
1985	Mont.-S.F.	1B	145	493	53	120	26	0	9	47	2	.243
	Totals		1676	5379	734	1440	277	23	151	749	154	.268

ATLEE HAMMAKER 28 6-2 195 — Bats L Throws L

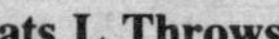

Showed signs of making a successful comeback, missing only a few starts last year . . . But he wasn't the same pitcher he had been prior to shoulder and elbow surgery . . . Plunged from best young lefty in NL in 1983 to a question mark . . . Born Jan. 24, 1958, in Carmel, Cal. . . . An Army brat, he bounced around as a youngster . . . Attended East Tennessee State on a basketball scholarship . . . Pitched three no-hitters in college . . . Royals' first choice in June 1979 draft . . . Traded to Giants in Vida Blue deal prior to 1982 season . . . Promptly won a dozen games as rookie and grabbed NL ERA crown in 1983 . . . Injured down the stretch that year, he hasn't recaptured that old magic.

Year	Club	G	IP	W	L	Pct.	SO	BB	H	ERA
1981	Kansas City	10	39	1	3	.250	11	12	44	5.54
1982	San Francisco	29	175	12	8	.600	102	28	189	4.11
1983	San Francisco	23	172⅓	10	9	.526	127	32	147	2.25
1984	San Francisco	6	33	2	0	1.000	24	9	32	2.18
1985	San Francisco	29	170⅔	5	12	.294	100	47	151	3.74
	Totals	97	590	30	32	.484	364	128	573	3.45

MIKE KRUKOW 34 6-4 205 — Bats R Throws R

Injury bug bit down the stretch, but he was Giants' most dependable starter . . . Also named club's most inspirational player by teammates . . . Got off to great start with 2-0 record and 0.53 ERA in April, when he yielded two runs in 34 innings . . . Born Jan. 21, 1952, in Long Beach, Cal. . . . Attended Cal Poly at San Luis Obispo . . . Had control batters as a youth . . . Once fired a no-hitter in which he walked 17 . . . Cubs' eighth-round selection in June 1973 draft . . . Traded to Phillies for Keith Moreland after 1981 season . . . One year later, he was swapped to Giants in offseason deal that sent Joe Morgan and Al Holland to Philadelphia . . . Great ability belies fact he has been pretty much a .500 pitcher most of his career . . . Owns one of best curves in NL.

Year	Club	G	IP	W	L	Pct.	SO	BB	H	ERA
1976	Chicago (NL)	2	4	0	0	.000	1	2	6	9.00
1977	Chicago (NL)	34	172	8	14	.364	106	61	195	4.40
1978	Chicago (NL)	27	138	9	3	.750	81	53	125	3.91
1979	Chicago (NL)	28	165	9	9	.500	119	81	172	4.20
1980	Chicago (NL)	34	205	10	15	.400	130	80	200	4.39
1981	Chicago (NL)	25	144	9	9	.500	101	55	146	3.69
1082	Philadelphia	33	208	13	11	.542	138	82	211	3.12
1983	San Francisco	31	184⅓	11	11	.500	136	76	189	3.95
1984	San Francisco	35	199⅓	11	12	.478	141	78	234	4.56
1985	San Francisco	28	194⅔	8	11	.419	150	49	170	3.30
	Totals	277	1614⅓	88	95	.481	1103	617	1654	3.96

VIDA BLUE 36 6-0 200 **Bats S Throws L**

Made club as spring longshot last year and was a .500 pitcher for a team that finished 38 games under .500 . . . Used as spot starter until he entered rotation down the stretch . . . Fell one victory shy of 200th, but did register his 2,000th career strikeout in 1985 . . . Was 2-1 with 2.30 ERA in June . . . Went the distance for the first time in three years in his last start . . . Born July 28, 1949, in Mansfield, La. . . . Picked by Kansas City A's in second round of June 1967 draft . . . His sensational major-league debut included a no-hitter against Twins in 1970 . . . Named AL MVP and Cy Young Award winner in first full major-league season as he captivated baseball world in 1971 . . . Acquired by Giants for first time in 1978 . . . Revived career, but his involvement in Kansas City drug scandal forced him to make second comeback after spending 1984 season out of the game.

Year	Club	G	IP	W	L	Pct.	SO	BB	H	ERA
1969	Oakland	12	42	1	1	.500	24	18	49	6.21
1970	Oakland	6	39	2	0	1.000	35	12	20	2.08
1971	Oakland	39	312	24	8	.750	301	88	209	1.82
1972	Oakland	25	151	6	10	.375	111	48	117	2.80
1973	Oakland	37	264	20	9	.690	158	105	214	3.27
1974	Oakland	40	282	17	15	.531	174	98	246	3.26
1975	Oakland	39	278	22	11	.667	189	99	243	3.01
1976	Oakland	37	298	18	13	.581	166	63	268	2.35
1977	Oakland	38	280	14	19	.424	157	86	284	3.83
1978	San Francisco	35	258	18	10	.643	171	70	233	2.79
1979	San Francisco	34	237	14	14	.500	138	111	246	5.01
1980	San Francisco	31	224	14	10	.583	129	61	202	2.97
1981	San Francisco	18	125	8	6	.571	63	54	97	2.45
1982	Kansas City	31	181	13	12	.520	103	80	163	3.78
1983	Kansas City	19	85⅓	0	5	.000	53	35	96	6.01
1984						Did Not Play				
1985	San Francisco	33	131	8	8	.500	103	80	115	4.47
	Totals	474	3187⅓	199	151	.569	2075	1108	2802	3.26

SCOTT GARRELTS 24 6-4 195 **Bats R Throws R**

The most pleasant surprise in a dismal season for Giants . . . Fastballer developed into one of NL's best relievers after failing as starter in 1984 . . . Replaced Greg Minton as right-handed stopper in bullpen . . . Giants' only All-Star Game representative . . . Kept ERA under 2.00 much of the season . . . Went 2-3 with 1.06 ERA and three saves in May . . . Allowed one earned run in 24⅔ innings in June . . . Went 6-0 with seven saves in July and August . . . Born Oct. 30, 1961, in Urbana, Ill. . . . Once struck out 22 batters in a seven-inning prep game . . . Giants' first-round selection in June 1979 draft . . . Minor-league career was plagued by control problems, but everything came together in 1985 when he led Giants with 13 saves.

Year	Club	G	IP	W	L	Pct.	SO	BB	H	ERA
1982	San Francisco	1	2	0	0	.000	4	2	3	13.50
1983	San Francisco	5	35⅔	2	2	.500	16	19	33	2.52
1984	San Francisco	21	43	2	3	.400	32	34	45	5.65
1985	San Francisco	74	105⅔	9	6	.600	106	58	76	2.30
	Totals	101	186⅓	13	11	.542	158	113	157	3.24

TOP PROSPECT

ROGER MASON 27 6-6 225 **Bats R Throws R**

Acquired from Tigers in trade for Alex Sanchez last year, he was sent to Phoenix and became Giants' top Triple-A pitcher . . . Posted 12-1 record and 3.33 ERA in Triple-A and 1-3 mark with 2.12 ERA for Giants in 1985 . . . Was reunited with Roger Craig when former Detroit pitching coach was named Giants' manager . . . Fired impressive shutout against Braves in final major-league start . . . Born Sept. 18, 1958, in Bellaire, Mich. . . . Attended Saginaw Valley State and was signed as free agent by Tigers in 1980 . . . Topped Southern League with 2.06 ERA for Birmingham (AA) in 1983.

MANAGER ROGER CRAIG: Signed a long-term contract to lead Giants out of the wilderness . . . Guided club to 6-12 record after replacing Jim Davenport in mid-September . . . Brings expertise as pitching instructor to new job and hopes to teach members of his staff the split-fingered fastball, his speciality . . . As Tigers' pitching coach in 1984, he received much of the credit for club's climb to world championship . . . Prior to that, he had his first taste of big-league managing with the Padres in 1978-79, compiling a 152-171 mark . . . As a rookie skipper in 1978, he posted 84-78 mark, the best in Padres' history . . . Born Feb. 17, 1931, in Durham, N.C. . . . Came up through Dodgers' system and reached majors with Brooklyn in 1955 . . . Capped rookie year with a victory over Yankees in World Series . . . Had the ignominious distinction of losing 46 games in two

years as right-handed ace of expansion Mets in 1962 and 1963 . . . Pitched dozen years in majors, compiling a 74-98 record and two World Series wins.

GREATEST SHORTSTOP

Hall of Famer Travis Jackson is a runaway choice as the Giants' greatest shortstop because of his longevity and excellence at the position. Jackson played with New York from 1922 until he concluded his career in 1936 and was equally distinguished with his bat and his glove.

Jackson must have been good because he ousted fellow Hall of Famer Davey Bancroft from the starting job in 1924. Prior to Bancroft, the Giants had an excellent shortstop in Art Fletcher and Alvin Dark made his mark with the clubs of the early '50s. There has been no outstanding all-around shortstop in the San Francisco era, though Johnnie LeMaster's fielding was outstanding.

Jackson was at his best from 1924-31, batting more than .300 five times en route to a .291 lifetime average. He hit a career-high .339 in 1930, belted 21 home runs in 1929, knocked in 101 runs in 1933 and hit 35 doubles in 1928. Jackson, an Arkansas native, led National League shortstops in fielding percentage with a .969 mark in 1929 and a .970 mark in 1931.

ALL-TIME GIANT SEASON RECORDS

BATTING: Bill Terry, .401, 1930
HRs: Willie Mays, 52, 1965
RBIs: Mel Ott, 151, 1929
STEALS: George Burns, 62, 1914
WINS: Christy Mathewson, 37, 1908
STRIKEOUTS: Christy Mathewson, 267, 1903

Willie Mays has Giant one-season homer mark (52).

INSIDE THE AMERICAN LEAGUE

By TOM VERDUCCI
Newsday

	East	West
PREDICTED ORDER OF FINISH	New York Yankees	Kansas City Royals
	Detroit Tigers	Seattle Mariners
	Toronto Blue Jays	Chicago White Sox
	Baltimore Orioles	Minnesota Twins
	Milwaukee Brewers	California Angels
	Boston Red Sox	Oakland A's
	Cleveland Indians	Texas Rangers

Playoff winner: **New York**

EAST DIVISION

	Team	Owner	1985	Morning Line Manager
1	**YANKEES** Navy blue pinstripes New mount has firm hand on frisky thoroughbred	George Steinbrenner	W 97 L 64	5-2 Lou Piniella
2	**TIGERS** Navy, orange & white Will regain 1984 form	John Fetzer	W 84 L 77	3-1 Sparky Anderson
3	**BLUE JAYS** Blue & white Tough field to repeat in	R. Howard Webster	W 99 L 62	4-1 Jimy Williams
4	**ORIOLES** Black & orange Will break fast from gate	Edward Bennett Williams	W 83 L 78	8-1 Earl Weaver
5	**BREWERS** Blue, gold & white Will sneak up in stretch run	Bud Selig	W 71 L 90	10-1 George Bamberger
6	**RED SOX** Red, white & blue No staying power	Jean Yawkey	W 81 L 81	15-1 John McNamara
7	**INDIANS** Red, white & blue Would be better off in other field	Pat O'Neill	W 60 L 102	45-1 Pat Corrales

Five-year scramble comes full circle with **YANKEES** regaining winning form. Will be hard-pressed by **TIGERS** and **BLUE JAYS**, who have what it takes if leader breaks stride. **ORIOLES** will make a late move. **BREWERS** will finish out of money, but will surprise. Back of pack belongs to aging **RED SOX** and stumbling **INDIANS**.

PINSTRIPED DERBY

86th Running. American League Race. Distance: 162 games plus playoff. Payoff (based on '85) $76,341 per winning player, World Series; $54,921 per losing player, World Series. A field of 14 entered in two divisions.

Track Record: 111 wins—Cleveland, 1954

WEST DIVISION

	Team	Owner	1985	Morning Line / Manager
1	**ROYALS** Royal blue & white Still the leader of the pack	Ewing Kauffman	W 91 L 71	**7-5** Dick Howser
2	**MARINERS** Blue, gold & white Young and frisky surprise	George Argyros	W 74 L 88	**4-1** Chuck Cottier
3	**WHITE SOX** Navy, white & scarlet Will put on a good chase	E. Einhorn/J. Reinsdorf	W 85 L 77	**5-1** Tony LaRussa
4	**TWINS** Scarlet, white & blue Should be improved over last run	Carl Pohlad	W 77 L 85	**10-1** Ray Miller
5	**ANGELS** Red, white & navy Not the horse it used to be	Gene Autry	W 90 L 72	**15-1** Gene Mauch
6	**A's** Forest green, gold & white Still at bottom of weak field	Roy Eisenhardt	W 77 L 85	**20-1** Jackie Moore
7	**RANGERS** Red, white & blue A good bet to finish last	Eddie Chiles	W 62 L 99	**50-1** Bobby Valentine

There's still no one in field strong enough to challenge **ROYALS**. **MARINERS** are likely to make a surprise run, but won't have enough left for the finish. A bunched field follows, led by the **WHITE SOX**, who'll finish a neck in front of the **TWINS**. Fading **ANGELS** have seen their better days. A's will make early run, but won't challenge thereafter. **RANGERS** bring up the rear.

BALTIMORE ORIOLES

TEAM DIRECTORY: Chairman: Edward Bennett Williams; Exec. VP-GM: Hank Peters; VP: Jack Dunn III; VP: Joseph P. Hamper, Jr.; Asst. GM: Jim Russo; Dir. Scouting-Play. Dev.: Tom Giordano; Dir. Pub. Rel.: Bob Brown; Trav. Sec.: Philip Itzoe; Mgr.: Earl Weaver. Home: Memorial Stadium (53,208). Field distances: 309, l.f. line; 385, l.c.; 405, c.f.; 385, r.c.; 309, r.f. line. Spring training: Miami, Fla.

SCOUTING REPORT

HITTING: No problem here. The Orioles' .430 slugging percentage was the best in the league in 1985 and no team hit more home runs than Baltimore's 214. Of course, most of the punch again came from Eddie Murray (.297, 31 homers, 124 RBI) and Cal Ripken Jr. (.282, 26 homers, 110 RBI). Fred Lynn contributed 23 homers and 68 RBI, but was plagued by injuries as usual. Lee Lacy, the other big 1985 addition, hit .293, but was limited to 121 games because of a broken thumb.

Injuries aside, the Orioles' greatest problem the past few years has been a lack of speed. They have needed a leadoff hitter and a No. 2 man who could advance more than one base at a time in front of Ripken and Murray. They helped themselves somewhat in that respect last season with the acquisition of Alan Wiggins, who stole 30 bases but scored only 43 runs in 76 games. Speedy John Shelby, a defensive specialist, may get more playing time.

The good news is that the Orioles are developing more good young hitters—namely, Mike Young (.273, 28 homers, 81 RBI). His tremendous second-half surge last season indicated he could be ready to put together an entire season of Murray-like production. There's also Larry Sheets (.262, 17 homers, 50 RBI), who was a pleasant surprise as a rookie last year.

PITCHING: The Orioles have traditionally been known for their pitching and defense, but tradition took a beating in 1985, when the Baltimore pitching staff ranked ninth in the AL with a 4.38 ERA. It was only the 10th time in the last 29 years that the Orioles did not finish in the top three. The best ERA among Baltimore pitchers who qualified for the ERA title was Ken Dixon's 3.67.

The biggest disappointments were Mike Boddicker (12-17, 4.07) and Scott McGregor (14-14, 4.81). However, Baltimore basically will go with the same names and hope for better numbers this year. Rich Bordi, acquired in the deal that sent Gary Roenicke to

Eddie Murray is a rare Bird: A slugger who's selective.

the Yankees, should help. Bordi (6-8, 3.21) is valuable in relief and as a starter. After two straight dismal seasons, Tippy Martinez (3-3, 5.40) no longer can be counted on to be the stopper he once was.

FIELDING: If pitching and defense go hand in hand, the Orioles had a pair of bad hands last year. In 1984, the Orioles led the AL with a .981 fielding percentage, marking the 19th time in 25 years that the Orioles ranked first or second. However, in 1985, they slumped to ninth with a .979 percentage.

Murray bequeathed his Gold Glove to the Yankees' Don Mattingly. There was little doubt that Mattingly had a superior defensive season, especially in light of Murray's 19 errors, easily the most among AL first basemen. There were some new problems at second base, where Wiggins replaced Rich Dauer, and some old problems at third base, where former Red Sox shortstop Jackie Gutierrez might wind up.

The strength of the Baltimore defense is up the middle. Catcher Rick Dempsey is a steady force behind the plate and Lynn, when healthy, can still cover a lot of ground in center.

OUTLOOK: Even the return of Earl Weaver as manager during last season failed to shake the Orioles from the doldrums they have been in since winning the world championship in 1983. They managed only 85 wins in 1984 and slipped to 83 in 1985. Another dip is possible if the pitching isn't greatly improved.

Weaver believes he can win with the pitchers he has. But Baltimore still needs a stopper to emerge from the bullpen and Boddicker to return to his 1984 form in order to contend.

BALTIMORE ORIOLES 1986 ROSTER

MANAGER Earl Weaver
Coaches—Terry Crowley, Elrod Hendricks, Cal Ripken Sr., Frank Robinson, Ken Rowe, Jimmy Williams

PITCHERS

No.	Name	1985 Club	W-L	IP	SO	ERA	B-T	Ht.	Wt.	Born
41	Aase, Don	Baltimore	10-6	88	67	3.78	R-R	6-3	222	9/8/54 Orange, CA
47	Bell, Eric	Hagerstown	11-6	158	162	3.13	L-L	6-0	165	10/27/63 Modesto, CA
		Baltimore	0-0	6	4	4.76				
52	Boddicker, Mike	Baltimore	12-17	203	135	4.07	R-R	5-11	172	8/23/57 Cedar Rapids, IA
—	Bordi, Rich	New York (AL)	6-8	98	64	3.21	R-R	6-7	220	4/18/59 S. San Francisco, CA
34	Davis, Storm	Baltimore	10-8	175	93	4.53	R-R	6-4	196	12/26/61 Dallas, TX
39	Dixon, Ken	Baltimore	8-4	162	108	3.67	B-R	5-11	192	10/17/60 Monroe, VA
46	Flanagan, Mike	Hagerstown	0-0	6	5	0.00	L-L	6-0	194	12/16/51 Manchester, NH
		Baltimore	4-5	86	42	5.13				
54	Habyan, John	Charlotte	13-5	190	123	3.27	R-R	6-1	195	1/29/64 Bayshore, NY
		Baltimore	1-0	3	2	0.00				
31	Havens, Brad	Rochester	8-10	134	130	4.85	L-L	6-1	196	11/17/59 Highland Park, MI
		Baltimore	0-1	14	19	8.79				
48	Huffman, Phil	Rochester	10-10	152	78	3.49	R-R	6-2	205	1/20/58 Freeport, TX
		Baltimore	0-0	5	2	15.43				
—	Leiter, Mark	Hagerstown	2-8	83	82	3.46	R-R	6-3	221	4/13/63 Joliet, IL
30	Martinez, Dennis	Baltimore	13-11	180	68	5.15	R-R	6-1	180	5/14/55 Nicaragua
23	Martinez, Tippy	Baltimore	3-3	70	47	5.40	L-L	5-10	179	5/31/50 LaJunta, CO
16	McGregor, Scott	Baltimore	14-14	204	86	4.81	B-L	6-1	190	1/18/54 Inglewood, CA
—	Skinner, Mike	Hagerstown	5-4	74	70	4.50	R-R	6-1	193	8/5/64 Teaneck, NJ
		Charlotte	11-1	111	70	2.51				
36	Snell, Nate	Baltimore	3-2	100	41	2.69	R-R	6-4	185	9/2/55 Orangeburg, SC
		Rochester	0-0	5	3	0.00				
32	Swaggerty, Bill	Rochester	11-13	189	58	3.24	R-R	6-2	200	12/5/56 Sanford, FL
		Baltimore	0-0	2	2	5.40				

CATCHERS

No.	Name	1985 Club	H	HR	RBI	Pct.	B-T	Ht.	Wt.	Born
24	Dempsey, Rick	Baltimore	92	12	52	.254	R-R	6-0	184	9/13/49 Fayetteville, TN
—	Nichols, Carl	Charlotte	78	2	37	.236	R-R	6-0	184	10/14/62 Los Angeles, CA
26	Pardo, Al	Rochester	49	8	35	.253	B-R	6-2	195	9/8/62 Spain
		Baltimore	10	0	1	.133				

INFIELDERS

No.	Name	1985 Club	H	HR	RBI	Pct.	B-T	Ht.	Wt.	Born
25	*Dauer, Rich	Baltimore	42	2	14	.202	R-R	6-0	180	7/27/52 San Bernardino, CA
14	Gross, Wayne	Baltimore	51	11	18	.235	L-R	6-2	221	1/14/52 Riverside, CA
—	Gutierrez, Jackie	Boston	60	2	21	.218	R-R	6-1	185	6/27/60 Colombia
—	Hudler, Rex	Columbus	95	3	18	.250	R-R	6-1	180	9/2/60 Tempe, AZ
		New York (AL)	8	0	1	.157				
—	Jones, Ricky	Rochester	9	0	4	.173	R-R	6-3	186	6/4/59 Tupelo, MS
		Charlotte	108	22	64	.280				
33	Murray, Eddie	Baltimore	173	31	124	.297	B-R	6-2	200	2/24/56 Los Angeles, CA
17	O'Malley, Tom	Nashville	39	1	12	.305	L-R	6-0	190	12/25/60 Orange, NJ
		Rochester	108	10	44	.302				
		Baltimore	1	1	2	.071				
21	Paris, Kelly	Rochester	121	18	67	.275	R-R	6-0	175	10/17/57 Encinada, CA
		Baltimore	0	0	0	.000				
6	Rayford, Floyd	Baltimore	110	18	48	.306	R-R	5-10	220	7/27/57 Memphis, TN
8	Ripken, Cal	Baltimore	181	26	110	.282	R-R	6-4	200	8/24/60 Havre de Grace, MD
12	*Sakata, Lenn	Baltimore	22	3	6	.227	R-R	5-9	160	6/8/53 Honolulu, HI
2	Wiggins, Alan	San Diego	2	0	0	.054	B-R	6-2	160	2/17/58 Los Angeles, CA
		Las Vegas	2	0	1	.250				
		Rochester	4	0	1	.182				
		Baltimore	85	0	21	.285				

OUTFIELDERS

No.	Name	1985 Club	H	HR	RBI	Pct.	B-T	Ht.	Wt.	Born
9	Dwyer, Jim	Baltimore	58	7	36	.249	L-L	5-10	175	1/3/50 Evergreen Park, IL
15	Ford, Dan	Baltimore	14	1	1	.187	R-R	6-1	197	5/19/52 Los Angeles, CA
—	Gerhart, Ken	Charlotte	62	17	50	.279	R-R	6-0	185	5/19/61 Charleston, SC
27	Lacy, Lee	Baltimore	144	9	48	.293	R-R	6-1	185	4/10/48 Longview, TX
19	Lynn, Fred	Baltimore	118	23	68	.263	L-L	6-1	190	2/3/52 Chicago, IL
18	Sheets, Larry	Baltimore	86	17	50	.262	L-R	6-3	217	12/6/59 Staunton, VA
37	Shelby, John	Rochester	59	8	21	.286	B-R	6-1	178	2/23/58 Lexington, KY
		Baltimore	58	7	27	.283				
—	Traber, Jim	Rochester	74	7	37	.265	L-L	6-0	194	12/26/61 Columbus, OH
43	Young, Mike	Baltimore	123	28	81	.273	B-R	6-2	194	3/20/60 Oakland, CA

*Free agent unsigned at press time

ORIOLE PROFILES

EDDIE MURRAY 30 6-2 200 **Bats S Throws R**

Had a typical Eddie Murray season in 1985, which is to say terrific . . . Hit .297, just missing his fourth straight .300 year . . . Had 31 homers and his career-high 124 RBI ranked him second in AL behind Yanks' Don Mattingly . . . Finished third in runs scored (111), fourth in slugging percentage (.523), fifth in on-base percentage (.383) and tied for fifth with teammate Cal Ripken Jr. in game-winning RBI (15) . . . Has driven in at least 100 runs in five of the last six seasons . . . His 78 RBI led AL in strike-shortened 1981 . . . Passed Ken Singleton and moved into third place on all-time home-run list for switch-hitters, trailing only Mickey Mantle (536) and Reggie Smith (314) . . . A natural right-handed hitter who began switch-hitting in 1975 . . . Hit .305 left-handed and .281 right-handed last year . . . Three-time Gold Glove winner at first base slumped defensively in '85, committing a career-high 19 errors . . . His four brothers also played pro baseball . . . Born Feb. 24, 1956, in Los Angeles . . . A high-school teammate of Cards' shortstop Ozzie Smith . . . Orioles' third-round pick in June 1973 draft.

Year	Club	Pos.	G	AB	R	H	2B	3B	HR	RBI	SB	Avg.
1977	Baltimore	OF-1B	160	611	81	173	29	2	27	88	0	.283
1978	Baltimore	1B-3B	161	610	85	174	32	3	27	95	6	.285
1979	Baltimore	1B	159	606	90	179	30	2	25	99	10	.295
1980	Baltimore	1B	158	621	100	186	36	2	32	116	7	.300
1981	Baltimore	1B	99	378	57	111	21	2	22	78	2	.294
1982	Baltimore	1B	151	550	87	174	30	1	32	110	7	.316
1983	Baltimore	1B	156	582	115	178	30	3	33	111	5	.306
1984	Baltimore	1B	162	588	97	180	26	3	29	110	10	.306
1985	Baltimore	1B	156	583	111	173	37	1	31	124	5	.297
	Totals		1362	5129	823	1528	271	19	258	931	52	.298

CAL RIPKEN Jr. 25 6-4 200 **Bats R Throws R**

Dropped 22 points from 1984 level to .284, but belted 26 homers and drove in career-high 110 runs . . . Played every inning of every game again last year . . . Has played in 603 straight games, representing 5,445 consecutive innings, since May 30, 1982 . . . During one four-game stretch in May, he went 12-for-19 with three homers and 10 RBI . . . Finished second in AL in runs scored (116) . . . Has cut down on his strikeout totals and had only 68 in 642 at-bats in 1985 . . . Committed 26 errors at shortstop last year . . . Was third baseman until being moved to shortstop July 1, 1982 . . . Born Aug. 24, 1960, in Havre de Grace, Md. . . . Grew up in a baseball atmosphere . . . Father Cal Sr. was minor-league manager in Baltimore system and is now Orioles' third-base coach . . . Was excellent pitcher for Aberdeen (Md.) High School, compiling 7-2 record and 0.70 ERA as a senior with 100 strikeouts in 60 innings.

Year	Club	Pos.	G	AB	R	H	2B	3B	HR	RBI	SB	Avg.
1981	Baltimore.	SS-3B	23	39	1	5	0	0	0	0	0	.128
1982	Baltimore.	SS-3B	160	598	90	158	32	5	28	93	3	.264
1983	Baltimore.	SS	162	663	121	211	47	2	27	102	0	.318
1984	Baltimore.	SS	162	641	103	195	37	7	27	86	2	.304
1985	Baltimore.	SS	161	642	116	181	32	5	26	110	2	.282
	Totals		668	2583	431	750	148	19	108	391	7	.290

LARRY SHEETS 26 6-3 217 — Bats L Throws R

Led AL rookies with 50 RBI and was second to Rangers' rookie Oddibe McDowell in home runs with 17 . . . Hit .309 the last six weeks of 1985 season with 21 hits in 68 at-bats . . . Played right field in first week of season, then was used exclusively as a designated hitter against right-handed pitching . . . Impressed club officials when he hit .400 on Orioles' exhibition tour of Japan following 1984 season . . . Orioles' second-round pick in June 1978 draft . . . Has had an outstanding pro career, though it has been interrupted by school and injuries . . . Led Appalachian Rookie League in RBI with 48 for Bluefield in 1978, but chose not to return to baseball the next spring in order to attend Eastern Mennonite College . . . Finally reported to Bluefield for the final three games of 1979 season . . . Had bone chips removed from right elbow in October 1980 and did not play at all in 1981 . . . Missed spring training in 1982 before reporting to Hagerstown (A) in June . . . Born Dec. 9, 1959, in Staunton, Va.

Year	Club	Pos.	G	AB	R	H	2B	3B	HR	RBI	SB	Avg.
1984	Baltimore.	OF	8	16	3	7	1	0	1	2	0	.438
1985	Baltimore.	OF	113	328	43	86	8	0	17	50	0	.262
	Totals		121	344	46	93	9	0	18	52	0	.270

ALAN WIGGINS 28 6-2 160 — Bats S Throws R

Padres gave up on this second baseman because of his recurring problems with drugs . . . Orioles dealt for him early last season and he became the leadoff hitter they've needed since departure of Al Bumbry . . . Began slowly with Baltimore, but hit .310 over last 60 games . . . Had 30 stolen bases from July 5 through end of season, more than any player in AL except Yanks' Rickey Henderson . . . Was a much better hitter right-handed

(.314) than left-handed (.269) . . . A singles hitter who has four lifetime homers . . . A converted outfielder who is still learning how to handle himself around second base, he committed 14 errors last season . . . Born Feb. 17, 1958, in Los Angeles . . . Padres drafted him out of Dodgers organization . . . Tied major-league record for stolen bases in a game with five, May 17, 1984 . . . Hit .316 for Padres in 1984 NLCS and .364 in World Series . . . Angels made him the seventh overall pick in January 1977 draft . . . Was placed on suspended list and then released by Angels' Quad Cities club in 1978.

Year	Club	Pos.	G	AB	R	H	2B	3B	HR	RBI	SB	Avg.
1981	San Diego	OF	15	14	4	5	0	0	0	0	2	.357
1982	San Diego	OF-2B	72	254	40	65	3	3	1	15	33	.256
1983	San Diego	OF-1B	144	503	83	139	20	2	0	22	66	.276
1984	San Diego	2B	158	596	106	154	19	7	3	34	70	.258
1985	San Diego	2B	10	37	3	2	1	0	0	0	0	.054
1985	Baltimore	2B	76	298	43	85	11	4	0	21	30	.285
	Totals		475	1702	279	450	54	16	4	92	201	.264

LEE LACY 37 6-1 185 Bats R Throws R

This re-entry free-agent acquisition failed to hit .300 for the first time in four years, though his .293 average was better than his lifetime mark going into 1985 . . . Seemed to be a lock for fourth straight .300 season when he was hitting .332 July 19, but went into downward trend . . . Hit nine home runs through Aug. 25, then did not hit another the rest of the season . . . Had problems swinging bat due to injured thumb . . . Suffered torn ligaments in thumb during spring training and was not activated until May 13 . . . Injury bothered him again in August . . . Regarded as a pure hitter whose outfield defense is weak . . . Born April 10, 1948, in Longview, Tex., he grew up in Oakland . . . Spent two tenures with Dodgers, who picked him in second round of June 1969 draft . . . A two-time free agent who left Dodgers to sign with Pittsburgh prior to 1979 season.

Year	Club	Pos.	G	AB	R	H	2B	3B	HR	RBI	SB	Avg.
1972	Los Angeles	2B	60	243	34	63	7	3	0	12	5	.259
1973	Los Angeles	2B	57	135	14	28	2	0	0	8	2	.207
1974	Los Angeles	2B-3B	48	78	13	22	6	0	0	8	2	.282
1975	Los Angeles	SS-2B-OF	101	306	44	96	11	5	7	40	5	.314
1976	Atl.-L.A.	2B-OF-3B	103	338	42	91	11	3	3	34	3	.269
1977	Los Angeles	OF-2B-3B	75	169	28	45	7	0	6	21	4	.266
1978	Los Angeles	OF-2B-3B	103	245	29	64	16	4	13	40	7	.261
1979	Pittsburgh	OF-2B	84	182	17	45	9	3	5	15	6	.247
1980	Pittsburgh	OF-3B	109	278	45	93	20	4	7	33	18	.335
1981	Pittsburgh	OF-3B	78	213	31	57	11	4	2	10	24	.268
1982	Pittsburgh	OF-3B	121	359	66	112	16	3	5	31	40	.312
1983	Pittsburgh	OF	108	288	40	87	12	3	4	13	31	.302
1984	Pittsburgh	OF-2B	138	474	66	152	26	3	12	70	21	.321
1985	Baltimore	OF	121	492	69	144	22	4	9	48	10	.293
	Totals		1306	3800	538	1099	176	39	73	383	178	.289

FRED LYNN 34 6-1 190 **Bats L Throws L**

Injuries continued to plague this center fielder . . . Career has fallen short of fulfilling promise offered by his spectacular 1975 season, when he became only player in history to be named MVP and Rookie of the Year . . . Played in every game for Baltimore prior to All-Star break last season, but then suffered torn ligaments in ankle in mid-July . . . Also missed some games late in the year with muscle spasms in his back . . . Played great defense, committing only two errors and crashing into wall so many times that the fenceposts had to be changed . . . Signed by Orioles as a re-entry free agent prior to last season after playing out his contract with California . . . Boston's second-round pick in June 1973 draft . . . Red Sox traded him to Angels with Steve Renko for Frank Tanana, Jim Dorsey and Joe Rudi prior to 1981 season . . . Born Feb. 3, 1952, in Chicago, but he grew up in El Monte, Cal.

Year	Club	Pos.	G	AB	R	H	2B	3B	HR	RBI	SB	Avg.
1974	Boston	OF	15	43	5	18	2	2	2	10	0	.419
1975	Boston	OF	145	528	103	175	47	7	21	105	10	.331
1976	Boston	OF	132	507	76	159	32	8	10	65	14	.314
1977	Boston	OF	129	497	81	129	29	5	18	76	2	.260
1978	Boston	OF	150	541	75	161	33	3	22	82	3	.298
1979	Boston	OF	147	531	116	177	42	1	39	122	2	.333
1980	Boston	OF	110	415	67	125	32	3	12	61	12	.301
1981	California	OF	76	256	28	56	8	1	5	31	1	.219
1982	California	OF	138	472	89	141	38	1	21	86	7	.299
1983	California	OF	117	437	56	119	20	3	22	74	2	.272
1984	California	OF	142	517	84	140	28	4	23	79	2	.271
1985	Baltimore	OF	124	448	59	118	12	1	23	68	7	.263
	Totals		1425	5192	839	1518	323	39	218	859	62	.292

MIKE YOUNG 26 6-2 194 **Bats S Throws R**

Enjoyed a tremendous second-half surge in first full season with Orioles, showing the potential that had prompted people to compare him to Eddie Murray, another switch-hitter with power . . . Drove in club-record 32 runs in August . . . In 50 games from July 12 until Sept. 10, he hit 20 homers and drove in 50 runs . . . Flourished as an everyday player under Earl Weaver after playing part-time role under Joe Altobelli . . . Until June 9, he was hitting .216 with four homers and 13 RBI in 40 games . . . Hit .284 with 24 homers and 68 RBI the rest of the way . . . Born March 20, 1960, in Oakland . . . Indians drafted him out of high school, but he did not sign . . . Played one season at St. Mary's

College and a fall season at Chabot Junior College before Orioles made him a first-round pick in secondary phase of January 1980 draft . . . Excellent defensive outfielder.

Year	Club	Pos.	G	AB	R	H	2B	3B	HR	RBI	SB	Avg.
1982	Baltimore.	OF	6	2	2	0	0	0	0	0	0	.000
1983	Baltimore.	DH	24	36	5	6	2	1	0	2	1	.167
1984	Baltimore.	OF	123	401	59	101	17	2	17	52	6	.252
1985	Baltimore.	OF	139	450	72	123	22	1	28	81	1	.273
	Totals		292	889	138	230	41	4	45	135	7	.259

RICK DEMPSEY 36 6-0 184 Bats R Throws R

Enjoyed probably the best offensive season of his 13-year major-league career . . . His 12 home runs and 52 RBI represented career highs . . . Durable catcher played in 132 games, the second-highest total of his career . . . Had four homers, 17 RBI and .305 average in April . . . Committed eight errors after making total of 12 in previous four seasons . . . One of the most colorful players in the game, whose impromptu portrayal of Babe Ruth during a rain delay has become as well-known as his World Series MVP performance in 1983 . . . Has done some television commentating . . . Twins' 12th-round selection in June 1967 draft . . . Traded to Yankees for outfielder Danny Walton prior to 1973 season . . . Came to Orioles in famous deal at June 1976 trading deadline that also sent Rudy May, Tippy Martinez, Dave Pagan and Scott MacGregor to Baltimore for Elrod Hendricks, Grant Jackson, Ken Holtzman and Doyle Alexander . . . Born Sept. 13, 1949, in Fayetteville, Tenn., but he grew up in Southern California.

Year	Club	Pos.	G	AB	R	H	2B	3B	HR	RBI	SB	Avg.
1969	Minnesota	C	5	6	1	3	1	0	0	0	0	.500
1970	Minnesota	C	5	7	1	0	0	0	0	0	0	.000
1971	Minnesota	C	6	13	2	4	1	0	0	0	0	.308
1972	Minnesota	C	25	40	0	8	1	0	0	0	0	.200
1973	New York (AL)	C	6	11	0	2	0	0	0	0	0	.182
1974	New York (AL)	C-OF	43	109	12	26	3	0	2	12	1	.239
1975	New York (AL)	C-OF-3B	71	145	18	38	8	0	1	11	0	.262
1976	N.Y.-Balt. (AL)	C-OF	80	216	12	42	2	0	0	12	1	.194
1977	Baltimore.	C	91	270	27	61	7	4	3	34	2	.226
1978	Baltimore.	C	136	441	41	114	25	0	6	32	7	.259
1979	Baltimore.	C	124	368	48	88	23	0	6	41	0	.239
1980	Baltimore.	C-OF-1B	119	362	51	95	26	3	9	40	3	.262
1981	Baltimore.	C	92	251	24	54	10	1	6	15	0	.215
1982	Baltimore.	C	125	344	35	88	15	1	5	36	0	.256
1983	Baltimore.	C	128	347	33	80	16	2	4	32	1	.231
1984	Baltimore.	C	109	330	37	76	11	0	11	34	1	.230
1985	Baltimore.	C	132	362	54	92	19	0	12	52	0	.254
	Totals		1297	3622	396	871	168	11	65	351	16	.240

SCOTT McGREGOR 32 6-1 190 Bats S Throws L

His season began with a bizarre attack of double vision . . . Doctors discovered that his diet was poor and that he was drinking too much coffee, which made him dizzy . . . After he started the year by going 1-4, Orioles gave him a strength test and discovered that his left arm had suffered a 10-percent loss in strength since 1984 season . . . Pitched well in his final seven starts, winning four of six decisions to boost his record to 14-14 . . . Made one relief appearance, his first since 1981 . . . Has spent entire nine-year major-league career with Orioles . . . First-round pick by Yankees in June 1972 draft came to Baltimore in June 1976 blockbuster . . . Born Jan. 18, 1954, in Inglewood Cal. . . . Prior to last season, he signed a four-year contract extension that carries through 1989 with options for 1990 and 1991.

Year	Club	G	IP	W	L	Pct.	SO	BB	H	ERA
1976	Baltimore	3	15	0	1	.000	6	5	17	3.60
1977	Baltimore	29	114	3	5	.375	55	30	119	4.42
1978	Baltimore	35	233	15	13	.536	94	47	217	3.32
1979	Baltimore	27	175	13	6	.684	81	23	165	3.34
1980	Baltimore	36	252	20	8	.714	119	58	254	3.32
1981	Baltimore	24	160	13	5	.722	82	40	167	3.26
1982	Baltimore	37	226⅓	14	12	.538	84	52	238	4.61
1983	Baltimore	36	260	18	7	.720	86	45	271	3.18
1984	Baltimore	30	196⅓	15	12	.556	67	54	216	3.94
1985	Baltimore	35	204	14	14	.500	86	65	226	4.81
	Totals	292	1835⅔	125	83	.601	760	418	1890	3.76

MIKE BODDICKER 28 5-11 172 Bats R Throws R

Appeared to be headed toward a second straight 20-win season when he got off to 6-1 start in 1985 . . . But he slumped miserably, losing 16 of his last 22 decisions . . . Did not have the good control that has marked his career, walking more batters and yielding more hits than he did in 1984, despite pitching 58 fewer innings . . . Was bothered by tendinitis in his left knee in September . . . Lost his last four starts and did not pitch after Sept. 19 because of the injury . . . Was a disappointment after strong 1983 season, when he was AL Rookie of the Year, and even better 1984, when he posted the lowest ERA in AL . . . Born Aug. 23, 1957, in Cedar Rapids, Iowa . . . Was drafted by Montreal out of high school, but chose to attend Iowa . . . Orioles' sixth-round pick in June 1978 draft progressed from college ball to Rochester (AAA) in 15 weeks . . . Raised and still lives in Norway, Iowa, where he has worked as a grain elevator operator during offseasons.

Year	Club	G	IP	W	L	Pct.	SO	BB	H	ERA
1980	Baltimore	1	7	0	1	.000	4	5	6	6.43
1981	Baltimore	2	6	0	0	.000	2	2	6	4.50
1982	Baltimore	7	25⅔	1	0	1.000	20	12	25	3.51
1983	Baltimore	27	179	16	8	.667	120	52	141	2.77
1984	Baltimore	34	261⅓	20	11	.645	128	81	218	2.79
1985	Baltimore	32	203⅓	12	17	.414	135	89	227	4.07
	Totals	103	682⅓	49	37	.570	409	241	623	3.24

TOP PROSPECTS

JOHN HABYAN 22 6-1 195 **Bats R Throws R**

Orioles have high hopes for this hard-throwing right-hander, who was youngest player on their 40-man roster last season at 21 . . . Had 13-5 record, 3.27 ERA and 123 strikeouts in 190 innings for Charleston (AA) in 1985 . . . Has been a strikeout pitcher since his high school days, when he fanned 226 in 148 innings during his last two years . . . Born Jan. 29, 1964, in Bayshore, N.Y. . . . Orioles' third-round pick in June 1982 draft . . . Made an instant impression, tying for Appalachian Rookie League lead in wins in 1982, when he went 9-2 with 3.54 ERA in 12 starts for Bluefield.

AL PARDO 23 6-2 187 **Bats S Throws R**

This switch-hitting catcher was given his first trial in majors last season . . . Hit .133 on 10-for-75, with no homers and one RBI in 34 games with Baltimore . . . Played 60 games for Rochester (AAA) and hit .253 with eight homers and 35 RBI . . . Led Southern League in game-winning RBI with 17 for Charlotte (AA) in 1984 . . . Orioles tabbed him in second round of June 1980 draft . . . Born Sept. 8, 1962, in Oviedo, Spain . . . His family moved to New York shortly after his birth . . . Played for Tampa's Hillsborough High School, the same school that produced Dwight Gooden and Floyd Youmans.

MANAGER EARL WEAVER: "The Earl of Baltimore" returned June 14, after Joe Altobelli was dismissed in the wake of a 30-26 start . . . Didn't do any better with an Oriole club uncharacteristically beset by pitching problems . . . His record through the remainder of the season was 53-52 . . . Retired after 1982 season to work as a special assignment scout and consultant . . . Also did baseball commentary for ABC-TV . . . His

No. 4 is one of three numbers that have been retired by Orioles. The others are Frank Robinson's No. 20 and Brooks Robinson's No. 5 . . . Served long managerial apprenticeship in Baltimore system, beginning in 1956 at Knoxville . . . Went 65-74 with Fitzgerald the next season—his last season without a winning record . . . Took over Orioles midway through 1968 season, replacing Hank Bauer, and led them to pennant in 1969 . . . That marked start of streak that saw Orioles win five titles in six years . . . Has won three AL East titles, four pennants and one world championship . . . Born Aug. 14, 1930, in St. Louis . . . Major-league managerial record is 1,407-971.

GREATEST SHORTSTOP

A .228 hitter who choked up on the bat and hit only 20 lifetime home runs, Mark Belanger did not represent a fearsome force in the batter's box. But Belanger played 18 major-league seasons—all but one of them with Baltimore—because of the wondrous talents he displayed in the field.

Belanger upheld Baltimore's long tradition of outstanding defensive players by winning eight Gold Gloves. He played in 1,962 games for the Orioles and only Brooks Robinson appeared in more games for Baltimore. Belanger played 1,942 games at shortstop, the 13th-highest figure of any shortstop.

But, more than durable, Belanger was consistent. His .977 lifetime fielding average is an American League record. In addition to keeping his fielding average high, he also exhibited great range, especially toward the third-base hole. Along with Robinson, he provided the Baltimore teams of the late '60s and '70s with one of the greatest left sides of an infield in history. Belanger completed his career with the Dodgers in 1982 and he is now active with the Major-League Baseball Players Association.

ALL-TIME ORIOLE SEASON RECORDS

BATTING: Ken Singleton, .328, 1977
HRs: Frank Robinson, 49, 1966
RBIs: Jim Gentile, 141, 1961
STEALS: Luis Aparicio, 57, 1964
WINS: Steve Stone, 25, 1980
STRIKEOUTS: Dave McNally, 202, 1968

BOSTON RED SOX

TEAM DIRECTORY: Pres.: Jean R. Yawkey; Chief Exec. Off.-Chief Oper. Off.: Haywood Sullivan; Exec. VP-Adm.: Edward (Buddy) LeRoux; VP-Baseball Oper.: Lou Gorman; VP-Dir. Play. Dev.: Edward Kenney; Dir. Scouting: Eddie Kasko; Dir. Pub. Rel.: Dick Bresciani; Trav. Sec.: Jack Rogers; Mgr.: John McNamara. Home: Fenway Park (33,583). Field distances: 315, l.f. line; 379, l.c.; 390, c.f.; 420, r.c. corner; 380, r.c.; 302, r.f. line. Spring training: Winter Haven, Fla.

SCOUTING REPORT

HITTING: No team in baseball has a more threatening lineup from one through nine. The Red Sox easily led the league with a .282 average and a .347 on-base percentage in 1985. There was no one better than Wade Boggs, who won his second league batting title by hitting .368. Boggs rapped 240 hits and reached base 339 times. It's no wonder Jim Rice (.291, 27 homers, 103 RBI) and Bill Buckner (.299, 16 homers, 110 RBI) have so many opportunities to drive in runs.

Still, for all their hitting ability, the Red Sox continued to be

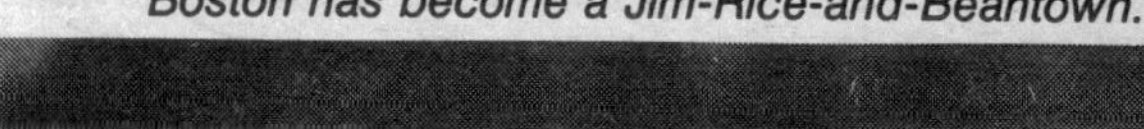

Boston has become a Jim-Rice-and-Beantown.

plagued by the same bad reputations that have stuck with them over the years. Traditionally, the Red Sox lack speed and tend to hit into too many double plays. They were doubled up 164 times last season and no other team hit into more than 147 double plays. The Red Sox also did nothing to dispel their reputation for being trouble at home and troubled on the road. They were 43-37 in cozy Fenway Park and 38-44 everywhere else last year.

PITCHING: The Red Sox' 81-81 record reflected their mediocre staff. The ace, Dennis "Oil Can" Boyd, began the season as if he was about to become one of the better pitchers in the AL. But he slumped in the second half to finish at 15-13 with a 3.70 ERA while proving he can be as temperamental as he is entertaining.

Bruce Hurst (11-13, 4.51) was the only other Boston pitcher in double figures in victories. Al Nipper (9-12, 4.06) was expected to be, but never found his form after a spring-training stomach disorder.

At least the Red Sox are not standing pat. They sent Bob Ojeda to the Mets for promising young pitchers Calvin Schiraldi and Wes Gardner and got Sammy Stewart from the Orioles in the offseason.

FIELDING: The Red Sox are improving at the corners of the infield. Buckner set a major-league record for a first baseman with 184 assists. Of course, that figure was largely due to Buckner's tendency to flip the ball to a pitcher covering first rather than make the putout himself. But his ability to handle low throws cannot be disregarded. And Boggs, once a defensive liability, has worked himself into a better-than-average third baseman.

The strengths of the Boston defense are in right, the home of perennial Gold Glove winner Dwight Evans, and at second base, where steady Marty Barrett plays. Boston, though, still needs help at shortstop. Jackie Gutierrez was one of only three players in the league with more errors than RBI (23 errors, 21 RBI). Gutierrez was dealt, so ex-Brewer Ed Romero will probably get a shot at the job.

OUTLOOK: The Red Sox may be gradually leaving their staid ways behind. They appear to be developing some good, young pitchers rather than pinning their hopes on winning a lot of 10-9 slugfests. And perhaps manager John McNamara will get more out of his players in August and September by resting them more during the summer. Last season, he couldn't resist the temptation to stick with the same awesome lineup day after day. Boston will be better than a .500 club in 1986, but how much better may depend on the young pitchers.

BOSTON RED SOX 1986 ROSTER

MANAGER John McNamara

Coaches—Bill Fischer, Walt Hriniak, Rene Lachemann, Joe Morgan

PITCHERS

No.	Name	1985 Club	W-L	IP	SO	ERA	B-T	Ht.	Wt.	Born
23	Boyd, Dennis	Boston	15-13	272	154	3.70	R-R	6-1	155	10/6/59 Meridian, MS
—	Brown, Mike	Boston	0-0	3	3	21.60	R-R	6-2	195	3/4/59 Haddon Township, NJ
		Pawtucket	2-5	71	51	5.60				
21	Clemens, Roger	Boston	7-5	98	74	3.29	R-R	6-4	215	8/4/62 Dayton, OH
28	Crawford, Steve	Boston	6-5	91	58	3.76	R-R	6-5	236	4/29/58 Pryor, OK
—	Gardner, Wes	Tidewater	7-6	77	75	2.82	R-R	6-4	175	4/29/61 Benton, AR
		New York (NL)	0-2	12	11	5.25				
47	Hurst, Bruce	Boston	11-13	229	189	4.51	L-L	6-3	207	3/24/58 St. George, UT
—	Johnson, Mitch	Pawtucket	5-13	157	63	4.48	R-R	6-5	218	8/2/62 Columbia, PA
29	Kison, Bruce	Boston	5-3	92	56	4.11	R-R	6-4	180	2/18/50 Pasco, WA
48	Lollar, Tim	Chi. (AL)-Bos.	8-10	150	105	4.62	L-L	6-3	204	3/17/56 Poplar Bluff, MO
49	Nipper, Al	Boston	9-12	162	85	4.06	R-R	6-0	194	4/2/59 San Diego, CA
—	Rochford, Mike	New Britain	8-5	93	42	2.99	L-L	6-4	203	3/14/63 Methuen, MA
		Pawtucket	5-2	72	47	4.13				
—	Schiraldi, Calvin	Tidewater	4-5	100	76	3.50	R-R	6-4	200	6/16/62 Houston, TX
		New York (NL)	2-1	26	21	8.89				
27	Sellers, Jeff	New Britain	14-7	185	115	2.78	R-R	6-0	181	5/11/54 Compton, CA
		Boston	2-0	22	6	3.63				
46	Stanley, Bob	Boston	6-6	88	40	2.87	R-R	6-4	220	11/10/54 Portland, ME
53	Stewart, Sammy	Baltimore	5-7	130	77	3.61	R-R	6-3	223	10/28/54 Asheville, NC
45	Trujillo, Mike	Boston	4-4	84	19	4.82	R-R	6-1	180	1/12/60 Denver, CO
42	Woodward, Rob	New Britain	7-5	86	54	3.54	R-R	6-3	202	9/28/62 Hanover, NH
		Pawtuucket	3-8	83	70	4.46				
		Boston	1-0	27	16	1.69				

CATCHERS

No.	Name	1985 Club	H	HR	RBI	Pct.	B-T	Ht.	Wt.	Born
10	Gedman, Rich	Boston	147	18	80	.295	L-R	6-0	215	9/26/59 Worcester, MA
15	Sullivan, Marc	Pawtucket	1	0	0	.250	R-R	6-4	213	7/25/58 Quincy, MA
		Boston	12	2	3	.174				

INFIELDERS

No.	Name	1985 Club	H	HR	RBI	Pct.	B-T	Ht.	Wt.	Born
17	Barrett, Marty	Boston	142	5	56	.266	R-R	5-10	175	6/23/58 Arcadia, CA
26	Boggs, Wade	Boston	240	8	78	.368	L-R	6-2	190	6/15/58 Omaha, NE
6	Buckner, Bill	Boston	201	16	110	.299	L-L	6-1	185	12/14/49 Vallejo, CA
18	Hoffman, Glenn	Boston	77	6	34	.276	R-R	6-2	188	7/7/58 Orange, CA
—	Horn, Sam	New Britain	129	11	82	.282	L-L	6-5	215	11/2/63 Dallas, TX
22	Jurak, Ed	Pawtucket	68	6	38	.259	R-R	6-2	187	10/24/57 Los Angeles, CA
		Boston	3	0	0	.231				
—	Quinonez, Ray	New Britain	113	9	50	.257	R-R	5-11	185	11/11/63 Puerto Rico
—	Romero, Ed	Milwaukee	61	0	21	.251	R-R	5-11	150	12/9/57 Puerto Rico
11	Stapleton, Dave	Pawtucket	3	0	0	.214	R-R	6-1	180	1/16/54 Fairhope, AL
—	Stenhouse, Mike	Minnesota	40	5	21	.223	L-R	6-1	195	5/29/58 Pueblo, CO

OUTFIELDERS

No.	Name	1985 Club	H	HR	RBI	Pct.	B-T	Ht.	Wt.	Born
20	Armas, Tony	Boston	102	23	64	.265	R-R	6-1	200	7/2/53 Venezuela
—	Benzinger, Todd	Pawtucket	64	11	47	.250	B-R	6-1	180	2/11/63 Dayton, KY
—	Burks, Ellis	New Britain	121	10	61	.254	R-R	6-2	175	9/11/64 Vicksburg, MS
—	Christensen, John	New York (NL)	21	3	13	.186	R-R	6-0	180	9/5/60 Downey, CA
		Tidewater	88	1	13	.212				
7	Easler, Mike	Boston	149	16	74	.262	L-R	6-1	196	11/29/50 Cleveland, OH
24	Evans, Dwight	Boston	162	29	78	.263	R-R	6-3	205	11/3/51 Santa Monica, CA
39	Greenwell, Mike	Pawtucket	107	13	52	.256	L-R	6-0	189	7/18/63 Louisville, KY
		Boston	10	4	8	.323				
12	Lyons, Steve	Boston	98	5	30	.264	L-R	6-3	192	6/3/60 Tacoma, WA
3	*Miller, Rick	Boston	15	0	9	.333	L-L	6-0	180	4/19/48 Grand Rapids, MI
14	Rice, Jim	Boston	159	27	103	.291	R-R	6-2	205	3/8/53 Anderson, SC
50	Romine, Kevin	Pawtucket	98	5	33	.243	R-R	5-11	191	5/23/61 Exeter, NH
		Boston	6	0	1	.214				
—	Williams, Dana	New Britain	139	1	39	.309	R-R	5-10	170	3/20/63 Weirton, WV

*Free agent unsigned at press time

RED SOX PROFILES

WADE BOGGS 27 6-2 190 **Bats L Throws R**

A hitting machine . . . Led majors in average (.368), hits (240), on-base percentage (.450) and multiple-hit games (72) . . . His 187 singles broke the AL record of 184, set by Royals' Willie Wilson in 1980 . . . Tied major-league record set by Chuck Klein in 1930 by hitting safely in 135 games . . . Batted .400 in 111 games after May 27 . . . Had the most hits of any player since Bill Terry had 253 in 1930 . . . Reached base 339 times, the most since Ted Williams reached 358 times in 1949 . . . Hit .397 with men in scoring position . . . Hit .418 at Fenway last season to give him .383 career average there . . . Had 28-game hitting streak . . . Born June 15, 1958, in Omaha, Neb. . . . Selected in seventh round of June 1976 draft . . . Third baseman went into starting lineup June 25, 1982, replacing injured Carney Lansford, and hit .361 the rest of the season, prompting Red Sox to trade Lansford.

Year	Club	Pos.	G	AB	R	H	2B	3B	HR	RBI	SB	Avg.
1982	Boston	1B-3B-OF	104	338	51	118	14	1	5	44	1	.349
1983	Boston	3B	153	582	100	210	44	7	5	74	3	.361
1984	Boston	3B	158	625	109	203	31	4	6	55	3	.325
1985	Boston	3B	161	653	107	240	42	3	8	78	2	.368
	Totals		576	2198	367	771	131	15	24	251	9	.351

JIM RICE 33 6-2 205 **Bats R Throws R**

Drove in 100 or more runs for third straight season, despite suffering a knee injury Aug. 12 . . . Left fielder missed four games, then was in and out of the lineup until he suffered a pulled thigh muscle Sept. 10 . . . Did not play in final 15 games and then underwent arthroscopic surgery . . . Hit .525 in September . . . Had an 11-game hitting streak in 1985 . . . Has hit 308 homers in the past 10 years, second only to 365 by Phillies' Mike Schmidt . . . Had .487 slugging percentage last season, the second-best mark on club . . . Born March 8, 1953, in Anderson, S.C. . . . Boston's first pick in June 1971 draft . . . Hit .309 in his first full major-league season in 1975 . . . Became only player to notch three straight seasons with at least 35 homers and 200 hits, from 1977-79 . . . Three-time AL home-run champion . . . Has tremendous power and most of his homers are line drives . . . Hits a golf ball almost as hard as he hits a baseball.

Year	Club	Pos.	G	AB	R	H	2B	3B	HR	RBI	SB	Avg.
1974	Boston	OF	24	67	6	18	2	1	1	13	0	.269
1975	Boston	OF	144	564	92	174	29	4	22	102	10	.309
1976	Boston	OF	153	581	75	164	25	8	25	85	8	.282
1977	Boston	OF	160	644	104	206	29	15	39	114	5	.320
1978	Boston	OF	163	677	121	213	25	15	46	139	7	.315
1979	Boston	OF	158	619	117	201	39	6	39	130	9	.325
1980	Boston	OF	124	504	81	148	22	6	24	86	8	.294
1981	Boston	OF	108	451	51	128	18	1	17	62	2	.284
1982	Boston	OF	145	573	86	177	24	5	24	97	0	.309
1983	Boston	OF	155	626	90	191	34	1	39	126	0	.305
1984	Boston	OF	159	657	98	184	25	7	28	122	4	.280
1985	Boston	OF	140	546	85	159	20	3	27	103	2	.291
	Totals		1633	6509	1006	1963	292	72	331	1179	55	.302

BILL BUCKNER 36 6-1 185 — Bats L Throws L

Finished his first full season in Boston with a flourish, hitting .533 in his last six games, but still fell a hair short of .300 at .299 for season . . . Hit safely in his final 11 games . . . His 201 hits broke mark for hits by a Red Sox first basemen, set by Jimmie Foxx with 198 in 1938 . . . Combined with Wade Boggs to give club its first pair of 200-hit players . . . Broke his own major-league record for assists by a first baseman with 184 . . . Second in AL in doubles and tied for sixth in total bases . . . Second-round pick by Dodgers in June 1968 draft . . . Played in one World Series with Los Angeles, hitting .250 in 1974, before being dealt to Cubs in 1977 . . . Traded to Red Sox for Dennis Eckersley and Mike Brumley, May 25, 1984 . . . Born Dec. 14, 1949, in Vallejo, Cal. . . . Stole 31 bases for Dodgers in 1974, but lost much of his speed after severely spraining left ankle in 1975.

Year	Club	Pos.	G	AB	R	H	2B	3B	HR	RBI	SB	Avg.
1969	Los Angeles	PH	1	1	0	0	0	0	0	0	0	.000
1970	Los Angeles	OF-1B	28	68	6	13	3	1	0	4	0	.191
1971	Los Angeles	OF-1B	108	358	37	99	15	1	5	41	4	.277
1972	Los Angeles	OF-1B	105	383	47	122	14	3	5	37	10	.319
1973	Los Angeles	1B-OF	140	575	68	158	20	0	8	40	12	.275
1974	Los Angeles	OF-1B	145	580	83	182	30	3	7	58	31	.314
1975	Los Angeles	OF	92	288	30	70	11	2	6	31	8	.243
1976	Los Angeles	1B-OF	154	642	76	193	28	4	7	60	28	.301
1977	Chicago (NL)	1B	122	426	40	121	27	0	11	60	7	.284
1978	Chicago (NL)	1B	117	446	47	144	26	1	5	74	7	.323
1979	Chicago (NL)	1B	149	591	72	168	34	7	14	66	9	.284
1980	Chicago (NL)	1B-OF	145	578	69	187	41	3	10	68	1	.324
1981	Chicago (NL)	1B	106	421	45	131	35	3	10	75	5	.311
1982	Chicago (NL)	1B	161	657	93	201	34	5	15	105	15	.306
1983	Chicago (NL)	1B-OF	153	626	79	175	38	6	16	66	12	.280
1984	Chicago (NL)	1B-OF	21	43	3	9	0	0	0	2	0	.209
1984	Boston	1B	114	439	51	122	21	2	11	67	2	.278
1985	Boston	1B	162	673	89	201	46	3	16	110	18	.299
	Totals		2023	7795	935	2296	423	44	146	970	169	.295

MIKE EASLER 35 6-1 196 **Bats L Throws R**

"The Hit Man" missed a lot in 1985 . . . Average went from .313 in 1984 to .262 last year, homers declined from 27 to 16 and RBI total dropped from 91 to 74 . . . Best month was June, when he hit .316 . . . Worst month was October, when he hit .215 . . . Played 130 games as a designated hitter and 20 games as an outfielder . . . Hit 16 homers at Fenway in 1984, but managed only four at home in 1985 . . . A classic late bloomer . . . Spent 10 years in minors with four organizations before finally spending an entire year in big leagues with Pittsburgh in 1979 . . . Sixth-round pick by Astros in June 1969 draft . . . Born Nov. 29, 1950, in Cleveland . . . Played in 1981 All-Star Game in his hometown . . . Hit for the cycle in 1980 . . . Acquired by Red Sox from Pittsburgh for John Tudor after the 1983 season . . . Wife Brenda is sister of Blue Jays' Cliff Johnson.

Year	Club	Pos.	G	AB	R	H	2B	3B	HR	RBI	SB	Avg.
1973	Houston	OF	6	7	1	0	0	0	0	0	0	.000
1974	Houston	PH	15	15	0	1	0	0	0	0	0	.067
1975	Houston	PH	5	5	0	0	0	0	0	0	0	.000
1976	California	DH	21	54	6	13	1	1	0	4	1	.241
1977	Pittsburgh	OF	10	18	3	8	2	0	1	5	0	.444
1979	Pittsburgh	OF	55	54	8	15	1	1	2	11	0	.278
1980	Pittsburgh	OF	132	393	66	133	27	3	21	74	5	.338
1981	Pittsburgh	OF	95	339	43	97	18	5	7	42	4	.286
1982	Pittsburgh	OF	142	475	52	131	27	2	15	58	1	.276
1983	Pittsburgh	OF	115	381	44	117	17	2	10	54	4	.307
1984	Boston	1B	156	601	87	188	31	5	27	91	1	.313
1985	Boston	OF	155	568	71	149	29	4	16	74	0	.262
	Totals		907	2910	381	852	153	23	99	413	16	.293

TONY ARMAS 32 6-1 200 **Bats R Throws R**

Limited to 103 games in 1985 because of a torn calf muscle in left leg suffered June 1 . . . Didn't play again until last week in July . . . His 14 homers and 30 RBI at the time of the injury ranked him among AL leaders . . . Slugged 200th career homer May 12 . . . Led Red Sox in slugging percentage at .514 . . . Hit at least 20 homers for sixth straight year, but injury prevented him from defending his home-run and RBI titles of 1984 . . . Born July 2, 1953, in Anzoatequi, Venezuela . . . Originally signed as free agent by Pittsburgh in 1971 . . . Traded from Oakland to Boston with Jeff Newman for Carney Lansford, Garry Hancock and Jerome King prior to 1983 season . . . Set major-league records for most chances (12) and most putouts (11) by a right fielder in one game during 1982 . . . Committed only three errors in center in 1985.

Year	Club	Pos.	G	AB	R	H	2B	3B	HR	RBI	SB	Avg.
1976	Pittsburgh	OF	4	6	0	2	0	0	0	1	0	.333
1977	Oakland.	OF-SS	118	363	26	87	8	2	13	53	1	.240
1978	Oakland.	OF	91	239	17	51	6	1	2	13	1	.213
1979	Oakland.	OF	80	278	29	69	9	3	11	34	1	.248
1980	Oakland.	OF	158	628	87	175	18	8	35	109	5	.279
1981	Oakland.	OF	109	440	51	115	24	3	22	76	5	.261
1982	Oakland.	OF	138	536	58	125	19	2	28	89	2	.233
1983	Boston	OF	145	574	77	125	23	2	36	107	0	.218
1984	Boston	OF	157	639	107	171	29	5	43	123	1	.268
1985	Boston	OF	103	385	50	102	17	5	23	64	0	.265
	Totals		1103	4088	502	1022	153	31	213	669	16	.250

RICH GEDMAN 26 6-0 215 — Bats L Throws R

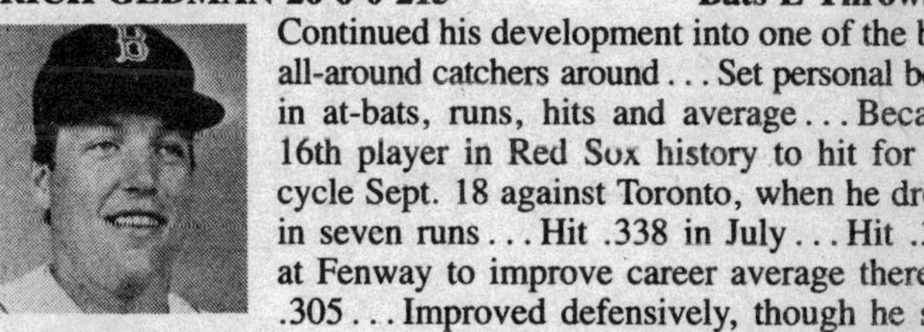

Continued his development into one of the best all-around catchers around . . . Set personal bests in at-bats, runs, hits and average . . . Became 16th player in Red Sox history to hit for the cycle Sept. 18 against Toronto, when he drove in seven runs . . . Hit .338 in July . . . Hit .335 at Fenway to improve career average there to .305 . . . Improved defensively, though he still committed 15 errors . . . Threw out 47-of-103 runners who attempted to steal on him after getting only 80-of-266 in previous four years . . . Signed as a free agent by Boston in 1977 . . . Was a pitcher and first baseman in high school . . . Was switched to catcher in first pro season . . . Born Sept. 26, 1959, in Worcester, Mass. . . . Suffered broken collarbone in 1982 and had surgery on his left wrist in 1980.

Year	Club	Pos.	G	AB	R	H	2B	3B	HR	RBI	SB	Avg.
1980	Boston	C	9	24	2	5	0	0	0	1	0	.208
1981	Boston	C	62	205	22	59	15	0	5	26	0	.288
1982	Boston	C	92	289	30	72	17	2	4	26	0	.249
1983	Boston	C	81	204	21	60	16	1	2	18	0	.294
1984	Boston	C	133	449	54	121	26	4	24	72	0	.269
1985	Boston	C	144	498	66	147	30	5	18	80	2	.295
	Totals		521	1669	195	464	104	12	53	223	2	.278

DWIGHT EVANS 34 6-3 205 — Bats R Throws R

Another Boston player who slipped dramatically in 1985 . . . His average dropped 32 points from 1984 level to .263 . . . Hit three less homers and drove in 26 less runs than in previous campaign . . . Managed to draw a career-high 114 walks, leading majors . . . Finished eighth in AL in on-base percentage at .378 . . . Led club with 13 game-winning RBI . . . Hit at least

22 homers for fifth straight year . . . Nineteen of his homers tied the score or put Red Sox ahead . . . Owns one of the best arms of any outfielder in the game . . . Committed only three errors in right in 1985 . . . Born Nov. 3, 1951, in Santa Monica, Cal. . . . Picked by Red Sox in fifth round of June 1969 draft . . . Missed much of 1977 season because of knee surgery . . . Had a streak of 191 straight errorless games spanning 1973 and 1974.

Year	Club	Pos.	G	AB	R	H	2B	3B	HR	RBI	SB	Avg.
1972	Boston	OF	18	57	2	15	3	1	1	6	0	.263
1973	Boston	OF	119	282	46	63	13	1	10	32	5	.223
1974	Boston	OF	133	463	60	130	19	8	10	70	4	.281
1975	Boston	OF	128	412	61	113	24	6	13	56	3	.274
1976	Boston	OF	146	501	61	121	34	5	17	62	6	.242
1977	Boston	OF	73	230	39	66	9	2	14	36	4	.287
1978	Boston	OF	147	497	75	123	24	2	24	63	8	.247
1979	Boston	OF	152	489	69	134	24	1	21	58	6	.274
1980	Boston	OF	148	463	72	123	37	5	18	60	3	.266
1981	Boston	OF	108	412	84	122	19	4	22	71	3	.296
1982	Boston	OF	162	609	122	178	37	7	32	98	3	.292
1983	Boston	OF	126	470	74	112	19	4	22	58	3	.238
1984	Boston	OF	162	630	121	186	37	8	32	104	3	.295
1985	Boston	OF	159	617	110	162	29	1	29	78	7	.263
	Totals		1781	6132	996	1648	328	55	265	852	58	.269

MARTY BARRETT 27 5-10 175 Bats R Throws R

AL pitchers must have learned how to pitch to this second baseman, who hit .303 as a rookie in 1984 . . . Hit only .266 in an inconsistent sophomore season . . . Strikeouts doubled from 25 in 1984 to 50 last year . . . Improved his numbers in runs, homers and RBI . . . Experienced no tailspin defensively . . . Led AL second baseman in putouts and double plays and was second to Royals' Frank White in assists and chances . . . Finished fourth in fielding percentage at .987, matching his league-leading mark of 1984 . . . Batted .275 at Fenway . . . Became regular Red Sox second baseman May 6, 1984 . . . Boston's first pick in secondary phase of June 1979 draft . . . Played one year at Arizona State after playing two years at Mesa Community College . . . Born June 23, 1958, in Arcadia, Cal. . . . Brother Tom is highly-rated second baseman in Yankees' system.

Year	Club	Pos.	G	AB	R	H	2B	3B	HR	RBI	SB	Avg.
1982	Boston	2B	8	18	0	1	0	0	0	0	0	.056
1983	Boston	2B	33	44	7	10	1	1	0	2	0	.227
1984	Boston	2B	139	475	56	144	23	3	3	45	5	.303
1985	Boston	2B	156	534	59	142	26	0	5	56	7	.266
	Totals		336	1071	122	297	50	4	8	103	12	.277

BOB STANLEY 31 6-4 220 **Bats R Throws R**

Was limited to career-low 87⅔ innings by a finger injury . . . Did not pitch after Aug. 28 and underwent surgery Sept. 12 . . . Had only 10 saves, his lowest total since 1981 . . . Has club-record 107 career saves . . . Ranks ninth in club history with 94 wins . . . Has appeared in most games of any pitcher in Red Sox history with 437 appearances . . . His 68 relief wins represent Red Sox record . . . Was chosen in first round of secondary phase of January 1974 draft . . . Had been drafted by Dodgers in 1973, but didn't sign . . . Was an all-state pitcher and shortstop in high school and pitched a perfect game in New Jersey championship tournament . . . Born Nov. 10, 1954, in Portland, Me . . . Jumped from Winter Haven (AA) to Red Sox in 1977 and pitched in 41 games, the most by a Red Sox rookie since Sparky Lyle's 49 in 1968.

Year	Club	G	IP	W	L	Pct.	SO	BB	H	ERA
1977	Boston	41	151	8	7	.533	44	43	176	3.99
1978	Boston	52	142	15	2	.882	38	34	142	2.60
1979	Boston	40	217	16	12	.571	56	44	250	3.98
1980	Boston	52	175	10	8	.556	71	52	186	3.39
1981	Boston	35	99	10	8	.556	28	38	110	3.82
1982	Boston	48	168⅓	12	7	.632	83	50	161	3.10
1983	Boston	64	145⅓	8	10	.444	65	38	145	2.85
1984	Boston	57	106⅔	9	10	.474	52	23	113	3.54
1985	Boston	48	87⅔	6	6	.500	46	30	76	2.87
	Totals	437	1292	94	70	.573	483	352	1359	3.39

DENNIS BOYD 26 6-1 155 **Bats R Throws R**

This lively and controversial character, blessed with a good fastball, moved into spotlight . . . Pitched 272⅓ innings, second in AL to Bert Blyleven . . . Hurled 13 complete games, tying for fourth in AL in that category . . . Three shutouts also tied him for fourth in league . . . Had outstanding first half before tailing off . . . Was 11-7 with 3.15 ERA at All-Star break and was miffed about spending it at home . . . Won only four times in second half as ERA rose to 3.70 . . . Involved in scuffle with teammate Jim Rice after complaining about a lack of offensive support from teammates . . . Born Oct. 6, 1959, in Meridian, Miss. . . . Nickname of "Oil Can" derived from what the locals called their beer bottles . . . A 16th-round pick in June 1980 draft . . . Father played for the Homestead Grays.

Year	Club	G	IP	W	L	Pct.	SO	BB	H	ERA
1982	Boston	3	8	0	1	.000	2	2	11	5.40
1983	Boston	15	99	4	8	.333	43	23	103	3.28
1984	Boston	29	197⅔	12	12	.500	134	53	207	4.37
1985	Boston	35	272⅓	15	13	.536	154	67	273	3.70
	Totals	82	577	31	34	.477	333	145	594	3.88

TOP PROSPECTS

MIKE GREENWELL 22 6-0 170 Bats L Throws R

Impressed Red Sox after being called up from Pawtucket (AAA) . . . Hit .323 with eight RBI in 17 games with Boston . . . Four of his 10 hits were home runs . . . Hit .256 for Pawtucket with 13 homers and 52 RBI . . . Had never played above Class A before 1985 . . . Sixth-round pick by Red Sox in June 1982 . . . Hit .269 for Elmira that year, then was limited to 48 games with Winston-Salem because of a knee injury in 1983 . . . Played third base for most of 1984 before being switched to left field in late June . . . Born July 18, 1963, in Louisville, Ky. . . . Played quarterback in high school.

ROB WOODWARD 23 6-3 185 Bats R Throws R

Began 1985 season with New Britain (AA) and finished it with Red Sox . . . Pitched in five games for Boston, including two starts, and was 1-0 with 1.69 ERA . . . Walked nine and struck out 16 in 26⅓ innings . . . Had been 7-5 with 3.54 ERA for New Britain before he was promoted to Pawtucket, where he was a deceptive 3-8 with 4.46 ERA . . . A hard thrower who has improved his control over last two seasons . . . Boston's third pick in June 1981 draft . . . Pitched three consecutive three-hitters for Winston-Salem in 1983 . . . Born Sept. 28, 1962, in Hanover, N.H. . . . Played center on his basketball team and defensive end in football during high school.

MANAGER JOHN McNAMARA: In his first year as skipper, he led Red Sox to mediocrity—an 81-81 record . . . That represented five less wins than Ralph Houk's club posted in 1984 . . . Last season marked only the second time since 1966 that the Red Sox did not have a winning record . . . Named Red Sox' 36th manager after Houk retired . . . Was a minor-league catcher who hit .239 in 1,120 career games . . . Was a minor-

league manager for nine years in Kansas City A's organization before being named a coach for the A's in 1968, when they moved to Oakland . . . Made managerial debut with Oakland in 1969, when he replaced Hank Bauer . . . Has also managed San Diego, Cincinnati and California . . . Led Reds to NL West titles in 1979 and 1980 . . . Born June 4, 1932, in Sacramento, Cal. . . . Composite record is 832-896 . . . Has managed current AL managers Tony LaRussa and Pat Corrales.

GREATEST SHORTSTOP

On Oct. 26, 1934, the Boston Red Sox traded a player named Lyn Lary and the very large sum of $225,000 to Washington to obtain a 28-year-old shortstop named Joe Cronin. Cronin, who had been a player-manager for the Senators the previous two seasons, including a pennant winning year in 1933, served as Boston's everyday shortstop for the next seven years, never hitting below .281, and managed the Red Sox through 1947. He played sparingly in his last four seasons with the Red Sox, but hit well enough to raise his average for 20 major-league seasons to .301 before retiring after the 1945 season.

Few players in the history of baseball have enjoyed careers that encompassed so many aspects of the game. As a player, Cronin was one of the best-hitting shortstops of all time. As a manager, he compiled a .540 winning percentage in 15 seasons and he brought the Red Sox to the World Series in 1946. Cronin later became president of the American League and was inducted into the Hall of Fame in 1956.

In 1969, Cronin was chosen by the Boston fans as the team's all-time best shortstop. A similar poll in 1982 revealed new results and shorter memories. Rick Burleson, who won a Gold Glove in 1975, was voted to the first team. Johnny Pesky, whose .335 average is a record for Red Sox shortstops, was voted to the second team.

ALL-TIME RED SOX SEASON RECORDS

BATTING: Ted Williams, .406, 1941
HRs: Jimmy Foxx, 50, 1938
RBIs: Jimmy Foxx, 175, 1938
STEALS: Tommy Harper, 54, 1973
WINS: Joe Wood, 34, 1912
STRIKEOUTS: Joe Wood, 258, 1912

CLEVELAND INDIANS

TEAM DIRECTORY: Chairman: Pat O'Neill; Pres.-Chief Exec. Officer: Peter Bavasi; Sr. VP Baseball Adm./Player Rel.: Dan O'Brien; VP-Baseball Adm.: Joe Klein; Dir. Publ. Rel.: Bob DiBiasio; Trav. Sec.: Mike Seghi; Mgr.: Pat Corrales. Home: Cleveland Municipal Stadium (74,280). Field distances: 320, l.f., line; 377, l.c.; 400, c.f.; 395, r.c.; 320, r.f. line. Spring training: Tucson, Ariz.

SCOUTING REPORT

HITTING: Okay, so the Indians are doomed to finish at the bottom of the pack again in the tough AL East. But this is a good-hitting club. Cleveland finished fourth in the AL in batting last year at .265 and is likely to do even better this season thanks to developing young talents like Brook Jacoby (.274, 20 homers, 87 RBI) and Julio Franco (.288, 6 homers, 90 RBI).

The Indians also have one of the finest leadoff hitters in the game in Brett Butler. There's no reason not to expect another outstanding year from Butler, who hit .311, scored 106 runs and stole 47 bases in 1985. The Indians also have big hopes for Andre Thornton (22 homers, 88 RBI), whose second-half tear showed he is completely recovered from his knee troubles.

What the Indians need most is a boost in run production from talented Joe Carter (.262, 15 homers, 59 RBI) and some sock out of the right-field position.

PITCHING: While the Indians have a great ability to score runs, they have an even greater knack for giving them up. All that offensive production in 1985 was squandered by a pitching staff whose 4.91 ERA was by far the worst in the league. You know there's something wrong with a staff when Neal Heaton's nine wins make him the ace.

Heaton (9-17, 4.90) was a disappointment. The talented left-hander has enough ability to turn those numbers around, though it will take more consistency and better control. Now that Bert Blyleven is gone to Minnesota, the Indians are starting from scratch with a bevy of young, unproven arms. Tom Waddell, who has gone 15-10 over the past two seasons, may be one answer in a rotation full of question marks—if his elbow is sound.

FIELDING: It's no secret that the Indians' fielding is terrible. But part of the reason may be because their field is often terrible, especially in the cold and wet weather of April and May. The

Give Brett Butler a step and he's gone with the wind.

Indians and their opponents often complain about bad hops and slippery footing.

That may be the excuse Franco might offer for his erratic play at shortstop. How else can he explain why he committed 21 errors in the first 55 games, then made only 15 in the last 105 games? Sixty of his 100 career errors have come before the All-Star break. Tony Bernazard, the other half of a shaky double-play combination, has made more errors over the past two seasons (36) than any other AL second baseman. The outfield is more sure-handed, especially with the speedy Butler in center. His .998 fielding percentage was the best in the AL.

OUTLOOK: The Indians can be a fun team to watch. They are never out of a game because of their offense and they are never safely in front because of their pitching. They play an aggressive brand of baseball under manager Pat Corrales and aren't afraid to make mistakes—and they make plenty. They could conceivably lose 100 games for the second straight year and fourth time in club history. However, the Indians can expect some improvement from their pitching staff. It can't get any worse.

CLEVELAND INDIANS 1986 ROSTER

MANAGER Pat Corrales
Coaches—Jack Aker, Bobby Bonds, Doc Edwards, Johnny Goryl, Fred Koenig

PITCHERS

No.	Name	1985 Club	W-L	IP	SO	ERA	B-T	Ht.	Wt.	Born
49	Barkley, Jeff	Cleveland	0-3	41	390	5.27	B-R	6-3	178	11/21/59 Hickory, NC
		Maine	1-4	39	34	1.62				
60	Bailes, Scott	Nashua	3-3	47	40	2.85	L-L	6-2	175	12/18/61 Chillicothe, OH
		Waterbury	6-3	79	53	2.62				
13	Camacho, Ernie	Cleveland	0-1	3	2	8.10	R-R	6-1	180	2/1/56 Salinas, CA
40	Creel, Keith	Maine	7-7	124	58	3.70	R-R	6-2	180	2/4/59 Dallas, TX
		Cleveland	2-5	62	31	4.79				
36	Easterly, Jamie	Cleveland	4-1	99	58	3.92	L-L	5-10	180	2/17/53 Houston, TX
44	Heaton, Neal	Cleveland	9-17	208	82	4.90	L-L	6-1	205	3/3/60 Jamaica, NY
51	Oelkers, Bryan	Orlando	2-3	33	15	6.00	L-L	6-3	205	3/11/61 Spain
		Toledo	0-4	48	30	6.75				
51	Pippin, Craig	Waterbury	3-3	39	47	2.97	R-R	6-2	180	8/4/57 Bristol, TN
		Maine	7-3	60	52	2.70				
35	Reed, Jerry	Maine	8-5	95	47	3.40	R-R	6-1	190	10/8/55 Bryson City, NC
		Cleveland	3-5	72	37	4.11				
53	Ritter, Reggie	Waterbury	7-6	101	31	3.21	L-$	6-2	195	1/23/60 Malvern, AR
		Maine	4-3	53	24	4.25				
34	Roman, Jose	Cleveland	0-4	16	12	6.61	R-R	6-0	175	5/21/63 Dominican Republic
		Maine	4-1	49	27	3.65				
18	Schrom, Ken	Minnesota	9-12	161	74	4.99	R-R	6-2	195	11/23/54 Orangeville, ID
37	Schulze, Don	Maine	6-4	115	45	2.65	R-R	6-3	225	9/27/62 Roselle, IL
		Cleveland	4-10	94	37	6.01				
38	Von Ohlen, Dave	Maine	2-1	24	7	3.80	L-L	6-2	200	10/25/58 Flushing, NY
		Cleveland	3-2	43	12	2.91				
54	Waddell, Tom	Cleveland	8-6	113	53	4.87	R-R	6-1	190	9/17/58 Scotland
31	Wardle, Curt	Minn.-Cle.	8-9	115	84	6.18	L-L	6-5	220	11/16/60 Downey, CA
42	Yett, Rich	Minnesota	0-0	.1	0	27.00	R-R	6-1	170	10/6/62 Pomona, Cal.
		Toledo	9-11	165	99	4.15				

CATCHERS

No.	Name	1985 Club	H	HR	RBI	Pct.	B-T	Ht.	Wt.	Born
67	Allanson, Andy	Waterbury	131	0	47	.312	R-R	6-5	215	11/22/61 Richmond, VA
23	Bando, Chris	Cleveland	24	0	13	.139	B-R	6-0	195	2/4/56 Cleveland, OH
59	Buckley, Kevin	Maine	65	15	45	.221	R-R	6-1	210	1/16/59 Quincy, MA
16	Willard, Jerry	Maine	9	1	4	.225	L-R	6-2	196	3/14/60 Oxnard, CA
		Cleveland	81	7	36	.270				

INFIELDERS

No.	Name	1985 Club	H	HR	RBI	Pct.	B-T	Ht.	Wt.	Born
4	Bernazard, Tony	Cleveland	137	11	59	.274	B-R	5-9	160	8/24/56 Puerto Rico
14	Franco, Julio	Cleveland	183	6	90	.288	R-R	6-0	160	8/23/61 Dominican Republic
21	*Hargrove, Mike	Cleveland	81	1	27	.285	L-L	6-0	195	10/26/49 Perryton, TX
26	Jacoby, Brook	Cleveland	166	20	87	.274	R-R	5-11	175	11/23/59 Philadelphia, PA
17	Noboa, Junior	Maine	116	5	32	.288	R-R	5-9	160	11/10/64 Dom. Republic
15	Rohn, Dan	Maine	116	9	56	.261	L-R	5-7	166	1/10/56 Alpena, WI
10	Tabler, Pat	Cleveland	111	5	59	.275	R-R	6-2	198	2/2/58 Hamilton, OH
29	Thornton, Andre	Cleveland	109	22	88	.236	R-R	6-2	205	8/13/49 Tuskegee, AL
—	Williams, Eddie	Cedar Rapids	106	20	83	.261	R-R	6-0	175	11/1/64 Shreveport, LA
11	Wilson, Jim	Maine	150	26	101	.287	R-R	6-3	225	12/29/60 Corvallis, OR
		Cleveland	5	0	4	.357				

OUTFIELDERS

No.	Name	1985 Club	H	HR	RBI	Pct.	B-T	Ht.	Wt.	Born
12	*Ayala, Benny	Cleveland	19	2	15	.250	R-R	6-1	195	2/7/51 Puerto Rico
63	Brito, Bernardo	Waterloo	128	29	78	.257	R-R	6-1	190	12/4/63 Dominican Republic
2	Butler, Brett	Cleveland	184	5	50	.311	L-L	5-10	160	6/15/57 Los Angeles, CA
30	Carter, Joe	Cleveland	128	15	59	.262	R-R	6-3	215	3/7/60 Oklahoma City, OK
8	Castillo, Carmen	Maine	23	2	18	.240	R-R	6-1	185	6/8/58 Dominican Republic
		Cleveland	45	11	25	.245				
56	Clark, Dave	Waterbury	140	12	64	.302	L-R	6-2	198	9/3/62 Tupelo, MS
27	Hall, Mel	Cleveland	21	0	12	.318	L-L	6-1	185	9/16/60 Lyons, NY
20	Nixon, Otis	Cleveland	38	3	9	.235	B-R	6-2	180	1/9/59 Evergreen, NC
69	Roman, Miguel	Waterloo	144	19	76	.263	R-R	6-2	170	6/18/64 Dominican Republic
61	Washington, Randy	Waterbury	138	14	84	.307	R-R	5-11	190	8/7/63 Stockton, CA
28	Weaver, Jim	Detroit	1	0	0	.143	L-L	6-4	200	10/10/59 Kingston, NY
		Toledo	53	10	34	.237				

*Free agent unsigned at press time

INDIAN PROFILES

JULIO FRANCO 24 6-0 160 Bats R Throws R

Continued to be one of baseball's most productive shortstops—and the most enigmatic ... Led AL in batting from April 11 until May 7 ... Disappeared April 20 during a road trip to New York and later was discovered at a relative's home in the Bronx that he claimed did not have a telephone ... Posted career highs in average (.288), runs (97), doubles (33), RBI (90) and walks (54) ... Had a team-high 16-game hitting streak that began July 30 ... His 90 RBI represented the most by an Indian shortstop since Lou Boudreau had 106 in 1948 ... Had 180 or more hits for second straight year, becoming first Indian to accomplish that since Dale Mitchell in 1948-49 ... Made 21 errors in his first 55 games and 15 in his last 105 games ... Born Aug. 23, 1961, in San Pedro de Macoris, Dominican Republic ... Was signed by Philadelphia as free agent in 1978 ... Phillies sent him, George Vukovich, Jerry Willard, Jay Baller and Manny Trillo to Cleveland for Von Hayes prior to 1983 season.

Year	Club	Pos.	G	AB	R	H	2B	3B	HR	RBI	SB	Avg.
1982	Philadelphia	SS-3B	16	29	3	8	1	0	0	3	0	.276
1983	Cleveland	SS	149	560	68	153	24	8	8	80	32	.273
1984	Cleveland	SS	160	658	82	188	22	5	3	79	19	.286
1985	Cleveland	SS-2B	160	636	97	183	33	4	6	90	13	.288
	Totals		485	1883	250	532	80	17	17	252	64	.283

ANDRE THORNTON 36 6-2 205 Bats R Throws R

Comeback Player of the Year in 1982 had to come back from an injury once again in 1985 ... Returned April 25 after March 26 surgery to repair cartilage in left knee and might have been rushing things a bit ... Didn't start hitting until July 4, then was as hot as a firecracker ... In 76 games from July 4 until the end of the season, he hit .290 with 19 homers and 71 RBI ... Designated hitter raised his average from .149 to .236 during that span ... Averaged 1.523 RBI per at-bat, the fourth-best ratio in AL ... Got his 600th RBI as an Indian June 3 ... Moved into 10th place on Cleveland's all-time RBI list ... Born Aug. 13, 1949, in Tuskegee, Ala. ... Originally signed as free agent by Philadelphia in 1967 ... Traded four times, including deal that sent him from Montreal to Cleveland for Jackie Brown prior to 1977 season . . . Has co-authored the book, "Triumph Born of Tragedy."

Year	Club	Pos.	G	AB	R	H	2B	3B	HR	RBI	SB	Avg.
1973	Chicago (NL)	1B	17	35	3	7	3	0	0	2	0	.200
1974	Chicago (NL)	1B-3B	107	303	41	79	16	4	10	46	2	.261
1975	Chicago (NL)	1B-3B	120	372	70	109	21	4	18	60	3	.293
1976	Chi. (NL)-Mont. . . .	1B-OF	96	268	28	52	11	2	11	38	4	.194
1977	Cleveland.	1B	131	433	77	114	20	5	28	70	3	.263
1978	Cleveland.	1B	145	508	97	133	22	4	33	105	4	.262
1979	Cleveland.	1B	143	515	89	120	31	1	26	93	5	.233
1980	Cleveland.				Disabled List							
1981	Cleveland.	1B	69	226	22	54	12	0	6	30	3	.239
1982	Cleveland.	1B	161	589	90	161	26	1	32	116	6	.273
1983	Cleveland.	1B	141	508	78	143	27	1	17	77	4	.281
1984	Cleveland.	1B	155	587	91	159	26	0	33	99	6	.271
1985	Cleveland.	1B	124	461	49	109	13	0	22	88	3	.236
	Totals		1409	4805	735	1240	228	22	236	824	43	.258

JOE CARTER 26 6-3 215 — Bats R Throws R

Left fielder salvaged a respectable season after a terrible start . . . Over the final four months, he hit .282 with 12 of his 15 homers and 41 of his 59 RBI . . . His seven game-winning hits and 24 stolen bases were career highs . . . Also had a career-high hitting streak of 15 games . . . Hit Indians' first inside-the-park homer in more than two years . . . Hit two homers in a game for fourth time in his career . . . Born March 7, 1960, in Oklahoma City, Okla. . . . Had All-American career at Wichita State . . . Cubs made him second player picked in June 1981 draft . . . Traded to Indians in June 13, 1984 swap that also brought Mel Hall, Don Schulze and Darryl Banks from Cubs for Rick Sutcliffe, George Frazier and Ron Hassey . . . Deal helped give Cubs the 1984 NL East title . . . Like Brett Butler, he grew up idolizing Pete Rose and Hank Aaron.

Year	Club	Pos.	G	AB	R	H	2B	3B	HR	RBI	SB	Avg.
1983	Chicago (NL)	OF	23	51	6	9	1	1	0	1	1	.176
1984	Cleveland.	OF-1B	66	244	32	67	6	1	13	41	2	.275
1985	Cleveland.	OF	143	489	64	128	27	0	15	59	24	.262
	Totals		232	784	102	204	34	2	28	101	27	.260

BRETT BUTLER 28 5-10 160 — Bats L Throws L

Indians' leadoff hitter and center fielder had best season of his career . . . Posted career highs in average (.311), hits (184), doubles (28), triples (14), RBI (50) and game-winning RBI (6) . . . Tied career best with five homers . . . Led AL outfielders with a .998 fielding percentage, committing only one error . . . Was second in AL in triples, third in stolen bases (47), fifth in hitting, eighth in runs scored (106) and eighth in hits . . . Had career-high 11-game hitting streak . . . Became first Indian to score 100 runs in consecutive seasons since Al Smith in 1954-55 . . . Was on base in 87 percent of games in which he batted . . . Hit a team-high .355 with runners in scoring position . . . Had 20 bunt hits . . . Born June 15, 1957, in Los Angeles . . . Selected by Atlanta in 23rd round of June 1979 draft . . . Traded to Indians with Brook Jacoby and Rick Behenna for Len Barker at conclusion of 1983 season . . . One of his career highlights was meeting his idol, Pete Rose.

Year	Club	Pos.	G	AB	R	H	2B	3B	HR	RBI	SB	Avg.
1981	Atlanta	OF	40	126	17	32	2	3	0	4	9	.254
1982	Atlanta	OF	89	240	35	52	2	0	0	7	21	.217
1983	Atlanta	OF	151	549	84	154	21	13	5	37	39	.281
1984	Cleveland.	OF	158	602	108	162	25	9	3	49	52	.269
1985	Cleveland.	OF	152	591	106	184	28	14	5	50	47	.311
	Totals		590	2108	350	584	78	39	13	147	168	.277

BROOK JACOBY 26 5-11 175 **Bats R Throws R**

Established himself as a dependable third baseman, offensively and defensively . . . Set career bests in average (.274), games (161), at-bats (606), runs scored (72), hits (166), doubles (26), homers (20) and RBI (87) . . . Hit his first major-league grand slam May 7 . . . Through 70 games, he had 10 homers and 41 RBI, surpassing his totals for all of 1984 . . . Hit .333 with three homers and 14 RBI in May . . . Also had good June, when he was runnerup for AL Player of the Month with .290 average, six homers and 21 RBI . . . Made 19 errors . . . Born Nov. 23, 1959, in Philadelphia . . . Selected by Atlanta in seventh round of June 1979 draft and was acquired by Cleveland in five-for-one trade that sent Von Hayes to Phillies . . . Father Brook Sr. played in Phillies' and Indians' organizations, too.

Year	Club	Pos.	G	AB	R	H	2B	3B	HR	RBI	SB	Avg.
1981	Atlanta	3B	11	10	0	2	0	0	0	1	0	.200
1983	Atlanta	3B	4	8	0	0	0	0	0	0	0	.000
1984	Cleveland.	3B-SS	126	439	64	116	19	3	7	40	3	.264
1985	Cleveland.	3B	161	606	72	166	26	3	20	87	2	.274
	Totals		302	1063	136	284	45	6	27	128	5	.267

TONY BERNAZARD 29 5-9 160 **Bats S Throws R**

Enjoyed one of his best major-league seasons . . . Set career highs in games (153), doubles (26), RBI (59) and walks (69) . . . Also tied a career high with 11 homers, the most by Indians' second baseman since Larry Brown hit 12 in 1964 . . . Hit so well that the Brewers checked his bat for cork . . . Had nine-game hitting streak, the second-longest of his career, from Aug. 30 to Sept. 7 . . . Was much more productive batting left-handed, hitting .283 with all of his 11 homers and 49 of his 59 RBI from that side . . . Came to Indians in deal that sent Gorman Thomas and Jack Perconte to Mariners prior to 1984 season . . . Born Aug. 24, 1956, in Caguas, Puerto Rico . . . Originally signed as free agent by Montreal in 1973.

Year	Club	Pos.	G	AB	R	H	2B	3B	HR	RBI	SB	Avg.
1979	Montreal	2B	22	40	11	12	2	0	1	8	1	.300
1980	Montreal	2B-SS	82	183	26	41	7	1	5	18	9	.224
1981	Chicago (AL)	2B-SS	106	384	53	106	14	4	6	34	4	.276
1982	Chicago (AL)	2B-SS	137	540	90	138	25	9	11	56	11	.256
1983	Chicago (AL)-Seattle	2B	139	533	65	141	34	3	8	56	23	.265
1984	Cleveland	2B	140	439	44	97	15	4	2	38	20	.221
1985	Cleveland	2B	153	500	73	137	26	3	11	59	17	.274
	Totals		769	2619	362	672	123	24	44	269	85	.257

MIKE HARGROVE 36 6-0 195 Bats L Throws L

Called "The Human Rain Delay" for his lengthy ritual in batter's box prior to each pitch . . . Used mostly as a pinch-hitter and defensive specialist in 1985 before starting at first base the last month . . . Gave indications that he may still be most useful as a regular player . . . Caught fire in last 34 games, batting .348 to raise average from .244 to .288 . . . Did not fare well as a pinch-hitter with three hits and one RBI in 21 at-bats . . . Had an 11-game hitting streak and had four hits in one game . . . Who says the legs are the first to go? He stole his first base in three years Oct. 2 . . . Full name is Dudley Michael Hargrove . . . Born Oct. 26, 1949, in Perryton, Tex. . . . Played at Northwest Oklahoma State before Rangers took him in 25th round of June 1972 draft . . . Traded to San Diego with Kurt Bevacqua and Bill Fahey for Oscar Gamble and Dave Roberts prior to 1979 season . . . Padres shipped him to Cleveland for Paul Dade, June 14, 1979.

Year	Club	Pos.	G	AB	R	H	2B	3B	HR	RBI	SB	Avg.
1974	Texas	1B-OF	131	415	57	134	18	6	4	66	0	.323
1975	Texas	1B-OF	145	519	82	157	22	2	11	62	4	.303
1976	Texas	1B	151	541	80	155	30	1	7	58	2	.287
1977	Texas	1B	153	525	98	160	28	4	18	69	2	.305
1978	Texas	1B	146	494	63	124	24	1	7	40	2	.251
1979	San Diego	1B	52	125	15	24	5	0	0	8	0	.192
1979	Cleveland	OF-1B	100	338	60	110	21	4	10	56	2	.325
1980	Cleveland	1B	160	589	86	179	22	2	11	85	4	.304
1981	Cleveland	1B	94	322	43	102	21	0	2	49	5	.317
1982	Cleveland	1B	160	591	67	160	26	1	4	65	2	.271
1983	Cleveland	1B	134	469	57	134	21	4	3	57	0	.286
1984	Cleveland	1B	133	352	44	94	14	2	2	44	0	.267
1985	Cleveland	1B	107	284	31	81	14	1	1	27	1	.285
	Totals		1666	5564	783	1614	266	28	80	686	24	.290

NEAL HEATON 25 6-1 205 **Bats L Throws L**

Dropped below double figures in wins for first time in his three full seasons with Indians, but no Cleveland pitcher won as many as 10 games in 1985 . . . A disappointment, although he did pitch well at times and didn't get any offensive support . . . Had 3-3 record and 2.44 ERA through May 18, then fell into slump that continued through rest of season . . . Was 6-14 with a 5.80 ERA after that date . . . August was his best month as he had 3-2 record with three complete-game victories . . . Suffered through six-game losing streak between June 7 and July 3 . . . Born March 3, 1960, in Jamaica, N.Y. . . . Once struck out 20 batters in seven-inning high-school game . . . Mets made him first player selected in June 1979 draft, but he chose to attend Miami, where he compiled 41-6 record . . . Selected by Indians in second round of June 1981 draft.

Year	Club	G	IP	W	L	Pct.	SO	BB	H	ERA
1982	Cleveland	8	31	0	2	.000	14	16	32	5.23
1983	Cleveland	39	149⅓	11	7	.611	75	44	157	4.16
1984	Cleveland	38	198⅔	12	15	.444	75	75	231	5.21
1985	Cleveland	36	207⅔	9	17	.346	82	80	244	4.90
	Totals	121	586⅔	32	41	.438	246	215	664	4.83

TOM WADDELL 27 6-1 190 **Bats R Throws R**

Had never started a major-league game before beating Yankees July 31 . . . Threw his first complete game Aug. 19, also against Yankees . . . Attended Manhattan College in the Bronx, which happens to be the Yankees' address . . . Worked out of Indians' bullpen until July 31, then remained in rotation the rest of the way, but his nine saves still led club . . . Had 4-1 record as starter . . . Change in role was result of elbow injury that made it difficult for him to come back the next day after pitching in relief . . . As a starter, he could rest elbow between starts . . . Finally underwent surgery to remove bone spurs Sept. 23 . . . Born Sept. 17, 1958, in Dundee, Scotland, but grew up in New Jersey . . . Originally signed by Hank Aaron and Braves as free agent in 1981 . . . Plucked by Cleveland out of Atlanta organization in minor-league draft prior to 1984 season.

Year	Club	G	IP	W	L	Pct.	SO	BB	H	ERA
1984	Cleveland	58	97	7	4	.636	59	37	68	3.06
1985	Cleveland	49	112⅔	8	6	.571	53	39	104	4.87
	Totals	107	209⅔	15	10	.600	112	76	172	4.03

Tony Bernazard flashed some muscle, hitting 11 homers.

TOP PROSPECTS

CORY SNYDER 23 6-3 175 **Bats R Throws R**

Indians' No. 1 pick and fourth overall in June 1984 draft... Named Most Valuable Player of Eastern League last season... Third baseman hit .281 and led league with 28 homers and 94 RBI for Waterbury (AA)... Indians planned to try him in the outfield during Florida Instructional League, where he won triple crown with .390 average, 14 homers and 53 RBI in 1984...

Played on 1984 U.S. Olympic team and hit .400 with two homers and seven RBI . . . Born Nov. 11, 1962, in Inglewood, Cal. . . . Attended Brigham Young and hit home runs on first three pitches he saw in his first collegiate game.

JIM WILSON 25 6-3 225 **Bats R Throws R**
Impressed Indians so much that he will be given a good chance to make club as first baseman in 1986 . . . Hit 26 homers and drove in 101 runs for Maine (AAA) last year, marking the second straight season that he led the International League in RBI . . . Was given September trial by Indians and hit .357 with four RBI in 14 at-bats . . . Born Dec. 29, 1960, in Corvallis, Ore. . . . Has steadily progressed through Cleveland system since being picked in second round of June 1982 draft.

MANAGER PAT CORRALES: Was rewarded with a perpetual contract after 60-102 season in 1985 . . . Has managed three major-league teams after playing for three . . . Managerial career began in 1975 with Alexandria of Texas League . . . Took over Rangers in 1979, after three seasons as a coach . . . Was dismissed by Texas after 1980 and was hired by Philadelphia in 1982 . . . Completed an unusual double in 1983, when he was fired by Phillies and hired by Indians . . . Joined John McGraw, Rogers Hornsby and Bill Virdon as only men to manage in both leagues during a single season . . . Born March 20, 1941, in Los Angeles . . . Was a catcher for Cardinals, Reds and Padres . . . Of Mexican-Indian descent . . . Composite major-league managerial record stands at 457-500.

GREATEST SHORTSTOP

At the young age of 25, Lou Boudreau was not only playing shortstop for the Indians, he was managing them. He continued in that dual role for Cleveland for eight more years.

The player-manager was at his best in 1948, when the Indians won 97 games and the world championship. Boudreau played 151 games at shortstop—he actually caught one game—and he hit .355 with 18 home runs and 106 RBI, both career-high figures. He was selected as the AL Most Valuable Player.

One of Boudreau's greatest games was the playoff game against Boston that year, the first such showdown in American League history. The teams had finished the season tied with 96-58 records. Boudreau went 4-for-4 with two home runs and three runs scored as the Indians won, 8-3, at Fenway Park.

Boudreau is remembered as one of the greatest all-around shortstops. He led the league in doubles three times—each time with 45—and won the batting title in 1944 with a .327 average. During that same season, Boudreau turned 134 double plays, the fourth-highest total in history. His 1,180 career double plays rank him 11th on the all-time list.

Boudreau retired in 1952 with a .295 lifetime average. Eighteen years later, he was inducted into the Hall of Fame and the Indians retired his No. 5.

ALL-TIME INDIAN SEASON RECORDS

BATTING: Joe Jackson, .408, 1911
HRs: Al Rosen, 43, 1953
RBIs: Hal Trosky, 162, 1936
STEALS: Miguel Dilone, 61, 1980
WINS: Jim Bagby, 31, 1920
STRIKEOUTS: Bob Feller, 348, 1946

DETROIT TIGERS

TEAM DIRECTORY: Chairman: John Fetzer; Vice-Chairman: Tom Monaghan; Pres.-Chief Exec. Off.: Jim Campbell; Exec. VP-Chief Oper. Off.: William Haase; VP-GM: William Lajoie; Dir. Minor League Oper.: Dave Miller; Dir. Pub. Rel.: Dan Ewald; Trav. Sec.: Bill Brown; Mgr.: Sparky Anderson. Home: Tiger Stadium (52,806). Field distances: 340, l.f. line; 365, l.c.; 440, c.f.; 370, r.c.; 325, r.f. line. Spring training: Lakeland, Fla.

SCOUTING REPORT

HITTING: While Darrell Evans showed he had learned how to hit AL pitchers in 1985, the rest of the Tigers seemed to forget how. Many Tigers boosted their batting numbers in the final month, when Detroit was well out of the pennant pursuit. The disappointments included Alan Trammell (.258, 13 homers, 57 RBI), Chet Lemon (.265, 18 homers, 68 RBI) and Lou Whitaker (.279, 21 homers, 73 RBI), who looked like a sure bet to hit .300 until he started swinging for the fences.

Evans surprised everyone by reaching the fences 40 times. He

Jack Morris stares down hitters with eye of the Tiger.

led the AL in homers, becoming the first Tiger to do so since Hank Greenberg in 1946. Kirk Gibson (29 homers, 97 RBI) did his part, but there wasn't enough support from the right side of the plate, outside of Lance Parrish (.273, 28 homers, 98 RBI).

The Tigers had to rethink some of their offensive philosophies. Manager Sparky Anderson realized that it is difficult to score runs by moving one base at a time, so the Tigers improved their team speed by acquiring Dave Collins from the A's for Barbaro Garbey during the offseason.

PITCHING: Why did the Tigers put 15-game winner Walt Terrell on the block during the winter? Terrell was one of the most consistent Tiger pitchers in 1985 and would have won 18 games if the Detroit bullpen hadn't squandered three of his leads. Anderson, though, had ideas of a balanced rotation of right-handers Jack Morris (16-11, 3.33) and Dan Petry (15-13, 3.36) and left-handers Frank Tanana (12-14, 4.27) and Dave LaPoint (7-17, 3.57), the former Giant.

It is a veteran staff that will give Anderson a lot of innings. If needed, he also has youngsters Randy O'Neal and Chuck Cary to start or relieve. If there was one big difference between the 1984 Tigers, who were world champions, and the 1985 Tigers, who finished 15 games out, it was the bullpen. Willie Hernandez had a nearly perfect season in 1984, but "slumped" to 31 saves in 40 opportunities in 1985.

FIELDING: The Tigers' strength is up the middle, as it has been for the past several years. With Mike Heath going from Oakland to St. Louis, Parrish may have the best throwing arm of any catcher in the AL. The double-play combination of Trammell and Whitaker is as fundamentally sound as any in the game. Center fielder Lemon may not be as orthodox—he catches everything one-handed—but he catches almost everything.

Is this the year that Chris Pittaro nails down a job at third base? The hot shot of last spring fizzled in his first try amid great publicity. If he's still not ready, Anderson can call on steady Tom Brookens or former Mariner prospect Darnell Coles.

OUTLOOK: The Tigers won 84 games in 1985, 20 fewer than they did in 1984. They were far from bad, but they were a group of underachieving star players. Players such as Trammell and Whitaker can be expected to rebound. The Tigers, then, are likely to be better than they were last year, but not as terrific as they were in 1984. If they can reach a balance point in 1986—say, 10 wins better than last year—they could win the tough AL East.

DETROIT TIGERS 1986 ROSTER

MANAGER Sparky Anderson

Coaches—Billy Consolo, Alex Grammas, Billy Muffett, Vada Pinson, Dick Tracewski

PITCHERS

No.	Name	1985 Club	W-L	IP	SO	ERA	B-T	Ht.	Wt.	Born
22	Barlow, Ricky	Lakeland	1-7	50	35	5.54	R-R	6-2	170	3/21/63 Woodville, TX
		Birmingham	1-5	63	39	8.38				
43	Cary, Chuck	Nashville	2-1	66	54	3.00	L-L	6-4	210	3/3/60 Whittier, CA
		Detroit	0-1	24	22	3.42				
48	Conner, Jeff	Birmingham	1-0	20	12	2.29	L-L	6-1	185	6/26/59 Biloxi, MS
		Nashville	8-7	105	57	2.74				
44	Denman, Brian	Nashville	10-8	182	65	4.06	R-R	6-4	210	2/12/56 Minneapolis, MN
42	Dotson, Wayne	Lakeland	6-8	101	71	5.44	R-R	6-1	175	3/18/65 Lubbock, TX
		Birmingham	1-5	43	20	4.85				
21	Hernandez, Willie	Detroit	8-10	107	76	2.70	L-L	6-2	185	11/14/54 Puerto Rico
45	Kelly, Bryan	Nashville	8-8	113	93	3.75	R-R	6-2	195	2/24/59 Silver Springs, MD
25	King, Eric	Shreveport	5-3	105	80	2.32	R-R	6-2	180	4/10/64 Oxnard, CA
40	LaPoint, Dave	San Francisco	7-17	207	74	3.57	L-L	6-3	215	7/29/59 Glens Falls, NY
29	*Lopez, Aurelio	Detroit	3-7	86	53	4.80	R-R	6-0	225	10/5/48 Mexico
47	Morris, Jack	Detroit	16-11	257	191	3.33	R-R	6-3	200	5/16/55 St. Paul, MN
49	O'Neal, Randy	Nashville	5-4	68	44	3.59	R-R	6-2	195	8/30/60 Ashland, KY
		Detroit	5-5	94	52	3.24				
46	Petry, Dan	Detroit	15-13	239	109	3.36	R-R	6-4	200	11/13/58 Palo Alto, CA
17	Scherrer, Bill	Detroit	3-2	66	46	4.36	L-L	6-4	170	1/20/58 Tonawanda, NY
26	Tanana, Frank	Tex.-Det.	12-14	215	159	4.27	L-L	6-3	195	7/3/53 Detroit, MI
35	Terrell, Walt	Detroit	15-10	229	130	3.85	L-R	6-2	205	5/11/58 Jeffersonville, IN
38	Voigt, Paul	Nashville	11-9	176	95	3.17	R-R	6-2	185	12/8/58 Bellrose, NY

CATCHERS

No.	Name	1985 Club	H	HR	RBI	Pct.	B-T	Ht.	Wt.	Born
8	Castillo, Marty	Detroit	10	2	5	.119	R-R	6-1	205	1/16/57 Long Beach, CA
18	Madison, Scotti	Birmingham	39	5	25	.322	B-R	5-11	185	9/12/58 Pensacola, FL
		Nashville	108	16	54	.341				
		Detroit	0	0	1	.000				
33	Nokes, Matt	Shreveport	101	14	56	.294	L-R	6-1	185	10/31/63 San Diego, CA
		San Francisco	11	2	5	.208				
13	Parrish, Lance	Detroit	150	28	98	.273	R-R	6-3	220	6/15/56 Clairton, PA

INFIELDERS

No.	Name	1985 Club	H	HR	RBI	Pct.	B-T	Ht.	Wt.	Born
9	Baker, Doug	Nashville	71	2	30	.218	B-R	5-9	165	4/3/61 Fullerton, CA
		Detroit	5	0	1	.185				
14	Bergman, Dave	Detroit	25	3	7	.179	L-L	6-2	180	6/6/53 Evanston, IL
16	Brookens, Tom	Detroit	115	7	47	.237	R-R	5-10	170	8/10/53 Chambersburg, PA
—	Coles, Darnell	Calgary	31	4	24	.320	R-R	6-1	185	6/22/62 San Bernardino, CA
		Seattle	14	1	5	.237				
24	Earl, Scott	Nashville	90	7	44	.236	R-R	5-11	165	9/18/60 Seymour, IN
41	Evans, Darrell	Detroit	125	40	94	.248	L-R	6-2	205	5/26/47 Pasadena, CA
20	Flynn, Doug	Montreal	1	0	0	.167	R-R	5-11	170	4/18/51 Lexington, KY
		Detroit	13	0	2	.255				
4	Laga, Mike	Nashville	113	20	79	.263	L-L	6-2	210	6/14/60 Ridgewood, NJ
		Detroit	6	2	6	.167				
12	Pittaro, Chris	Detroit	15	0	7	.242	B-R	5-11	170	9/16/61 Trenton, NJ
		Nashville	34	3	19	.194				
3	Trammell, Alan	Detroit	156	13	57	.258	R-R	6-0	175	2/21/58 Garden Grove, CA
1	Whitaker, Lou	Detroit	170	21	73	.279	L-R	5-11	160	5/12/57 New York, NY

OUTFIELDERS

No.	Name	1985 Club	H	HR	RBI	Pct.	B-T	Ht.	Wt.	Born
29	Collins, Dave	Oakland	95	4	29	.251	B-L	5-10	175	10/20/52 Rapid City, SD
23	Gibson, Kirk	Detroit	167	29	97	.287	L-L	6-3	215	5/28/57 Pontiac, MI
30	Grubb, John	Detroit	38	5	25	.245	L-R	6-3	180	8/4/48 Richmond, VA
31	Herndon, Larry	Detroit	108	12	37	.244	R-R	6-3	200	11/3/53 Sunflower, MS
34	Lemon, Chet	Detroit	137	18	68	.265	R-R	6-1	190	2/12/55 Jackson, MS
32	Sanchez, Alex	Nashville	9	2	5	.237	R-R	6-0	185	2/26/59 Dominican Republic
		Detroit	33	6	12	.248				
37	Simmons, Nelson	Detroit	60	10	33	.239	B-R	6-1	195	6/27/63 Washington, DC
		Nashville	46	9	26	.245				

*Free agent unsigned at press time

TIGER PROFILES

DARRELL EVANS 38 6-2 205 **Bats L Throws R**

First baseman turned up the power and had outstanding season while most of Tigers tumbled . . . Became oldest player to lead league in homers, with 40 . . . Became seventh major leaguer to hit 30 or more homers for three different teams . . . Was first Tiger to lead league in homers since Hank Greenberg hit 44 in 1946 . . . Was first left-handed-hitting Tiger to win home-run title since Ty Cobb in 1909 . . . Hit only two homers in first 72 at-bats, through May 14, then he embarked on pace of one homer per 11 at-bats . . . Finished fifth in AL in slugging percentage (.519) . . . Born May 26, 1947, in Pasadena, Cal. . . . Signed by Kansas City Athletics in secondary phase of June 1967 draft . . . Had already been drafted by Cubs, Yankees, Tigers and Phillies . . . Signed by Tigers as a re-entry free agent prior to 1984 season, after he had hit 30 homers, had driven in 82 runs and had been named Giants' MVP in 1983.

Year	Club	Pos.	G	AB	R	H	2B	3B	HR	RBI	SB	Avg.
1969	Atlanta	3B	12	26	3	6	0	0	0	1	0	.231
1970	Atlanta	3B	12	44	4	14	1	1	0	9	0	.318
1971	Atlanta	3B-OF	89	260	42	63	11	1	12	38	2	.242
1972	Atlanta	3B	125	418	67	106	12	0	19	71	4	.254
1973	Atlanta	3B-1B	161	595	114	167	25	8	41	104	6	.281
1974	Atlanta	3B	160	571	99	137	21	3	25	79	4	.240
1975	Atlanta	3B-1B	156	567	82	138	22	2	22	73	12	.243
1976	Atl.-S.F.	1B-3B	136	396	53	81	9	1	11	46	9	.205
1977	San Francisco...	OF-1B-3B	144	461	64	117	18	3	17	72	9	.254
1978	San Francisco...	3B	159	547	82	133	24	2	20	78	4	.243
1979	San Francisco...	3B	160	562	68	142	23	2	17	70	6	.253
1980	San Francisco...	3B-1B	154	556	69	147	23	0	20	78	17	.264
1981	San Francisco...	3B-1B	102	357	51	92	13	4	12	48	2	.258
1982	San Francisco...	3B-1B-SS	141	465	64	119	20	4	16	61	5	.256
1983	San Francisco...	1B-3B-SS	142	523	94	145	29	3	30	82	6	.277
1984	Detroit	3B-1B	131	401	60	93	11	1	16	63	2	.232
1985	Detroit	1B-3B	151	505	81	125	17	0	40	94	0	.248
	Totals		2135	7254	1097	1825	279	35	318	1067	88	.252

KIRK GIBSON 28 6-3 215 **Bats L Throws L**

For a second straight season, he fulfilled the great expectations that the Tigers held for him when they made him their first-round pick in June 1978 draft . . . Right fielder fell one home run short of becoming first Tiger to hit 30 homers and steal 30 bases in same season . . . His 29 homers and 97 RBI were career highs . . . Had 30 stolen bases in 34 attempts in 1985 . . .

Named MVP of 1984 ALCS with .417 average and .750 slugging percentage . . . Hit two homers in final game of 1984 World Series . . . Born May 28, 1957, in Pontiac, Mich. . . . Was an All-American flanker for Michigan State . . . Signed with Tigers after playing only one year of baseball in college . . . Promoted to Tigers toward end of 1979 season, his second year in pro ball . . . Has rare combination of speed and power . . . Became free agent at end of last season.

Year	Club	Pos.	G	AB	R	H	2B	3B	HR	RBI	SB	Avg.
1979	Detroit	OF	12	38	3	9	3	0	1	4	3	.237
1980	Detroit	OF	51	175	23	46	2	1	9	16	4	.263
1981	Detroit	OF	83	290	41	95	11	3	9	40	17	.328
1982	Detroit	OF	69	266	34	74	16	2	8	35	9	.278
1983	Detroit	OF	128	401	60	91	12	9	15	51	14	.227
1984	Detroit	OF	149	531	92	150	23	10	27	91	29	.282
1985	Detroit	OF	154	581	96	167	37	5	29	97	30	.287
	Totals		646	2282	349	632	104	30	98	334	106	.277

DAVE COLLINS 33 5-10 175 **Bats S Throws L**

Tigers sent Barbaro Garbey to A's to get this left fielder, who had asked out of Oakland after miserable first season there . . . His 1985 season began with a bang as, in his first at-bat in Oakland Coliseum as a member of the A's, he hit a home run off Angels' Tommy John . . . But his year went downhill from there . . . Arrived from Toronto amidst great expectations following 1984 season in which he hit .308 and stole 60 bases for Blue Jays . . . Came to Oakland, hit .251, his lowest average since 1978, and stole only 29 bases, his lowest total since 1981 . . . A's acquired him from Blue Jays with Alfredo Griffin for Bill Caudill prior to last season . . . Hit his first career grand slam in 1985 off Angels' Mike Witt . . . Born Oct. 20, 1952, in Rapid City, S.D., an appropriate birthplace for a stolen-base threat . . . Chosen by Angels in secondary phase of June 1972 draft . . . Hit .357 for Cincinnati in 1979 NLCS against Pittsburgh.

Year	Club	Pos.	G	AB	R	H	2B	3B	HR	RBI	SB	Avg.
1975	California	OF	93	319	41	85	13	4	3	29	24	.266
1976	California	OF	99	365	45	96	12	1	4	28	32	.263
1977	Seattle	OF	120	402	46	96	9	3	5	28	25	.239
1978	Cincinnati	OF	102	102	13	22	1	0	0	7	7	.216
1979	Cincinnati	OF-1B	122	396	59	126	16	4	3	35	16	.318
1980	Cincinnati	OF	144	551	94	167	20	4	3	35	79	.303
1981	Cincinnati	OF	95	360	63	98	18	6	3	23	26	.272
1982	New York (AL)	OF-1B	111	348	41	88	12	3	3	25	13	.253
1983	Toronto	OF-1B	118	402	55	109	12	4	1	34	31	.271
1984	Toronto	OF-1B	128	441	59	136	24	15	2	44	60	.308
1985	Oakland	OF	112	370	52	95	16	4	4	29	29	.251
	Totals		1244	4065	568	1118	153	48	31	317	342	.275

ALAN TRAMMELL 28 6–0 175 Bats R Throws R

Another big reason Tigers did not contend in 1985 . . . Suffered through disappointing season after winning World Series MVP award in 1984 . . . Batted .258 after two consecutive years of averages no lower than .314 . . . Struck out career-high 71 times and scored 79 runs, his lowest total since 1982 . . . Shortstop committed 15 errors—that's five more than he made in 1984 and it represents his worst figure since 1982 . . . Underwent surgery on his left knee and right shoulder after 1984 season . . . Hit .450 with two homers against Padres in 1984 World Series . . . Voted best defensive infielder and smartest player in poll of AL managers in 1984 . . . Tigers' second-round pick in June 1976 draft . . . Born Feb. 21, 1958, in Garden Grove, Cal. . . . Made major-league debut, Sept. 9, 1977, in same game that middle-infield partner Lou Whitaker made his first appearance.

Year	Club	Pos.	G	AB	R	H	2B	3B	HR	RBI	SB	Avg.
1977	Detroit	SS	19	43	6	8	0	0	0	0	0	.186
1978	Detroit	SS	139	448	49	120	14	6	2	34	3	.268
1979	Detroit	SS	142	460	68	127	11	4	6	50	17	.276
1980	Detroit	SS	146	560	107	168	21	5	9	65	12	.300
1981	Detroit	SS	105	392	52	101	15	3	2	31	10	.258
1982	Detroit	SS	157	489	66	126	34	3	9	57	19	.258
1983	Detroit	SS	142	505	83	161	31	2	14	66	30	.319
1984	Detroit	SS	139	555	85	174	34	5	14	69	19	.314
1985	Detroit	SS	149	605	79	156	21	7	13	57	14	.258
	Totals		1138	4057	595	1141	181	35	69	429	124	.281

LOU WHITAKER 28 5-11 160 Bats L Throws R

"Sweet Lou" was enjoying an outstanding season until Aug. 13, when he was informed that he could set Tiger record for homers by a second baseman . . . Sacrificed average for power the rest of the way . . . Was hitting .317 with 17 homers and 55 RBI after 106 games . . . During his final 46 games, his season average dipped to .279 and he had only four homers and 18 RBI . . . His 21 homers did set club record for second baseman . . . Drove in career-high 73 runs . . . Walked 80 times and struck out only 56 times . . . Hit homer over Tiger Stadium roof, against Rangers' Burt Hooton May 13 . . . Hit another homer on the roof, off Red Sox' Al Nipper June 17 . . . Four of his homers began Tigers' first inning . . . Tigers' fifth-round choice in June 1975 draft . . . Began career as a third baseman, but was switched to second in 1976 . . . Voted Tiger of the Year in 1983, when he became first left-handed-hitting Tiger to get 200 hits since Dick Wakefield in 1943 . . . Named AL Rookie of the Year in 1978 . . .

Born May 12, 1957, in Brooklyn, N.Y., but grew up in Martinsville, Va.

Year	Club	Pos.	G	AB	R	H	2B	3B	HR	RBI	SB	Avg.
1977	Detroit	2B	11	32	5	8	1	0	0	2	0	.250
1978	Detroit	2B	139	484	71	138	12	7	3	58	7	.285
1979	Detroit	2B	127	423	75	121	14	8	3	42	20	.286
1980	Detroit	2B	145	477	68	111	19	1	1	45	8	.233
1981	Detroit	2B	109	335	48	88	14	4	5	36	5	.263
1982	Detroit	2B	152	560	76	160	22	8	15	65	11	.286
1983	Detroit	2B	161	643	94	206	40	6	12	72	17	.320
1984	Detroit	2B	143	558	90	161	25	1	13	56	6	.289
1985	Detroit	2B	152	609	102	170	29	8	21	73	6	.279
	Totals		1139	4121	629	1163	176	43	73	449	80	.282

LANCE PARRISH 29 6-3 220 Bats R Throws R

Suffered through periods during which his back bothered him, but still wound up with 28 homers and team-leading 98 RBI . . . Missed 17 games in mid-July . . . Led Tigers with 16 game-winning RBI, one short of club record set by Kirk Gibson in 1984 . . . Recognized as one of the best defensive catchers in the game . . . Had a 38-percent success rate in nailing would-be base-stealers last year . . . Threw out 33 runners in 88 attempts after gunning down 33 in 79 tries in 1984 . . . Hit 32 homers in 1982, setting a since-broken record for AL catchers . . . Tigers' first-round pick in June 1974 draft as a third baseman . . . Switched to catcher, his high school position, in 1975 . . . Turned down football scholarship from UCLA to sign with Detroit . . . Born June 15, 1956, in Clairton, Pa.

Year	Club	Pos.	G	AB	R	H	2B	3B	HR	RBI	SB	Avg.
1977	Detroit	C	12	46	10	9	2	0	3	7	0	.196
1978	Detroit	C	85	288	37	63	11	3	14	41	0	.219
1979	Detroit	C	143	493	65	136	26	3	19	65	6	.276
1980	Detroit	C-1B-OF	144	553	79	158	34	6	24	82	6	.286
1981	Detroit	C	96	348	39	85	18	2	10	46	2	.244
1982	Detroit	C-OF	133	486	75	138	19	2	32	87	3	.284
1983	Detroit	C	155	605	80	163	42	3	27	114	1	.269
1984	Detroit	C	147	578	75	137	16	2	33	98	2	.237
1985	Detroit	C	140	549	64	150	27	1	28	98	2	.273
	Totals		1055	3946	524	1039	195	22	190	638	22	.263

JACK MORRIS 30 6-3 200 Bats R Throws R

Prevailed as ace of Tigers' staff again, although he was slightly off his 1984 form . . . Led club in wins for seventh straight season, a Detroit record . . . Led Tigers in innings pitched for seventh straight year, another club mark . . . Finished third in AL in strikeouts (191), tied for fourth in complete games (13) and tied for second in shutouts with four, the most by a Tiger since Jack Billingham in 1978 . . . However, he was much more inconsistent than in 1984 until finding a groove in June . . . Won seven of eight decisions between June 5 and Aug. 14 . . . Has outstanding split-fingered fastball . . . Born May 16, 1955, in St. Paul, Minn. . . . Picked by Tigers in fifth round of June 1976 draft . . . Threw a no-hitter against White Sox in 1984 . . . Became first pitcher under Sparky Anderson to throw a complete game in post-season play with two during 1984 World Series.

Year	Club	G	IP	W	L	Pct.	SO	BB	H	ERA
1977	Detroit	7	46	1	1	.500	28	23	38	3.72
1978	Detroit	28	106	3	5	.375	48	49	107	4.33
1979	Detroit	27	198	17	7	.708	113	59	179	3.27
1980	Detroit	36	250	16	15	.516	112	87	252	4.18
1981	Detroit	25	198	14	7	.667	97	78	153	3.05
1982	Detroit	37	266⅓	17	16	.515	135	96	247	4.06
1983	Detroit	37	293⅔	20	13	.606	232	83	257	3.34
1984	Detroit	35	240⅓	19	11	.633	148	87	221	3.60
1985	Detroit	35	257	16	11	.593	191	110	212	3.33
	Totals	267	1855⅓	123	86	.589	1104	672	1666	3.61

WILLIE HERNANDEZ 31 6-2 185 Bats L Throws L

Many fingers were pointed at this guy by those analyzing Tigers' failure to contend in 1985 after winning World Series in 1984 . . . Had 31 saves—one fewer than in 1984, when he became sixth pitcher and second reliever to win both Cy Young Award and MVP award in same season . . . Had 32 saves in 33 opportunities in 1984 . . . Ranked third in AL with 31 saves in 40 opportunities in 1985 . . . Became first Tiger to record 30 or more saves in back-to-back seasons . . . Walked only 14 batters in 106⅔ innings and struck out 76 . . . Threw 13 gopher balls after being tagged for only six homers in 1984 . . . Born Nov. 14, 1954, in Aguada, Puerto Rico . . . Acquired from Philadelphia with Dave Bergman for John Wockenfuss and Glenn Wilson prior to 1984 season . . . Originally signed as free agent by Phillies in 1974, he was chosen by Cubs in December 1976 minor-league draft . . . Known for his tricky screwball . . . Was on the mound when Tigers clinched AL East, ALCS and World Series titles in 1984.

Year	Club	G	IP	W	L	Pct.	SO	BB	H	ERA
1977	Chicago (NL)	67	110	8	7	.533	78	28	94	3.03
1978	Chicago (NL)	54	60	8	2	.800	38	35	57	3.75
1979	Chicago (NL)	51	79	4	4	.500	53	39	85	5.01
1980	Chicago (NL)	53	108	1	9	.100	75	45	115	4.42
1981	Chicago (NL)	12	14	0	0	.000	13	8	14	3.86
1982	Chicago (NL)	75	75	4	6	.400	54	24	74	3.00
1983	Chi (NL)-Phil.	74	115⅓	9	4	.692	93	32	109	3.28
1984	Detroit	80	140⅓	9	3	.750	112	36	96	1.92
1985	Detroit	74	106⅔	8	10	.444	76	14	82	2.70
	Totals	540	808⅓	51	45	.531	592	261	726	3.27

DAN PETRY 27 6-4 200 **Bats R Throws R**

Qualified as Tigers' hard-luck pitcher of 1985 ... Finished at 15-13, but deserved better ... In 10 of his 13 losses, the Tigers scored two runs or less ... Was 0-2 and had two no-decisions in games in which the Tigers were shut out ... During one four-start stretch of bad fortune, he threw three complete games but was 1-2 with a no-decision ... Tigers didn't score a run for him in 25 straight innings ... Twice pitched into 10th inning of scoreless games ... Has won at least 15 games for four straight seasons and has been in double figures in victories since 1980 ... Born Nov. 13, 1958, in Palo Alto, Cal. ... Fourth-round pick by Tigers in June 1976 draft ... Recognized as a fierce competitor.

Year	Club	G	IP	W	L	Pct.	SO	BB	H	ERA
1979	Detroit	15	98	6	5	.545	43	33	90	3.95
1980	Detroit	27	165	10	9	.526	88	83	145	3.93
1981	Detroit	23	141	10	9	.526	79	57	115	3.00
1982	Detroit	35	246	15	9	.625	132	100	220	3.22
1983	Detroit	38	266⅓	19	11	.633	122	99	256	3.92
1984	Detroit	35	233⅓	18	8	.692	144	66	231	3.24
1985	Detroit	34	238⅔	15	13	.536	109	81	190	3.36
	Totals	207	1388⅓	93	64	.592	717	519	1258	3.49

WALT TERRELL 27 6-2 205 **Bats L Throws R**

Has gained a reputation as a bulldog of a pitcher ... Had a typical year as he was unspectacular, but consistently good ... Set career highs with 15 wins, 34 starts, 229 innings pitched, 130 strikeouts and three shutouts ... Total of five complete games might have been biggest surprise ... Had clashed with Dave Johnson, his former manager with Mets, about finishing games and was expected to be lifted just as quickly by Sparky Anderson, alias "Captain Hook" ... Acquired from Mets for Howard Johnson prior to last season ... Won his first four games as a Tiger ... Threw two shutouts against AL East champion Blue Jays ... Sinkerballer who benefitted from the high infield grass at Tiger Stadium, where he posted 9-2 record ... Hit two homers off Cubs' Ferguson Jenkins in 1983 game ... Originally a 33rd-round pick by Rangers in June 1980 draft ... Mets got him and Ron Darling for Lee Mazzilli on April Fools Day, 1982 . . . Born May 11, 1958, in Jeffersonville, Ind.

Year	Club	G	IP	W	L	Pct.	SO	BB	H	ERA
1982	New York (NL)	3	21	0	3	.000	8	14	22	3.43
1983	New York (NL)	21	133⅔	8	8	.500	59	55	123	3.57
1984	New York (NL)	33	215	11	12	.478	114	80	232	3.52
1985	Detroit	34	229	15	10	.600	130	95	221	3.85
	Totals	91	598⅔	34	33	.507	311	244	598	3.65

TOP PROSPECTS

NELSON SIMMONS 22 6-1 195 **Bats S Throws R**

Tigers have high hopes for this speedy outfielder . . . Was forced to serve mostly as DH in his 75 games with Tigers, because of crowded outfield . . . Hit .239 with 10 homers and 33 RBI. . . . Hit .433 in nine games with Tigers during his first major-league trial in 1984 . . . Signed by Detroit as second-round pick in June 1981 draft . . . Rated the outfielder with best arm in Southern League when he played for Birmingham (AA) in 1983 . . . Born June 27, 1963, in Washington, D.C. . . . Led American Association with 41 doubles for Evansville (AAA) in 1984.

CHUCK CARY 25 6-4 210 **Bats L Throws L**

Earned first promotion to majors and made 16 relief appearances for Tigers . . . Was 0-1 with 3.42 ERA and two saves . . . Not regarded as overpowering, he has outstanding control of all his pitches . . . Walked only eight and struck out 22 in his 23⅔ innings with Tigers . . . Spent 1984 season with Birmingham (AA), where he was used primarily as a starter . . . Walked 46 and struck out 62 in 108⅓ innings while going 6-4 with 4.82 ERA that season . . . Posted 2-1 record with 3.00 ERA and eight saves for Nashville (AAA) in 1985.

MANAGER SPARKY ANDERSON: Saw his defending world

champions slip to third place, 15 games behind Toronto . . . Tigers' 84-77 mark represented a dropoff of 20 victories from 1984 . . . Became first manager to win 100 or more games with two different teams and the first to win a World Series in both leagues in 1984 . . . Composite major-league record is 1,426-1,047 . . . Joined Tigers on June 14, 1979 . . . Has contract that runs through 1986 season . . . Known for his outrageous and exaggerated opinions . . . Once called an at-bat by Dave Bergman against the Blue Jays in May 1984 "the greatest at-bat in the history of baseball" . . . Said Howard Johnson had a "mortal lock" on third-base spot, then Tigers traded him weeks later . . . Guided Reds to 863-586 record from 1970-78, winning two World Series, four pennants and five NL West titles . . . Born Feb. 22, 1934, in Bridgewater, S.D. . . . Played in minors for six seasons before joining Phillies as an infielder in 1959, when he hit .218 in his only major-league season . . . Played four more years in minors . . . Managed for four years in minors and coached for San Diego in 1969.

GREATEST SHORTSTOP

A panel of experts recently convened in Detroit to select the Tigers' all-time team. When it was time to pick the club's greatest shortstop, these gentlemen did not have to delve deep into their memories or research books. Their choice was Alan Trammell.

The Tigers made Trammell a second-round pick in the June 1976 draft. On Sept. 9, 1977, he played in the majors for the first time, in the second game of a doubleheader in Boston. He singled in his first at-bat and has been the Tigers' shortstop ever since.

Trammell is regarded as one of the smartest defensive players in the game. His instincts and strong arm have helped him win four Gold Gloves. He is dangerous at bat, too. Trammell has hit .300 or better in three seasons. He hit .364 during the 1984 American League playoffs, then hit .450 with two home runs and six RBI as the Tigers beat San Diego in the World Series. Trammell was selected as the World Series MVP.

Trammell's consistent defensive play and productive hitting have helped him supplant Billy Rogell as the club's greatest shortstop. Rogell was given that honor in a vote by Tigers' fans in 1969. Rogell was the regular Detroit shortstop from 1932-38 and he retired in 1940 with a .267 lifetime average.

ALL-TIME TIGER SEASON RECORDS

BATTING: Ty Cobb, .420, 1911
HRs: Hank Greenberg, 58, 1938
RBIs: Hank Greenberg, 183, 1937
STEALS: Ty Cobb, 96, 1915
WINS: Denny McLain, 31, 1968
STRIKEOUTS: Mickey Lolich, 308, 1971

MILWAUKEE BREWERS

TEAM DIRECTORY: Pres.: Allan (Bud) Selig; Exec. VP-GM: Harry Dalton; Asst. GM: Walter Shannon; Spec. Assts. to GM: Dee Fondy, Sal Bando; Farm Dir.: Bruce Manno; Dir. Publ.: Tom Skibosh; Trav. Sec.: Jimmy Bank; Mgr.: George Bamberger. Home: Milwaukee County Stadium (53,192). Field distances: 315, l.f. line; 362, l.f.; 392, l.c.; 402, c.f.; 392, r.c.; 362, r.f.; 315, r.f. line. Spring training: Sun City, Ariz.

SCOUTING REPORT

HITTING: The Brewer bats weren't exactly terrifying last year, but they awakened after a deep slumber in 1984. The most heartening developments for Milwaukee fans were the comebacks of Paul Molitor (.297, 93 runs, 21 stolen bases) and Cecil Cooper (.293, 16 homers, 99 RBI). The Brew Crew, though, still has to conquer the effects of time on its big hitters. The heart of the order includes Cooper, 36, Ben Oglivie, 37, and Ted Simmons, 36.

The Brewers can always count on steady Robin Yount (.277, 15 homers, 68 RBI) and have high hopes for continued improvement by youngsters Earnest Riles (.286 as a rookie) at shortstop and Bill Schroeder (.242 in an injury-filled season) behind the plate. But Milwaukee is still one big bat away from having the kind of lineup it wants. The Brewers need an outfielder who can hit 25 homers and the re-acquired David Green isn't the answer.

PITCHING: Manager George Bamberger, who helped develop some great pitching staffs in Baltimore, is going to have some fun this season. Moose Haas (8-8, 3.84) and Danny Darwin (8-18, 3.80) appear to be the only veterans in the starting rotation. That gives Bamberger the opportunity to develop some of the finest young arms in the league. At the head of the class is Teddy Higuera (15-8, 3.90) who, in just one season, has already developed into the ace of the staff and the closest thing to Fernando Valenzuela.

The Brewers may have this season's top rookie pitcher, too, in 21-year-old Juan Nieves, who is likely to find a spot on the staff. If Nieves is something of a prodigy, then former Met Tim Leary is a late bloomer. Leary, 27, may finally be putting his outstanding ability to full use based on his showing late in the 1985 season. If rookie Bill Wegman also develops as expected, the Brewers will have a staff that will grow together and win together. Unfortunately, even with the addition of Mark Clear, there is not enough help in the bullpen.

Brewers know they can count on Sockin' Robin Yount.

FIELDING: Perhaps the Brewers should have some reservations about moving Yount to center. The former shortstop showed a good arm in left last season, but is it strong enough for center? The defense is strong in the middle infield, where Riles and second baseman Jim Gantner cover a lot of ground. However, Cooper is not the first baseman he used to be and Molitor's 19 errors were the third-most among AL third basemen.

OUTLOOK: The Brewers' mixture of age and youth is curious, because it is so extreme. On one hand, there are questions about the productivity of Milwaukee's aging position players. On the other hand, the Brewers' pitching staff is an unknown quantity because of its inexperience. The Brewers aren't ready to challenge the elite of the AL East, but they may be only a year away. It all depends on the pitching staff, which is much like the young Mets staff of two seasons ago. Bamberger would be happy if his kids develop as quickly as those Mets did.

MILWAUKEE BREWERS 1986 ROSTER

MANAGER George Bamberger
Coaches—Andy Etchebarren, Larry Haney, Frank Howard, Tony Muser, Herm Starrette

PITCHERS

No.	Name	1985 Club	W-L	IP	SO	ERA	B-T	Ht.	Wt.	Born
—	Birkbeck, Mike	El Paso	9-10	158	106	3.53	R-R	6-2	185	3/10/61 Orrville, OH
—	Bosio, Chris	El Paso	11-6	181	154	3.82	R-R	6-3	220	4/3/63 Carmichael, CA
48	Burris, Ray	Milwaukee	9-13	170	81	4.81	R-R	6-5	210	8/22/50 Idabel, OK
—	Ciardi, Mark	Stockton	10-6	129	119	3.69	R-R	6-0	180	8/19/61 New Brunswick, NJ
		El Paso	8-1	68	50	2.66				
—	Clear, Mark	Boston	1-3	56	55	3.72	R-R	6-4	204	5/27/56 Los Angeles, CA
47	Cocanower, Jaime	Milwaukee	6-8	116	44	4.33	R-R	6-4	190	2/14/57 Puerto Rico
—	Clutterbuck, Bryan	Vancouver	11-7	148	101	3.53	R-R	6-4	225	12/17/59 Detroit, MI
59	Grim, Chuck	Vancouver	3-6	107	68	4.56	R-R	6-0	170	7/23/61 Van Nuys, CA
18	Darwin, Danny	Milwaukee	8-18	218	125	3.80	R-R	6-3	190	10/25/55 Bonham, TX
—	Duquette, Bryan	Vancouver	5-3	64	48	3.25	L-L	6-0	190	11/24/61 Inglewood, CA
40	Gibson, Bob	Milwaukee	6-7	92	53	3.90	R-R	6-0	195	6/19/57 Philadelphia, PA
30	Haas, Moose	Milwaukee	8-8	162	78	3.84	R-R	6-0	170	4/22/56 Baltimore, MD
40	Higuera, Ted	Milwaukee	15-8	212	127	3.90	B-L	5-10	178	11/9/58 Mexico
39	Leary, Tim	Vancouver	10-7	178	133	4.00	R-R	6-3	190	12/23/58 Santa Monica, CA
		Milwaukee	1-4	33	29	4.05				
10	McClure, Bob	Milwaukee	4-1	86	57	4.31	B-L	5-11	170	4/29/53 Oakland, CA
—	Murphy, Dan	Stockton	9-7	132	157	3.95	R-R	6-2	195	9/18/64 Artesia, CA
20	Nieves, Juan	El Paso	8-2	120	91	3.53	L-L	6-3	175	1/5/65 Puerto Rico
		Vancouver	8-3	69	54	3.80				
—	Plesac, Dan	El Paso	12-5	150	128	5.03	L-L	6-5	210	2/4/62 Gary, IN
43	Porter, Chuck	Beloit	1-0	14	12	3.29	R-R	6-3	188	1/12/56 Baltimore, MD
		Milwaukee	0-0	14	8	1.98				
41	Searage. Ray	Vancouver	2-0	26	31	2.42	L-L	6-1	180	5/1/55 Freeport, NY
		Milwaukee	1-4	38	36	5.92				
46	Wegman, Bill	Vancouver	10-11	188	113	4.02	R-R	6-5	200	12/19/62 Cincinnati, OH
		Milwaukee	2-0	18	6	3.57				

CATCHERS

No.	Name	1985 Club	H	HR	RBI	Pct.	B-T	Ht.	Wt.	Born
22	Moore, Charlie	Milwaukee	81	0	31	.232	R-R	5-11	180	6/21/53 Birmingham, AL
21	Schroeder, Bill	Milwaukee	47	8	25	.242	R-R	6-2	200	9/7/58 Baltimore, MD
23	Simmons, Ted	Milwaukee	144	12	76	.273	B-R	6-0	200	8/9/49 Highland Park, MI

INFIELDERS

No.	Name	1985 Club	H	HR	RBI	Pct.	B-T	Ht.	Wt.	Born
9	Adduci, Jim	Vancouver	109	20	76	.277	L-L	6-4	200	8/9/59 Chicago, IL
3	Castillo, Juan	Vancouver	119	1	32	.270	B-R	5-11	155	1/25/62 Dominican Republic
15	Cooper, Cecil	Milwaukee	185	16	99	.293	L-L	6-2	190	12/20/49 Brenham, TX
—	Diaz, Edgar	El Paso	134	0	55	.267	R-R	6-0	160	2/8/64 Puerto Rico
17	Gantner, Jim	Milwaukee	133	5	44	.254	L-R	5-11	175	1/5/54 Eden, WI
4	Molitor, Paul	Milwaukee	171	10	48	.297	R-R	6-0	175	8/22/56 St. Paul, MN
1	Riles, Ernest	Vancouver	41	2	20	.347	L-R	6-1	180	10/2/60 Whigham, GA
		Milwaukee	128	5	45	.286				
13	Robidoux, Billy Joe	El Paso	176	23	132	.342	L-R	6-1	200	1/13/64 Ware, MA
		Milwaukee	9	3	8	.180				
—	Sveum, Dale	Vancouver	98	6	48	.236	B-R	6-3	185	11/23/63 Richmond, CA

OUTFIELDERS

No.	Name	1985 Club	H	HR	RBI	Pct.	B-T	Ht.	Wt.	Born
—	Braggs, Glenn	El Paso	139	20	103	.310	R-R	6-3	210	10/17/62 San Bernardino, CA
—	Deer, Rob	San Francisco	30	8	20	.185	R-R	6-3	210	9/29/60 Orange, CA
—	Green, David	San Francisco	73	5	20	.248	R-R	6-3	185	12/4/60 Nicaragua
16	Felder, Mike	Vancouver	177	2	43	.314	B-R	5-8	160	11/18/62 Richmond, CA
		Milwaukee	11	0	0	.196				
7	Householder, Paul	Milwaukee	77	11	34	.258	B-R	6-0	185	9/4/58 Columbus, OH
14	James, Dion	Vancouver	4	0	5	.108	L-L	6-1	175	11/9/62 Philadelphia, PA
		Milwaukee	11	0	3	.224				
28	Manning, Rick	Milwaukee	47	2	18	.218	L-R	6-1	180	9/2/54 Niagara Falls, NY
24	Oglivie, Ben	Milwaukee	99	10	61	.290	L-L	6-2	170	2/11/49 Panama
2	Ready, Randy	Vancouver	62	4	29	.326	R-R	5-11	180	1/8/60 San Mateo, CA
		Milwaukee	48	1	21	.265				
19	Yount, Robin	Milwaukee	129	15	68	.277	R-R	6-0	180	9/16/55 Danville, IL

BREWER PROFILES

CECIL COOPER 36 6-2 190 **Bats L Throws L**

First baseman rebounded from a disappointing 1984 season with a more typical performance . . . Boosted home-run total from 11 to 16, RBI total from 67 to 99 and average from .275 to .293 . . . Missed shot at .300 season and 100 RBI when bad elbow during last two weeks helped limit him to one hit in final 31 at-bats . . . Played in 154 games, tops on club . . . Led Brewers in slugging percentage (.456), homers and RBI . . . Batted .302 with runners in scoring position . . . Hit .373 from the seventh inning on . . . One of game's most consistent hitters in 1980s . . . Born Dec. 20, 1949, in Brenham, Tex. . . . Traded from Boston to Milwaukee for George Scott and Bernie Carbo prior to 1977 season . . . Resides in Sealy, Tex., hometown of NFL star Eric Dickerson.

Year	Club	Pos.	G	AB	R	H	2B	3B	HR	RBI	SB	Avg.
1971	Boston	1B	14	42	9	13	4	1	0	3	1	.310
1972	Boston	1B	12	17	0	4	1	0	0	2	0	.235
1973	Boston	1B	30	101	12	24	2	0	3	11	1	.238
1974	Boston	1B	121	414	55	114	24	1	8	43	2	.275
1975	Boston	1B	106	305	49	95	17	6	14	44	1	.311
1976	Boston	1B	123	451	66	127	22	6	15	78	7	.282
1977	Milwaukee	1B	160	643	86	193	31	7	20	78	13	.300
1978	Milwaukee	1B	107	407	60	127	23	2	13	54	3	.312
1979	Milwaukee	1B	150	590	83	182	44	1	24	106	15	.308
1980	Milwaukee	1B	153	622	96	219	33	4	25	122	17	.352
1981	Milwaukee	1B	106	416	70	133	35	1	12	60	5	.320
1982	Milwaukee	1B	155	654	104	205	38	3	32	121	2	.313
1983	Milwaukee	1B	160	661	106	203	37	3	30	126	2	.307
1984	Milwaukee	1B	148	603	63	166	28	3	11	67	8	.275
1985	Milwaukee	1B	154	631	82	185	39	8	16	99	10	.293
	Totals		1699	6557	941	1990	378	46	223	1014	87	.303

PAUL MOLITOR 29 6-0 175 **Bats R Throws R**

"The Ignitor" made great comeback in 1985 . . . Underwent serious surgery May 21, 1984, when a ligament in his right elbow was replaced by a tendon from his left forearm and a muscle that had torn away from the bone was reattached . . . After hitting .217 in 13 games in 1984, he rebounded with a team-high .297 average in 140 games last year . . . Led Brewers in runs scored with 93 . . . Third baseman hit safely in 24 of his last 25 games . . . Had a nine-game hitting streak, went hitless in a pinch-hitting appearance, then hit in 16 consecutive games . . .

Missed three weeks with a sprained ankle . . . No. 1 overall pick in June 1977 draft . . . Spent only one season in minors and won Midwest League batting title and MVP award for Burlington (A) in 1977 . . . Born Aug. 22, 1956, in St. Paul, Minn. . . . Hit .355 in the 1982 World Series and had five hits in one game against St. Louis.

Year	Club	Pos.	G	AB	R	H	2B	3B	HR	RBI	SB	Avg.
1978	Milwaukee	2B-SS-3B	125	521	73	142	26	4	6	45	30	.273
1979	Milwaukee	2B-SS	140	584	88	188	27	16	9	62	33	.322
1980	Milwaukee	2B-SS-3B	111	450	81	137	29	2	9	37	34	.304
1981	Milwaukee	OF	64	251	45	67	11	0	2	19	10	.267
1982	Milwaukee	3B-SS	160	666	136	201	26	8	19	71	41	.302
1983	Milwaukee	3B	152	608	95	164	28	6	15	47	41	.269
1984	Milwaukee	3B	13	46	3	10	1	0	0	6	1	.217
1985	Milwaukee	3B	140	576	93	171	28	3	10	48	21	.297
	Totals		905	3702	614	1080	176	39	70	335	211	.292

EARNEST RILES 25 6-1 180 — Bats L Throws R

Had never played a game in majors before 1985, but earned raves with his smooth play at shortstop and his hitting ability . . . Toll of his first full season may have been evident in September, when he hit .241 . . . Started that month with .305 average . . . Hit .368 with 16 RBI in August . . . Hit .408 with men on base that month . . . Began last season platooning with Ed Romero, but played well enough to become a regular player in June . . . Born Oct. 10, 1960, in Whigham, Ga. . . . Brewers selected him third in secondary phase of January 1981 draft . . . Does not have the perfect nickname for a baseball player: "E" . . . Committed 21 of those at shortstop.

Year	Club	Pos.	G	AB	R	H	2B	3B	HR	RBI	SB	Avg.
1985	Milwaukee	SS	116	448	54	128	12	7	5	45	2	.286

BEN OGLIVIE 37 6-2 170 — Bats L Throws L

Outfielder hit .290 but was hampered by sore right thumb all season . . . Did not play at all after Sept. 19 . . . His average was third-best on club and he led Brewers with .363 on-base percentage . . . Hit .326 with men on base and .298 with runners in scoring position . . . Best month was July, when he hit .417 with three homers and 20 RBI . . . Answers to any of three nicknames: Benji, B.O. or Spiderman . . . Born Feb. 11, 1949, in Colon, Panama . . . Seventh-round choice by Red Sox in June 1968 draft . . . Traded from Boston to Detroit for Dick McAuliffe prior to 1974 season . . . Traded from Detroit to Milwaukee for Jim Slaton and Rich Folkers prior to 1978 season.

Year	Club	Pos.	G	AB	R	H	2B	3B	HR	RBI	SB	Avg.
1971	Boston	OF	14	38	2	10	3	0	0	4	0	.263
1972	Boston	OF	94	253	27	61	10	2	8	30	1	.241
1973	Boston	OF	58	147	16	32	9	1	2	9	1	.218
1974	Detroit	OF-1B	92	252	28	68	11	3	4	29	12	.270
1975	Detroit	OF-1B	100	332	45	95	14	1	9	36	11	.286
1976	Detroit	OF-1B	115	305	36	87	12	3	15	47	9	.285
1977	Detroit	OF	132	450	63	118	24	2	21	61	9	.262
1978	Milwaukee	OF-1B	128	469	71	142	29	4	18	72	11	.303
1979	Milwaukee	OF-1B	139	514	88	145	30	4	29	81	12	.282
1980	Milwaukee	OF	156	592	94	180	26	2	41	118	11	.304
1981	Milwaukee	OF	107	400	53	97	15	2	14	72	2	.243
1982	Milwaukee	OF	159	602	92	147	22	1	34	102	3	.244
1983	Milwaukee	OF	125	411	49	115	19	3	13	66	4	.280
1984	Milwaukee	OF	131	461	49	121	16	2	12	60	0	.262
1985	Milwaukee	OF	101	341	40	99	17	2	10	61	0	.290
	Totals		1651	5567	753	1517	257	32	230	848	86	.272

TED SIMMONS 36 6-0 200 — Bats S Throws R

Rebounded from a .221 season in 1984 by hitting .273 in 1985 . . . Posted .307 mark right-handed . . . Designated hitter led Brewers in game-winning RBI with 13 and averaged one strikeout per 16.5 at-bats . . . Hit .290 with men on base . . . Of his 76 RBI, 44 came with score tied or with Brewers facing chance to tie . . . First-round pick by Cardinals in June 1967 draft . . . Obtained by Brewers with Pete Vuckovich and Rollie Fingers for David Green, Sixto Lezcano, Dave LaPoint and Lary Sorenson prior to 1981 season . . . Nicknamed "Simba" because of his long mane . . . Works as a banker in offseason . . . Born Aug. 9, 1949, in Highland Park, Mich.

Year	Club	Pos.	G	AB	R	H	2B	3B	HR	RBI	SB	Avg.
1968	St. Louis	C	2	3	0	1	0	0	0	0	0	.333
1969	St. Louis	C	5	14	0	3	0	1	0	3	0	.214
1970	St. Louis	C	82	284	29	69	8	2	3	24	2	.243
1971	St. Louis	C	133	510	64	155	32	4	7	77	1	.304
1972	St. Louis	C-1B	152	594	70	180	36	6	16	96	1	.303
1973	St. Louis	OF-1B-C	161	619	62	192	36	2	13	91	2	.310
1974	St. Louis	C-1B	152	599	66	163	33	6	20	103	0	.272
1975	St. Louis	C-1B-OF	157	581	80	193	32	3	18	100	1	.332
1976	St. Louis	C-1B-OF-3B	150	546	60	159	35	3	5	75	0	.291
1977	St. Louis	C-OF	150	516	82	164	25	3	21	95	2	.318
1978	St. Louis	C-OF	152	516	71	148	40	5	22	80	1	.287
1979	St. Louis	C	123	448	68	127	22	0	26	87	0	.283
1980	St. Louis	C-OF	145	495	84	150	33	2	21	98	1	.303
1981	Milwaukee	C-1B	100	380	45	82	13	3	14	61	0	.216
1982	Milwaukee	C	137	539	73	145	29	0	23	97	0	.269
1983	Milwaukee	C	153	600	76	185	39	3	13	108	4	.308
1984	Milwaukee	1B-3B	132	497	44	110	23	2	4	52	4	.221
1985	Milwaukee	1B-DH-C	143	528	60	144	28	2	12	76	1	.273
	Totals.		2229	8269	1034	2370	464	47	238	1323	19	.287

ROBIN YOUNT 30 6-0 180 **Bats R Throws R**

Played left field in 1985 and is projected as Brewers' center fielder this season . . . Underwent shoulder surgery to remove calcium deposits during first week of September . . . Led Brewers by hitting .327 with men on base . . . His .442 slugging percentage was second-best on club . . . His .277 average, 15 homers and 68 RBI were his lowest totals since 1981 . . . Played only one season in minors after Brewers chose him in first round of June 1973 draft . . . Born Sept. 16, 1955, in Danville, Ill. . . . Was Brewers' regular shortstop at age 19 . . . Named AL MVP in 1982, when he became first shortstop to lead league in slugging percentage and total bases.

Year	Club	Pos.	G	AB	R	H	2B	3B	HR	RBI	SB	Avg.
1974	Milwaukee	SS	107	344	48	86	14	5	3	26	7	.250
1975	Milwaukee	SS	147	558	67	149	28	2	8	52	12	.267
1976	Milwaukee	SS-OF	161	638	59	161	19	3	2	54	16	.252
1977	Milwaukee	SS	154	605	66	174	34	4	4	49	16	.288
1978	Milwaukee	SS	127	502	66	147	23	9	9	71	16	.293
1979	Milwaukee	SS	149	577	72	154	26	5	8	51	11	.267
1980	Milwaukee	SS	143	611	121	179	49	10	23	87	20	.293
1981	Milwaukee	SS	96	377	50	103	15	5	10	49	4	.273
1982	Milwaukee	SS	156	635	129	210	46	12	29	114	14	.331
1983	Milwaukee	SS	149	578	102	178	42	10	17	80	12	.308
1984	Milwaukee	SS	160	624	105	186	27	7	16	80	14	.298
1985	Milwaukee	OF	122	466	76	129	26	3	15	68	10	.277
	Totals		1671	6515	961	1856	349	75	144	781	152	.285

JIM GANTNER 32 5-11 175 **Bats L Throws R**

Signed big contract prior to last season, then endured one of his worst years . . . Batted .254, his lowest average since 1978 . . . Committed 11 errors at second base . . . Played third base at times . . . Remained one of toughest Brewers to strike out, fanning once per 12.5 at-bats . . . Was second on club in games played with 143 . . . Led Milwaukee with 10 sacrifice hits . . . Born Jan. 5, 1954, in Eden, Wisc. . . . Was selected by Brewers in 12th round of June 1974 draft.

Year	Club	Pos.	G	AB	R	H	2B	3B	HR	RBI	SB	Avg.
1976	Milwaukee	3B	26	69	6	17	1	0	0	7	1	.246
1977	Milwaukee	3B	14	47	4	14	1	0	1	2	2	.298
1978	Milwaukee	INF	43	97	14	21	1	0	1	8	2	.216
1979	Milwaukee	INF-P	70	208	29	59	10	3	2	22	3	.284
1980	Milwaukee	3B-2B-SS	132	415	47	117	21	3	4	40	11	.282
1981	Milwaukee	2B	107	352	35	94	14	1	2	33	3	.267
1982	Milwaukee	2B	132	447	48	132	17	2	4	43	6	.295
1983	Milwaukee	2B	161	603	85	170	23	8	11	74	5	.282
1984	Milwaukee	2B	153	613	61	173	27	1	3	56	6	.282
1985	Milwaukee	2B	143	523	63	133	15	4	5	44	11	.254
	Totals		981	3374	392	930	130	22	33	329	50	.276

TED HIGUERA 27 5-10 178 — Bats S Throws L

Invites comparison to Dodgers' Fernando Valenzuela . . . He's a native of Mexico and his middle name is Valenzuela . . . From July 2 through end of season, this rookie won 11 of 14 decisions . . . Established Milwaukee record for wins by a rookie with 15, two more than Bill Parsons . . . Came up with five pitches, but Brewers' coaches thought that was two too many and limited him to fastball, breaking ball and screwball . . . Has good velocity on fastball . . . Won six straight games between July 29 and Sept. 11, the longest winning streak by a Brewer since Moose Haas won eight in a row in 1983 . . . Started his streak with 7-6 record and 5.01 ERA and ended it with 13-6 record and 4.09 ERA . . . Born Nov. 9, 1958, in Los Mochis, Sinaloa, Mexico . . . Brewers purchased his contract from Juarez of Mexican League, where he led all pitchers with 222 innings and 165 strikeouts in 1983 . . . Finished second in voting for AL Rookie of the Year award.

Year	Club	G	IP	W	L	Pct.	SO	BB	H	ERA
1985	Milwaukee	32	212⅓	15	8	.652	127	63	186	3.90

MOOSE HAAS 29 6-0 170 — Bats R Throws R

Appeared to be on his way to outstanding season when he threw a one-hitter against Yankees June 29 . . . At the time, he was 7-3 with 2.33 ERA . . . But he was bothered by tendinitis in his arm the rest of the season and won only once more as his ERA rose to 3.84 . . . Threw a three-hitter against Toronto . . . Best month was May, when he was 4-0 with 2.67 ERA . . . Led AL with .813 winning percentage in 1983 . . . Full name is Bryan Edmond Haas . . . Born April 22, 1956, in Baltimore . . . Selected by Brewers in second round of June 1974 draft . . . An avid tennis player, he has black belt in Tae Kwon Do and is an amateur magician and certified locksmith.

Year	Club	G	IP	W	L	Pct.	SO	BB	H	ERA
1976	Milwaukee	5	16	0	1	.000	9	12	12	3.94
1977	Milwaukee	32	198	10	12	.455	113	84	195	4.32
1978	Milwaukee	7	31	2	3	.400	32	8	33	6.10
1979	Milwaukee	29	185	11	11	.500	95	59	198	4.77
1980	Milwaukee	33	252	16	15	.516	146	56	246	3.11
1981	Milwaukee	24	137	11	7	.611	64	40	145	4.47
1982	Milwaukee	32	193⅓	11	8	.579	104	39	232	4.47
1983	Milwaukee	25	179	13	3	.813	75	42	170	3.27
1984	Milwaukee	31	189⅓	9	11	.450	84	43	205	3.99
1985	Milwaukee	27	161⅔	8	8	.500	78	25	166	3.84
	Totals	245	1542⅓	91	79	.535	800	408	1602	4.03

Cecil Cooper fell one short of notching 100 RBI.

TOP PROSPECTS

JUAN NIEVES 21 6-3 175 **Bats L Throws L**
One of the most sought-after players in the country when he signed with Brewers as free agent in 1983 . . . Born Jan. 5, 1965, in Santurce, Puerto Rico, he went to prep school in Avon, Conn., where he was 19-1 with 1.05 ERA and 288 strikeouts in 196 innings . . . Threw a six-inning no-hitter in first pro start for Beloit (A) in 1983 . . . Started 1985 season at El Paso (AA), where he went 8-2 with 3.53 ERA . . . Was promoted to Vancouver (AAA), where he was 8-3 with 3.80 ERA . . . Has composite record of 33-9 in three-year pro career . . . Will be given a good chance to make Brewers in 1986.

MIKE FELDER 23 5-8 160 **Bats S Throws R**
Was called up in September after hitting .314 at Vancouver (AAA) and stealing 61 bases to win his fourth stolen-base title in five-year minor-league career . . . Speedy, switch-hitting outfielder hit .196 in 15 games with Brewers and stole four bases in five attempts . . . Born Nov. 18, 1962, in Richmond, Cal. . . . Brewers selected him in third round of January 1981 draft . . . Lists his hobbies as dancing and bowling.

MANAGER GEORGE BAMBERGER: Returned for his second tenure with Brewers and pulled them out of last place . . . Finished with 71-91 record, an improvement of four wins over 1984 finish under Rene Lachemann . . . Has retired twice in his career, leaving Milwaukee Sept. 8, 1980 and leaving the Mets June 2, 1983 . . . During his first stint with Brewers, he underwent a heart bypass operation . . . Played 18 years of pro baseball as a pitcher, but made only 10 major-league appearances, spanning 14 innings . . . Retired as player after 1963 . . . Harry Dalton, Milwaukee executive vice president, signed him to first managerial contract in 1978 with Brewers . . . Compiled .566 winning percentage on 235-180 record during first stay with Brewers . . . Laid groundwork for Brewers' pennant-winning team of 1982 . . . Born Aug. 1, 1925, in Staten Island, N.Y. . . . One of the most well-liked and colorful persons in baseball . . . Overall major-league managerial record is 388-398 . . . Served lengthy apprenticeship as Orioles' pitching coach.

GREATEST SHORTSTOP

In 1973, the Brewers used their first pick and the third selection overall in the June draft on a shortstop from Taft High School in Woodland Hills, Cal. That summer, he hit .285 for Newark in the New York-Penn League. He was voted the player most likely to make the majors. Robin Yount never played in another minor-league game after that.

Yount jumped from Class A to the Brewers in 1974. Since then, all he has done is establish himself as the Brewers' leader in games, at-bats, runs, hits, doubles, triples, extra-base hits and total bases.

Yount was never better than in 1982, when he was named the AL MVP and the Brewers won the pennant. Yount led the league in hits (210), doubles (46) and slugging percentage (.578) and batted .331 with 29 home runs and 114 RBI. He was the first shortstop in AL history to hit better than .300, belt more than 20 homers and drive in more than 100 runs. He excelled defensively, too, that season. Yount won his first Gold Glove while leading AL shortstops in assists.

Now 30, Yount has already played 12 full major-league seasons. The Brewers have relocated him to the outfield due to shoulder trouble, but Yount has easily established himself as the club's all-time best shortstop.

ALL-TIME BREWER SEASON RECORDS

BATTING: Cecil Cooper, .352, 1980
HRs: Gorman Thomas, 45, 1979
RBIs: Cecil Cooper, 126, 1983
STEALS: Paul Molitor, 41, 1982, 1983
WINS: Mike Caldwell, 22, 1978
STRIKEOUTS: Marty Pattin, 161, 1971

NEW YORK YANKEES

TEAM DIRECTORY: Principal Owner: George Steinbrenner III; Pres.: Eugene McHale; Adm. VP-Treas.: David Weidler; VP-GM: Clyde King; VP-Baseball Oper.: Woody Woodward; Dir. Minor League Oper.: Bobby Hofman; Dir. Scouting: Doug Melvin; Dir. Media Rel.: Joseph Safety; Trav. Sec.: Bill Kane; Mgr.: Lou Piniella. Home: Yankee Stadium (57,545). Field distances: 312, l.f. line; 379, l.f.; 411, l.c.; 410, c.f.; 385, r.c.; 310, r.f. line. Spring training: Fort Lauderdale, Fla.

SCOUTING REPORT

HITTING: With the legs of Rickey Henderson and the bats of Don Mattingly and Dave Winfield, no team can beat you in more ways than the Yankees. Henderson (.314, 24 homers, 80 stolen bases) is the catalyst, a leadoff hitter with that rare combination of speed and power. Mattingly (.324, 35 homers, 145 RBI) is merely the best overall hitter in the game. Another AL MVP season is not out of the question for the hard-working first baseman.

AL MVP Don Mattingly keeps getting more awesome.

Winfield (.275, 26 homers, 114 RBI) is still going strong at 34.

The Yankees pose a terrific lineup on paper, but have still some questions to answer. Can Mike Pagliarulo develop into a full-time third baseman by learning how to hit left-handers? Is Dan Pasqua (9 homers in 148 at-bats) ready for a full season in the big leagues? Can new manager Lou Piniella keep his overstocked bench happy? Piniella has to find time for Ken Griffey and former Oriole Gary Roenicke, among others.

PITCHING: Left-handed pitching has always been important in Yankee Stadium, where the deep dimensions in left center frustrate right-handed hitters. That was one of the reasons the Yankees were so intent on acquiring Britt Burns from the White Sox. Burns (18-11, 3.96) and Ron Guidry (22-6, 3.27) were two of the winningest left-handers in the AL last year. Guidry has learned how to mix in off-speed pitches with his fastball, which he can still pop at times. Phil Niekro (16-12, 4.09) and Joe Niekro (11-13 with Astros and Yanks) can still make hitters knuckle under.

One of Piniella's first moves as manager will be to give Dave Righetti a more clearly defined role out of the bullpen. Righetti (12-7, 2.78 ERA, 29 saves) was used for as much as four innings and as little as one batter by Billy Martin last year. Righetti will pitch no more than two innings per outing in 1986. If Brian Fisher (4-4, 2.38 ERA, 14 saves) continues to develop, the Yankees will have the best lefty-righty relief tandem in the AL.

FIELDING: Mattingly gained deserved recognition for his outstanding defense, winning the first of what will be many Gold Gloves for the first baseman. Second baseman Willie Randolph may have lost a step, but he still turns one of the smoothest double plays you'll ever see. Shortstop Bobby Meacham has great range, but tends to be erratic with his sidearm throws. Pagliarulo has soft hands and a good arm at third.

Winfield remains one of the premier outfielders in the game and his arm is rarely challenged. Henderson can outrun a lot of his mistakes in center, but teams do not hesitate to run on his arm. Butch Wynegar, plagued by injuries last season, is only adequate behind the plate.

OUTLOOK: The Yankees' story is a familiar one. They have the talent to win the division, based on the fact that they are slightly better than last year, when they won 97 games. But can they avoid self-destructing? No one knows how good a manager Piniella will be in his first managerial try. He is blessed with a talented club in his maiden year, but cursed by the pressures imposed by the club's owner and its fans.

NEW YORK YANKEES 1986 ROSTER

MANAGER Lou Piniella

Coaches—Joe Altobelli, Sammy Ellis, Stump Merrill, Gene Michael, Jeff Torborg, Roy White

PITCHERS

No.	Name	1985 Club	W-L	IP	SO	ERA	B-T	Ht.	Wt.	Born
53	Allen, Neil	St. Louis	1-4	29	10	5.59	R-R	6-2	190	1/24/58 Kansas City, KS
		New York (AL)	1-0	29	16	2.76				
36	Armstrong, Mike	Columbus	2-2	41	40	6.64	R-R	6-3	195	3/17/54 Glen Cove, NY
		New York (AL)	0-0	15	11	3.07				
40	Burns, Britt	Chicago (AL)	18-11	227	172	3.96	R-L	6-5	217	6/8/59 Houston, TX
50	Bystrom, Marty	Columbus	2-0	24	16	1.88	R-R	6-5	210	7/26/58 Coral Gables, FL
		New York (AL)	3-2	41	16	5.71				
46	Drabek, Doug	Albany	13-7	193	153	2.99	R-R	6-1	185	7/25/62 Victoria, TX
54	Fisher, Brian	Columbus	0-0	11	12	2.38	R-R	6-4	210	3/18/62 Honolulu, HI
		New York (AL)	4-4	98	85	2.38				
57	Fulton, Bill	Ft. Lauderdale	11-2	112	71	1.61	R-R	6-3	195	10/22/63 Pittsburgh, PA
52	George, Steve	Ft. Lauderdale	13-7	165	141	1.75	B-L	6-0	160	10/18/61 St. Louis, MO
49	Guidry, Ron	New York (AL)	22-6	259	143	3.27	L-L	5-11	157	8/28/50 Lafayette, LA
20	Niekro, Joe	Houston	9-12	213	117	3.72	R-R	6-1	195	11/7/44 Martins Ferry, OH
		New York (AL)	2-1	12	4	5.84				
35	Niekro, Phil	New York (AL)	16-12	220	149	4.09	R-R	6-1	193	4/1/39 Blaine, OH
45	Rasmussen, Dennis	Columbus	0-3	45	43	3.80	L-L	6-7	225	4/18/59 Los Angeles, CA
		New York (AL)	3-5	102	63	3.98				
19	Righetti, Dave	New York (AL)	12-7	107	92	2.78	L-L	6-3	198	11/28/58 San Jose, CA
28	Scurry, Rod	Pittsburgh	0-1	48	43	3.21	L-L	6-2	195	3/17/56 Sacramento, CA
		New York (AL)	1-0	13	17	2.84				
29	Shirley, Bob	New York (AL)	5-5	109	55	2.64	R-L	6-0	180	6/25/54 Cushing, OK
39	Tewksbury, Bob	Albany	6-5	107	63	3.54	R-R	6-4	180	11/30/60 Concord, NH
		Columbus	3-0	44	21	1.02				
38	Whitson, Ed	New York (AL)	10-8	159	89	4.88	R-R	6-3	195	5/19/55 Johnson City, TN

CATCHERS

No.	Name	1985 Club	H	HR	RBI	Pct.	B-T	Ht.	Wt.	Born
34	Bradley, Scott	Albany	3	0	2	.125	L-R	5-11	185	3/22/60 Essex Fells, NJ
		Columbus	49	4	27	.301				
		New York (AL)	8	0	1	.163				
58	Espino, Juan	Columbus	56	3	20	.250	R-R	6-1	190	3/16/56 Dominican Republic
		New York (AL)	4	0	0	.364				
22	Lombardi, Phil	Albany	64	5	32	.256	R-R	6-2	200	2/20/63 Abilene, TX
59	Lyden, Mitch	Ft. Lauderdale	102	10	58	.255	R-R	6-3	200	12/14/64 Portland, OR
27	Wynegar, Butch	New York (AL)	69	5	32	.223	B-R	6-1	194	3/14/56 York, PA

INFIELDERS

No.	Name	1985 Club	H	HR	RBI	Pct.	B-T	Ht.	Wt.	Born
2	Berra, Dale	New York (AL)	25	1	8	.230	R-R	6-0	190	12/13/56 Ridgewood, NJ
55	Bonilla, Juan	Columbus	128	1	52	.330	R-R	5-9	170	2/12/56 Puerto Rico
		New York (AL)	2	0	2	.125				
61	Destrade, Orestes	Albany	119	23	72	.253	B-R	6-4	210	5/8/62 Cuba
—	Fischlin, Mike	Cleveland	12	0	2	.200	R-R	6-1	166	9/13/55 Sacramento, CA
23	Mattingly, Don	New York (AL)	211	35	145	.324	L-L	5-11	185	4/20/61 Evansville, IN
20	Meacham, Bobby	New York (AL)	105	1	47	.218	B-R	6-1	180	8/25/60 Los Angeles, CA
6	Pagliarulo, Mike	New York (AL)	91	19	62	.239	L-R	6-2	195	3/15/60 Medford, MA
30	Randolph, Willie	New York (AL)	137	5	40	.276	R-R	5-11	166	7/6/54 Holly Hill, SC
18	Robertson, Andre	Columbus	11	0	1	.393	R-R	5-10	162	10/2/57 Orange, TX
		New York (AL)	41	2	17	.328				
—	Sosa, Miguel	Richmond	83	14	49	.192	R-R	5-10	165	5/15/60 Dominican Republic

OUTFIELDERS

No.	Name	1985 Club	H	HR	RBI	Pct.	B-T	Ht.	Wt.	Born
25	Baylor, Don	New York (AL)	110	23	91	.231	R-R	6-1	210	6/28/48 Austin, TX
46	Cotto, Henry	Columbus	70	7	36	.257	R-R	6-2	178	1/5/61 Bronx, NY
		New York (AL)	17	1	6	.304				
33	Griffey, Ken	New York (AL)	120	10	69	.274	L-L	6-0	200	4/10/50 Donora, PA
24	Henderson, Rickey	Ft. Lauderdale	1	0	3	.167	R-L	5-10	195	12/25/58 Chicago, IL
		New York (AL)	172	24	72	.314				
3	Hernandez, Leo	Rochester	128	17	69	.269	R-R	5-11	220	11/6/59 Venezuela
		Baltimore	1	0	0	.048				
17	Mata, Vic	New York (AL)	1	0	0	.143	R-R	6-1	165	6/17/61Dominican Republic
		Columbus	98	3	27	.261				
21	Pasqua, Dan	Columbus	92	18	69	.321	L-L	6-0	203	10/17/61 Yonkers, NY
		New York (AL)	31	9	25	.209				
—	Roenicke, Gary	Baltimore	49	15	43	.218	R-R	6-3	201	12/5/54 Covina, CA
31	Winfield, Dave	New York (AL)	174	26	114	.275	R-R	6-6	220	10/3/51 St. Paul, MN

YANKEE PROFILES

DON MATTINGLY 24 5-11 185 Bats L Throws L

Felt he was given raw deal when owner George Steinbrenner exercised right to renew his contract after a long negotiating battle prior to last season . . . It didn't stop him from enjoying a tremendous 1984 campaign . . . Led majors in RBI (145) and doubles (48) . . . Finished third in AL batting race (.324), fourth in homers (35), second in slugging percentage (.567), second in hits (211), first in game-winning RBI (21) and first in fielding percentage among first basemen (.995) . . . His RBI total was most by a Yankee since Joe DiMaggio drove in 155 in 1948 and he was first Yankee to lead league in RBI since Roger Maris in 1961 . . . Had most hits by a Yankee since Red Rolfe had 213 in 1939 . . . Became first Yankee to collect 200 hits in consecutive seasons since DiMaggio in 1936-37 . . . Became first AL player to lead majors in doubles for two straight seasons since Tris Speaker did it from 1920-23 . . . Blessed with natural hitting ability, he also is one of hardest workers around . . . Was not chosen until 19th round of June 1979 draft, because most organizations had assumed he would attend college . . . Born April 20, 1961, in Evansville, Ind. . . . Brother Randy was pro football player . . . Named AL MVP last season, outdistancing Royals' George Brett . . . Edged teammate Dave Winfield for AL batting title in 1984 by collecting four hits in season finale.

Year	Club	Pos.	G	AB	R	H	2B	3B	HR	RBI	SB	Avg.
1982	New York (AL)	OF-1B	7	12	0	2	0	0	0	1	0	.167
1983	New York (AL)	OF-1B-2B	91	279	34	79	15	4	4	32	0	.283
1984	New York (AL)	1B-OF	153	603	91	207	44	2	23	110	1	.343
1985	New York (AL)	1B	159	652	107	211	48	3	35	145	2	.324
	Totals		410	1546	232	499	107	9	62	288	3	.323

DAVE WINFIELD 34 6-6 220 Bats R Throws R

Enjoyed truce in war of words with George Steinbrenner, until Yankees' owner popped off during key September series against Toronto and called him "Mr. May" . . . His average dipped 65 points from 1984 level, but he drove in 114 runs, the third-highest total in AL . . . Became first Yankee to drive in 100 or more runs in four consecutive seasons since Yogi Berra in 1953-56 . . . Became first Yankee to drive in 100 runs and score 100 runs in two straight seasons since Joe DiMaggio in 1941-42

. . . Committed only three errors in right field for a .991 fielding percentage, the fourth-best mark among outfielders who played at least 140 games, and had 13 assists . . . Never played a minor-league game . . . San Diego made him fourth player picked overall in June 1973 draft . . . Signed a 10-year contract with Yankees as a re-entry free agent prior to the 1981 season . . . Helped Yankees to AL pennant in 1981, but hit .045 in six World Series games . . . Born Oct. 3, 1951, in St. Paul, Minn. . . . Attended Minnesota . . . Was drafted by Padres in baseball, Minnesota Vikings (NFL) in football, Utah Stars (ABA) and Atlanta Hawks (NBA) in basketball . . . Had 19 game-winning RBI in 1985.

Year	Club	Pos.	G	AB	R	H	2B	3B	HR	RBI	SB	Avg.
1973	San Diego	OF-1B	56	141	9	39	4	1	3	12	0	.277
1974	San Diego	OF	145	498	57	132	18	4	20	75	9	.265
1975	San Diego	OF	143	509	74	136	20	2	15	76	23	.267
1976	San Diego	OF	137	492	81	139	26	4	13	69	26	.283
1977	San Diego	OF	157	615	104	169	29	7	25	92	16	.275
1978	San Diego	OF-1B	158	587	88	181	30	5	24	97	21	.308
1979	San Diego	OF	159	597	97	184	27	10	34	118	15	.308
1980	San Diego	OF	162	558	89	154	25	6	20	87	23	.276
1981	New York (AL) . .	OF	105	388	52	114	25	1	13	68	11	.294
1982	New York (AL) . .	OF	140	539	84	151	24	8	37	106	5	.280
1983	New York (AL) . .	OF	152	598	99	169	26	8	32	116	15	.283
1984	New York (AL) . .	OF	141	567	106	193	34	4	19	100	6	.340
1985	New York (AL) . .	OF	155	633	105	174	34	6	26	114	18	.275
	Totals		1810	6722	1045	1935	322	66	281	1130	188	.288

RICKEY HENDERSON 27 5-10 195 Bats R Throws L

Yankees gave up five players to get this offensive catalyst and he responded with his best season . . . Stole 80 bases to lead AL and break Yankee record of 74, set by Fritz Maisel in 1914 . . . Missed the first 10 games while recovering from an ankle sprain suffered in spring training . . . Struggled at the plate in his first month, then took off on a tear that carried through All-Star break . . . Was AL Player of the Month in June, when he hit .416 with 31 runs, six homers, 17 RBI and 22 stolen bases . . . Was hitting .357 at All-Star break, then tailed off . . . His 24 homers and 72 RBI were career highs . . . Finished fourth in AL in batting (.314), first in runs (146), fourth in on-base percentage (.419) and fourth in walks (99) . . . Moved from left field to center in 1985 and his defense went from Gold Glove quality to slightly better than adequate, as he committed nine errors . . . Acquired from Oakland with Bert Bradley for Jay Howell, Tim Birtsas, Eric Plunk, Jose Rijo and Stan Javier prior to last season . . . Born Christmas Day, 1958, in Chicago . . . Has led AL in stolen bases five straight seasons . . . An All-Star selection in five of his six full seasons . . . Holds all-time single-season stolen-base record with 130 in 1982

... Was an outstanding running back in high school, receiving numerous scholarship offers.

Year	Club	Pos.	G	AB	R	H	2B	3B	HR	RBI	SB	Avg.
1979	Oakland..........	OF	89	351	49	96	13	3	1	26	33	.274
1980	Oakland..........	OF	158	591	111	179	22	4	9	53	100	.303
1981	Oakland..........	OF	108	423	89	135	18	7	6	35	56	.319
1982	Oakland..........	OF	149	536	119	143	24	4	10	51	130	.267
1983	Oakland..........	OF	145	513	105	150	25	7	9	48	108	.292
1984	Oakland..........	OF	142	502	113	147	27	4	16	58	66	.293
1985	New York (AL)	OF	143	547	146	172	28	5	24	72	80	.314
	Totals		934	3463	732	1022	157	34	75	343	573	.295

WILLIE RANDOLPH 31 5-11 166 — Bats R Throws R

Smooth second baseman enjoyed another consistent season, hitting .276 ... Finished sixth in AL in on-base percentage and tied for seventh in walks ... Hit five homers and drove in 40 runs, his best output in production departments since 1980 ... Hit two of those homers in one game, against Oakland Sept. 5 ... Committed 11 errors, but none after July 30 ... Missed 13 games in September with pulled hamstring ... One of the classiest acts in baseball, on the field and in the clubhouse ... Born July 6, 1954, in Holly Hill, S.C., but grew up in Brooklyn, N.Y. ... Has .158 average in 57 at-bats during three World Series ... Brother Terry was drafted by Green Bay Packers and played for Jets.

Year	Club	Pos.	G	AB	R	H	2B	3B	HR	RBI	SB	Avg.
1975	Pittsburgh	2B-3B	30	61	9	10	1	0	0	3	1	.164
1976	New York (AL) ..	2B	125	430	59	115	15	4	1	40	37	.267
1977	New York (AL) ..	2B	147	551	91	151	28	11	4	40	13	.274
1978	New York (AL) ..	2B	134	499	87	139	18	6	3	42	36	.279
1979	New York (AL) ..	2B	153	574	98	155	15	13	5	61	33	.270
1980	New York (AL) ..	2B	138	513	99	151	23	7	7	46	30	.294
1981	New York (AL) ..	2B	93	357	59	83	14	3	2	24	14	.232
1982	New York (AL) ..	2B	144	553	85	155	21	4	3	36	16	.280
1983	New York (AL) ..	2B	104	420	73	117	21	1	2	38	12	.279
1984	New York (AL) ..	2B	142	564	86	162	24	2	2	31	10	.287
1985	New York (AL) ..	2B	143	497	75	137	21	2	5	40	16	.276
	Totals		1353	5019	821	1375	201	53	34	401	218	.274

KEN GRIFFEY 35 6-0 200 — Bats L Throws L

His 1985 season will be remembered for his terrific, wall-climbing, game-saving robbery of apparent home run off bat of Red Sox' Marty Barrett Aug. 19 ... A career .300 hitter, although he has failed to reach that mark in three of his four seasons with Yankees ... Left fielder began last season by hitting in first eight games and enjoyed a good May, when his average reached .310 . . . Hit a grand slam May 14 . . . Average tailed off to .274 . . . Brooded at times and requested a trade . . . Bothered by sore knees . . . Drove in 69 runs, his best total since 1980 . . . Impending free agency prompted Reds to deal him for Brian Ryder and Fred Toliver prior to 1982 season . . . Was not picked until 29th round of June 1969 draft, when Reds tabbed him . . . Has played in two World Series, posting .186 average in 11 games . . . Born April 10, 1950, in Donora, Pa., the birthplace of Stan Musial.

Year	Club	Pos.	G	AB	R	H	2B	3B	HR	RBI	SB	Avg.
1973	Cincinnati	OF	25	86	19	33	5	1	3	14	4	.384
1974	Cincinnati	OF	88	227	24	57	9	5	2	19	9	.251
1975	Cincinnati	OF	132	463	95	141	15	9	4	46	16	.305
1976	Cincinnati	OF	148	562	111	189	28	9	6	74	34	.336
1977	Cincinnati	OF	154	585	117	186	35	8	12	57	17	.318
1978	Cincinnati	OF	158	614	90	177	33	8	10	63	23	.288
1979	Cincinnati	OF	95	380	62	120	27	4	8	32	12	.316
1980	Cincinnati	OF	146	544	89	160	28	10	13	85	23	.294
1981	Cincinnati	OF	101	396	65	123	21	6	2	34	12	.311
1982	New York (AL)	OF	127	484	70	134	23	2	12	54	10	.277
1983	New York (AL)	OF-1B	118	458	60	140	21	3	11	46	6	.306
1984	New York (AL)	OF-1B	120	399	44	109	20	1	7	56	2	.273
1985	New York (AL)	OF-1B	127	438	68	120	28	4	10	69	7	.274
	Totals		1539	5636	914	1689	293	70	100	649	175	.300

RON GUIDRY 35 5-11 157 **Bats L Throws L**

Enjoyed successful comeback season after altering his pitching style to include more off-speed pitches . . . Still has a good fastball at times, but it's not the consistently hard one that helped him to a unanimous selection as AL Cy Young Award winner in 1978, when he was 25-3 . . . Had first losing season of career in 1984, but rebounded with 22-6 record last season . . . Led AL in wins and winning percentage (.786) . . . Was fifth in innings pitched (259) and seventh in ERA (3.27) . . . Reeled off 12 straight victories between May 4 and July 31 . . . Was 10-0 with 2.42 ERA during the day and 12-6 with 3.63 ERA at night . . . Went 13-2 with 2.82 ERA at home and 9-4 with 3.77 ERA on the road . . . Flourished under Billy Martin, just as he has done his entire career . . . Has gone 84-25 under Martin and 70-43 under other Yankee managers . . . Became first Yankee to win 20 games three times since Mel Stottlemyre in 1965, 1968 and 1969 . . . Recognized as an outstanding athlete, he has won two Gold Gloves and plays a mean center field during batting practice . . . "Louisiana Lightning" was born Aug. 28, 1950, in Lafayette, La . . . Yankees'

third-round pick in June 1971 draft . . . Has 5-2 record in post-season play and extraordinary 154-68 career mark.

Year	Club	G	IP	W	L	Pct.	SO	BB	H	ERA
1975	New York (AL)	10	16	0	1	.000	15	9	15	3.38
1976	New York (AL)	7	16	0	0	.000	12	4	20	5.63
1977	New York (AL)	31	211	16	7	.696	176	65	174	2.82
1978	New York (AL)	35	274	25	3	.893	248	72	187	1.74
1979	New York (AL)	33	236	18	8	.692	201	71	203	2.78
1980	New York (AL)	37	220	17	10	.630	166	80	215	3.56
1981	New York (AL)	23	127	11	5	.688	104	26	100	2.76
1982	New York (AL)	34	222	14	8	.636	162	69	216	3.81
1983	New York (AL)	31	250⅓	21	9	.700	156	60	232	3.42
1984	New York (AL)	29	195⅔	10	11	.476	127	44	223	4.51
1985	New York (AL)	34	259	22	6	.786	143	42	243	3.27
	Totals	304	2027	154	68	.694	1510	542	1828	3.17

DAVE RIGHETTI 27 6-3 198 **Bats L Throws L**

Turned in another outstanding season in his second year as a reliever . . . Saved 29 games, two fewer than in 1984, but his total was fifth-best in AL last season . . . Appeared in club-record 74 games, third-highest figure in league . . . Suffered dislocated toe in Anaheim May 17 and promptly went into a slump . . . In 13 games between May 25 and June 20, he was 1-4 with two saves while allowing 14 earned runs in 17⅓ innings . . . During that span, he allowed four of the five homers he surrendered in 1985 . . . His ERA at the end of that stretch was 3.66 . . . Lost only one more game after that and lowered ERA to 2.78 . . . Allowed no earned runs from Aug. 9 to Aug. 31, a stretch spanning 13 games and 17⅔ innings . . . Remains center of controversy as debate rages about whether he should start or relieve . . . Showed great potential as a starter in 1983, when he was 14-8 and threw a no-hitter vs. Red Sox on July 4, the birthday of the nation and George Steinbrenner . . . Was teammate of Blue Jays' Dave Stieb at San Jose City College . . . Born Nov. 28, 1958, in San Jose, Cal. . . . Rangers made him ninth player selected overall in January 1977 draft . . . Traded to Yankees with Mike Griffin, Paul Mirabella, Juan Beniquez and Greg Jemison for Sparky Lyle, Larry McCall and Dave Rajsich prior to 1979 season.

Year	Club	G	IP	W	L	Pct.	SO	BB	H	ERA
1979	New York (AL)	3	17	0	1	.000	13	10	10	3.71
1981	New York (AL)	15	105	8	4	.667	89	38	75	2.06
1982	New York (AL)	33	183	11	10	.524	163	108	155	3.79
1983	New York (AL)	31	217	14	8	.636	169	67	194	3.44
1984	New York (AL)	64	96⅓	5	6	.455	90	37	79	2.34
1985	New York (AL)	74	107	12	7	.632	92	45	96	2.78
	Totals	220	725⅓	50	36	.581	616	305	609	3.09

BRITT BURNS 26 6-5 217 **Bats R Throws L**

The lefty pitcher the Yankees had sought since the end of the '85 season, Burns came from the White Sox with minor leaguers Mike Soper and Glen Braxton in deal for Joe Cowley and Ron Hassey . . . Fell two wins short of 20 victories when he lost his last three starts, allowing 17 earned runs in 11 innings . . . His 18 wins still represented a career high . . . Had four shutouts, tying him for second spot in AL in that department . . . Had three shutouts against Cleveland and combined for another against Indians . . . Went 21⅓ innings without giving up a run during one stretch . . . Bothered by sore hip most of the season, though he did not miss any starts because of the injury . . . Born June 8, 1959, in Houston . . . Selected by White Sox in third round of June 1978 draft . . . Sox learned about him when a former Chicago Tribune book critic read an article about his high-school heroics in Birmingham, Ala., and mailed it to White Sox president Bill Veeck . . . Was 35-2 with 0.12 ERA in high school . . . Pitched in only 37 minor-league games before sticking with White Sox for good in 1980.

Year	Club	G	IP	W	L	Pct.	SO	BB	H	ERA
1978	Chicago (AL)	2	8	0	2	.000	3	3	14	12.38
1979	Chicago (AL)	6	5	0	0	.000	2	1	10	5.40
1980	Chicago (AL)	34	238	15	13	.536	133	63	213	2.84
1981	Chicago (AL)	24	157	10	6	.625	108	49	139	2.64
1982	Chicago (AL)	28	169	13	5	.722	116	67	168	4.04
1983	Chicago (AL)	29	174	10	11	.476	115	55	165	3.58
1984	Chicago (AL)	34	117	4	12	.250	85	45	130	5.00
1985	Chicago (AL)	36	227	18	11	.621	172	79	206	3.96
	Totals	193	1095	70	60	.538	734	362	1045	3.66

PHIL NIEKRO 46 6-1 193 **Bats R Throws R**

After four failed attempts, he finally notched career victory No. 300 on final day of last season, with a shutout against Toronto . . . Did not throw his famed knuckleball until striking out Jeff Burroughs for final out of that game . . . Was his only shutout of season and 45th of his career as he became oldest player ever to throw one . . . Became 18th pitcher to reach 300 club . . . Gave up 29 homers in 1985, nearly double his 1984 total of 15 . . . Won 16 games for second straight season . . . Atlanta owner Ted Turner figured he was through after 1983, but Turner has since admitted his mistake, retired the pitcher's No. 35 and erected a statue in his honor . . . His career record is 300-250 . . . Has won four Gold Gloves . . . Threw a no-hitter against San Diego in 1973 . . . Born on April Fools' Day, 1939, in Blaine, Ohio . . . Signed as free agent by Milwaukee Braves in 1958 . . . Was a high-school teammate of former Boston Celtics great John Havlicek . . . Has often been mentioned as a managerial candidate . . . Destroyed phone booth after one of his unsuccessful attempts at No. 300.

Year	Club	G	IP	W	L	Pct.	SO	BB	H	ERA
1964	Milwaukee	10	15	0	0	.000	8	7	15	4.80
1965	Milwaukee	41	75	2	3	.400	40	26	73	2.88
1966	Atlanta	28	50	4	3	.571	17	23	48	4.14
1967	Atlanta	46	207	11	9	.550	129	55	164	1.87
1968	Atlanta	37	257	14	12	.538	140	45	228	2.50
1969	Atlanta	40	284	23	13	.639	193	57	235	2.57
1970	Atlanta	34	230	12	18	.400	168	68	222	4.27
1971	Atlanta	42	269	15	14	.517	173	70	248	2.98
1972	Atlanta	38	282	16	12	.571	164	53	254	3.06
1973	Atlanta	42	245	13	10	.565	131	89	214	3.31
1974	Atlanta	41	302	20	13	.606	195	88	249	2.38
1975	Atlanta	39	276	15	15	.500	144	72	285	3.20
1976	Atlanta	38	271	17	11	.607	173	101	249	3.29
1977	Atlanta	44	330	16	20	.444	262	164	315	4.04
1978	Atlanta	44	334	19	18	.514	248	102	295	2.88
1979	Atlanta	44	342	21	20	.512	208	113	311	3.39
1980	Atlanta	40	275	15	18	.455	176	85	256	3.63
1981	Atlanta	22	139	7	7	.500	62	56	120	3.11
1982	Atlanta	35	234⅓	17	4	.810	144	73	225	3.61
1983	Atlanta	34	201⅔	11	10	.524	128	105	212	3.97
1984	New York (AL)	32	215⅔	16	8	.667	136	76	219	3.09
1985	New York (AL)	33	220	16	12	.571	149	120	203	4.09
	Totals	804	5054⅔	300	250	.545	3197	1648	4640	3.23

BRIAN FISHER 23 6-4 210 — Bats R Throws R

Opened eyes in spring training with his 93-mph fastball and hard slider . . . Shipped to Columbus (AAA) to start season, he was soon recalled and came through with an outstanding rookie year . . . Collected 14 saves and allowed only four homers in 98⅓ innings as Yankee . . . Had control problems as starter in Atlanta organization, but they vanished when he was switched to bullpen by Yankees last season . . . Struck out 85 and walked only 29 . . . Opponents hit only .216 against him, the best mark among Yankee pitchers . . . In his last 14 games, he was 0-1 with seven saves, allowing six runs in 23⅔ innings . . . All those runs came in ninth inning of disastrous outing against Cleveland Sept. 16 . . . Born March 18, 1962, in Honolulu, Hawaii . . . Grew up in Colorado . . . Was obtained from Braves for Rick Cerone prior to last season . . . Became first Yankee to wear uniform No. 54 since Rich Gossage—and it fit him nicely.

Year	Club	G	IP	W	L	Pct.	SO	BB	H	ERA
1985	New York (AL)	55	98⅓	4	4	.500	85	29	77	2.38

TOP PROSPECTS

SCOTT BRADLEY 25 5-11 185 Bats L Throws R

Voted the outstanding rookie in spring camp last year, when he made Yankees because of his versatility and consistent hitting . . . But his season received a jolt when he broke a finger in a collision at home plate in May . . . Was put on minor-league rehabilitation program before being recalled by Yankees late in the season . . . Hit .163 in 19 games with Yankees . . . Primarily a catcher, he can play first base, third base and outfield . . . Was named International League MVP in 1984, when he hit .335 with 84 RBI for Columbus (AAA) . . . Does not have home-run power, but has a good, short stroke and rarely strikes out . . . Born March 22, 1960, in Essex Fells, N.J. . . . Attended North Carolina and was second-round pick by Yankees in June 1981 draft.

DAN PASQUA 24 6-0 205 Bats L Throws L

Shuttled between Columbus (AAA) and Yankees in 1985, though he may have earned a permanent 1986 spot on big club with his power . . . Hit .321 with 18 homers and 69 RBI in 287 at-bats for Columbus last year . . . Crushed nine homers and drove in 25 runs in 148 at-bats with Yankees . . . Batted only .209 for Yanks, but club believes left fielder has the swing to hit for decent average, too . . . Has stroke that is tailor-made for Yankee Stadium's short porch in right . . . Born Oct. 17, 1961, in Yonkers, N.Y. . . . Picked by Yankees in third round of June 1982 draft . . . Hit 33 homers for Nashville (AA) in 1984.

MANAGER LOU PINIELLA: Although he has no managerial

experience, he took over the hottest seat in baseball when he replaced Billy Martin following 97-64 finish last season . . . George Steinbrenner insisted that general manager Clyde King and vice president Woody Woodward made decision to hire this guy without consulting the Boss . . . Retired as player June 17, 1984 . . . Hit .291 in 1,747 career games . . . Signed by Cleveland in 1962, he was drafted by Washington Senators later that year . . . Traded to Baltimore in 1964 and then to Cleveland in 1966 . . . Selected by expansionist Seattle Pilots in 1968 and traded by Pilots to Royals in 1969 . . . Finally, in his first full major-league season, he won AL Rookie of the Year Award for KC in 1969 . . . Outfielder was traded to Yankees with Ken Wright for Lindy McDaniel prior to 1974 season . . . Spent his last 11 years with New York and hit .295 . . . "Sweet Lou" won hearts of fans with animated play . . . Batted .305 in five ALCS and .319 in four World Series . . . Born Aug. 28, 1943, in Tampa . . . Won Steinbrenner's admiration as player, but can he keep it as Yankee manager?

GREATEST SHORTSTOP

Phil Rizzuto played all 13 of his major-league seasons in a New York Yankee uniform. In nine of those seasons, the Yankees reached the World Series. The club's success was in large part due to the leadership of Rizzuto, a small man who played a large role.

Rizzuto, who was 5-6, 150 pounds, was nicknamed "The Scooter." He hit .273 in his career and was never better than in 1950, when he was named the AL MVP. Rizzuto hit a career-high .324 with 66 RBI that year.

Rizzuto won the shortstop job in 1941 from Frank Crosetti, also one of the finest Yankee shortstops. Crosetti played on seven pennant-winning clubs in his 17-year career, all with the Yankees. He finished with a .245 lifetime batting average and played 1,515 games at shortstop. Neither Crosetti nor Rizzuto has been elected to the Hall of Fame, though Rizzuto has received lots of support in recent years.

ALL-TIME YANKEE SEASON RECORDS

BATTING: Babe Ruth, .393, 1923
HRs: Roger Maris, 61, 1961
RBIs: Lou Gehrig, 184, 1931
STEALS: Rickey Henderson, 80, 1985
WINS: Jack Chesbro, 41, 1904
STRIKEOUTS: Ron Guidry, 248, 1978

TORONTO BLUE JAYS

TEAM DIRECTORY: Chairman: R. Howard Webster; Vice-Chairman/Chief Exec. Off: N.E. (Peter) Hardy; Exec. VP-Baseball: Pat Gillick; VP-Bus. Oper.: Paul Beeston; VP-Baseball: Al LaMacchia; VP-Baseball: Bob Mattick; VP-Finance: Bob Nicholson; Dir. Pub. Rel.: Howard Starkman; Trav. Sec.: Ken Carson; Mgr.: Jimy Williams. Home: Exhibition Stadium (43,737). Field Distances: 330, l.f. line; 375, l.c.; 400, c.f.; 375, r.c.; 330, r.f. line. Spring training: Dunedin, Fla.

SCOUTING REPORT

HITTING: The important thing to remember about the Blue Jays is that, although they won the AL East, most of their players have yet to reach their potential. Outside of Ernie Whitt (.245, 19 homers, 64 RBI), few players had career years in 1985. There were even some disappointments, including first baseman Willie Upshaw (.275, 15 homers, 65 RBI). So the Blue Jays may actually be a better hitting team in 1986, especially if young players like Tony Fernandez (.289) continue to develop.

The third-base platoon of Rance Mulliniks (.295) and Garth

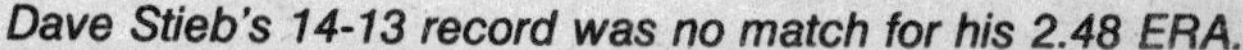

Dave Stieb's 14-13 record was no match for his 2.48 ERA.

Iorg (.313) has worked out just fine. It may even convince new manager Jimy Williams to give more playing time to right-handed-hitting Cecil Fielder (.311 in 30 games) at first base. Toronto could benefit from Fielder's home-run power in Exhibition Stadium. The Blue Jays can expect continued production from outfielders George Bell (.275, 28 homers, 95 RBI), Jesse Barfield (.289, 27 homers, 84 RBI) and Lloyd Moseby (.259, 18 homers, 70 RBI). Toronto has a well-balanced offense, the kind that helps avoid long losing streaks because the burden of run production is shared by so many players.

PITCHING: Why doesn't Dave Stieb win more? It's fast becoming the mystery of two countries. Stieb won the AL ERA title with a 2.48 mark, but was 14-13 in 1985. He has one of the best sliders in the game, but has not been able to control his emotions as well as his pitches.

By contrast, some are wondering why Doyle Alexander wins so often. He was 17-10 with a 3.45 ERA last year with his variety of junk pitches, including a knuckler. Jimmy Key (14-6, 3.00) and Jim Clancy (9-6, 3.78) give Toronto solid front-line pitching. But the Blue Jays' improvement last year was due mainly to their bullpen, although imports Gary Lavelle and Bill Caudill hardly produced what was expected from them. The pleasant surprises included Dennis Lamp (11-0, 3.32), Jim Acker (7-2, 3.23, 10 saves) and Tom Henke (3-3, 2.03 ERA, 13 saves). Toronto's weakness has quickly developed into one of its greatest strengths.

FIELDING: Fernandez has fast gained a reputation as one of the smoothest fielding shortstops in the AL. So why did he commit 30 errors last year? Fernandez tends to sling the ball underhanded and he sometimes rushes throws unnecessarily. The tools are there, though. Look for his error totals to decrease as he matures.

The Blue Jays are strong at third base, where Mulliniks led all players with a .971 fielding percentage, and in right, where the strong-armed Barfield led all outfielders with 22 assists. The biggest question is at catcher, where Buck Martinez must battle back from a broken leg.

OUTLOOK: Five years, five different winners—that's the way it has been in the AL East. Past history dictates that the Blue Jays can't be favored, but Toronto does have strong enough pitching to repeat. This is a team with very few holes. The most glaring question is in the dugout, where Williams takes over for Bobby Cox. If Stieb develops into a winner and the bullpen duplicates the job it did in 1985, the Blue Jays can make it two straight titles.

TORONTO BLUE JAYS 1986 ROSTER

MANAGER Jimy Williams

Coaches—Cito Gaston, John McLaren, Billy Smith, John Sullivan, Al Widmar

PITCHERS

No.	Name	1985 Club	W-L	IP	SO	ERA	B-T	Ht.	Wt.	Born
31	Acker, Jim	Toronto	7-2	86	42	3.23	R-R	6-2	212	9/24/58 Freer, TX
33	Alexander, Doyle	Toronto	17-10	261	142	3.45	R-R	6-3	200	9/4/50 Cordova, AL
32	Aquino, Luis	Knoxville	5-7	83	82	2.60	R-R	6-0	155	5/19/65 Puerto Rico
36	Caudill, Bill	Toronto	4-6	69	46	2.99	R-R	6-1	225	7/13/56 Santa Monica, CA
55	Cerutti, John	Syracuse	11-9	182	110	2.97	L-L	6-2	195	4/28/60 Albany, NY
		Toronto	0-2	7	5	5.40				
18	Clancy, Jim	Knoxville	1-0	8	2	3.38	R-R	6-4	215	12/18/55 Chicago, IL
		Toronto	9-6	129	66	3.78				
34	Clarke, Stan	Syracuse	14-4	118	98	3.37	R-L	6-1	180	8/9/60 Toledo, OH
		Toronto	0-0	4	2	4.50				
25	Davis, Steve	Knoxville	17-6	154	107	2.45	L-L	6-1	170	8/4/60 San Antonio, TX
		Syracuse	3-2	36	34	2.50				
		Toronto	2-1	28	22	3.54				
—	DeJesus, Jose	Fort Myers	8-10	130	94	4.30	R-R	6-5	177	1/6/65 Brooklyn, NY
49	Filer, Tom	Syracuse	7-2	78	31	2.53	R-R	6-1	198	12/1/56 Philadelphia, PA
		Toronto	7-0	49	24	3.88				
—	Gordon, Don	Syracuse	8-5	113	43	2.07	R-R	6-1	175	10/10/59 New York, NY
50	Henke, Tom	Syracuse	2-1	51	60	0.88	R-R	6-5	215	12/21/57 Kansas City, MO
		Toronto	3-3	40	42	2.03				
22	Key, Jimmy	Toronto	14-6	213	85	3.00	R-L	6-1	185	4/22/61 Huntsville, AL
53	Lamp, Dennis	Toronto	11-0	106	68	3.32	R-R	6-3	215	9/23/52 Los Angeles, CA
46	Lavelle, Gary	Toronto	5-7	73	50	3.10	R-L	6-1	217	1/3/49 Scranton, PA
48	Leal, Luis	Toronto	3-6	67	33	5.75	R-R	6-3	220	3/21/57 Venezuela
		Syracuse	6-2	69	43	3.91				
37	Stieb, Dave	Toronto	14-13	265	167	2.48	R-R	6-1	195	7/22/57 Santa Ana, CA

CATCHERS

No.	Name	1985 Club	H	HR	RBI	Pct.	B-T	Ht.	Wt.	Born
27	DeWillis, Jeff	Kinston	16	1	8	.184	R-R	6-2	170	4/13/65 Houston, TX
		Knoxville	43	2	22	.219				
		Syracuse	11	1	3	.229				
54	Hearron, Jeff	Knoxville	29	5	14	.223	R-R	6-1	195	11/19/61 Long Beach, CA
		Toronto	1	0	0	.143				
13	Martinez, Buck	Toronto	16	4	14	.162	R-R	5-11	200	11/7/48 Redding, CA
38	*Nicosia, Steve	Montreal	12	0	1	.169	R-R	5-10	185	8/6/55 Paterson, NJ
		Toronto	4	0	1	.267				
12	Whitt, Ernie	Toronto	101	19	64	.245	L-R	6-2	200	6/13/52 Detroit, MI

INFIELDERS

No.	Name	1985 Club	H	HR	RBI	Pct.	B-T	Ht.	Wt.	Born
1	Fernandez, Tony	Toronto	163	2	51	.289	B-R	6-2	165	8/6/62 Dominican Republic
23	Fielder, Cecil	Knoxville	106	18	81	.294	R-R	6-3	217	9/21/63 Los Angeles, CA
		Toronto	23	4	16	.311				
7	Garcia, Damaso	Toronto	169	8	65	.282	R-R	6-0	175	2/7/57 Dominican Republic
17	Gruber, Kelly	Syracuse	118	21	69	.249	R-R	6-0	180	2/26/62 Houston, TX
		Toronto	3	0	1	.231				
16	Iorg, Garth	Toronto	90	7	37	.313	R-R	5-11	170	10/12/54 Arcata, CA
14	Infante, Alexis	Syracuse	109	2	39	.241	R-R	5-10	175	12/4/62 Venezuela
00	Johnson, Cliff	Tex.-Tor.	96	13	66	.260	R-R	6-4	225	7/22/47 San Antonio, TX
4	Lee, Manny	Toronto	8	0	0	.200	B-R	5-9	150	6/17/65 Dominican Republic
19	McGriff, Fred	Syracuse	40	5	20	.227	L-L	6-3	200	10/31/63 Tampa, FL
5	Mulliniks, Rance	Toronto	109	10	57	.295	L-R	6-0	170	1/15/56 Tulare, CA
10	Sharperson, Mike	Syracuse	155	1	59	.289	R-R	6-1	175	10/4/61 Orangeburg, SC
26	Upshaw, Willie	Toronto	138	15	65	.275	L-L	6-0	185	4/27/57 Blanco, TX

OUTFIELDERS

No.	Name	1985 Club	H	HR	RBI	Pct.	B-T	Ht.	Wt.	Born
29	Barfield, Jesse	Toronto	156	27	84	.289	R-R	6-1	200	10/29/59 Joliet, IL
11	Bell, George	Toronto	167	28	95	.275	R-R	6-1	190	10/21/60 Dominican Rep.
44	*Burroughs, Jeff	Toronto	49	6	28	.257	R-R	6-0	200	3/7/51 Long Beach, CA
—	Green, Otis	Knoxville	128	11	68	.290	L-L	6-2	180	3/11/64 Miami, FL
—	Hill, Glenallen	Kinston	98	20	56	.210	R-R	6-2	190	3/22/65 Santa Cruz, CA
15	Moseby, Lloyd	Toronto	151	18	70	.259	L-R	6-3	205	11/5/59 Portland, OR
0	*Oliver, Al	Los Angeles	20	0	8	.253	L-L	6-1	185	10/14/46 Portsmouth, OH
		Toronto	47	5	23	.251				
21	Shepherd, Ron	Syracuse	41	2	16	.308	R-R	6-4	175	10/27/60 Longview, TX
		Toronto	4	0	1	.114				
28	Thornton, Lou	Toronto	17	1	8	.236	L-R	6-0	175	4/26/63 Montgomery, AL

*Free agent unsigned at press time

BLUE JAY PROFILES

GEORGE BELL 26 6-1 190 Bats R Throws R

Only a September tailspin marred his best season in majors . . . Attained career highs in at-bats (607), runs (87), triples (6), homers (28), RBI (95) and stolen bases (21) . . . Hit .239 in September with one homer and eight RBI . . . Charged Boston pitcher Bruce Kison June 23 and was suspended for two games, ending his consecutive-game streak at 120 . . . Hit .304 in June and .307 in August . . . Belted his first career grand slam July 9 and hit another Aug. 2 . . . Set club record by homering in four straight games in August . . . Committed 11 errors in left . . . Born Oct. 21, 1959, in San Pedro de Macoris, Dominican Republic . . . Signed by Phillies as free agent in 1978 . . . Plucked out of Philadelphia organization in minor-league draft after 1980 season . . . Spent 1981 season with Toronto, but was optioned to minors in 1982, when he was plagued by mononucleosis, a sore left knee and a broken jaw.

Year	Club	Pos.	G	AB	R	H	2B	3B	HR	RBI	SB	Avg.
1981	Toronto	OF	60	163	19	38	2	1	5	12	3	.233
1983	Toronto	OF	39	112	5	30	5	4	2	17	1	.268
1984	Toronto	OF-3B	159	606	85	177	39	4	26	88	11	.292
1985	Toronto	OF	157	607	87	167	28	6	28	95	21	.275
	Totals		415	1488	196	412	74	15	61	212	36	.277

JESSE BARFIELD 26 6-1 200 Bats R Throws R

Given a full-time job in right field in 1985, he responded with career highs in at-bats (539), RBI (84), hits (156), doubles (34) and triples (9) and he tied his career high in homers (27) . . . He and George Bell became first Blue Jays to hit 20 homers and steal 20 bases in single season . . . A streaky hitter with good power . . . Hit .314 in May and .365 in August, but only .218 in June . . . Had a 16-game hitting streak in May . . . Set club records with 70 extra-base hits and 143 strikeouts . . . Has one of the best throwing arms of any AL outfielder . . . His 21 assists led league and set club record . . . Born Oct. 29, 1959, in Joliet, Ill., the town that produced Larry Gura, Bill Gullickson and Jack Perconte . . . Blue Jays' ninth-round pick in June 1977 draft . . . Spent five years in minors, never hitting more than 16 homers in a season.

Year	Club	Pos.	G	AB	R	H	2B	3B	HR	RBI	SB	Avg.
1981	Toronto	OF	25	95	7	22	3	2	2	9	4	.232
1982	Toronto	OF	139	394	54	97	13	2	18	58	1	.246
1983	Toronto	OF	128	388	58	98	13	3	27	68	2	.253
1984	Toronto	OF	110	320	51	91	14	1	14	49	8	.284
1985	Toronto	OF	155	539	94	156	34	9	27	84	22	.289
	Totals		557	1736	264	464	77	17	88	268	37	.267

LLOYD MOSEBY 26 6-3 205 **Bats L Throws R**

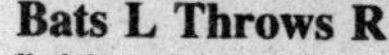

Provided stability in center field and in second spot of Blue Jays' batting order . . . However, his average dropped from .280 in 1984 to .259 last year, marking his second straight year of decline . . . Has hit 18 homers in each of the last three years . . . Led Blue Jays with 37 stolen bases, but was caught 15 times . . . Hit .301 in August . . . Led Blue Jays with 76 walks . . . Born Nov. 5, 1959, in Portland, Ark. . . . Blue Jays made him second selection overall in June 1978 draft . . . Played two seasons of Class-A ball and one in Triple-A before his promotion to Blue Jays in 1980 . . . Had five hits, including a homer, in his first nine at-bats . . . Became first Blue Jay ever to score 100 runs in 1983 . . . Was a high-school All-American basketball player and was so elusive that he earned the nickname "Shaker."

Year	Club	Pos.	G	AB	R	H	2B	3B	HR	RBI	SB	Avg.
1980	Toronto	OF	114	389	44	89	24	1	9	46	4	.229
1981	Toronto	OF	100	378	36	88	16	2	9	43	11	.233
1982	Toronto	OF	147	487	51	115	20	9	9	52	11	.236
1983	Toronto	OF	151	539	104	170	31	7	18	81	27	.315
1984	Toronto	OF	158	592	97	166	28	15	18	92	39	.280
1985	Toronto	OF	152	584	92	151	30	7	18	70	37	.259
	Totals		822	2969	424	779	149	41	81	384	129	.262

WILLIE UPSHAW 28 6-0 185 **Bats L Throws L**

Again failed to match his great season of 1983, when he hit .306 with 27 homers and 104 RBI . . . His average, homers and RBI have dropped in each of the two years since then . . . Started with a .270 average in April, but his best months were July, when he hit .326, and August, when he hit .346 . . . Hit 10 of his 15 homers against right-handers . . . Stole eight bases and was caught an equal number of times . . . Born April 27, 1957, in Blanco, Tex. . . . Fifth-round pick of Yanks in June 1975 draft . . . Selected by Blue Jays in minor-league draft after 1977 season . . . Made his major-league debut the next season, without benefit of any

Triple-A experience . . . First cousin of former NFL players Gene and Marvin Upshaw.

Year	Club	Pos.	G	AB	R	H	2B	3B	HR	RBI	SB	Avg.
1978	Toronto	OF	95	224	26	53	8	2	1	17	4	.237
1980	Toronto	1B-OF	34	61	10	13	3	1	1	5	1	.213
1981	Toronto	1B-OF	61	111	15	19	3	1	4	10	2	.171
1982	Toronto	1B	160	580	77	155	25	7	21	75	8	.267
1983	Toronto	1B	160	579	99	177	26	7	27	104	10	.306
1984	Toronto	1B	152	569	79	158	31	9	19	84	9	.278
1985	Toronto	1B	148	501	79	138	31	5	15	65	8	.275
	Totals		810	2625	385	713	127	32	88	360	42	.272

ERNIE WHITT 33 6-2 200 **Bats L Throws R**

A pleasant surprise for Blue Jays, he enjoyed a productive 1985 season . . . Established career highs in games (139), at-bats (412), runs (55), hits (101), doubles (21), homers (19) and RBI (64) . . . Also had a career-high 10-game hitting streak . . . Hit 17 of his 19 homers off right-handers . . . Hit first career grand slam . . . Hit .344 in May . . . A workhorse down the stretch . . . Because of an injury to Buck Martinez, he started 27 of last 29 games . . . One of three remaining Blue Jays from the 1976 expansion draft, he was plucked from Red Sox organization . . . A 15th-round pick by Boston in June 1972 draft . . . Born June 13, 1952, in Detroit . . . Hit a home run in his first major-league game as a member of the Red Sox, Sept. 21, 1976.

Year	Club	Pos.	G	AB	R	H	2B	3B	HR	RBI	SB	Avg.
1976	Boston	C	8	18	4	4	2	0	1	3	0	.222
1977	Toronto	C	23	41	4	7	3	0	0	6	0	.171
1978	Toronto	C	2	4	0	0	0	0	0	0	0	.000
1980	Toronto	C	106	295	23	70	12	2	6	34	1	.237
1981	Toronto	C	74	195	16	46	9	0	1	16	5	.236
1982	Toronto	C	105	284	28	74	14	2	11	42	3	.261
1983	Toronto	C	123	344	53	88	15	2	17	56	1	.256
1984	Toronto	C	124	315	35	75	12	1	15	46	0	.238
1985	Toronto	C	139	412	55	101	21	2	19	64	2	.245
	Totals		704	1908	218	465	88	9	70	267	12	.244

TONY FERNANDEZ 23 6-2 165 **Bats S Throws R**

Responded to his first chance to play every day with a consistent season . . . Hit .294 right-handed and .286 left-handed . . . Was only Blue Jay to appear in every game in 1985 . . . Best month was June, when he hit .358 with one homer and 13 RBI . . . Also had a good August, when he hit .320 . . . Posted single-game career highs with four hits and four RBI Sept. 29 against Milwaukee . . . Has developed into one of game's smoothest-fielding shortstops, though his 30 errors in 1985 indicated some inconsistency . . . Likes to throw with a slingshot style . . . Born Aug. 6, 1962, in San Pedro de Macoris, Dominican Republic . . . Signed as a free agent in 1979.

Year	Club	Pos.	G	AB	R	H	2B	3B	HR	RBI	SB	Avg.
1983	Toronto	SS	15	34	5	9	1	1	0	2	0	.265
1984	Toronto	SS-3B	89	234	29	63	5	3	3	19	5	.269
1985	Toronto	SS	161	564	71	163	31	10	2	51	13	.289
	Totals		265	832	105	235	37	14	5	72	18	.282

DAMASO GARCIA 28 6-0 175 **Bats R Throws R**

Put together solid season, despite sluggish start and nagging injuries . . . Hit .209 in April . . . Suffered jammed right wrist and bruised right instep in June, twisted right knee in August and damaged left knee in September collision with Yankees' Rickey Henderson . . . Still managed to attain career highs in homers (8), RBI (65) and game-winning RBI (10) . . . Set single-game career high with six RBI against Seattle May 10 . . . Stole third base three times to stretch string of successes to 22 in a row, dating back to 1981 . . . Known as one of the true free-swingers in the game . . . Walked only 15 times, tying a career low for a full season . . . Born Feb. 7, 1957, in Moca, Dominican Republic . . . Signed as free agent by Yankees in 1975 . . . Traded to Toronto with Paul Mirabella and Chris Chambliss for Tom Underwood, Rick Cerone and Ted Wilborn prior to 1980 season . . . Played in only 29 games with Yankees, but managed to hit into a triple play during 1979 game against Blue Jays.

Year	Club	Pos.	G	AB	R	H	2B	3B	HR	RBI	SB	Avg.
1978	New York (AL)	SS-2B	18	41	5	8	0	0	0	1	1	.195
1979	New York (AL)	SS-3B	11	38	3	10	1	0	0	4	2	.263
1980	Toronto	2B	140	543	50	151	30	7	4	46	13	.278
1981	Toronto	2B	64	250	24	63	8	1	1	13	13	.252
1982	Toronto	2B	147	597	89	185	32	3	5	42	54	.310
1983	Toronto	2B	131	525	84	161	23	6	3	38	31	.307
1984	Toronto	2B	152	633	79	180	32	5	5	46	46	.284
1985	Toronto	2B	146	600	70	169	25	4	8	65	28	.282
	Totals		809	3227	404	927	151	26	26	255	188	.287

DAVE STIEB 28 6-1 195 **Bats R Throws R**

Somehow his record always fails to reflect his talents . . . Was 14-13 in 1985, despite AL-leading 2.48 ERA . . . Was third in league in innings pitched with 265 . . . Set club record with 26 consecutive scoreless innings in May and June . . . Named AL Pitcher of the Month in May, when he was 4-1 with five complete games and a 1.69 ERA . . . Was 9-5 with 1.87 ERA at All-Star break and he pitched in his third straight All-Star Game

... Won only one of his first five starts after break, when he was plagued by a tender elbow ... Won only one of his last six decisions ... Fields his position very well ... Was an outfielder and pitcher at Southern Illinois ... Born July 22, 1957, in Santa Ana, Cal. ... Toronto's fifth-round pick in June 1978 draft ... Pitched in only 19 minor-league games before making Blue Jays in 1979.

Year	Club	G	IP	W	L	Pct.	SO	BB	H	ERA
1979	Toronto	18	129	8	8	.500	52	48	139	4.33
1980	Toronto	34	243	12	15	.444	108	83	232	3.70
1981	Toronto	25	184	11	10	.524	89	61	148	3.18
1982	Toronto	38	288⅓	17	14	.548	141	75	271	3.25
1983	Toronto	36	278	17	12	.586	187	93	223	3.04
1984	Toronto	35	267	16	8	.667	198	88	215	2.83
1985	Toronto	36	265	14	13	.519	167	96	206	2.48
	Totals	222	1654⅓	95	80	.543	942	544	1434	3.17

JIMMY KEY 24 6-1 185 **Bats L Throws L**

Provided the left-handed starting pitching that the Blue Jays had craved ... His victory May 1 broke club's string of 614 games without a win by a left-handed starter, a drought that dated back to Oct. 4, 1980 ... His 14 wins set club record for victories by a left-hander ... Won six straight games during May and June ... Finished year with four straight wins ... Pitched in 63 games as a reliever in 1984, his first year with Blue Jays ... Born April 22, 1961, in Huntsville, Ala. ... Third-round selection in June 1982 draft ... Attended Clemson, where he was a pitcher and a .300 hitter as a DH ... Was starter in first two years of pro ball until assuming a relief role in 1984.

Year	Club	G	IP	W	L	Pct.	SO	BB	H	ERA
1984	Toronto	63	62	4	5	.444	44	32	70	4.65
1985	Toronto	35	212⅔	14	6	.700	85	50	188	3.00
	Totals	98	274⅔	18	11	.621	129	82	258	3.38

DOYLE ALEXANDER 35 6-3 200 **Bats R Throws R**

Continued to baffle hitters with off-speed pitches and fastballs while toying with a knuckleball ... Set club record with career-high 17 wins in 1985 ... Also attained a career best with 142 strikeouts ... Had career-high 11 strikeouts vs. Seattle July 23, passing 1,000th mark for his career ... Won first four games at start of year ... Had five-game streak from July 10 to Aug. 24, then, after one loss, he went on another four-game streak ... Has 41-23 record as Blue Jay, including 15-3 mark in games in September and October ... Born Sept. 4, 1950, in Cordova, Ala. ... Started career as Dodgers' 44th-round choice in June 1968 draft . . . Has pitched for Dodgers, Orioles, Yankees (twice), Rangers, Braves, Giants and Blue Jays . . . Released by Yankees June 1, 1983 and signed by Toronto 21 days later . . . One of only four pitchers to record wins over all 26 major-league teams.

Year	Club	G	IP	W	L	Pct.	SO	BB	H	ERA
1971	Los Angeles	17	92	6	6	.500	30	18	105	3.82
1972	Baltimore	35	106	6	8	.429	49	30	78	2.46
1973	Baltimore	29	175	12	8	.600	63	52	169	3.84
1974	Baltimore	30	174	6	9	.400	40	43	127	4.03
1975	Baltimore	32	133	8	8	.500	46	47	127	3.05
1976	Balt.-N.Y. (AL)	30	201	13	9	.591	58	63	172	3.36
1977	Texas	34	237	17	11	.607	82	82	221	3.65
1978	Texas	31	191	9	10	.474	81	71	198	3.86
1979	Texas	23	113	5	7	.417	50	69	114	4.46
1980	Atlanta	35	232	14	11	.560	114	74	227	4.19
1981	San Francisco	24	152	11	7	.611	77	44	156	2.90
1982	New York (AL)	16	66⅔	1	7	.125	26	14	81	6.08
1983	New York (AL)-Toronto	25	145	7	8	.467	63	33	157	4.41
1984	Toronto	36	261⅔	17	6	.739	139	59	238	3.13
1985	Toronto	36	260⅔	17	10	.630	142	67	268	3.45
	Totals	433	2480	149	125	.544	1060	766	2438	3.67

TOP PROSPECTS

CECIL FIELDER 22 6-3 230 — Bats R Throws R

Jumped from Knoxville (AA) to majors and made an instant impression . . . Made his major-league debut July 20 and went on to hit safely in his first five games . . . Used primarily as first baseman against left-handed pitching, he hit .311 with four homers and 16 RBI in 30 games . . . Was Toronto organization's Player of Month in May, when he hit .363 with 10 homers and 37 RBI in 20 games for Knoxville . . . Posted combined totals of 28 homers and 93 RBI while splitting 1984 season between Knoxville and Kinston (A) . . . Traded to Blue Jays in 1983 for Leon Roberts after being Royals' fourth-round pick in secondary phase of June 1982 draft . . . Born Sept. 21, 1963, in Los Angeles.

STEVE DAVIS 25 6-1 170 — Bats L Throws L

May be the left-handed starter the Blue Jays need to complement Jimmy Key . . . Began 1985 season in Double-A, but was in majors by Aug. 25 . . . Was 2-1 with 3.54 ERA in 10 games, including five starts, for Blue Jays . . . Tied a Knoxville record with 17 wins before his promotion to Syracuse (AAA) last year . . . Was 6-0 in July and won 11 of his last 13 decisions for Knoxville . . . Struck out 10 for Syracuse, his season high, just before joining Toronto . . . Born Aug. 4, 1960, in San Antonio, Tex. . . . First pitcher in Toronto organization to have a 20 victory season . . . Was 21st-round draft pick in June 1982 draft.

MANAGER JIMY WILLIAMS: Named to replace Bobby Cox, who left to take GM post with Atlanta . . . Last year marked his sixth season as Blue Jays' third-base coach . . . Had been mentioned for openings in Oakland after 1982 season and in Seattle after 1983 season . . . Managerial experience consists of six seasons in minors, as he spent 1974-79 in California organization . . . Was a shortstop who hit .214 in 14 career major-league games with Cardinals in 1966 and 1967 . . . Traded to Cincinnati along with Pat Corrales, now the Cleveland manager, for Johnny Edwards prior to 1968 season . . . Selected by Expos in 1968 expansion draft . . . Injured his shoulder while moving furniture the next season and played only 35 games for Vancouver . . . Spent two more years in minors before assuming first managing job with Quad Cities in 1971 . . . In 1975, when he was manager at El Paso, he batted 17 times and got two hits . . . Born Oct. 4, 1943, in Arroyo Grande, Cal. . . . Attended Fresno State.

GREATEST SHORTSTOPS

The Blue Jays opened their first season in 1977 with Hector Torres at shortstop. The following season, their Opening Day shortstop was Luis Gomez. Then, after the 1978 season, they solved their shortstop problem in a trade with the Indians. The Blue Jays sent pitcher Victor Cruz to Cleveland for third baseman Phil Lansford and Alfredo Griffin, who became the best shortstop in club history.

Griffin had such an outstanding season the next year that he shared AL Rookie-of-the-Year honors with Minnesota third baseman John Castino. In 1979, Griffin set club marks for hits (179), runs (81), triples (10) and stolen bases (21). His .287 average was the best of any shortstop in the league. In 1980, Griffin tied for the league lead in triples with 15, an American League record for a switch-hitter.

Griffin brought stability and durability to a key position. He played every game in 1982 and 1983 and paced AL shortstops in putouts each of those years. He hit .241 in 1984 before the Blue Jays sent him and Dave Collins to Oakland for Bill Caudill. Toronto was able to make the deal because of its high regard for Tony Fernandez, who may eventually supplant Griffin as the best shortstop in club history.

ALL-TIME BLUE JAY SEASON RECORDS

BATTING: Lloyd Moseby, .315, 1983
HRs: John Mayberry, 30, 1980
RBIs: Willie Upshaw, 104, 1983
STEALS: Damaso Garcia, 54, 1982
WINS: Doyle Alexander, 17, 1984, 1985
STRIKEOUTS: Dave Stieb, 198, 1984

George Bell rang up team-leading 95 RBI.

CALIFORNIA ANGELS

TEAM DIRECTORY: Chairman-Pres.: Gene Autry; VP: Jackie Autry; GM: Mike Port; Dir. Scouting-Play. Dev.: Larry Himes; Dir. Minor League Oper.: Bill Bavasi; Dir. Pub. Rel.: Tim Mead; Trav. Sec.: Frank Sims; Mgr.: Gene Mauch. Home: Anaheim Stadium (65,158). Field distances: 333, l.f. line; 386, l.c.; 404, c.f.; 386, r.c.; 333, r.f. line. Spring training: Palm Springs, Cal.

SCOUTING REPORT

HITTING: In a dramatic departure from their previous big-spending approach toward free agents, the Angels are in the process of replacing their aging stars with prospects from their system. The rise of young center fielder Gary Pettis (.257, 56 stolen bases) and third baseman Jack Howell (.197 in 43 games) has coincided with the decline and departure of veteran Rod Carew. Still, the Angels are counting heavily upon Reggie Jackson, 39, Bob Boone, 38, George Hendrick, 36, and Doug DeCinces, 35.

Jackson's days as an outfielder are over. Manager Gene Mauch intends to use him strictly as a DH, though Jackson hit .199 as a DH and .282 as an outfielder last year. Mauch is also counting on a strong comeback by DeCinces (.244, 20 homers, 78 RBI), who has been plagued by back problems. However, Mauch's biggest hope is that Hendrick (.122 in 16 games with the Angels) will emerge as his regular right fielder. Mauch calls Hendrick "my sleeper." The manager may be disappointed to find out exactly how right he is. The Angels' other project is Pettis, who must cut down on his strikeouts and establish a better command of the strike zone in order to become a solid leadoff hitter.

PITCHING: Again, Mauch has a combination of experience and youth, with not much in between. His stalwarts are John Candelaria (7-3, 3.80 ERA with the Angels) and Don Sutton (15-10, 3.86 ERA), who should gain entry into the 300-win club in 1986. But the Angels also rely heavily on youngsters Mike Witt (15-9, 3.56), Urbano Lugo (3-4, 3.69), Stewart Cliburn (9-3, 2.09), Kirk McCaskill (12-12, 4.70) and Ron Romanick (14-9, 4.11). Their progress should be speeded by the presence of Sutton.

The Angels strengthened themselves last year with the addition of Donnie Moore, who set a club record with 31 of the staff's total of 41 saves. If the Angels can notch a similar number of saves in 1986, they should remain a title contender.

Will 1986 season be Reggie's curtain call?

FIELDING: The Angels were stronger defensively up the middle than even the Tigers last year. Boone helped limit opponents to only 79 stolen bases in 135 attempts. Bobby Grich led all AL second basemen with a .997 fielding percentage. Shortstop Dick Schofield Jr. committed 25 errors, but helped the Angels turn 202 double plays — only 15 short of the major-league record. Acrobatic center fielder Pettis has become the baseball equivalent of basketball's Dominique Wilkins, "The Human Highlight Film."

There are questions, though, for California in 1986. DeCinces will be tried at first base, though his back problems may hinder his mobility and make it difficult for him to catch low throws. If DeCinces can handle the move, Howell will be given a shot at the third-base job. Hendrick must prove he is the player he once was before the Angels' outfield can be considered solid.

OUTLOOK: The reinforcements aren't arriving quick enough for the Angels to survive their aging process. This is their transitional year and transitional years hardly ever result in pennants. But the AL West is weak enough so that California will not be far from contention. The Angels' title hopes will hinge on another strong season from the bullpen and an improbable revitalization by Hendrick. It doesn't look like Mauch will win that elusive first pennant this season.

CALIFORNIA ANGELS 1986 ROSTER

MANAGER Gene Mauch
Coaches—Bob Clear, Bobby Knoop, Marcel Lachemann, Jimmie Reese, Moose Stubing

PITCHERS

No.	Name	1985 Club	W-L	IP	SO	ERA	B-T	Ht.	Wt.	Born
45	Candelaria, John	Pittsburgh	2-4	54	22	3.64	L-L	6-6	225	11/6/53 New York, NY
		California	7-3	71	53	3.80				
—	Chadwick, Ray	Redwood	0-1	14	10	6.43	R-R	6-2	180	11/17/62 Durham, NC
		Midland	5-2	60	44	5.25				
		Edmonton	1-1	12	9	3.09				
33	Cliburn, Stew	Edmonton	0-0	4	2	0.00	R-R	6-0	187	12/19/56 Jackson, MI
		California	9-3	99	48	2.09				
23	Corbett, Doug	California	3-3	46	24	4.89	R-R	6-1	185	11/4/52 Sarasota, FL
		Edmonton	0-1	3	1	3.00				
46	Fowlkes, Alan	Edmonton	9-8	142	69	3.79	R-R	6-2	185	8/8/58 Brawley, CA
		California	0-0	7	5	9.00				
19	*Holland, Al	Phi.-Pit.	1-4	63	48	3.45	R-L	5-11	210	8/16/52 Roanoke, VA
		California	0-1	24	14	1.48				
31	LaCorte, Frank	California	Disabled list				R-R	6-1	180	10/31/51 San Jose, CA
—	Lucas, Gary	W. Palm Beach	0-0	5	3	7.20	L-L	6-5	200	11/8/54 Riverside, CA
		Indianapolis	0-0	2	2	0.00				
		Montreal	6-2	68	31	3.19				
18	Lugo, Urbano	Edmonton	2-0	26	19	4.56	R-R	6-0	190	8/12/62 Venezuela
		California	3-4	83	42	3.69				
15	McCaskill, Kirk	Edmonton	1-1	18	18	2.04	R-R	6-1	190	4/9/61 Canada
		California	12-12	190	102	4.70				
37	Moore, Donnie	California	8-8	103	72	1.92	L-R	6-0	185	2/13/54 Lubbock, TX
10	Romanick, Ron	California	14-9	195	64	4.11	R-R	6-4	203	11/6/60 Burley, ID
41	Slaton, Jim	California	6-10	148	60	4.37	R-R	6-0	188	6/19/50 Long Beach, CA
35	Smith, D. W.	Edmonton	6-7	72	29	3.75	R-R	6-1	196	8/30/57 Tomball, TX
		California	0-0	5	3	7.20				
27	Sutton, Don	Oak.-Cal.	15-10	226	107	3.86	R-R	6-1	190	4/2/45 Clio, AL
—	Willis, Carl	Cincinnati	1-0	14	6	9.22	L-R	6-3	210	12/28/60 Danville, VA
39	Witt, Mike	California	15-9	250	180	3.56	R-R	6-7	192	7/20/60 Fullerton, CA

CATCHERS

No.	Name	1985 Club	H	HR	RBI	Pct.	B-T	Ht.	Wt.	Born
8	Boone, Bob	California	114	5	55	.248	R-R	6-2	210	11/19/47 San Diego, CA
34	Narron, Jerry	California	29	5	14	.220	L-R	6-2	190	1/15/56 Goldsboro, NC

INFIELDERS

7	Burleson, Rick	California	Disabled list				R-R	5-10	160	4/29/51 Lynwood, CA
11	DeCinces, Doug	California	104	20	78	.244	R-R	6-2	195	8/29/50 Burbank, CA
2	Gerber, Craig	California	24	0	6	.264	L-R	6-0	175	1/8/59 Chicago, IL
4	Grich, Bobby	California	116	13	53	.242	R-R	6-2	190	1/15/49 Muskegon, MI
16	Howell, Jack	Edmonton	106	13	48	.373	L-R	6-0	192	8/18/61 Tucson, AZ
		California	27	5	18	.197				
—	Joyner, Wally	Edmonton	135	12	73	.283	L-L	6-2	185	6/16/62 Atlanta, GA
36	Keedy, Pat	Edmonton	101	17	61	.277	R-R	6-4	223	1/10/59 Birmingham, AL
28	McLemore, Mark	Midland	124	2	46	.271	B-R	5-11	175	10/4/64 San Diego, CA
—	Merrifield, Bill	Midland	142	15	83	.280	R-R	6-4	195	5/7/62 Waukegan, IL
56	Polidor, Gus	Edmonton	131	2	51	.285	R-R	6-0	170	10/26/61 Venezuela
		California	1	0	0	1.000				
22	Schofield, Dick	California	96	8	41	.219	R-R	5-10	176	11/21/62 Springfield, IL
6	Sconiers, Daryl	Midland	13	1	10	.224	L-L	6-2	205	10/3/58 San Bernardino, CA
		Edmonton	7	0	4	.350				
		California	28	2	12	.286				
9	Wilfong, Bob	California	41	4	13	.189	L-R	6-1	179	9/1/53 Pasadena, CA

OUTFIELDERS

12	*Beniquez, Juan	California	125	8	42	.304	R-R	5-11	175	5/13/50 Puerto Rico
5	Downing, Brian	California	137	20	85	.263	R-R	5-10	200	10/9/50 Los Angeles, CA
25	Hendrick, George	Pittsburgh	59	2	25	.230	R-R	6-3	195	10/18/49 Los Angeles, CA
		California	5	2	6	.122				
44	Jackson, Reggie	California	116	27	85	.252	L-L	6-0	208	5/18/46 Wyncote, PA
13	Jones, Ruppert	California	90	21	67	.231	L-L	5-10	189	3/12/55 Dallas, TX
24	Linares, Rufino	Edmonton	119	16	65	.311	R-R	6-1	166	2/28/51 Dominican Republic
		California	11	3	11	.256				
32	Miller, Darrell	California	18	2	7	.375	R-R	6-2	200	2/26/59 Washington, DC
		Edmonton	20	1	6	.282				
—	Montgomery, Reggie	Midland	130	22	101	.289	R-R	6-4	220	8/4/62 Los Angeles, CA
20	Pettis, Gary	California	114	1	32	.257	B-R	6-1	159	4/3/58 Oakland, CA
30	White, Devon	Midland	77	4	35	.296	B-R	6-1	175	12/29/62 Jamaica
		Edmonton	70	4	39	.253				
		California	1	0	0	.140				

*Free agent unsigned at press time

ANGEL PROFILES

REGGIE JACKSON 39 6-0 208 **Bats L Throws L**

Vaulted over five players into eighth place on all-time home-run list in 1985 . . . Hit No. 513 June 20 to pass Eddie Matthews and Ernie Banks and belted No. 522 Aug. 17 to pass Willie McCovey and Ted Williams . . . Always known for his great sense for dramatics, he hit home run No. 521 at exactly 5:21 P.M. . . . Collected his 1,000th extra-base hit Aug. 30 . . . Hit his first sacrifice fly since 1983 . . . Started season in right field as manager Gene Mauch hoped to sharpen slugger's concentration following a .194 season in 1983 and a .223 year in 1984 . . . Responded well, hitting .282 as an outfielder and only .199 as DH . . . Played right only once between Sept. 14 and the final weekend . . . Was benched during important October showdown against Royals . . . Born May 18, 1946, in Wyncote, Pa. . . . Was second player selected overall in June 1966 draft, by Kansas City A's . . . Recognized as "Mr. October" for his World Series heroics . . . Has hit .357 with 10 homers and 24 RBI in five World Series . . . Collects rare cars . . . Has worked as television commentator.

Year	Club	Pos.	G	AB	R	H	2B	3B	HR	RBI	SB	Avg.
1967	Kansas City	OF	35	118	13	21	4	4	1	6	1	.178
1968	Oakland	OF	154	553	82	138	13	6	29	74	14	.250
1969	Oakland	OF	152	549	123	151	36	3	47	118	13	.275
1970	Oakland	OF	149	426	57	101	21	2	23	66	26	.237
1971	Oakland	OF	150	567	87	157	29	3	32	80	16	.277
1972	Oakland	OF	135	499	72	132	25	2	25	75	9	.265
1973	Oakland	OF	151	539	99	158	28	2	32	117	22	.293
1974	Oakland	OF	148	506	90	146	25	1	29	93	25	.289
1975	Oakland	OF	157	593	91	150	39	3	36	104	17	.253
1976	Baltimore	OF	134	498	84	138	27	2	27	91	28	.277
1977	New York (AL) . . .	OF	146	525	93	150	39	2	32	110	17	.286
1978	New York (AL) . . .	OF	139	511	82	140	13	5	27	97	14	.274
1979	New York (AL) . . .	OF	131	465	78	138	24	2	29	89	9	.297
1980	New York (AL) . . .	OF	143	514	94	154	22	4	41	111	1	.300
1981	New York (AL) . . .	OF	94	334	33	79	17	1	15	54	0	.237
1982	California	OF	153	530	92	146	17	1	39	101	4	.275
1983	California	OF	116	397	43	77	14	1	14	49	0	.194
1984	California	OF	143	525	67	117	17	2	25	81	8	.223
1985	California	OF	143	460	64	116	27	0	27	85	1	.252
	Totals		2573	9109	1444	2409	437	46	530	1601	225	.264

BRIAN DOWNING 35 5-10 200 **Bats R Throws R**

Salvaged a productive season following a miserable start . . . Was batting .194 June 21, then he took off on a .368 hitting tear over the next two months to raise his average to .278 . . . Had five straight two-hit games in August . . . Scored 600th career run . . . Committed an error in left field July 21, snapping string of 229 consecutive errorless games, 15 short of his own major-league record . . . Finished season with two errors . . . Became first Angel and 27th player in history to hit a ball on Comiskey Park roof . . . Hit in every spot in the order, except eighth and ninth . . . Was especially successful batting leadoff, hitting .341 . . . Born Oct. 9, 1950, in Los Angeles . . . Acquired from White Sox with Dave Frost and Chris Knapp for Bobby Bonds, Thad Bosley and Richard Dotson prior to 1978 season . . . First major-league hit was inside-the-park homer off Mickey Lolich in 1973 . . . An avid weight lifter who has earned the nickname "The Incredible Hulk."

Year	Club	Pos.	G	AB	R	H	2B	3B	HR	RBI	SB	Avg.
1973	Chicago (AL)	OF-C-3B	34	73	5	13	1	0	2	4	0	.178
1974	Chicago (AL)	C-OF	108	293	41	66	12	1	10	39	0	.225
1975	Chicago (AL)	C	138	420	58	101	12	1	7	41	13	.240
1976	Chicago (AL)	C	104	317	38	81	14	0	3	30	7	.256
1977	Chicago (AL)	C-OF	69	169	28	48	4	2	4	25	1	.284
1978	California	C	133	412	42	105	15	0	7	46	3	.255
1979	California	C	148	509	87	166	27	3	12	75	3	.326
1980	California	C	30	93	5	27	6	0	2	25	0	.290
1981	California	OF-C	93	317	47	79	14	0	9	41	1	.249
1982	California	OF	158	623	109	175	37	2	28	84	2	.281
1983	California	OF	113	403	68	99	15	1	19	53	1	.246
1984	California	OF	156	539	65	148	28	2	23	91	0	.275
1985	California	OF	150	520	80	137	23	1	20	85	5	.263
	Totals		1434	4688	673	1245	208	13	146	639	36	.266

GARY PETTIS 27 6-1 159 — Bats S Throws R

Showed improvement offensively to complement his outstanding defense and excellent speed . . . Center fielder made several leaping catches of apparent home runs . . . Had 13 assists, most by a California outfielder since Leroy Stanton had 16 in 1975 . . . Had 12 putouts in an extra-inning game, tying major-league record . . . Stole 56 bases, ranking him second in AL to Yanks' Rickey Henderson . . . Became second Angel to steal 40 or more bases two straight years . . . Set club record by swiping 22 consecutive bases without being caught . . . Stole home twice . . . Hit .293 right-handed . . . Born April 3, 1958, in Oakland . . . Angels' sixth-round pick in January 1979 draft . . . Biggest snag in career has been inability to make contact consistently . . . Struck out 125 times in 443 at-bats in 1985 after fanning 115 times in 397 at-bats the previous season.

Year	Club	Pos.	G	AB	R	H	2B	3B	HR	RBI	SB	Avg.
1982	California	OF	10	5	5	1	0	0	1	1	0	.200
1983	California	OF	22	85	19	25	2	3	3	6	8	.294
1984	California	OF	140	[illegible]	[illegible]	[illegible]	11	6	2	[illegible]	[illegible]	[illegible]
1985	California	OF	125	443	67	114	10	8	1	32	56	.257
	Totals		297	930	154	230	23	17	7	68	112	.247

BOBBY GRICH 37 6-2 190 Bats R Throws R

Became Angels' all-time home-run leader when he cracked his 142nd homer for California Sept. 12 . . . Played in his 1,000th game as Angel and scored his 500th run as Angel, ranking him second in franchise history in both departments . . . Had an 11-game hitting streak during which he hit .425 from June 28 through July 9 . . . Marked his longest streak since 1981 . . . Hit homers in consecutive games against Yankees after hitting only two in his prior 73 games . . . Played first base, second base and third base . . . Played all three positions in a game against Chicago Sept. 18 . . . Born Jan. 15, 1949, in Muskegon, Mich. . . . Angels signed him as re-entry free agent prior to 1977 season . . . First-round pick and 18th player selected overall in June 1967 draft, by Baltimore . . . Passed up several football and baseball scholarship offers to sign with Orioles . . . Established major-league record for putouts by a second baseman with 484 in 1974.

Year	Club	Pos.	G	AB	R	H	2B	3B	HR	RBI	SB	Avg.
1970	Baltimore.	SS-2B-3B	30	95	11	20	1	3	0	8	1	.211
1971	Baltimore.	SS-2B	7	30	7	9	0	0	1	6	1	.300
1972	Baltimore.	SS-2B-1B-3B	133	460	66	128	21	3	12	50	13	.278
1973	Baltimore.	2B	162	581	82	146	29	7	12	50	17	.251
1974	Baltimore.	2B	160	582	92	153	29	6	19	82	17	.263
1975	Baltimore.	2B	150	524	81	136	26	4	13	57	14	.262
1976	Baltimore.	2B-3B	144	518	93	138	31	4	13	54	14	.266
1977	California.	SS	52	181	24	44	6	0	7	23	6	.243
1978	California.	2B	144	487	68	122	16	2	6	42	4	.251
1979	California.	2B	153	534	78	157	30	5	30	101	1	.294
1980	California.	2B-1B	150	498	60	135	22	2	14	62	3	.271
1981	California.	2B	100	352	56	107	14	2	22	61	2	.304
1982	California.	2B	145	500	74	132	20	5	19	65	0	.261
1983	California.	2B-SS	120	387	65	113	17	0	16	62	2	.292
1984	California.	2B-1B-3B	116	363	60	93	15	1	18	58	2	.256
1985	California.	2B-1B-3B	144	479	74	116	17	3	13	53	4	.242
	Totals		1910	6577	991	1749	302	47	215	834	104	.266

DOUG DeCINCES 35 6-2 195 Bats R Throws R

Third baseman's 1985 season was marred by nagging back spasms that have plagued him since he suffered torn muscles in his lower back in 1979 . . . Visited disabled list from May 20 through June 3 . . . Bothered again by back spasms from Aug. 17 to Sept. 13, when he did not start a game and appeared only five times as a pinch-hitter . . . May be moved to first base this season to alleviate some of the pain . . . Best month was July, when he hit .286 with five homers and 19 RBI . . . Belted two homers off Toronto's Jimmy Key July 18, the 17th multi-homer game of his career . . . Scored his 600th career run . . . Hit 20 homers for second straight year . . . Born Aug. 29, 1950, in Burbank,

Cal. . . . Acquired from Baltimore with Jeff Schneider for Dan Ford prior to 1982 season . . . Hit home run in first World Series at-bat in 1979 . . . Has started two triple plays in his career.

Year	Club	Pos.	G	AB	R	H	2B	3B	HR	RBI	SB	Avg.
1973	Baltimore.	3B-2B-SS	10	18	2	2	0	0	0	3	0	.111
1974	Baltimore.	3B	1	1	0	0	0	0	0	0	0	.000
1975	Baltimore.	3B-SS-2B-1B	61	167	20	42	6	3	4	23	0	.251
1976	Baltimore.	3B-2B-SS-1B	129	440	36	103	17	2	11	42	8	.234
1977	Baltimore.	3B-2B-1B	150	522	63	135	28	3	19	69	8	.259
1978	Baltimore.	3B-2B	142	511	72	146	37	1	28	80	7	.286
1979	Baltimore.	3B	120	422	67	97	27	1	16	61	5	.230
1980	Baltimore.	3B-1B	145	489	64	122	23	2	16	64	11	.249
1981	Baltimore.	3B-1B-OF	100	346	49	91	23	2	13	55	0	.263
1982	California.	3B-SS	153	575	94	173	42	5	30	97	7	.301
1983	California.	3B	95	370	49	104	19	3	18	65	2	.281
1984	California.	3B	146	547	77	147	23	3	20	82	4	.269
1985	California.	3B	120	427	50	104	22	1	20	78	1	.244
	Totals		1372	4835	643	1266	267	26	195	719	53	.262

DON SUTTON 40 6-1 190 — Bats R Throws R

Moved to within five victories of 300 club . . . Conquered some uncharacteristic control problems early in season and had a consistent second half . . . In his last 23 starts, he walked only 28 and allowed more than three earned runs only four times . . . Reached 100 strikeouts for major-league-record 20th straight season . . . Was 2-2 with 3.69 ERA for Angels after being acquired from Oakland for pennant run . . . Born April 2, 1945, in Clio, Ala. . . . Spent his first 16 pro seasons in Dodgers' organization . . . Has 4-1 record and 2.04 ERA in five League Championship Series games . . . Member of five World Series teams . . . Has 2-3 record and 5.26 ERA in eight World Series starts.

Year	Club	G	IP	W	L	Pct.	SO	BB	H	ERA
1966	Los Angeles.	37	226	12	12	.500	209	52	192	2.99
1967	Los Angeles.	37	233	11	15	.423	169	57	223	3.94
1968	Los Angeles.	35	208	11	15	.423	162	59	179	2.60
1969	Los Angeles.	41	293	17	18	.486	217	91	269	3.47
1970	Los Angeles.	38	260	15	13	.536	201	78	251	4.08
1971	Los Angeles.	38	265	17	12	.586	194	55	231	2.55
1972	Los Angeles.	33	273	19	9	.679	207	63	186	2.08
1973	Los Angeles.	33	256	18	10	.643	200	56	196	2.43
1974	Los Angeles.	40	276	19	9	.679	179	80	241	3.23
1975	Los Angeles.	35	254	16	13	.552	175	62	202	2.87
1976	Los Angeles.	35	268	21	10	.677	161	82	231	3.06
1977	Los Angeles.	33	240	14	8	.636	150	69	207	3.19
1978	Los Angeles.	34	238	15	11	.577	154	54	228	3.55
1979	Los Angeles.	33	226	12	15	.444	146	61	201	3.82
1980	Los Angeles.	32	212	13	5	.722	128	47	163	2.21
1981	Houston	23	159	11	9	.550	104	29	132	2.60
1982	Houston	27	195	13	8	619	139	46	169	3.00
1982	Milwaukee.	7	54⅔	4	1	.800	36	18	55	3.29
1983	Milwaukee.	31	220⅓	8	13	.381	134	54	209	4.08
1984	Milwaukee.	33	212⅔	14	12	.538	143	51	224	3.77
1985	Oak.-Cal.	34	226	15	10	.600	107	59	221	3.86
	Totals.	689	4795⅔	295	228	.564	3315	1223	4210	3.17

JOHN CANDELARIA 32 6-6 225 Bats S Throws L

Bolstered Angels' starting rotation after being acquired with Al Holland and George Hendrick in Aug. 2 trade that sent Pat Clements, Mike Brown and Bob Kipper to Pirates . . . Pitched well for the Angels after finally making his long-awaited escape from Pittsburgh . . . Improved his career record in September to 20-10 . . . Won five of his seven games with Angels on road . . . Pitched well in his first two outings with California, then was bombed for 11 earned runs in his next 3⅓ innings as his ERA ballooned from 3.38 to 7.49 . . . Allowed only four earned runs in next 33 innings to lower ERA to 3.59 . . . Hurled a no-hitter against Dodgers in 1976 . . . Won 20 games and had NL-leading 2.34 ERA in 1977 . . . Born Nov. 6, 1953, in New York City . . . A high-school All-American in basketball . . . Pirates' second-round pick in June 1972 draft.

Year	Club	G	IP	W	L	Pct.	SO	BB	H	ERA
1975	Pittsburgh	18	121	8	6	.571	95	36	95	2.75
1976	Pittsburgh	32	220	16	7	.696	138	60	173	3.15
1977	Pittsburgh	33	231	20	5	.800	133	50	197	2.34
1978	Pittsburgh	30	189	12	11	.522	94	49	191	3.24
1979	Pittsburgh	33	207	14	9	.609	101	41	201	3.22
1980	Pittsburgh	35	233	11	14	.440	97	50	246	4.02
1981	Pittsburgh	6	41	2	2	.500	14	11	42	3.51
1982	Pittsburgh	31	174⅔	12	7	.632	133	37	166	2.94
1983	Pittsburgh	33	197⅔	15	8	.652	157	45	191	3.23
1984	Pittsburgh	33	185⅓	12	11	.522	133	34	179	2.72
1985	Pittsburgh	37	54⅓	2	4	.333	47	14	57	3.64
1985	California	13	71	7	3	.700	53	24	70	3.80
	Totals	334	1925	131	87	.601	1195	451	1808	3.14

DONNIE MOORE 32 6-0 185 Bats L Throws R

Plucked from the free-agent compensation pool prior to last season, he became first pitcher to be named Angels' MVP since Nolan Ryan . . . Saved 31 games, three more than he had amassed in his previous six years in majors . . . Set Angels' single-season save record, surpassing 25 recorded by Dave LaRoche in 1978 . . . Failed in only eight save situations . . . Was tagged with a loss in his first appearance, but then did not allow an earned run in his next 26 innings . . . Was 2-0 with seven saves and 0.54 ERA in May . . . His 1.92 ERA was lowest among AL relievers with 80 or more innings pitched . . . Born Feb. 13, 1954, in Lubbock, Tex. . . . Has had many stops in pro career that began in 1972 . . . Signed by Red Sox as 12th-round choice in June 1972 draft . . . Signed as a free agent by Cubs in June 1973 . . . Traded to Cardinals for Mike Tyson in 1979 . . . Sold to Brewers in September 1981, he was returned to St. Louis one month later . . . Finally traded to Braves in 1982 . . . First cousin of Expos' Hubie Brooks . . . Became very attractive re-entry free agent at conclusion of 1985 season.

Year	Club	G	IP	W	L	Pct.	SO	BB	H	ERA
1975	Chicago (NL)	4	9	0	0	.000	8	4	12	4.00
1977	Chicago (NL)	27	49	4	2	.667	34	18	51	4.04
1978	Chicago (NL)	71	103	9	7	.563	50	31	117	4.11
1979	Chicago (NL)	39	73	1	4	.200	43	25	95	5.18
1980	St. Louis	11	22	1	1	.500	10	5	25	6.14
1981	Milwaukee	3	4	0	0	.000	2	4	4	6.75
1982	Atlanta	16	27⅔	3	1	.750	17	7	32	4.23
1983	Atlanta	43	68⅔	2	3	.400	41	10	72	3.67
1984	Atlanta	47	64⅓	4	5	.444	47	18	63	2.94
1985	California	65	103	8	8	.500	72	21	91	1.92
	Totals	326	523⅔	32	31	.508	324	143	562	3.73

MIKE WITT 25 6-7 192 **Bats R Throws R**

Won 15 games for second straight season . . . Has more wins over the past two years than any other Angel . . . Had two five-game winning streaks in 1985 . . . Strikeout high was 10, accomplished twice, both times against the Yankees . . . Was 4-1 with 2.82 ERA in June and 4-0 with 2.87 ERA in August . . . Threw his only shutout of the season April 25 . . . Born July 20, 1960, in Fullerton, Cal. . . . Has outstanding breaking pitches . . . Put everything together on last day of 1984 season, when he hurled a perfect game against Texas . . . Angels' fourth-round pick in June 1978 draft . . . Wife Lisa is former secretary in Angels' organization . . . Brother Steve is pitcher in Phillies' organization . . . Jumped from El Paso (AA) to majors in 1981, after only 68 minor-league appearances.

Year	Club	G	IP	W	L	Pct.	SO	BB	H	ERA
1981	California	22	129	8	9	.471	75	47	123	3.28
1982	California	33	179⅔	8	6	.571	85	47	177	3.51
1983	California	43	154	7	14	.333	77	75	173	4.91
1984	California	34	246⅔	15	11	.577	196	84	227	3.47
1985	California	35	250	15	9	.625	180	98	228	3.56
	Totals	167	959⅓	53	49	.520	613	351	928	3.71

TOP PROSPECTS

JACK HOWELL 24 6-0 185 **Bats L Throws R**

Enjoyed such an outstanding season for Edmonton (AAA) in 1985 that Angels are thinking of moving Doug DeCinces to first base and installing this youngster at third in 1986 . . . Hit .373 with 13 homers and 48 RBI in 79 games for Edmonton . . . Also played in 43 games with Angels, because DeCinces was often sidelined by back spasms . . . Hit only .197 with five homers and 18 RBI in 137 at-bats with California . . . Last year was only his second full season in pro ball . . . Signed by Angels as a free agent in 1983 . . . Led California League third basemen in fielding percentage (.943), assists (259) and double plays (23) with Redwood (A) in 1984 . . . Born Aug. 18, 1961, in Tucson, Ariz.

WALLY JOYNER 23 6-2 185 **Bats L Throws L**

Had solid season for Edmonton in his third year of pro ball . . . Will get a crack at majors, although he may need another year of Triple-A seasoning before becoming Angels' first baseman . . . Hit .283 with 12 homers and 73 RBI in 126 games last year . . . Walked 60 times and struck out 64 times . . . Outstanding defensive first baseman . . . Batted .328 for Peoria (A) in 1983 and .317 for Waterbury (AA) in 1984 . . . Born June 16, 1962, in Atlanta . . . Angels' third-round pick in June 1983 draft.

MANAGER GENE MAUCH: Credited with doing an outstanding job in 1985, when he kept Angels in pennant picture until last week of the season despite handicap of inexperienced pitching staff . . . Guided Angels to second-best mark in club's 25-year history at 90-72 . . . Carries dubious record of 24 years of managing without winning a pennant . . . Remembered for overworking starters Jim Bunning and Chris Short during Phils' great collapse in 1964 . . . Led California to AL West title in 1982, but resigned under pressure after Angels blew 2-0 lead in best-of-five ALCS against Milwaukee . . . Known for stressing fundamentals and his affection for the sacrifice bunt . . . Started as a shortstop in Brooklyn Dodger organization . . . Played for six major-league teams from 1944-57, batting .239 . . . Took first managerial job at age 28, piloting Atlanta Crackers of Southern Association in 1953 . . . Has managed Phillies, Expos, Twins and Angels . . . Born Nov. 18, 1925, in Salina, Kan. . . . On all-time managerial list, he is tied for sixth in years of service (24), ranks eighth in games (3,616) and ninth in wins (1,736) . . . His composite major-league record is 1,736-1,880.

GREATEST SHORTSTOP

Jim Fregosi is regarded as the best and certainly the most popular shortstop in Angels' history—and not because he was part of the trade that brought Nolan Ryan to California from the New York Mets.

Fregosi played behind Joe Koppe in 1961 and 1962, the first two seasons of the Angels' franchise. Fregosi won the job in 1963, at the age of 21, and held the position until the Angels traded him to New York following the 1971 season. Fregosi made the All-Star team six times during that span.

Fregosi provided stability while the franchise suffered through its growing pains. He is the Angels' all-time leader in games (1,429), at-bats (5,244), runs (691), hits (1,408), doubles (219), triples (70), RBI (546), extra-base hits (404) and total bases (2,112).

Fregosi, who also played for the Texas Rangers and Pittsburgh Pirates, ended his playing career in 1978 with a lifetime .265 average. He returned to manage the Angels for four seasons, winning the AL West title in 1979. Last season, he was the manager of the Cardinals' Triple-A franchise in Louisville and he has a son playing professional baseball.

ALL-TIME ANGEL SEASON RECORDS

BATTING: Rod Carew, .339, 1983
HRs: Reggie Jackson, 39, 1982
RBIs: Don Baylor, 139, 1979
STEALS: Mickey Rivers, 70, 1975
WINS: Clyde Wright, 22, 1970
Nolan Ryan, 22, 1974
STRIKEOUTS: Nolan Ryan, 383, 1973

CHICAGO WHITE SOX

TEAM DIRECTORY: Chairman: Jerry Reinsdorf; Pres.: Eddie Einhorn; Spec. Asst.: Roland Hemond; Exec. VP-Baseball Oper.: Ken Harrelson; Exec. VP-Howard Pizer; VP-Baseball Adm.: Jack Gould; Dir. Minor Leagues/Play. Dev.: Alvin Dark; Dir. Pub. Rel.: Paul Jensen; Trav. Sec.: Glen Rosenbaum; Mgr.: Tony LaRussa. Home: Comiskey Park (44,087). Field distances: 341, l.f. line; 374, l.c.; 401, c.f.; 374, r.c.; 341, r.f. line. Spring training: Sarasota, Fla.

SCOUTING REPORT

HITTING: As long as the White Sox have Harold Baines, they have the basis for a dangerous lineup. Baines (.309, 22 homers, 113 RBI) has developed into one of the toughest outs in the game, especially in clutch situations. However, it is important that the White Sox protect his bat by placing a couple of good hitters behind him.

Greg Walker (.258, 24 homers, 92 RBI) may be ready to hit for a higher average without sacrificing any power, but the rest of the White Sox hitters are going to have to do better. In 1985, only Kansas City and California finished with a worse batting average than Chicago's .252 mark. Carlton Fisk, the veteran catcher who hit 37 homers and drove in 107 runs at age 37 last season, may end up in left field, with some punch expected from the new

Harold Baines is one of Bill Veeck's legacies to White Sox.

catching platoon of Joel Skinner (.341 in 22 games) and former Yankee Ron Hassey (.296 and a career-high 13 homers). Chicago hopes that Darryl Boston (.228 in 95 games) may finally be ready to make an impact and that Ozzie Guillen (.273) continues to mature as a hitter.

PITCHING: It seemed a bit odd that the White Sox would be willing to give up a quality pitcher like 18-game winner Britt Burns. Good left-handed pitchers are a rare commodity. But Chicago's willingness to trade Burns to the Yankees reflects the confidence the White Sox have in Joe Cowley, who was acquired in the deal along with Hassey. Cowley (12-6, 3.95) was 21-8 in less than two full seasons with the Yankees and the White Sox are hoping he can win at least 15 games for them in 1986.

The White Sox would be satisfied with another 16-11 season from Tom Seaver, who reached the 300-win milestone in 1985. Now if they can only straighten out Floyd Bannister, who continues to baffle the experts by posting losing records. How could someone with so much ability finish 1985 with a 10-14 record and a 4.87 ERA? Bannister struck out 198 batters in 210⅔ innings, despite being four games under .500. At least the White Sox can feel assured about their bullpen situation this season. Bob James filled a long-standing gap there with 32 saves in 1985.

FIELDING: Everyone is raving about Guillen, the rookie who solidified the entire Chicago defense. He led all AL shortstops with a .980 fielding percentage and the White Sox tied for the overall league lead with a .982 percentage. Guillen committed only 12 errors and only one of them led to an unearned run. His only problem was that he occasionally missed the second-base bag on force plays, a small flaw on a gem of a player.

The White Sox still need help at third base. Scott Fletcher, Tim Hulett and Luis Salazar made a total of 36 errors, so the White Sox acquired versatile infielder Wayne Tolleson from Texas during the offseason.

OUTLOOK: The White Sox have dealt away LaMarr Hoyt, Britt Burns and Tim Lollar since the end of the 1984 season—and it's not as if they have a surplus of pitching. They need too many pieces to fit together for their staff to hold up this season. The job of manager Tony LaRussa always seems to be on the line, but LaRussa always finds a way to save it. In recent seasons, the White Sox have managed to field a winning team, but not one that can win the AL West. Hiring a new general manager in Ken Harrelson is not the sort of personnel move that will make the difference. Adding some starting pitchers would be a bigger help.

CHICAGO WHITE SOX 1986 ROSTER

MANAGER Tony La Russa
Coaches—Ed Brinkman, Moe Drabowsky, Dave Duncan, Willie Horton, Art Kusnyer, Doug Rader

PITCHERS

No.	Name	1985 Club	W-L	IP	SO	ERA	B-T	Ht.	Wt.	Born
50	Agosto, Juan	Buffalo	0-0	13	11	2.13	L-L	6-2	187	2/23/58 Puerto Rico
		Chicago (AL)	4-3	60	39	3.58				
19	Bannister, Floyd	Chicago (AL)	10-14	211	198	4.87	L-L	6-1	203	6/10/55 Pierre, SD
40	Cowley, Joe	New York (AL)	12-6	160	97	3.95	R-R	6-5	210	8/15/58 Lexington, KY
52	Davis, Joel	Glens Falls	1-1	25	20	2.84	L-R	6-5	210	1/30/65 Jacksonville, FL
		Buffalo	2-5	56	31	4.79				
		Chicago (AL)	3-3	71	37	4.16				
34	Dotson, Richard	Chicago (AL)	3-4	52	33	4.47	R-R	6-0	204	1/10/59 Cincinnati, OH
27	Fallon, Bob	Buffalo	3-8	80	60	4.39	L-L	6-3	211	2/18/60 New York, NY
		Chicago (AL)	0-0	16	17	6.19				
46	Gleaton, Jerry Don	Buffalo	8-2	55	37	2.44	L-L	6-3	210	9/14/57 Brownwood, TX
		Chicago (AL)	1-0	30	22	5.76				
43	James, Bob	Chicago (AL)	8-7	110	88	2.13	R-R	6-4	230	8/15/58 Glendale, CA
49	Jones, Al	Chicago (AL)	1-0	6	2	1.50	R-R	5-11	165	2/10/59 Charleston, MS
		Buffalo	0-1	3	1	10.13				
36	Long, Bill	Buffalo	13-6	151	71	3.51	R-R	6-0	185	2/29/60 Cincinnati, OH
		Chicago (AL)	0-1	14	13	10.29				
61	McKeon, Joel	Buffalo	6-4	82	62	3.72	L-L	6-0	185	2/25/63 Covington, KY
30	Nelson, Gene	Chicago (AL)	10-10	146	101	4.26	R-R	6-0	175	12/3/60 Tampa, FL
41	Seaver, Tom	Chicago (AL)	16-11	239	134	3.17	R-R	6-1	221	11/17/44 Fresno, CA
24	Schmidt, Dave	Texas	7-6	86	46	3.15	R-R	6-1	185	4/22/57 Niles, MI
37	*Spillner, Dan	Chicago (AL)	4-3	92	41	3.44	R-R	6-1	190	11/27/51 Casper, WY
31	Tanner, Bruce	Buffalo	5-7	109	49	3.46	L-R	6-3	220	12/9/61 New Castle, PA
		Chicago (AL)	1-2	27	9	5.33				
51	Wehrmeister, Dave	Buffalo	5-8	126	89	5.77	R-R	6-4	195	11/9/52 La Grange, IL
		Chicago (AL)	2-2	39	32	3.43				

CATCHERS

No.	Name	1985 Club	H	HR	RBI	Pct.	B-T	Ht.	Wt.	Born
72	Fisk, Carlton	Chicago (AL)	129	37	107	.238	R-R	6-2	217	12/26/47 Bellows Falls, VT
14	Hassey, Ron	New York (AL)	79	13	42	.296	L-R	6-2	195	2/27/53 Tucson, AZ
7	Hill, Marc	Chicago (AL)	10	0	4	.133	R-R	6-3	240	2/18/52 Elsberry, MO
53	Karkovice, Ron	Glens Falls	70	11	37	.216	R-R	6-1	215	8/8/63 Union, NJ
22	Skinner, Joel	Buffalo	94	12	59	.240	R-R	6-4	204	2/21/61 LaJolla, CA
		Chicago (AL)	15	1	5	.341				

INFIELDERS

No.	Name	1985 Club	H	HR	RBI	Pct.	B-T	Ht.	Wt.	Born
26	Bonilla, Bobby	Prince William	34	3	11	.262	R-R	6-3	210	2/23/63 New York, NY
—	Cochrane, Dave	Jackson	23	4	20	.223	B-R	6-2	180	1/31/63 Riverside, CA
12	Cruz, Julio	Chicago (AL)	46	00	15	.197	B-R	5-9	180	12/2/54 Brooklyn, NY
38	De Sa, Joe	Buffalo	105	17	66	.287	L-L	5-11	170	7/27/59 Honolulu, HI
		Chicago (AL)	8	2	7	.182				
13	Guillen, Ozzie	Chicago (AL)	134	1	33	.273	L-R	5-11	150	1/20/64 Venezuela
32	Hulett, Tim	Chicago (AL)	106	5	37	.268	R-R	6-0	185	1/12/60 Springfield, IL
47	Little, Bryan	Buffalo	56	1	20	.306	B-R	5-10	160	10/8/59 Houston, TX
		Chicago (AL)	47	2	27	.250				
25	Morman, Russ	Glens Falls	131	17	81	.310	R-R	6-4	215	4/28/62 Independence, MO
		Buffalo	19	7	14	.297				
6	Salazar, Luis	Chicago (AL)	80	10	45	.245	R-R	5-9	180	5/19/56 Venezuela
—	Tolleson, Wayne	Texas	101	1	18	.313	B-R	5-9	160	11/22/55 Spartanburg, SC
29	Walker, Greg	Chicago (AL)	155	24	92	.258	L-R	6-3	210	10/6/60 Douglas, GA

OUTFIELDERS

No.	Name	1985 Club	H	HR	RBI	Pct.	B-T	Ht.	Wt.	Born
3	Baines, Harold	Chicago (AL)	198	22	113	.309	L-L	6-2	195	3/15/59 Easton, MD
8	Boston, Daryl	Buffalo	65	10	35	.271	L-L	6-3	193	1/4/63 Cincinnati, OH
		Chicago (AL)	53	3	15	.228				
33	Cangelosi, John	Buffalo	58	1	21	..238	B-L	5-8	150	3/10/63 Brooklyn, NY
		Chicago (AL)	0	0	0	.000				
17	Hairston, Jerry	Chicago (AL)	34	2	20	.243	B-R	5-10	190	2/16/52 Birmingham, AL
42	Kittle, Ron	Chicago (AL)	87	26	58	.230	R-R	6-4	220	1/5/58 Gary, IN
		Buffalo	7	2	5	.333				
23	Law, Rudy	Chicago (AL)	101	4	36	.259	L-L	6-2	176	10/7/56 Waco, TX
20	Nichols, Reid	Bos.-Chi. (AL)	41	2	18	.273	R-R	5-11	172	8/5/58 Ocala, TX
16	Williams, Ken	Glens Falls	130	16	66	.250	R-R	6-1	184	4/6/64 Berkeley, CA

*Free agent unsigned at press time

WHITE SOX PROFILES

HAROLD BAINES 27 6-2 195 **Bats L Throws L**

One of the finest clutch hitters around and he keeps getting better . . . Set career highs with a .309 average and 113 RBI . . . Missed 200 hits by two when he went hitless in his final three games . . . Had a team-leading 14-game hitting streak in April . . . Also suffered through 0-for-26 drought in May . . . A notoriously slow starter, he broke tradition and hit .356 in April before slumping to .188 in May last season . . . Right fielder had nine homers through Aug. 22, then hit 13 in his last 45 games . . . Shared club lead in game-winning RBI with 13 . . . Born March 15, 1959, in Easton, Md. . . . Was first pick in nation in June 1977 draft . . . Had been scouted since he was 12 by former White Sox owner Bill Veeck when both lived on Maryland Eastern Shore . . . Led AL in slugging percentage in 1984 with .541 mark . . . Ranks as all-time home-run leader among White Sox' left-handed batters.

Year	Club	Pos.	G	AB	R	H	2B	3B	HR	RBI	SB	Avg.
1980	Chicago (AL)	OF	141	491	55	125	23	6	13	49	2	.255
1981	Chicago (AL)	OF	82	280	42	80	11	7	10	41	6	.286
1982	Chicago (AL)	OF	161	608	89	165	29	8	25	105	10	.271
1983	Chicago (AL)	OF	156	596	76	167	32	2	20	99	7	.280
1984	Chicago (AL)	OF	147	569	72	173	28	10	29	94	1	.304
1985	Chicago (AL)	OF	160	640	86	198	29	3	22	113	1	.309
	Totals		847	3184	420	908	152	36	119	501	27	.285

CARLTON FISK 38 6-2 217 **Bats R Throws R**

"Pudge" had one of his finest seasons . . . Set career highs with 37 homers, the second-best figure in AL, and 107 RBI . . . Hit 33 homers as a catcher, breaking AL record set by Lance Parrish . . . His 37 homers tied club record set by Dick Allen in 1972 . . . Played in career-high 153 games . . . The grind took its toll over last two months as he hit only five homers after Aug. 14. . . . Credited offseason weight training program for his increased power . . . Matched his career high with 17 stolen bases, ranking second on club . . . Rebounded from disappointing 1984 season in which he suffered an abdominal muscle pull . . . Born Dec. 26, 1947, in Bellows Falls, Vt. . . . Signed by Red Sox as fourth player picked in June 1967 draft . . . Hit dramatic 12th-inning homer in Game 6 of 1975 World Series against Cincinnati . . . Signed with White Sox as veteran free agent prior to 1981 season and decided to test market again after last season . . .

Second to Yogi Berra in career homers by an AL catcher... Brother-in-law of Rick Miller.

Year	Club	Pos.	G	AB	R	H	2B	3B	HR	RBI	SB	Avg.
1969	Boston	C	2	5	0	0	0	0	0	0	0	.000
1971	Boston	C	14	48	7	15	2	1	2	6	0	.313
1972	Boston	C	131	457	74	134	28	9	22	61	4	.293
1973	Boston	C	135	508	65	125	21	0	26	71	7	.246
1974	Boston	C	52	187	36	56	12	1	11	26	5	.299
1975	Boston	C	79	263	47	87	14	4	10	52	4	.331
1976	Boston	C	134	487	76	124	17	5	17	58	12	.255
1977	Boston	C	152	536	106	169	26	3	26	102	7	.315
1978	Boston	C-OF	157	571	94	162	39	5	20	88	7	.284
1979	Boston	C-OF	91	320	49	87	23	2	10	42	3	.272
1980	Boston	C-OF-1B-3B	131	478	73	138	25	3	18	62	11	.289
1981	Chicago (AL) ..	C-1B-3B-OF	96	338	44	89	12	0	7	46	3	.263
1982	Chicago (AL) ..	C-1B	135	476	66	127	17	3	14	65	17	.267
1983	Chicago (AL) ..	C	138	488	85	141	26	4	26	86	9	.289
1984	Chicago (AL) ..	C	102	359	54	83	20	1	21	43	6	.231
1985	Chicago (AL) ..	C	153	543	85	129	23	1	37	107	17	.238
	Totals		1702	6064	961	1666	305	42	267	915	113	.275

RON KITTLE 28 6-4 220 **Bats R Throws R**

Suffered through miserable first half after injuring his right shoulder by running into left-field wall on first weekend of season... Tried to play with the injury before White Sox finally put him on disabled list July 4... On Aug. 8, he was hitting .191 with eight homers and 17 RBI... From that point on, he hit 18 homers, drove in 41 runs and raised his average to .230 ... Hit two homers in a game five times... Born Jan. 5, 1958, in Gary, Ind.... Signed by Dodgers as a free agent in 1977... Underwent spinal fusion after first pro season and was released in 1978 ... Signed by White Sox after a special tryout in September 1978 that was arranged by former Chicago pitcher Billy Pierce ... Was an iron construction worker at the time... Chosen Minor League Player of the Year in 1982, when he hit .345 with 50 homers and 144 RBI for Edmonton (AAA).

Year	Club	Pos.	G	AB	R	H	2B	3B	HR	RBI	SB	Avg.
1982	Chicago (AL)	OF	20	29	3	7	2	0	1	7	0	.241
1983	Chicago (AL)	OF	145	520	75	132	19	3	35	100	8	.254
1984	Chicago (AL)	OF	139	466	67	100	15	0	32	74	3	.215
1985	Chicago (AL)	OF	116	379	51	87	12	0	26	58	1	.230
	Totals		420	1394	196	326	48	3	94	239	12	.234

GREG WALKER 26 6-3 210 **Bats L Throws R**

Tied a career high with 24 homers, though a September slump pulled his average down to career-low .258... Tied club record by playing in 163 games, including a rain-curtailed seven-inning tie against Red Sox... Tied with Carlton Fisk and Harold Baines for club lead in game-winning RBI with 13... Had an 11-game hitting streak in September, his career high...

Has worked hard on his defensive work at first base, making himself into a better-than-average fielder . . . Committed 11 errors in 1985 . . . Born Oct. 6, 1959, in Douglas, Ga. . . . Signed by Phillies as 20th-round pick in June 1977 draft . . . Drafted by White Sox in minor-league draft after 1979 season . . . Has big swing, leading to club-leading 100 strikeouts in 1985.

Year	Club	Pos.	G	AB	R	H	2B	3B	HR	RBI	SB	Avg.
1982	Chicago (AL)	DH	11	17	3	7	2	1	2	7	0	.412
1983	Chicago (AL)	1B	118	307	32	83	16	3	10	55	2	.270
1984	Chicago (AL)	1B	136	442	62	130	29	2	24	75	8	.294
1985	Chicago (AL)	1B	163	601	77	155	38	4	24	92	5	.258
	Totals		428	1367	174	375	85	10	60	229	15	.274

WAYNE TOLLESON 30 5-9 160 **Bats S Throws R**

White Sox acquired this second baseman from Rangers along with Dave Schmidt for Scott Fletcher and Ed Correa during offseason . . . In 123 games in 1985, he batted .313, a full 100 points higher than his 1984 average . . . Boasted the fifth-best average in AL among players with 200 or more at-bats . . . Stole 21 bases, marking third straight season in which he has had at least 20 . . . Improved tremendously against right-handed pitching, hitting .333 from left side in 1985, a big improvement over his .189 mark in 1984 . . . Born Nov. 22, 1955, in Spartanburg, S.C. . . . Selected by Texas in eighth round of June 1978 draft . . . Was high-school football teammate of NFL quarterback Steve Fuller . . . Was wide receiver who led NCAA in pass receptions in his senior year at Western Carolina.

Year	Club	Pos.	G	AB	R	H	2B	3B	HR	RBI	SB	Avg.
1981	Texas	3B-SS	14	24	6	4	0	0	0	1	2	.167
1982	Texas	SS-3B-2B	38	70	6	8	1	0	0	2	1	.114
1983	Texas	2B-SS	134	470	64	122	13	2	3	20	33	.260
1984	Texas	2B-SS-3B-OF	118	338	35	72	9	2	0	9	22	.213
1985	Texas	2B-SS-3B	123	323	45	101	9	5	1	18	21	.313
	Totals		427	1225	156	307	32	9	4	50	79	.251

OZZIE GUILLEN 22 5-11 150 **Bats L Throws R**

Staked reputation as one of the finest fielding shortstops in the game during outstanding rookie season . . . Committed only 12 errors, a White Sox record for shortstops and the fewest errors made by any starting shortstop in majors last year . . . Has great instincts and range . . . An aggressive hitter who walked only 12 times . . . Hit .276 in April, then slumped and was hitting .210 June 13 . . . Rallied to finish at .273 . . . Hit .308 in four minor-league seasons . . . Born Jan. 20, 1964, in Oculare del Tuy, Venezuela . . . Signed by San Diego as free agent in 1980 . . . Traded from Padres to White Sox with Tim Lollar, Bill Long and Luis

Salazar for LaMarr Hoyt, Todd Simmons and Kevin Kristan prior to 1985 season . . . Third Venezuelan shortstop for White Sox, following Chico Carrasquel and Luis Aparicio . . . Originally a switch-hitter, he has hit exclusively from left side the past three years . . . Named AL Rookie of the Year.

Year	Club	Pos.	G	AB	R	H	2B	3B	HR	RBI	SB	Avg.
1985	Chicago (AL)	SS	150	491	71	134	21	9	1	33	7	.273

FLOYD BANNISTER 30 6-1 203 **Bats L Throws L**

After posting winning records in previous two seasons with White Sox, he came under heavy criticism for his 10-14 season in 1985 . . . Had to win his last four starts just to reach double figures in victories . . . Lost seven straight decisions from June 10 to Aug. 25 . . . Won one game, then lost three more in a row to drop his record to 6-14 . . . Win streak at end of season pushed his ERA below 5.00 . . . His 198 strikeouts were second-best in AL and second-best in his career . . . Born June 10, 1955, in Pierre, S.D. . . . Houston made him first player picked in country in June 1976 draft . . . Was 38-6 at Arizona State . . . Had only seven games of minor-league experience before being promoted to Astros in 1977 . . . Posted 11-18 record over two years before Houston traded him to Seattle for Craig Reynolds before 1979 season . . . Chosen by 16 teams in re-entry draft before signing with White Sox prior to 1983 season.

Year	Club	G	IP	W	L	Pct.	SO	BB	H	ERA
1977	Houston	24	143	8	9	.471	112	68	138	4.03
1978	Houston	20	110	3	0	.250	94	63	120	4.83
1979	Seattle	30	182	10	15	.400	115	68	185	4.05
1980	Seattle	32	218	9	13	.409	155	66	200	3.47
1981	Seattle	21	121	9	9	.500	85	39	128	4.46
1982	Seattle	35	247	12	13	.480	209	77	225	3.43
1983	Chicago (AL)	34	217⅓	16	10	.615	193	71	191	3.35
1984	Chicago (AL)	34	218	14	11	.560	152	80	211	4.83
1985	Chicago (AL)	34	210⅔	10	14	.417	198	100	211	4.87
	Totals	272	1667	91	103	.469	1313	632	1609	4.08

TOM SEAVER 41 6-1 221 **Bats R Throws R**

Gained membership into "300 Club" with victory at Yankee Stadium Aug. 4 . . . Set a major-league record with his 15th Opening Day start, April 9 in Milwaukee . . . Ranks third on the all-time strikeout list with 3,537 strikeouts . . . Missed two starts, because of back spasms and a flu bug, marking the first time since 1982 that he missed a turn . . . Born Nov. 17, 1944, in Fresno, Cal. . . . Signed by Atlanta in 1966, but commissioner William Eckert ruled the signing violated rules and Mets subsequently won a special drawing for rights to him . . . Won NL Rookie of the Year Award in 1967 and NL Cy Young Award in 1969, 1973 and 1975 . . . Acquired from Mets in compensation pool prior to 1984 season . . . Considered to be a gaffe by Mets, who gambled and left him unprotected because they believed his age and prohibitive contract would make him undesirable.

Year	Club	G	IP	W	L	Pct.	SO	BB	H	ERA
1967	New York (NL)	35	251	16	13	.552	170	78	224	2.76
1968	New York (NL)	36	278	16	12	.571	205	48	224	2.20
1969	New York (NL)	36	273	25	7	.781	208	82	202	2.21
1970	New York (NL)	37	291	18	12	.600	283	83	230	2.81
1971	New York (NL)	36	286	20	10	.667	289	61	210	1.76
1972	New York (NL)	35	262	21	12	.636	249	77	215	2.92
1973	New York (NL)	36	290	19	10	.655	251	64	219	2.07
1974	New York (NL)	32	236	11	11	.500	201	75	199	3.20
1975	New York (NL)	36	280	22	9	.710	243	88	217	2.38
1976	New York (NL)	35	271	14	11	.560	235	77	211	2.59
1977	NY (NL)-Cin.	33	261	21	6	.778	196	66	199	2.59
1978	Cincinnati	36	260	16	14	.533	226	89	218	2.87
1979	Cincinnati	32	215	16	6	.727	131	61	187	3.14
1980	Cincinnati	26	168	10	8	.556	101	59	140	3.64
1981	Cincinnati	23	166	14	2	.875	87	66	120	2.55
1982	Cincinnati	21	111⅓	5	13	.278	62	44	136	5.50
1983	New York (NL)	34	231	9	14	.391	135	86	201	3.55
1984	Chicago (AL)	34	236⅔	15	11	.577	131	61	216	3.95
1985	Chicago (AL)	35	238⅔	16	11	.593	134	69	223	3.17
	Totals	628	4605⅔	304	192	.613	3537	1334	3791	2.82

BOB JAMES 27 6-4 230 **Bats R Throws R**

Set White Sox record with 32 saves, despite missing nearly a month with a knee injury . . . Broke record of 30 set by Ed Farmer in 1980 . . . Blew only nine of 41 save opportunities . . . Injured his knee July 11 . . . Came back July 31, but was not 100 percent . . . Won Rolaids Relief Award for September . . . Allowed only five homers in 110 innings . . . Owns one of the best fastballs in AL . . . Born Aug. 15, 1958, in Glendale, Cal. . . . Expos made him ninth player picked in June 1976 draft . . . In 1984, he spent his first full season in majors as he shared bullpen load with Jeff Reardon . . . Traded to White Sox for Vance Law prior to 1985 season . . . Did not pitch regularly until his senior year in high school, when he threw two no-hitters . . . Had been a catcher.

Year	Club	G	IP	W	L	Pct.	SO	BB	H	ERA
1978	Montreal	4	4	0	1	.000	3	4	4	9.00
1979	Montreal	2	2	0	0	.000	1	3	2	13.50
1982	Montreal	7	9	0	0	.000	11	8	10	6.00
1982	Detroit	12	19⅔	0	2	.000	20	8	22	5.03
1983	Detroit	4	4	0	0	.000	4	3	5	11.25
1983	Montreal	27	50	1	0	1.000	56	23	37	2.88
1984	Montreal	62	96	6	6	.500	91	45	92	3.66
1985	Chicago (AL)	69	110	8	7	.533	88	23	90	2.13
	Totals	187	294⅔	15	16	.484	274	117	262	3.36

JUAN AGOSTO 28 6-2 187 **Bats L Throws L**

Carried burden of being the only left-hander out of the White Sox bullpen for most of the season . . . Struggled a bit early and was sent to Buffalo (AAA) for 10 days to work out his problems . . . Came back and pitched well the rest of the season . . . Has a good breaking ball that is tough on left-handed hitters . . . Allowed only 45 hits in 60⅓ innings . . . Has surrendered only five homers during the last two years . . . Born Feb. 23, 1958, in Rio Piedras, Puerto Rico . . . A successful reclamation project . . . Signed with Red Sox as free agent in 1974 at age 16 . . . Experienced arm trouble and was released in 1978 . . . Sat out entire 1979 season . . . Signed by White Sox as free agent in 1980, on recommendation of former major-leaguer Orlando Cepeda, then a White Sox coach . . . Converted from a starter into a reliever.

Year	Club	G	IP	W	L	Pct.	SO	BB	H	ERA
1981	Chicago (AL)	2	6	0	0	.000	3	0	5	4.50
1982	Chicago (AL)	1	2	0	0	.000	1	0	7	18.00
1983	Chicago (AL)	39	41⅔	2	2	.500	29	11	41	4.10
1984	Chicago (AL)	49	55⅓	2	1	.667	26	34	54	3.09
1985	Chicago (AL)	54	60⅓	4	3	.571	39	23	45	3.58
	Totals	145	165⅓	8	6	.571	98	68	152	3.76

TOP PROSPECTS

JOEL DAVIS 21 6-5 210 **Bats R Throws R**

Has made fast progression through White Sox system since being selected in first round of June 1983 draft as the 13th player chosen overall . . . Started 1985 with Glens Falls (AA) and finished the season in White Sox rotation . . . Made major-league debut Aug. 27 and beat Milwaukee . . . Made 11 starts in 12 appearances for Chicago, going 3-3 with 4.16 ERA and one complete game . . . Was 1-1 with 2.84 ERA for Glens Falls after getting a late start due to an injury . . . Was 2-5 with 4.79 ERA in 10 games for Buffalo (AAA) before earning his promotion to White Sox . . . Born Jan. 30, 1965, in Jacksonville, Fla.

RUSS MORMAN 23 6-4 215 **Bats R Throws R**

White Sox have ideas of playing him at third base to enable him to reach majors more quickly . . . Originally a first baseman, he was second-round pick by White Sox in June 1983 draft . . . Hit .310 for Glens Falls with 17 homers and 81 RBI in 119 games last season . . . Promoted to Buffalo and hit .297 with seven homers and 14 RBI in 21 games . . . Born April 28, 1962, in Independence, Mo.

MANAGER TONY LaRUSSA: His job always seems to be on the line, but he always saves it . . . Led White Sox to 85-77 record and third-place finish, six games behind AL West titlist Kansas City . . . Rebounded from tough 1984 season, when White Sox suffered biggest dropoff in victories by any defending champion in history, dipping from 99 in 1983 to 74 . . . Replaced Don Kessinger as White Sox manager Aug. 2, 1979 after serving as a coach with White Sox for half of 1978 season . . . Had managed parts of two seasons in minors . . . Signed as a shortstop with Kansas City A's in 1962 . . . Spent parts of six years in majors, hitting .199 in career that spanned 1962-77 . . . Holds a law degree from Florida State . . . Born Oct. 4, 1944, in Tampa . . . Has composite major-league record of 496-472 . . . An American Legion teammate of Yankee manager Lou Piniella.

GREATEST SHORTSTOP

Luis Aparicio and Luke Appling are listed consecutively in the Baseball Encyclopedia. They are just as close when it comes to selecting the greatest shortstop in White Sox history. Appling was known for the great hitting ability that gave him a .310 average over 20 seasons. Aparicio was one of the finest defensive shortstops in history and a devastating threat on the basepaths.

This is how close the careers of Aparicio and Appling were: Aparicio played the most games at shortstop in history (2,581) and Appling is second (2,218); Aparicio is sixth in putouts (4,548), Appling is seventh (4,398); Aparicio is first in assists (8,016), Appling is fourth (7,218); Aparicio is first in double plays (1,553), Appling is second (1,424).

Aparicio led the American League in stolen bases in each of his first nine seasons, beginning in 1956. Appling, who retired after the 1950 season following a career spent entirely with the White Sox, won the league batting title in 1936 and 1943. Both players are in the Hall of Fame. Aparicio, known as "Little Looie," was inducted in 1984. Appling, known as "Old Aches and Pains," was enshrined 20 years earlier. There they are, forever linked in baseball history.

ALL-TIME WHITE SOX SEASON RECORDS

BATTING: Luke Appling, .388, 1936
HRs: Dick Allen, 37, 1972
Carlton Fisk, 37, 1985
RBIs: Zeke Bonura, 138, 1936
STEALS: Rudy Law, 77, 1983
WINS: Ed Walsh, 40, 1908
STRIKEOUTS: Ed Walsh, 269, 1908

KANSAS CITY ROYALS

TEAM DIRECTORY: Chairman: Ewing Kauffman; Vice-Chairman: Avron Fogelman; Pres.: Joe Burke; Exec. VP-GM: John Schuerholz; Exec. VP-Adm.: Spencer Robinson; Dir. Scouting/Play. Dev.: Art Stewart; VP-Pub. Rel.: Dean Vogelaar; Trav. Sec.: Will Rudd; Mgr.: Dick Howser. Home: Royals Stadium (40,625). Field distances: 330, l.f. line; 385, l.c.; 410, c.f.; 385, r.c.; 330, r.f. line. Spring training: Fort Myers, Fla.

SCOUTING REPORT

HITTING: With their pitching staff, the Royals don't need much offense and they have just enough to get by. But any lineup that includes George Brett (.335, 30 homers, 112 RBI) deserves some respect. Brett enjoyed one of his finest seasons in 1985, thanks to a rigorous offseason conditioning program and a lack of injuries. Willie Wilson also avoided physical problems—except for a severe reaction to a penicillin shot—and hit .278 with 43 stolen bases.

The Royals will be a better offensive club in 1986 because they'll have Lonnie Smith for the entire season. Smith (.257, 40 steals), who was acquired from St. Louis, combined with Wilson to give Kansas City one of the most dangerous one-two combinations at the top of any AL lineup. They figure to give Brett and ageless DH Hal McRae (.259, 14 homers, 70 RBI) plenty of RBI opportunities. The Royals have learned to tolerate the strikeouts and streaky hitting of Steve Balboni (36 homers, 88 RBI). He has developed into a true power threat and that is a much-needed commodity in this lineup.

PITCHING: AL Cy Young Award winner Bret Saberhagen (20-6, 2.87) had a Cinderella year at the age of 21. He won 20 games in the regular season, won two games in the World Series and fathered his first child in 1985. For an encore, Saberhagen said he'd like to win 21 games, win three World Series games and have twins. He is the ace of a young, deep pitching staff that is the best in the AL.

The Royals boasted four other pitchers who won at least 10 games—Bud Black (10-15, 4.33 ERA), who figures to reverse those numbers; Danny Jackson (14-12, 3.42 ERA); Charlie Leibrandt (17-9, 2.69 ERA) and Mark Gubicza (14-10, 4.06 ERA). As if that isn't enough pitching, the Royals also have Dan Quisenberry (8-9, 2.37 ERA and 37 saves) in the bullpen.

Buddy Biancalana was out here, but Royals were '85 champs.

FIELDING: With Buddy Bell out of the league, Brett finally landed his first Gold Glove. He earned it. Brett has worked hard over the years to turn himself from a below-average third baseman into a consistent and even spectacular one at times. Second baseman Frank White has slowed a bit. His 17 errors were the most by any AL second baseman last year.

The Royals have Buddy Biancalana to provide smooth defense at shortstop, but they are still wrestling with the need for more offensive punch at that position. Smith is a liability in left and he is removed from close games in the late innings. But the speedy Wilson still plays one of the shallowest and steadiest center fields in the league.

OUTLOOK: Why mess with success? The world champions will use the same formula in 1986. They have a pitching staff that is the envy of the AL. They play good defense and have just enough hitting to win by a run. Last year, they were one game better than California and needed to come back from 3-1 postseason deficits to beat Toronto and St. Louis. The Royals should repeat, at least in the AL West, which they've won seven times in the past 10 years.

KANSAS CITY ROYALS 1986 ROSTER

MANAGER Dick Howser

Coaches—Gary Blaylock, Mike Ferraro, Jose Martinez, Lee May, Jim Schaffer

PITCHERS

No.	Name	1985 Club	W-L	IP	SO	ERA	B-T	Ht.	Wt.	Born
27	Beckwith, Joe	Kansas City	1-5	95	80	4.07	L-R	6-2	200	1/28/55 Auburn, AL
40	Black, Bud	Kansas City	10-15	206	122	4.33	L-L	6-2	180	6/30/57 San Mateo, CA
13	Cone, David	Omaha	9-15	159	113	4.65	L-R	6-1	180	1/2/63 Kansas City, MO
26	Farr, Steve	Omaha	10-4	134	98	2.02	R-R	5-11	190	12/12/56 Cheverly, MD
		Kansas City	2-1	38	36	3.11				
51	Ferreira, Tony	Omaha	11-10	174	105	3.21	L-L	6-1	160	10/4/62 Riverside, CA
		Kansas City	0-0	6	5	7.94				
23	Gubicza, Mark	Kansas City	14-10	177	99	4.06	R-R	6-6	215	8/14/62 Philadelphia, PA
—	Hargesheimer, Al	Omaha	11-10	152	91	2.91	R-R	6-3	200	11/21/56 Chicago, IL
38	Huismann, Mark	Omaha	4-5	88	70	2.04	R-R	6-3	195	5/11/58 Lincoln, NE
		Kansas City	1-0	19	9	1.93				
25	Jackson, Danny	Kansas City	14-12	208	114	3.42	R-L	6-0	190	1/5/62 San Antonio, TX
17	Jones, Mike	Kansas City	3-3	64	32	4.78	L-L	6-5	230	7/39/59 Rochester, NY
37	Leibrandt, Charlie	Kansas City	17-9	238	108	2.69	R-L	6-3	200	10/4/56 Chicago, IL
22	Leonard, Dennis	Ft. Myers	2-0	16	10	1.10	R-R	6-1	195	5/8/51 Brooklyn, NY
		Memphis	0-0	5	1	7.20				
		Kansas City	0-0	2	1	0.00				
29	Quisenberry, Dan	Kansas City	8-9	129	54	2.37	R-R	6-2	180	2/7/53 Santa Monica, CA
31	Saberhagen, Bret	Kansas City	20-6	235	158	2.87	R-R	6-1	160	4/11/64 Chicago Heights, IL

CATCHERS

No.	Name	1985 Club	H	HR	RBI	Pct.	B-T	Ht.	Wt.	Born
8	Sundberg, Jim	Kansas City	90	10	35	.245	R-R	6-0	195	5/18/51 Galesburg, IL
18	Quirk, Jamie	Kansas City	16	0	4	.281	L-R	6-4	200	10/22/54 Whittier, CA
12	Wathan, John	Kansas City	34	1	9	.234	R-R	6-2	205	10/4/49 Cedar Rapids, IA

INFIELDERS

No.	Name	1985 Club	H	HR	RBI	Pct.	B-T	Ht.	Wt.	Born
45	Balboni, Steve	Kansas City	146	36	88	.243	R-R	6-3	225	1/16/57 Brockton, MA
1	Biancalana, Buddy	Kansas City	26	1	6	.188	B-R	5-11	160	2/2/60 Larkspur, CA
5	Brett, George	Kansas City	184	30	112	.335	L-R	6-0	195	5/15/53 Glendale, WV
—	Citari, Joe	Memphis	124	22	64	.253	R-R	6-2	195	8/31/63 Oak Park, IL
2	Concepcion, Onix	Kansas City	64	2	20	.204	R-R	5-6	180	10/5/58 Puerto Rico
4	Pryor, Greg	Kansas City	25	1	3	.219	R-R	6-0	185	10/2/49 Marietta, OH
16	Scranton, Jim	Omaha	74	1	29	.196	R-R	6-0	175	5/5/60 Torrance, CA
		Kansas City	0	0	0	.000				
20	White, Frank	Kansas City	140	22	69	.249	R-R	5-11	175	9/4/50 Greenville, MS

OUTFIELDERS

No.	Name	1985 Club	H	HR	RBI	Pct.	B-T	Ht.	Wt.	Born
—	Brewer, Mike	Maine	97	17	53	.235	R-R	6-5	190	10/24/59 Shreveport, LA
9	*Iorg, Dane	Kansas City	29	1	21	.223	L-R	6-0	180	5/11/50 Eureka, CA
35	Jones, Lynn	Kansas City	32	0	9	.211	R-R	5-9	170	1/1/53 Meadville, PA
—	Kingery, Mike	Omaha	113	2	49	.255	L-L	6-0	180	3/29/61 St. James, MN
36	Leeper, Dave	Omaha	106	10	52	.279	L-L	5-11	170	10/30/59 Santa Ana, CA
		Kansas City	3	0	4	.088				
11	McRae, Hal	Kansas City	83	14	70	.259	R-R	5-11	185	7/10/46 Avon Park, FL
24	Motley, Darryl	Kansas City	85	17	49	.222	R-R	5-9	196	1/21/60 Muskogee, OK
3	Orta, Jorge	Kansas City	80	4	45	.267	L-R	5-10	175	11/26/50 Mexico
15	Sheridan, Pat	Kansas City	47	3	17	.228	L-R	6-3	175	12/4/57 Ann Arbor, MI
21	Smith, Lonnie	St. Louis	25	0	7	.260	R-R	5-9	170	12/22/55 Chicago, IL
		Kansas City	115	6	41	.257				
48	Snider, Van	Memphis	69	8	39	.236	L-R	6-3	180	8/11/63 Birmingham, AL
—	Thurman, Gary	Fort Myers	137	0	45	.302	R-R	5-10	165	11/12/64 Indianapolis, IN
6	Wilson, Willie	Kansas City	168	4	43	.278	B-R	6-3	195	7/9/55 Montgomery, AL

*Free agent unsigned at press time

ROYAL PROFILES

GEORGE BRETT 32 6-0 195 **Bats L Throws R**

Strict offseason conditioning program was rewarded by injury-free season in 1985 . . . Was second in AL in batting (.335), total bases (322), on-base percentage (.436) and extra-base hits (73) . . . Led AL in slugging percentage (.585) . . . Was third in league in walks (103) and game-winning RBI (16) and fifth in doubles (38), runs (108) and RBI (112) . . . Played in 155 games, the most since 1976 . . . Homered in each of his last four games . . . AL Player of the Month in May, when he hit .350 with six homers and 22 RBI . . . His 31 intentional walks led majors . . . Had .967 fielding percentage, second among AL third basemen who played at least 100 games . . . Born May 15, 1953, in Glendale, W. Va. . . . Selected in second round of June 1971 draft . . . Has batted over .300 in nine of his 12 seasons . . . Starting third baseman for AL in 10 straight All-Star Games . . . Hit the infamous "Pine Tar" home run off Goose Gossage, July 24, 1983 . . . Also homered off Gossage in Game 3 of AL Championship Series in 1980, giving Royals their first pennant . . . Named MVP of 1985 AL Championship Series against Toronto.

Year	Club	Pos.	G	AB	R	H	2B	3B	HR	RBI	SB	Avg.
1973	Kansas City	3B	13	40	2	5	2	0	0	0	0	.125
1974	Kansas City	3B-SS	133	457	49	129	21	5	2	47	8	.282
1975	Kansas City	3B-SS	159	634	84	195	35	13	11	89	13	.308
1976	Kansas City	3B-SS	159	645	94	215	34	14	7	67	21	.333
1977	Kansas City	3B-SS	139	564	105	170	32	13	22	88	14	.312
1978	Kansas City	3B-SS	128	510	79	150	45	8	9	62	23	.294
1979	Kansas City	3B-1B	154	645	119	212	42	20	23	107	17	.329
1980	Kansas City	3B-1B	117	449	87	175	33	9	24	118	15	.390
1981	Kansas City	3B	89	347	42	109	27	7	6	43	14	.314
1982	Kansas City	3B-OF	144	552	101	166	32	9	21	82	6	.301
1983	Kansas City	3B-1B-OF	123	464	90	144	38	2	25	93	0	.310
1984	Kansas City	3B	104	377	42	107	21	3	13	69	0	.284
1985	Kansas City	3B	155	550	108	184	38	5	30	112	9	.335
	Totals		1617	6234	1002	1967	400	108	193	977	140	.316

STEVE BALBONI 29 6-3 225 **Bats R Throws**

A true power hitter who generally hits the ball a long way or not at all . . . Slugged club-record 36 homers in 1985 . . . Has hit 64 homers in last two years . . . Hit a record 16 homers at Royals Stadium in 1985 . . . Hit home runs in four straight games in July . . . Royals were 28-4 in games in which he homered . . . First baseman also set a club record with 166 strikeouts . . . Hit second grand slam of his career April 30 against Cleveland

...Born Jan. 16, 1957, in Brockton, Mass....Obtained from Yankees with Roger Erickson for Mike Armstrong and Duane Dewey prior to 1984 season...Was a Yankee yo-yo, going up and down between Columbus (AAA) and majors...Hit 27 or more homers in four straight minor-league seasons before the trade ...A fourth-round pick by Yankees in June 1978 draft...Had several key hits en route to .320 World Series average, but went entire 1985 postseason without getting an extra-base hit.

Year	Club	Pos.	G	AB	R	H	2B	3B	HR	RBI	SB	Avg.
1981	New York (AL)	1B	4	7	2	2	1	1	0	2	0	.286
1982	New York (AL)	1B	33	107	8	20	2	1	2	4	0	.187
1983	New York (AL)	1B	32	86	8	20	2	0	5	17	0	.233
1984	Kansas City	1B	126	438	58	107	23	2	28	77	0	.244
1985	Kansas City	1B	160	600	74	146	28	2	36	88	1	.243
	Totals		355	1238	150	295	56	6	71	188	1	.238

JIM SUNDBERG 34 6-0 195 — Bats R Throws R

After playing for non-contenders in Texas and Milwaukee, he saw first postseason action of his 12-year career...Scored winning run in Game 6 of 1985 World Series on head-first slide in ninth inning...Tied a career high with 10 homers...Hit only .213 in April, but rebounded by hitting in 10 straight games starting May 12...Missed 24 games after having cartilage pull away from his lower left rib cage during batting practice Aug. 18...Has won six Gold Gloves, but his throwing efficiency has eroded somewhat...Threw out 18-of-70 would-be basestealers last season after gunning down 41-of-82 in 1984...Ranked third among AL catchers with .992 fielding percentage...Born May 18, 1951, in Galesburg, Ill....Obtained from Milwaukee in four-team deal prior to 1985 season in which Royals surrendered catcher Don Slaught and pitcher Frank Willis...Played 10 years with Texas without spending time on the disabled list...Iowa grad was chosen by Rangers in second round of January 1973 draft.

Year	Club	Pos.	G	AB	R	H	2B	3B	HR	RBI	SB	Avg.
1974	Texas	C	132	368	45	91	13	3	3	36	2	.247
1975	Texas	C	155	472	45	94	9	0	6	36	3	.199
1976	Texas	C	140	448	33	102	24	2	3	34	0	.228
1977	Texas	C	149	453	61	132	20	3	6	65	2	.291
1978	Texas	C	149	518	54	144	23	6	6	58	2	.278
1979	Texas	C	150	495	50	136	23	4	5	64	3	.275
1980	Texas	C	151	505	59	138	24	1	10	63	2	.273
1981	Texas	C-OF	102	339	42	94	17	2	3	28	2	.277
1982	Texas	C-OF	139	470	37	118	22	5	10	47	2	.251
1983	Texas	C	131	378	30	76	14	0	2	28	0	.201
1984	Milwaukee	[illegible]	110	[illegible]	[illegible]	91	19	4	7	43	1	.261
1985	Kansas City	C	115	367	38	90	12	4	10	35	0	.245
	Totals		1623	5161	537	1306	220	34	71	537	19	.253

WILLIE WILSON 30 6-3 195 **Bats S Throws R**

Center fielder had a unique season . . . Missed 18 games in September after a penicillin shot in his buttocks caused swelling and necessitated minor surgery . . . Missed two games when a throw from catcher Carlton Fisk hit him in back of neck . . . Hit four balls out of the park in 1985 . . . Only eight of his 21 career homers have gone over the wall . . . Led the club in steals for eighth straight year with 43 . . . Stole 400th base of his career . . . Drove in deciding run in 10th inning of 5-4 victory Oct. 5 that gave the Royals the AL West title . . . Born July 9, 1955, in Montgomery, Ala. . . . Selected in first round of June 1974 draft . . . Was a football star in high school and had accepted a scholarship offer to Maryland before signing with Royals . . . Began switch-hitting at Omaha (AAA) in 1977 . . . Had 11 hits and .367 average in 1985 World Series against Cardinals to get large monkey off his back . . . Had been 4-for-26 (.154) with 12 strikeouts in 1980 World Series against Phillies.

Year	Club	Pos.	G	AB	R	H	2B	3B	HR	RBI	SB	Avg.
1976	Kansas City	OF	12	6	0	1	0	0	0	0	2	.167
1977	Kansas City	OF	13	34	10	11	2	0	0	1	6	.324
1978	Kansas City	OF	127	198	43	43	8	2	0	16	46	.217
1979	Kansas City	OF	154	588	113	185	18	13	6	49	83	.315
1980	Kansas City	OF	161	705	133	230	28	15	3	49	79	.326
1981	Kansas City	OF	102	439	54	133	10	7	1	32	34	.303
1982	Kansas City	OF	136	585	87	194	19	15	3	46	37	.332
1983	Kansas City	OF	137	576	90	159	22	8	2	33	59	.276
1984	Kansas City	OF	128	541	81	163	24	9	2	44	47	.301
1985	Kansas City	OF	141	605	87	168	25	21	4	43	43	.278
	Totals		1111	4277	090	1207	150	90	21	010	400	.001

LONNIE SMITH 30 5-9 170 **Bats R Throws R**

Has achieved a rare triple, winning three World Series rings with three different teams . . . Also won championships with 1980 Phillies and 1982 Cardinals . . . Obtained from St. Louis for outfielder John Morris May 17 of last season . . . Stole a combined 52 bases, including 40 for the Royals . . . His .257 batting average was the lowest in his six-year career . . . Hit .318 in September . . . Batted mostly in No. 2 position, behind Willie Wilson, until manager Dick Howser decided to flip-flop the two speedsters Sept. 29 . . . Turned out to be a winning combination in World Series as each player hit above .300 . . . Born Dec. 22, 1955, in Chicago . . . Nicknamed "Skates" because of his unsteady play in left field . . . Committed nine errors with Royals . . . Led NL outfielders in errors in 1984 with 11 . . . Finished second to Bill Madlock in NL batting race in 1983 . . . First-round pick by Phillies in June 1974 draft.

Year	Club	Pos.	G	AB	R	H	2B	3B	HR	RBI	SB	Avg.
1978	Philadelphia	OF	17	4	6	0	0	0	0	0	4	.000
1979	Philadelphia	OF	17	30	4	5	2	0	0	3	2	.167
1980	Philadelphia	OF	100	298	69	101	14	4	3	20	33	.339
1981	Philadelphia	OF	62	176	40	57	14	3	2	11	21	.324
1982	St. Louis	OF	156	592	120	182	35	8	8	69	68	.307
1983	St. Louis	OF	130	492	83	158	31	5	8	45	43	.321
1984	St. Louis	OF	145	504	77	126	20	4	6	49	50	.250
1985	St. Louis	OF	28	96	15	25	2	2	0	7	12	.260
1985	Kansas City	OF	120	448	77	115	23	4	6	41	40	.257
	Totals		775	2640	511	769	141	30	33	245	273	.291

FRANK WHITE 35 5-11 175 **Bats R Throws R**

Hit a career-high 22 homers and batted fourth in Royals' lineup during World Series because of DH Hal McRae's unavailability . . . Fifteen of his homers tied the score or put Royals ahead last season . . . Led all AL second basemen in homers . . . Played in 149 games, his highest total since 1980 . . . Started Kansas City's first triple play since 1972 on May 3 at Yankee Stadium . . . Born Sept. 4, 1950, in Greenville, Miss. . . . Signed by Royals as a free agent in 1970 . . . In 1973, he became the first graduate of Royals Academy to reach majors . . . Only second baseman in AL history to win six Gold Gloves . . . Played football and basketball at Kansas City's Lincoln High, but school did not field a baseball team.

Year	Club	Pos.	G	AB	R	H	2B	3B	HR	RBI	SB	Avg.
1973	Kansas City . . .	SS-2B	51	139	20	31	6	1	0	5	3	.223
1974	Kansas City . . .	2B-SS-3B	99	204	19	45	6	3	1	18	3	.221
1975	Kansas City . . .	2B-3B-SS-C	111	304	43	76	10	2	7	36	11	.250
1976	Kansas City . . .	2B-SS	152	446	39	102	17	6	2	46	20	.229
1977	Kansas City . . .	2B-SS	152	474	59	116	21	5	5	50	23	.245
1978	Kansas City . . .	2B	143	461	66	127	24	6	7	50	13	.275
1979	Kansas City . . .	2B	127	467	73	124	26	4	10	48	28	.266
1980	Kansas City . . .	2B	154	560	70	148	23	4	7	60	19	.264
1981	Kansas City . . .	2B	94	364	35	91	17	1	9	38	4	.250
1982	Kansas City . . .	2B	145	524	71	156	45	6	11	56	10	.298
1983	Kansas City . . .	2B	146	549	52	143	35	6	11	77	13	.260
1984	Kansas City . . .	2B	129	479	58	130	22	5	17	56	5	.271
1985	Kansas City . . .	2B	149	563	62	140	25	1	22	69	10	249
	Totals		1652	5534	667	1429	277	50	109	609	162	258

HAL McRAE 39 5-11 185 **Bats R Throws R**

Re-emerged as a threat as a designated hitter, though he was limited to pinch-hitting appearances in non-DH World Series . . . After becoming full-time DH July 22, he hit .291 with seven homers and 46 RBI in 56 games . . . Hit .300 in June . . . Started only 12 times in Royals' first 46 games . . . Collected his 1,000th RBI and 2,000th hit . . . Son Brian was drafted by Royals in first round of June 1985 draft . . . Believed to be first time a father and son have played in same organization at same time . . . Born July 10, 1946, in Avon Park, Fla. . . . Obtained from Reds with Wayne Simpson for Roger Nelson and Richie Scheinblum prior to 1973 season . . . Originally signed with Reds as sixth-round pick in June 1965 draft . . . Hit .332 in 1976, but was edged for the batting crown by teammate George Brett on the last day of the season . . . Has appeared in four World Series . . . May be the most prolific DH in history.

Year	Club	Pos.	G	AB	R	H	2B	3B	HR	RBI	SB	Avg.
1968	Cincinnati	2B	17	51	1	10	1	0	0	2	1	.196
1970	Cincinnati	OF-3B-2B	70	165	18	41	6	1	8	23	0	.248
1971	Cincinnati	OF	99	337	39	89	24	2	9	34	3	.264
1972	Cincinnati	OF-3B	62	97	9	27	4	0	5	26	0	.278
1973	Kansas City	OF-3B	106	338	36	79	18	3	9	50	2	.234
1974	Kansas City	OF-3B	148	539	71	167	36	4	15	88	11	.310
1975	Kansas City	OF-3B	126	480	58	147	38	6	5	71	11	.306
1976	Kansas City	OF	149	527	75	175	34	5	8	73	22	.332
1977	Kansas City	OF	162	641	104	191	54	11	21	92	18	.298
1978	Kansas City	OF	156	623	90	170	39	5	16	72	17	.273
1979	Kansas City	DH	101	393	55	113	32	4	10	74	5	.288
1980	Kansas City	OF	124	489	73	145	39	5	14	83	10	.297
1981	Kansas City	OF	101	389	38	106	23	2	7	36	3	.272
1982	Kansas City	OF	159	613	91	189	46	8	27	133	4	.308
1983	Kansas City	DH	157	589	84	183	41	6	12	82	2	.311
1984	Kansas City	DH	106	317	30	96	13	4	3	42	0	.303
1985	Kansas City	DH	112	320	41	83	19	0	14	70	0	.259
	Totals		1954	6908	913	2011	467	66	183	1051	109	.291

DAN QUISENBERRY 33 6-2 180 — Bats R Throws R

Enduring some rocky outings early, he put together another outstanding season out of the Royals' bullpen . . . Won his fourth straight Fireman of the Year Award . . . Led AL with 37 saves . . . Broke his own club records for appearances (84) and games finished (77) . . . Posted 10 saves in July . . . Has excellent control . . . Did not walk a batter in 69 of his 84 appearances and walked 16 all season . . . Born Feb. 7, 1953, in Santa Monica, Cal. . . . Signed by Royals as a free agent in 1975 . . . Runnerup to Willie Hernandez for 1984 AL Cy Young Award . . . Made only one start in 280 appearances as a minor-leaguer . . . Won Game 6 of 1985 World Series . . . One of the wittiest players in the game . . . Has 217 career saves, ranking fifth on all-time list.

Year	Club	G	IP	W	L	Pct.	SO	BB	H	ERA
1979	Kansas City	32	40	3	2	.600	13	7	42	3.15
1980	Kansas City	75	128	12	7	.632	37	27	129	3.09
1981	Kansas City	40	62	1	4	.200	20	15	59	1.74
1982	Kansas City	72	136⅔	0	7	.563	46	12	126	2.57
1983	Kansas City	69	139	5	3	.625	48	11	118	1.94
1984	Kansas City	72	129⅓	6	3	.667	41	12	121	2.64
1985	Kansas City	84	129	8	9	471	54	16	142	2.37
	Totals	444	764	44	35	557	259	100	737	2.49

BRET SABERHAGEN 21 6-1 160 Bats R Throws R

Had a storybook season in his third year out of high school . . . Won 20 games, then won two more in the World Series while earning MVP honors . . . Was presented with his first child the day before pitching a five-hit shutout in Game 7 . . . Finished third in AL with 2.87 ERA . . . Was the fifth-youngest pitcher ever to win 20 games . . . Became youngest pitcher to win AL Cy Young Award . . . Was AL Pitcher of the Month in July, when he was 5-1 with 2.05 ERA . . . Walked only 38 and struck out 158, one of the best ratios in majors . . . Won 10 of his last 11 decisions, 13 of his last 15 and 18 of his last 21 . . . Born April 11, 1964, in Chicago Heights, Ill. . . . Chosen in 19th round of June 1982 draft . . . Compiled a 21-2 record in three high-school seasons and threw a no-hitter during senior year in city championship game at Dodger Stadium . . . Has a great knack for locating his pitches and setting up a hitter and has a lively fastball that tends to be underrated.

Year	Club	G	IP	W	L	Pct.	SO	BB	H	ERA
1984	Kansas City	38	157⅔	10	11	.476	73	36	138	3.48
1985	Kansas City	32	235⅓	20	6	.769	158	38	211	2.87
	Totals	70	393	30	17	.638	231	74	349	3.11

CHARLIE LEIBRANDT 29 6-3 200 Bats R Throws L

Was Royals' hard-luck pitcher of 1985 World Series . . . Lost Game 2 when his two-hit shutout dissolved into 4-2 defeat in ninth inning . . . Was brilliant again in Game 6, but got no decision after pitching 7⅔ innings in which he allowed one run on four hits . . . Emerged as one of AL's best left-handers during season that was the best of his career . . . His 2.69 ERA was second in AL . . . Led Kansas City pitchers with 237⅔ innings pitched . . . Named AL Pitcher of the Month in April (3-0 with 1.69 ERA) and in September (4-1 with 0.91 ERA) . . . Won seven of his last 10 starts . . . Pitched into the seventh inning in 28 of his 33 starts . . . Born Oct. 4, 1956, in Chicago . . . Obtained from Reds for Bob Tufts, June 7, 1983 . . . Had been 16-17 with 4.42 ERA with Cincinnati . . . A graduate of Miami of Ohio, where he set school records for innings pitched and strikeouts while compiling 23-17 record.

Year	Club	G	IP	W	L	Pct.	SO	BB	H	ERA
1979	Cincinnati	3	4	0	0	.000	1	2	2	0.00
1980	Cincinnati	36	174	10	9	.526	62	54	200	4.24
1981	Cincinnati	7	30	1	1	.500	9	15	28	3.60
1982	Cincinnati	36	107⅔	5	7	.417	34	48	30	5.10
1984	Kansas City	23	143⅔	11	7	.611	53	38	158	3.63
1985	Kansas City	33	237⅔	17	9	.654	108	68	223	2.69
	Totals	138	697	44	33	.571	267	225	741	3.67

TOP PROSPECTS

DAVID LEEPER 26 5-11 170 Bats L Throws L

Outfielder was recalled three times from Omaha (AAA) because of injuries to Royals . . . Hit .088 with no homers and four RBI in 15 games for Royals . . . Hit .279 with 10 homers and 52 RBI in 98 games with Omaha . . . Born Oct. 30, 1959, in Santa Ana, Cal. . . . Royals' first pick in June 1981 draft . . . Hit .257 with 16 homers and 70 RBI for Omaha in 1984 . . . Made major-league debut toward end of 1984 season, but had no hits in six at-bats . . . Not a base-stealer or a power threat, so he must improve hitting consistency to stick with Royals.

ALAN HARGESHEIMER 29 6-3 200 Bats R Throws R

Royals are hoping for a continued comeback from this big righthander, though he'll have a tough time cracking the staff . . . Was 11-10 with a 2.91 ERA for Omaha after undergoing arm surgery in May 1984 . . . Was acquired from Cubs for pitcher Derek Botelho and catcher Don Werner prior to 1984 season . . . Originally signed as a free agent by Giants in 1978 . . . Born Nov. 21, 1956, in Chicago . . . Attended Mayfair Junior College in Chicago and Northeastern Illinois . . . Has 5-8 record and 4.50 ERA in 26 major-league games with Giants and Cubs.

MANAGER DICK HOWSER: His much-publicized 0-11 post-season record changed drastically as Royals rallied to win AL Championship Series and World Series . . . On both occasions, the Royals overcame 3-1 deficits in best-of-seven series . . . None of his teams have finished lower than second in five-plus seasons as a manager . . . Won 103 games in his first managerial job, with Yankees in 1980, becoming the fourth manager to win

100 games or more in his first season . . . Had been a Yankee coach for 10 years . . . Fired after a three-game sweep by Royals in ALCS . . . Named Royals' manager Aug. 31, 1981 and led club to second-half title in split season . . . Club was 10 games under .500, but finished with 20 wins in last 33 games under him . . . Won AL West title in 1984 . . . Posted 91-71 record in 1985 . . . Born May 14, 1936, in Miami . . . Played at Florida State before signing with Kansas City A's . . . An infielder who was a member of All-Star team as a rookie with A's in 1961 . . . Also played for Indians . . . Hit .248 in 789 major-league games . . . Has a composite managerial record of 467-376 and is 364-317 with Royals.

GREATEST SHORTSTOP

Freddie Patek was best known for his small stature. He stood only 5-5 and weighed 148 pounds, which accounted for his nickname, "The Flea." But Patek provided the Royals with solid play at shortstop for nine years after he was acquired in a trade with Pittsburgh following the 1970 season.

Perhaps the best measure of Patek's contribution during those years is that the Royals won three AL West titles. Patek and second baseman Cookie Rojas provided Kansas City with the sort of stable middle infield that is so important for championship clubs.

Patek hit only 41 homers in his 14 major-league seasons and never more than six in a single season, but his value was in his ability to get on base and his consistent defense. Patek starred in the 1976 and 1977 ALCS, when he hit .389 for the Royals. Often in such big moments, the small shortstop did not go unnoticed.

ALL-TIME ROYAL SEASON RECORDS

BATTING: George Brett, .390, 1980
HRs: Steve Balboni, 36, 1985
RBIs: Hal McRae, 133, 1982
STEALS: Willie Wilson, 83, 1979
WINS: Steve Busby, 22, 1974
STRIKEOUTS: Dennis Leonard, 244, 1977

MINNESOTA TWINS

TEAM DIRECTORY: Owner: Carl Pohlad; Pres.: Howard T. Fox, Jr.: VPs: Dave Moore, Andy MacPhail, Jim McHenry, Don Schiel; Dir. Media Rel.: Tom Mee; Mgr.: Ray Miller. Home: Hubert H. Humphrey Metrodome (55,244). Field distances: 343, l.f. line; 408, c.f.; 327, r.f. line. Spring training: Orlando, Fla.

SCOUTING REPORT

HITTING: What happened to all those solid, young Twins hitters in 1985? Minnesota batted .264 as a team, ranking in the middle of the pack in AL. No Twin finished among the top 15 hitters in the league. The leading hitter on the club who qualified for the batting title was Kirby Puckett, who hit .288. Perhaps that explains why Minnesota, which was not eliminated until the final week of the 1984 season, was never a factor in the 1985 race.

The biggest disappointment was Kent Hrbek, whose average dipped to .278, though he did finish with 21 homers and 93 RBI. The Twins need better production out of Hrbek and Gary Gaetti (.246, 20 homers, 63 RBI). They'll take the same power stats

Friendly confines of Metrodome suit Tom Brunansky to an HR.

from Tom Brunansky (.242, 27 homers, 90 RBI), but would like him to hit for a higher average.

The Twins figure to improve their offense at second base with the addition of rookie Steve Lombardozzi (.370 in 28 games with the Twins) and they appear to have stumbled upon a bargain when they snatched catcher Mark Salas (.300, 9 homers, 41 RBI) from the St. Louis organization prior to last season.

PITCHING: Frank Viola won 18 games for Minnesota last season and yet he had an inconsistent year (18-14, 4.09). That's an indication that he can become the best left-hander in the league. Viola is part of the one of the most durable rotations in baseball. The staff includes Bert Blyleven (17-16, 3.16 ERA), Mike Smithson (15-14, 4.34 ERA) and John Butcher (11-14, 4.98). All four pitchers made at least 33 starts in 1985.

The Twins, though, need to shore up their bullpen. They used an assortment of pitchers in middle relief last year to set up Ron Davis, who still may not be the answer as a closer. Davis (2-6, 3.48 ERA, 25 saves) rescued himself from a miserable year with a good second half, but he may be best suited for a set-up role. Trouble is, the Twins have no one else to take the finisher's load off Davis. Only Seattle, Cleveland and Texas had a worse team ERA than the Twins' mark of 4.48 last year.

FIELDING: The Twins expect a big improvement at second base, where Lombardozzi replaces Tim Teufel, who was en route to breaking his own major-league record for completing the fewest double plays until an injury sidelined him. There remains a very large gap at shortstop. Minnesota has discovered that Roy Smalley is inadequate and Alvaro Espinoza and Ron Washington aren't the answers, either.

The Twins, though, are a sound defensive club, especially at the Metrodome. Hrbek is gaining a reputation as one of the finest-fielding first basemen in either league. Center fielder Puckett had 19 assists last season, establishing himself as one of the league's best throwers.

OUTLOOK: Manager Ray Miller will be working his first spring training with the Twins. He would like the club to run more, but Puckett is his only real threat to steal a base. The Twins were one of baseball's big disappointments last season. They seemed on the verge of winning a title, but slumped to 77-85 instead. Miller, who gained a reputation in Baltimore as a pitching expert, should get the most out of a reliable starting pitching corps. If he can find a reliever or two and the young Twins show their hitting ability in 1986, perhaps Minnesota can challenge.

MINNESOTA TWINS 1986 ROSTER

MANAGER Ray Miller

Coaches—Tom Kelly, Tony Oliva, Rick Stelmaszek, Dick Such, Wayne Terwilliger

PITCHERS

No.	Name	1985 Club	W-L	IP	SO	ERA	B-T	Ht.	Wt.	Born
52	Anderson, Allan	Toledo	7-11	176	94	3.43	L-L	5-11	169	1/7/64 Lancaster, OH
28	Blyleven, Bert	Cle.-Min.	17-16	294	206	3.16	R-R	6-3	205	4/6/51 Holland
58	Broersma, Eric	Toledo	4-5	79	63	3.74	R-R	6-4	235	1/24/60 Davis, CA
—	Burns, Tom	Lynch	2-0	52	48	1.04	R-R	6-3	200	9/30/61 Jacksonville, FL
17	Burtt, Dennis	Toledo	14-8	172	95	4.13	B-R	6-0	187	11/29/57 San Diego, CA
		Minnesota	2-2	28	9	3.81				
32	Butcher, John	Minnesota	11-14	208	92	4.98	R-R	6-4	190	3/8/57 Glendale, CA
39	Davis, Ron	Minnesota	2-6	65	72	3.48	R-R	6-4	196	8/6/55 Houston, TX
26	Eufemia, Frank	Toledo	3-1	36	23	1.49	R-R	5-11	180	12/23/59 Bronx, NY
		Minnesota	4-2	62	30	3.79				
23	Filson, Pete	Minnesota	4-5	96	42	3.67	B-L	6-2	185	9/28/58 Darby, PA
37	Hodge, Ed	Toledo	9-7	152	80	4.50	L-L	6-2	192	4/19/58 Bellflower, CA
19	Lysander, Rick	Toledo	1-0	10	8	0.87	R-R	6-2	198	2/21/53 Huntington Park, CA
		Minnesota	0-2	51	26	6.05				
—	Mitchell, Charlie	Pawtucket	5-9	112	65	2.90	R-R	6-3	169	6/24/62 Dickson, TN
		Boston	0-0	2	2	16.20				
36	Portugal, Mark	Toledo	8-5	129	89	3.78	R-R	6-0	190	10/30/62 Los Angeles, CA
		Minnesota	1-3	24	12	5.55				
—	Romero, Ramon	Maine	0-2	42	23	3.00	L-L	6-4	170	1/8/59 Dominican Republic
		Cleveland	2-3	64	38	6.58				
33	Smith, Roy	Maine	10-4	109	65	2.39	R-R	6-3	200	9/6/61 Mt. Vernon, NY
		Cleveland	1-4	62	28	5.34				
48	Smithson, Mike	Minnesota	15-14	257	127	4.34	L-R	6-8	215	1/21/55 Centerville, TN
57	Straker, Les	Orlando	16-6	193	106	3.08	R-R	6-1	178	10/10/59 Venezuela
16	Viola, Frank	Minnesota	18-14	251	135	4.09	L-L	6-4	209	4/19/60 Hempstead, NY

CATCHERS

No.	Name	1985 Club	H	HR	RBI	Pct.	B-T	Ht.	Wt.	Born
20	Engle, Dave	Minnesota	44	7	25	.256	R-R	6-3	216	11/30/56 San Diego, CA
15	Laudner, Tim	Minnesota	39	7	19	.238	R-R	6-3	208	6/7/58 Mason City, IA
10	Reed, Jeff	Toledo	100	5	36	.248	L-R	6-2	190	11/12/62 Joliet, IL
12	Salas, Mark	Minnesota	108	9	41	.300	L-R	6-0	205	3/8/61 Montebello, CA

INFIELDERS

No.	Name	1985 Club	H	HR	RBI	Pct.	B-T	Ht.	Wt.	Born
1	Espinoza, Alvaro	Toledo	61	1	33	.229	R-R	6-0	170	2/19/62 Venezuela
		Minnesota	15	0	9	.263				
8	Gaetti, Gary	Minnesota	138	20	63	.246	R-R	6-0	193	8/19/58 Centralia, IL
31	Gagne, Greg	Minnesota	66	2	23	.225	R-R	5-11	185	11/12/61 Fall River, MA
14	Hrbek, Kent	Minnesota	165	21	93	.278	L-R	6-4	229	5/21/60 Minneapolis, MN
4	Lombardozzi, Steve	Toledo	119	14	48	.264	R-R	6-0	175	4/26/60 Malden, MA
		Minnesota	20	0	6	.370				
5	Smalley, Roy	Minnesota	100	12	45	.258	B-R	6-1	182	10/25/52 Los Angeles, CA
11	Teufel, Tim	Minnesota	113	10	50	.260	R-R	6-0	175	7/7/58 Greenwich, CT
38	Washington, Ron	Minnesota	37	1	14	.274	R-R	5-11	169	4/29/52 New Orleans, LA

OUTFIELDERS

No.	Name	1985 Club	H	HR	RBI	Pct.	B-T	Ht.	Wt.	Born
24	Brunansky, Tom	Minnesota	137	27	90	.242	R-R	6-4	211	8/20/60 Covina, CA
25	Bush, Randy	Minnesota	56	10	35	.239	L-L	6-1	186	10/5/58 Dover, DE
21	David, Andre	Toledo	[illegible]	0	40	.266	L-L	6-0	186	5/18/58 Hollywood, CA
27	Davidson, Mark	Orlando	137	25	106	.302	R-R	6-2	180	2/15/61 Knoxville, TN
40	Funderburk, Mark	Orlando	148	34	116	.283	R-R	6-5	230	5/16/57 Charlotte, NC
		Minnesota	22	2	13	.314				
49	Hart, Mike	Toledo	133	24	83	.268	L-L	5-11	185	2/17/58 Milwaukee, WI
9	Hatcher, Mickey	Minnesota	125	3	49	.282	R-R	6-2	199	3/15/55 Cleveland, OH
50	Marte, Alex	Orlando	171	0	33	.320	L-L	6-0	160	12/12/62 Dominican Rep.
7	Meier, Dave	Minnesota	27	1	8	.260	R-R	6-0	185	8/8/59 Helena, MT
34	Puckett, Kirby	Minnesota	199	4	74	.288	R-R	5-8	175	3/14/61 Chicago, IL

TWIN PROFILES

KENT HRBEK 25 6-4 229 **Bats L Throws R**

One of the brightest young stars in the game dimmed a bit in 1985 as the victim of a sluggish start . . . Prior to last season, he signed five-year contract that Twins claimed made him the highest-paid athlete in Minnesota sports history . . . Was hitting .230 with seven homers and 33 RBI through June 15 . . . Had trouble with left-handers in those first 57 games . . . Rebounded to hit .309 in his last 101 games to finish at .278, the lowest mark in his career . . . Considered an outstanding defensive first baseman, he committed eight errors in 1985 . . . Runnerup to Tigers' Willie Hernandez in 1984 AL MVP voting . . . Born May 21, 1960, in Minneapolis . . . Went to Bloomington High School, in shadow of Metropolitan Stadium, Twins' former home . . . Signed by Twins as 17th-round pick in June 1978 draft . . . Jumped from Class-A ball to majors after hitting .379 for Visalia in 1981 . . . Has battled a weight problem throughout his career.

Year	Club	Pos.	G	AB	R	H	2B	3B	HR	RBI	SB	Avg.
1981	Minnesota	1B	24	67	5	16	5	0	1	7	0	.239
1982	Minnesota	1B	140	532	82	160	21	4	23	92	3	.301
1983	Minnesota	1B	141	515	75	153	41	5	16	84	4	.297
1984	Minnesota	1B	149	559	80	174	31	3	27	107	1	.311
1985	Minnesota	1B	158	593	78	165	31	2	21	93	1	.278
	Totals		612	2266	320	668	129	14	88	383	9	.295

KIRBY PUCKETT 25 5-8 175 **Bats R Throws R**

Followed outstanding rookie season with another solid year . . . Led majors with 691 at-bats, a club record . . . Missed 200 hits by one . . . Led Twins with 13 triples and 21 stolen bases . . . Figures to run more in 1986 under manager Ray Miller . . . Has ended Twins' long search for a leadoff hitter . . . However, he hits the ball to right field so often that the club feels he may be an even better No. 2 hitter if a speedy No. 1 hitter can be found . . . Drove in 74 runs, tops among all leadoff batters . . . Led AL in assists in 1984 with 16 and finished second to Blue Jays' Jesse Barfield in 1985 with 19 . . . Has good throwing arm and gets a good jump on hits, but committed eight errors in center . . . Became ninth player in modern history to collect four hits in his major-league debut, May 8, 1984 . . . Hit safely in first seven games and 20 of first 21 . . . Twins' first-round pick in June 1982 draft . . . Played a little more than two seasons in minors before his promotion . . . In his first pro season, he led Appalachian League in batting (.382), runs, hits, total bases, at-bats, stolen bases and outfield assists for Elizabethton (A) . . . Born March 14, 1961, in Chicago . . . Youngest of nine children.

Year	Club	Pos.	G	AB	R	H	2B	3B	HR	RBI	SB	Avg.
1984	Minnesota	OF	128	557	63	165	12	5	0	31	14	.296
1985	Minnesota	OF	161	691	80	199	29	13	4	74	21	.288
	Totals		289	1248	143	364	41	18	4	105	35	.292

TOM BRUNANSKY 25 6-4 211 Bats R Throws R

Led club in homers for a third straight season with 27, but struggled through a poor second half . . . Through May 24, he was hitting .345 in 40 games . . . Hit .206 the remainder of season as overall average slipped to .242 . . . Was Twins' representative at the All-Star Game, which was played at the Metrodome . . . Won home-run contest on day prior to the All-Star Game, when he belted three as the last contestant to bat . . . Led Twins with 10 game-winning RBI and 13 sacrifice flies . . . Drove in 90 runs . . . His RBI production has increased each year since his arrival in majors . . . Born Aug. 20, 1960, in Covina, Cal. . . . Signed with Angels as a first-round pick in June 1978 draft, turning down a football scholarship to Stanford as a wide receiver . . . Acquired from the Angels with Mike Walters for Doug Corbett and Rob Wilfong, May 11, 1982 . . . Right fielder has developed into a solid defensive player with an excellent throwing arm.

Year	Club	Pos.	G	AB	R	H	2B	3B	HR	RBI	SB	Avg.
1981	California	OF	11	33	7	5	0	0	3	6	1	.152
1982	Minnesota	OF	127	463	77	126	30	1	20	46	1	.272
1983	Minnesota	OF	151	542	70	123	24	5	28	82	2	.227
1984	Minnesota	OF	155	567	75	144	21	0	32	85	4	.254
1985	Minnesota	OF	157	567	71	137	28	4	27	90	5	.242
	Totals		601	2172	300	535	103	10	110	309	13	.246

MARK SALAS 25 6-0 205  **Bats L Throws R**

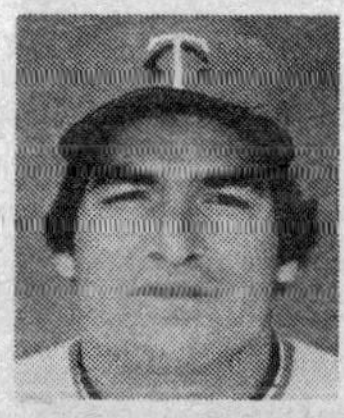

Catcher turned out to be a big bonus after Twins drafted him off roster of Cardinals' Louisville (AAA) farm team in December 1984 . . . Figured to be the backup to Tim Laudner while heir apparent Jeff Reed was fine-tuned in minors . . . But, after Laudner began season in a slump, Billy Gardner tried this guy, who started hitting and never stopped . . . Finished year at .300 . . . Improved his defense, though it was still lacking . . . Threw out only 23-of-86 would-be base-stealers . . . Born March 8, 1961, in Montebello, Cal. . . . Doubled in first major-league at-bat in 1984 . . . Originally a 17th-round pick by Cardinals in June 1979 draft . . . Also played outfield during minor-league career . . . Came into his own with Arkansas (AA) in 1983, when he hit .304 with 20 homers and 82 RBI . . . Nicknamed "The Chief."

Year	Club	Pos.	G	AB	R	H	2B	3B	HR	RBI	SB	Avg.
1984	St. Louis	C-OF	14	20	1	2	1	0	0	1	0	.100
1985	Minnesota	C	120	360	51	108	20	5	9	41	0	.300
	Totals		134	380	52	110	21	5	9	42	0	.289

ROY SMALLEY 33 6-1 182 Bats S Throws R

Returned to Minnesota after a three-year absence . . . Had a mediocre year with .258 average, 12 homers and 45 RBI . . . Started season as regular shortstop, but Twins soon learned that he did not have the range to play the position, especially on artificial turf . . . Acquired from White Sox for Randy Johnson and Ron Scheer prior to 1985 season . . . Hit .233 right-handed with no homers and eight RBI . . . Drafted by Expos, Red Sox (twice) and Cardinals before signing with Texas as first player picked in January 1974 draft . . . Received a reported $100,000 bonus to sign with Rangers . . . Traded to Twins with Bill Singer, Jim Gideon and Mike Cubbage for Bert Blyleven and Danny Thompson, June 1, 1976 . . . Played for Yankees and White Sox before returning . . . Born Oct. 25, 1952, in Los Angeles . . . Father Roy played shortstop for 11 years with Cubs, Braves and Phillies . . . California manager Gene Mauch is his uncle . . . Bothered by a back problem since 1981.

Year	Club	Pos.	G	AB	R	H	2B	3B	HR	RBI	SB	Avg.
1975	Texas	SS-2B-C	78	250	22	57	8	0	3	33	4	.228
1976	Texas-Minnesota . . .	SS-2B	144	513	61	133	18	3	3	44	2	.259
1977	Minnesota	SS	150	584	93	135	21	5	6	56	5	.231
1978	Minnesota	SS	158	586	80	160	31	3	19	77	2	.273
1979	Minnesota	SS-1B	162	621	94	168	28	3	24	95	2	.271
1980	Minnesota	SS-1B	133	486	64	135	24	1	12	63	3	.278
1981	Minnesota	2B-1B	56	167	24	44	7	1	7	22	0	.263
1982	Minn.-NY (AL)	SS-3B-2B	146	499	57	127	15	2	20	67	0	.255
1983	New York (AL)	SS-3B-1B	130	451	70	124	24	1	18	62	3	.275
1984	NY (AL)-Chi. (AL) . .	3B-1B-SS	114	344	32	73	12	1	11	39	3	.212
1985	Minnesota	SS-3B-1B	129	388	57	100	20	0	12	45	0	.258
	Totals		1400	4889	654	1256	208	20	135	603	24	.257

GARY GAETTI 27 6-0 193 Bats R Throws R

Has missed total of only two games during last two seasons . . . Matched his career average at .246, but rebounded from a power shortage . . . Hit 20 homers, 15 more than in 1984 . . . Tied Kent Hrbek for club lead in doubles with 31 . . . Second on club in steals with career-high 13 . . . Made 17 errors at third base . . . Also made some appearances in left field . . . Hit home run in first major-league at-bat in 1981 . . . Tied record with 123 sacrifice flies as a rookie in 1982 . . . Led AL third basemen in putouts, assists and total chances in 1984 . . . Drafted by Cardinals and White Sox before signing with the Twins as their first-round pick in June 1979 draft . . . Born Aug. 19, 1958, in Centralia, Ill. . . . Attended Lake Land College in Mattoon, Ill. and Northwest Missouri State.

Year	Club	Pos.	G	AB	R	H	2B	3B	HR	RBI	SB	Avg.
1981	Minnesota	3B	9	26	4	5	0	0	2	3	0	.192
1982	Minnesota	3B-SS	145	508	59	117	25	4	25	84	0	.230
1983	Minnesota	3B-SS	157	584	81	143	30	3	21	78	7	.245
1984	Minnesota	3B-OF-SS	162	588	55	154	29	4	5	65	11	.262
1985	Minnesota	3B-OF	160	560	71	138	31	0	20	63	13	.246
	Totals		633	2266	270	557	115	11	73	293	31	.246

FRANK VIOLA 25 6-4 209 **Bats L Throws L**

Matched his victory total of 1984 with 18, but was somewhat of a disappointment . . . Suffered through a four-game losing streak in August . . . After Chicago had roughed him up in only one inning of work Sept. 11, he was 13-14 with an ERA approaching 5.00 . . . However, after new pitching coach Dick Such corrected a mechanical flaw in this lefty's delivery, he won his last five starts . . . Pitched complete games in his last four outings . . . Tied for third in AL in wins . . . Born April 19, 1960, in Hempstead, N.Y. . . . Attended St. John's, where he beat Yale's Ron Darling in a classic 1-0, 12-inning duel in 1981 NCAA regional play . . . Signed as Twins' second-round pick in 1981 . . . Pitched in only 25 minor-league games before joining Twins rotation in June 1982 . . . Signed by scout Herb Stein, who also discovered Rod Carew.

Year	Club	G	IP	W	L	Pct.	SO	BB	H	ERA
1982	Minnesota	22	126	4	10	.286	84	38	152	5.21
1983	Minnesota	35	210	7	15	.318	127	92	242	5.49
1984	Minnesota	35	257⅔	18	12	.600	149	73	225	3.21
1985	Minnesota	36	250⅔	18	14	.563	135	68	262	4.09
	Totals	128	844⅓	47	51	.480	495	271	881	4.34

BERT BLYLEVEN 34 6-3 205 **Bats R Throws R**

Rejoined Twins, his original team, Aug. 1 of last season in deal that sent Curt Wardle, Richard Yett, Jay Bell and Jim Weaver to Indians . . . Was 8-5 with 3.00 ERA for Minnesota and 17-16 with 3.16 ERA overall . . . Finished fifth in AL in ERA, first in strikeouts (206), first in innings pitched (293⅔), first in complete games (24), first in shutouts (5) and tied for first in starts (37)... Born April 6, 1951, in Zeist, Holland... Full name is Rik Aalbert Blyleven... Was selected by Twins in third round of June 1969 draft... Spent only 21 games in minors before making it to the Twins at end of 1970 season... Pitched for Rangers, Pirates and Indians before coming back to Minnesota ... Has won 20 games once, in 1973, and has come within three wins of 20 four other times... Noted for having one of best curves in game... Threw a no-hitter against Angels, Sept. 27, 1977... Finished third in AL Cy Young Award voting last season.

Year	Club	G	IP	W	L	Pct.	SO	BB	H	ERA
1970	Minnesota	27	164	10	9	.526	135	47	143	3.18
1971	Minnesota	38	278	16	15	.516	224	59	267	2.82
1972	Minnesota	39	287	17	17	.500	228	69	247	2.73
1973	Minnesota	40	325	20	17	.541	258	67	296	2.52
1974	Minnesota	37	281	17	17	.500	249	77	244	2.66
1975	Minnesota	35	276	15	10	.600	233	84	219	3.00
1976	Minn.-Tex.	36	298	13	16	.448	219	81	283	2.87
1977	Texas	30	235	14	12	.538	182	69	181	2.72
1978	Pittsburgh	34	244	14	10	.583	182	66	217	3.02
1979	Pittsburgh	37	237	12	5	.706	172	92	238	3.61
1980	Pittsburgh	34	217	8	13	.381	168	59	219	3.82
1981	Cleveland	20	159	11	7	.611	107	40	145	2.89
1982	Cleveland	4	20⅓	2	2	.500	19	11	16	4.87
1983	Cleveland	24	156⅓	7	10	.412	123	44	160	3.91
1984	Cleveland	33	245	19	7	.731	170	74	204	2.87
1985	Clev.-Minn.	37	293⅔	17	16	.515	206	75	264	3.16
	Totals	505	3716⅓	212	183	.537	2875	1014	3343	3.01

MIKE SMITHSON 30 6-8 215 — Bats L Throws R

The tallest player in baseball... Tied for major-league lead in starts for second straight year with 37... Won six decisions in a row from June 19 to July 30, the longest streak by a Twins pitcher in 1985... Lost four in a row at the conclusion of his winning streak... Continued his streakiness by winning three in a row, losing three in a row and then winning his last start ... Was 10-7 with 3.65 ERA in his last 22 games... Has 30-27 record since being acquired from Texas with John Butcher and Sam Sorce for Gary Ward prior to 1984 season... Born Jan. 21, 1955, in Centerville, Tenn.... Selected by Red Sox in fifth round of June 1976 draft... Traded to Texas for John Henry Johnson prior to 1982 season... Led AL with 35 home runs allowed in 1984, but that number dropped to 25 in 1985... Likes to pitch inside and hit a club-high 15 batters with pitches last season.

Year	Club	G	IP	W	L	Pct.	SO	BB	H	ERA
1982	Texas	8	46⅔	3	4	.429	24	13	51	5.01
1983	Texas	33	223⅓	10	14	.417	135	71	233	3.91
1984	Minnesota	36	252	15	13	.536	144	54	246	3.68
1985	Minnesota	37	257	15	14	.517	127	78	264	4.34
	Totals	114	779	43	45	.489	430	216	794	4.04

RON DAVIS 30 6-4 196 **Bats R Throws R**

Season reached low point May 13, when he gave up a ninth-inning homer to Yanks' Don Mattingly to cap a 9-8 loss in game the Twins had led, 8-0 . . . Broke into tears in clubhouse after the game . . . It marked third straight appearance in which he had given up a game-winning homer . . . Strangely, he was welcomed home in Minnesota May 16 with a standing ovation that seemed to turn his season around . . . Had been 1-4 with 6.92 ERA May 13 . . . Was 1-2 with 2.61 ERA for the rest of the season, blowing only one save opportunity . . . Installment of Ray Miller as manager also was instrumental in his turnaround . . . Finished with 25 saves, his fourth straight year with 22 or more, but his second consecutive decline since saving 30 in 1983 . . . Acquired from Yankees with Paul Boris and Greg Gagne for Roy Smalley in April 1982 . . . Began career with Cubs, who picked him in third round of June 1976 draft . . . Traded to Yankees for Ken Holtzman, June 10, 1978 . . . Set rookie relief record with 14 wins in 1979 as advance man for Goose Gossage . . . In 1982, he struck out nine consecutive batters to set a major-league record for a reliever, striking out eight Angels in one game and the first Seattle hitter to face him in his next game . . . Born Aug. 6, 1955, in Houston . . . Had 23.14 ERA in four World Series games against Dodgers in 1981 . . . Has 128 career saves.

Year	Club	G	IP	W	L	Pct.	SO	BB	H	ERA
1978	New York (AL)	4	2	0	0	.000	0	3	3	13.50
1979	New York (AL)	44	85	14	2	.875	43	28	84	2.86
1980	New York (AL)	53	131	9	3	.750	65	32	121	2.95
1981	New York (AL)	43	73	4	5	.444	83	25	47	2.71
1982	Minnesota	63	106	3	9	.250	89	47	106	4.42
1983	Minnesota	66	89	5	8	.385	84	33	89	3.34
1984	Minnesota	64	83	7	11	.389	74	41	79	4.55
1985	Minnesota	57	64⅔	2	6	.250	72	35	55	3.48
	Totals	394	633⅔	44	44	.500	510	244	584	3.51

TOP PROSPECTS

DENNIS BURTT 28 6-0 187 **Bats S Throws R**

Called up toward the end of last season, he made his major-league debut after 10 seasons in the minors . . . In five games with Twins, he was 2-2 with 3.81 ERA . . . Led International League with career-high 14 wins before his promotion . . . Went 14-8 with 4.13 ERA for Toledo (AAA) last season . . . Second-round choice by Red Sox in June 1976 draft . . . Signed as free agent by Twins in December 1984 . . . Born Nov. 29, 1957, in San Diego . . . Is he a late bloomer or is he running out of chances?

STEVE LOMBARDOZZI 25 6-0 175 Bats R Throws R
May inherit Twins' second-base job, if only because he can turn a double play . . . Incumbent Tim Teufel set an AL record for fewest double plays by a second baseman who played at least 150 games in 1984 . . . Was a shortstop in high school, college and pros until being moved to second at Toledo in 1984 . . . Hit .264 with 14 homers and 48 RBI for Toledo last year . . . Was called up to Twins in July for four games . . . Returned toward end of season and hit .370 in 28 games . . . Born April 26, 1960, in Malden, Mass. . . . Ninth-round pick by Twins in June 1981 draft.

MANAGER RAY MILLER: Replaced Billy Gardner June 21 . . . Twins finished with 77-85 record, but he posted a break-even mark at 50-50 . . . Had been pitching coach for Baltimore for more than six seasons before getting his first major-league managerial job . . . Managed in Puerto Rican Winter League for three seasons . . . Spent 10 years in pros as a pitcher without making it to the majors . . . Allowed only 848 hits in 1,003 career innings and averaged nearly one strikeout an inning . . . Had 60-65 career record as pitcher . . . Originally signed by San Francisco, he was drafted by Cleveland after the 1964 season . . . Joined Rochester of Baltimore organization in 1971 . . . Remained in Baltimore system until accepting Twins' post . . . Is credited with aiding development of Mike Flanagan, Dennis Martinez, Scott McGregor and Sammy Stewart while those pitchers were in the minors . . . Nicknamed "Rabbit" . . . Born April 30, 1945, in Takoma Park, Md.

GREATEST SHORTSTOP

His numbers were not typical of a league MVP selection, but Zoilo Versalles was indeed the 1965 AL MVP. He hit .273 that season with 19 homers and 77 RBI. He also made 39 errors. But the Minnesota Twins won the AL pennant that season, largely because of Versalles' daily contributions at shortstop.

Versalles was spectacular defensively. The high number of errors he committed resulted from his extraordinary range, which allowed him to reach balls that most shortstops could not. He led the league in doubles (45), triples (12) and runs scored (126). The 5-10, 146-pounder, known as "Zorro," was the heart of a championship club.

Versalles never had another year like 1965. His average dipped to .249 in 1966 and then to .200 in 1967 before the Twins traded him to the Los Angeles Dodgers, ending his seven-year tenure in Minnesota. Versalles finished his career with Atlanta in 1971. He was a lifetime .242 hitter who will be remembered for his unlikely MVP year of 1965.

ALL-TIME TWIN SEASON RECORDS

BATTING: Rod Carew, .388, 1977
HRs: Harmon Killebrew, 49, 1964, 1969
RBIs: Harmon Killebrew, 140, 1969
STEALS: Rod Carew, 49, 1976
WINS: Jim Kaat, 25, 1966
STRIKEOUTS: Bert Blyleven, 258, 1973

OAKLAND A's

TEAM DIRECTORY: Pres.: Roy Eisenhardt; Exec. VP: Wally Haas; VP-Baseball Oper.: Sandy Alderson; Dir. Play. Dev.: Karl Kuehl; Dir. Scouting: Dick Bogard; Dir. Baseball Adm.: Walt Jocketty; Dir. Publ.-Trav. Sec.: Mickey Morabito; Mgr.: Jackie Moore. Home: Oakland Coliseum (50,219). Field distances: 330, l.f. line; 372, l.c.; 397, c.f.; 372, r.c.; 330, r.f. line. Spring training: Phoenix, Ariz.

SCOUTING REPORT

HITTING: Oakland can't wait to see if Jose Canseco will be everything his minor-league credentials have promised. From all reports, he is one of the great hitting prospects to come along in recent years. Canseco (.302, 5 homers, 13 RBI in 29 games with Oakland) is being counted on to complement slugging DH Dave Kingman (30 homers, 91 RBI), assuming Kingman signs.

The A's retained veterans Dusty Baker (.268, 14 homers, 52 RBI) and Bruce Bochte (.295, 14 homers, 60 RBI). They'll need improved numbers from center fielder Dwayne Murphy (.233, 20 homers, 59 RBI), who apparently will never cut down on his mighty swing. Alfredo Griffin, who drove in a career-high 64 runs while batting .270, and Mike Davis (.287, 24 homers, 82 RBI) will be hoping to equal their surprising 1985 production.

Oakland used to be known as the swinging A's. Call this group the free-swinging A's. Davis struck out 99 times and Murphy 123 times. Even Canseco struck out an average of once per three at-bats. He'll fit in nicely.

PITCHING: The A's were so desperate for pitching that they were willing to gamble on Joaquin Andujar, who is 33 and won only once in the last two months of last season. Andujar (21-12, 3.40) brings with him from St. Louis a troublesome temperament and a 10-day suspension at the start of the season for his antics in the World Series finale. On the plus side, he is the only pitcher in baseball to win 20 games each of the past two seasons. A switch in leagues may be good for him.

The best of the rest were all plucked out of the Yankees' system in the Rickey Henderson trade prior to last season. Leading the way in the bullpen is Jay Howell (9-8, 2.85 ERA, 29 saves). Tim Birtsas (10-6, 4.01 ERA) has cemented himself in the rotation. Hard-throwing Jose Rijo (6-4, 3.53 ERA and 65 strikeouts in 63⅔ innings) may be learning how to pitch. However, the A's

Slugging Dwayne Murphy hopes to boost .233 average.

still need more help. Only Seattle's pitchers issued more walks than the Oakland staff's 607 in 1985.

FIELDING: Murphy won another Gold Glove for his outstanding defensive work in center. With Davis in right, the A's have a solid outfield. To get Andujar, the A's had to give up catcher Mike Heath and his throwing ability will be missed. Few teams even attempted to run with Heath behind the plate. But curiously, the ERA of Oakland pitchers was more than a full run higher when Heath was catching than when Mickey Tettleton was the catcher.

Griffin, who didn't miss a game, added some stability to an otherwise average Oakland infield at shortstop. Carney Lansford was leading the league in fielding July 25 when he was hit by a pitch and suffered a fractured wrist. The A's need this third baseman's bat and glove in the lineup every day.

OUTLOOK: It will take more than one tough Dominican to solve the A's pitching problems. Give Jackie Moore credit. The Oakland manager kept a below-average team in the AL West race until late August. But the A's shouldn't expect to be contenders just yet. They should aim for a .500 season first while developing their young pitchers. A break-even season would represent an improvement of four wins over 1985 and the A's should accomplish at least that much.

OAKLAND A's 1986 ROSTER

MANAGER Jackie Moore
Coaches—Bob Didier, Dave McKay, Jeff Newman, Ron Plaza, Wes Stock

PITCHERS

No.	Name	1985 Club	W-L	IP	SO	ERA	B-T	Ht.	Wt.	Born
58	Akerfelds, Darrel	Huntsville	9-6	96	56	3.46	R-R	6-2	210	6/12/62 Denver, CO
—	Andujar, Joaquin	St. Louis	21-12	270	112	3.40	B-R	6-0	180	12/21/52 Dom. Republic
55	Atherton, Keith	Oakland	4-7	105	77	4.30	R-R	6-4	200	2/19/59 Matthews, VA
48	Birtsas, Tim	Tacoma	2-2	27	25	3.04	L-L	6-7	225	9/5/60 Pontiac, MI
		Oakland	10-6	141	94	4.01				
23	Codiroli, Chris	Oakland	14-14	226	111	4.46	R-R	6-1	160	3/26/58 Oxnard, CA
59	Dozier, Tom	Huntsville	5-2	60	54	3.17	R-R	6-2	190	9/5/61 Richmond, CA
		Tacoma	0-0	34	22	4.24				
50	Howell, Jay	Oakland	9-8	98	68	2.85	R-R	6-3	205	11/26/55 Miami, FL
25	*John, Tommy	Cal.-Oak.	4-10	86	25	5.53	R-L	6-3	200	5/22/43 Terre Haute, IN
32	Krueger, Bill	Tacoma	0-1	10	10	9.31	L-L	6-5	205	4/24/58 McMinnville, OR
		Oakland	9-10	151	56	4.52				
47	Kyles, Stan	Tacoma	1-7	72	31	5.13	R-R	6-1	165	2/26/61 Chicago, IL
21	Langford, Rick	Modesto	0-0	6	3	6.00	R-R	6-0	180	3/20/52 Farmville, VA
		Oakland	3-5	59	21	3.51				
54	*McCatty, Steve	Oakland	4-4	86	36	5.57	R-R	6-3	210	3/20/54 Detroit, MI
35	Mooneyham, Bill	Modesto	2-0	14	13	1.26	R-R	6-0	175	8/16/60 Los Angeles, CA
		Huntsville	2-1	36	28	1.98				
		Tacoma	2-6	60	49	4.18				
61	Ontiveros, Steve	Tacoma	3-0	34	30	2.94	R-R	6-0	180	3/5/61 Tularosa, NM
		Oakland	1-3	75	36	1.93				
51	Plunk, Eric	Huntsville	8-2	79	68	3.40	R-R	6-5	210	9/3/63 Wilmington, CA
		Tacoma	0-5	53	43	5.77				
38	Rijo, Jose	Tacoma	7-10	149	179	2.90	R-R	6-2	180	5/13/65 Dominican Republic
		Oakland	6-4	64	65	3.53				
29	Young, Curt	Modesto	0-0	6	3	4.76	R-L	6-1	175	10/18/59 Saginaw, MI
		Tacoma	2-0	15	8	3.60				
		Oakland	0-4	45	19	7.35				

CATCHERS

No.	Name	1985 Club	H	HR	RBI	Pct.	B-T	Ht.	Wt.	Born
57	Dorsett, Brian	Modesto	43	2	30	.267	R-R	6-4	215	4/9/61 Terre Haute, IN
		Huntsville	84	11	42	.268				
9	O'Brien, Charlie	Modesto	8	1	2	.296	R-R	6-2	195	5/1/60 Tulsa, OK
		Huntsville	24	7	16	.209				
		Tacoma	9	0	7	.158				
		Oakland	3	0	1	.273				
6	Tettleton, Mickey	Modesto	3	0	2	.214	B-R	6-2	200	9/16/60 Oklahoma City, OK
		Oakland	53	3	15	.251				

INFIELDERS

No.	Name	1985 Club	H	HR	RBI	Pct.	B-T	Ht.	Wt.	Born
20	Bochte, Bruce	Oakland	125	14	60	.295	L-L	6-3	205	11/12/50 Pasadena, CA
53	Garbey, Barbaro	Detroit	61	6	29	.257	R-R	5-10	170	12/4/56 Cuba
3	Griffin, Alfredo	Oakland	166	2	64	.270	B-R	5-11	165	3/6/57 Dominican Republic
25	Hill, Donnie	Oakland	112	3	48	.285	B-R	5-10	160	11/12/60 Pomona, CA
10	*Kingman, Dave	Oakland	141	30	91	.238	R-R	6-6	215	12/21/48 Pendleton, OR
4	Lansford, Carney	Oakland	111	13	46	.277	R-R	6-2	195	2/7/57 San Jose, CA
49	Nelson, Rob	Huntsville	116	32	98	.232	L-L	6-4	215	5/17/64 Pasadena, CA
18	Phillips, Tony	Tacoma	9	0	5	.130	B-R	5-10	160	11/9/59 Atlanta, GA
		Oakland	45	4	17	.280				
8	*Picciolo, Rob	Oakland	28	1	8	.275	R-R	6-2	178	2/4/53 Santa Monica, CA

OUTFIELDERS

No.	Name	1985 Club	H	HR	RBI	Pct.	B-T	Ht.	Wt.	Born
12	Baker, Dusty	Oakland	92	14	52	.268	R-R	6-2	200	6/15/49 Riverside, CA
33	Canseco, Jose	Huntsville	67	25	80	.318	R-R	6-3	195	7/2/64 Cuba
		Tacoma	81	11	47	.348				
		Oakland	29	5	13	.302				
16	Davis, Mike	Oakland	157	24	82	.287	L-L	6-3	185	6/11/59 San Diego, CA
5	Henderson, Steve	Oakland	58	3	31	.301	R-R	6-1	185	11/18/52 Houston, TX
30	Javier, Stan	Huntsville	138	9	64	.284	B-R	6-0	180	9/1/65 Dominican Republic
21	Murphy, Dwayne	Oakland	122	20	59	.233	L-R	6-1	185	3/18/55 Merced, CA

*Free agent unsigned at press time

A's PROFILES

MIKE DAVIS 26 6-3 185 **Bats L Throws L**

Blossomed into a star in his third full season with A's . . . Set career highs in every offensive category . . . His 34 doubles represented third-best total in Oakland history, exceeded only by Reggie Jackson and Joe Rudi . . . Became sixth "20-20" player in Oakland history with 24 homers and 24 stolen bases . . . A's won 17 of 22 games in which he homered in 1985 . . . His emergence actually began in September 1984, when he hit .375 with three homers and 12 RBI . . . Born June 11, 1959, in San Diego . . . Selected by A's in third round of June 1977 draft . . . Younger brother Mark plays baseball at Stanford . . . Cousin Dave Grayson is former NFL defensive back . . . Right fielder committed eight errors in 1985 . . . Interested in a real-estate career after his baseball career ends.

Year	Club	Pos.	G	AB	R	H	2B	3B	HR	RBI	SB	Avg.
1980	Oakland.	OF-1B	51	95	11	20	2	1	1	8	2	.211
1981	Oakland.	OF-1B	17	20	0	1	1	0	0	0	0	.050
1982	Oakland.	OF-1B	23	75	12	30	4	0	1	10	3	.400
1983	Oakland.	OF	128	443	61	122	24	4	8	62	32	.275
1984	Oakland.	OF	134	382	47	88	18	3	9	46	14	.230
1985	Oakland.	OF	154	547	92	157	34	1	24	82	24	.287
	Totals		507	1562	223	418	83	9	43	208	75	.268

CARNEY LANSFORD 29 6-2 195 **Bats R Throws R**

Failed to hit .300 for first time in five seasons . . . Was hit by a pitch from Brewers' Peter Ladd July 25 and suffered hairline fracture of right wrist . . . Played in only five of Oakland's final 67 games . . . At the time of his injury, he had committed only four errors, the fewest of any regular AL third baseman, and he finished season with five . . . Had one streak of 47 consecutive errorless games . . . Came to A's in trade with Red Sox, who had to create a space for the emerging Wade Boggs . . . Boston sent him, Gary Hancock and Jerome King to Oakland for Tony Armas and Jeff Newman prior to 1983 season . . . Born Feb. 7, 1957, in San Jose, Cal. . . . A direct descendant of Sir Francis

Drake, the 16th-century British admiral . . . Third-round pick by Angels in June 1975 draft.

Year	Club	Pos.	G	AB	R	H	2B	3B	HR	RBI	SB	Avg.
1978	California	3B	121	453	63	133	23	2	8	52	20	.294
1979	California	3B	157	654	114	188	30	5	19	79	20	.287
1980	California	3B	151	602	87	157	27	3	15	80	14	.261
1981	Boston	3B	102	399	61	134	23	3	4	52	15	.336
1982	Boston	3B	128	482	65	145	28	4	11	63	9	.301
1983	Oakland	3B-SS	80	299	43	92	16	2	10	45	3	.308
1984	Oakland	3B	151	597	70	179	31	5	14	74	9	.300
1985	Oakland	3B	98	401	51	111	18	2	13	46	2	.277
	Totals		988	3887	554	1139	196	26	94	491	92	.293

DUSTY BAKER 36 6-2 200 **Bats R Throws R**

Cut loose by Giants prior to 1985 season, he provided A's with needed experience and a strong first half . . . Drove in 52 runs in 111 games . . . Excelled as pinch-hitter with .412 average on seven hits in 17 at-bats and four RBI . . . Outfielder who played first base at times . . . Has played for four major-league teams since Braves picked him in 26th round of June 1967 draft . . . Traded to Dodgers with Ed Goodson for Jimmy Wynn, Lee Lacy, Tom Paciorek and Jerry Royster prior to 1976 season . . . Dodgers waived him prior to 1984 season and Giants signed him . . . Played in three World Series with Los Angeles, hitting .232 in 18 games . . . Also played in All-Star Games in 1981 and 1982 . . . Born June 15, 1949, in Riverside, Cal. . . . Attended American River Junior College . . . Full name is Johnnie B. Baker Jr.

Year	Club	Pos.	G	AB	R	H	2B	3B	HR	RBI	SB	Avg.
1968	Atlanta	OF	6	5	0	2	0	0	0	0	0	.400
1969	Atlanta	OF	3	7	0	0	0	0	0	0	0	.000
1970	Atlanta	OF	13	24	3	7	0	0	0	4	0	.292
1971	Atlanta	OF	29	62	2	14	2	0	0	4	0	.226
1972	Atlanta	OF	127	446	62	143	27	2	17	76	4	.321
1973	Atlanta	OF	159	604	101	174	29	4	21	99	24	.288
1974	Atlanta	OF	149	574	80	147	35	0	20	69	18	.256
1975	Atlanta	OF	142	494	63	129	18	2	19	72	12	.261
1976	Los Angeles	OF	112	384	36	93	13	0	4	39	2	.242
1977	Los Angeles	OF	153	533	86	155	26	1	30	86	2	.291
1978	Los Angeles	OF	149	522	62	137	24	1	11	66	12	.262
1979	Los Angeles	OF	151	544	86	152	29	1	23	88	11	.274
1980	Los Angeles	OF	153	579	80	170	26	4	29	97	12	.294
1981	Los Angeles	OF	103	400	48	128	17	3	9	49	10	.320
1982	Los Angeles	OF	147	570	80	171	19	1	23	88	17	.300
1983	Los Angeles	OF	149	531	71	138	25	1	15	73	7	.260
1984	San Francisco	OF	100	243	31	71	7	2	3	32	4	.292
1985	Oakland	OF	111	343	48	92	15	1	14	52	2	.268
	Totals		1956	6875	939	1923	312	23	238	994	137	.280

BRUCE BOCHTE 35 6-3 205 **Bats L Throws L**

Swung the most consistent bat in Oakland lineup in 1985 . . . First baseman kept average over .300 mark last season until falling into 0-for-15 tailspin just prior to year's end . . . Had three hits in nine at-bats as a pinch-hitter . . . Had at least two hits in 27 games . . . His 14 homers represented the second-best total of his career . . . Perhaps best known for his one-year "retirement" from baseball during 1983 . . . Ended that retirement when he signed with A's as a re-entry free agent prior to 1984 season . . . Second-round pick of the Angels in June 1972 draft . . . Traded to Cleveland with Sid Monge for Dave LaRoche and Dave Schuler, May 11, 1977 . . . Hit .301 in 1977, then was signed by Mariners as a re-entry free agent that winter . . . Holds many all-time Mariner batting records . . . Born Nov. 12, 1950, in Pasadena, Cal. . . . Attended Santa Clara.

Year	Club	Pos.	G	AB	R	H	2B	3B	HR	RBI	SB	Avg.
1974	California	OF-1B	57	196	24	53	4	1	5	26	6	.270
1975	California	1B	107	375	41	107	19	3	3	48	3	.285
1976	California	OF-1B	146	466	53	120	17	1	2	49	4	.258
1977	Cal.-Clev	OF-1B	137	492	64	148	23	1	7	51	7	.301
1978	Seattle	OF-1B	140	486	58	128	25	3	11	51	3	.263
1979	Seattle	1B	150	554	81	175	38	6	16	100	2	.316
1980	Seattle	1B	148	520	62	156	34	4	13	78	2	.300
1981	Seattle	1B-OF	99	335	39	87	16	0	6	30	1	.260
1982	Seattle	1B-OF	144	509	58	151	21	0	12	70	8	.297
1983	. . . .				Did Not Play							
1984	Oakland	1B	148	469	58	124	23	0	5	52	2	.264
1985	Oakland	1B	137	424	48	125	17	1	14	60	3	.295
	Totals		1413	4826	586	1374	237	20	94	615	40	.285

ALFREDO GRIFFIN 29 5-11 165 **Bats S Throws R**

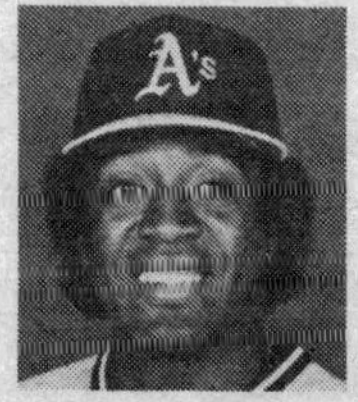

Kept the Bill Caudill trade from being a complete bust . . . Dave Collins was a disappointment, but the other Toronto import was a pleasant surprise . . . Shortstop drove in 64 runs, although he had never driven in more than 48 in any previous season as a pro . . . Played in 162 games for third time in his career . . . Led A's with 614 at-bats and 166 hits . . . Stole 24 bases in 32 attempts . . . Was signed as free agent by Indians in 1973 at age 16, but his first pro season was 1974 . . . In 1976, he moved from San Jose (A) to Williamsport (AA) to Toledo (AAA) to the Indians . . . In his debut for Cleveland, vs. Milwaukee, he hit the first pitch he saw for a single . . . Traded to Toronto with Phil Lansford for Victor Cruz after the 1978 season . . . Born March 6,

1957, in Santo Domingo, Dominican Republic . . . Lives in San Pedro de Macoris, "the cradle of shortstops."

Year	Club	Pos.	G	AB	R	H	2B	3B	HR	RBI	SB	Avg.
1976	Cleveland	SS	12	4	0	1	0	0	0	0	0	.250
1977	Cleveland	SS	14	41	5	6	1	0	0	3	2	.146
1978	Cleveland	SS	5	4	1	2	1	0	0	0	0	.500
1979	Toronto	SS	153	624	81	179	22	10	2	31	20	.287
1980	Toronto	SS	155	653	63	166	26	15	2	41	18	.254
1981	Toronto	SS-3B-2B	101	388	30	81	19	6	0	21	8	.209
1982	Toronto	SS	162	539	57	130	20	8	1	48	10	.241
1983	Toronto	SS-2B	162	528	62	132	22	9	4	47	8	.250
1984	Toronto	SS-2B	140	419	53	101	8	2	4	30	11	.241
1985	Oakland	SS-2B	162	614	75	166	18	7	2	64	24	.270
	Totals		1066	3814	427	964	137	57	15	285	101	.253

DWAYNE MURPHY 31 6-1 185 Bats L Throws R

Has one of the longest and most powerful swings in the game, which helps account for his team-leading 123 strikeouts . . . Also walked a team-leading 84 times . . . Hit two homers off Baltimore's Scott McGregor last season, marking the fourth two-homer game of his career . . . His 59 RBI represented his lowest total since 1979 . . . Moved into third place on all-time Oakland home-run list with 136, trailing only Reggie Jackson and Sal Bando . . . A 12th-round pick by A's in June 1973 draft . . . Turned down football scholarship from Arizona State to sign with Oakland . . . Born March 18, 1955, in Merced, Cal. . . . Won four straight Gold Gloves from 1980-83 . . . Has one of the strongest throwing arms among AL center fielders and made only five errors in 1985.

Year	Club	Pos.	G	AB	R	H	2B	3B	HR	RBI	SB	Avg.
1978	Oakland	OF	60	52	15	10	2	0	0	5	0	.192
1979	Oakland	OF	121	388	57	99	10	4	11	40	15	.255
1980	Oakland	OF	159	573	86	157	18	2	13	68	26	.274
1981	Oakland	OF	107	390	58	98	10	3	15	60	10	.251
1982	Oakland	OF-SS	151	543	84	129	15	1	27	94	26	.238
1983	Oakland	OF	130	471	55	107	17	2	17	75	7	.227
1984	Oakland	OF	153	559	93	143	18	2	33	88	4	.256
1985	Oakland	OF	152	523	77	122	21	3	20	59	4	.233
	Totals		1033	3499	525	865	111	17	136	489	92	.247

JOAQUIN ANDUJAR 33 6-0 180 Bats S Throws R

A postseason bust after notching second straight 20-win year for the Cards, he was traded to A's at winter meetings for Mike Heath and Tim Conroy . . . Troubles down the stretch spilled over to NLCS (0-1, 6.97 ERA) and World Series (0-1, 9.00 ERA) . . . Ejected from Game 7 of World Series after tantrum concerning ball-strike calls . . . Won 12 of first 13 starts before being replaced by John Tudor as staff ace . . . Biggest winner in majors at All-Star break with 5-4 record, but refused invitation to All-Star Game because NL manager Dick Williams indicated he wasn't going to start . . . Became majors' first 20-game winner Aug. 23 but won only once thereafter . . . Fiery temper has made him target of critics . . . Born Dec. 21, 1952, in San Pedro de Macoris, Dominican Republic . . . Originally signed by Astros, he salvaged career after June 6, 1981 trade to Cardinals for Tony Scott.

Year	Club	G	IP	W	L	Pct.	SO	BB	H	ERA
1976	Houston	28	172	9	10	.474	59	75	163	3.61
1977	Houston	26	159	11	8	.579	69	64	149	3.68
1978	Houston	35	111	5	7	.417	55	58	88	3.41
1979	Houston	46	194	12	12	.500	77	88	168	3.43
1980	Houston	35	122	3	8	.273	75	43	132	3.91
1981	Hou.-St.L.	20	79	8	4	.667	37	23	85	4.10
1982	St. Louis	38	265⅔	15	10	.600	137	50	237	2.47
1983	St. Louis	39	225	6	16	.273	125	75	215	4.16
1984	St. Louis	36	261⅓	20	14	.588	147	70	218	3.34
1985	St. Louis	38	269⅔	21	12	.636	112	82	265	3.40
	Totals	341	1858⅔	110	101	.521	893	628	1720	3.46

JAY HOWELL 30 6-3 205 — Bats R Throws R

When Yankees included this fastballer in trade for Rickey Henderson, they had some doubts about whether he could cut it as a closer . . . Immediately answered those questions by having a great year in that role for Oakland . . . Ranked fifth in AL with 29 saves in 36 save opportunities . . . Posted second-best save total in Oakland history, exceeded only by Bill Caudill's 36 in 1984 . . . Led AL in strikeouts per innings pitched in 1984, fanning 109 in 103⅔ innings . . . That ratio fell to 68 strikeouts in 98 innings last season . . . Bothered throughout 1985 season by allergy problem . . . One of his allergies was to a strain of grass in Oakland Coliseum infield . . . Signed by Cincinnati as 31st-round pick in June 1976 draft . . . Had rejected an offer from Reds three years earlier, when they made him a 12th round pick . . . Attended Colorado . . . Born Nov. 26, 1955, in Miami . . . Thanks to him, nobody missed Caudill in 1985.

Year	Club	G	IP	W	L	Pct.	SO	BB	H	ERA
1980	Cincinnati	5	3	0	0	.000	1	0	8	15.00
1981	Chicago (NL)	10	22	2	0	1.000	10	10	23	4.91
1982	New York (AL)	6	28	2	3	.400	21	13	42	7.71
1983	New York (AL)	19	82	1	5	.167	61	35	89	5.38
1984	New York (AL)	61	103⅔	9	4	.692	109	34	86	2.69
1985	Oakland	63	98	9	8	.529	68	31	98	2.85
	Totals	164	336⅔	23	20	.535	270	123	346	4.06

TIM BIRTSAS 25 6-7 225 **Bats L Throws L**

Had only Class-A experience prior to 1985, but he pitched well enough for Tacoma (AAA) to earn a trip to majors May 2 . . . Continued his success with A's, posting 10-6 record and amassing 94 strikeouts, the second-highest total on club . . . His 10 wins were third-best on staff . . . Known as "Big Bird" . . . Attended Michigan State and played on junior varsity basketball team when the varsity, led by Magic Johnson, won NCAA championship . . . A close friend and former college teammate of Kirk Gibson, he accidentally struck Gibson in the face with a pitch in 1985 . . . Born Sept. 5, 1960, in Pontiac, Mich. . . . Originally signed by Yankees, who selected him in second round of June 1982 draft . . . Yankees sent him, Jay Howell, Jose Rijo, Eric Plunk and Stan Javier to Oakland for Rickey Henderson and Bert Bradley prior to last season . . . Lists sailing and poetry among his hobbies.

Year	Club	G	IP	W	L	Pct.	SO	BB	H	ERA
1985	Oakland	29	141⅓	10	6	.625	94	91	124	4.01

TOP PROSPECTS

JOSE CANSECO 21 6-3 185 **Bats R Throws R**

A's think they have a future star in this slugging outfielder . . . Was named MVP of Southern League in 1985, despite playing in only 58 games for Huntsville (AA) . . . His composite production numbers for Huntsville, Tacoma (AAA) and Oakland were 41 home runs and 140 RBI in 146 games . . . Hit .318 for Huntsville, .348 for Tacoma and .302 in 29 games with A's . . . Hit five homers and drove in 13 runs for Oakland in 96 at-bats . . . Born July 2, 1964, in Havana, Cuba . . . Oakland's 15th-round selection in June 1982 draft . . . Twin brother Osvaldo is a right-handed pitcher in Yankee organization.

JOSE RIJO 20 6-2 180 **Bats R Throws R**

Had 7-10 record and 2.90 ERA for Tacoma (AAA) to earn promotion to A's Aug. 11 . . . Compiled 6-4 record and 3.53 ERA in 12 games, including nine starts, for Oakland . . . Struck out 65 batters in 63⅔ innings . . . Signed as free agent in 1981 by Yankees, who rushed him to majors in 1984 as their answer to

Mets' Dwight Gooden . . . Went north with parent club at start of season, but soon was sent to Columbus (AAA) . . . Had 2-8 record and 4.76 ERA for Yankees in 1984 . . . Traded to A's as part of package for Rickey Henderson . . . Born May 13, 1965, in San Cristobal, Dominican Republic . . . Has excellent velocity and movement on his fastball.

MANAGER JACKIE MOORE: Retained by A's after leading club to 77-85 finish in his first full season as manager in 1985 . . . Kept A's in scrambled AL West title chase until club's abrupt September fadeout . . . Took over reins May 24, 1984, after Steve Boros was fired . . . Inherited 20-24 club and posted 57-61 record the rest of the way in 1984 . . . In his first game as manager, the A's and Yankees were involved in a brawl . . . Had only 2½ years of minor-league managerial experience when the A's hired him . . . Spent 14 years as coach in majors, making stops with Brewers, Rangers (twice), Blue Jays and A's . . . Born Feb. 19, 1939, in Jay, Fla. . . . Caught for 11 years in minors . . . Major-league career consisted of 21 games with Tigers in 1965, when he hit .094 in 53 at-bats . . . Works for a car dealership in Arlington, Tex., in winter . . . Has never posted a winning record in five years of managing . . . Has 134-146 overall mark in majors.

GREATEST SHORTSTOP

Bert Campaneris seemed destined for a special career when he socked two home runs in his first major-league game in 1964, when the A's were still based in Kansas City. The next season, Campaneris became the first player in history to play all nine positions in one game. He went on to become the greatest shortstop in Oakland A's history.

"Campy" led the A's to five straight AL West titles in the '70s. The A's won three world championships in that span. The Cuban-born shortstop holds Oakland career records for games, at-bats, runs, hits, doubles, triples and total bases.

Campaneris led the league in stolen bases six times and finished his career with 649. He also played for Texas, California and the Yankees, with whom he ended his major-league career. At the age of 39, Campaneris hit .322 in 60 games for the Yankees. He finished his 19-year career with a .259 average and he played 2,097 games at shortstop, the sixth-highest amount in history. He took part in 1,186 double plays, which placed him ninth among shortstops on the all-time list.

ALL-TIME A's SEASON RECORDS

BATTING: Napoleon Lajoie, .422, 1901
HRs: Jimmie Foxx, 58, 1932
RBIs: Jimmie Foxx, 169, 1932
STEALS: Rickey Henderson, 130, 1982
WINS: John Coombs, 31, 1910
Lefty Grove, 31, 1931
STRIKEOUTS: Rube Waddell, 349, 1904

SEATTLE MARINERS

TEAM DIRECTORY: Owner: George Argyros; Pres.: Chuck Armstrong; VP-Baseball Oper.: Dick Balderson; Dir. Play. Dev.: Bill Haywood; Dir. Publ.: Bob Porter; Trav. Sec.: Lee Pelekoudas; Mgr.: Chuck Cottier. Home: Kingdome (59,438). Field distances: 316, l.f. line; 357, l.c.; 410, c.f.; 357, r.c.; 316, r.f. line. Spring training: Tempe, Ariz.

SCOUTING REPORT

HITTING: Phil Bradley represents all that's right with the Mariners. The team has developed young players at the expense of growing pains along the way. Now, Bradley has blossomed into a star and the Mariners may be ready to win. In addition to Bradley (.300, 26 homers, 88 RBI), the Mariners also boast good hitters in Alvin Davis (.287, 18 homers, 78 RBI), Jim Presley (.275, 28 homers, 84 RBI) and rookie Danny Tartabull (.328 in 19 games with the Mariners).

Alvin Davis showed his great rookie season was no fluke.

Seattle had the most prolific attack in its short history last year. This season, the Mariners' offense should be even better, if only because all those young hitters have another year under their belts. The Mariners, though, could use a boost in production out of the catching spot. Seattle has two fine defensive catchers in ex-Dodger Steve Yeager and Bob Kearney, but neither offers much pop. However, if infielder Tartabull fulfills his promise, the Mariners may be willing to sacrifice some offense behind the plate.

PITCHING: If only the Seattle pitchers would pick the same season to have a good year. In 1984, Mark Langston emerged as the best pitcher on the staff and led the league in strikeouts. In 1985, while the injury-plagued Langston slumped to 7-14, former No. 1 draft pick Mike Moore finally realized his potential, compiling a 17-10 record.

Behind Langston and Moore, there is Matt Young, who somehow lost 19 games while winning 12 last year. Jim Beattie (5-6, 7.29 ERA) is expected to rebound from a miserable season in which he pitched just 70 innings. The next young arm to step into the Seattle rotation will probably be Billy Swift (6-10, 4.77 ERA), who showed great promise and an outstanding sinker last year. Now all the Mariners need to do is stay healthy and find help for top reliever Edwin Nunez (7-3, 3.09 ERA, 16 saves).

FIELDING: The Mariners have not been satisfied with the way Kearney has handled the young pitchers. So Seattle gave up reliever Ed Vande Berg to get Yeager. Seattle won't be disappointed if Yeager hits .210, which he probably will. The veteran was acquired to be a pitching coach behind the plate.

The Mariners like Spike Owen's work at shortstop and Bradley's glove in left. The rest of the defense is unspectacular, but solid. The Mariners finished third in fielding percentage, behind California and Chicago, last year.

OUTLOOK: The Mariners should have done better than 74-88 last year, but they were decimated by injuries to their pitching staff. A healthy staff would be worth at least 10 more wins this season and that would automatically put the Mariners into contention in the weak AL West. How far Seattle goes from there will depend on the continued development of the young hitters and getting some help for Nunez in the bullpen. Manager Chuck Cottier's club has been playing aggressively and confidently. Seattle no longer expects to find a way to lose. Don't be surprised if the Mariners are playing meaningful games in late September this season.

SEATTLE MARINERS 1986 ROSTER

MANAGER Chuck Cottier

Coaches—Deron Johnson, Jim Mahoney, Marty Martinez, Phil Regan, Phil Roof

PITCHERS

No.	Name	1985 Club	W-L	IP	SO	ERA	B-T	Ht.	Wt.	Born
31	Barojas, Salome	Seattle	0-5	53	27	5.98	R-R	5-9	198	6/16/57 Mexico
45	Beattie, Jim	Seattle	5-6	70	45	7.29	R-R	6-6	225	7/14/54 Hampton, VA
39	Best, Karl	Calgary	0-0	5	8	0.00	R-R	6-4	210	3/6/59 Aberdeen, MA
		Seattle	2-1	32	32	1.95				
36	Guetterman, Lee	Calgary	5-8	110	48	5.79	L-L	6-8	225	11/22/58 Chattanooga, TN
12	Langston, Mark	Seattle	7-14	127	72	5.47	R-L	6-2	180	8/20/60 San Diego, CA
52	Mirabella, Paul	Calgary	5-4	68	42	4.08	L-L	6-2	196	3/20/54 Bellville, NJ
		Seattle	0-0	14	8	1.32				
—	Monteleone, Rich	Nashville	6-12	145	97	5.08	R-R	6-2	205	3/22/63 Tampa, FL
25	Moore, Mike	Seattle	17-10	247	155	3.46	R-R	6-4	205	11/26/59 Eakly, OK
35	Morgan, Mike	Seattle	1-1	6	2	12.00	R-R	6-2	185	10/8/59 Tulare, CA
		Calgary	0-0	2	0	4.50				
30	Nunez, Edwin	Seattle	7-3	90	58	3.09	R-R	6-5	235	5/27/63 Puerto Rico
18	Swift, Bill	Chattanooga	2-1	39	21	3.69	R-R	6-0	170	10/27/61 S. Portland, ME
		Seattle	6-10	121	55	4.77				
47	Taylor, Terry	Chattanooga	4-15	165	107	5.28	R-R	6-1	180	7/28/64 Crestview, FL
49	Thomas, Roy	Calgary	2-2	30	40	4.55	R-R	6-6	200	6/22/53 Quantico, VA
		Seattle	7-0	94	70	3.36				
51	Wilkinson, Bill	Salinas	6-1	60	75	2.72	R-L	5-10	160	8/19/64 Greybull, WY
		Calgary	5-1	57	42	2.67				
		Seattle	0-2	6	5	13.50				
43	Wills, Frank	Calgary	4-3	46	31	4.47	R-R	6-2	200	10/26/58 New Orleans, LA
		Seattle	5-11	123	67	6.00				
40	Young, Matt	Seattle	12-19	218	136	4.91	L-L	6-3	205	8/9/58 Pasadena, CA

CATCHERS

No.	Name	1985 Club	H	HR	RBI	Pct.	B-T	Ht.	Wt.	Born
11	Kearney, Bob	Seattle	74	6	27	.243	R-R	6-0	185	10/3/56 San Antonio, TX
2	Scott, Donnie	Calgary	12	0	9	.462	B-R	5-11	185	8/16/61 Dunedin, FL
		Seattle	41	4	23	.222				
5	Valle, David	Calgary	45	6	26	.344	R-R	6-2	200	10/30/60 Bayside, NY
		Seattle	11	0	4	.157				
—	Yeager, Steve	Los Angeles	25	0	9	.207	R-R	6-0	207	11/24/48 Huntington, WV

INFIELDERS

No.	Name	1985 Club	H	HR	RBI	Pct.	B-T	Ht.	Wt.	Born
21	Davis, Alvin	Seattle	166	18	78	.287	L-R	6-1	190	9/9/60 Riverside, CA
7	Owen, Spike	Seattle	91	6	37	.259	R-R	5-10	166	4/10/61 Cleburne, TX
11	Perconte, Jack	Calgary	15	0	9	.288	L-R	5-10	165	8/31/54 Joliet, IL
		Seattle	128	2	23	.264				
44	Phelps, Ken	Seattle	24	9	24	.207	L-L	6-1	204	8/6/54 Seattle, WA
17	Presley, Jim	Seattle	157	28	84	.275	R-R	6-1	185	10/23/61 Pensacola, FL
3	Ramos, Domingo	Seattle	33	1	15	.196	R-R	5-10	154	3/29/58 Dominican Republic
24	Reynolds, Harold	Seattle	15	0	6	.144	B-R	5-11	165	11/26/60 Eugene, OR
		Calgary	77	5	30	.363				
38	Tartabull, Danny	Calgary	142	43	109	.300	R-R	6-1	185	10/20/62 Puerto Rico
		Seattle	20	1	7	.328				

OUTFIELDERS

No.	Name	1985 Club	H	HR	RBI	Pct.	B-T	Ht.	Wt.	Born
9	Bonnell, Barry	Seattle	37	1	10	.243	R-R	6-3	208	10/27/53 Milford, OH
29	Bradley, Phil	Seattle	192	26	88	.300	R-R	6-0	178	3/11/59 Bloomington, IN
55	Brantley, Mickey	Calgary	68	11	45	.244	R-R	5-10	185	6/17/61 Catskill, NY
22	Calderon, Ivan	Seattle	60	0	20	.286	R-R	6-1	205	3/19/62 Puerto Rico
23	Chambers, Al	Calgary	109	9	64	.308	L-L	6-4	215	3/24/61 Harrisburg, PA
		Seattle	0	0	0	.000				
16	Cowens, Al	Seattle	120	14	69	.265	R-R	6-2	205	10/25/51 Los Angeles, CA
42	Henderson, Dave	Seattle	121	14	68	.241	R-R	6-2	212	7/21/58 Dos Palos, CA
53	Hengel, Dave	Chattanooga	132	17	89	.287	R-R	6-0	195	12/18/61 Oakland, CA
		Calgary	2	0	3	.087				
26	Moses, John	Calgary	152	5	47	.321	B-L	5-10	170	8/9/57 Los Angeles, CA
		Seattle	12	0	3	.194				
48	Nixon, Donell	Seattle	Disabled list				R-R	6-1	185	12/31/61 Evergreen, NC
20	Thomas, Gorman	Seattle	104	32	87	.215	R-R	6-2	215	12/12/50 Charleston, SC
50	Wishnevski, Mike	Salinas	125	13	91	.302	L-L	6-0	205	3/29/61 Johnstown, PA

MARINER PROFILES

GORMAN THOMAS 35 6-2 215 Bats R Throws R

Named AL Comeback Player of the Year... Designated hitter made amazing recovery from rotator-cuff surgery, which he had undergone June 8, 1984... Finished fifth in AL with club-record 32 homers, representing his biggest power surge since he tied for AL home-run title with 39 in 1982... Notched 250th career homer Sept. 9... Set club records with 11 homers in July and two or more homers in five games... Cracked three homers, including a grand slam, April 11... Missed 19 games with a strained muscle in his side... Finished season in 2-for-29 slump... Never one to hit for high average... Hit .163 in May and .165 in August... Born Dec. 12, 1950, in Charleston, S.C. ... Acquired from Cleveland with Jack Perconte for Tony Bernazard prior to 1984 season... Played in first 35 games in 1984 before being placed on disabled list with a torn rotator cuff... First draft pick ever by Seattle Pilots, who chose him in first round in June 1969... Drafted as a shortstop and played the infield during the early part of his minor-league career.

Year	Club	Pos.	G	AB	R	H	2B	3B	HR	RBI	SB	Avg.
1973	Milwaukee	OF-3B	59	155	16	29	7	1	2	11	5	.187
1974	Milwaukee	OF	17	46	10	12	4	0	2	11	4	.261
1975	Milwaukee	OF	121	240	34	43	12	2	10	28	4	.179
1976	Milwaukee	OF-3B	99	227	27	45	9	2	8	36	2	.198
1978	Milwaukee	OF-INF	137	452	70	111	24	1	32	86	3	.246
1979	Milwaukee	OF	156	557	97	136	29	0	45	123	1	.244
1980	Milwaukee	OF	162	628	78	150	26	3	38	105	8	.239
1981	Milwaukee	OF	103	363	54	94	22	0	21	65	4	.259
1982	Milwaukee	OF	158	567	96	139	29	1	*39	112	3	.245
1983	Mil.-Clev.	OF	152	535	72	112	23	1	22	69	10	.209
1984	Seattle	OF	35	108	6	17	3	0	1	13	0	.157
1985	Seattle	DH	135	484	76	104	16	1	32	87	3	.215
	Totals		1334	4362	636	992	204	12	252	746	47	.227

PHIL BRADLEY 27 6-0 178 Bats R Throws R

Blossomed into star in second full season in majors... Set club records with 714 plate appearances, 192 hits, 319 total bases, five hits in a game, 67 extra-base hits and 129 strikeouts ... Surprised everyone with his power... Had 26 homers after hitting only three in 340 minor-league at-bats and none in first 398 major-league at-bats... Won five games with a homer during Mariners' final at-bat... Was seventh in AL in batting (.300), sixth in hits, third in total bases, tied for seventh in triples (8) and ninth in slugging percentage (.498) . . . His .298 career average is best in club history among players who have appeared in at least 300 games . . . Born March 11, 1959, in Bloomington, Ind. . . . Selected in third round of June 1981 draft . . . Was an All-Big Eight quarterback at Missouri . . . Led AL rookies by hitting .301 in 1984 . . . There are few things he can't do . . . Excellent left fielder . . . Has speed, can hit for average and can hit for power.

Year	Club	Pos.	G	AB	R	H	2B	3B	HR	RBI	SB	Avg.
1983	Seattle	OF	23	67	8	18	2	0	0	5	3	.269
1984	Seattle	OF	124	322	49	97	12	4	0	24	21	.301
1985	Seattle	OF	159	641	100	192	33	8	26	88	22	.300
	Totals		306	1030	157	307	47	12	26	117	46	.298

ALVIN DAVIS 25 6-1 190 **Bats L Throws R**

Appeared to be suffering from sophomore jinx in first half of last season . . . But, after hitting .266 through All-Star break, he hit .310 for the remainder of season to finish at .287 . . . Hit 11 of his 18 homers and drove in 45 of his 78 runs in second half . . . Hit .346 in July and .350 in August . . . Had a career-high 11-game hitting streak Aug. 31 through Sept. 11 . . . Had his average up to .296 Oct. 1, but went hitless in his final 17 at-bats . . . Born Sept. 9, 1960, in Riverside, Cal. . . . Selected by Mariners in sixth round of June 1982 draft . . . Graduated from Arizona State . . . Began 1984 season in Triple-A but was recalled April 7, after Ken Phelps suffered a broken finger . . . Homered in his second at-bat and then again in his next game . . . Had already amassed 18 homers and 65 RBI when he represented the Mariners at the 1984 All-Star Game . . . Set club records in RBI (116), walks (97) and grand slams (2) and won AL Rookie of the Year Award in 1984 . . . Broke major-league mark with 16 intentional walks as a rookie.

Year	Club	Pos.	G	AB	R	H	2B	3B	HR	RBI	SB	Avg.
1984	Seattle	1B	152	567	80	161	34	3	27	116	5	.284
1985	Seattle	1B	155	578	78	166	33	1	18	78	1	.287
	Total		307	1145	158	327	67	4	45	194	6	.286

DAVE HENDERSON 27 6-2 212 **Bats R Throws R**

His average dipped to .241, his lowest figure in four full seasons with Mariners . . . Became club's all-time home-run leader Sept. 27, when he belted his 65th career homer . . . Had a career-high 14-game hitting streak April 29 through May 19, batting .463 . . . Hit .291 with runners in scoring position and drove in a career-high 68 runs . . . Hit .303 in May and

.188 in July . . . Born July 21, 1958, in Dos Palos, Cal. . . . First-round pick by Seattle in June 1977 draft . . . Hit .315 in first pro season at Bellingham (A) . . . Was Mariners' starting center fielder on Opening Night in 1981, but was later sent back to Spokane (AAA) . . . Recalled in September by Seattle and has stayed with club since . . . Uncle Joe Henderson pitched for White Sox in 1974.

Year	Club	Pos.	G	AB	R	H	2B	3B	HR	RBI	SB	Avg.
1981	Seattle	OF	59	126	17	21	3	0	6	13	2	.167
1982	Seattle	OF	104	324	47	82	17	1	14	48	2	.253
1983	Seattle	OF	137	484	50	130	24	5	17	55	9	.269
1984	Seattle	OF	113	350	42	98	23	0	14	43	5	.280
1985	Seattle	OF	139	502	70	121	28	2	14	68	6	.241
	Totals		552	1786	226	452	95	8	65	227	24	.253

JIM PRESLEY 24 6-1 185 — Bats R Throws R

Established himself as a streaky power hitter in his first full major-league season . . . Finished second on the club in homers (28) and third in RBI (84) and hits (157) . . . Tied for team lead with 33 doubles . . . Homered in four straight games twice during 1985 . . . Hit six homers and drove in 13 runs in Mariners' first nine games . . . Hit .246 with 20 homers and 58 RBI against right-handers and batted .358 with eight homers and 26 RBI against left-handers . . . Committed 17 errors at third base . . . Struck out 100 times, one of four Mariners to reach century mark . . . Best month was July, when he hit .327 with seven homers and 13 RBI . . . Born Oct. 23, 1961, in Pensacola, Fla. . . . Fourth-round pick in June 1979 draft . . . Led his team to the 1974 Little League World Series in Williamsport, Pa. . . . Ended 1984 season with seven-game hitting streak and topped that with 10-game streak in 1985 . . . Hit .196 for Bellingham (A) in first pro season.

Year	Club	Pos.	G	AB	R	H	2B	3B	HR	RBI	SB	Avg.
1984	Seattle	3B	70	251	27	57	12	1	10	36	1	.227
1985	Seattle	3B	155	570	71	157	33	1	28	84	2	.275
	Totals		225	821	98	214	45	2	38	120	3	.261

JACK PERCONTE 31 5-10 165 — Bats L Throws R

After tying club record with 180 hits in 1984, this second baseman found himself in minors . . . Sent to Calgary (AAA) July 9 after a 7-for-66 nightmare of a slump . . . Recalled Aug. 2 and hit .302 for the remainder of season . . . Ended the longest homerless streak in the majors at 990 at-bats by cracking one to lead off a game against Baltimore May 17 . . . Hit another homer Sept. 11 . . . Tied a club record with five hits in a game Sept. 1 . . . Had career-high 15-game hitting streak, beginning May 31 . . . Ended season with 27 consecutive successful stolen-base attempts . . . Stole 31 bases in 33 tries . . . Born Aug. 31, 1954, in Joliet, Ill. . . . Acquired from Cleveland with Gorman Thomas for Tony Bernazard prior to 1984 season . . . A 16th-round pick by Dodgers in June 1976 draft . . . Played at Murray State.

Year	Club	Pos.	G	AB	R	H	2B	3B	HR	RBI	SB	Avg.
1980	Los Angeles	2B	14	17	2	4	0	0	0	2	3	.235
1981	Los Angeles	2B	8	9	2	2	0	1	0	1	1	.222
1982	Cleveland	2B	93	219	27	52	4	4	0	15	9	.237
1983	Cleveland	2B	14	26	1	7	1	0	0	0	0	.260
1984	Seattle	2B	155	612	93	180	24	4	0	31	29	.294
1985	Seattle	2B	125	485	60	128	17	7	2	23	31	.264
	Totals		409	1368	185	373	46	16	2	72	76	.273

MARK LANGSTON 25 6-2 180 Bats R Throws L

After finishing second to teammate Alvin Davis in race for 1984 AL Rookie of the Year, he slumped during injury-plagued second season . . . Was on disabled list from June 7 through July 22 with a strained flexor muscle in his left elbow . . . Got off to a 5-3 start, but went 2-11 after May 21 . . . Lost six straight decisions from May 21 to Aug. 8 before winning back-to-back starts . . . Lost his last five decisions in seven starts . . . Did not pitch after an 11-4 loss to the Rangers Sept. 23 . . . Born Aug. 20, 1960, in San Diego . . . Third-round pick by Mariners in June 1981 draft . . . Jumped from Double-A to majors in 1984, when he became only the fourth rookie to lead AL in strikeouts with 204 . . . Struck out 12 in a game three times and 11 once . . . Set club records for wins (17), highest winning percentage for a starter (.630), most consecutive wins (7), walks (118), consecutive shutout innings by a starter (21) and consecutive strikeouts (7).

Year	Club	G	IP	W	L	Pct.	SO	BB	H	ERA
1984	Seattle	35	225	17	10	.630	204	118	188	3.40
1985	Seattle	24	126⅔	7	14	.333	72	91	122	5.47
	Totals	59	351⅔	24	24	500	276	209	310	4.15

MIKE MOORE 26 6-4 205 Bats R Throws R

Finally emerged as the sort of pitcher the Mariners had hoped he would be when they made him first player picked overall in June 1981 draft . . . Tied club records for wins (17), winning percentage (.630) and innings pitched (247) . . . Set club record with 14 complete games, ranking in second in AL . . . Was 10th in AL with 155 strikeouts . . . Had longest no-hit bid by a Mariner pitcher, holding the Brewers hitless for eight innings May 8 . . . Placed on the disabled list June 5 with a strained right thigh muscle . . . Won six straight games beginning Aug. 31 . . . Born Nov. 26, 1959, in Eakly, Okla. . . . Was the first right-handed pitcher to be No. 1 pick in the nation . . . Was 12-2 at Oral Roberts in 1981 . . . Made Mariners in 1982 after only 13 games in Double-A . . . His 17 losses in 1984 matched a Mariner record.

Year	Club	G	IP	W	L	Pct.	SO	BB	H	ERA
1982	Seattle	28	144⅓	7	14	.333	73	79	159	5.36
1983	Seattle	22	128	6	8	.429	108	60	130	4.71
1984	Seattle	34	212	7	17	.292	158	85	236	4.97
1985	Seattle	35	247	17	10	.630	155	70	230	3.46
	Totals	119	731⅓	37	49	.430	494	294	755	4.49

MATT YOUNG 27 6-3 205 **Bats L Throws L**

May have considered himself lucky because he was only one of Mariners' five starters not to spend time on the disabled list in 1985 . . . On the other hand, he lost a club-record 19 games . . . Had a six-game losing streak June 30 through Aug. 15 . . . Won his next four starts, including his first shutout since 1983 . . . Lost his last four starts . . . Allowed 23 homers, the most of any Seattle pitcher . . . Born Aug. 9, 1958, in Pasadena, Cal. . . . Second-round pick by Mariners in June 1980 draft . . . Pitched at Pasadena City College and UCLA . . . Overcame control problems in first two pro seasons . . . Represented Mariners at 1983 All-Star Game . . . Especially difficult for left-handers to hit.

Year	Club	G	IP	W	L	Pct.	SO	BB	H	ERA
1983	Seattle	33	203⅔	11	15	.423	130	79	178	3.27
1984	Seattle	22	113⅓	6	8	.429	73	57	141	5.72
1985	Seattle	37	218⅓	12	19	.387	136	76	242	4.91
	Totals	92	535⅓	29	42	.408	339	212	561	4.46

EDWIN NUNEZ 22 6-5 235 **Bats R Throws R**

Was successful as Mariners' short reliever in his first full season in majors . . . Finished ninth in AL with 16 saves and fifth with 70 appearances . . . Picked up a save in his first three appearances and allowed only two earned runs in April, when he was 1-0 with a 1.08 ERA . . . Did not allow an earned run in 15 appearances from June 8 to July 12 . . . May have suffered from toll of his first long season . . . Posted 12 of his 16 saves before All-Star break . . . Had 4.82 ERA in August and 4.11 mark in September and October . . . Born May 27, 1963, in Humacao, Puerto Rico . . . Signed as free agent at age 15, he turned 16 just prior to first pro season in 1979, when he stood 6-3 and weighed

170 pounds . . . Was originally a starting pitcher . . . Worked exclusively in short relief beginning with stay in Arizona Instructional League after 1983 season . . . Once broke his left hand on a clubhouse door after being removed from a game.

Year	Club	G	IP	W	L	Pct.	SO	BB	H	ERA
1982	Seattle	8	35⅓	1	2	.333	27	16	36	4.58
1983	Seattle	14	37	0	4	.000	35	22	40	4.38
1984	Seattle	37	67⅔	2	2	.500	57	21	55	3.19
1985	Seattle	70	90⅓	7	3	.700	58	34	79	3.09
	Totals	129	230⅓	10	11	.476	177	93	210	3.56

TOP PROSPECTS

DANNY TARTABULL 23 6-1 185 **Bats R Throws R**

Infielder was having an impressive season for Calgary (AAA) before Mariners recalled him . . . Led all of professional baseball with 43 homers and was named Pacific Coast League MVP . . . Led Calgary with 109 RBI, 12 game-winning RBI, 102 runs and 291 total bases . . . Hit .300 and stole 17 bases . . . Hit .328 with one homer and seven RBI in 19 games for Seattle . . . Born Oct. 20, 1962, in San Juan, Puerto Rico . . . Selected from Reds in 1983 compensation pool . . . Hit .300 in 10-game trial with Mariners in 1984 . . . Father Jose was major-league outfielder.

BILL SWIFT 24 6-0 170 **Bats R Throws R**

Was assigned to Chattanooga (AA) out of spring training before making the quickest jump to big leagues in Mariner history . . . Spent only two months and five days in minors . . . Made major-league debut June 7 at Cleveland, winning in relief . . . Started in 21 of his next 22 appearances . . . Won two of his last three games with Mariners to finish at 6-10 with 4.77 ERA . . . Was 2-1 with 3.69 ERA for Chattanooga . . . Has a very good sinker . . . Born Oct. 27, 1961, in South Portland, Maine . . . Seattle's first pick in June 1984 draft . . . Was a member of U.S. Olympic team . . . One of 15 children.

MANAGER CHUCK COTTIER: Had disappointing 74-88 record in first full season as Seattle manager . . . Plagued by injuries to his pitching staff throughout season . . . Highlight of his season came at Yankee Stadium, where he tore first base from ground and hurled it into right field during an argument with umpires . . . Named interim manager Sept. 1, 1984 and finished with a 15-12 record . . . Had managed for five years in

minors, compiling 287-197 record before becoming fifth Mariner skipper . . . Served as third-base and infield coach for Mets from 1979-81 . . . Was Mariners' third-base coach for four seasons prior to being named manager . . . Born Jan. 8, 1936, in Delta, Colo. . . . Spent five years in minors as an infielder before making it to Milwaukee Braves in 1959 . . . Spent his first four seasons in majors with Washington . . . Hit .220 in 580 major-league games before an injury to his Achilles tendon ended his playing career . . . Composite major-league managerial record is 89-100.

GREATEST SHORTSTOP

In the nine-year history of the Mariners, no shortstop has started on Opening Day for more than two consecutive seasons. The list includes Craig Reynolds, Mario Mendoza, Jim Anderson, Todd Cruz and Spike Owen. However, the Mariners' best shortstop is still their first: Reynolds.

Reynolds was acquired in the club's first trade. The Mariners sent pitcher Grant Jackson to Pittsburgh for Reynolds and infielder Jimmy Sexton. Reynolds, who had played a total of only 38 games in his first two seasons with the Pirates, immediately became the Mariners' starting shortstop. He hit .248 in the club's first season in 1977, then hit .292 in 1978, when he was the Mariners' representative at the All-Star Game.

Reynolds also distinguished himself in his departure from Seattle. When the Mariners traded him to Houston following his fine 1978 season, they received left-hander Floyd Bannister, who became one of the club's most dependable pitchers.

ALL-TIME MARINER SEASON RECORDS

BATTING: Tom Paciorek, .326, 1981
HRs: Gorman Thomas, 32, 1985
RBIs: Alvin Davis, 116, 1984
STEALS: Julio Cruz, 59, 1978
WINS: Mark Langston, 17, 1984
Mike Moore, 17, 1985
STRIKEOUTS: Floyd Bannister, 209, 1982

TEXAS RANGERS

TEAM DIRECTORY: Chairman: Eddie Chiles; Pres.: Mike Stone; VP-GM: Tom Grieve; VP-Adm.: Larry Schmittou; VP-Fin.: Charles Wangner; Asst. GM-Play. Pers./Scouting: Sandy Johnson; Dir. Play. Dev.: Marty Scott; Media Rel. Dir.: John Blake; Trav. Sec.: Dan Schimek; Mgr.: Bobby Valentine. Home: Arlington Stadium (43,508). Field distances: 330, l.f. line; 380, l.c.; 400, c.f.; 380, r.c.; 330, r.f. line. Spring training: Pompano Beach, Fla.

Thanks to Oddibe McDowell, Bobby Valentine can take heart.

SCOUTING REPORT

HITTING: The Rangers are so strapped for offense that they may be willing to give outfielder Pete Incaviglia the chance to jump directly from Oklahoma State University to the pros. It's a risk that a 62-99 team can afford to take. Oddibe McDowell, the Rangers' center fielder, made the jump with only a minimal amount of minor-league experience. McDowell (.239, 18 homers, 42 RBI) showed good power, but also a big strike zone for a small man in his 111 games with the Rangers last season.

Texas benefitted from the 1985 renaissance of Toby Harrah (.270, 9 homers, 44 RBI, 113 walks), whose escape from New York was a blessing. Now the Rangers are hoping for a comeback from Larry Parrish (.249, 17 homers, 51 RBI), who underwent knee surgery during last season. Texas' other big bats belong to Gary Ward (.287, 15 homers, 70 RBI) and Pete O'Brien (.267, 22 homers, 92 RBI). Newcomer Tom Paciorek is a proven hitter, too.

PITCHING: Twenty pitchers appeared in games for the Rangers last year. Outside of Charlie Hough, none won more than eight games. Hough (14-16, 3.31 ERA) was a workhorse again, but, after him, there's little help. Next best is Mike Mason, who was 8-15. Where are Mike Smithson, John Butcher, Ron Darling, Walt Terrell and Tom Henke now that the Rangers need them?

The Rangers must hope that one of the young pitchers they haven't traded away will emerge. The staff has so many open spots that the Rangers might carry as many as three rookie pitchers. One pleasant surprise last season was the work of reliever Greg Harris (2.47, 11 saves), who has one of the best curves in the league.

FIELDING: With all their young pitchers, the Rangers would greatly benefit from having a solid infield. Unfortunately, they don't have one; it's average at best. The left side is unsettled and Harrah is sure-handed, but has limited range at second base. There is little to be excited about in the outfield, too, except for the speed and grace of McDowell in center. Parrish has a strong arm in right, but his range is not the best.

OUTLOOK: Will Bobby Valentine's Rangers ever see their way out of last place? He took over as manager with the team in last place and it remained there for the remainder of last season. Valentine has a shortage of pitching, no catching and a mediocre infield. In short, it looks like another long, hard summer in Texas.

TEXAS RANGERS 1986 ROSTER

MANAGER Bobby Valentine

Coaches—Joe Ferguson, Tim Foli, Tom House, Art Howe, Tom Robson

PITCHERS

No.	Name	1985 Club	W-L	IP	SO	ERA	B-T	Ht.	Wt.	Born
33	Cook, Glen	Oklahoma City	9-6	121	78	3.21	R-R	5-11	180	9/8/59 Buffalo, NY
		Texas	2-3	40	19	9.45				
—	Correa, Ed	Glens Falls	1-5	40	34	6.75	R-R	6-2	192	4/29/66 Puerto Rico
		Appleton	13-3	139	128	2.53				
		Chicago (AL)	1-0	10	10	6.97				
—	Ferlenda, Greg	Florence	12-5	165	160	3.27	R-R	6-1	185	8/7/64 Syracuse, NY
23	Guzman, Jose	Oklahoma City	10-5	150	76	3.13	R-R	6-3	185	4/9/63 Puerto Rico
		Texas	3-2	33	24	2.76				
27	Harris, Greg	Texas	5-4	113	111	2.47	B-R	6-0	165	11/2/55 Lynwood, CA
45	Henry, Dwayne	Tulsa	7-6	81	97	2.66	R-R	6-3	205	2/16/62 Elkton, MD
		Texas	2-2	21	20	2.57				
46	Hooton, Burt	Texas	5-8	124	62	5.23	R-R	6-1	210	2/7/50 Greenville, TX
49	Hough, Charlie	Texas	14-16	250	141	3.31	R-R	6-2	190	1/5/48 Honolulu, HI
16	Mason, Mike	Texas	8-15	179	92	4.83	L-L	6-2	205	11/21/58 Faribault, MN
—	Patterson, Scott	Albany	7-2	46	35	1.55	R-R	6-2	180	9/11/58 Philadelphia, PA
		Columbus	5-2	38	26	3.35				
—	Rogers, Kenny	Daytona Beach	0-1	10	9	7.20	L-L	6-1	185	11/10/64 Savannah, GA
		Burlington	2-5	95	96	2.84				
30	Rozema, Dave	Texas	3-7	88	42	4.19	R-R	6-4	200	8/5/56 Grand Rapids, MI
40	Russell, Jeff	Den.-Okla. City	7-4	115	94	4.06	R-R	6-4	195	9/2/61 Cincinnati, OH
		Texas	3-6	62	44	7.55				
44	Surhoff, Rich	Portland	7 8	111	91	3.17	R-R	6-3	215	10/3/62 Bronx, NY
		Philadelphia	1-0	1	1	0.00				
		Texas	0-1	8	8	7.56				
31	Taylor, Billy	Tulsa	3-9	104	87	3.47	B-R	6-8	220	10/16/61 Monticello, FL
29	Williams, Matt	Syracuse	7-12	136	100	4.43	R-R	6-1	200	7/25/59 Houston, TX
		Oklahoma City	0-0	4	4	2.25				
		Texas	2-1	26	22	2.42				
—	Williams, Mitch	Salem	6-9	99	138	5.45	L-L	6-4	200	11/17/64 Santa Ana, CA
		Tulsa	2-2	33	37	4.64				
38	Wright, Ricky	Oklahoma City	5-4	83	55	2.72	L-L	6-3	175	11/22/58 Paris, TX
		Texas	0-0	8	7	4.70				

CATCHERS

No.	Name	1985 Club	H	HR	RBI	Pct.	B-T	Ht.	Wt.	Born
—	Mercado, Orlando	Oklahoma City	52	8	29	.252	R-R	6-0	195	11/7/61 Puerto Rico
12	Petralli, Geno	Maine	1	0	1	.143	B-R	6-1	180	9/25/59 Sacramento, CA
		Oklahoma City	21	1	5	.263				
		Texas	27	0	11	.270				
4	Slaught, Don	Texas	96	8	35	.280	R-R	6-1	190	9/11/58 Long Beach, CA

INFIELDERS

No.	Name	1985 Club	H	HR	RBI	Pct.	B-T	Ht.	Wt.	Born
—	Browne, Jerry	Salem	123	3	58	.267	B-R	5-10	165	2/13/66 Virgin Islands
22	Buechele, Steve	Oklahoma City	104	9	64	.297	R-R	6-2	190	9/26/61 Lancaster, PA
		Texas	48	6	21	.219				
—	Fletcher, Scott	Chicago (AL)	77	2	31	.256	R-R	5-11	173	7/30/58 Ft. Walton Beach, FL
11	Harrah, Toby	Texas	107	9	44	.270	R-R	6-0	180	10/26/48 Sissonville, WV
20	Kunkel, Jeff	Oklahoma City	72	5	43	.195	R-R	6-2	180	3/25/62 West Palm Beach, FL
		Texas	1	0	0	.250				
9	O'Brien, Pete	Texas	153	22	92	.267	L-L	6-1	198	2/9/58 Santa Monica, CA
19	Wilkerson, Curtis	Texas	88	0	22	.244	B-R	5-9	158	4/26/61 Petersburg, VA

OUTFIELDERS

No.	Name	1985 Club	H	HR	RBI	Pct.	B-T	Ht.	Wt.	Born
—	Brower, Bob	Oklahoma City	111	5	50	.249	R-R	6-0	190	1/10/60 Queens, NY
13	Dunbar, Tommy	Texas	21	1	5	.202	L-L	6-2	195	11/24/59 Aiken, SC
		Oklahoma City	37	0	16	.226				
—	Incaviglia, Pete	College					R-R	6-1	220	4/2/64 Pebble Beach, CA
0	McDowell, Oddibe	Oklahoma City	50	2	18	.400	L-L	5-9	160	8/24/62 Hollywood FL
		Texas	97	18	42	.400				
—	Paciorek, Tom	Chicago (AL)	30	0	9	.246	R-R	6-4	204	11/2/46 Detroit, MI
		New York (NL)	33	1	11	.284				
15	Parrish, Larry	Texas	86	17	51	.249	R-R	6-3	215	11/10/53 Winter Haven, FL
—	Sierra, Ruben	Tulsa	137	13	74	.251	B-R	6-1	175	10/6/65 Puerto Rico
32	Ward, Gary	Texas	170	15	70	.287	R-R	6-2	202	12/6/53 Los Angeles, CA
26	Wright, George	Texas	69	2	18	.190	B-R	5-11	180	12/22/58 Oklahoma City, OK
		Oklahoma City	36	8	27	.254				

RANGER PROFILES

ODDIBE McDOWELL 23 5-9 160 **Bats L Throws L**

Center fielder proved to be an exciting player after being called up from minors May 18 . . . Little guy showed good power, belting 18 homers, the most of any rookie in majors . . . Also led AL rookies with 25 stolen bases in 32 attempts . . . Became the first player in Rangers' history to hit for the cycle, July 23 against Cleveland . . . Opened eyes at Rangers' spring-training camp, but started season in Oklahoma City (AAA) . . . Texas signed him as first-round pick in June 1984 draft . . . Was scheduled to report to Tulsa after playing for U.S. Olympic team, but he sustained hairline fracture of his left ring finger in fall at his home Aug. 9 and did not make his pro debut until 1985 . . . Born Aug. 25, 1962, in Hollywood, Fla. . . . Excelled at Arizona State, winning Golden Spikes Award as the outstanding amateur player in U.S. . . . Had been drafted by Yankees, Blue Jays and Twins, but did not sign until Rangers courted him . . . Survived a serious car accident in which he suffered a ruptured spleen in 1979 . . . Wears "O" as in Oddibe.

Year	Club	Pos.	G	AB	R	H	2B	3B	HR	RBI	SB	Avg.
1985	Texas	OF	111	406	63	97	14	5	18	42	25	.239

PETE O'BRIEN 28 6-1 198 **Bats L Throws L**

Slugged team-leading 22 homers, the most ever by a left-handed-hitting Ranger . . . Started slowly, with .167 average, but hit .292 in his last 124 games in 1985 . . . Committed only eight errors last season and had the second-highest fielding percentage (.995) among AL first basemen, trailing only Yanks' Don Mattingly . . . Led Rangers with 92 RBI, nine sacrifice flies and 10 game-winning RBI . . . Good strikeout ratio for a power hitter, fanning only 53 times in 573 at-bats . . . Tied his career high with five stolen bases, but was caught stealing twice that many times . . . Born Feb. 9, 1958, in Santa Monica, Cal. . . . Selected in 15th round of June 1979 draft . . . Was an All-Big Eight first baseman for Nebraska in 1979.

Year	Club	Pos.	G	AB	R	H	2B	3B	HR	RBI	SB	Avg.
1982	Texas	OF-1B	20	67	13	16	4	1	4	13	1	.239
1983	Texas	1B-OF	154	524	53	124	24	5	8	53	5	.237
1984	Texas	1B-OF	142	520	57	149	26	2	18	80	3	.287
1985	Texas	1B-OF	159	573	69	153	34	3	22	92	5	.267
	Totals		475	1684	192	442	88	11	52	238	14	.262

LARRY PARRISH 32 6-3 215 **Bats R Throws R**

Missed 57 games between July 3 and Sept. 1 after undergoing arthroscopic surgery on his left knee in 1985 . . . Right fielder still managed to hit 17 homers and drive in 51 runs . . . Became fifth player in history to hit three homers in one game in each league when he connected vs. Yankees April 29 . . . It marked the fourth time he had hit three homers in one game, as he had accomplished the feat three times for the Expos . . . Posted his lowest average in four seasons as a Ranger . . . Was acquired by Texas from Montreal with Dave Hostetler in trade for Al Oliver prior to 1982 season . . . Was originally signed by Expos as a free agent in 1972 . . . Born Nov. 10, 1953, in Winter Haven, Fla. . . . Owns a 140-acre ranch outside of Haines City, Fla. and has 50 head of cattle.

Year	Club	Pos.	G	AB	R	H	2B	3B	HR	RBI	SB	Avg.
1974	Montreal	3B	25	69	9	14	5	0	0	4	0	.203
1975	Montreal	3B-2B-SS	145	532	50	146	32	5	10	65	4	.274
1976	Montreal	3B	154	543	65	126	28	5	11	61	2	.232
1977	Montreal	3B	123	402	50	99	19	2	11	46	2	.246
1978	Montreal	3B	144	520	68	144	39	4	15	70	2	.277
1979	Montreal	3B	153	544	83	167	39	2	30	82	5	.307
1980	Montreal	3B	126	452	55	115	27	3	15	72	2	.254
1981	Montreal	3B	97	349	41	85	19	3	8	44	0	.244
1982	Texas	OF-3B	128	440	59	116	15	0	17	62	5	.264
1983	Texas	OF	145	555	76	151	26	4	26	88	0	.272
1984	Texas	OF-3B	156	613	72	175	42	1	22	101	2	.285
1985	Texas	OF	94	346	44	86	11	1	17	51	0	.249
	Totals		1490	5365	672	1424	303	30	182	746	24	.265

DON SLAUGHT 27 6-1 190 **Bats R Throws R**

Showed improvement offensively by hitting a career-high eight homers and batting .280, the third-best mark among AL players who caught at least 100 games . . . Missed 50 games during midseason with a pulled hamstring . . . Recovered to hit .322 in his last 34 games . . . Was acquired from Kansas City before the 1985 season in a complicated, four-team trade that sent Jim Sundberg to Kansas City . . . Selected by Royals in seventh round of June 1980 draft . . . Born Sept. 11, 1958, in Long Beach, Cal. . . . Enjoyed outstanding career at UCLA . . . Hit his only career grand slam in 1984, off current teammate Mike Mason.

Year	Club	Pos.	G	AB	R	H	2B	3B	HR	RBI	SB	Avg.
1982	Kansas City	C	43	115	14	32	6	0	3	8	0	.270
1983	Kansas City	C	83	276	21	86	13	4	0	28	3	.312
1984	Kansas City	C	124	409	48	108	27	4	4	42	0	.264
1985	Texas	C	102	343	34	96	17	4	8	35	5	.280
	Totals		352	1143	117	322	63	12	15	113	8	.282

GARY WARD 32 6-2 202 Bats R Throws R

Outfielder wielded one of the most consistent bats in Rangers' lineup last season . . . Led Rangers' qualifiers for batting title with .287 average . . . Hit .379 in his last 20 games . . . Traditionally is much better hitter after All-Star break . . . Led Texas in runs (77), hits (170), triples (7) and stolen bases (26) . . . His triples total tied a club record and his steals represented a career high . . . Was the only Texas player selected to the All-Star Game, his second . . . Acquired from Minnesota with catcher Sam Sorce for John Butcher and Mike Smithson prior to the 1984 season . . . Originally signed as a free agent by Minnesota in 1972 . . . Born Dec. 6, 1953, in Los Angeles.

Year	Club	Pos.	G	AB	R	H	2B	3B	HR	RBI	SB	Avg.
1979	Minnesota	DH	10	14	2	4	0	0	0	1	0	.286
1980	Minnesota	OF	13	41	11	19	6	2	1	10	0	.463
1981	Minnesota	OF	85	295	42	78	7	6	3	29	5	.264
1982	Minnesota	OF	152	570	85	165	33	7	28	91	13	.289
1983	Minnesota	OF	157	623	76	173	34	5	19	88	8	.278
1984	Texas	OF	155	602	97	171	21	7	21	79	7	.284
1985	Texas	OF	154	593	77	170	28	7	15	70	26	.287
	Totals		726	2738	390	780	129	34	87	368	59	.285

GREG HARRIS 30 6-0 165 Bats S Throws R

Had quietly outstanding season out of the Rangers' bullpen . . . Led all AL pitchers in strikeout ratio with 111 strikeouts in 113 innings . . . Allowed only 74 hits in those 113 innings, the best ratio among AL relievers who pitched at least 75 innings . . . Was third in AL in innings pitched among relievers and was 12th in AL with 58 appearances . . . Led the Rangers in saves with 11 and in ERA with 2.47 mark . . . Acquired from Padres for cash just prior to 1985 season . . . Born Nov. 2, 1955, in Lynwood, Cal. . . . Has pitched for the Mets, Reds, Expos, Padres and Rangers . . . Signed as a free agent by Mets in 1976 . . . Was involved in George Foster deal, going to Cincinnati with Alex Trevino and Jim Kern prior to 1982 season . . . Pitched in one NLCS game for Padres in 1984, allowing eight runs in two innings . . . However, in his lone World Series appearance, he threw 5⅓ scoreless innings.

Year	Club	G	IP	W	L	Pct.	SO	BB	H	ERA
1981	New York (NL)	16	69	3	5	.375	54	28	65	4.43
1982	Cincinnati	34	91⅓	2	6	.250	67	37	96	4.83
1983	Cincinnati	1	1	0	0	.000	1	3	2	27.00
1984	Mont.-S.D.	34	54⅓	2	2	.500	45	25	38	2.48
1985	Texas	58	113	5	4	.556	111	43	74	2.47
	Totals	143	328⅔	12	17	.414	278	136	275	3.61

TOBY HARRAH 37 6-0 180 **Bats R Throws R**

Rescued from unhappy stay in New York, he responded to his homecoming with strong season . . . Drew 113 walks, the second-highest total in majors, and had .432 on-base percentage, the third-highest figure in baseball . . . Finished second among AL second basemen with .989 fielding percentage in 1985 . . . Committed only six errors . . . Average had dipped to career-low .217 with Yankees in 1984 . . . Bettered that mark by 53 points last year, after spring trade that sent him back to Texas for outfielder Billy Sample . . . Started his major-league career with Washington Senators, who drafted him out of Philadelphia organization in 1967 . . . Played for Texas from 1972-78 enjoying his best season in 1975, when he hit .293 with 20 homers and 93 RBI . . . Traded to Cleveland for Buddy Bell prior to 1979 season . . . Traded to Yankees with Rick Browne for George Frazier, Guy Elston and Otis Nixon prior to 1984 season . . . Born Oct. 26, 1948, in Sissonville, W. Va. . . . Has been selected to four AL All-Star teams . . . Attended Ohio Northern for one year on a football scholarship.

Year	Club	Pos.	G	AB	R	H	2B	3B	HR	RBI	SB	Avg.
1969	Washington	SS	8	1	4	0	0	0	0	0	0	.000
1971	Washington	SS-3B	127	383	45	88	11	3	2	22	10	.230
1972	Texas	SS	116	374	47	97	14	3	1	31	16	.259
1973	Texas	3B-SS	118	461	64	120	16	1	10	50	10	.260
1974	Texas	SS-3B	161	573	79	149	23	2	21	74	15	.260
1975	Texas	SS-3B-2B	151	522	81	153	24	1	20	93	23	.293
1076	Texas	SS-3B	155	584	64	152	21	1	15	67	8	.260
1977	Texas	3B-SS	159	539	90	142	25	5	27	87	27	.263
1978	Texas	SS-3B	139	450	56	103	17	3	12	59	31	.229
1979	Cleveland	3B-SS	149	527	99	147	25	1	20	77	20	.279
1980	Cleveland	3B-SS	160	561	100	150	22	4	11	72	17	.267
1981	Cleveland	SS-3B	103	361	64	105	12	4	5	44	12	.291
1982	Cleveland	3B-2B-SS	162	602	100	183	29	4	25	78	17	.304
1983	Cleveland	3B-2B	138	526	81	140	23	1	9	53	16	.266
1984	New York (AL)	3B-2B-OF	88	253	40	55	9	4	1	26	3	.217
1985	Texas	2B-SS-3B	126	396	65	107	18	1	9	44	11	.270
	Totals		2060	7113	1079	1891	289	38	188	877	236	.266

CHARLIE HOUGH 38 6-2 190 **Bats R Throws R**

Only Texas pitcher to reach double figures in wins last season with 14 . . . Led Rangers in virtually all pitching departments and tied for second in AL in complete games with 14 . . . Ranked eighth in AL in ERA at 3.31 . . . Has led Texas in wins for the past four seasons . . . Suffered a career-high 16 losses in 1985 . . . He goes as his knuckleball goes, which means he can be streaky . . . Lost six decisions in a row in June, then went 9-2 in July and August . . . Uncorked 11 wild pitches and hit seven batters, both tops among Rangers pitchers . . . Born Jan. 5, 1948, in Honolulu, Hawaii . . . Was eighth-round pick by Dodgers in June 1966 draft, as a third baseman . . . Hurt his arm in Albuquerque (AAA) in 1969 and learned knuckleball from Dodger scout Goldie Holt in Arizona Instructional League . . . Was purchased by Rangers from Los Angeles, July 11, 1980 . . . Father Richard was a minor-league third baseman and later received a Silver Star with three clusters during World War II.

Year	Club	G	IP	W	L	Pct.	SO	BB	H	ERA
1970	Los Angeles..........	8	17	0	0	.000	8	11	18	5.29
1971	Los Angeles..........	4	4	0	0	.000	4	3	3	4.50
1972	Los Angeles..........	2	3	0	0	.000	4	2	2	3.00
1973	Los Angeles..........	37	72	4	2	.667	70	45	52	2.75
1974	Los Angeles..........	49	96	9	4	.692	63	40	65	3.75
1975	Los Angeles..........	38	61	3	7	.300	34	34	43	2.95
1976	Los Angeles..........	77	143	12	8	.600	81	77	102	2.20
1977	Los Angeles..........	70	127	6	12	.333	105	70	98	3.33
1978	Los Angeles..........	55	93	5	5	.500	66	48	69	3.29
1979	Los Angeles..........	42	151	7	5	.583	76	66	152	4.77
1980	Los Angeles..........	19	32	1	3	.250	25	21	37	5.63
1980	Texas..............	16	61	2	2	.500	47	37	54	3.98
1981	Texas..............	21	82	4	1	.800	69	31	61	2.96
1982	Texas..............	34	228	16	13	.552	128	72	217	3.95
1983	Texas..............	34	252	15	13	.536	152	95	219	3.18
1984	Texas..............	36	266	16	14	.533	164	94	260	3.76
1985	Texas..............	34	250⅓	14	16	.467	141	83	198	3.31
	Totals..............	576	1938⅓	114	105	.521	1237	829	1650	3.51

MIKE MASON 27 6-2 205 **Bats L Throws L**

Suffered through 8-15 season that dropped his career record to 18-32 . . . Rangers' No. 2 starter, behind Charlie Hough, finished second on the club in wins, starts and innings pitched and third in strikeouts . . . ERA jumped by more than a run from 1984 mark . . . Though recognized as more of an off-speed pitcher than a hard thrower, he set Texas record for strikeouts in game by a left-hander with 11 against Seattle . . . Recorded his first major-league shutout in same game . . . Born Nov. 21, 1958, in Faribault, Minn. . . . Selected by Texas in first round of June 1980 draft . . . Pitched two years at Normandale Community College in Minnesota and one season at Oral Roberts . . . Was drafted by Tigers, Twins and Cards before signing with Texas.

Year	Club	G	IP	W	L	Pct.	SO	BB	H	ERA
1982	Texas..............	4	23	1	2	.333	8	9	21	5.09
1983	Texas..............	5	10⅔	0	2	.000	9	6	10	5.91
1984	Texas..............	36	184⅓	9	13	.409	113	51	159	3.61
1985	Texas..............	38	179	8	15	.348	92	73	212	4.83
	Totals..............	83	397	18	32	.360	222	139	402	4.31

TOP PROSPECTS

JOSE GUZMAN 22 6-3 185 Bats R Throws R
Made impressive debut in majors that may lead to spot in Rangers' rotation in 1986 . . . Came up in September to make five starts . . . Compiled 3-2 record and 2.76 ERA . . . Won his last three starts, allowing only two earned runs in 22⅔ innings . . . Was 10-5 with 3.13 ERA for Oklahoma City (AAA) prior to recall . . . It was his fifth minor-league season, but his first in Triple-A . . . Born April 9, 1963, in Santa Isabel, Puerto Rico . . . Rangers signed him as a free agent in 1981, when he was 17 . . . Has 37-29 lifetime minor-league record.

DWAYNE HENRY 24 6-3 205 Bats R Throws R
Pitched well out of the Texas bullpen during trial that began in mid-August . . . Will be a candidate for Rangers' short-relief role . . . Had 2-2 record, three saves and 2.57 ERA in 16 appearances for Texas, striking out 20 batters in 21 innings . . . Compiled 7-6 record and nine saves for Tulsa (AA) before being called up . . . Second-round pick by Rangers in June 1980 draft . . . Switched from starter to reliever after ulnar-nerve surgery on his right elbow in 1982, the same sort of procedure Tommy John underwent in 1974 . . . Born Feb. 16, 1962, in Elkton, Md.

MANAGER BOBBY VALENTINE: Was Mets' third-base coach until Rangers selected him to replace Doug Rader in May . . . Had no managerial experience, though he had been mentioned for several job openings . . . An aggressive third-base coach for Mets, he is trying to instill that same spirit in Rangers. Inherited 9-23 club and compiled 53-76 mark the rest of the way . . . Retired as a player in 1979, ending a career that was marred by a broken right leg he suffered while playing center for Angels in 1973 . . . Was hitting .302 in 32 games at time of injury . . . Started his career with Dodgers as first-round pick in 1968 draft . . . Later played for Angels, Padres, Mets and Mariners . . . Hit .260 in 639 career games . . . Served as the Padres' infield instructor in 1980 and 1981 and as Mets' minor league instructor in 1982 . . . Born May 13, 1950, in Stamford, Conn. . . . Owns three res-

taurants in Connecticut . . . Wife Mary is daughter of former Dodgers pitcher Ralph Branca.

GREATEST SHORTSTOP

The first shortstop in the history of the Texas Rangers was Toby Harrah, who had been the regular shortstop for the Washington Senators in 1971, the year before the move to Arlington. Harrah remains the best shortstop in Texas Rangers history.

Harrah was the Rangers' regular shortstop until 1977, when the club moved him to third base. After 1978, the Rangers moved him all the way to Cleveland in a deal for Buddy Bell. Harrah established himself as a shortstop who could provide uncommon offensive production. He twice hit more than 20 homers as the Texas shortstop and has topped the 20-homer mark five times in his career. He enjoyed his best season in 1975, when he belted 20 homers, drove in 93 runs, hit .293 and was the AL All-Star shortstop. Harrah also led AL shortstops with 281 putouts in 1974 and tied for lead with 290 in 1976.

Harrah has carved a place for himself in baseball history in more dubious ways, too. On June 25, 1976, he set a record for shortstops when he played both games of a doubleheader without getting a chance in the field. In 1976, his 36 errors were the most of any shortstop in the league. He is also one of the few players whose name is spelled the same backwards and forwards. The oddity mirrors the course of his 16-year career, because, after stops in Cleveland and New York, Harrah is back with the Rangers, this time as their second baseman.

ALL-TIME RANGER SEASON RECORDS

BATTING: Mickey Rivers, .333, 1980
HRs: Jeff Burroughs, 30, 1973
RBIs: Jeff Burroughs, 118, 1974
STEALS: Bump Wills, 52, 1978
WINS: Ferguson Jenkins, 25, 1974
STRIKEOUTS: Gaylord Perry, 233, 1975

ALL-TIME MAJOR LEAGUE RECORDS

National	American
Batting (Season)	
Average	
.438 Hugh Duffy, Boston, 1894	.422 Napoleon Lajoie, Phila., 1901
.424 Rogers Hornsby, St. Louis, 1924	
At Bat	
701 Juan Samuel, Phila., 1984	705 Willie Wilson, Kansas City, 1980
Runs	
196 William Hamilton, Phila., 1894	177 Babe Ruth, New York, 1921
158 Chuck Klein, Phila., 1930	
Hits	
254 Frank J. O'Doul, Phila., 1929	257 George Sisler, St. Louis, 1920
254 Bill Terry, New York, 1930	
Doubles	
64 Joseph M. Medwick, St. L., 1936	67 Earl W. Webb, Boston, 1931
Triples	
36 J. Owen Wilson, Pitts., 1912	26 Joseph Jackson, Cleve., 1912
	26 Samuel Crawford, Detroit, 1914
Home Runs	
56 Hack Wilson, Chicago, 1930	61 Roger Maris, New York, 1961 (162-game schedule)
	60 Babe Ruth, New York, 1927
Runs Batted In	
190 Hack Wilson, Chicago, 1930	184 Lou Gehrig, New York, 1931
Stolen Bases	
118 Lou Brock, St. Louis, 1974	130 Rickey Henderson, Oakland, 1982
Bases on Balls	
148 Eddie Stanky, Brooklyn, 1945	170 Babe Ruth, New York, 1923
148 Jim Wynn, Houston, 1969	
Strikeouts	
189 Bobby Bonds, S.F., 1970	175 Dave Nicholson, Chicago, 1963
	175 Gorman Thomas, Milwaukee, 1979
Pitching (Season)	
Games	
106 Mike Marshall, L.A., 1974	88 Wilbur Wood, Chicago, 1968
Innings Pitched	
434 Joseph J. McGinnity, N.Y., 1903	464 Edward Walsh, Chicago, 1908
Victories	
37 Christy Mathewson, N.Y., 1908	41 Jack Chesbro, New York, 1904
Losses	
29 Victor Willis, Boston, 1905	26 John Townsend, Wash., 1904
	26 Robert Groom, Wash., 1909
Strikeouts (Lefthander)	
382 Sandy Koufax, Los Angeles, 1965	343 Rube Waddell, Phila., 1904
(Righthander)	
313 J.R. Richard, Houston, 1979	383 Nolan Ryan, Cal., 1973
Bases on Balls	
185 Sam Jones, Chicago, 1955	208 Bob Feller, Cleveland, 1938
Earned-Run Average (Minimum 200 Innings)	
1.12 Bob Gibson, St. L., 1968	1.01 Hubert Leonard, Boston, 1914
Shutouts	
16 Grover C. Alexander, Phila., 1916	13 John W. Coombs, Phila., 1910

MAJOR LEAGUE YEAR-BY-YEAR LEADERS

NATIONAL LEAGUE MVP

Year	Player, Club
1931	Frank Frisch, St. Louis Cardinals
1932	Chuck Klein, Philadelphia Phillies
1933	Carl Hubbell, New York Giants
1934	Dizzy Dean, St. Louis Cardinals
1935	Gabby Hartnett, Chicago Cubs
1936	Carl Hubbell, New York Giants
1937	Joe Medwick, St. Louis Cardinals
1938	Ernie Lombardi, Cincinnati Reds
1939	Bucky Walters, Cincinnati Reds
1940	Frank McCormick, Cincinnati Reds
1941	Dolph Camilli, Brooklyn Dodgers
1942	Mort Cooper, St. Louis Cardinals
1943	Stan Musial, St. Louis Cardinals
1944	Marty Marion, St. Louis Cardinals
1945	Phil Cavarretta, Chicago Cubs
1946	Stan Musial, St. Louis Cardinals
1947	Bob Elliott, Boston Braves
1948	Stan Musial, St. Louis Cardinals
1949	Jackie Robinson, Brooklyn Dodgers
1950	Jim Konstanty, Philadelphia Phillies
1951	Roy Campanella, Brooklyn Dodgers
1952	Hank Sauer, Chicago Cubs
1953	Roy Campanella, Brooklyn Dodgers
1954	Willie Mays, New York Giants
1955	Roy Campanella, Brooklyn Dodgers
1956	Don Newcombe, Brooklyn Dodgers
1957	Hank Aaron, Milwaukee Braves
1958	Ernie Banks, Chicago Cubs
1959	Ernie Banks, Chicago Cubs

The Cardinals' Stan Musial was a three-time MVP.

Year	Player, Club
1960	Dick Groat, Pittsburgh Pirates
1961	Frank Robinson, Cincinnati Reds
1962	Maury Wills, Los Angeles Dodgers
1963	Sandy Koufax, Los Angeles Dodgers
1964	Ken Boyer, St. Louis Cardinals
1965	Willie Mays, San Francisco Giants
1966	Roberto Clemente, Pittsburgh Pirates
1967	Orlando Cepeda, St. Louis Cardinals
1968	Bob Gibson, St. Louis Cardinals
1969	Willie McCovey, San Francisco Giants
1970	Johnny Bench, Cincinnati Reds
1971	Joe Torre, St. Louis Cardinals
1972	Johnny Bench, Cincinnati Reds
1973	Pete Rose, Cincinnati Reds
1974	Steve Garvey, Los Angeles Dodgers
1975	Joe Morgan, Cincinnati Reds
1976	Joe Morgan, Cincinnati Reds
1977	George Foster, Cincinnati Reds
1978	Dave Parker, Pittsburgh Pirates
1979	Keith Hernandez, St. Louis Cardinals
	Willie Stargell, Pittsburgh Pirates
1980	Mike Schmidt, Philadelphia Phillies
1981	Mike Schmidt, Philadelphia Phillies
1982	Dale Murphy, Atlanta Braves
1983	Dale Murphy, Atlanta Braves
1984	Ryne Sandberg, Chicago Cubs
1985	Willie McGee, St. Louis Cardinals

AMERICAN LEAGUE MVP

Year	Player, Club
1931	Lefty Grove, Philadelphia Athletics
1932	Jimmy Foxx, Philadelphia Athletics
1933	Jimmy Foxx, Philadelphia Athletics
1934	Mickey Cochrane, Detroit Tigers
1935	Hank Greenberg, Detroit Tigers
1936	Lou Gehrig, New York Yankees
1937	Charley Gehringer, Detroit Tigers
1938	Jimmy Foxx, Boston Red Sox
1939	Joe DiMaggio, New York Yankees
1940	Hank Greenberg, Detroit Tigers
1941	Joe DiMaggio, New York Yankees

As a Minnesota Twin, Rod Carew had his MVP year in 1077.

Year	Player, Club
1942	Joe Gordon, New York Yankees
1943	Spud Chandler, New York Yankees
1944	Hal Newhouser, Detroit Tigers
1945	Hal Newhouser, Detroit Tigers

Year	Player, Club
1946	Ted Williams, Boston Red Sox
1947	Joe DiMaggio, New York Yankees
1948	Lou Boudreau, Cleveland Indians
1949	Ted Williams, Boston Red Sox
1950	Phil Rizzuto, New York Yankees
1951	Yogi Berra, New York Yankees
1942	Bobby Shantz, Philadelphia Athletics
1953	Al Rosen, Cleveland Indians
1954	Yogi Berra, New York Yankees
1955	Yogi Berra, New York Yankees
1956	Mickey Mantle, New York Yankees
1957	Mickey Mantle, New York Yankees
1958	Jackie Jensen, Boston Red Sox
1959	Nellie Fox, Chicago White Sox
1960	Roger Maris, New York Yankees
1961	Roger Maris, New York Yankees
1962	Mickey Mantle, New York Yankees
1963	Elston Howard, New York Yankees
1964	Brooks Robinson, Baltimore Orioles
1965	Zoilo Versalles, Minnesota Twins
1966	Frank Robinson, Baltimore Orioles
1967	Carl Yastrzemski, Boston Red Sox
1968	Dennis McLain, Detroit Tigers
1969	Harmon Killebrew, Minnesota Twins
1970	Boog Powell, Baltimore Orioles
1971	Vida Blue, Oakland A's
1972	Dick Allen, Chicago White Sox
1973	Reggie Jackson, Oakland A's
1974	Jeff Burroughs, Texas Rangers
1975	Fred Lynn, Boston Red Sox
1976	Thurman Munson, New York Yankees
1977	Rod Carew, Minnesota Twins
1978	Jim Rice, Boston Red Sox
1979	Don Baylor, California Angels
1980	George Brett, Kansas City Royals
1981	Rollie Fingers, Milwaukee Brewers
1982	Robin Yount, Milwaukee Brewers
1983	Cal Ripken Jr., Baltimore Orioles
1984	Willie Hernandez, Detroit Tigers
1985	Don Mattingly, New York Yankees

CY YOUNG AWARD WINNERS

(Prior to 1967 there was a single overall major league award.)

Year	Player, Club
1956	Don Newcombe, Brooklyn Dodgers
1957	Warren Spahn, Milwaukee Braves
1958	Bob Turley, New York Yankees
1959	Early Wynn, Chicago White Sox
1960	Vernon Law, Pittsburgh Pirates
1961	Whitey Ford, New York Yankees
1962	Don Drysdale, Los Angeles Dodgers
1963	Sandy Koufax, Los Angeles Dodgers
1964	Dean Chance, Los Angeles Angels
1965	Sandy Koufax, Los Angeles Dodgers
1966	Sandy Koufax, Los Angeles Dodgers

Dodger Sandy Koufax won the Cy Young Award three times.

AL CY YOUNG

Year	Player, Club
1967	Jim Lonborg, Boston Red Sox
1968	Dennis McLain, Detroit Tigers
1969	Mike Cuellar, Baltimore Orioles
	Dennis McLain, Detroit Tigers
1970	Jim Perry, Minnesota Twins
1971	Vida Blue, Oakland A's
1972	Gaylord Perry, Cleveland Indians
1973	Jim Palmer, Baltimore Orioles
1974	Jim Hunter, Oakland A's
1975	Jim Palmer, Baltimore Orioles
1976	Jim Palmer, Baltimore Orioles
1977	Sparky Lyle, New York Yankees
1978	Ron Guidry, New York Yankees
1979	Mike Flanagan, Baltimore Orioles
1980	Steve Stone, Baltimore Orioles
1981	Rollie Fingers, Milwaukee Brewers
1982	Pete Vuckovich, Milwaukee Brewers
1983	LaMarr Hoyt, Chicago White Sox
1984	Willie Hernandez, Detroit Tigers
1985	Bret Saberhagen, Kansas City

NL CY YOUNG

Year	Player, Club
1967	Mike McCormick, San Francisco Giants
1968	Bob Gibson, St. Louis Cardinals
1969	Tom Seaver, New York Mets
1970	Bob Gibson, St. Louis Cardinals
1971	Ferguson Jenkins, Chicago Cubs
1972	Steve Carlton, Philadelphia Phillies
1973	Tom Seaver, New York Mets
1974	Mike Marshall, Los Angeles Dodgers
1975	Tom Seaver, New York Mets
1976	Randy Jones, San Diego Padres
1977	Steve Carlton, Philadelphia Phillies
1978	Gaylord Perry, San Diego Padres
1979	Bruce Sutter, Chicago Cubs
1980	Steve Carlton, Philadelphia Phillies
1981	Fernando Valenzuela, Los Angeles Dodgers
1982	Steve Carlton, Philadelphia Phillies
1983	John Denny, Philadelphia Phillies
1984	Rick Sutcliffe, Chicago Cubs
1985	Dwight Gooden, New York Mets

Fernando Valenzuela: Rookie of Year, Cy Young winner in '81.

AMERICAN LEAGUE
Rookie of Year

Year	Player, Club
1949	Roy Sievers, St. Louis Browns
1950	Walt Dropo, Boston Red Sox
1951	Gil McDougald, New York Yankees
1952	Harry Byrd, Philadelphia Athletics
1953	Harvey Kuenn, Detroit Tigers
1954	Bob Grim, New York Yankees
1955	Herb Score, Cleveland Indians
1956	Luis Aparicio, Chicago White Sox
1957	Tony Kubek, New York Yankees
1958	Albie Pearson, Washington Senators
1959	Bob Allison, Washington Senators
1960	Ron Hansen, Baltimore Orioles
1961	Don Schwall, Boston Red Sox
1962	Tom Tresh, New York Yankees
1963	Gary Peters, Chicago White Sox
1964	Tony Oliva, Minnesota Twins
1965	Curt Blefary, Baltimore Orioles
1966	Tommie Agee, Chicago White Sox
1967	Rod Carew, Minnesota Twins
1968	Stan Bahnsen, New York Yankees
1969	Lou Piniella, Kansas City Royals
1970	Thurman Munson, New York Yankees
1971	Chris Chambliss, Cleveland Indians
1972	Carlton Fisk, Boston Red Sox
1973	Al Bumbry, Baltimore Orioles
1974	Mike Hargrove, Texas Rangers
1975	Fred Lynn, Boston Red Sox
1976	Mark Fidrych, Detroit Tigers
1977	Eddie Murray, Baltimore Orioles
1978	Lou Whitaker, Detroit Tigers
1979	John Castino, Minnesota Twins
	Alfredo Griffin, Toronto Blue Jays
1980	Joe Charboneau, Cleveland Indians
1981	Dave Righetti, New York Yankees
1982	Cal Ripken, Jr., Baltimore Orioles
1983	Ron Kittle, Chicago White Sox
1984	Alvin Davis, Seattle Mariners
1985	Ozzie Guillen, Chicago White Sox

NATIONAL LEAGUE
Rookie of Year

Year	Player, Club
1947	Jackie Robinson, Brooklyn Dodgers
1948	Al Dark, Boston Braves
1949	Don Newcombe, Brooklyn Dodgers
1950	Sam Jethroe, Boston Braves
1951	Willie Mays, New York Giants
1952	Joe Black, Brooklyn Dodgers
1953	Junior Gilliam, Brooklyn Dodgers
1954	Wally Moon, St. Louis Cardinals
1955	Bill Virdon, St. Louis Cardinals
1956	Frank Robinson, Cincinnati Reds
1957	Jack Sanford, Philadelphia Phillies
1958	Orlando Cepeda, San Francisco Giants
1959	Willie McCovey, San Francisco Giants
1960	Frank Howard, Los Angeles Dodgers
1961	Billy Williams, Chicago Cubs
1962	Kenny Hubbs, Chicago Cubs
1963	Pete Rose, Cincinnati Reds
1964	Richie Allen, Philadelphia Phillies
1965	Jim Lefebvre, Los Angeles Dodgers
1966	Tommy Helms, Cincinnati Reds
1967	Tom Seaver, New York Mets
1968	Johnny Bench, Cincinnati Reds
1969	Ted Sizemore, Los Angeles Dodgers
1970	Carl Morton, Montreal Expos
1971	Earl Williams, Atlanta Braves
1972	Jon Matlack, New York Mets
1973	Gary Matthews, San Francisco Giants
1974	Bake McBride, St. Louis Cardinals
1975	John Montefusco, San Francisco Giants
1976	Pat Zachry, Cincinnati Reds
	Butch Metzger, San Diego Padres
1977	Andre Dawson, Montreal Expos
1978	Bob Horner, Atlanta Braves
1979	Rick Sutcliffe, Los Angeles Dodgers
1980	Steve Howe, Los Angeles Dodgers
1981	Fernando Valenzuela, Los Angeles Dodgers
1982	Steve Sax, Los Angeles Dodgers
1983	Darryl Strawberry, New York Mets
1984	Dwight Gooden, New York Mets
1985	Vince Coleman, St. Louis Cardinals

AMERICAN LEAGUE
Batting Champions

Year	Player, Club	Avg.
1901	Napoleon Lajoie, Philadelphia Athletics	.422
1902	Ed Delahanty, Washington Senators	.376
1903	Napoleon Lajoie, Cleveland Indians	.355
1904	Napoleon Lajoie, Cleveland Indians	.381
1905	Elmer Flick, Cleveland Indians	.306
1906	George Stone, St. Louis Browns	.358
1907	Ty Cobb, Detroit Tigers	.350
1908	Ty Cobb, Detroit Tigers	.324
1909	Ty Cobb, Detroit Tigers	.377
1910	Ty Cobb, Detroit Tigers	.385
1911	Ty Cobb, Detroit Tigers	.420
1912	Ty Cobb, Detroit Tigers	.410
1913	Ty Cobb, Detroit Tigers	.390
1914	Ty Cobb, Detroit Tigers	.368
1915	Ty Cobb, Detroit Tigers	.370
1916	Tris Speaker, Cleveland Indians	.386
1917	Ty Cobb, Detroit Tigers	.383
1918	Ty Cobb, Detroit Tigers	.382
1919	Ty Cobb, Detroit Tigers	.384
1920	George Sisler, St. Louis Browns	.407
1921	Harry Heilmann, Detroit Tigers	.393
1922	George Sisler, St. Louis Browns	.420
1923	Harry Heilmann, Detroit Tigers	.398
1924	Babe Ruth, New York Yankees	.378
1925	Harry Heilmann, Detroit Tigers	.393
1926	Heinie Manush, Detroit Tigers	.377
1927	Harry Heilmann, Detroit Tigers	.398
1928	Goose Goslin, Washington Senators	.379
1929	Lew Fonseca, Cleveland Indians	.369
1930	Al Simmons, Philadelphia Athletics	.381
1931	Al Simmons, Philadelphia Athletics	.390
1932	David Alexander, Detroit Tigers-Boston Red Sox	.367
1933	Jimmy Foxx, Philadelphia Athletics	.356
1934	Lou Gehrig, New York Yankees	.365
1935	Buddy Myer, Washington Senators	.349
1936	Luke Appling, Chicago White Sox	.388
1937	Charlie Gehringer, Detroit Tigers	.371
1938	Jimmy Foxx, Boston Red Sox	.349
1939	Joe DiMaggio, New York Yankees	.381
1940	Joe DiMaggio, New York Yankees	.352
1941	Ted Williams, Boston Red Sox	.406

Four-time batting champ Ted Williams hit .406 in 1941.

Year	Player, Club	Avg.
1942	Ted Williams, Boston Red Sox	.356
1943	Luke Appling, Chicago White Sox	.328
1944	Lou Boudreau, Cleveland Indians	.327
1945	Snuffy Stirnweiss, New York Yankees	.309
1946	Mickey Vernon, Washington Senators	.353
1947	Ted Williams, Boston Red Sox	.343
1948	Ted Williams, Boston Red Sox	.369
1949	George Kell, Detroit Tigers	.343
1950	Billy Goodman, Boston Red Sox	.354
1951	Ferris Fain, Philadelphia Athletics	.344

Year	Player, Club	Avg.
1952	Ferris Fain, Philadelphia Athletics	.327
1953	Mickey Vernon, Washington Senators	.337
1954	Bobby Avila, Cleveland Indians	.341
1955	Al Kaline, Detroit Tigers	.340
1956	Mickey Mantle, New York Yankees	.353
1957	Ted Williams, Boston Red Sox	.388
1958	Ted Williams, Boston Red Sox	.328
1959	Harvey Kuenn, Detroit Tigers	.353
1960	Pete Runnels, Boston Red Sox	.320
1961	Norm Cash, Detroit Tigers	.361
1962	Pete Runnels, Boston Red Sox	.326
1963	Carl Yastrzemski, Boston Red Sox	.321
1964	Tony Oliva, Minnesota Twins	.323
1965	Tony Oliva, Minnesota Twins	.321
1966	Frank Robinson, Baltimore Orioles	.316
1967	Carl Yastrzemski, Boston Red Sox	.326
1968	Carl Yastrzemski, Boston Red Sox	.301
1969	Rod Carew, Minnesota Twins	.332
1970	Alex Johnson, California Angels	.329
1971	Tony Oliva, Minnesota Twins	.337
1972	Rod Carew, Minnesota Twins	.318
1973	Rod Carew, Minnesota Twins	.350
1974	Rod Carew, Minnesota Twins	.364
1975	Rod Carew, Minnesota Twins	.359
1976	George Brett, Kansas City Royals	.333
1977	Rod Carew, Minnesota Twins	.388
1978	Rod Carew, Minnesota Twins	.333
1979	Fred Lynn, Boston Red Sox	.333
1980	George Brett, Kansas City Royals	.390
1981	Carney Lansford, Boston Red Sox	.336
1982	Willie Wilson, Kansas City Royals	.332
1983	Wade Boggs, Boston Red Sox	.361
1984	Don Mattingly, New York Yankees	.343
1985	Wade Boggs, Boston Red Sox	.368

NATIONAL LEAGUE
Batting Champions

Year	Player, Club	Avg.
1876	Roscoe Barnes, Chicago	.403
1877	James White, Boston	.385
1878	Abner Dalrymple, Milwaukee	.356
1879	Cap Anson, Chicago	.407
1880	George Gore, Chicago	.365
1881	Cap Anson, Chicago	.399
1882	Dan Brouthers, Buffalo	.367
1883	Dan Brouthers, Buffalo	.371
1884	Jim O'Rourke, Buffalo	.350
1885	Roger Connor, New York	.371
1886	Mike Kelly, Chicago	.388
1887	Cap Anson, Chicago	.421
1888	Cap Anson, Chicago	.343
1889	Dan Brouthers, Boston	.373
1890	Jack Glassock, New York	.336
1891	Billy Hamilton, Philadelphia	.338
1892	Cupid Childs, Cleveland	.335
	Dan Brouthers, Brooklyn	.335
1893	Hugh Duffy, Boston	.378
1894	Hugh Duffy, Boston	.438
1895	Jesse Burkett, Cleveland	.423
1896	Jesse Burkett, Cleveland	.410
1897	Willie Keeler, Baltimore	.432
1898	Willie Keeler, Baltimore	.379
1899	Ed Delahanty, Philadelphia	.408
1900	Honus Wagner, Pittsburgh	.380
1901	Jesse Burkett, St. Louis Cardinals	.382
1902	C.H. Beaumont, Pittsburgh Pirates	.357
1903	Honus Wagner, Pittsburgh Pirates	.355
1904	Honus Wagner, Pittsburgh Pirates	.349
1905	J. Bentley Seymour, Cincinnati Reds	.377
1906	Honus Wagner, Pittsburgh Pirates	.339
1907	Honus Wagner, Pittsburgh Pirates	.350
1908	Honus Wagner, Pittsburgh Pirates	.354
1909	Honus Wagner, Pittsburgh Pirates	.339
1910	Sherwood Magee, Philadelphia Phillies	.331
1911	Honus Wagner, Pittsburgh Pirates	.334
1912	Heinie Zimmerman, Chicago Cubs	.372
1913	Jake Daubert, Brooklyn Dodgers	.350
1914	Jake Daubert, Brooklyn Dodgers	.329
1915	Larry Doyle, New York Giants	.320

Year	Player, Club	Avg.
1916	Hal Chase, Cincinnati Reds	.339
1917	Edd Roush, Cincinnati Reds	.341
1918	Zack Wheat, Brooklyn Dodgers	.335
1919	Edd Roush, Cincinnati Reds	.321
1920	Rogers Hornsby, St. Louis Cardinals	.370
1921	Rogers Hornsby, St. Louis Cardinals	.397
1922	Rogers Hornsby, St. Louis Cardinals	.401
1923	Rogers Hornsby, St. Louis Cardinals	.384
1924	Rogers Hornsby, St. Louis Cardinals	.424
1925	Rogers Hornsby, St. Louis Cardinals	.403
1926	Bubbles Hargrave, Cincinnati Reds	.353
1927	Paul Waner, Pittsburgh Pirates	.380
1928	Rogers Hornsby, Boston Braves	.387
1929	Lefty O'Doul, Philadelphia Phillies	.398
1930	Bill Terry, New York Giants	.401
1931	Chick Hafey, St. Louis Cardinals	.349
1932	Lefty O'Doul, Brooklyn Dodgers	.368
1933	Chuck Klein, Philadelphia Phillies	.368
1934	Paul Waner, Pittsburgh Pirates	.362
1935	Arky Vaughan, Pittsburgh Pirates	.385
1936	Paul Waner, Pittsburgh Pirates	.373
1937	Joe Medwick, St. Louis Cardinals	.374
1938	Ernie Lombardi, Cincinnati Reds	.342
1939	Johnny Mize, St. Louis Cardinals	.349
1940	Debs Garms, Pittsburgh Pirates	.355
1941	Pete Reiser, Brooklyn Dodgers	.343
1942	Ernie Lombardi, Boston Braves	.330
1943	Stan Musial, St. Louis Cardinals	.330
1944	Dixie Walker, Brooklyn Dodgers	.357
1945	Phil Cavarretta, Chicago Cubs	.355
1946	Stan Musial, St. Louis Cardinals	.365
1947	Harry Walker, St. L. Cardinals-Phila. Phillies	.363
1948	Stan Musial, St. Louis Cardinals	.376
1949	Jackie Robinson, Brooklyn Dodgers	.342
1950	Stan Musial, St. Louis Cardinals	.346
1951	Stan Musial, St. Louis Cardinals	.355
1952	Stan Musial, St. Louis Cardinals	.336
1953	Carl Furillo, Brooklyn Dodgers	.344
1954	Willie Mays, New York Giants	.345
1955	Richie Ashburn, Philadelphia Phillies	.338
1956	Hank Aaron, Milwaukee Braves	.328
1957	Stan Musial, St. Louis Cardinals	.351
1958	Richie Ashburn, Philadelphia Phillies	.350
1959	Hank Aaron, Milwaukee Braves	.328

Year	Player, Club	Avg.
1960	Dick Groat, Pittsburgh Pirates	.325
1961	Roberto Clemente, Pittsburgh Pirates	.351
1962	Tommy Davis, Los Angeles Dodgers	.346
1963	Tommy Davis, Los Angeles Dodgers	.326
1964	Roberto Clemente, Pittsburgh Pirates	.339
1965	Roberto Clemente, Pittsburgh Pirates	.329
1966	Matty Alou, Pittsburgh Pirates	.342
1967	Roberto Clemente, Pittsburgh Pirates	.357
1968	Pete Rose, Cincinnati Reds	.335
1969	Pete Rose, Cincinnati Reds	.348
1970	Rico Carty, Atlanta Braves	.366
1971	Joe Torre, St. Louis Cardinals	.363
1972	Billy Williams, Chicago Cubs	.333
1973	Pete Rose, Cincinnati Reds	.338
1974	Ralph Garr, Atlanta Braves	.353
1975	Bill Madlock, Chicago Cubs	.354
1976	Bill Madlock, Chicago Cubs	.339
1977	Dave Parker, Pittsburgh Pirates	.338
1978	Dave Parker, Pittsburgh Pirates	.334
1979	Keith Hernandez, St. Louis Cardinals	.344
1980	Bill Buckner, Chicago Cubs	.324
1981	Bill Madlock, Pittsburgh Pirates	.341
1982	Al Oliver, Montreal Expos	.331
1983	Bill Madlock, Pittsburgh Pirates	.323
1984	Tony Gwynn, San Diego Padres	.351
1985	Willie McGee, St. Louis Cardinals	.353

AMERICAN LEAGUE
Home Run Leaders

Year	Player, Club	HRs
1901	Napoleon Lajoie, Philadelphia Athletics	13
1902	Ralph Seybold, Philadelphia Athletics	16
1903	John Freeman, Boston Pilgrims	13
1904	Harry Davis, Philadelphia Athletics	10
1905	Harry Davis, Philadelphia Athletics	8
1906	Harry Davis, Philadelphia Athletics	12
1907	Harry Davis, Philadelphia Athletics	8
1908	Sam Crawford, Detroit Tigers	7
1909	Ty Cobb, Detroit Tigers	9
1910	Garland Stahl, Boston Red Sox	10
1911	Frank (Home Run) Baker, Philadelphia Athletics	9
1912	Frank (Home Run) Baker, Philadelphia Athletics	10
1913	Frank (Home Run) Baker, Philadelphia Athletics	12
1914	Frank (Home Run) Baker, Philadelphia Athletics	8
	Sam Crawford, Detroit Tigers	8
1915	Bob Roth, Cleveland Indians	7
1916	Wally Pipp, New York Yankees	12
1917	Wally Pipp, New York Yankees	9
1918	Babe Ruth, Boston Red Sox	11
	Clarence Walker, Philadelphia Athletics	11
1919	Babe Ruth, Boston Red Sox	29
1920	Babe Ruth, New York Yankees	54
1921	Babe Ruth, New York Yankees	59
1922	Ken Williams, St. Louis Browns	39
1923	Babe Ruth, New York Yankees	41
1924	Babe Ruth, New York Yankees	46
1925	Bob Meusel, New York Yankees	33
1926	Babe Ruth, New York Yankees	47
1927	Babe Ruth, New York Yankees	60
1928	Babe Ruth, New York Yankees	54
1929	Babe Ruth, New York Yankees	46
1930	Babe Ruth, New York Yankees	49
1931	Babe Ruth, New York Yankees	46
	Lou Gehrig, New York Yankees	46
1932	Jimmy Foxx, Philadelphia Athletics	58
1933	Jimmy Foxx, Philadelphia Athletics	48
1934	Lou Gehrig, New York Yankees	49
1935	Hank Greenberg, Detroit Tigers	36
	Jimmy Fox, Philadelphia Athletics	36
1936	Lou Gehrig, New York Yankees	49

Year	Player, Club	HRs
1937	Joe DiMaggio, New York Yankees	46
1938	Hank Greenberg, Detroit Tigers	58
1939	Jimmy Foxx, Boston Red Sox	35
1940	Hank Greenberg, Detroit Tigers	41
1941	Ted Williams, Boston Red Sox	37
1942	Ted Williams, Boston Red Sox	36
1943	Rudy York, Detroit Tigers	34
1944	Nick Etten, New York Yankees	22
1945	Vern Stephens, St. Louis Browns	24
1946	Hank Greenberg, Detroit Tigers	44
1947	Ted Williams, Boston Red Sox	32
1948	Joe DiMaggio, New York Yankees	39
1949	Ted Williams, Boston Red Sox	43
1950	Al Rosen, Cleveland Indians	37
1951	Gus Zernial, Philadelphia Athletics	33
1952	Larry Doby, Cleveland Indians	32
1953	Al Rosen, Cleveland Indians	43
1954	Larry Doby, Cleveland Indians	32
1955	Mickey Mantle, New York Yankees	37
1956	Mickey Mantle, New York Yankees	52
1957	Roy Sievers, Washington Senators	42
1958	Mickey Mantle, New York Yankees	42
1959	Rocky Colavito, Cleveland Indians	42
	Harmon Killebrew, Washington Senators	42
1960	Mickey Mantle, New York Yankees	40
1961	Roger Maris, New York Yankees	61
1962	Harmon Killebrew, Minnesota Twins	48
1963	Harmon Killebrew, Minnesota Twins	45
1964	Harmon Killebrew, Minnesota Twins	49
1965	Tony Conigliaro, Boston Red Sox	32
1966	Frank Robinson, Baltimore Orioles	49
1967	Carl Yastrzemski, Boston Red Sox	44
	Harmon Killebrew, Minnesota Twins	44
1968	Frank Howard, Washington Senators	44
1969	Harmon Killebrew, Minnesota Twins	49
1970	Frank Howard, Washington Senators	44
1971	Bill Melton, Chicago White Sox	33
1972	Dick Allen, Chicago White Sox	37
1973	Reggie Jackson, Oakland A's	32
1974	Dick Allen, Chicago White Sox	32
1975	George Scott, Milwaukee Brewers	36
	Reggie Jackson, Oakland A's	36
1976	Graig Nettles, New York Yankees	32
1977	Jim Rice, Boston Red Sox	39

Year	Player, Club	HRs
1978	Jim Rice, Boston Red Sox	46
1979	Gorman Thomas, Milwaukee Brewers	45
1980	Ben Oglivie, Milwaukee Brewers	41
	Reggie Jackson, New York Yankees	41
1981	Bobby Grich, California Angels	22
	Eddie Murray, Baltimore Orioles	22
	Dwight Evans, Boston Red Sox	22
	Tony Armas, Oakland A's	22
1982	Reggie Jackson, California Angels	39
	Gorman Thomas, Milwaukee Braves	39
1983	Jim Rice, Boston Red Sox	39
1984	Tony Armas, Boston Red Sox	43
1985	Darrell Evans, Detroit Tigers	40

Harmon Killebrew won or shared AL HR crown six times.

NATIONAL LEAGUE
Home Run Leaders

Year	Player, Club	HRs
1900	Herman Long, Boston Nationals	12
1901	Sam Crawford, Cincinnati Reds	16
1902	Tom Leach, Pittsburgh Pirates	6
1903	Jim Sheckard, Brooklyn Dodgers	9
1904	Harry Lumley, Brooklyn Dodgers	9
1905	Fred Odwell, Cincinnati Reds	9
1906	Tim Jordan, Brooklyn Dodgers	12
1907	Dave Brian, Boston Nationals	10
1908	Tim Jordan, Brooklyn Dodgers	12
1909	Jim Murray, New York Giants	7
1910	Fred Beck, Boston Nationals	10
	Frank Schulte, Chicago Cubs	10
1911	Frank Schulte, Chicago Cubs	21
1912	Heinie Zimmerman, Chicago Cubs	14
1913	Gavvy Cravath, Philadelphia Phillies	19
1914	Gavvy Cravath, Philadelphia Phillies	19
1915	Gavvy Cravath, Philadelphia Phillies	24
1916	Dave Robertson, New York Giants	12
	Cy Williams, Chicago Cubs	12
1917	Gavvy Cravath, Philadelphia Phillies	12
	Dave Robertson, New York Giants	12
1918	Gavvy Cravath, Philadelphia Phillies	8
1919	Gavvy Cravath, Philadelphia Phillies	12
1920	Cy Williams, Philadelphia Phillies	15
1921	George Kelly, New York Giants	23
1922	Rogers Hornsby, St. Louis Cardinals	42
1923	Cy Williams, Philadelphia Phillies	41
1924	Jack Fournier, Brooklyn Dodgers	27
1925	Rogers Hornsby, St. Louis Cardinals	39
1926	Hack Wilson, Chicago Cubs	21
1927	Cy Williams, Philadelphia Phillies	30
	Hack Wilson, Chicago Cubs	30
1928	Jim Bottomley, St. Louis Cardinals	31
	Hack Wilson, Chicago Cubs	31
1929	Chuck Klein, Philadelphia Phillies	43
1930	Hack Wilson, Chicago Cubs	56
1931	Chuck Klein, Philadelphia Phillies	31
1932	Chuck Klein, Philadelphia Phillies	38
	Mel Ott, New York Giants	38

Year	Player, Club	HRs
1933	Chuck Klein, Philadelphia Phillies	28
1934	Rip Collins, St. Louis Cardinals	35
	Mel Ott, New York Giants	35
1935	Wally Berger, Boston Braves	34
1936	Mel Ott, New York Giants	33
1937	Joe Medwick, St. Louis Cardinals	31
	Mel Ott, New York Giants	31
1938	Mel Ott, New York Giants	36
1939	Johnny Mize, St. Louis Cardinals	28
1940	Johnny Mize, St. Louis Cardinals	43
1941	Dolph Camilli, Brooklyn Dodgers	34
1942	Mel Ott, New York Giants	30
1943	Bill Nicholson, Chicago Cubs	29
1944	Bill Nicholson, Chicago Cubs	33
1945	Tommy Holmes, Boston Braves	28
1946	Ralph Kiner, Pittsburgh Pirates	23
1947	Ralph Kiner, Pittsburgh Pirates	51
	Johnny Mize, New York Giants	51
1948	Ralph Kiner, Pittsburgh Pirates	40
	Johnny Mize, New York Giants	40
1949	Ralph Kiner, Pittsburgh Pirates	54
1950	Ralph Kiner, Pittsburgh Pirates	47
1951	Ralph Kiner, Pittsburgh Pirates	42
1952	Ralph Kiner, Pittsburgh Pirates	37
	Hank Sauer, Chicago Cubs	37
1953	Eddie Mathews, Milwaukee Braves	47
1954	Ted Kluszewski, Cincinnati Reds	49
1955	Willie Mays, New York Giants	51
1956	Duke Snider, Brooklyn Dodgers	43
1957	Hank Aaron, Milwaukee Braves	44
1958	Ernie Banks, Chicago Cubs	47
1959	Eddie Mathews, Milwaukee Braves	46
1960	Ernie Banks, Chicago Cubs	41
1961	Orlando Cepeda, San Francisco Giants	46
1962	Willie Mays, San Francisco Giants	49
1963	Hank Aaron, Milwaukee Braves	44
	Willie McCovey, San Francisco Giants	44
1964	Willie Mays, San Francisco Giants	47
1965	Willie Mays, San Francisco Giants	52
1966	Hank Aaron, Atlanta Braves	44
1967	Hank Aaron, Atlanta Braves	39
1968	Willie McCovey, San Francisco Giants	36
1969	Willie McCovey, San Francisco Giants	45
1970	Johnny Bench, Cincinnati Reds	45
1971	Willie Stargell, Pittsburgh Pirates	48

This was after Hank Aaron hit his record-breaking 715th HR.

Year	Player, Club	HRs
1972	Johnny Bench, Cincinnati Reds	40
1973	Willie Stargell, Pittsburgh Pirates	44
1974	Mike Schmidt, Philadelphia Phillies	36
1975	Mike Schmidt, Philadelphia Phillies	38
1976	Mike Schmidt, Philadelphia Phillies	38
1977	George Foster, Cincinnati Reds	52
1978	George Foster, Cincinnati Reds	40
1979	Dave Kingman, Chicago Cubs	48
1980	Mike Schmidt, Philadelphia Phillies	48
1981	Mike Schmidt, Philadelphia Phillies	31
1982	Dave Kingman, New York Mets	37
1983	Mike Schmidt, Philadelphia Phillies	40
1984	Mike Schmidt, Philadelphia Phillies	36
1984	Dale Murphy, Atlanta Braves	36
1985	Dale Murphy, Atlanta Braves	37

WORLD SERIES WINNERS

Year	A. L. Champion	N. L. Champion	World Series Winner
1903	Boston Red Sox	Pittsburgh Pirates	Boston, 5-3
1905	Philadelphia Athletics	New York Giants	New York, 4-1
1906	Chicago White Sox	Chicago Cubs	Chicago (AL), 4-2
1907	Detroit Tigers	Chicago Cubs	Chicago, 4-0-1
1908	Detroit Tigers	Chicago Cubs	Chicago, 4-1
1909	Detroit Tigers	Pittsburgh Pirates	Pittsburgh, 4-3
1910	Philadelphia Athletics	Chicago Cubs	Philadelphia, 4-1
1911	Philadelphia Athletics	New York Giants	Philadelphia, 4-2
1912	Boston Red Sox	New York Giants	Boston, 4-3-1
1913	Philadelphia Athletics	Boston Braves	Boston, 4-0
1914	Philadelphia Athletics	New York Giants	Philadelphia, 4-1
1915	Boston Red Sox	Philadelphia Phillies	Boston, 4-1
1916	Boston Red Sox	Philadelphia Phillies	Boston, 4-1
1917	Chicago White Sox	New York Giants	Chicago, 4-2
1918	Boston Red Sox	Chicago Cubs	Boston, 4-2
1919	Chicago White Sox	Cincinnati Reds	Cincinnati, 5-2
1920	Cleveland Indians	Brooklyn Dodgers	Cleveland, 5-2
1921	New York Yankees	New York Giants	New York (NL), 5-3
1922	New York Yankees	New York Giants	New York (NL), 4-0-1
1923	New York Yankees	New York Giants	New York (AL), 4-2
1924	Washington Senators	New York Giants	Washington, 4-2
1925	Washington Senators	Pittsburgh Pirates	Pittsburgh, 4-3
1926	New York Yankees	St. Louis Cardinals	St. Louis, 4-3
1927	New York Yankees	Pittsburgh Pirates	New York, 4-0
1928	New York Yankees	St. Louis Cardinals	New York, 4-0
1929	Philadelphia Athletics	Chicago Cubs	Philadelphia, 4-2
1930	Philadelphia Athletics	St. Louis Cardinals	Philadelphia, 4-2
1931	Philadelphia Athletics	St. Louis Cardinals	St. Louis, 4-3
1932	New York Yankees	Chicago Cubs	New York, 4-0
1933	Washington Senators	New York Giants	New York, 4-1
1934	Detroit Tigers	St. Louis Cardinals	St. Louis, 4-3
1935	Detroit Tigers	Chicago Cubs	Detroit, 4-2
1936	New York Yankees	New York Giants	New York (AL), 4-2
1937	New York Yankees	New York Giants	New York (AL), 4-1
1938	New York Yankees	Chicago Cubs	New York, 4-0
1939	New York Yankees	Cincinnati Reds	New York, 4-0
1940	Detroit Tigers	Cincinnati Reds	Cincinnati, 4-3
1941	New York Yankees	Brooklyn Dodgers	New York, 4-1
1942	New York Yankees	St. Louis Cardinals	St. Louis, 4-1
1943	New York Yankees	St. Louis Cardinals	New York, 4-1
1944	St. Louis Browns	St. Louis Cardinals	St. Louis (NL), 4-2
1945	Detroit Tigers	Chicago Cubs	Detroit, 4-3
1946	Boston Red Sox	St. Louis Cardinals	St. Louis, 4-3
1947	New York Yankees	Brooklyn Dodgers	New York, 4-3
1948	Cleveland Indians	Boston Braves	Cleveland, 4-2
1949	New York Yankees	Brooklyn Dodgers	New York, 4-1
1950	New York Yankees	Philadelphia Phillies	New York, 4-0
1951	New York Yankees	New York Giants	New York (AL), 4-2
1952	New York Yankees	Brooklyn Dodgers	New York, 4-3
1953	New York Yankees	Brooklyn Dodgers	New York, 4-2
1954	Cleveland Indians	New York Giants	New York, 4-0
1955	New York Yankees	Brooklyn Dodgers	Brooklyn, 4-3

Dodger Duke Snider homers against White Sox in '59 Series.

Year	A. L. Champion	N. L. Champion	World Series Winner
1956	New York Yankees	Brooklyn Dodgers	New York, 4-3
1957	New York Yankees	Milwaukee Braves	Milwaukee, 4-3
1958	New York Yankees	Milwaukee Braves	New York, 4-3
1959	Chicago White Sox	Los Angeles Dodgers	Los Angeles, 4-2
1960	New York Yankees	Pittsburgh Pirates	Pittsburgh, 4-3
1961	New York Yankees	Cincinnati Reds	New York, 4-1
1962	New York Yankees	San Francisco Giants	New York, 4-3
1963	New York Yankees	Los Angeles Dodgers	Los Angeles, 4-0
1964	New York Yankees	St. Louis Cardinals	St. Louis, 4-3
1965	Minnesota Twins	Los Angeles Dodgers	Los Angeles, 4-3

Alan Trammell was MVP of '84 Series, won by the Tigers.

Year	A. L. Champion	N. L. Champion	World Series Winner
1966	Baltimore Orioles	Los Angeles Dodgers	Baltimore, 4-0
1967	Boston Red Sox	St. Louis Cardinals	St. Louis, 4-3
1968	Detroit Tigers	St. Louis Cardinals	Detroit, 4-3
1969	Baltimore Orioles	New York Mets	New York, 4-1
1970	Baltimore Orioles	Cincinnati Reds	Baltimore, 4-1
1971	Baltimore Orioles	Pittsburgh Pirates	Pittsburgh, 4-3
1972	Oakland A's	Cincinnati Reds	Oakland, 4-3
1973	Oakland A's	New York Mets	Oakland, 4-3
1974	Oakland A's	Los Angeles Dodgers	Oakland, 4-1
1975	Boston Red Sox	Cincinnati Reds	Cincinnati, 4-3
1976	New York Yankees	Cincinnati Reds	Cincinnati, 4-0
1977	New York Yankees	Los Angeles Dodgers	New York, 4-2
1978	New York Yankees	Los Angeles Dodgers	New York, 4-2
1979	Baltimore Orioles	Pittsburgh Pirates	Pittsburgh, 4-3
1980	Kansas City Royals	Philadelphia Phillies	Philadelphia, 4-2
1981	New York Yankees	Los Angeles Dodgers	Los Angeles, 4-2
1982	Milwaukee Brewers	St. Louis Cardinals	St. Louis, 4-3
1983	Baltimore Orioles	Philadelphia Phillies	Baltimore, 4-1
1984	Detroit Tigers	San Diego Padres	Detroit, 4-1
1985	Kansas City Royals	St. Louis Cardinals	Kansas City, 4-3

It's goodbye for Whitey Herzog and Cards in '85 Series.

1985 WORLD SERIES

ST. LOUIS CARDINALS

BATTER	AVG	G	AB	R	H	2B	3B	HR	RBI	GW	SH	SF	HB	BB	SO	SB	CS	E
Braun	.000	1	1	0	0	0	0	0	0	0	0	0	0	0	0	0	0	0
Cedeno	.133	5	15	1	2	1	0	0	1	1	0	0	0	2	2	0	0	0
Clark	.240	7	25	1	6	2	0	0	4	0	0	0	0	3	9	0	0	0
DeJesus	.000	1	1	0	0	0	0	0	0	0	0	0	0	0	0	0	0	0
Harper	.250	4	4	0	1	0	0	0	1	0	0	0	0	0	1	0	0	0
Herr	.154	7	26	2	4	2	0	0	0	0	0	0	0	2	2	0	0	0
Jorgensen	.000	2	3	0	0	0	0	0	0	0	0	0	0	0	0	0	0	0
Landrum	.360	7	25	3	9	2	0	1	1	1	0	0	0	0	2	0	0	0
Lawless		1	0	0	0	0	0	0	0	0	0	0	0	0	0	0	0	0
McGee	.259	7	27	2	7	2	0	1	2	0	0	0	0	1	3	1	2	0
Nieto	.000	2	5	0	0	0	0	0	1	0	1	0	0	1	2	0	0	0
Pendleton	.261	7	23	3	6	1	1	0	3	1	0	0	0	3	2	0	0	1
Porter	.133	5	15	0	2	0	0	0	0	0	0	0	0	2	5	0	0	0
Smith	.087	7	23	1	2	0	0	0	0	0	1	0	0	4	0	1	1	1
Van Slyke	.091	6	11	0	1	0	0	0	0	0	0	0	0	0	5	0	0	0
Pitchers	.000	7	12	0	0	0	0	0	0	0	1	0	0	0	9	0	0	0
TOTALS	.185		216	13	40	10	1	2	13	3	3	0	0	18	42	2	3	2

PITCHER		W	L	ERA	G	GS	CG	SHO	SV	IP	AB	H	R	ER	HR	HB	BB	SO	WP
Andujar	R	0	1	9.00	2	1	0	0	0	4.0	19	10	4	4	1	0	4	3	0
Campbell	R	0	0	2.25	3	0	0	0	0	4.0	15	4	1	1	0	0	2	5	0
Cox	R	0	0	1.29	2	2	0	0	0	14.0	49	14	2	2	0	0	4	13	0
Dayley	L	1	0	.00	4	0	0	0	0	6.0	19	1	0	0	0	0	3	5	0
Forsch	R	0	1	12.00	2	1	0	0	0	3.0	14	6	4	4	0	0	1	3	1
Horton	L	0	0	6.75	3	0	0	0	0	4.0	16	4	3	3	0	0	5	5	0
Lahti	R	0	0	12.27	3	0	0	0	1	3.2	20	10	6	5	0	0	0	2	0
Tudor	L	2	1	3.00	3	3	1	1	0	18.0	66	15	6	6	1	1	7	14	0
Worrell	R	0	1	3.86	3	0	0	0	1	4.2	18	4	2	2	0	0	2	6	0
TOTALS		3	4	3.96	25	7	1	1	2	61.1	236	68	28	27	2	1	28	56	1

GAME 1
at KANSAS CITY
Saturday, October 19

										R	H	E
St. Louis	0	0	1	1	0	0	0	0	1	3	7	1
Kansas City	0	1	0	0	0	0	0	0	0	1	8	0

TUDOR, Worrell (7) (S), and Porter
JACKSON, Quisenberry (8), Black (9), and Sundberg
HR: None
T-2:48; A-41,650

GAME 2
at KANSAS CITY
Sunday, October 20

										R	H	E
St. Louis	0	0	0	0	0	0	0	0	4	4	6	0
Kansas City	0	0	0	2	0	0	0	0	0	2	9	0

Cox, DAYLEY (8), Lahti (9) (S), and Porter
LEIBRANDT, Quisenberry (9), and Sundberg
HR: None
T-2:44; A-41,656

GAME 3
at ST. LOUIS
Tuesday, October 22

										R	H	E
Kansas City	0	0	0	2	2	0	2	0	0	6	11	0
St. Louis	0	0	0	0	0	1	0	0	0	1	6	0

SABERHAGEN, and Sundberg
ANDUJAR, Campbell (5), Horton (6), Dayley (8), and Porter
HR: Kansas City (1)—White
T-3:00; A-53,634

GAME 4
at ST. LOUIS
Wednesday, October 23

										R	H	E
Kansas City	0	0	0	0	0	0	0	0	0	0	5	1
St. Louis	0	1	1	0	1	0	0	0	X	3	6	0

BLACK, Beckwith (6), Quisenberry (8), and Sundberg
TUDOR, and Nieto
HR: St. Louis (2)—Landrum, McGee
T-2:19; A-53,634

KANSAS CITY ROYALS

BATTER	AVG	G	AB	R	H	2B	3B	HR	RBI	GW	SH	SF	HB	BB	SO	SB	CS	E
Balboni	.320	7	25	2	8	0	0	0	3	0	0	0	0	5	4	0	0	0
Biancalana	.278	7	18	2	5	0	0	0	2	1	0	0	0	5	4	0	0	0
Brett.............	.370	7	27	5	10	1	0	0	1	0	0	0	0	4	7	1	0	1
Concepcion		3	0	1	0	0	0	0	0	0	0	0	0	0	0	0	0	0
Iorg	.500	2	2	0	1	0	0	0	2	1	0	0	0	0	0	0	0	0
Jones L	.667	5	3	0	2	1	1	0	0	0	0	0	0	0	0	0	0	0
McRae............	.000	3	1	0	0	0	0	0	0	0	0	0	1	1	0	0	0	0
Motley............	.364	5	11	1	4	0	0	1	3	1	0	0	0	0	1	0	1	0
Orta..............	.333	3	3	0	1	0	0	0	0	0	0	0	0	0	0	0	0	0
Pryor		1	0	0	0	0	0	0	0	0	0	0	0	0	0	0	0	0
Sheridan	.222	5	18	0	4	2	0	0	1	0	0	0	0	0	7	0	0	0
Smith.............	.333	7	27	5	9	3	0	0	4	1	0	0	0	3	8	2	2	0
Sundberg.........	.250	7	24	6	6	2	0	0	1	0	0	0	0	6	4	0	0	0
Wathan	.000	2	1	0	0	0	0	0	0	0	0	0	0	0	1	0	0	0
White............	.250	7	28	4	7	3	0	1	6	0	0	0	0	3	4	1	1	0
Wilson...........	.367	7	30	1	11	0	1	0	3	0	0	0	0	1	4	3	0	0
Pitchers..........	.000	7	18	1	0	0	0	0	0	0	3	0	0	0	12	0	0	2
TOTALS	.288		236	28	68	12	2	2	26	4	3	0	1	28	56	7	4	3

PITCHER		W	L	ERA	G	GS	CG	SHO	SV	IP	AB	H	R	ER	HR	HB	BB	SO	WP
Beckwith	R	0	0	.00	1	0	0	0	0	2.0	7	1	0	0	0	0	0	3	0
Black..................	L	0	1	5.06	2	1	0	0	0	5.1	17	4	3	3	2	0	5	4	0
Jackson................	L	1	1	1.69	2	2	1	0	0	16.0	55	9	3	3	0	0	5	12	0
Leibrandt..............	L	0	1	2.76	2	2	0	0	0	16.1	58	10	5	5	0	0	4	10	0
Quisenberry............	R	1	0	2.08	4	0	0	0	0	4.1	15	5	1	1	0	0	3	3	1
Saberhagen............	R	2	0	.50	2	2	2	1	0	18.0	64	11	1	1	0	0	1	10	0
TOTALS		4	3	1.89	13	7	3	1	0	62	216	40	13	13	2	0	18	42	1

GAME 5
at ST. LOUIS
Thursday, October 24

Kansas City ...	1	3	0	0	0	0	0	1	1	6	11	2
St. Louis	1	0	0	0	0	0	0	0	0	1	5	1

JACKSON, and Sundberg
FORSCH, Horton (2), Campbell (4), Worrell (6), Lahti (8), and Nieto
HR: None
T-2:52; A-53,634

GAME 6
at KANSAS CITY
Saturday, October 26

St. Louis	0	0	0	0	0	0	0	1	0	1	5	0
Kansas City ...	0	0	0	0	0	0	0	0	2	2	10	0

Cox, Dayley (8), WORRELL (9), and Porter
Leibrandt, QUISENBERRY (8), and Sundberg
HR: None
T-2:48; A-41,628

GAME 7
at KANSAS CITY
Sunday, October 27

St. Louis	0	0	0	0	0	0	0	0	0	0	5	0
Kansas City ...	0	2	3	0	6	0	0	0	X	11	14	0

TUDOR, Campbell (3), Lahti (5), Horton (5), Andujar (5), Forsch (5), Dayley (7), and Porter
SABERHAGEN, and Sundberg
HR: Kansas City (1)—Motley
T-2:46; A-41,658

SCORE BY INNINGS

Kansas City .	1	6	3	4	8	0	2	1	3	28	68	3
St. Louis ...	1	1	2	1	1	1	0	1	5	13	40	2

E—Pendleton, Black, Jackson, Brett, O. Smith
DP—Kansas City (3), St. Louis (9)
LOB—Kansas City (56), St. Louis (38)
SB—O. Smith, White, Wilson (3), McGee, L. Smith (2), Brett
S—Tudor, Leibrandt (2), Saberhagen, Nieto, O. Smith
SF—None

WP—Quisenberry
Balk—Horton
PB—Sundberg, Porter
HBP—McRae (by Tudor)
ATT—327,494

Official 1985 National League Records

(Compiled by Elias Sports Bureau, New York)

1985 FINAL STANDINGS

EASTERN DIVISION

	W	L	PCT.	GB
St. Louis	101	61	.623	
New York	98	64	.605	3
Montreal	84	77	.522	16.5
Chicago	77	84	.478	23.5
Philadelphia	75	87	.463	26
Pittsburgh	57	104	.354	43.5

WESTERN DIVISION

	W	L	PCT.	GB
Los Angeles	95	67	.586	
Cincinnati	89	72	.553	5.5
Houston	83	79	.512	12
San Diego	83	79	.512	12
Atlanta	66	96	.407	29
San Francisco	62	100	.383	33

TIE GAME: Cincinnati at Chicago, September 8, 9 innings (5-5)

Championship Series: St. Louis defeated Los Angeles, 4 games to 2

BATTING

INDIVIDUAL BATTING LEADERS

Batting Average	.353	McGee, St.L.
Games	162	Garvey, S.D. & Murphy, Atl.
At Bats	663	Samuel, Phil.
Runs	118	Murphy, Atl.
Hits	216	McGee, St.L.
Total Bases	350	Parker, Cin.
Singles	162	McGee, St.L.
Doubles	42	Parker, Cin.
Triples	18	McGee, St.L.
Home Runs	37	Murphy, Atl.
Runs Batted In	125	Parker, Cin.
Game-Winning RBI	24	Hernandez, N.Y.
Sacrifice Hits	14	Backman, N.Y. & Ryan, Hou.
Sacrifice Flies	13	Herr, St.L.
Hit by Pitch	11	Brown, S.F.
Bases on Balls	90	Murphy, Atl.
Intentional Bases on Balls	24	Durham, Chi., Parker, Cin. & Templeton, S.D.
Strikeouts	141	Murphy, Atl. & Samuel, Phil.
Stolen Bases	110	Coleman, St.L.
Caught Stealing	25	Coleman, St.L.
Grounded into Double Plays	26	Parker, Cin.
Slugging Percentage	.577	Guerrero, L.A.
On-Base Percentage	.422	Guerrero, L.A.
Longest Batting Streak, Games	18	Sandberg, Chi. (June 18-July 6)
	18	Moreland, Chi. (Sept. 12-29)

Montreal's Tim Raines was NL's third-leading hitter.

TOP FIFTEEN QUALIFIERS FOR BATTING CHAMPIONSHIP
(* Left-Handed Batter # Switch-Hitter)

Player, Club	AVG.	G	AB	R	H	TB	2B	3B	HR	RBI	GW RBI	BB	SO	SB	SLG
#McGee, Willie, St.L.	.353	152	612	114	216	308	26	18	10	82	17	34	86	56	.503
Guerrero, Pedro, L.A.	.320	137	487	99	156	281	22	2	33	87	16	83	68	12	.577
#Raines, Timothy, Mtl.	.320	150	575	115	184	273	30	13	11	41	4	81	60	70	.475
*Gwynn, Anthony, S.D.	.317	154	622	90	197	254	29	5	6	46	8	45	33	14	.408
*Parker, David, Cin.	.312	160	635	88	198	350	42	4	34	125	18	52	80	5	.551
*Hernandez, Keith, N.Y.	.309	158	593	87	183	255	34	4	10	91	24	77	59	3	.430
Moreland, B. Keith, Chi.	.307	161	587	74	180	258	30	3	14	106	12	68	58	12	.440
Sandberg, Ryne, Chi.	.305	153	609	113	186	307	31	6	26	83	10	57	97	54	.504
#Herr, Thomas, St.L.	.302	159	596	97	180	248	38	3	8	110	14	80	55	31	.416
Murphy, Dale, Atl.	.300	162	616	118	185	332	32	2	37	111	14	90	141	10	.539
*Cruz, Jose, Hou.	.300	141	544	69	163	232	34	4	9	79	9	43	74	16	.426
*Scioscia, Michael, L.A.	.296	141	429	47	127	180	26	3	7	53	4	77	21	3	.420
#Oester, Ronald, Cin.	.295	152	526	59	155	190	26	3	1	34	4	51	65	5	.361
Marshall, Michael, L.A.	.293	135	518	72	152	267	27	2	28	95	12	37	137	3	.515
#Doran, William, Hou.	.287	148	578	84	166	251	31	6	14	59	6	71	69	23	.434

ALL PLAYERS LISTED ALPHABETICALLY
(* Left-Handed Batter # Switch-Hitter)

Player, Club	AVG.	G	AB	R	H	TB	2B	3B	HR	RBI	GW RBI	BB	SO	SB	SLG
Abrego, Johnny, Chi.	.000	6	9	0	0	0	0	0	0	1	0	0	2	0	.000
Adams, Ricky, S.F.	.190	54	121	12	23	34	3	1	2	10	2	5	23	1	.281
Aguayo, Luis, Phil.	.279	91	165	27	46	77	7	3	6	21	4	22	26	1	.467
Aguilera, Richard, N.Y.	.278	22	36	1	10	12	2	0	0	2	0	1	5	0	.333
Allen, Neil, St.L.	.000	23	2	0	0	0	0	0	0	0	0	0	2	0	.000
Almon, William, Pitt.	.270	88	244	33	66	101	17	0	6	29	1	22	61	10	.414
Andersen, Larry, Phil.	.000	57	4	1	0	0	0	0	0	0	0	0	0	0	.000
Anderson, David, L.A.	.199	77	221	24	44	62	6	0	4	18	4	35	42	5	.281
#Andujar, Joaquin, St.L.	.106	38	94	2	10	12	2	0	0	8	0	5	50	3	.128
#Ashby, Alan, Hou.	.280	65	189	20	53	85	8	0	8	25	4	24	27	0	.450
#Backman, Walter, N.Y.	.273	145	520	77	142	179	24	5	1	38	3	36	72	30	.344
#Bailey, J. Mark, Hou.	.265	114	332	47	88	132	14	0	10	45	4	67	70	0	.398
Bailor, Robert, L.A.	.246	74	118	8	29	34	3	1	0	7	1	3	5	1	.288
Bair, C. Douglas, St.L.	---	2	0	0	0	0	0	0	0	0	0	0	0	0	---
Baller, Jay, Chi.	.000	20	8	0	0	0	0	0	0	0	0	0	6	0	.000
Barker, Leonard, Atl.	.000	20	17	0	0	0	0	0	0	0	0	0	7	0	.000
Barnes, William, Mtl.	.154	19	26	0	4	5	1	0	0	0	0	0	2	0	.192
#Bass, Kevin, Hou.	.269	150	539	72	145	230	27	5	16	68	6	31	63	19	.427
Beane, William, N.Y.	.250	8	8	0	2	3	1	0	0	1	0	0	3	0	.375
*Beard, David, Chi.	---	9	0	0	0	0	0	0	0	0	0	0	0	0	---
Bedrosian, Stephen, Atl.	.078	37	64	3	5	5	0	0	0	1	0	1	22	0	.078
Bell, David, Cin.	.219	67	247	28	54	91	15	2	6	36	4	34	27	0	.368
Belliard, Rafael, Pitt.	.200	17	20	1	4	4	0	0	0	1	0	0	5	0	.200
Benedict, Bruce, Atl.	.202	70	208	12	42	48	6	0	0	20	1	22	12	0	.231
Berenyi, Bruce, N.Y.	.250	3	4	1	1	2	1	0	0	1	0	0	2	0	.500
Bevacqua, Kurt, S.D.	.239	71	138	17	33	48	6	0	3	25	3	25	17	0	.348
Bielecki, Michael, Pitt.	.000	13	10	1	0	0	0	0	0	0	0	1	5	0	.000
Bilardello, Dann, Cin.	.167	42	102	6	17	20	0	0	1	9	2	4	15	0	.196
*Blocker, Terry, N.Y.	.067	18	15	1	1	1	0	0	0	0	0	1	2	0	.067
#Blue, Vida, S.F.	.133	33	30	0	4	5	1	0	0	0	0	3	12	0	.167
Bochy, Bruce, S.D.	.268	48	112	16	30	50	2	0	6	13	1	6	30	0	446
Boever, Joseph, St.L.	---	13	0	0	0	0	0	0	0	0	0	0	0	0	---
Booker, Gregory, S.D.	.000	17	1	0	0	0	0	0	0	0	0	0	0	0	.000
*Bosley, Thaddis, Chi.	.328	108	180	25	59	92	6	3	7	27	3	20	29	5	.511
Botelho, Derek, Chi.	.143	11	14	2	2	2	0	0	0	0	0	1	[illegible]	0	.143
#Bowa, Lawrence, Chi.-N.Y.	.234	86	214	15	50	65	7	4	0	15	4	13	22	5	.304
*Braun, Stephen, St.L.	.239	64	67	7	16	23	4	0	1	6	2	10	9	0	.343
*Bream, Sidney, L.A.-Pitt.	.230	50	148	18	34	59	7	0	6	21	3	18	24	0	.399
Brenly, Robert, S.F.	.220	133	440	41	97	172	16	1	19	56	5	57	62	1	.391
Brennan, Thomas, L.A.	.125	12	8	0	1	1	0	0	0	0	0	0	1	0	.125
*Brock, Gregory, L.A.	.251	129	438	64	110	192	19	0	21	66	4	54	72	4	.438
Brooks, Hubert, Mtl.	.269	156	605	67	163	250	34	7	13	100	13	34	79	6	.413
Brown, J. Christopher, S.F.	.271	131	432	50	117	191	20	3	16	61	10	38	78	2	.442
Brown, Michael C., Pitt.	.332	57	205	29	68	105	18	2	5	33	2	22	27	2	.512
#Brown, Rogers, S.D.	.155	79	84	8	13	16	3	0	0	6	0	5	20	6	.190
*Browning, Thomas, Cin.	.193	39	88	4	17	21	2	1	0	2	0	4	29	0	.239
Brusstar, Warren, Chi.	.143	51	7	0	1	1	0	0	0	0	0	1	5	0	.143
*Bryant, Ralph, L.A.	.333	6	6	0	2	2	0	0	0	1	0	0	2	0	.333
*Buchanan, Robert, Cin.	.000	14	1	0	0	0	0	0	0	0	0	0	0	0	.000
*Bullock, Eric, Hou.	.280	18	25	3	7	9	2	0	0	2	1	1	3	0	.360

Mets' Darryl Strawberry: 29 HRs, 79 RBI in 111 games.

Player, Club	AVG.	G	AB	R	H	TB	2B	3B	HR	RBI	GW RBI	BB	SO	SB	SLG
*Bumbry, Alonza, S.D.	.200	68	95	6	19	25	3	0	1	10	1	7	9	2	.263
Burke, Timothy, Mtl.	.100	78	10	0	1	1	0	0	0	0	0	1	5	0	.100
Butera, Salvatore, Mtl.	.200	67	120	11	24	34	1	0	3	12	0	13	12	0	.283
Cabell, Enos, Hou.-L.A.	.272	117	335	40	91	118	19	1	2	36	7	30	36	9	.352
*Calhoun, Jeffrey, Hou.	.000	44	5	0	0	0	0	0	0	1	0	1	2	0	.000
Camp, Rick, Atl.	.231	66	13	1	3	6	0	0	1	2	0	1	5	0	.462
Campbell, William, St.L.	.333	50	6	2	2	2	0	0	0	1	0	3	2	0	.333
#Candelaria, John, Pitt.	.000	37	1	0	0	0	0	0	0	0	0	0	1	0	.000
*Carlton, Steven, Phil.	.179	16	28	2	5	6	1	0	0	3	0	1	8	0	.214
*Carman, Donald, Phil.	.000	71	3	0	0	0	0	0	0	0	0	0	1	0	.000
Carter, Gary, N.Y.	.281	149	555	83	156	271	17	1	32	100	18	69	46	1	.488
Castillo, Robert, L.A.	.100	36	10	0	1	1	0	0	0	0	0	1	4	0	.100
Cedeno, Cesar, Cin.-St.L.	.291	111	296	38	86	131	16	1	9	49	8	24	42	14	.443
Cerone, Richard, Atl.	.216	96	282	15	61	79	9	0	3	25	2	29	25	0	.280
Cey, Ronald, Chi.	.232	145	500	64	116	204	18	2	22	63	4	58	106	1	.408
*Chambliss, C. Christopher, Atl.	.235	101	170	16	40	56	7	0	3	21	2	18	22	0	.329
Chapman, Kelvin, N.Y.	.174	62	144	16	25	28	3	0	0	7	1	9	15	5	.194
Childress, Rodney, Phil.	.167	16	6	0	1	1	0	0	0	0	0	0	2	0	.167
Christensen, John, N.Y.	.186	51	113	10	21	36	4	1	3	13	0	19	23	1	.319
Clark, Jack, St.L.	.281	126	442	71	124	222	26	3	22	87	7	83	88	1	.502
Clements, Patrick, Pitt.	.333	27	3	0	1	1	0	0	0	0	0	0	2	0	.333
#Coleman, Vincent, St.L.	.267	151	636	107	170	213	20	10	1	40	3	50	115	110	.335
Concepcion, David, Cin.	.252	155	560	59	141	185	19	2	7	48	7	50	67	16	.330
*Corcoran, Timothy, Phil.	.214	103	182	11	39	47	6	1	0	22	2	29	20	0	.258
Cox, Danny, St.L.	.152	35	79	3	12	13	1	0	0	6	0	4	24	0	.165
*Cruz, Jose, Hou.	.300	141	544	69	163	232	34	4	9	79	9	43	74	16	.426
Darling, Ronald, N.Y.	.171	42	76	9	13	17	4	0	0	0	0	4	25	1	.224
*Daulton, Darren, Phil.	.204	36	103	14	21	38	3	1	4	11	0	16	37	3	.369
#Davis, Charles, S.F.	.270	136	481	53	130	198	25	2	13	56	3	62	74	15	.412
Davis, Eric, Cin.	.246	56	122	26	30	63	3	3	8	18	4	7	39	16	.516
Davis, Gerald, S.D.	.293	44	58	10	17	22	3	1	0	2	1	5	7	0	.379
Davis, Glenn, Hou.	.271	100	350	51	95	166	11	0	20	64	7	27	68	0	.474
Davis, Jody, Chi.	.232	142	482	47	112	193	30	0	17	58	8	48	83	1	.400
*Davis, Mark, S.F.	.250	77	12	0	3	5	0	1	0	0	0	0	5	0	.417
*Davis, Trench, Pitt.	.143	2	7	1	1	1	0	0	0	0	0	0	0	1	.143
Dawley, William, Hou.	.200	49	10	1	2	2	0	0	0	0	0	1	3	0	.200
Dawson, Andre, Mtl.	.255	139	529	65	135	235	27	2	23	91	12	29	92	13	.444
Dayett, Brian, Chi.	.231	22	26	1	6	9	0	0	1	4	1	0	6	0	.346
*Dayley, Kenneth, St.L.	.400	57	5	0	2	2	0	0	0	0	0	0	1	0	.400
*Dedmon, Jeffrey, Atl.	.111	60	9	0	1	1	0	0	0	1	0	1	3	0	.111
Deer, Robert, S.F.	.185	78	162	22	30	61	5	1	8	20	2	23	71	0	.377
DeJesus, Ivan, St.L.	.222	59	72	11	16	21	5	0	0	7	0	4	16	2	.292
DeLeon, Jose, Pitt.	.056	31	36	1	2	2	0	0	0	0	0	3	19	0	.056
DeLeon, Luis, S.D.	.200	29	5	1	1	1	0	0	0	0	0	0	1	0	.200
Denny, John, Phil.	.123	33	81	2	10	11	1	0	0	4	0	4	19	2	.136
Dernier, Robert, Chi.	.254	121	469	63	119	148	20	3	1	21	3	40	44	31	.316
*Deshaies, James, Hou.	----	2	0	0	0	0	0	0	0	0	0	0	0	0	----
Diaz, Baudilio, Phil.-Cin.	.245	77	237	21	58	88	13	1	5	31	1	21	25	0	.371
Diaz, Carlos, L.A.	.000	46	4	0	0	0	0	0	0	0	0	0	1	0	.000
#Dilone, Miguel, Mtl.-S.D.	.200	78	130	18	26	32	0	3	0	7	2	10	19	17	.246
*DiPino, Frank, Hou.	.167	54	12	1	2	2	0	0	0	1	0	0	7	0	.167
*Dopson, John, Mtl.	.000	4	4	0	0	0	0	0	0	0	0	2	3	0	.000
#Doran, William, Hou.	.287	148	578	84	166	251	31	6	14	59	6	71	69	23	.434
Dravecky, David, S.D.	.116	34	69	5	8	11	1	1	0	1	0	4	20	0	.159
*Driessen, Daniel, Mtl.-S.	.243	145	493	53	120	173	26	0	9	47	6	50	51	2	.351
#Duncan, Mariano, L.A.	.244	142	562	74	137	191	24	6	6	39	5	38	113	38	.340
Dunston, Shawon, Chi.	.260	74	250	40	65	97	12	4	4	18	2	19	42	11	.388
*Durham, Leon, Chi.	.282	153	542	58	153	252	32	2	21	75	6	64	99	7	.465
Dybzinski, Jerome, Pitt.	.000	5	4	0	0	0	0	0	0	0	0	0	0	0	.000
*Dykstra, Leonard, N.Y.	.254	83	236	40	60	78	9	3	1	19	3	30	24	15	.331
Eckersley, Dennis, Chi.	.125	26	56	1	7	10	0	0	1	1	0	7	25	0	.179
Engel, Steven, Chi.	.188	11	16	1	3	6	0	0	1	4	0	3	7	0	.375
Esasky, Nicholas, Cin.	.262	125	413	61	108	192	21	0	21	66	9	41	102	3	.465
*Fernandez, C. Sidney, N.Y.	.212	26	52	2	11	13	0	1	0	1	0	0	26	0	.250
Fitzgerald, Michael, Mtl.	.207	108	295	25	61	85	7	1	5	34	6	38	55	5	.288
*Flannery, Timothy, S.D.	.281	126	384	50	108	131	14	3	1	40	6	58	39	2	.341
Flynn, R. Douglas, Mtl.	.167	9	6	0	1	1	0	0	0	0	0	0	0	0	.167
*Foley, Thomas, Cin.-Phil.	.240	89	250	24	60	84	13	1	3	23	4	19	34	2	.336
Foli, Timothy, Pitt.	.189	19	37	1	7	7	0	0	0	2	0	4	2	0	.189
*Fontenot, S. Ray, Chi.	.049	38	41	2	2	2	0	0	0	0	0	0	18	0	.049
*Ford, Curtis, St.L.	.500	11	12	2	6	8	2	0	0	3	1	4	1	1	.667
Forsch, Robert, St.L.	.244	34	45	3	11	18	2	1	1	4	1	0	10	0	.400
*Forster, Terry, Atl.	.000	46	4	0	0	0	0	0	0	0	0	0	0	0	.000
Foster, George, N.Y.	.263	129	452	57	119	208	24	1	21	77	10	46	87	0	.460
*Franco, John, Cin.	.333	67	6	1	2	2	0	0	0	1	0	0	0	0	.333
*Francona, Terry, Mtl.	.267	107	281	19	75	98	15	1	2	31	4	12	12	5	.349
Frazier, George, Chi.	.000	51	6	0	0	0	0	0	0	0	0	0	4	0	.000
*Frobel, Douglas, Pitt.-Mtl.	.189	65	132	17	25	34	6	0	1	11	2	21	30	4	.258

Cardinals' Vince Coleman led majors in stolen bases (110).

Player, Club	AVG.	G	AB	R	H	TB	2B	3B	HR	RBI	GW RBI	BB	SO	SB	SLG
*Gainey, Telmanch, Hou.	.162	13	37	5	6	6	0	0	0	0	0	2	9	0	.162
Galarraga, Andres, Mtl.	.187	24	75	9	14	21	1	0	2	4	1	3	18	1	.280
Garber, H. Eugene, Atl.	.200	59	5	1	1	1	0	0	0	1	0	0	1	0	.200
Garcia, Alfonso, Phil.	.000	4	3	0	0	0	0	0	0	0	0	0	1	0	.000
Gardenhire, Ronald, N.Y.	.179	26	39	5	7	11	2	1	0	2	0	8	11	0	.282
Gardner, Wesley, N.Y.	---	9	0	0	0	0	0	0	0	0	0	0	0	0	---
Garner, Philip, Hou.	.268	135	463	65	124	185	23	10	6	51	9	34	72	4	.400
Garrelts, Scott, S.F.	.222	74	9	1	2	3	1	0	0	2	0	1	4	0	.333
Garvey, Steven, S.D.	.281	162	654	80	184	281	34	6	17	81	11	35	67	0	.430
Gladden, C. Daniel, S.F.	.243	142	502	64	122	174	15	8	7	41	6	40	78	32	.347
Glynn, Edward, Mtl.	---	3	0	0	0	0	0	0	0	0	0	0	0	0	---
Gonzalez, Denio, Pitt.	.226	35	124	11	28	44	4	0	4	12	2	13	27	2	.355
Gonzalez, Jose, L.A.	.273	23	11	6	3	5	2	0	0	0	0	1	3	1	.455
Gooden, Dwight, N.Y.	.226	35	93	11	21	26	2	0	1	9	0	5	15	0	.280
*Gorman, Thomas, N.Y.	.000	34	5	0	0	0	0	0	0	0	0	0	3	0	.000
Gossage, Richard, S.D.	.000	50	11	1	0	0	0	0	0	0	0	2	5	0	.000
Gott, James, S.F.	.196	26	51	6	10	21	2	0	3	3	0	1	30	0	.412
Grapenthin, Richard, Mtl.	1.000	5	1	0	1	1	0	0	0	0	0	0	0	0	1.000
Green, David, S.F.	.248	106	294	36	73	102	10	2	5	20	7	22	58	6	.347
*Gross, Gregory, Phil.	.260	93	169	21	44	53	5	2	0	14	1	32	9	1	.314
Gross, Kevin, Phil.	.138	39	65	1	9	14	2	0	1	6	1	2	23	0	.215
Guante, Cecilio, Pitt.	.059	63	17	0	1	1	0	0	0	0	0	0	12	0	.059
Guerrero, Pedro, L.A.	.320	137	487	99	156	281	22	2	33	87	16	83	68	12	.577
Gullickson, William, Mtl.	.188	29	64	2	12	16	4	0	0	6	0	0	17	0	.250
Gumpert, David, Chi.	.000	9	1	0	0	0	0	0	0	0	0	0	1	0	.000
*Gura, Lawrence, Chi.	.000	5	6	0	0	0	0	0	0	0	0	1	4	0	.000
*Gwynn, Anthony, S.D.	.317	154	622	90	197	254	29	5	6	46	8	45	33	14	.408
#Hall, Albert, Atl.	.149	54	47	5	7	9	0	1	0	3	1	9	12	1	.191
#Hammaker, C. Atlee, S.F.	.085	29	47	0	4	4	0	0	0	0	0	0	17	0	.085
Harper, Brian, St.L.	.250	43	52	5	13	17	4	0	0	8	1	2	3	0	.327
Harper, Terry, Atl.	.264	138	492	58	130	200	15	2	17	72	7	44	76	9	.407
*Hassler, Andrew, St.L.	---	10	0	0	0	0	0	0	0	0	0	0	0	0	---
Hatcher, William, Chi.	.245	53	163	24	40	60	12	1	2	10	1	8	12	2	.368
Hawkins, M. Andrew, S.D.	.078	33	77	1	6	6	0	0	0	3	1	3	16	0	.078
*Hayes, Von, Phil.	.263	152	570	76	150	227	30	4	13	70	9	61	99	21	.398
Heathcock, R. Jeffery, Hou.	.063	14	16	1	1	1	0	0	0	0	0	4	11	0	.063
*Hebner, Richard, Chi.	.217	83	120	10	26	37	2	0	3	22	3	7	15	0	.308
*Heep, Daniel, N.Y.	.280	95	271	26	76	114	17	0	7	42	3	27	27	2	.421
Hendrick, George, Pitt.	.230	69	256	23	59	80	15	0	2	25	4	18	42	1	.313
*Hernandez, Keith, N.Y.	.309	158	593	87	183	255	34	4	10	91	24	77	59	3	.430
#Herr, Thomas, St.L.	.302	159	596	97	180	248	38	3	8	110	14	80	55	31	.416
Hershiser, Orel, L.A.	.197	37	76	5	15	16	1	0	0	4	0	4	20	1	.211
*Hesketh, Joseph, Mtl.	.091	26	44	0	4	4	0	0	0	1	0	4	30	0	.091
Holland, Alfred, Phil.-Pitt.	.400	41	5	1	2	4	0	1	0	0	0	1	2	0	.800
Holton, Brian, L.A.	---	3	0	0	0	0	0	0	0	0	0	0	0	0	---
*Honeycutt, Frederick, L.A.	.132	32	38	5	5	6	1	0	0	1	1	3	6	0	.158
Horner, J. Robert, Atl.	.267	130	483	61	129	241	25	3	27	89	6	50	57	1	.499
*Horton, Ricky, St.L.	.063	49	16	1	1	1	0	0	0	0	0	3	5	0	.063
Howe, Arthur, St.L.	.000	4	3	0	0	0	0	0	0	0	0	0	0	0	.000
*Howe, Steven, L.A.	---	19	0	0	0	0	0	0	0	0	0	0	0	0	---
Howell, Kenneth, L.A.	.000	56	4	0	0	0	0	0	0	0	0	0	2	0	.000
Hoyt, D. LaMarr, S.D.	.063	31	64	4	4	4	0	0	0	2	0	1	21	0	.063
Hubbard, Glenn, Atl.	.232	142	439	51	102	138	21	0	5	39	5	56	54	4	.314
#Hudson, Charles, Phil.	.140	38	57	2	8	8	0	0	0	3	0	1	18	0	.140
Hume, Thomas, Cin.	.000	56	5	0	0	0	0	0	0	0	0	0	2	0	.000
Hunt, J. Randall, St.L.	.158	14	19	1	3	3	0	0	0	1	0	0	5	0	.158
*Hurdle, Clinton, N.Y.	.195	43	82	7	16	29	4	0	3	7	1	13	20	0	.354
Jackson, Darrin, Chi.	.091	5	11	0	1	1	0	0	0	0	0	0	3	0	.091
Jackson, Roy Lee, S.D.	.000	22	5	0	0	0	0	0	0	0	0	0	3	0	.000
*Jeffcoat, J. Michael, S.F.	.000	19	1	0	0	0	0	0	0	0	0	1	0	0	.000
Jeltz, L. Steven, Phil.	.189	89	196	17	37	43	4	1	0	12	1	26	55	1	.219
#Johnson, Howard, N.Y.	.242	126	389	38	94	153	18	4	11	46	8	34	78	6	.393
Johnson, Joseph, Atl.	.043	15	23	0	1	2	1	0	0	2	0	3	8	0	.087
*Johnson, Roy, Mtl.	.000	3	5	0	0	0	0	0	0	0	0	0	3	0	.000
*Johnstone, John, L.A.	.133	17	15	0	2	3	1	0	0	2	1	1	2	0	.200
*Jones, Christopher, Hou.	.200	31	25	0	5	5	0	0	0	1	0	3	7	0	.200
*Jorgensen, Michael, St.L.	.196	72	112	14	22	28	6	0	0	11	2	31	27	2	.250
*Kemp, Steven, Pitt.	.250	92	236	19	59	82	13	2	2	21	3	25	54	1	.347
*Kennedy, Terrence, S.D.	.261	143	532	54	139	198	27	1	10	74	9	31	102	0	.372
Keough, Matthew, St.L.	.000	4	2	0	0	0	0	0	0	0	0	0	0	0	.000
*Kepshire, Kurt, St.L.	.118	32	51	6	6	9	3	0	0	2	0	1	18	0	.176
Kerfeld, Charles, Hou.	.000	11	14	0	0	0	0	0	0	0	0	0	9	0	.000
Khalifa, Sam, Pitt.	.238	95	320	30	76	102	14	3	2	31	3	34	56	5	.319
Kipper, Robert, Pitt.	.250	5	8	1	2	2	0	0	0	0	0	0	3	0	.250
*Knepper, Robert, Hou.	.141	38	78	5	11	15	1	0	1	5	0	2	38	0	.192
Knicely, Alan, Cin.-Phil.	.242	55	165	17	40	64	9	0	5	26	2	16	38	0	.388
Knight, C. Ray, N.Y.	.218	90	271	22	59	89	12	0	6	36	2	13	32	1	.328
Knudson, Mark, Hou.	.000	2	2	0	0	0	0	0	0	0	0	1	2	0	.000

Pedro Guerrero: No. 1 in slugging and on-base percentage.

Tommy Herr's .302 was second-highest on the Cards.

Player, Club	AVG.	G	AB	R	H	TB	2B	3B	HR	RBI	GW RBI	BB	SO	SB	SLG
Komminsk, Brad, Atl.	.227	106	300	52	68	98	12	3	4	21	2	38	71	10	.327
Koosman, Jerome, Phil.	.088	19	34	1	3	3	0	0	0	4	1	1	9	0	.088
Krawczyk, Raymond, Pitt.	---	8	0	0	0	0	0	0	0	0	0	0	0	0	---
*Krenchicki, Wayne, Cin.	.272	90	173	16	47	68	9	0	4	25	1	28	20	0	.393
Krukow, Michael, S.F.	.218	28	55	2	12	19	4	0	1	3	0	1	15	1	.345
*Kuiper, Duane, S.F.	.600	9	5	0	3	3	0	0	0	0	0	1	0	0	.600
Lahti, Jeffrey, St.L.	.000	52	9	0	0	0	0	0	0	0	0	0	5	0	.000
*LaPoint, David, S.F.	.167	31	60	4	10	11	1	0	0	6	1	6	11	0	.183
Lake, Steven, Chi.	.151	58	119	5	18	23	2	0	1	11	1	3	21	1	.193
*Landreaux, Kenneth, L.A.	.268	147	482	70	129	195	26	2	12	50	10	33	37	15	.405
Landrum, Terry, St.L.	.280	85	161	21	45	69	8	2	4	21	3	19	30	1	.429
Laskey, William, S.F.-Mtl.	.135	30	37	2	5	5	0	0	0	2	0	3	16	0	.135
*Latham, William, N.Y.	.333	7	3	1	1	1	0	0	0	1	0	1	0	0	.333
*Lavalliere, Michael, St.L.	.147	12	34	2	5	6	1	0	0	6	0	7	3	0	.176
Law, Vance, Mtl.	.266	147	519	75	138	210	30	6	10	52	5	86	96	6	.405
Lawless, Thomas, St.L.	.207	47	58	8	12	17	3	1	0	8	2	5	4	2	.293
Leach, Terry, N.Y.	.167	22	12	1	2	3	1	0	0	0	0	1	8	0	.250
*Lefferts, Craig, S.D.	.250	60	4	0	1	1	0	0	0	0	0	0	2	0	.250
LeMaster, Johnnie, S.F.-Pitt.	.122	34	74	5	9	12	0	0	1	6	0	6	17	1	.162
Leonard, Jeffrey, S.F.	.241	133	507	49	122	199	20	3	17	62	7	21	107	11	.393
Lezcano, Sixto, Pitt.	.207	72	116	16	24	35	2	0	3	9	0	35	17	0	.302
Lopes, David, Chi.	.284	99	275	52	78	122	11	0	11	44	6	46	37	47	.444
Loucks, Scott, Pitt.	.286	4	7	1	2	4	2	0	0	1	0	2	2	0	.571
*Lucas, Gary, Mtl.	.000	49	5	0	0	0	0	0	0	0	0	0	4	0	.000
Lynch, Edward, N.Y.	.077	31	52	1	4	4	0	0	0	0	0	3	30	0	.077
*Madden, Michael, Hou.	---	13	0	0	0	0	0	0	0	0	0	0	0	0	---
Maddox, Garry, Phil.	.239	105	218	22	52	74	8	1	4	23	3	13	26	1	.339
Madlock, Bill, Pitt.-L.A.	.275	144	513	69	141	206	27	1	12	56	6	49	53	10	.402
#Mahler, Michael, Mtl.	.188	9	16	2	3	5	0	1	0	0	0	0	5	0	.313
Mahler, Richard, Atl.	.156	39	90	9	14	15	1	0	0	8	3	3	18	0	.167
Maldonado, Candido, L.A.	.225	121	213	20	48	72	7	1	5	19	2	19	40	1	.338
Manrique, Fred, Mtl.	.308	9	13	5	4	10	1	1	1	1	0	1	3	0	.769
Marshall, Michael, L.A.	.293	135	518	72	152	267	27	2	28	95	12	37	137	3	.515
Martinez, Carmelo, S.D.	.253	150	514	64	130	223	28	1	21	72	13	87	82	0	.434
Mason, Roger, S.F.	.091	5	11	1	1	1	0	0	0	0	0	0	5	0	.091
Mathis, Ronald, Hou.	.071	23	14	0	1	1	0	0	0	0	0	1	6	0	.071
Matthews, Gary, Chi.	.235	97	298	45	70	121	12	0	13	40	3	59	64	2	.406
*Matuszek, Leonard, L.A.	.222	43	63	10	14	27	2	1	3	13	2	8	14	0	.429
#Mazzilli, Lee, Pitt.	.282	92	117	20	33	44	8	0	1	9	1	29	17	4	.376
#McCullers, Lance, S.D.	.000	21	4	0	0	0	0	0	0	0	0	0	4	0	.000
McDowell, Roger, N.Y.	.158	62	19	1	3	4	1	0	0	1	0	1	7	0	.211
McGaffigan, Andrew, Cin.	.034	15	29	0	1	2	1	0	0	1	1	1	18	0	.069
#McGee, Willie, St.L.	.353	152	612	114	216	308	26	18	10	82	17	34	86	56	.503
McMurtry, J. Craig, Atl.	.071	17	14	0	1	1	0	0	0	0	0	0	7	0	.071
McReynolds, W. Kevin, S.D.	.234	152	564	61	132	209	24	4	15	75	12	43	81	4	.371
*McWilliams, Larry, Pitt.	.125	32	40	2	5	6	1	0	0	2	0	1	19	0	.150
*Meridith, Ronald, Chi.	.250	32	4	0	1	1	0	0	0	0	0	1	1	0	.250
*Milner, Eddie, Cin.	[illegible]	145	453	[illegible]	[illegible]	[illegible]	19	7	3	33	4	61	31	35	.347
#Minton, Gregory, S.F.	.000	68	8	1	0	0	0	0	0	1	0	1	6	0	.000
*Mizerock, John, Hou.	.237	15	38	6	9	13	4	0	0	6	2	2	8	0	.342
Moore, Robert, S.F.	.000	11	2	0	0	0	0	0	0	0	0	0	0	0	.000
Moreland, B. Keith, Chi.	.307	161	587	74	180	258	30	3	14	106	12	68	58	12	.440
Morrison, James, Pitt.	.254	92	244	17	62	84	10	0	4	22	0	8	44	3	.344
#Mumphrey, Jerry, Hou.	.277	130	444	52	123	176	25	2	8	61	3	37	57	6	.396
Murphy, Dale, Atl.	.300	162	616	118	185	332	32	2	37	111	14	90	141	10	.539
*Murphy, Robert, Cin.	---	2	0	0	0	0	0	0	0	0	0	0	0	0	---
*Myers, Randall, N.Y.	---	1	0	0	0	0	0	0	0	0	0	0	0	0	---
*Nettles, Graig, S.D.	.261	137	440	66	115	185	23	1	15	61	4	72	59	0	.420
#Newman, Albert, Mtl.	.172	25	29	7	5	6	1	0	0	1	1	3	4	2	.207
Nicosia, Steven, Mtl.	.169	42	71	4	12	14	2	0	0	1	0	7	11	1	.197
Niedenfuer, Thomas, L.A.	.111	64	9	0	1	1	0	0	0	0	0	0	3	0	.111
Niekro, Joseph, Hou.	.250	32	68	6	17	18	1	0	0	6	1	1	16	0	.265
*Niemann, Randy, N.Y.	---	4	0	0	0	0	0	0	0	0	0	0	0	0	---
Nieto, Thomas, St.L.	.225	95	253	15	57	71	10	2	0	34	5	26	37	0	.281
*Nokes, Matthew, S.F.	.208	19	53	3	11	19	2	0	2	5	0	1	9	0	.358
*Oberkfell, Kenneth, Atl.	.272	134	412	30	112	148	19	4	3	35	2	51	38	1	.359
O'Berry, P. Michael, Mtl.	.190	20	21	2	4	4	0	0	0	0	0	4	3	1	.190
*O'Connor, Jack, Mtl.	---	20	0	0	0	0	0	0	0	0	0	0	0	0	---
#Oester, Ronald, Cin.	.295	152	526	59	155	190	26	3	1	34	4	51	65	5	.361
*Oliver, Albert, L.A.	.253	35	79	1	20	25	5	0	0	8	2	5	11	1	.316
*O'Neill, Paul, Cin.	.333	5	12	1	4	5	1	0	0	1	0	0	2	0	.417
Orosco, Jesse, N.Y.	.429	54	7	0	3	3	0	0	0	0	0	0	1	0	.429
*Orsulak, Joseph, Pitt.	.300	121	397	54	119	145	14	6	0	21	0	26	27	24	.365
Ortiz, Adalberto, Pitt.	.292	23	72	4	21	26	2	0	1	5	1	3	17	1	.361
#Owen, Dave, Chi.	.368	22	19	6	7	7	0	0	0	1	0	1	5	1	.368
Owen, Lawrence, Atl.	.239	26	71	7	17	26	3	0	2	12	0	8	17	0	.366
Paciorek, Thomas, N.Y.	.284	46	116	14	33	41	3	1	1	11	1	6	14	1	.353
Palmer, David, Mtl.	.111	24	36	1	4	5	1	0	0	0	0	0	10	0	.139

Player, Club	AVG.	G	AB	R	H	TB	2B	3B	HR	RBI	GW RBI	BB	SO	SB	SLG
Pankovits, James, Hou.	.244	75	172	24	42	57	3	0	4	14	2	17	29	1	.331
*Parker, David, Cin.	.312	160	635	88	198	350	42	4	34	125	18	52	80	5	.551
Pastore, Frank, Cin.	.143	17	14	1	2	3	1	0	0	0	0	0	6	0	.214
*Patterson, Reginald, Chi.	.100	8	10	1	1	1	0	0	0	0	0	1	4	0	.100
Patterson, Robert, S.D.	---	3	0	0	0	0	0	0	0	0	0	0	0	0	---
*Pederson, Stuart, L.A.	.000	8	4	1	0	0	0	0	0	1	0	0	2	0	.000
Pena, Adalberto, Hou.	.276	20	29	7	8	10	2	0	0	4	1	1	6	0	.345
Pena, Alejandro, L.A.	.000	2	1	0	0	0	0	0	0	0	0	0	0	0	.000
Pena, Antonio, Pitt.	.249	147	546	53	136	197	27	2	10	59	7	29	67	12	.361
#Pendleton, Terry, St.L.	.240	149	559	56	134	171	16	3	5	69	12	37	75	17	.306
Perez, Atanasio, Cin.	.328	72	183	25	60	86	8	0	6	33	4	22	22	0	.470
Perez, Pascual, Atl.	.120	22	25	0	3	3	0	0	0	1	1	3	13	0	.120
*Perlman, Jonathan, Chi.	.000	6	1	0	0	0	0	0	0	0	0	0	1	0	.000
*Perry, Gerald, Atl.	.214	110	238	22	51	65	5	0	3	13	3	23	28	9	.273
*Perry, W. Patrick, St.L.	.500	6	2	0	1	1	0	0	0	0	0	0	0	0	.500
*Porter, Darrell, St.L.	.221	84	240	30	53	99	12	2	10	36	6	41	48	6	.413
Powell, Dennis, L.A.	.000	16	3	0	0	0	0	0	0	0	0	0	2	0	.000
Power, Ted, Cin.	---	64	0	0	0	0	0	0	0	0	0	1	0	0	---
Price, Joseph, Cin.	.000	26	14	0	0	0	0	0	0	0	0	1	7	0	.000
*Puhl, Terrance, Hou.	.284	57	194	34	55	81	14	3	2	23	1	18	23	6	.418
Rabb, John, Atl.	.000	3	2	0	0	0	0	0	0	0	0	0	1	0	.000
#Raines, Timothy, Mtl.	.320	150	575	115	184	273	30	13	11	41	4	81	60	70	.475
*Rajsich, Gary, S.F.	.165	51	91	5	15	21	6	0	0	10	2	17	22	0	.231
Ramirez, Mario, S.D.	.283	37	60	6	17	23	0	0	2	5	0	3	11	0	.383
Ramirez, Rafael, Atl.	.248	138	568	54	141	189	25	4	5	58	5	20	63	2	.333
#Ramsey, Michael, L.A.	.133	9	15	1	2	3	1	0	0	0	0	2	4	0	.200
Rawley, Shane, Phil.	.138	36	58	3	8	9	1	0	0	6	0	5	21	0	.155
#Ray, Johnny, Pitt.	.274	154	594	67	163	223	33	3	7	70	5	46	24	13	.375
Reardon, Jeffrey, Mtl.	.286	63	7	0	2	2	0	0	0	1	0	0	4	0	.286
Redus, Gary, Cin.	.252	101	246	51	62	102	14	4	6	28	4	44	52	48	.415
Reuschel, Ricky, Pitt.	.169	31	59	8	10	15	2	0	1	7	1	3	17	1	.254
*Reuss, Jerry, L.A.	.135	34	74	1	10	10	0	0	0	7	2	2	28	0	.135
Reyes, Gilberto, L.A.	.000	6	1	0	0	0	0	0	0	0	0	1	1	0	.000
*Reynolds, G. Craig, Hou.	.272	107	379	43	103	149	18	8	4	32	7	12	30	4	.393
#Reynolds, Robert, L.A.-Pitt.	.282	104	337	44	95	133	15	7	3	42	8	22	49	18	.395
Reynolds, Ronn, N.Y.	.209	28	43	4	9	11	2	0	0	1	0	0	18	0	.256
Rhoden, Richard, Pitt.	.189	37	74	2	14	17	3	0	0	6	3	2	7	0	.230
Rivera, German, Hou.	.194	13	36	3	7	11	2	1	0	2	0	4	8	0	.306
Roberge, Bertrand, Mtl.	.000	42	1	0	0	0	0	0	0	0	0	0	1	0	.000
Robinson, Don, Pitt.	.238	44	21	2	5	10	2	0	1	4	0	0	11	0	.476
Robinson, Jeffrey, S.F.	---	8	0	0	0	0	0	0	0	0	0	0	0	0	---
Robinson, Ronald, Cin.	.091	33	22	0	2	2	0	0	0	1	0	0	8	0	.091
Rodriguez, Edwin, S.D.	.000	1	1	0	0	0	0	0	0	0	0	0	0	0	.000
#Roenicke, Ronald, S.F.	.256	65	133	23	34	54	9	1	3	13	1	35	27	6	.406
Rogers, Stephen, Mtl.	.143	8	14	1	2	3	1	0	0	1	0	0	1	0	.214
#Rose, Peter, Cin.	.264	119	405	60	107	129	12	2	2	46	6	86	35	8	.319
Ross, Mark, Hou.	.000	8	1	0	0	0	0	0	0	1	0	0	0	0	.000
Rowdon, Wade, Cin.	.222	5	9	2	2	2	0	0	0	2	0	2	1	0	.222
Royster, Jeron, S.D.	.281	90	249	31	70	102	13	2	5	31	4	32	31	6	.410
*Rucker, David, Phil.	.333	41	12	2	4	5	1	0	0	0	0	1	5	0	.417
Runge, Paul, Atl.	.218	50	87	15	19	25	3	0	1	5	0	18	18	0	.287
#Runnells, Thomas, Cin.	.200	28	35	3	7	8	1	0	0	0	0	3	4	0	.229
Russell, John, Phil.	.218	81	216	22	47	86	12	0	9	23	1	18	72	2	.398
Russell, William, L.A.	.260	76	169	19	44	52	6	1	0	13	2	18	9	4	.308
Ruthven, Richard, Chi.	.208	20	24	1	5	5	0	0	0	1	0	0	7	0	.208
Ryan, L. Nolan, Hou.	.111	35	63	2	7	9	2	0	0	4	0	4	21	0	.143
St. Claire, Randy, Mtl.	.200	42	5	1	1	1	0	0	0	0	0	2	3	0	.200
*Sambito, Joseph, N.Y.	---	8	0	0	0	0	0	0	0	0	0	0	0	0	---
Samuel, Juan, Phil.	.264	161	663	101	175	289	31	13	19	74	13	33	141	53	.436
Sandberg, Ryne, Chi.	.305	153	609	113	186	307	31	6	26	83	10	57	97	54	.504
Sanderson, Scott, Chi.	.065	19	31	1	2	2	0	0	0	1	0	1	17	0	.065
Santana, Rafael, N.Y.	.257	154	529	41	136	160	19	1	1	29	6	29	54	1	.302
Sax, Stephen, L.A.	.279	136	488	62	136	155	8	4	1	42	6	54	43	27	.318
*Schatzeder, Daniel, Mtl.	.194	24	31	4	6	13	1	0	2	5	1	1	10	0	.419
Schiraldi, Calvin, N.Y.	.125	10	8	0	1	1	0	0	0	0	0	0	4	0	.125
Schmidt, Michael, Phil.	.277	158	549	89	152	292	31	5	33	93	8	87	117	1	.532
Schu, Richard, Phil.	.252	112	416	54	105	155	21	4	7	24	2	38	78	8	.373
Schuler, David, Atl.	---	9	0	0	0	0	0	0	0	0	0	0	0	0	---
*Scioscia, Michael, L.A.	.296	141	429	47	127	180	26	3	7	53	4	77	21	3	.420
Scott, Michael, Hou.	.153	36	72	7	11	17	3	0	1	11	1	4	24	1	.236
*Scurry, Rodney, Pitt.	.000	30	4	0	0	0	0	0	0	0	0	0	2	0	.000
Shields, Stephen, Atl.	.111	23	18	0	2	2	0	0	0	0	0	1	6	0	.111
#Shines, A. Raymond, Mtl.	.120	47	50	0	6	6	0	0	0	3	1	4	9	0	.120
Shipanoff, David, Phil.	.000	26	3	0	0	0	0	0	0	0	0	0	3	0	.000
Show, Eric, S.D.	.127	35	79	3	10	13	0	0	1	6	0	0	30	0	.165
Sisk, Douglas, N.Y.	.000	42	12	1	0	0	0	0	0	1	0	0	7	0	.000
Smith, Bryn, Mtl.	.194	32	72	6	14	18	1	0	1	4	0	3	24	0	.250
Smith, David, Hou.	.000	64	3	1	0	0	0	0	0	1	0	1	2	0	.000

Player, Club	AVG.	G	AB	R	H	TB	2B	3B	HR	RBI	GW RBI	BB	SO	SB	SLG
Smith, Lee, Chi.	.000	65	6	0	0	0	0	0	0	0	0	1	5	0	.000
Smith, Lonnie, St.L.	.260	28	96	15	25	31	2	2	0	7	1	15	20	12	.323
Smith, Michael, Cin.	---	2	0	0	0	0	0	0	0	0	0	0	0	0	---
#Smith, Osborne, St.L.	.276	158	537	70	148	194	22	3	6	54	5	65	27	31	.361
*Smith, Zane, Atl.	.162	43	37	1	6	6	0	0	0	3	1	1	5	0	.162
Solano, Julio, Hou.	.000	20	2	0	0	0	0	0	0	0	0	0	1	0	.000
Sorensen, Lary, Chi.	.000	45	6	1	0	0	0	0	0	0	0	1	4	0	.000
Soto, Mario, Cin.	.133	37	83	3	11	13	0	1	0	4	1	1	24	0	.157
Speier, Chris, Chi.	.243	106	218	16	53	76	11	0	4	24	6	17	34	1	.349
*Spilman, W. Harry, Hou.	.136	44	66	3	9	13	1	0	1	4	0	3	7	0	.197
*Staub, Daniel, N.Y.	.267	54	45	2	12	18	3	0	1	8	0	10	4	0	.400
Stewart, David, Phil.	---	4	0	0	0	0	0	0	0	0	0	0	0	0	---
Stoddard, Timothy, S.D.	.000	44	5	0	0	0	0	0	0	0	0	0	1	0	.000
*Stone, Jeffery, Phil.	.265	88	264	36	70	89	4	3	3	11	1	15	50	15	.337
*Strawberry, Darryl, N.Y.	.277	111	393	78	109	219	15	4	29	79	8	73	96	26	.557
*Stubbs, Franklin, L.A.	.222	10	9	0	2	2	0	0	0	2	0	0	3	0	.222
Stuper, John, Cin.	.059	33	17	0	1	1	0	0	0	1	1	3	10	1	.059
Surhoff, Richard, Phil.	---	2	0	0	0	0	0	0	0	0	0	0	0	0	---
*Sutcliffe, Richard, Chi.	.233	20	43	4	10	13	0	0	1	3	0	2	10	0	.302
Sutter, H. Bruce, Atl.	.000	58	4	0	0	0	0	0	0	0	0	0	1	0	.000
Tekulve, Kenton, Pitt.-Phil.	.000	61	3	0	0	0	0	0	0	0	0	0	1	0	.000
#Templeton, Garry, S.D.	.282	148	546	63	154	206	30	2	6	55	5	41	88	16	.377
Thomas, Andres, Atl.	.278	15	18	6	5	5	0	0	0	2	0	0	2	0	.278
#Thomas, Derrel, Phil.	.207	63	92	16	19	33	2	0	4	12	2	11	14	2	.359
*Thompson, Jason, Pitt.	.241	123	402	42	97	152	17	1	12	61	6	84	58	0	.378
*Thompson, Milton, Atl.	.302	73	182	17	55	66	7	2	0	6	1	7	36	9	.363
*Thompson, V. Scot, S.F.-Mtl.	.224	98	143	10	32	38	6	0	0	10	3	5	17	0	.266
Thon, Richard, Hou.	.251	84	251	26	63	89	6	1	6	29	5	18	50	8	.355
*Thurmond, Mark, S.D.	.088	36	34	2	3	3	0	0	0	2	1	1	10	0	.088
Tibbs, Jay, Cin.	.092	36	65	3	6	6	0	0	0	3	0	2	33	0	.092
Toliver, Freddie, Phil.	.500	11	4	0	2	2	0	0	0	0	0	0	1	0	.500
Tolman, Timothy, Hou.	.140	31	43	4	6	13	1	0	2	8	2	1	10	0	.302
*Tomlin, David, Pitt.	---	1	0	0	0	0	0	0	0	0	0	0	0	0	---
Trevino, Alejandro, S.F.	.217	57	157	17	34	64	10	1	6	19	0	20	24	0	.408
Trillo, J. Manuel, S.F.	.224	125	451	36	101	130	16	2	3	25	4	40	44	2	.288
*Trout, Steven, Chi.	.109	24	46	2	5	6	1	0	0	2	0	2	13	0	.130
*Tudor, John, St.L.	.138	37	94	9	13	20	3	2	0	2	1	5	25	0	.213
Tunnell, B. Lee, Pitt.	.085	24	47	2	4	6	0	1	0	1	0	1	20	0	.128
#Uribe, Jose, S.F.	.237	147	476	46	113	150	20	4	3	26	3	30	57	8	.315
*Valenzuela, Fernando, L.A.	.216	35	97	7	21	26	2	0	1	7	0	0	9	0	.268
Van Gorder, David, Cin.	.238	73	151	12	36	49	7	0	2	24	3	9	19	0	.325
*Van Slyke, Andrew, St.L.	.259	146	424	61	110	186	25	6	13	55	7	47	54	34	.439
*Venable, W. McKinley, Cin.	.289	77	135	21	39	57	12	3	0	10	3	6	17	11	.422
Virgil, Osvaldo, Phil.	.246	131	426	47	105	184	16	3	19	55	7	49	85	0	.432
Walk, Robert, Pitt.	.000	9	17	0	0	0	0	0	0	0	0	0	9	0	.000
#Walker, Cleotha, Chi.	.083	21	12	3	1	1	0	0	0	0	0	0	5	1	.083
Walker, Duane, Cin.	.167	37	48	5	8	18	2	1	2	8	0	6	18	1	.375
Wallach, Timothy, Mtl.	.260	155	569	70	148	256	36	3	22	81	8	38	79	9	.450
Walling, Dennis, Hou.	.270	119	345	44	93	136	20	1	7	45	4	25	26	5	.394
Walter, Gene, S.D.	.000	15	1	0	0	0	0	0	0	0	0	1	0	0	.000
Ward, Colin, S.F.	.000	6	2	0	0	0	0	0	0	0	0	0	1	0	.000
Washington, Claudell, Atl.	.276	122	398	62	110	181	14	6	15	43	2	40	66	14	.455
Washington, U.L., Mtl.	.249	68	193	24	48	68	9	4	1	17	1	15	33	6	.352
Webster, Mitchell, Mtl.	.274	74	212	32	58	103	8	2	11	30	2	20	33	15	.486
Welch, Robert, L.A.	.180	25	50	4	9	10	1	0	0	4	0	3	13	0	.200
Wellman, Brad, S.F.	.236	71	174	16	41	54	11	1	0	16	2	4	33	5	.310
Whitfield, Terry, L.A.	.260	79	104	8	27	43	7	0	3	16	2	6	27	0	.413
Wiggins, Alan, S.D.	.054	10	37	3	2	3	1	0	0	0	0	2	4	0	.081
Williams, Frank, S.F.	.000	49	3	0	0	0	0	0	0	0	0	0	0	0	.000
Williams, Reginald, L.A.	.333	22	9	4	3	3	0	0	0	0	0	0	4	1	.333
Willis, Carl, Cin.	.000	11	1	0	0	0	0	0	0	0	0	1	0	0	.000
Wilson, Glenn, Phil.	.275	161	608	73	167	258	39	5	14	102	12	35	117	7	.424
Wilson, William, N.Y.	.276	93	337	56	93	143	16	8	6	26	1	28	52	24	.424
Winn, James, Pitt.	.111	30	18	2	2	3	1	0	0	0	0	1	8	0	.167
Winningham, Herman, Mtl.	.237	125	312	30	74	99	6	5	3	21	3	28	72	20	.317
Wockenfuss, Johnny, Phil.	.162	32	37	1	6	6	0	0	0	2	0	8	7	0	.162
Wohlford, James, Mtl.	.192	70	125	7	24	34	5	1	1	15	6	16	18	0	.272
Wojna, Edward, S.D.	.167	15	12	0	2	2	0	0	0	0	0	0	8	0	.167
Woodard, Michael, S.F.	.244	24	82	12	20	21	1	0	0	9	0	5	3	6	.256
Woods, Gary, Chi.	.244	81	82	11	20	23	3	0	0	4	0	14	18	0	.280
Worrell, Todd, St.L.	.000	17	1	0	0	0	0	0	0	0	0	0	1	0	.000
Wynne, Marvell, Pitt.	.205	103	337	21	69	87	6	3	2	18	2	18	48	10	.258
Yeager, Stephen, L.A.	.207	53	121	4	25	31	4	1	0	9	2	7	24	0	.256
Yost, Edgar, Mtl.	.182	5	11	1	2	2	0	0	0	0	0	0	2	0	.182
Youmans, Floyd, Mtl.	.053	14	19	1	1	1	0	0	0	0	0	3	10	0	.053
Youngblood, Joel, S.F.	.270	95	230	24	62	80	6	0	4	24	1	30	37	3	.348
Zachry, Patrick, Phil.	.000	10	1	0	0	0	0	0	0	0	0	0	1	0	.000
Zuvella, Paul, Atl.	.253	81	190	16	48	58	8	1	0	4	0	16	14	2	.305

CLUB BATTING

Club	AVG.	G	AB	R	H	TB	2B	3B	HR	RBI	GW RBI	BB	SO	SB	LOB	SLG
St. Louis	.264	162	5467	747	1446	2070	245	59	87	687	94	586	853	314	1105	.379
Houston	.261	162	5582	706	1457	2165	261	42	121	666	77	477	873	96	1117	.388
Los Angeles	.261	162	5502	682	1434	2103	226	28	129	632	87	539	846	136	1187	.382
New York	.257	162	5549	695	1425	2136	239	35	134	651	90	546	872	117	1149	.385
San Diego	.255	162	5507	650	1405	2029	241	28	109	611	81	513	809	60	1156	.368
Cincinnati	.255	162	5431	677	1385	2044	249	34	114	634	84	576	856	159	1134	.376
Chicago	.254	162	5492	686	1397	2142	239	28	150	640	72	562	937	182	1147	.390
Montreal	.247	161	5429	633	1342	2036	242	49	118	593	76	492	880	169	1061	.375
Pittsburgh	.247	161	5436	568	1340	1887	251	28	80	535	56	514	842	110	1132	.347
Atlanta	.246	162	5526	632	1359	2006	213	28	126	598	58	553	849	72	1163	.363
Philadelphia	.245	162	5477	667	1343	2098	238	47	141	628	71	527	1095	122	1099	.383
San Francisco	.233	162	5420	556	1263	1887	217	31	115	517	58	488	962	99	1090	.348
Totals	.252	971	65818	7899	16596	24603	2861	437	1424	7392	904	6373	10674	1636	13540	.374

PITCHING

INDIVIDUAL PITCHING LEADERS

Games Won	24	Gooden, N.Y.
Games Lost	19	DeLeon, Pitt.
Won-Lost Percentage	.864	Hershiser, L.A.
Earned Run Average	1.53	Gooden, N.Y.
Games	78	Burke, Mtl.
Games Started	39	Mahler, Atl.
Complete Games	16	Gooden, N.Y.
Games Finished	57	Smith, Chi.
Shutouts	10	Tudor, St.L.
Saves	41	Reardon, Mtl.
Innings	276.2	Gooden, N.Y.
Hits	272	Mahler, Atl.
Batsmen Faced	1127	Andujar, St.L.
Runs	119	Knepper, Hou. & Rhoden, Pitt.
Earned Runs	106	Rhoden, Pitt.
Home Runs	30	Soto, Cin.
Sacrifice Hits	16	Smith, Atl.
Sacrifice Flies	12	Hawkins, S.D., Niekro & Ryan, Hou.
Hit Batsmen	11	Andujar, St.L.
Bases on Balls	114	Darling, N.Y.
Intentional Bases on Balls	18	Minton, S.F.
Strikeouts	268	Gooden, N.Y.
Wild Pitches	21	Niekro, Hou.
Balks	5	Roberge, Mtl.
Games Won, Consecutive	14	Gooden, N.Y. (May 30 - Aug. 25)
Games Lost, Consecutive	11	DeLeon, Pitt. (June 19 - Oct. 4 2g)

Reds' Tom Browning didn't look green en route to 20 wins.

TOP FIFTEEN QUALIFIERS FOR EARNED RUN AVERAGE CHAMPIONSHIP
(* Left-Handed Pitcher)

Pitcher, Club	W	L	PCT.	ERA	G	GS	CG	GF	SHO	SV	IP	H	TBF	R	ER	HR	SH	SF	HB	BB	IB	SO	WP	BK
Gooden, Dwight, N.Y.	24	4	.857	1.53	35	35	16	0	8	0	276.2	198	1065	51	47	13	6	2	2	69	4	268	6	2
*Tudor, John, St.L.	21	8	.724	1.93	36	36	14	0	10	0	275.0	209	1062	68	59	14	4	3	5	49	4	169	4	0
Hershiser, Orel, L.A.	19	3	.864	2.03	36	34	9	1	5	0	239.2	179	953	72	54	8	5	4	6	68	5	157	5	0
Reuschel, Ricky, Pitt.	14	8	.636	2.27	31	26	9	4	1	1	194.0	153	773	58	49	7	5	3	3	52	10	138	4	0
Welch, Robert, L.A.	14	4	.778	2.31	23	23	8	0	3	0	167.1	141	675	49	43	16	6	2	6	35	2	96	7	4
*Valenzuela, Fernando, L.A.	17	10	.630	2.45	35	35	14	0	5	0	272.1	211	1109	92	74	14	13	8	1	101	5	208	10	1
*Fernandez, C. Sidney, N.Y.	9	9	.500	2.80	26	26	3	0	0	0	170.1	108	685	56	53	14	4	3	2	80	3	180	3	2
Cox, Danny, St.L.	18	9	.667	2.88	35	35	10	0	4	0	241.0	226	989	91	77	19	12	9	3	64	5	131	3	1
Darling, Ronald, N.Y.	16	6	.727	2.90	36	35	4	1	2	0	248.0	214	1043	93	80	21	13	4	3	114	1	167	7	1
Smith, Bryn, Mtl.	18	5	.783	2.91	32	32	4	0	2	0	222.1	193	890	85	72	12	13	4	1	41	3	127	1	1
*Reuss, Jerry, L.A.	14	10	.583	2.92	34	33	5	0	3	0	212.2	210	883	78	69	13	8	6	3	58	7	84	5	0
*Dravecky, David, S.D.	13	11	.542	2.93	34	31	7	1	2	0	214.2	200	876	79	70	18	13	3	1	57	5	105	2	2
Eckersley, Dennis, Chi.	11	7	.611	3.08	25	25	6	0	2	0	169.1	145	664	61	58	15	6	2	3	19	4	117	0	3
Show, Eric, S.D.	12	11	.522	3.09	35	35	5	0	2	0	233.0	212	977	95	80	27	9	5	5	87	7	141	4	0
Hawkins, M. Andrew, S.D.	18	8	.692	3.15	33	33	5	0	2	0	228.2	229	953	88	80	18	13	12	4	65	8	69	3	3

ALL PITCHERS LISTED ALPHABETICALLY
(* Left-Handed Pitcher)

Pitcher, Club	W	L	PCT.	ERA	G	GS	CG	GF	SHO	SV	IP	H	TBF	R	ER	HR	SH	SF	HB	BB	IB	SO	WP	BK
Abrego, Johnny, Chi.	1	1	.500	6.38	6	5	0	0	0	0	24.0	32	109	18	17	3	5	1	0	12	1	13	0	0
Aguilera, Richard, N.Y.	10	7	.588	3.24	21	19	2	1	0	0	122.1	118	507	49	44	8	7	4	2	37	2	74	5	2
Allen, Neil, St.L.	1	4	.200	5.59	23	1	0	13	0	2	29.0	32	135	22	18	3	1	3	1	17	6	10	1	1
Andersen, Larry, Phil.	3	3	.500	4.32	57	0	0	19	0	3	73.0	78	318	41	35	5	3	1	3	26	4	50	1	1
Andujar, Joaquin, St.L.	21	12	.636	3.40	38	38	10	0	2	0	269.2	265	1127	113	102	15	11	4	11	82	12	112	2	0
Bair, C. Douglas, St.L.	0	0	---	0.00	2	0	0	1	0	0	2.0	1	8	0	0	0	0	0	0	2	0	0	0	0
Baller, Jay, Chi.	2	3	.400	3.46	20	4	0	4	0	1	52.0	52	223	21	20	8	4	1	1	17	7	31	2	0
Barker, Leonard, Atl.	2	9	.182	6.35	20	18	0	1	0	0	73.2	84	335	55	52	10	4	1	1	37	1	47	3	0
Beard, David, Chi.	0	0	---	6.39	9	0	0	5	0	0	12.2	16	59	9	9	2	1	0	0	7	2	4	0	0
Bedrosian, Stephen, Atl.	7	15	.318	3.83	37	37	0	0	0	0	206.2	198	907	101	88	17	6	7	5	111	6	134	6	0
Berenyi, Bruce, N.Y.	1	0	1.000	2.63	3	3	0	0	0	0	13.2	8	58	6	4	0	0	0	1	10	0	10	3	0
Bielecki, Michael, Pitt.	2	3	.400	4.53	12	7	0	1	0	0	45.2	45	211	26	23	5	4	0	1	31	1	22	1	1
*Blue, Vida, S.F.	8	8	.500	4.47	33	20	1	5	0	0	131.0	115	574	70	65	17	11	3	1	80	1	103	8	2

Outgoing Card Joaquin Andujar led NL in hit batsmen (11).

Pitcher, Club	W	L	PCT.	ERA	G	GS	CG	GF	SHO	SV	IP	H	TBF	R	ER	HR	SH	SF	HB	BB	IB	SO	WP	BK
Boever, Joseph, St.L.	0	0	---	4.41	13	0	0	5	0	0	16.1	17	69	8	8	3	1	1	0	4	1	20	1	0
Booker, Gregory, S.D.	0	1	.000	6.85	17	0	0	9	0	0	22.1	20	102	17	17	3	1	2	1	17	2	7	5	0
Botelho, Derek, Chi.	1	3	.250	5.32	11	7	1	0	0	0	44.0	52	203	27	26	8	4	0	2	23	1	23	2	0
Brennan, Thomas, L.A.	1	3	.250	7.39	12	4	0	2	0	0	31.2	41	144	26	26	2	5	5	0	11	4	17	0	3
*Browning, Thomas, Cin.	20	9	.690	3.55	38	38	6	0	4	0	261.1	242	1083	111	103	29	13	7	3	73	8	155	2	0
Brusstar, Warren, Chi.	4	3	.571	6.05	51	0	0	20	0	4	74.1	87	346	55	50	8	4	5	3	36	11	34	3	0
*Buchanan, Robert, Cin.	1	0	1.000	8.44	14	0	0	3	0	0	16.0	25	77	15	15	4	0	0	0	9	1	3	1	0
Burke, Timothy, Mtl.	9	4	.692	2.39	78	0	0	31	0	8	120.1	86	483	32	32	9	8	3	7	44	14	87	7	0
Butera, Salvatore, Mtl.	0	0	---	0.00	1	0	0	1	0	0	1.0	0	3	0	0	0	0	0	0	0	0	0	0	0
*Calhoun, Jeffrey, Hou.	2	5	.286	2.54	44	0	0	21	0	4	63.2	56	259	21	18	2	3	2	0	24	4	47	4	1
Camp, Rick, Atl.	4	6	.400	3.95	66	2	0	23	0	3	127.2	130	569	72	56	8	4	4	5	61	11	49	4	0
Campbell, William, St.L.	5	3	.625	3.50	50	0	0	18	0	4	64.1	55	270	32	25	5	5	3	2	21	9	41	1	0
*Candelaria, John, Pitt.	2	4	.333	3.64	37	0	0	26	0	9	54.1	57	229	23	22	7	3	4	1	14	2	47	0	0
*Carlton, Steven, Phil.	1	8	.111	3.33	16	16	0	0	0	0	92.0	84	401	43	34	6	9	1	0	53	4	48	3	2
*Carman, Donald, Phil.	9	4	.692	2.08	71	0	0	33	0	7	86.1	52	342	25	20	6	5	5	2	38	3	87	1	0
Castillo, Robert, L.A.	2	2	.500	5.43	35	5	0	5	0	0	68.0	59	301	42	41	9	1	2	1	41	6	57	2	0
Childress, Rodney, Phil.	0	1	.000	6.21	16	1	0	3	0	0	33.1	45	151	23	23	3	2	2	0	9	3	14	1	0
*Clements, Patrick, Pitt.	0	2	.000	3.67	27	0	0	7	0	2	34.1	39	153	14	14	2	2	1	0	15	3	17	2	0
Cox, Danny, St.L.	18	9	.667	2.88	35	35	10	0	4	0	241.0	226	989	91	77	19	12	9	3	64	5	131	3	1
Darling, Ronald, N.Y.	16	6	.727	2.90	36	35	4	1	2	0	248.0	214	1043	93	80	21	13	4	3	114	1	167	7	1
*Davis, Mark, S.F.	5	12	.294	3.54	77	1	0	38	0	7	114.1	89	465	49	45	13	13	1	3	41	7	131	6	1
Dawley, William, Hou.	5	3	.625	3.56	49	0	0	19	0	2	81.0	76	347	35	32	7	12	4	0	37	7	48	2	0
*Dayley, Kenneth, St.L.	4	4	.500	2.76	57	0	0	27	0	11	65.1	65	271	24	20	2	4	2	0	18	9	62	4	0
Dedmon, Jeffrey, Atl.	6	3	.667	4.08	60	0	0	15	0	0	86.0	84	377	52	39	5	8	1	1	49	14	41	2	1
DeLeon, Jose, Pitt.	2	19	.095	4.70	31	25	1	5	0	3	162.2	138	700	93	85	15	7	4	3	89	3	149	7	1
DeLeon, Luis, S.D.	0	3	.000	4.19	29	0	0	13	0	3	38.2	39	163	18	18	6	3	1	3	10	4	31	1	0
Denny, John, Phil.	11	14	.440	3.82	33	33	6	0	2	0	230.2	252	998	112	98	15	11	8	3	83	5	123	8	0
*Deshaies, James, Hou.	0	0	---	0.00	2	0	0	0	0	0	3.0	1	10	0	0	0	0	0	0	0	0	2	0	0
*Diaz, Carlos, L.A.	6	3	.667	2.61	46	0	0	21	0	0	79.1	70	326	28	23	7	3	1	0	18	6	73	1	0
*DiPino, Frank, Hou.	3	7	.300	4.03	54	0	0	29	0	6	76.0	69	329	44	34	7	3	3	2	43	6	49	4	1
Dopson, John, Mtl.	0	2	.000	11.08	4	3	0	0	0	0	13.0	25	70	17	16	4	0	0	0	4	0	4	2	0
*Dravecky, David, S.D.	13	11	.542	2.93	34	31	7	1	2	0	214.2	200	876	79	70	18	13	3	1	57	5	105	2	2
Eckersley, Dennis, Chi.	11	7	.611	3.08	25	25	6	0	2	0	169.1	145	664	61	58	15	6	2	3	19	4	117	0	3
*Engel, Steven, Chi.	1	5	.167	5.57	11	8	1	1	0	1	51.2	61	237	36	32	10	5	1	0	26	1	29	2	1
*Fernandez, C. Sidney, N.Y.	9	9	.500	2.80	26	26	3	0	0	0	170.1	108	685	56	53	14	4	3	2	80	3	180	3	2
*Fontenot, S. Ray, Chi.	6	10	.375	4.36	38	23	0	5	0	0	154.2	177	661	86	75	23	12	2	0	45	4	70	3	2
Forsch, Robert, St.L.	9	6	.600	3.90	34	19	3	4	1	2	136.0	132	567	63	59	11	5	1	2	47	4	48	4	0
*Forster, Terry, Atl.	2	3	.400	2.28	46	0	0	19	0	1	59.1	49	253	22	15	7	2	2	0	28	4	37	1	0
*Franco, John, Cin.	12	3	.800	2.18	67	0	0	33	0	12	99.0	83	407	27	24	5	11	1	1	40	8	61	4	0
Frazier, George, Chi.	7	8	.467	6.39	51	0	0	17	0	2	76.0	88	357	57	54	11	7	1	3	52	9	46	4	2

Pitcher, Club	W	L	PCT.	ERA	G	GS	CG	GF	SHO	SV	IP	H	TBF	R	ER	HR	SH	SF	HB	BB	IB	SO	WP	BK
Garber, H. Eugene, Atl.	6	6	.500	3.61	59	0	0	31	0	1	97.1	98	409	41	39	8	9	1	2	25	8	66	1	0
Gardner, Wesley, N.Y.	0	2	.000	5.25	9	0	0	8	0	0	12.0	18	61	14	7	1	4	1	0	8	2	11	1	0
Garrelts, Scott, S.F.	9	6	.600	2.30	74	0	0	44	0	13	105.2	76	454	37	27	2	6	3	3	58	12	106	7	1
*Glynn, Edward, Mtl.	0	0	---	19.29	3	0	0	0	0	0	2.1	5	16	5	5	0	1	0	0	4	0	2	0	0
Gooden, Dwight, N.Y.	24	4	.857	1.53	35	35	16	0	8	0	276.2	198	1065	51	47	13	6	2	2	69	4	268	6	2
*Gorman, Thomas, N.Y.	4	4	.500	5.13	34	2	0	12	0	0	52.2	56	227	32	30	8	6	1	0	18	2	32	2	2
Gossage, Richard, S.D.	5	3	.625	1.82	50	0	0	38	0	26	79.0	64	308	21	16	1	3	4	1	17	1	52	0	0
Gott, James, S.F.	7	10	.412	3.88	26	26	2	0	0	0	148.1	144	629	73	64	10	6	4	1	51	3	78	3	2
Grapenthin, Richard, Atl.	0	0	---	14.14	5	0	0	1	0	0	7.0	13	43	11	11	0	0	1	1	8	2	4	0	0
Gross, Kevin, Phil.	15	13	.536	3.41	38	31	6	0	2	0	205.2	194	873	86	78	11	7	5	7	81	6	151	2	0
Guante, Cecilio, Pitt.	4	6	.400	2.72	63	0	0	31	0	5	109.0	84	445	34	33	5	4	3	5	40	9	92	5	0
Gullickson, William, Mtl.	14	12	.538	3.52	29	29	4	0	1	0	181.1	187	759	78	71	8	12	8	1	47	9	68	1	1
Gumpert, David, Chi.	1	0	1.000	3.48	9	0	0	3	0	0	10.1	12	52	7	4	0	0	2	0	7	1	4	0	0
*Gura, Lawrence, Chi.	0	3	.000	8.41	5	4	0	0	0	0	20.1	34	102	19	19	4	3	0	1	6	0	7	0	0
*Hammaker, C. Atlee, S.F.	5	12	.294	3.74	29	29	1	0	1	0	170.2	161	713	81	71	17	8	6	0	47	5	100	4	4
*Hassler, Andrew, St.L.	0	1	.000	1.80	10	0	0	4	0	0	10.0	9	45	5	2	0	0	1	0	4	0	5	0	0
Hawkins, M. Andrew, S.D.	18	8	.692	3.15	33	33	5	0	2	0	228.2	229	953	88	80	18	13	12	4	65	8	69	3	3
Heathcock, R. Jeffery, Hou.	3	1	.750	3.36	14	7	1	5	0	1	56.1	50	226	25	21	9	2	1	1	13	0	25	2	0
Hershiser, Orel, L.A.	19	3	.864	2.03	36	34	9	1	5	0	239.2	179	953	72	54	8	5	4	6	68	5	157	5	0
*Hesketh, Joseph, Mtl.	10	5	.667	2.49	25	25	2	0	1	0	155.1	125	618	52	43	10	8	2	0	45	2	113	3	3
*Holland, Alfred, Phil.-Pitt.	1	4	.200	3.45	41	0	0	22	0	5	62.2	53	256	24	24	5	5	4	0	21	8	48	0	1
Holton, Brian, L.A.	1	1	.500	9.00	3	0	0	0	0	0	4.0	9	21	7	4	0	0	0	0	1	0	1	1	0
*Honeycutt, Frederick, L.A.	8	12	.400	3.42	31	25	1	2	0	1	142.0	141	600	71	54	9	5	4	1	49	7	67	2	0
*Horton, Ricky, St.L.	3	2	.600	2.91	49	3	0	10	0	1	89.2	84	382	30	29	5	8	3	3	34	13	59	3	2
*Howe, Steven, L.A.	1	1	.500	4.91	19	0	0	14	0	3	22.0	30	104	17	12	2	2	2	1	5	2	11	2	0
Howell, Kenneth, L.A.	4	7	.364	3.77	56	0	0	31	0	12	86.0	66	356	41	36	8	4	0	0	35	3	85	4	2
Hoyt, D. LaMarr, S.D.	16	8	.667	3.47	31	31	8	0	3	0	210.1	210	839	85	81	20	9	3	2	20	2	83	0	4
Hudson, Charles, Phil.	8	13	.381	3.78	38	26	3	7	0	0	193.0	188	833	92	81	23	8	4	1	74	7	122	4	3
Hume, Thomas, Cin.	3	5	.375	3.26	56	0	0	15	0	3	80.0	65	331	33	29	7	2	1	3	35	5	50	3	1
Jackson, Roy Lee, S.D.	2	3	.400	2.70	22	2	0	6	0	2	40.0	32	163	13	12	4	4	2	1	13	1	28	0	1
*Jeffcoat, J. Michael, S.F.	0	2	.000	5.32	19	1	0	7	0	0	22.0	27	99	13	13	4	2	1	2	6	3	10	1	0
Johnson, Joseph, Atl.	4	4	.500	4.10	15	14	1	0	0	0	85.2	95	367	44	39	9	4	3	3	24	5	34	2	0
Keough, Matthew, St.L.	0	1	.000	4.50	4	1	0	0	0	0	10.0	10	43	5	5	0	2	0	1	4	1	10	0	0
Kepshire, Kurt, St.L.	10	9	.526	4.75	32	29	0	0	0	0	153.1	155	671	89	81	16	5	7	0	71	3	67	6	2
Kerfeld, Charles, Hou.	4	2	.667	4.06	11	6	0	2	0	0	44.1	44	193	22	20	2	1	3	0	25	2	30	1	0
*Kipper, Robert, Pitt.	1	2	.333	5.11	5	4	0	1	0	0	24.2	21	104	16	14	4	1	1	0	7	0	13	0	0
*Knepper, Robert, Hou.	15	13	.536	3.55	37	37	4	0	0	0	241.0	253	1016	119	95	21	15	9	3	54	5	131	4	0
Knudson, Mark, Hou.	0	2	.000	9.00	2	2	0	0	0	0	11.0	21	53	11	11	0	1	0	0	3	0	4	0	0
*Koosman, Jerome, Phil.	6	4	.600	4.62	19	18	3	0	1	0	99.1	107	433	56	51	14	5	4	3	34	3	60	2	2
Krawczyk, Raymond, Pitt.	0	2	.000	14.04	8	0	0	3	0	0	8.1	20	51	13	13	1	0	0	1	6	3	9	1	0

Pirate Rick Reuschel had fourth-lowest NL ERA (2.27).

Pitcher, Club	W	L	PCT.	ERA	G	GS	CG	GF	SHO	SV	IP	H	TBF	R	ER	HR	SH	SF	HB	BB	IB	SO	WP	BK
Krukow, Michael, S.F.	8	11	.421	3.38	28	28	6	0	1	0	194.2	176	804	80	73	19	10	3	3	49	10	150	10	3
Lahti, Jeffrey, St.L.	5	2	.714	1.84	52	0	0	31	0	19	68.1	63	279	15	14	3	2	0	0	26	10	41	1	0
*LaPoint, David, S.F.	7	17	.292	3.57	31	31	2	0	1	0	206.2	215	886	99	82	18	7	5	0	74	6	122	10	0
Laskey, William, S.F -Mtl.	5	16	.238	4.91	30	26	0	3	0	0	148.1	165	656	91	81	19	13	5	2	53	1	60	3	1
*Latham, William, N.Y.	1	3	.250	3.97	7	3	0	1	0	0	22.2	21	93	10	10	1	1	1	0	7	1	10	1	1
Leach, Terry, N.Y.	3	4	.429	2.91	22	4	1	4	1	1	55.2	48	226	19	18	3	5	2	1	14	3	30	0	0
*Lefferts, Craig, S.D.	7	6	.538	3.35	60	0	0	24	0	2	83.1	75	345	34	31	7	7	1	0	30	4	48	2	0
*Lucas, Gary, Mtl.	6	2	.750	3.19	49	0	0	18	0	1	67.2	63	284	29	24	6	7	2	0	24	8	31	5	0
Lynch, Edward, N.Y.	10	8	.556	3.44	31	29	6	1	1	0	191.0	188	777	76	73	19	9	5	1	27	1	65	0	0
*Madden, Michael, Hou.	0	0	---	4.26	13	0	0	4	0	0	19.0	29	92	15	9	1	0	1	0	11	0	16	1	0
*Mahler, Michael, Mtl.	1	4	.200	3.54	9	7	1	2	1	1	48.1	40	203	22	19	3	2	1	1	24	1	32	3	0
Mahler, Richard, Atl.	17	15	.531	3.48	39	39	6	0	1	0	266.2	272	1110	116	103	24	10	5	2	79	8	107	3	1
Mason, Roger, S.F.	1	3	.250	2.12	5	5	1	0	1	0	29.2	28	128	13	7	1	2	0	0	11	1	26	0	0
Mathis, Ronald, Hou.	3	5	.375	6.04	23	8	0	5	0	1	70.0	83	319	54	47	7	4	4	1	27	1	34	1	0
McCullers, Lance, S.D.	0	2	.000	2.31	21	0	0	11	0	5	35.0	23	142	15	9	3	7	0	1	16	3	27	0	1
McDowell, Roger, N.Y.	6	5	.545	2.83	62	2	0	36	0	17	127.1	108	516	43	40	9	6	2	1	37	8	70	6	2
McGaffigan, Andrew, Cin.	3	3	.500	3.72	15	15	2	0	0	0	94.1	88	392	40	39	4	4	0	2	30	4	83	2	0
McMurtry, J. Craig, Atl.	0	3	.000	6.60	17	6	0	3	0	1	45.0	56	220	36	33	6	7	2	1	27	1	28	3	0
*McWilliams, Larry, Pitt.	7	9	.438	4.70	30	19	2	2	0	0	126.1	139	568	70	66	9	4	3	7	62	11	52	4	0
*Meridith, Ronald, Chi.	3	2	.600	4.47	32	0	0	8	0	1	46.1	53	209	24	23	3	5	3	1	24	6	23	0	0
Minton, Gregory, S.F.	5	4	.556	3.54	68	0	0	36	0	4	96.2	98	424	42	38	6	6	4	0	54	18	37	2	0
Moore, Robert, S.F.	0	0	---	3.24	11	0	0	4	0	0	16.2	18	78	6	6	1	1	0	0	10	2	10	0	1
*Murphy, Robert, Cin.	0	0	---	6.00	2	0	0	2	0	0	3.0	2	12	2	2	1	0	0	0	2	0	1	0	0
*Myers, Randall, N.Y.	0	0	---	0.00	1	0	0	1	0	0	2.0	0	7	0	0	0	0	0	0	1	0	2	0	0
Niedenfuer, Thomas, L.A.	7	9	.438	2.71	64	0	0	43	0	19	106.1	86	415	32	32	6	1	3	1	24	5	102	0	0
Niekro, Joseph, Hou.	9	12	.429	3.72	32	32	4	0	1	0	213.0	197	925	100	88	21	10	12	5	99	6	117	21	1
*Niemann, Randy, N.Y.	0	0	---	0.00	4	0	0	0	0	0	4.2	5	18	0	0	0	0	0	0	0	0	2	0	0
*O'Connor, Jack, Mtl.	0	2	.000	4.94	20	1	0	7	0	0	23.2	21	106	14	13	1	3	2	0	13	7	16	1	1
*Orosco, Jesse, N.Y.	8	6	.571	2.73	54	0	0	39	0	17	79.0	66	331	26	24	6	1	1	0	34	7	68	4	0
Palmer, David, Mtl.	7	10	.412	3.71	24	23	0	0	0	0	135.2	128	588	60	56	5	5	2	3	67	5	106	9	0
Pastore, Frank, Cin.	2	1	.667	3.83	17	6	1	3	0	0	54.0	60	232	23	23	1	3	3	1	16	1	29	2	0
Patterson, Reginald, Chi.	3	0	1.000	3.00	8	5	1	0	0	0	39.0	36	157	13	13	2	2	1	0	10	1	17	1	0
*Patterson, Robert, S.D.	0	0	---	24.75	3	0	0	2	0	0	4.0	13	26	11	11	2	0	0	0	3	0	1	0	1
Pena, Alejandro, L.A.	0	1	.000	8.31	2	1	0	0	0	0	4.1	7	23	5	4	1	0	0	0	3	1	2	0	0
Perez, Pascual, Atl.	1	13	.071	6.14	22	22	0	0	0	0	95.1	115	453	72	65	10	5	3	1	57	10	57	2	2
Perlman, Jonathan, Chi.	1	0	1.000	11.42	6	0	0	1	0	0	8.2	10	42	11	11	3	1	1	0	8	2	4	1	0
*Perry, W. Patrick, St.L.	1	0	1.000	0.00	6	0	0	1	0	0	12.1	3	42	0	0	0	0	0	0	3	1	6	1	0
*Powell, Dennis, L.A.	1	1	.500	5.22	16	2	0	6	0	1	29.1	30	133	19	17	7	4	1	1	13	3	19	3	0
Power, Ted, Cin.	8	6	.571	2.70	64	0	0	50	0	27	80.0	65	342	27	24	2	6	4	1	45	8	42	1	0
*Price, Joseph, Cin.	2	2	.500	3.90	26	8	0	5	0	1	64.2	59	274	35	28	10	2	5	0	23	7	52	2	0

Pitcher, Club	W	L	PCT.	ERA	G	GS	CG	GF	SHO	SV	IP	H	TBF	R	ER	HR	SH	SF	HB	BB	IB	SO	WP	BK
*Rawley, Shane, Phil.	13	8	.619	3.31	36	31	6	1	2	0	198.2	188	849	82	73	16	6	5	2	81	6	106	7	0
Reardon, Jeffrey, Mtl.	2	8	.200	3.18	63	0	0	50	0	41	87.2	68	356	31	31	7	3	1	1	26	4	67	2	0
Reuschel, Ricky, Pitt.	14	8	.636	2.27	31	26	9	4	1	1	194.0	153	773	58	49	7	5	3	3	52	10	138	4	0
*Reuss, Jerry, L.A.	14	10	.583	2.92	34	33	5	0	3	0	212.2	210	883	78	69	13	8	6	3	58	7	84	5	0
Rhoden, Richard, Pitt.	10	15	.400	4.47	35	35	2	0	0	0	213.1	254	944	119	106	18	10	0	6	69	3	128	8	3
Roberge, Bertrand, Mtl.	3	3	.500	3.44	42	0	0	15	0	2	68.0	58	280	28	26	5	6	0	2	22	5	34	1	5
Robinson, Don, Pitt.	5	11	.313	3.87	44	6	0	22	0	3	95.1	95	418	49	41	6	2	0	2	42	11	65	2	0
Robinson, Jeffrey, S.F.	0	0	---	5.11	8	0	0	0	0	0	12.1	16	59	11	7	2	0	1	0	10	1	8	1	0
Robinson, Ronald, Cin.	7	7	.500	3.99	33	12	0	9	0	1	108.1	107	453	53	48	11	3	4	1	32	3	76	3	0
Rogers, Stephen, Mtl.	2	4	.333	5.68	8	7	1	1	0	0	38.0	51	179	25	24	1	2	2	0	20	1	18	0	1
Ross, Mark, Hou.	0	2	.000	4.85	8	0	0	4	0	1	13.0	12	52	7	7	2	0	0	0	2	0	3	2	0
*Rucker, David, Phil.	3	2	.600	4.31	39	3	0	11	0	1	79.1	83	350	42	38	6	4	6	2	40	6	41	2	0
Ruthven, Richard, Chi.	4	7	.364	4.53	20	15	0	3	0	0	87.1	103	392	49	44	6	5	6	0	37	3	26	0	0
Ryan, L. Nolan, Hou.	10	12	.455	3.80	35	35	4	0	0	0	232.0	205	983	108	98	12	11	12	9	95	8	209	14	2
St. Claire, Randy, Mtl.	5	3	.625	3.93	42	0	0	14	0	0	68.2	69	294	32	30	3	6	1	1	26	7	25	1	0
*Sambito, Joseph, N.Y.	0	0	---	12.66	8	0	0	2	0	0	10.2	21	60	18	15	1	1	1	0	8	0	3	0	0
Sanderson, Scott, Chi.	5	6	.455	3.12	19	19	2	0	0	0	121.0	100	480	49	42	13	7	7	0	27	4	80	1	0
*Schatzeder, Daniel, Mtl.	3	5	.375	3.80	24	15	1	2	0	0	104.1	101	431	52	44	13	7	3	0	31	0	64	4	0
Schiraldi, Calvin, N.Y.	2	1	.667	8.89	10	4	0	2	0	0	26.1	43	131	27	26	4	0	0	3	11	0	21	2	1
*Schuler, David, Atl.	0	0	---	6.75	9	0	0	5	0	0	10.2	19	50	8	8	4	0	0	0	3	0	10	0	0
Scott, Michael, Hou.	18	8	.692	3.29	36	35	4	1	2	0	221.2	194	922	91	81	20	6	6	3	80	4	137	7	2
*Scurry, Rodney, Pitt.	0	1	.000	3.21	30	0	0	13	0	2	47.2	42	210	22	17	4	2	2	0	28	1	43	3	0
Shields, Stephen, Atl.	1	2	.333	5.16	23	6	0	3	0	0	68.0	86	311	46	39	9	6	3	1	32	6	29	6	0
Shines, A. Raymond, Mtl.	0	0	---	0.00	1	0	0	1	0	0	1.0	1	4	0	0	0	0	0	0	0	0	0	0	0
Shipanoff, David, Phil.	1	2	.333	3.22	26	0	0	12	0	3	36.1	33	162	15	13	3	0	2	1	16	3	26	0	1
Show, Eric, S.D.	12	11	.522	3.09	35	35	5	0	2	0	233.0	212	977	95	80	27	9	5	5	87	7	141	4	0
Sisk, Douglas, N.Y.	4	5	.444	5.30	42	0	0	22	0	2	73.0	86	341	48	43	3	3	0	2	40	2	26	1	1
Smith, Bryn, Mtl.	18	5	.783	2.91	32	32	4	0	2	0	222.1	193	890	85	72	12	13	4	1	41	3	127	1	1
Smith, David, Hou.	9	5	.643	2.27	64	0	0	46	0	27	79.1	69	315	26	20	3	3	1	1	17	5	40	4	1
Smith, Lee, Chi.	7	4	.636	3.04	65	0	0	57	0	33	97.2	87	397	35	33	9	3	1	1	32	6	112	4	0
Smith, Michael, Cin.	0	0	---	5.40	2	0	0	1	0	0	3.1	2	13	2	2	2	0	0	0	1	0	2	0	0
*Smith, Zane, Atl.	9	10	.474	3.80	42	18	2	3	2	0	147.0	135	631	70	62	4	16	1	3	80	5	85	2	0
Solano, Julio, Hou.	2	2	.500	3.48	20	0	0	9	0	0	33.2	34	144	13	13	5	1	0	0	13	2	17	2	0
Sorensen, Lary, Chi.	3	7	.300	4.26	45	3	0	18	0	0	82.1	86	355	44	39	8	11	2	4	24	10	34	0	2
Soto, Mario, Cin.	12	15	.444	3.58	36	36	9	0	1	0	256.2	196	1055	109	102	30	13	9	2	104	3	214	8	2
Stewart, David, Phil.	0	0	---	6.23	4	0	0	3	0	0	4.1	5	22	4	3	0	0	0	0	4	0	2	2	0
Stoddard, Timothy, S.D.	1	6	.143	4.65	44	0	0	20	0	1	60.0	63	279	35	31	3	6	2	0	37	7	42	5	0
Stuper, John, Cin.	8	5	.615	4.55	33	13	1	11	0	0	99.0	116	432	60	50	8	5	7	0	37	3	38	1	1
Surhoff, Richard, Phil.	1	0	1.000	0.00	2	0	0	0	0	0	1.0	2	4	0	0	0	0	0	0	0	0	1	0	0
Sutcliffe, Richard, Chi.	8	8	.500	3.18	20	20	6	0	3	0	130.0	119	549	51	46	12	3	4	3	44	3	102	6	0

Pitcher, Club	W	L	PCT.	ERA	G	GS	CG	GF	SHO	SV	IP	H	TBF	R	ER	HR	SH	SF	HB	BB	IB	SO	WP	BK
Sutter, H. Bruce, Atl.	7	7	.500	4.48	58	0	0	50	0	23	88.1	91	382	46	44	13	7	2	3	29	4	52	0	0
Tekulve, Kenton, Pitt.-Phil.	4	10	.286	3.57	61	0	0	42	0	14	75.2	74	327	35	30	5	6	2	2	30	10	40	0	0
*Thurmond, Mark, S.D.	7	11	.389	3.97	36	23	1	4	1	2	138.1	154	592	70	61	9	12	4	3	44	5	57	0	0
Tibbs, Jay, Cin.	10	16	.385	3.92	35	34	5	0	2	0	218.0	216	928	111	95	14	11	8	0	83	10	98	12	1
Toliver, Freddie, Phil.	0	4	.000	4.68	11	3	0	4	0	1	25.0	27	117	15	13	2	0	1	0	17	1	23	0	0
*Tomlin, David, Pitt.	0	0	---	0.00	1	0	0	0	0	0	1.0	1	4	0	0	0	0	0	0	1	0	0	1	0
*Trout, Steven, Chi.	9	7	.563	3.39	24	24	3	0	1	0	140.2	142	601	57	53	8	7	5	1	63	7	44	2	1
*Tudor, John, St.L.	21	8	.724	1.93	36	36	14	0	10	0	275.0	209	1062	68	59	14	4	3	5	49	4	169	4	0
Tunnell, B. Lee, Pitt.	4	10	.286	4.01	24	23	0	1	0	0	132.1	126	565	70	59	11	3	2	1	57	4	74	3	0
*Valenzuela, Fernando, L.A.	17	10	.630	2.45	35	35	14	0	5	0	272.1	211	1109	92	74	14	13	8	1	101	5	208	10	1
Walk, Robert, Pitt.	2	3	.400	3.68	9	9	1	0	1	0	58.2	60	248	27	24	3	3	1	0	18	2	40	2	3
*Walter, Gene, S.D.	0	2	.000	2.05	15	0	0	7	0	3	22.0	12	86	6	5	0	1	1	0	8	1	18	0	0
*Ward, Colin, S.F.	0	0	---	4.38	6	2	0	0	0	0	12.1	10	52	6	6	0	1	1	0	7	0	8	0	0
Welch, Robert L.A.	14	4	.778	2.31	23	23	8	0	3	0	167.1	141	675	49	43	16	6	2	6	35	2	96	7	4
Williams, Frank, S.F.	2	4	.333	4.19	49	0	0	15	0	0	73.0	65	318	39	34	5	4	4	6	35	7	54	3	1
Willis, Carl, Cin.	1	0	1.000	9.22	11	0	0	6	0	1	13.2	21	69	18	14	3	1	2	0	5	0	6	1	0
Winn, James, Pitt.	3	6	.333	5.23	30	7	0	10	0	0	75.2	77	326	45	44	4	2	1	2	31	2	22	5	2
Wojna, Edward, S.D.	2	4	.333	5.79	15	7	0	1	0	0	42.0	53	198	35	27	6	3	3	3	19	0	18	1	2
Worrell, Todd, St.L.	3	0	1.000	2.91	17	0	0	11	0	5	21.2	17	88	7	7	2	0	2	0	7	2	17	2	0
Youmans, Floyd, Mtl.	4	3	.571	2.45	14	12	0	2	0	0	77.0	57	331	27	21	3	2	2	1	49	1	54	5	0
Zachry, Patrick, Phil.	0	0	---	4.26	10	0	0	1	0	0	12.2	14	61	7	6	1	0	0	0	11	1	8	1	0

CLUB PITCHING

Club	W	L	ERA	G	CG	SHO	SV	IP	H	TBF	R	ER	HR	SH	SF	HB	BB	IB	SO	WP	BK
Los Angeles	95	67	2.96	162	37	21	36	1465.0	1280	6043	579	482	102	57	38	21	462	56	979	42	10
St. Louis	101	61	3.10	162	37	20	44	1464.0	1343	6048	572	505	98	60	39	28	453	80	798	33	6
New York	98	64	3.11	162	32	19	37	1488.0	1306	6146	568	514	111	66	27	18	515	36	1039	41	14
San Diego	83	79	3.40	162	26	19	44	1451.1	1399	6049	622	549	127	91	43	25	443	50	727	23	14
Montreal	84	77	3.55	161	13	13	53	1457.0	1346	6109	636	574	99	87	35	21	509	70	870	46	12
San Francisco	62	100	3.61	162	13	5	24	1448.0	1348	6168	674	581	125	88	40	19	572	76	985	57	16
Houston	83	79	3.66	162	17	9	42	1458.0	1393	6185	691	593	119	72	58	25	543	50	909	69	8
Philadelphia	75	87	3.68	162	24	9	30	1447.0	1424	6241	673	592	115	66	47	26	596	63	899	34	9
Cincinnati	89	72	3.71	162	24	11	45	1451.1	1347	6100	666	598	131	74	51	14	535	61	910	42	5
Pittsburgh	57	104	3.97	161	15	6	29	1445.1	1406	6205	708	638	107	57	28	32	584	72	962	48	11
Chicago	77	84	4.16	162	20	8	42	1442.1	1492	6195	729	666	156	95	45	23	519	83	820	31	11
Atlanta	66	96	4.19	162	9	9	29	1457.1	1512	6374	781	679	134	88	35	28	642	83	776	35	4
Totals	970	970	3.59	971	267	149	455	17474.2	16596	73863	7899	6971	1424	901	486	280	6373	780	10674	501	120

OFFICIAL 1985 AMERICAN LEAGUE RECORDS

compiled by

SPORTS INFORMATION CENTER

FINAL STANDINGS OF CLUBS AT CLOSE OF 1985 SEASON

American League West

	Won	Lost	Pct.	Games Behind
Kansas City	91	71	.562	
California	90	72	.556	1
Chicago	85	77	.525	6
Minnesota	77	85	.475	14
Oakland	77	85	.475	14
Seattle	74	88	.457	17
Texas	62	99	.385	28½

American League East

	Won	Lost	Pct.	Games Behind
Toronto	99	62	.615	
New York	97	64	.602	2
Detroit	84	77	.522	15
Baltimore	83	78	.516	16
Boston	81	81	.500	18½
Milwaukee	71	90	.441	28
Cleveland	60	102	.370	39½

Championship Series: Kansas City defeated Toronto, 4 games to 3

BATTING

TOP FIFTEEN QUALIFIERS FOR BATTING CHAMPIONSHIP
(502 OR MORE PLATE APPEARANCES)

* BATS LEFTHANDED †SWITCH HITTER

BATTER AND CLUB	AVG	G	AB	R	H	TB	2B	3B	HR	RBI	GW RBI	SH	SF	HB	BB	IBB	SO	SB	CS	GI DP	SLG	OBP
BOGGS, WADE, BOS.*	.368	161	653	107	240	312	42	3	8	78	5	3	2	4	96	5	61	2	1	20	.478	.450
BRETT, GEORGE, K.C.*	.335	155	550	108	184	322	38	5	30	112	16	0	9	3	103	31	49	9	1	12	.585	.436
MATTINGLY, DON, N.Y.*	.324	159	652	107	211	370	48	3	35	145	21	2	15	2	56	13	41	2	2	15	.567	.371
HENDERSON, RICKEY, N.Y.	.314	143	547	146	172	282	28	5	24	72	6	0	5	3	99	1	65	80	10	8	.516	.419
BUTLER, BRETT, CLEV.*	.311	152	591	106	184	255	28	14	5	50	6	8	3	1	63	2	42	47	20	8	.431	.377
BAINES, HAROLD, CHI.*	.309	160	640	86	198	299	29	3	22	113	13	0	10	1	42	8	89	1	1	23	.467	.348
BRADLEY, PHIL, SEA	.300	159	641	100	192	319	33	8	26	88	12	4	2	12	55	4	129	22	9	14	.498	.365
BUCKNER, BILL, BOS.*	.299	162	673	89	201	301	46	3	16	110	11	2	11	2	30	5	36	18	4	16	.447	.325
MOLITOR, PAUL, MILW	.297	140	576	93	171	235	28	3	10	48	2	7	4	1	54	6	80	21	7	12	.408	.356
MURRAY, EDDIE, BALT.†	.297	156	583	111	173	305	37	1	31	124	15	0	8	2	84	12	68	5	2	8	.523	.383
GEDMAN, RICH, BOS.*	.295	144	498	66	147	241	30	5	18	80	10	3	2	3	50	11	79	2	0	12	.484	.362
COOPER, CECIL, MILW.*	.293	154	631	82	185	288	39	8	16	99	10	1	10	2	30	3	77	10	3	24	.456	.322
LACY, LEE, BALT	.293	121	492	69	144	201	22	4	9	48	5	1	6	2	39	0	95	10	3	10	.409	.343
RICE, JIM, BOS	.291	140	546	85	159	266	20	3	27	103	9	0	9	2	51	5	75	2	0	35	.487	.349
BARFIELD, JESSE, TOR	.289	155	539	94	156	289	34	9	27	84	12	0	3	4	66	5	143	22	8	14	.536	.369

INDIVIDUAL BATTING
(ALL PLAYERS LISTED ALPHABETICALLY)

* BATS LEFTHANDED †SWITCH HITTER

BATTER AND CLUB	AVG	G	AB	R	H	TB	2B	3B	HR	RBI	GW RBI	SH	SF	HB	BB	IBB	SO	SB	CS	GI DP	SLG	OBP
AIKENS, WILLIE, TOR.*	.200	12	20	2	4	8	1	0	1	5	1	0	1	0	3	0	6	0	0	1	.400	.292
ALLENSON, GARY, TOR	.118	14	34	2	4	5	1	0	0	3	0	0	0	0	0	0	10	0	0	1	.147	.118
ARMAS, TONY, BOS	.265	103	385	50	102	198	17	5	23	64	10	0	5	2	18	4	90	0	0	14	.514	.298
AYALA, BENNY, CLEV	.250	46	76	10	19	32	7	0	2	15	2	0	1	0	4	1	17	0	0	2	.421	.284
BAINES, HAROLD, CHI.*	.309	160	640	86	198	299	29	3	22	113	13	0	10	1	42	8	89	1	1	23	.467	.348
BAKER, DOUG, DET.†	.185	15	27	4	5	6	1	0	0	1	0	0	0	0	0	0	9	0	0	0	.222	.185

* BATS LEFTHANDED †SWITCH HITTER

BATTER AND CLUB	AVG	G	AB	R	H	TB	2B	3B	HR	RBI	GW RBI	SH	SF	HB	BB	IBB	SO	SB	CS	GI DP	SLG	OBP
BAKER, DUSTY, OAK	.268	111	343	48	92	151	15	1	14	52	4	0	3	0	50	0	47	2	1	12	.440	.359
BALBONI, STEVE, K.C	.243	160	600	74	146	286	28	2	36	88	9	0	5	5	52	4	166	1	1	14	.477	.307
BANDO, CHRIS, CLEV.†	.139	73	173	11	24	30	4	1	0	13	1	2	2	0	22	0	21	0	1	6	.173	.234
BANNISTER, ALAN, TEX	.262	57	122	17	32	41	4	1	1	6	0	1	0	0	14	0	17	8	2	1	.336	.338
BARFIELD, JESSE, TOR	.289	155	539	94	156	289	34	9	27	84	12	0	3	4	66	5	143	22	8	14	.536	.369
BARRETT, MARTY, BOS	.266	156	534	59	142	183	26	0	5	56	3	12	4	2	56	3	50	7	5	14	.343	.336
BAYLOR, DON, N.Y	.231	142	477	70	110	205	24	1	23	91	10	1	10	24	52	6	90	0	4	10	.430	.330
BELL, BUDDY, TEX	.236	84	313	33	74	105	13	3	4	32	3	0	4	1	33	1	21	3	2	14	.335	.308
BELL, GEORGE, TOR	.275	157	607	87	167	291	28	6	28	95	11	0	8	8	43	6	90	21	6	8	.479	.327
BENIQUEZ, JUAN, CAL	.304	132	411	54	125	172	13	5	8	42	5	9	1	5	34	3	47	4	3	16	.418	.364
BENTON, BUTCH, CLEV	.179	31	67	5	12	16	4	0	0	7	0	1	2	0	3	2	9	0	0	1	.239	.208
BERGMAN, DAVE, DET.*	.179	69	140	8	25	36	2	0	3	7	2	1	2	0	14	0	15	0	0	6	.257	.250
BERNAZARD, TONY, CLEV.†	.274	153	500	73	137	202	26	3	11	59	5	5	4	1	69	2	72	17	9	11	.404	.361
BERRA, DALE, N.Y	.229	48	109	8	25	35	5	1	1	8	1	2	0	0	7	0	20	1	1	2	.321	.276
BIANCALANA, BUDDY, K.C.†	.188	81	138	21	26	36	5	1	1	6	1	5	0	0	17	0	34	1	4	1	.261	.277
BOCHTE, BRUCE, OAK.*	.295	137	424	48	125	186	17	1	14	60	6	0	1	0	49	6	58	3	1	14	.439	.367
BODDICKER, MIKE, BALT	—	34	0	1	0	0	0	0	0	0	0	0	0	0	0	0	0	0	0	0	—	—
BOGGS, WADE, BOS.*	.368	161	653	107	240	312	42	3	8	78	5	3	2	4	96	5	61	2	1	20	.478	.450
BONILLA, JUAN, N.Y	.125	8	16	0	2	3	1	0	0	2	0	0	0	0	0	0	3	0	0	0	.188	.125
BONNELL, BARRY, SEA	.243	48	111	9	27	38	8	0	1	10	1	0	0	0	6	1	19	1	2	1	.342	.282
BOONE, BOB, CAL	.248	150	460	37	114	146	17	0	5	55	7	16	4	3	37	2	35	1	2	12	.317	.306
BOSTON, DARYL, CHI.*	.228	95	232	20	53	77	13	1	3	15	2	1	1	0	14	1	44	8	6	3	.332	.271
BRADLEY, PHIL, SEA	.300	159	641	100	192	319	33	8	26	88	12	4	2	12	55	4	129	22	9	14	.498	.365
BRADLEY, SCOTT, N.Y.*	.163	19	49	4	8	12	2	1	0	1	0	0	0	1	1	0	5	0	0	2	.245	.196
BRETT, GEORGE, K.C.*	.335	155	550	108	184	322	38	5	30	112	16	0	9	3	103	31	49	9	1	12	.585	.436
BROOKENS, TOM, DET	.237	156	485	54	115	182	34	6	7	47	5	9	1	0	27	0	78	14	5	8	.375	.277
BROUHARD, MARK, MILW	.259	37	108	11	28	42	7	2	1	13	1	1	0	1	5	1	26	0	0	2	.389	.298
BROWN, MIKE, CAL	.268	60	153	23	41	64	9	1	4	20	4	3	0	1	7	0	21	0	1	9	.418	.304
BRUMMER, GLENN, TEX	.278	49	108	7	30	34	4	0	0	5	0	0	0	2	11	1	22	1	5	2	.315	.355
BRUNANSKY, TOM, MINN	.242	157	567	71	137	254	28	4	27	90	10	0	13	0	71	7	86	5	3	12	.448	.320

Yanks' Rickey Henderson led AL in stolen bases (80).

* BATS LEFTHANDED †SWITCH HITTER

BATTER AND CLUB	AVG	G	AB	R	H	TB	2B	3B	HR	RBI	GW RBI	SH	SF	HB	BB	IBB	SO	SB	CS	GI DP	SLG	OBP
BUCKNER, BILL, BOS.*	.299	162	673	89	201	301	46	3	16	110	11	2	11	2	30	5	36	18	4	16	.447	.325
BUECHELE, STEVE, TEX.	.219	69	219	22	48	78	6	3	6	21	0	0	1	2	14	2	38	3	2	11	.356	.271
BURROUGHS, JEFF, TOR	.257	86	191	19	49	82	9	3	6	28	2	0	2	0	34	1	36	0	1	7	.429	.366
BUSH, RANDY, MINN.*	.239	97	234	26	56	105	13	3	10	35	4	0	2	5	24	1	30	3	0	3	.449	.321
BUTLER, BRETT, CLEV.*	.311	152	591	106	184	255	28	14	5	50	6	8	3	1	63	2	42	47	20	8	.431	.377
CALDERON, IVAN, SEA	.286	67	210	37	60	108	16	4	8	28	2	1	1	2	19	1	45	4	2	10	.514	.349
CANGELOSI, JOHN, CHI.†	.000	5	2	2	0	0	0	0	0	0	0	1	0	1	0	0	1	0	0	0	.000	.333
CANSECO, JOSE, OAK	.302	29	96	16	29	47	3	0	5	13	0	0	0	0	4	0	31	1	1	1	.490	.330
CAPRA, NICK, TEX	.125	8	8	1	1	1	0	0	0	0	0	0	0	0	0	0	0	0	0	0	.125	.125
CAREW, ROD, CAL.*	.280	127	443	69	124	153	17	3	2	39	4	9	1	1	64	9	47	5	5	8	.345	.371
CARTER, JOE, CLEV	.262	143	489	64	128	200	27	0	15	59	7	3	4	2	25	2	74	24	6	9	.409	.298
CASTILLO, CARMEN, CLEV	.245	67	184	27	45	85	5	1	11	25	1	0	0	3	11	0	40	3	0	6	.462	.298
CASTILLO, MARTY, DET	.119	57	84	4	10	18	2	0	2	5	0	0	1	0	2	0	19	0	2	1	.214	.138
CHAMBERS, AL, SEA.*	.000	4	4	0	0	0	0	0	0	0	0	0	0	0	0	0	2	0	0	0	.000	.000
CLARK, BOBBY, MILW	.226	29	93	6	21	24	3	0	0	8	1	0	1	0	7	0	19	1	1	3	.258	.277
COLES, DARNELL, SEA	.237	27	59	8	14	21	4	0	1	5	1	0	2	1	9	0	17	0	1	0	.356	.338
COLLINS, DAVE, OAK.†	.251	112	379	52	95	131	16	4	4	29	6	5	4	1	29	2	37	29	8	6	.346	.303
CONCEPCION, ONIX, K.C	.204	131	314	32	64	77	5	1	2	20	2	12	1	6	16	0	29	4	4	8	.245	.255
CONNALLY, FRITZ, BALT	.232	50	112	16	26	39	4	0	3	15	0	2	1	1	19	0	21	0	0	1	.348	.346
COOPER, CEÇIL, MILW.*	.293	154	631	82	185	288	39	8	16	99	10	1	10	2	30	3	77	10	3	24	.456	.322
COTTO, HENRY, N.Y	.304	34	56	4	17	21	1	0	1	6	0	1	0	0	3	0	12	1	1	1	.375	.339
COWENS, AL, SEA	.265	122	452	59	120	204	32	5	14	69	5	0	4	1	30	3	56	0	0	23	.451	.310
CRUZ, JULIO, CHI.†	.197	91	234	28	46	54	2	3	0	15	3	1	1	2	32	0	40	8	5	6	.231	.297
DAUER, RICH, BALT	.202	85	208	25	42	55	7	0	2	14	2	5	0	1	20	0	7	0	1	9	.264	.275
DAVIS, ALVIN, SEA.*	.287	155	578	78	166	255	33	1	18	78	7	0	7	2	90	7	71	1	2	14	.441	.381
DAVIS, MIKE, OAK.*	.287	154	547	92	157	265	34	1	24	82	8	3	2	2	50	8	99	24	10	10	.484	.348
DE SA, JOE, CHI.*	.182	28	44	5	8	16	2	0	2	7	0	1	0	0	3	1	6	0	0	0	.364	.234
DECINCES, DOUG, CAL	.244	120	427	50	104	188	22	1	20	78	9	5	7	2	47	11	71	1	4	18	.440	.317
DEMPSEY, RICK, BALT	.254	132	362	54	92	147	19	0	12	52	4	5	2	1	50	0	87	0	1	2	.406	.345
DIXON, KEN, BALT	—	37	0	0	0	0	0	0	0	0	0	0	0	0	0	0	0	0	0	0	—	—

DOWNING, BRIAN, CAL	.263	150	520	80	137	222	23	1	20	85	12	5	4	13	78	3	60	5	3	12	.427	.371
DUNBAR, TOMMY, TEX.*	.202	45	104	7	21	28	4	0	1	5	0	0	0	1	12	3	9	0	3	5	.269	.291
DWYER, JIM, BALT.*	.249	101	233	35	58	93	8	3	7	36	3	2	1	1	37	2	31	0	3	5	.399	.353
EASLER, MIKE, BOS.*	.262	155	568	71	149	234	29	4	16	74	7	0	7	3	53	1	129	0	1	15	.412	.325
ENGLE, DAVE, MINN	.256	70	172	28	44	77	8	2	7	25	3	0	2	0	21	1	28	2	2	3	.448	.333
ESPINO, JUAN, N.Y	.364	9	11	0	4	4	0	0	0	0	0	0	0	0	0	0	0	0	0	0	.364	.364
ESPINOZA, ALVARO, MINN	.263	32	57	5	15	17	2	0	0	9	0	3	0	1	1	0	9	0	1	2	.298	.288
EVANS, DARRELL, DET.*	.248	151	505	81	125	262	17	0	40	94	10	1	2	1	85	12	85	0	4	5	.519	.356
EVANS, DWIGHT, BOS	.263	159	617	110	162	280	29	1	29	78	13	1	7	5	114	4	105	7	2	16	.454	.378
FELDER, MIKE, MILW.†	.196	15	56	8	11	12	1	0	0	0	0	1	0	0	5	0	6	4	1	2	.214	.262
FERNANDEZ, TONY, TOR.†	.289	161	564	71	163	220	31	10	2	51	6	7	2	2	43	2	41	13	6	12	.390	.340
FIELDER, CECIL, TOR	.311	30	74	6	23	39	4	0	4	16	4	0	1	0	6	0	16	0	0	2	.527	.358
FISCHLIN, MIKE, CLEV	.200	73	60	12	12	18	4	1	0	2	0	4	0	0	5	0	7	0	1	0	.300	.262
FISK, CARLTON, CHI	.238	153	543	85	129	265	23	1	37	107	13	2	6	17	52	12	81	17	9	9	.488	.320
FLETCHER, SCOTT, CHI	.256	119	301	38	77	93	8	1	2	31	1	11	1	0	35	0	47	5	5	9	.309	.332
FLYNN, DOUG, DET	.255	32	51	2	13	17	2	1	0	2	0	3	1	0	0	0	3	0	0	1	.333	.250
FORD, DAN, BALT	.187	28	75	4	14	19	2	0	1	1	0	0	0	0	7	0	17	0	1	3	.253	.256
FRANCO, JULIO, CLEV	.288	160	636	97	183	242	33	4	6	90	9	0	9	4	54	2	74	13	9	26	.381	.343
FUNDERBURK, MARK, MINN	.314	23	70	7	22	37	7	1	2	13	1	0	2	0	5	0	12	0	1	4	.529	.351
GAETTI, GARY, MINN	.246	160	560	71	138	229	31	0	20	63	8	3	1	7	37	3	89	13	5	15	.409	.301
GAGNE, GREG, MINN	.225	114	293	37	66	93	15	3	2	23	4	3	3	3	20	0	57	10	4	5	.317	.279
GALLEGO, MIKE, OAK	.208	76	77	13	16	26	5	1	1	9	1	2	1	1	12	0	14	1	1	2	.338	.319
GAMBLE, OSCAR, CHI.*	.203	70	148	20	30	47	5	0	4	20	1	0	1	1	34	3	22	0	0	1	.318	.353
GANTNER, JIM, MILW.*	.254	143	523	63	133	171	15	4	5	44	5	10	4	3	33	7	42	11	8	13	.327	.300
GARBEY, BARBARO, DET	.257	86	237	27	61	90	9	1	6	29	3	0	4	3	15	1	37	3	2	7	.380	.305
GARCIA, DAMASO, TOR	.282	146	600	70	169	226	25	4	8	65	10	5	3	4	15	2	41	28	15	13	.377	.302
GEDMAN, RICH, BOS.*	.295	144	498	66	147	241	30	5	18	80	10	3	2	3	50	11	79	2	0	12	.484	.362
GERBER, CRAIG, CAL.*	.264	65	91	8	24	29	1	2	0	6	0	3	1	0	2	0	3	0	3	2	.319	.277
GIBSON, KIRK, DET.*	.287	154	581	96	167	301	37	5	29	97	8	3	10	5	71	16	137	30	4	5	.518	.364
GILBERT, MARK, CHI †	.273	7	22	3	6	7	1	0	0	3	0	0	0	0	4	0	5	0	0	1	.318	.385
GILES, BRIAN, MILW	.172	34	58	6	10	14	1	0	1	1	0	0	0	0	7	0	16	2	1	1	.241	.262
GREENWELL, MIKE, BOS.*	.323	17	31	7	10	23	1	0	4	8	2	0	0	0	3	1	4	1	0	0	.742	.382
GRICH, BOBBY, CAL	.242	144	479	74	116	178	17	3	13	53	5	8	0	3	81	3	77	3	5	18	.372	.355

* BATS LEFTHANDED †SWITCH HITTER

BATTER AND CLUB	AVG	G	AB	R	H	TB	2B	3B	HR	RBI	GW RBI	SH	SF	HB	BB	IBB	SO	SB	CS	GI DP	SLG	OBP
GRIFFEY, KEN, N.Y.*	.274	127	438	68	120	186	28	4	10	69	6	0	8	0	41	4	51	7	7	2	.425	.331
GRIFFIN, ALFREDO, OAK.†	.270	162	614	75	166	204	18	7	2	64	8	5	7	0	20	1	50	24	9	6	.332	.290
GROSS, WAYNE, BALT.*	.235	103	217	31	51	92	8	0	11	18	1	1	0	0	46	0	48	1	1	3	.424	.369
GRUBB, JOHN, DET.*	.245	78	155	19	38	62	7	1	5	25	2	0	4	1	24	0	25	0	1	5	.400	.342
GRUBER, KELLY, TOR	.231	5	13	0	3	3	0	0	0	1	1	0	0	0	0	0	3	0	0	0	.231	.231
GUILLEN, OZZIE, CHI.*	.273	150	491	71	134	176	21	9	1	33	3	8	1	1	12	1	36	7	4	5	.358	.291
GUTIERREZ, JACKIE, BOS	.218	103	275	33	60	75	5	2	2	21	2	9	1	0	12	0	37	10	2	9	.273	.250
HAIRSTON, JERRY, CHI.†	.243	95	140	9	34	48	8	0	2	20	2	0	4	2	29	3	18	0	0	3	.343	.371
HALL, MEL, CLEV.*	.318	23	66	7	21	27	6	0	0	12	0	0	1	0	8	0	12	0	1	2	.409	.387
HARGROVE, MIKE, CLEV.*	.285	107	284	31	81	100	14	1	1	27	0	2	1	0	39	2	29	1	0	8	.352	.370
HARRAH, TOBY, TEX	.270	126	396	65	107	154	18	1	9	44	6	2	6	4	113	2	60	11	4	4	.389	.432
HASSEY, RON, N.Y.*	.296	92	267	31	79	136	16	1	13	42	6	0	0	3	28	4	21	0	0	7	.509	.369
HATCHER, MICKEY, MINN	.282	116	444	46	125	162	28	0	3	49	5	3	2	2	16	1	23	0	0	15	.365	.308
HEARRON, JEFF, TOR	.143	4	7	0	1	1	0	0	0	0	0	0	0	0	0	0	2	0	0	0	.143	.143
HEATH, MIKE, OAK	.250	138	436	71	109	178	18	6	13	55	5	10	4	1	41	0	63	7	7	13	.408	.313
HEGMAN, BOB, K.C.	—	1	0	0	0	0	0	0	0	0	0	0	0	0	0	0	0	0	0	0	—	—
HENDERSON, DAVE, SEA	.241	139	502	70	121	195	28	2	14	68	7	1	2	3	48	2	104	6	1	11	.388	.310
HENDERSON, RICKEY, N.Y	.314	143	547	146	172	282	28	5	24	72	6	0	5	3	99	1	65	80	10	8	.516	.419
HENDERSON, STEVE, OAK	.301	85	193	25	58	81	8	3	3	31	4	1	1	0	18	0	34	0	0	10	.420	.358
HENDRICK, GEORGE, CAL	.122	16	41	5	5	12	1	0	2	6	0	0	1	0	4	1	8	0	0	4	.293	.196
HERNANDEZ, LEO, BALT	.048	12	21	0	1	1	0	0	0	0	0	0	0	0	0	0	4	0	0	2	.048	.048
HERNANDEZ, WILLIE, DET.*	.000	74	1	0	0	0	0	0	0	0	0	0	0	0	0	0	0	0	0	0	.000	.000
HERNDON, LARRY, DET	.244	137	442	45	108	170	12	7	12	37	5	1	1	1	33	1	79	2	1	9	.385	.298
HILL, DONNIE, OAK.†	.285	123	393	45	112	138	13	2	3	48	2	16	4	0	23	2	33	8	4	8	.351	.321
HILL, MARC, CHI	.133	40	75	5	10	12	2	0	0	4	1	8	0	0	12	0	9	0	0	2	.160	.253
HOFFMAN, GLENN, BOS	.276	96	279	40	77	116	17	2	6	34	3	9	3	5	25	0	40	2	2	6	.416	.343
HOUSEHOLDER, PAUL, MILW.†	.258	95	299	41	77	125	15	0	11	34	0	1	1	1	27	0	60	1	2	5	.418	.320
HOWELL, JACK, CAL.*	.197	43	137	19	27	46	4	0	5	18	2	4	1	0	16	2	33	1	1	1	.336	.279
HRBEK, KENT, MINN.*	.278	158	593	78	165	263	31	2	21	93	9	0	4	2	67	12	87	1	1	12	.444	.351
HUDLER, REX, N.Y	.157	20	51	4	8	10	0	1	0	1	0	5	0	0	1	0	9	0	1	0	.196	.173

Detroit's Darrell Evans topped majors in HRs with 40.

* BATS LEFTHANDED †SWITCH HITTER

BATTER AND CLUB	AVG	G	AB	R	H	TB	2B	3B	HR	RBI	GW RBI	SH	SF	HB	BB	IBB	SO	SB	CS	GI DP	SLG	OBP
HULETT, TIM, CHI	.268	141	395	52	106	148	19	4	5	37	2	4	3	4	30	1	81	6	4	8	.375	.324
HUPPERT, DAVE, MILW	.048	15	21	1	1	1	0	0	0	0	0	2	0	0	2	0	7	0	0	1	.048	.130
IORG, DANE, K.C.*	.223	64	130	7	29	43	9	1	1	21	4	0	0	0	8	2	16	0	1	6	.331	.268
IORG, GARTH, TOR	.313	131	288	33	90	135	22	1	7	37	0	2	1	0	21	3	26	2	6	6	.469	.358
JACKSON, REGGIE, CAL.*	.252	143	460	64	116	224	27	0	27	85	11	0	2	1	78	12	138	1	2	16	.487	.360
JACOBY, BROOK, CLEV	.274	161	606	72	166	258	26	3	20	87	4	1	7	0	48	3	120	2	3	17	.426	.324
JAMES, DION, MILW.*	.224	18	49	5	11	12	1	0	0	3	0	0	0	0	6	0	6	0	0	0	.245	.309
JOHNSON, CLIFF, TEX.-TOR	.260	106	369	35	96	154	17	1	13	66	2	1	4	3	40	2	59	0	0	4	.417	.334
JONES, BOBBY, TEX.*	.224	83	134	14	30	47	2	0	5	23	1	0	2	1	11	1	30	1	0	1	.351	.284
JONES, LYNN, K.C.	.211	110	152	12	32	39	7	0	0	9	1	4	2	3	8	0	15	0	1	6	.257	.261
JONES, RUPPERT, CAL.*	.231	125	389	66	90	174	17	2	21	67	9	8	2	0	57	2	82	7	4	5	.447	.328
JURAK, ED, BOS	.231	26	13	4	3	3	0	0	0	0	0	0	0	0	1	0	3	0	0	1	.231	.286
KEARNEY, BOB, SEA	.243	108	305	24	74	108	14	1	6	27	4	5	1	4	11	1	59	1	1	7	.354	.277
KEEDY, PAT, CAL	.500	3	4	1	2	6	1	0	1	1	0	0	0	0	0	0	0	0	1	0	1.500	.500
KEY, JIMMY, TOR	—	36	0	0	0	0	0	0	0	0	0	0	0	0	0	0	0	0	0	0	—	—
KIEFER, STEVE, OAK	.197	40	66	8	13	19	1	1	1	10	1	2	2	0	1	0	18	0	0	1	.288	.203
KINGMAN, DAVE, OAK	.238	158	592	66	141	247	16	0	30	91	9	2	8	2	62	6	114	3	2	17	.417	.309
KITTLE, RON, CHI	.230	116	379	51	87	177	12	0	26	58	8	0	2	5	31	1	92	1	4	12	.467	.295
KUNKEL, JEFF, TEX	.250	2	4	1	1	1	0	0	0	0	0	0	0	0	0	0	3	0	0	0	.250	.250
KUNTZ, RUSTY, DET	.000	5	5	0	0	0	0	0	0	0	0	0	0	0	2	0	2	0	1	0	.000	.286
LACY, LEE, BALT.	.293	121	492	69	144	201	22	4	9	48	5	1	6	2	39	0	95	10	3	10	.409	.343
LAGA, MIKE, DET.*	.167	9	36	3	6	13	1	0	2	6	0	0	0	0	0	0	9	0	0	1	.361	.167
LANSFORD, CARNEY, OAK	.277	98	401	51	111	172	18	2	13	46	7	4	5	4	18	1	27	2	3	6	.429	.311
LAUDNER, TIM, MINN	.238	72	164	16	39	65	5	0	7	19	2	4	1	1	12	0	45	0	1	2	.396	.292
LAW, RUDY, CHI.*	.259	125	390	62	101	146	21	6	4	36	3	6	1	3	27	0	40	29	6	4	.374	.311
LEACH, RICK, TOR.*	.200	16	35	2	7	9	0	1	0	1	0	0	0	0	3	1	9	0	0	0	.257	.263
LEE, MANNY, TOR.†	.200	64	40	9	8	8	0	0	0	0	0	1	0	0	2	0	9	1	4	2	.200	.238
LEEPER, DAVE, K.C.*	.088	15	34	1	3	3	0	0	0	4	2	0	0	0	1	0	3	0	0	0	.088	.114
LEMASTER, JOHNNIE, CLEV	.150	11	20	0	3	3	0	0	0	2	0	1	0	0	0	0	6	0	1	0	.150	.150
LEMON, CHET, DET	.265	145	517	69	137	227	28	4	18	68	9	0	3	10	45	3	93	0	2	5	.439	.334

LINARES, RUFINO, CAL	.256	18	43	7	11	22	2	0	3	11	3	0	1	0	2	0	5	2	0	1	.512	.283
LITTLE, BRYAN, CHI.†	.250	73	188	35	47	64	9	1	2	27	4	3	3	3	26	0	21	0	1	4	.340	.345
LOLLAR, TIM, CHI.-BOS.*	.000	35	1	0	0	0	0	0	0	0	0	0	0	0	0	0	0	0	0	0	.000	.000
LOMAN, DOUG, MILW*	.212	24	66	10	14	21	3	2	0	7	0	2	1	0	1	0	12	0	0	0	.318	.221
LOMBARDOZZI, STEVE, MINN.	.370	28	54	10	20	26	4	1	0	6	0	4	1	0	6	0	6	3	2	0	.481	.426
LOWENSTEIN, JOHN, BALT.*	.077	12	26	0	2	2	0	0	0	2	1	0	1	0	2	0	3	0	0	0	.077	.138
LYNN FRED, BALT.*	.263	124	448	59	118	201	12	1	23	68	8	0	6	1	53	6	100	7	3	7	.449	.339
LYONS, STEVE, BOS.*	.264	133	371	52	98	133	14	3	5	30	3	2	3	1	32	0	64	12	9	2	.358	.322
MADISON, SCOTTI, DET.†	.000	6	11	0	0	0	0	0	0	1	0	0	1	0	2	0	0	0	0	0	.000	.143
MANNING, RICK, MILW.*	.218	79	216	19	47	64	9	1	2	18	3	1	0	0	14	0	19	1	0	2	.296	.265
MARTINEZ, BUCK, TOR	.162	42	99	11	16	31	3	0	4	14	3	0	3	1	10	0	12	0	0	3	.313	.239
MATA, VIC, N.Y	.143	6	7	1	1	1	0	0	0	0	0	0	0	0	0	0	0	0	0	0	.143	.143
MATTINGLY, DON, N.Y.*	.324	159	652	107	211	370	48	3	35	145	21	2	15	2	56	13	41	2	2	15	.567	.371
MATUSZEK, LEONARD, TOR.*	.212	62	151	23	32	48	6	2	2	15	0	0	4	0	11	0	24	2	1	5	.318	.259
MCDOWELL, ODDIBE TEX.*	.239	111	406	63	97	175	14	5	18	42	7	5	2	3	36	2	85	25	7	6	.431	.304
MCRAE, HAL, K.C	.259	112	320	41	83	144	19	0	14	70	9	2	2	1	44	3	45	0	1	12	.450	.349
MEACHAM, BOBBY, N.Y.†	.218	156	481	70	105	128	16	2	1	47	3	23	3	5	54	1	102	25	7	7	.266	.302
MEIER, DAVE, MINN	.260	71	104	15	27	36	6	0	1	8	0	3	0	1	18	0	12	0	6	0	.346	.374
MELVIN, BOB, DET	.220	41	82	10	18	24	4	1	0	4	0	2	0	0	3	0	21	0	0	1	.293	.247
MEYER, DANNY, OAK.*	.000	14	12	2	0	0	0	0	0	0	0	0	0	0	1	0	0	0	0	1	.000	.077
MILLER, DARRELL, CAL	.375	51	48	8	18	28	2	1	2	7	0	0	0	1	1	0	10	0	1	0	.583	.400
MILLER, RICK, BOS.*	.333	41	45	5	15	17	2	0	0	9	0	0	1	0	5	0	6	1	0	1	.378	.392
MOLITOR, PAUL, MILW	.297	140	576	93	171	235	28	3	10	48	2	7	4	1	54	6	80	21	7	12	.408	.356
MOORE, CHARLIE, MILW	.232	105	349	35	81	102	13	4	0	31	8	3	1	1	27	0	53	4	0	12	.292	.288
MORENO, OMAR, N.Y.-K.C.*	.221	58	136	21	30	52	5	4	3	16	0	1	1	1	4	0	24	1	2	2	.382	.246
MORRIS, JACK, DET	—	36	0	0	0	0	0	0	0	0	0	0	0	0	0	0	0	0	0	0	—	—
MOSEBY, LLOYD, TOR.*	.259	152	584	92	151	249	30	7	18	70	10	1	5	4	76	4	91	37	15	12	.426	.345
MOSES, JOHN, SEA.*	.194	33	62	4	12	12	0	0	0	3	0	1	0	0	2	0	8	5	2	3	.194	.219
MOTLEY, DARRYL, K.C	.222	123	383	45	85	158	20	1	17	49	4	0	5	2	18	2	57	6	4	17	.413	.257
MULLINIKS, RANCE, TOR.*	.295	129	366	55	108	166	26	1	10	57	11	1	5	0	55	2	54	2	0	10	.454	.383
MURPHY, DWAYNE, OAK.*	.233	152	523	77	122	209	21	3	20	59	7	5	4	3	84	3	123	4	5	14	.400	.340
MURRAY, EDDIE, BALT.†	.297	156	583	111	173	305	37	1	31	124	15	0	8	2	84	12	68	5	2	8	.523	.383
NARRON, JERRY, CAL.*	.220	67	132	12	29	48	4	0	5	14	2	0	0	0	11	2	17	0	0	2	.364	.280

* BATS LEFTHANDED †SWITCH HITTER

BATTER AND CLUB	AVG	G	AB	R	H	TB	2B	3B	HR	RBI	GW RBI	SH	SF	HB	BB	IBB	SO	SB	CS	GI DP	SLG	OBP
NELSON, GENE, CHI	.000	47	1	0	0	0	0	0	0	0	0	0	0	0	0	0	0	0	0	0	.000	.000
NELSON, RICKY, SEA.*	.000	6	2	2	0	0	0	0	0	0	0	0	0	0	0	0	1	0	0	0	.000	.000
NICHOLS, REID, BOS.-CHI	.273	72	150	23	41	57	8	1	2	18	4	3	2	1	17	1	17	6	5	2	.380	.347
NICOSIA, STEVE, TOR	.267	6	15	0	4	4	0	0	0	1	0	0	0	0	0	0	0	0	0	0	.267	.267
NIXON, OTIS, CLEV.†	.235	104	162	34	38	51	4	0	3	9	1	4	0	0	8	0	27	20	11	2	.315	.271
NOLAN, JOE, BALT.*	.132	31	38	1	5	7	2	0	0	6	0	0	1	0	5	1	5	0	0	1	.184	.227
O'BRIEN, CHARLIE, OAK	.273	16	11	3	3	4	1	0	0	1	0	0	0	0	3	0	3	0	0	0	.364	.429
O'BRIEN, PETE, TEX.*	.267	159	573	69	153	259	34	3	22	92	10	3	9	1	69	4	53	5	10	18	.452	.342
O'MALLEY, THOMAS, BALT.*	.071	8	14	1	1	4	0	0	1	2	0	0	0	0	0	0	2	0	0	1	.286	.071
OGLIVIE, BEN, MILW.*	.290	101	341	40	99	150	17	2	10	61	7	4	10	2	37	3	51	0	2	8	.440	.354
OLIVER, AL, TOR.*	.251	61	187	20	47	70	6	1	5	23	3	0	0	1	7	2	13	0	0	8	.374	.282
ORTA, JORGE, K.C.*	.267	110	300	32	80	115	21	1	4	45	6	2	4	2	22	5	28	2	1	8	.383	.317
OWEN, SPIKE, SEA.†	.259	118	352	41	91	131	10	6	6	37	3	5	2	0	34	0	27	11	5	5	.372	.322
PACIOREK, TOM, CHI	.246	46	122	14	30	32	2	0	0	9	2	0	2	1	8	0	22	2	0	3	.262	.293
PAGLIARULO, MIKE, N.Y.*	.239	138	380	55	91	168	16	2	19	62	5	3	3	4	45	4	86	0	0	6	.442	.324
PARDO, AL, BALT.†	.133	34	75	3	10	11	1	0	0	1	0	0	0	0	3	0	15	0	0	0	.147	.167
PARIS, KELLY, BALT	.000	5	9	0	0	0	0	0	0	0	0	0	0	0	0	0	1	0	0	0	.000	.000
PARRISH, LANCE, DET	.273	140	549	64	150	263	27	1	28	98	16	3	5	2	41	5	90	2	6	10	.479	.323
PARRISH, LARRY, TEX	.249	94	346	44	86	150	11	1	17	51	4	0	2	1	33	2	77	0	2	13	.434	.314
PASQUA, DAN, N.Y.*	.209	60	148	17	31	63	3	1	9	25	1	0	1	1	16	4	38	0	0	1	.426	.289
PERCONTE, JACK, SEA.*	.264	125	485	60	128	165	17	7	2	23	2	2	2	3	50	0	36	31	2	9	.340	.335
PETRALLI, GENO, TEX.†	.270	42	100	7	27	29	2	0	0	11	1	3	4	1	8	0	12	1	0	4	.290	.319
PETTIS, GARY, CAL.†	.257	125	443	67	114	143	10	8	1	32	2	9	2	0	62	0	125	56	9	5	.323	.347
PHELPS, KEN, SEA.*	.207	61	116	18	24	54	3	0	9	24	3	0	0	0	24	2	33	2	0	1	.466	.343
PHILLIPS, TONY, OAK.†	.280	42	161	23	45	73	12	2	4	17	2	3	1	0	13	0	34	3	2	1	.453	.331
PICCIOLO, ROB, OAK	.275	71	102	19	28	33	2	0	1	8	0	0	0	0	2	0	17	3	2	1	.324	.288
PITTARO, CHRIS, DET.†	.242	28	62	10	15	20	3	1	0	7	1	1	0	0	5	0	13	1	1	0	.323	.299
POLIDOR, GUS, CAL	.000	2	1	1	1	1	0	0	0	0	0	0	0	0	0	0	0	0	0	0	1.000	1.000
PONCE, CARLOS, MILW	.161	21	62	4	10	15	2	0	1	5	0	1	2	0	1	0	9	0	0	4	.242	.169
PRESLEY, JIM, SEA	.275	155	570	71	157	276	33	1	28	84	6	1	9	1	44	9	100	2	2	29	.484	.324

PRYOR, GREG, K.C	.219	63	114	8	25	31	3	0	1	3	1	3	0	0	8	0	12	0	1	6	.272 .270
PUCKETT, KIRBY, MINN	.288	161	691	80	199	266	29	13	4	74	7	5	3	4	41	0	87	21	12	9	.385 .330
PUJOLS, LUIS, TEX	.000	1	1	0	1	1	0	0	0	0	0	0	0	0	0	0	0	0	0	0	1.000 1.000
QUIRK, JAMIE, K.C.*	.281	19	57	3	16	21	3	1	0	4	2	0	0	0	2	0	9	0	0	1	.368 .305
RAMOS, DOMINGO, SEA	.196	75	168	19	33	42	6	0	1	15	2	3	2	0	17	0	23	0	1	4	.250 .267
RANDOLPH, WILLIE, N.Y	.276	143	497	75	137	177	21	2	5	40	6	5	6	4	85	3	39	16	9	24	.356 .382
RAYFORD, FLOYD, BALT	.306	105	359	55	110	187	21	1	18	48	3	2	1	0	10	0	69	3	1	10	.521 .324
READY, RANDY, MILW	.265	48	181	29	48	70	9	5	1	21	3	2	2	1	14	0	23	0	0	6	.387 .318
REED, JEFF, MINN.*	.200	7	10	2	2	2	0	0	0	0	0	0	0	0	0	0	3	0	0	0	.200 .200
REYNOLDS, HAROLD, SEA.†	.144	67	104	15	15	20	3	1	0	6	0	1	0	0	17	0	14	3	2	0	.192 .264
RICE, JIM, BOS	.291	140	546	85	159	266	20	3	27	103	9	0	9	2	51	5	75	2	0	35	.487 .349
RILES, EARNEST, MILW.*	.286	116	448	54	128	169	12	7	5	45	3	6	3	2	36	0	54	2	2	16	.377 .339
RIPKEN, CAL, BALT	.282	161	642	116	181	301	32	5	26	110	15	0	8	1	67	1	68	2	3	32	.469 .347
ROBERTSON, ANDRE, N.Y	.328	50	125	16	41	52	5	0	2	17	0	2	2	1	6	0	24	1	2	3	.416 .358
ROBIDOUX, BILLY JOE, MILW.*	.176	18	51	5	9	20	2	0	3	8	3	0	0	0	12	0	16	0	0	1	.392 .333
ROENICKE, GARY, BALT	.218	113	225	36	49	103	9	0	15	43	5	2	3	0	44	1	36	2	2	5	.458 .342
ROMERO, ED, MILW	.251	88	251	24	63	76	11	1	0	21	1	5	0	0	26	0	20	1	1	3	.303 .321
ROMINE, KEVIN, BOS	.214	24	28	3	6	8	2	0	0	1	0	2	0	0	1	0	4	1	0	1	.286 .241
RYAL, MARK, CHI.*	.152	12	33	4	5	8	3	0	0	3	0	1	0	0	3	0	3	0	0	2	.242 .222
SAKATA, LENN, BALT	.227	55	97	15	22	34	3	0	3	6	1	1	0	1	6	0	15	3	2	3	.351 .279
SALAS, MARK, MINN.*	.300	120	360	51	108	165	20	5	9	41	7	0	3	1	18	5	37	0	1	7	.458 .332
SALAZAR, LUIS, CHI	.245	122	327	39	80	132	18	2	10	45	5	9	5	0	12	2	60	14	4	5	.404 .267
SAMPLE, BILLY, N.Y	.288	59	139	18	40	48	5	0	1	15	0	2	2	2	9	0	10	2	1	2	.345 .336
SANCHEZ, ALEJANDRO, DET	.248	71	133	19	33	61	6	2	6	12	2	0	0	0	0	0	39	2	2	4	.459 .248
SAX, DAVE, BOS	.306	22	36	2	11	14	3	0	0	6	0	3	1	0	3	0	3	0	1	0	.389 .350
SCHOFIELD, DICK, CAL	.219	147	438	50	96	145	19	3	8	41	4	12	3	8	35	0	70	11	4	8	.331 .287
SCHROEDER, BILL, MILW	.242	53	194	18	47	79	8	0	8	25	1	0	2	2	12	1	61	0	1	5	.407 .290
SCONIERS, DARYL, CAL.*	.286	44	98	14	28	42	6	1	2	12	1	0	3	0	15	0	18	2	1	2	.429 .371
SCOTT, DONNIE, SEA.†	.222	80	185	18	41	66	13	0	4	23	4	1	4	0	15	0	41	1	1	3	.357 .275
SCRANTON, JIM, K.C	.000	6	4	1	0	0	0	0	0	0	0	0	0	0	0	0	0	0	0	0	.000 .000
SHEETS, LARRY, BALT.*	.262	113	328	43	86	145	8	0	17	50	4	1	1	2	28	2	52	0	1	15	.442 .323
SHELBY, JOHN, BALT†	.283	69	205	28	58	89	6	2	7	27	4	2	0	0	7	0	44	5	1	4	.434 .307
SHEPHERD, RON, TOR	.114	38	35	7	4	6	2	0	0	1	0	0	0	0	2	0	12	3	0	1	.171 .162

DH Dave Kingman's 30 HRs give him a career total of 407.

* BATS LEFTHANDED †SWITCH HITTER

BATTER AND CLUB	AVG	G	AB	R	H	TB	2B	3B	HR	RBI	GW RBI	SH	SF	HB	BB	IBB	SO	SB	CS	GI DP	SLG	OBP
SHERIDAN, PAT, K.C.*	.228	78	206	18	47	69	9	2	3	17	3	3	1	1	23	2	38	11	3	4	.335	.307
SIMMONS, NELSON, DET.†	.239	75	251	31	60	101	11	0	10	33	4	0	4	0	26	5	41	1	0	4	.402	.306
SIMMONS, TED, MILW.†	.273	143	528	60	144	212	28	2	12	76	13	1	5	1	57	9	32	1	1	17	.402	.342
SKINNER, JOEL, CHI	.341	22	44	9	15	24	4	1	1	5	0	1	0	0	5	0	13	0	0	2	.545	.408
SLAUGHT, DON, TEX	.280	102	343	34	96	145	17	4	8	35	4	1	0	6	20	1	41	5	4	8	.423	.331
SMALLEY, ROY, MINN.†	.258	129	388	57	100	156	20	0	12	45	5	1	2	1	60	3	65	0	2	8	.402	.357
SMITH, KEITH, N.Y.†	—	4	0	1	0	0	0	0	0	0	0	0	0	0	0	0	0	0	0	0	—	—
SMITH, LONNIE, K.C	.257	120	448	77	115	164	23	4	6	41	6	0	5	4	41	0	69	40	7	2	.366	.321
SPILLNER, DAN, CHI	—	53	0	0	0	0	0	0	0	0	0	0	0	0	1	0	0	0	0	0	—	1.000
SQUIRES, MIKE, CHI.*	—	2	0	1	0	0	0	0	0	0	0	0	0	0	0	0	0	0	0	0	—	—
STAPLETON, DAVE, BOS	.227	30	66	4	15	21	6	0	0	2	0	1	0	0	4	0	11	0	0	1	.318	.271
STEIN, BILL, TEX	.253	44	79	5	20	28	3	1	1	12	1	0	0	1	1	1	15	0	0	2	.354	.272
STENHOUSE, MIKE, MINN.	.223	81	179	23	40	60	5	0	5	21	3	0	1	0	29	1	18	1	0	3	.335	.330
SULLIVAN, MARC, BOS	.174	32	69	10	12	20	2	0	2	3	0	2	0	0	6	0	15	0	0	0	.290	.240
SUNDBERG, JIM, K.C	.245	115	367	38	90	140	12	4	10	35	4	4	2	1	33	3	67	0	2	9	.381	.308
TABLER, PAT, CLEV	.275	117	404	47	111	150	18	3	5	59	5	2	3	2	27	2	55	0	6	15	.371	.321
TARTABULL, DANNY, SEA	.328	19	61	8	20	32	7	1	1	7	0	0	0	0	8	0	14	1	0	1	.525	.406
TETTLETON, MICKEY, OAK.†	.251	78	211	23	53	74	12	0	3	15	1	5	0	2	28	0	59	2	2	6	.351	.344
TEUFEL, TIM, MINN.	.260	138	434	58	113	173	24	3	10	50	4	7	4	3	48	2	70	4	2	14	.399	.335
THOMAS, GORMAN, SEA.	.215	135	484	76	104	218	16	1	32	87	10	2	3	1	84	6	126	3	2	11	.450	.330
THORNTON, ANDRE, CLEV	.236	124	461	49	109	188	13	0	22	88	6	0	6	0	47	1	75	3	2	14	.408	.304
THORNTON, LOUIS, TOR.*	.236	56	72	18	17	23	1	1	1	8	1	0	0	1	2	0	24	1	0	2	.319	.267
TOLLESON, WAYNE, TEX.†	.313	123	323	45	101	123	9	5	1	18	6	9	2	0	21	0	46	21	12	6	.381	.353
TRAMMELL, ALAN, DET	.258	149	605	79	156	230	21	7	13	57	5	11	9	2	50	4	71	14	5	6	.380	.312
UPSHAW, WILLIE, TOR.*	.275	148	501	79	138	224	31	5	15	65	7	1	3	4	48	7	71	8	8	6	.447	.342
VALENTINE, ELLIS, TEX.	.211	11	38	5	8	15	1	0	2	4	2	0	0	0	2	0	8	0	1	1	.395	.250
VALLE, DAVE, SEA.	.157	31	70	2	11	12	1	0	0	4	0	1	0	1	1	0	17	0	0	1	.171	.181
VUKOVICH, GEORGE, CLEV*	.244	149	434	43	106	152	22	0	8	45	4	1	4	1	30	6	75	2	2	9	.350	.292
WAITS, RICK, MILW	.000	24	1	0	0	0	0	0	0	0	0	0	0	0	0	0	1	0	0	0	.000	.000
WALKER, DUANE, TEX.*	.174	53	132	14	23	40	2	0	5	11	0	0	0	1	15	0	29	2	1	2	.303	.264

* BATS LEFTHANDED †SWITCH HITTER

BATTER AND CLUB	AVG	G	AB	R	H	TB	2B	3B	HR	RBI	GW RBI	SH	SF	HB	BB	IBB	SO	SB	CS	GI DP	SLG	OBP
WALKER, GREG, CHI.*	.258	163	601	77	155	273	38	4	24	92	13	0	3	2	44	6	100	5	2	16	.454	.309
WARD, GARY, TEX	.287	154	593	77	170	257	28	7	15	70	5	0	5	1	39	3	97	26	7	19	.433	.329
WASHINGTON, RON, MINN	.274	70	135	24	37	54	6	4	1	14	2	3	3	0	8	0	15	5	1	3	.400	.308
WATHAN, JOHN, K.C	.234	60	145	11	34	47	8	1	1	9	1	2	0	1	17	0	15	1	1	4	.324	.319
WEAVER, JIM, DET.*	.143	12	7	2	1	2	1	0	0	0	0	0	0	0	1	0	4	0	1	0	.286	.250
WEBSTER, MITCH, TOR.†	.000	4	1	0	0	0	0	0	0	0	0	0	0	0	0	0	0	0	1	0	.000	.000
WHITAKER, LOU, DET.*	.279	152	609	102	170	278	29	8	21	73	9	5	5	2	80	9	56	6	4	3	.456	.362
WHITE, DEVON, CAL.†	.143	21	7	7	1	1	0	0	0	0	0	0	0	1	1	0	3	3	1	0	.143	.333
WHITE, FRANK, K.C	.249	149	563	62	140	233	25	1	22	69	9	5	3	1	28	2	86	10	4	8	.414	.284
WHITT, ERNIE, TOR.*	.245	139	412	55	101	183	21	2	19	64	8	3	2	1	47	9	59	3	6	7	.444	.323
WIGGINS, ALAN, BALT.†	.285	76	298	43	85	104	11	4	0	21	0	6	0	2	29	0	16	30	13	2	.349	.353
WILFONG, ROB, CAL.*	.189	83	217	16	41	56	3	0	4	13	0	8	2	0	16	1	32	4	1	0	.258	.243
WILKERSON, CURTIS, TEX.†	.244	129	360	35	88	111	11	6	0	22	3	6	3	4	22	0	63	14	7	7	.308	.293
WILLARD, JERRY, CLEV.*	.270	104	300	39	81	115	13	0	7	36	6	4	1	1	28	1	59	0	0	3	.383	.333
WILSON, JIM, CLEV	.357	4	14	2	5	5	0	0	0	4	1	0	0	0	1	0	3	0	0	0	.357	.400
WILSON, WILLIE, K.C.†	.278	141	605	87	168	247	25	21	4	43	7	2	1	5	29	3	94	43	11	6	.408	.316
WINFIELD, DAVE, N.Y	.275	155	633	105	174	298	34	6	26	114	19	0	4	0	52	8	96	19	7	17	.471	.328
WRIGHT, GEORGE, TEX.†	.190	109	363	21	69	88	13	0	2	18	1	3	2	0	25	5	49	4	7	9	.242	.241
WYNEGAR, BUTCH, N.Y.†	.223	102	309	27	69	99	15	0	5	32	3	1	1	0	64	2	43	0	0	11	.320	.356
YOUNG, MIKE, BALT.†	.273	139	450	72	123	231	22	1	28	81	9	1	1	4	48	5	104	1	5	9	.513	.348
YOUNT, ROBIN, MILW	.277	122	466	76	129	206	26	3	15	68	3	1	9	2	49	3	56	10	4	8	.442	.342

TOP FIFTEEN DESIGNATED HITTERS

(BASED ON TIMES AT BAT)

BATTER	BATS	CLUB	AVG	G	AB	R	H	TB	2B	3B	HR	RBI	GW RBI	SH	SF	HB	BB	IBB	SO	SB	CS	GI DP	SLG	OBP
KINGMAN	R	OAK	.233	149	567	61	132	229	13	0	28	84	9	2	8	2	57	6	110	2	2	17	.404	.301
EASLER	L	BOS	.259	130	494	63	128	203	27	3	14	68	7	0	6	3	44	1	114	0	1	12	.411	.320
THOMAS G	R	SEA	.215	133	483	76	104	218	16	1	32	87	10	2	3	1	83	6	126	3	2	10	.451	.330

BAYLOR	R	N.Y.	.232	140	475	70	110	205	24	1	23	91	10	1	10	24	52	6	89	0	4	10	.432	.332
THORNTON	R	CLEV	.235	122	460	48	103	184	13	0	21	87	6	0	6	0	46	1	75	3	2	14	.400	.301
SIMMONS	S	MILW	.265	99	374	40	99	146	19	2	8	53	10	0	5	1	35	8	24	1	0	11	.390	.325
JOHNSON	R	TEX 82																						
		TOR 21	.264	103	360	35	95	153	17	1	13	65	2	1	4	3	39	2	56	0	0	4	.425	.337
MCRAE..........	R	K.C.	.264	106	314	41	83	144	19	0	14	70	9	2	2	1	44	3	43	0	1	11	.459	.355
SHEETS	L	BALT	.262	93	294	37	77	123	7	0	13	43	4	1	1	2	25	2	46	0	1	13	.418	.323
ORTA	L	K.C.	.263	85	281	30	74	108	20	1	4	40	5	2	4	2	19	3	25	2	1	8	.384	.310
KITTLE..........	R	CHI	.251	57	191	28	48	101	5	0	16	35	6	0	2	3	13	0	44	0	3	5	.529	.306
OLIVER	L	TOR	.253	59	186	20	47	70	6	1	5	23	3	0	0	1	5	0	13	0	0	8	.376	.276
BURROUGHS.....	R	TOR	.265	75	181	18	48	78	9	3	5	27	2	0	2	0	33	1	32	0	1	5	.431	.375
SMALLEY........	S	MINN	.244	56	180	23	44	67	11	0	4	23	4	0	1	0	29	0	26	0	1	2	.372	.348
JACKSON........	L	CAL	.196	52	168	25	33	65	8	0	8	26	3	0	2	1	35	9	65	0	2	6	.387	.335

CLUB BATTING

CLUB	AVG	G	AB	R	OR	H	TB	2B	3B	HR	GS	RBI	GW	SH	SF	HB	BB	IBB	SO	SB	CS	GIDP	LOB	SHO	SLG	OBP
BOSTON.......	.282	163	5720	800	720	1615	2455	292	3[illegible]	162	5	760	80	50	57	30	562	39	816	66	27	164	1241	8	.429	.347
TORONTO.....	.269	161	5508	759	588	1482	2343	281	53	158	3	714	90	21	44	38	503	44	807	143	77	121	1067	5	.425	.331
NEW YORK.....	.267	161	5458	839	660	1458	2320	272	31	176	3	793	87	48	60	50	620	50	771	155	53	119	1125	6	.425	.344
CLEVELAND....	.265	162	5527	729	861	1465	2129	254	31	116	4	689	58	38	48	15	492	26	817	132	72	139	1068	12	.385	.324
OAKLAND	.264	162	5581	757	787	1475	2238	230	34	155	2	690	71	63	47	15	508	29	861	116	58	129	1073	5	.401	.325
MINNESOTA....	.264	162	5509	705	782	1453	2240	282	41	141	5	678	74	39	47	31	502	36	779	68	44	117	1144	12	.407	.326
MILWAUKEE...	.263	161	5568	690	802	1467	2108	250	44	101	3	636	64	54	55	19	462	33	746	69	34	145	1130	10	.379	.319
BALTIMORE....	.263	161	5517	818	764	1451	2371	234	22	214	7	773	80	31	40	19	604	30	908	69	43	132	1124	7	.430	.336
SEATTLE	.255	162	5521	719	818	1410	2276	277	38	171	3	686	69	28	41	31	564	36	942	94	35	147	1143	8	.412	.326
TEXAS	.253	161	5361	617	785	1359	2041	213	41	129	1	578	56	34	45	33	530	30	819	130	76	136	1100	9	.381	.322
DETROIT	.253	161	5575	729	688	1413	2363	254	45	202	3	703	81	40	53	27	526	56	926	75	41	81	1142	6	.424	.318
CHICAGO.......	.253	163	5470	736	720	1386	2145	247	37	146	3	695	78	59	45	43	471	40	843	108	56	119	1009	7	.392	.315
KANSAS CITY...	.252	162	5500	687	639	1384	2205	261	39	154	3	657	87	44	41	36	473	57	840	128	48	125	1057	4	.401	.313
CALIFORNIA ..	.251	162	5442	732	703	1364	2100	215	31	153	6	685	80	99	35	39	648	51	902	106	51	139	1165	10	.386	.333
TOTALS	.261	1132	77257	10317	10317	20182	31334	3562	528	2178	51	9737	1055	648	658	419	7465	557	11777	1459	715	1813	15588	109	.406	.327

PITCHING

TOP FIFTEEN QUALIFIERS FOR EARNED-RUN LEADERSHIP
(162 OR MORE INNINGS)

*THROWS LEFTHANDED PITCHER AND CLUB	W	L	PCT	ERA	G	GS	CG	SHO	GF	SV	IP	H	TBF	R	ER	HR	SH	SF	HB	TBB	IBB	SO	WP	BK
STIEB, DAVE, TOR	14	13	.519	2.48	36	36	8	2	0	0	265.0	206	1087	89	73	22	14	2	9	96	3	167	4	1
LEIBRANDT, CHARLIE, K.C.*	17	9	.654	2.69	33	33	8	3	0	0	237.2	223	983	86	71	17	8	5	2	68	3	108	4	3
SABERHAGEN, BRET, K.C	20	6	.769	2.87	32	32	10	1	0	0	235.1	211	931	79	75	19	9	7	1	38	1	158	1	3
KEY, JIMMY, TOR.*	14	6	.700	3.00	35	32	3	0	0	0	212.2	188	856	77	71	22	5	5	2	50	1	85	6	1
BLYLEVEN, BERT, CLEV.-MINN	17	16	.515	3.16	37	37	24	5	0	0	293.2	264	1203	121	103	23	5	8	9	75	1	206	4	1
SEAVER, TOM, CHI	16	11	.593	3.17	35	33	6	1	0	0	238.2	223	993	103	84	22	7	8	8	69	6	134	10	0
GUIDRY, RON, N.Y.*	22	6	.786	3.27	34	33	11	2	0	0	259.0	243	1033	104	94	28	3	8	0	42	3	143	3	1
HOUGH, CHARLIE, TEX	14	16	.467	3.31	34	34	14	1	0	0	250.1	198	1018	102	92	23	1	7	7	83	1	141	11	3
MORRIS, JACK, DET	16	11	.593	3.33	35	35	13	4	0	0	257.0	212	1077	102	95	21	11	7	5	110	7	191	15	3
PETRY, DAN, DET	15	13	.536	3.36	34	34	8	0	0	0	238.2	190	962	98	89	24	0	2	3	81	9	109	6	0
JACKSON, DANNY, K.C.*	14	12	.538	3.42	32	32	4	3	0	0	208.0	209	893	94	79	7	5	4	6	76	2	114	4	2
ALEXANDER, DOYLE, TOR	17	10	.630	3.45	36	36	6	1	0	0	260.2	268	1090	105	100	28	6	3	6	67	0	142	9	0
MOORE, MIKE, SEA	17	10	.630	3.46	35	34	14	2	1	0	247.0	230	1016	100	95	18	2	7	4	70	2	155	10	3
WITT, MIKE, CAL	15	9	.625	3.56	35	35	6	1	0	0	250.0	228	1049	115	99	22	4	5	4	98	6	180	11	1
DIXON, KEN, BALT	8	4	.667	3.67	34	18	3	1	7	1	162.0	144	683	68	66	20	8	2	2	64	7	108	5	2

INDIVIDUAL PITCHING
(ALL PLAYERS LISTED ALPHABETICALLY)

*THROWS LEFTHANDED PITCHER AND CLUB	W	L	PCT	ERA	G	GS	CG	SHO	GF	SV	IP	H	TBF	R	ER	HR	SH	SF	HB	TBB	IBB	SO	WP	BK
AASE, DON, BALT	10	6	.625	3.78	54	0	0	0	43	14	88.0	83	366	44	37	6	5	3	1	35	7	67	0	1
ACKER, JIM, TOR	7	2	.778	3.23	61	0	0	0	26	10	86.1	86	370	35	31	7	1	2	3	43	1	42	2	0
AGOSTO, JUAN, CHI.*	4	3	.571	3.58	54	0	0	0	21	1	60.1	45	246	27	24	3	3	3	3	23	1	39	0	0
ALEXANDER, DOYLE, TOR	17	10	.630	3.45	36	36	6	1	0	0	260.2	268	1090	105	100	28	6	3	6	67	0	142	9	0
ALLEN, NEIL, N.Y	1	0	1.000	2.76	17	0	0	0	10	1	29.1	26	124	9	9	1	0	0	0	13	0	16	2	0

ARMSTRONG, MIKE, N.Y	0	0	—	3.07	9	0	0	0	8	0	14.2	9	54	5	5	4	0	0	0	2	0	11	1	0
ATHERTON, KEITH, OAK	4	7	.364	4.30	56	0	0	0	21	3	104.2	89	435	51	50	17	3	4	0	42	8	77	2	0
BAIR, DOUG, DET	2	0	1.000	6.24	21	3	0	0	4	0	49.0	54	224	38	34	3	2	4	1	25	5	30	6	1
BANNISTER, FLOYD, CHI.*	10	14	.417	4.87	34	34	4	1	0	0	210.2	211	928	121	114	30	9	8	4	100	5	198	11	0
BARKLEY, JEFF, CLEV	0	3	.000	5.27	21	0	0	0	6	1	41.0	37	174	26	24	5	5	2	0	15	3	30	2	1
BAROJAS, SALOME, SEA	0	5	.000	5.98	17	4	0	0	3	0	52.2	65	250	40	35	6	2	2	0	33	5	27	6	0
BEATTIE, JIM, SEA	5	6	.455	7.29	18	15	1	1	1	0	70.1	93	335	61	57	9	0	5	3	33	0	45	2	0
BECKWITH, JOE, K.C	1	5	.167	4.07	49	0	0	0	21	1	95.0	99	410	45	43	9	4	3	3	32	8	80	6	0
BEHENNA, RICK, CLEV	0	2	.000	7.78	4	4	0	0	0	0	19.2	29	91	17	17	3	0	1	0	8	0	4	1	0
BELL, ERIC, BALT.*	0	0	—	4.76	4	0	0	0	3	0	5.2	4	24	3	3	1	0	0	0	4	0	4	0	0
BERENGUER, JUAN, DET	5	6	.455	5.59	31	13	0	0	9	0	95.0	96	424	67	59	12	1	4	1	48	3	82	4	1
BEST, KARL, SEA	2	1	.667	1.95	15	0	0	0	7	4	32.1	25	128	9	7	1	0	0	1	6	0	32	0	0
BIRTSAS, TIM, OAK.*	10	6	.625	4.01	29	25	2	0	4	0	141.1	124	624	72	63	18	4	5	3	91	0	94	6	0
BLACK, BUD, K.C.*	10	15	.400	4.33	33	33	5	2	0	0	205.2	216	885	111	99	17	8	4	8	59	4	122	9	1
BLYLEVEN, BERT, CLEV.-MINN	17	16	.515	3.16	37	37	24	5	0	0	293.2	264	1203	121	103	23	5	8	9	75	1	206	4	1
BODDICKER, MIKE, BALT.	12	17	.414	4.07	32	32	9	2	0	0	203.1	227	899	104	92	13	9	2	5	89	7	135	5	0
BOGGS, TOMMY, TEX	0	0	—	11.57	4	0	0	0	0	0	7.0	13	36	9	9	3	0	0	0	2	0	6	0	0
BORDI, RICH, N.Y	6	8	.429	3.21	51	3	0	0	16	2	98.0	95	415	41	35	5	6	3	1	29	4	64	1	0
BOYD, DENNIS, BOS	15	13	.536	3.70	35	35	13	3	0	0	272.1	273	1132	117	112	26	9	7	4	67	3	154	1	1
BROWN, MARK, MINN	0	0	—	6.89	6	0	0	0	4	0	15.2	21	73	13	12	1	0	3	0	7	0	5	0	0
BROWN, MIKE, BOS	0	0	—	21.60	2	1	0	0	0	0	3.1	9	22	8	8	0	0	1	0	3	0	3	0	1
BURNS, BRITT, CHI.*	18	11	.621	3.96	36	34	8	4	1	0	227.0	206	944	105	100	26	6	5	2	79	1	172	2	0
BURRIS, RAY, MILW	9	13	.409	4.81	29	28	6	0	0	0	170.1	182	738	95	91	25	6	6	3	53	0	81	7	0
BURTT, DENNIS, MINN	2	2	.500	3.81	5	2	0	0	1	0	28.1	20	109	13	12	2	1	1	0	7	0	9	1	1
BUTCHER, JOHN, MINN.	11	14	.440	4.98	34	33	8	2	0	0	207.2	239	893	125	115	24	6	10	6	43	4	92	5	1
BYSTROM, MARTY, N.Y	3	2	.600	5.71	8	8	0	0	0	0	41.0	44	180	29	26	8	2	1	1	19	0	16	0	0
CAMACHO, ERNIE, CLEV	0	1	.000	8.10	2	0	0	0	1	0	3.1	4	15	3	3	0	0	2	0	1	0	2	1	0
CANDELARIA, JOHN, CAL.*	7	3	.700	3.80	13	13	1	1	0	0	71.0	70	301	33	30	7	4	3	3	24	1	53	2	0
CARY, CHUCK, DET.*	0	1	.000	3.42	16	0	0	0	6	2	23.2	16	95	9	9	2	0	1	2	8	1	22	0	0
CAUDILL, BILL, TOR	4	6	.400	2.99	67	0	0	0	51	14	69.1	53	297	26	23	9	3	4	2	35	6	46	0	0
CERUTTI, JOHN, TOR.*	0	2	.000	5.40	4	1	0	0	1	0	6.2	10	36	7	4	1	0	0	1	4	0	5	2	0
CLANCY, JIM, TOR	9	6	.600	3.78	23	23	1	0	0	0	128.2	117	527	54	54	15	0	5	0	37	0	66	2	0
CLARK, BRYAN, CLEV.*	3	4	.429	6.32	31	3	0	0	10	2	62.2	78	290	47	44	8	3	2	0	34	2	24	5	0
CLARKE, STAN, TOR.*	0	0	—	4.50	4	0	0	0	2	0	4.0	3	16	2	2	1	0	0	0	2	0	2	0	0
CLEAR, MARK, BOS.	1	3	.250	3.72	41	0	0	0	30	3	55.2	45	259	26	23	1	2	2	5	50	10	55	8	0
CLEMENS, ROGER, BOS	7	5	.583	3.29	15	15	3	1	0	0	98.1	83	407	38	36	5	1	2	3	37	0	74	1	3
CLEMENTS, PAT, CAL.*	[illegible]	0	1.000	3.34	41	0	0	0	12	1	62.0	47	247	23	23	4	4	0	2	25	2	19	1	0

*THROWS LEFTHANDED

PITCHER AND CLUB	W	L	PCT	ERA	G	GS	CG	SHO	GF	SV	IP	H	TBF	R	ER	HR	SH	SF	HB	TBB	IBB	SO	WP	BK
CLIBURN, STU, CAL	9	3	.750	2.09	44	0	0	0	26	6	99.0	87	395	25	23	5	5	2	1	26	6	48	2	0
COCANOWER, JAIME, MILW	6	8	.429	4.33	24	15	3	1	2	0	116.1	122	534	72	56	6	4	4	8	73	2	44	13	0
CODIROLI, CHRIS, OAK	14	14	.500	4.46	37	37	4	0	0	0	226.0	228	975	125	112	23	4	8	3	78	2	111	8	1
CONROY, TIM, OAK.*	0	1	.000	4.26	16	2	0	0	7	0	25.1	22	110	15	12	3	0	1	1	15	1	8	4	0
COOK, GLEN, TEX	2	3	.400	9.45	9	7	0	0	1	0	40.0	53	187	42	42	12	0	4	3	18	1	19	1	0
COOPER, DON, N.Y	0	0	—	5.40	7	0	0	0	2	0	10.0	12	44	6	6	2	0	1	0	3	0	4	1	0
CORBETT, DOUG, CAL	3	3	.500	4.89	30	0	0	0	11	0	46.0	49	203	33	25	7	2	1	1	20	3	24	0	0
CORREA, ED, CHI	1	0	1.000	6.97	5	1	0	0	3	0	10.1	11	51	9	8	2	0	0	0	11	0	10	1	0
COWLEY, JOE, N.Y.	12	6	.667	3.95	30	26	1	0	2	0	159.2	132	684	75	70	29	1	4	6	85	2	97	5	1
CRAWFORD, STEVE, BOS	6	5	.545	3.76	44	1	0	0	26	12	91.0	103	394	47	38	5	6	3	0	28	8	58	5	0
CREEL, KEITH, CLEV	2	5	.286	4.79	15	8	0	0	5	0	62.0	73	277	35	33	7	0	5	2	23	2	31	1	0
DARWIN, DANNY, MILW	8	18	.308	3.80	39	29	11	1	8	2	217.2	212	919	112	92	34	7	9	4	65	4	125	6	0
DAVIS, JOEL, CHI	3	3	.500	4.16	12	11	1	0	0	0	71.1	71	307	34	33	6	1	2	1	26	0	37	1	0
DAVIS, RON, MINN	2	6	.250	3.48	57	0	0	0	50	25	64.2	55	285	28	25	7	3	4	4	35	6	72	8	1
DAVIS, STEVE, TOR.*	2	1	.667	3.54	10	5	0	0	1	0	28.0	23	117	14	11	5	0	1	0	13	0	22	0	0
DAVIS, STORM, BALT	10	8	.556	4.53	31	28	8	1	0	0	175.0	172	750	92	88	11	3	3	1	70	5	93	2	1
DIXON, KEN, BALT	8	4	.667	3.67	34	18	3	1	7	1	162.0	144	683	68	66	20	8	2	2	64	7	108	5	2
DORSEY, JIM, BOS	0	1	.000	20.25	2	1	0	0	0	0	5.1	12	37	12	12	2	0	0	0	10	1	2	0	0
DOTSON, RICHARD, CHI	3	4	.429	4.47	9	9	0	0	0	0	52.1	53	226	30	26	5	1	2	3	17	1	33	0	0
EASTERLY, JAMIE, CLEV.*	4	1	.800	3.92	50	7	0	0	18	0	98.2	96	435	52	43	9	5	9	4	53	4	58	7	0
EUFEMIA, FRANK, MINN	4	2	.667	3.79	39	0	0	0	21	2	61.2	56	250	27	26	7	2	3	0	21	7	30	2	2
FALLON, BOB, CHI.*	0	0	—	6.19	10	0	0	0	4	0	16.0	25	79	11	11	5	0	1	0	9	2	17	1	0
FARR, STEVE, K.C	2	1	.667	3.11	16	3	0	0	5	1	37.2	34	164	15	13	2	1	2	2	20	4	36	3	0
FERREIRA, TONY, K.C.*	0	0	—	7.94	2	0	0	0	1	0	5.2	6	24	5	5	0	0	0	0	2	0	5	0	0
FILER, TOM, TOR.	7	0	1.000	3.88	11	9	0	0	0	0	48.2	38	192	21	21	6	2	1	0	18	0	24	0	1
FILSON, PETE, MINN.*	4	5	.444	3.67	40	6	1	0	12	2	95.2	93	406	42	39	13	3	2	0	30	4	42	1	1
FINGERS, ROLLIE, MILW	1	6	.143	5.04	47	0	0	0	37	17	55.1	59	241	33	31	9	4	1	0	19	5	24	1	0
FIREOVID, STEVE, CHI	0	0	—	5.14	4	0	0	0	2	0	7.0	17	38	4	4	0	0	0	0	2	0	2	0	0
FISHER, BRIAN, N.Y	4	4	.500	2.38	55	0	0	0	23	14	98.1	77	391	32	26	4	3	2	0	29	3	85	3	0
FLANAGAN, MIKE, BALT.*	4	5	.444	5.13	15	15	1	0	0	0	86.0	101	379	49	49	14	7	2	2	28	0	42	3	0
FOWLKES, ALAN, CAL	0	0	—	9.00	2	0	0	0	0	0	7.0	8	33	7	7	4	0	0	0	4	0	5	1	0
GEISEL, DAVE, SEA.*	0	0	—	6.33	12	0	0	0	1	0	27.0	35	128	21	19	3	0	0	0	15	3	17	0	1
GIBSON, BOB, MILW	6	7	.462	3.90	41	1	0	0	25	11	92.1	86	392	44	40	10	7	4	1	49	3	53	4	0
GLEATON, JERRY, CHI.*	1	0	1.000	5.76	31	0	0	0	9	1	29.2	37	135	19	19	3	4	1	0	13	3	22	3	0

GUBICZA, MARK, K.C	14	10	.583	4.06	29	28	0	0	0	0	177.1	160	760	88	80	14	1	6	5	77	0	99	12	0
GUIDRY, RON, N.Y.*	22	6	.786	3.27	34	33	11	2	0	0	259.0	243	1033	104	94	28	3	8	0	42	3	143	3	1
GURA, LARRY, K.C.*	0	0	—	12.46	3	0	0	0	2	1	4.1	7	23	6	6	1	0	0	0	4	0	2	1	0
GUZMAN, JOSE, TEX	3	2	.600	2.76	5	5	0	0	0	0	32.2	27	140	13	10	3	0	0	0	14	1	24	1	0
HAAS, MOOSE, MILW	8	8	.500	3.84	27	26	6	1	0	0	161.2	165	666	85	69	21	1	5	1	25	3	78	2	0
HABYAN, JOHN, BALT	1	0	1.000	.00	2	0	0	0	1	0	2.2	3	12	1	0	0	0	0	0	0	0	2	0	0
HARRIS, GREG, TEX	5	4	.556	2.47	58	0	0	0	35	11	113.0	74	450	35	31	7	3	2	5	43	3	111	2	1
HAVENS, BRADLEY, BALT.*	0	1	.000	8.79	8	1	0	0	3	0	14.1	20	70	14	14	4	0	0	0	10	1	19	0	0
HEATON, NEAL, CLEV.*	9	17	.346	4.90	36	33	5	1	2	0	207.2	244	921	119	113	19	7	8	7	80	2	82	2	2
HENKE, TOM, TOR.	3	3	.500	2.03	28	0	0	0	22	13	40.0	29	153	12	9	4	2	2	0	8	2	42	0	0
HENRY, DWAYNE, TEX	2	2	.500	2.57	16	0	0	0	10	3	21.0	16	86	7	6	0	2	1	0	7	0	20	1	0
HERNANDEZ, WILLIE, DET.*	8	10	.444	2.70	74	0	0	0	64	31	106.2	82	415	38	32	13	4	5	1	14	2	76	2	0
HIGUERA, TED, MILW.*	15	8	.652	3.90	32	30	7	2	2	0	212.1	186	874	105	92	22	5	10	3	63	0	127	4	3
HOLLAND, AL, CAL.*	0	1	.000	1.48	15	0	0	0	6	0	24.1	17	99	4	4	4	1	0	0	10	1	14	1	0
HOOTON, BURT, TEX	5	8	.385	5.23	29	20	2	0	2	0	124.0	149	546	78	72	18	0	5	0	40	2	62	2	0
HOUGH, CHARLIE, TEX	14	16	.467	3.31	34	34	14	1	0	0	250.1	198	1018	102	92	23	1	7	7	83	1	141	11	3
HOWE, STEVE, MINN.*	2	3	.400	6.16	13	0	0	0	5	0	19.0	28	94	16	13	1	0	3	0	7	2	10	1	0
HOWELL, JAY, OAK	9	8	.529	2.85	63	0	0	0	58	29	98.0	98	414	32	31	5	3	4	1	31	3	68	4	1
HUFFMAN, PHIL, BALT	0	0	—	15.43	2	1	0	0	0	0	4.2	7	26	8	8	1	1	0	0	5	1	2	0	0
HUISMANN, MARK, K.C	1	0	1.000	1.93	9	0	0	0	6	0	18.2	14	70	4	4	1	1	2	0	3	0	9	0	0
HURST, BRUCE, BOS.*	11	13	.458	4.51	35	31	6	1	0	0	229.1	243	973	123	115	31	6	4	3	70	4	189	3	4
JACKSON, DANNY, K.C.*	14	12	.538	3.42	32	32	4	3	0	0	208.0	209	893	94	79	7	5	4	6	76	2	114	4	2
JAMES, BOB, CHI	8	7	.533	2.13	69	0	0	0	60	32	110.0	90	436	31	26	5	7	5	2	23	4	88	3	2
JEFFCOAT, MIKE, CLEV.*	0	0	—	2.79	9	0	0	0	3	0	9.2	8	44	5	3	1	2	2	0	6	1	4	0	0
JOHN, TOMMY, CAL.-OAK.*	4	10	.286	5.53	23	17	0	0	2	0	86.1	117	397	59	53	9	9	4	2	28	1	25	7	0
JONES, AL, CHI	1	0	1.000	1.50	5	0	0	0	1	0	6.0	3	21	2	1	0	0	0	0	3	0	2	0	0
JONES, MIKE, K.C.*	3	3	.500	4.78	33	1	0	0	16	0	64.0	62	290	40	34	6	4	6	0	39	4	32	1	0
KAISER, JEFF, OAK.*	0	0	—	14.58	15	0	0	0	4	0	16.2	25	97	32	27	6	1	2	1	20	2	10	2	0
KERN, JIM, MILW	0	1	.000	6.55	5	0	0	0	1	0	11.0	14	50	8	8	1	1	0	0	5	1	3	3	0
KEY, JIMMY, TOR.*	14	6	.700	3.00	35	32	3	0	0	0	212.2	188	856	77	71	22	5	5	2	50	1	85	6	1
KIPPER, BOB, CAL.*	0	1	.000	21.60	2	1	0	0	0	0	3.1	7	20	8	8	1	0	2	0	3	0	0	0	0
KISON, BRUCE, BOS	5	3	.625	4.11	22	9	0	0	5	1	92.0	98	398	43	42	9	4	3	1	32	4	56	1	0
KLAWITTER, TOM, MINN.*	0	0	—	6.75	7	2	0	0	3	0	9.1	7	45	7	7	2	1	0	0	13	0	5	3	0
KRUEGER, BILL, OAK.*	9	10	.474	4.52	32	23	2	0	4	0	151.1	165	674	95	76	13	1	5	2	69	1	56	6	2
LACOSS, MIKE, K.C	1	1	.500	5.09	21	0	0	0	7	1	40.2	49	193	25	23	2	3	0	0	29	6	26	2	0
LADD, PETE, MILW	0	0	—	4.53	29	0	0	0	13	2	45.2	58	202	26	23	5	0	6	2	10	0	22	1	0
LAMP, DENNIS, TOR	11	0	1.000	3.32	53	1	0	0	11	2	105.2	96	426	42	39	7	5	6	0	27	3	68	5	0

*THROWS LEFTHANDED

PITCHER AND CLUB	W	L	PCT	ERA	G	GS	CG	SHO	GF	SV	IP	H	TBF	R	ER	HR	SH	SF	HB	TBB	IBB	SO	WP	BK
LANGFORD, RICK, OAK	3	5	.375	3.51	23	3	0	0	7	0	59.0	60	247	24	23	8	2	0	0	15	2	21	2	0
LANGSTON, MARK, SEA.*	7	14	.333	5.47	24	24	2	0	0	0	126.2	122	577	85	77	22	3	2	2	91	2	72	3	3
LAVELLE, GARY, TOR.*	5	7	.417	3.10	69	0	0	0	19	8	72.2	54	298	30	25	5	8	2	0	36	5	50	0	1
LAZORKO, JACK, SEA	0	0	—	3.54	15	0	0	0	4	1	20.1	23	92	10	8	[illegible]	2	0	3	8	1	7	0	0
LEAL, LUIS, TOR	3	6	.333	5.75	15	14	0	0	1	0	67.1	82	303	46	43	13	1	4	3	24	3	33	3	1
LEARY, TIM, MILW	1	4	.200	4.05	5	5	0	0	0	0	33.1	40	146	18	15	5	2	0	1	8	0	29	1	0
LEIBRANDT, CHARLIE, K.C.*	17	9	.654	2.69	33	33	8	3	0	0	237.2	223	983	86	71	17	8	5	2	68	3	108	4	3
LEONARD, DENNIS, K.C	0	0	—	.00	2	0	0	0	1	0	2.0	1	7	0	0	0	0	0	0	0	0	1	0	0
LESLEY, BRAD, MILW	1	0	1.000	9.95	5	0	0	0	0	0	6.1	8	29	7	7	2	0	0	0	2	0	5	0	0
LEWIS, JIM, SEA	0	1	.000	7.71	2	1	0	0	0	0	4.2	8	23	4	4	1	1	0	2	1	0	1	0	0
LOLLAR, TIM, CHI.-BOS.*	8	10	.444	4.62	34	23	1	0	7	1	150.0	140	669	85	77	19	4	5	2	98	1	105	10	2
LONG, BILL, CHI	0	1	.000	10.29	4	3	0	0	1	0	14.0	25	71	17	16	4	1	1	0	5	2	13	1	0
LONG, ROBERT, SEA	0	0	—	3.76	28	0	0	0	13	0	38.1	30	162	17	16	7	0	0	2	17	1	29	2	0
LOPEZ, AURELIO, DET	3	7	.300	4.80	51	0	0	0	22	5	86.1	82	379	50	46	15	3	6	1	41	9	53	4	0
LUGO, RAFAEL, CAL	3	4	.429	3.69	20	10	1	0	5	0	83.0	86	351	36	34	10	2	2	4	29	1	42	2	0
LYSANDER, RICK, MINN	0	2	.000	6.05	35	1	0	0	9	3	61.0	72	262	43	41	3	2	2	0	22	2	26	9	0
MACK, TONY, CAL	0	1	.000	15.43	1	1	0	0	0	0	2.1	8	14	4	4	0	0	0	0	0	0	0	0	0
MAHLER, MICKEY, DET.*	1	2	.333	1.74	3	2	0	0	0	0	20.2	19	84	8	4	2	1	0	0	4	2	14	4	0
MARTINEZ, DENNIS, BALT	13	11	.542	5.15	33	31	3	1	1	0	180.0	203	789	110	103	29	0	11	9	63	3	68	4	1
MARTINEZ, TIPPY, BALT.*	3	3	.500	5.40	49	0	0	0	20	4	70.0	70	312	48	42	8	3	4	0	37	8	47	5	0
MASON, MIKE, TEX.*	8	15	.348	4.83	38	30	1	1	1	0	179.0	212	800	113	96	22	4	10	3	73	4	92	4	1
MCCARTHY, TOM, BOS	0	0	—	10.80	3	0	0	0	2	0	5.0	7	25	6	6	1	0	1	0	4	0	2	1	0
MCCASKILL, KIRK, CAL	12	12	.500	4.70	30	29	6	1	0	0	189.2	189	807	105	99	23	2	5	4	64	1	102	5	0
MCCATTY, STEVE, OAK	4	4	.500	5.57	30	9	1	0	8	0	85.2	95	383	56	53	10	3	3	4	41	4	36	1	0
MCCLURE, BOB, MILW.*	4	1	.800	4.31	38	1	0	0	12	3	85.2	91	370	43	41	10	3	2	3	30	2	57	5	0
MCGREGOR, SCOTT, BALT.*	14	14	.500	4.81	35	34	8	1	0	0	204.0	226	884	118	109	34	10	8	1	65	2	86	2	1
MIRABELLA, PAUL, SEA.*	0	0	—	1.32	10	0	0	0	1	0	13.2	9	57	4	2	0	1	2	2	4	1	8	0	0
MITCHELL, CHARLIE, BOS	0	0	—	16.20	2	0	0	0	0	0	1.2	5	10	3	3	1	0	0	0	0	0	2	0	0
MONTEFUSCO, JOHN, N.Y	0	0	—	10.29	3	1	0	0	1	0	7.0	12	34	8	8	3	0	1	0	2	0	2	0	0
MOORE, DONNIE, CAL	8	8	.500	1.92	65	0	0	0	57	31	103.0	91	417	28	22	9	10	2	0	21	3	72	2	0
MOORE, MIKE, SEA	17	10	.630	3.46	35	34	14	2	1	0	247.0	230	1016	100	95	18	2	7	4	70	2	155	10	3
MORGAN, MIKE, SEA	1	1	.500	12.00	2	2	0	0	0	0	6.0	11	33	8	8	2	0	0	0	5	0	2	1	0
MORRIS, JACK, DET	16	11	.593	3.33	35	35	13	4	0	0	257.0	212	1077	102	95	21	11	7	5	110	7	191	15	3
MURA, STEVE, OAK	1	1	.500	4.13	23	1	0	0	10	1	48.0	41	209	25	22	3	1	1	0	25	4	29	0	0

MURRAY, DALE, N.Y.-TEX	0	0	—	15.00	4	0	0	0	2	0	3.0	7	15	5	5	0	1	0	0	0	0	0	1	0
MUSSELMAN, RON, TOR	3	0	1.000	4.47	25	4	0	0	9	0	52.1	59	236	28	26	2	0	4	0	24	2	29	3	0
NELSON, GENE, CHI	10	10	.500	4.26	46	18	1	0	11	2	145.2	144	643	74	69	23	9	2	7	67	4	101	11	1
NIEKRO, JOE, N.Y	2	1	.667	5.84	3	3	0	0	0	0	12.1	14	58	8	8	3	0	0	0	8	0	4	0	0
NIEKRO, PHIL, N.Y	16	12	.571	4.09	33	33	7	1	0	0	220.0	203	955	110	100	29	1	3	2	120	1	149	5	2
NIPPER, AL, BOS	9	12	.429	4.06	25	25	5	0	0	0	162.0	157	713	83	73	14	4	4	9	82	3	85	3	1
NOLES, DICKIE, TEX	4	8	.333	5.06	28	13	0	0	3	1	110.1	129	488	67	62	11	2	0	6	33	1	59	1	0
NUNEZ, EDWIN, SEA	7	3	.700	3.09	70	0	0	0	53	16	90.1	79	378	36	31	13	4	3	0	34	5	58	2	1
O'NEAL, RANDY, DET	5	5	.500	3.24	28	12	1	0	8	1	94.1	82	383	42	34	8	1	7	2	36	3	52	5	0
OJEDA, BOB, BOS.*	9	11	.450	4.00	39	22	5	0	10	1	157.2	166	671	74	70	11	10	3	2	48	9	102	3	3
ONTIVEROS, STEVE, OAK	1	3	.250	1.93	39	0	0	0	18	8	74.2	45	284	17	16	4	2	2	2	19	2	36	1	0
PETRY, DAN, DET	15	13	.536	3.36	34	34	8	0	0	0	238.2	190	962	98	89	24	0	2	3	81	9	109	6	0
PORTER, CHUCK, MILW	0	0	—	1.98	6	1	0	0	1	0	13.2	15	53	8	3	1	1	0	0	2	0	8	0	0
PORTUGAL, MARK, MINN	1	3	.250	5.55	6	4	0	0	0	0	24.1	24	105	16	15	3	0	2	0	14	0	12	1	1
QUISENBERRY, DAN, K.C.	8	9	.471	2.37	84	0	0	0	76	37	129.0	142	532	41	34	8	4	3	1	16	5	54	0	0
RASMUSSEN, DENNIS, N.Y.*	3	5	.375	3.98	22	16	2	0	1	0	101.2	97	429	56	45	10	1	5	1	42	1	63	3	1
REED, JERRY, CLEV	3	5	.375	4.11	33	5	0	0	19	8	72.1	67	301	41	33	12	2	4	3	19	2	37	4	0
RIGHETTI, DAVE, N.Y.*	12	7	.632	2.78	74	0	0	0	60	29	107.0	96	452	36	33	5	6	3	0	45	3	92	7	0
RIJO, JOSE, OAK	6	4	.600	3.53	12	9	0	0	1	0	63.2	57	272	26	25	6	5	0	1	28	2	65	0	0
ROMAN, JOSE, CLEV	0	4	.000	6.61	5	3	0	0	1	0	16.1	13	79	17	12	3	0	0	0	14	0	12	1	1
ROMANICK, RON, CAL	14	9	.609	4.11	31	31	6	1	0	0	195.0	210	831	101	89	29	4	10	4	62	1	64	2	3
ROMERO, RAMON, CLEV.*	2	3	.400	6.58	19	10	0	0	5	0	64.1	69	295	48	47	13	1	1	5	38	0	38	6	0
ROZEMA, DAVE, TEX	3	7	.300	4.19	34	4	0	0	16	7	88.0	100	374	45	41	10	1	1	2	22	3	42	1	0
RUHLE, VERN, CLEV	2	10	.167	4.32	42	16	1	0	7	3	125.0	139	532	65	60	16	4	4	2	30	6	54	2	0
RUSSELL, JEFF, TEX	3	6	.333	7.55	13	13	0	0	0	0	62.0	85	295	55	52	10	1	3	2	27	1	44	2	0
SABERHAGEN, BRET, K.C.	20	6	.769	2.87	32	32	10	1	0	0	235.1	211	931	79	75	19	9	7	1	38	1	158	1	3
SANCHEZ, LUIS, CAL	2	0	1.000	5.72	26	0	0	0	16	2	61.1	67	268	41	39	9	0	3	1	27	3	34	2	0
SCHERRER, BILL, DET.*	3	2	.600	4.36	48	0	0	0	14	0	66.0	62	299	35	32	10	5	2	1	41	13	46	5	0
SCHMIDT, DAVE, TEX	7	6	.538	3.15	51	4	1	1	35	5	85.2	81	356	36	30	6	3	2	0	22	8	46	2	1
SCHROM, KEN, MINN	9	12	.429	4.99	29	26	6	0	1	0	160.2	164	679	95	89	28	9	8	0	59	2	74	2	0
SCHULZE, DON, CLEV	4	10	.286	6.01	19	18	1	0	0	0	94.1	128	429	75	63	10	6	3	4	19	2	37	3	0
SCURRY, ROD, N.Y.*	1	0	1.000	2.84	5	0	0	0	2	1	12.2	5	51	4	4	2	1	0	0	10	1	17	0	0
SEARAGE, RAY, MILW.*	1	4	.200	5.92	33	0	0	0	18	1	38.0	54	169	27	25	2	4	1	0	24	4	36	0	0
SEAVER, TOM, CHI	16	11	.593	3.17	35	33	6	1	0	0	238.2	223	993	103	84	22	7	8	8	69	6	134	10	0
SEBRA, BOB, TEX	0	2	.000	7.52	7	4	0	0	0	0	20.1	26	102	17	17	4	0	2	1	14	2	13	0	0
SELLERS, JEFF, BOS	2	0	1.000	3.63	4	4	1	0	0	0	22.1	24	97	10	9	1	1	1	0	7	1	6	1	0
SHIRLEY, BOB, N.Y.*	5	5	.500	2.64	48	8	2	0	9	2	109.0	103	446	34	32	5	5	4	0	26	2	55	1	0

*THROWS LEFTHANDED

PITCHER AND CLUB	W	L	PCT	ERA	G	GS	CG	SHO	GF	SV	IP	H	TBF	R	ER	HR	SH	SF	HB	TBB	IBB	SO	WP	BK
SLATON, JIM, CAL	6	10	.375	4.37	29	24	1	0	3	1	148.1	162	645	82	72	22	5	5	2	63	1	60	8	0
SMITH, D.W., CAL	0	0	—	7.20	4	0	0	0	2	0	5.0	5	20	4	4	1	0	1	0	1	0	3	0	0
SMITH, ROY, CLEV	1	4	.200	5.34	12	11	1	0	0	0	62.1	84	285	40	37	8	1	4	1	17	0	28	[illegible]	0
SMITHSON, MIKE, MINN	15	14	.517	4.34	37	37	8	3	0	0	257.0	264	1088	134	124	25	10	7	15	78	1	127	6	1
SNELL, NATE, BALT	3	2	.600	2.69	43	0	0	0	15	5	100.1	100	421	44	30	4	4	1	1	30	5	41	1	0
SNYDER, BRIAN, SEA.*	1	2	.333	6.37	15	6	0	0	5	1	35.1	44	166	28	25	2	1	1	1	19	2	23	4	2
SPILLNER, DAN, CHI	4	3	.571	3.44	52	3	0	0	15	1	91.2	83	378	39	35	10	3	3	0	33	2	41	4	0
STANLEY, BOB, BOS	6	6	.500	2.87	48	0	0	0	41	10	87.2	76	360	30	28	7	3	4	2	30	10	46	1	0
STANTON, MIKE, SEA.-CHI	1	3	.250	6.42	35	0	0	0	16	1	40.2	47	200	34	29	6	1	1	3	29	3	29	3	0
STEWART, DAVE, TEX	0	6	.000	5.42	42	5	0	0	29	4	81.1	86	361	53	49	13	5	2	2	37	5	64	5	1
STEWART, SAMMY, BALT	5	7	.417	3.61	56	1	0	0	36	9	129.2	117	557	60	52	15	9	5	1	66	10	77	5	1
STIEB, DAVE, TOR	14	13	.519	2.48	36	36	8	2	0	0	265.0	206	1087	89	73	22	14	2	9	96	3	167	4	1
STODDARD, BOB, DET	0	0	—	6.75	8	0	0	0	3	1	13.1	15	61	11	10	3	0	0	0	5	0	11	2	0
SURHOFF, RICH, TEX	0	1	.000	7.56	7	0	0	0	5	2	8.1	12	39	7	7	2	1	0	0	3	0	8	0	0
SUTTON, DON, OAK.-CAL	15	10	.600	3.86	34	34	1	1	0	0	226.0	221	943	101	97	25	4	5	0	59	0	107	6	0
SWAGGERTY, BILL, BALT	0	0	—	5.40	1	0	0	0	0	0	1.2	3	10	1	1	0	0	0	0	2	1	2	0	0
SWIFT, BILL, SEA	6	10	.375	4.77	23	21	0	0	0	0	120.2	131	532	71	64	8	6	3	5	48	5	55	5	3
TANANA, FRANK, TEX.-DET.*	12	14	.462	4.27	33	33	4	0	0	0	215.0	220	907	112	102	28	5	8	3	57	8	159	5	1
TANNER, BRUCE, CHI	1	2	.333	5.33	10	4	0	0	3	0	27.0	34	128	17	16	1	2	1	2	13	3	9	0	0
TELLMANN, THOMAS, OAK	0	0	—	5.06	11	0	0	0	3	0	21.1	33	106	12	12	3	0	1	1	9	1	8	0	0
TERRELL, WALT, DET	15	10	.600	3.85	34	34	5	3	0	0	229.0	221	983	107	98	9	11	7	4	95	5	130	5	0
THOMAS, ROY, SEA	7	0	1.000	3.36	40	0	0	0	9	1	93.2	66	385	37	35	8	2	7	2	48	12	70	4	2
THOMPSON, RICH, CLEV	3	8	.273	6.30	57	0	0	0	24	5	80.0	95	379	63	56	8	5	6	6	48	6	30	6	2
TOBIK, DAVE, SEA	1	0	1.000	6.00	8	0	0	0	4	1	9.0	10	40	8	6	2	0	2	0	3	0	8	1	0
TRUJILLO, MIKE, BOS	4	4	.500	4.82	27	7	1	0	7	1	84.0	112	379	55	45	7	1	2	3	23	1	19	1	0
VANDE BERG, ED, SEA.*	2	1	.667	3.72	76	0	0	0	22	3	67.2	71	296	30	28	4	2	3	1	31	5	34	4	0
VIOLA, FRANK, MINN.*	18	14	.563	4.09	36	36	9	0	0	0	250.2	262	1059	136	114	26	5	5	2	68	3	135	6	2
VON OHLEN, DAVE, CLEV.*	3	2	.600	2.91	26	0	0	0	9	0	43.1	47	196	20	14	3	9	4	0	20	6	12	0	0
VUCKOVICH, PETE, MILW	6	10	.375	5.51	22	22	1	0	0	0	112.2	134	511	74	69	16	5	1	7	48	2	55	3	0
WADDELL, TOM, CLEV	8	6	.571	4.87	49	9	1	0	28	9	112.2	104	471	61	61	20	5	4	1	39	8	53	1	0
WAITS, RICK, MILW.*	3	2	.600	6.51	24	0	0	0	8	1	47.0	67	220	37	34	3	2	1	0	20	5	24	1	0
WARDLE, CURT, MINN.-CLEV.*	8	9	.471	6.18	50	12	0	0	13	1	115.0	127	523	83	79	20	6	6	2	62	0	84	3	1
WARREN, MIKE, OAK	1	4	.200	6.61	16	6	0	0	2	0	49.0	52	243	42	36	13	0	2	4	38	0	48	3	1
WEGMAN, BILL, MILW	2	0	1.000	3.57	3	3	0	0	0	0	17.2	17	73	8	7	3	0	1	0	3	0	6	0	1

WEHRMEISTER, DAVE, CHI	2	2	.500	3.43	23	0	0	0	4	2	39.1	35	159	15	15	4	1	0	3	10	0	32	0	0
WELSH, CHRIS, TEX.*	2	5	.286	4.13	25	6	0	0	4	0	76.1	101	351	40	35	11	1	1	4	25	3	31	5	0
WHITEHOUSE, LEN, MINN.*	0	0	—	11.05	5	0	0	0	2	1	7.1	12	36	9	9	4	0	0	0	2	0	4	1	0
WHITSON, ED, N.Y	10	8	.556	4.88	30	30	2	2	0	0	158.2	201	705	100	86	19	3	7	2	43	0	89	1	0
WILCOX, MILT, DET	1	3	.250	4.85	8	8	0	0	0	0	39.0	51	177	24	21	6	1	0	0	14	2	20	2	0
WILKINSON, BILL, SEA.*	0	2	.000	13.50	2	2	0	0	0	0	6.0	8	30	9	9	2	0	0	0	6	1	5	0	0
WILLIAMS, MATT, TEX	2	1	.667	2.42	6	3	0	0	1	0	26.0	20	106	7	7	3	1	0	0	10	0	22	2	0
WILLS, FRANK, SEA	5	11	.313	6.00	24	18	1	0	2	1	123.0	122	541	85	82	18	4	8	3	68	3	67	9	1
WITT, MIKE, CAL	15	9	.625	3.56	35	35	6	1	0	0	250.0	228	1049	115	99	22	4	5	4	98	6	180	11	1
WOODWARD, ROB, BOS	1	0	1.000	1.69	5	2	0	0	3	0	26.2	17	113	8	5	0	1	0	2	9	0	16	0	0
WRIGHT, RICKY, TEX.*	0	0	—	4.70	5	0	0	0	1	0	7.2	5	32	4	4	0	0	0	0	5	1	7	0	0
YETT, RICH, MINN	0	0	—	27.00	1	1	0	0	0	0	0.1	1	5	1	1	0	0	0	0	2	0	0	1	0
YOUNG, CURT, OAK.*	0	4	.000	7.24	19	7	0	0	5	0	46.0	57	214	38	37	15	0	1	1	22	0	19	1	0
YOUNG, MATT, SEA.*	12	19	.387	4.91	37	35	5	2	2	1	218.1	242	951	135	119	23	7	3	7	76	3	136	6	2
ZAHN, GEOFF, CAL.*	2	2	.500	4.38	7	7	1	1	0	0	37.0	44	154	19	18	5	2	1	0	14	0	14	1	0

CLUB PITCHING

CLUB	W	L	ERA	G	CG	SHO	REL	SV	IP	H	TBF	R	ER	HR	SH	SF	HB	TBB	IBB	SO	WP	BK
TORONTO	99	62	3.31	161	18	9	316	47	1448.0	1312	6004	588	532	147	47	41	26	484	26	823	36	5
KANSAS CITY	91	71	3.49	162	27	11	216	41	1461.0	1433	6165	639	566	103	48	42	28	463	37	846	43	9
NEW YORK	97	64	3.69	161	25	9	271	49	1440.1	1373	6065	660	590	157	32	42	13	518	20	907	34	5
DETROIT	84	77	3.78	161	31	11	250	40	1456.0	1313	6135	688	612	141	43	49	23	556	67	943	62	6
CALIFORNIA	90	72	3.91	162	22	8	250	41	1457.1	1453	6164	703	633	171	48	44	27	514	30	767	45	4
BOSTON	81	81	4.06	163	35	8	202	29	1461.1	1487	6281	720	659	130	49	38	35	540	54	913	34	13
CHICAGO	85	77	4.07	163	20	8	305	39	1451.2	1411	6221	720	656	161	57	47	36	569	35	1023	54	5
BALTIMORE	83	78	4.38	161	32	6	238	33	1427.1	1480	6182	764	694	160	59	41	23	568	57	793	32	7
MILWAUKEE	71	90	4.39	161	34	6	248	37	1437.0	1510	6212	802	701	175	52	51	33	499	31	777	51	4
OAKLAND	77	85	4.41	162	10	6	299	41	1453.0	1451	6327	787	712	172	39	46	25	607	32	785	48	5
MINNESOTA	77	85	4.48	162	41	7	237	34	1426.1	1468	6067	782	710	164	47	55	30	462	31	767	51	11
TEXAS	62	99	4.56	161	18	5	264	33	1411.2	1479	6112	785	715	173	28	44	36	501	38	863	43	7
SEATTLE	74	88	4.68	162	23	8	335	30	1432.0	1456	6260	818	744	154	38	48	41	637	54	868	61	18
CLEVELAND	60	102	4.91	162	24	7	306	28	1421.0	1556	6262	861	776	170	61	70	43	547	45	702	46	7
TOTALS	1131	1131	4.15	1132	360	109	3737	522	20184.0	20182	86457	10317	9300	2178	648	658	419	7465	557	11777	640	106

TV/RADIO ROUNDUP

NETWORK COVERAGE

NBC-TV: This is NBC's year for the World Series, plus the Saturday Game of the Week and two prime-time regular-season games. Vin Scully, Joe Garagiola, Bob Costas and Tony Kubek do the honors.

ABC-TV: Monday Night Baseball, the 1986 All-Star Game, the American and National League Championship Series and probably late-season Sunday afternoon games are on the ABC docket. Al Michaels, Jim Palmer and Tim McCarver are the likely announcing crew.

NATIONAL LEAGUE

ATLANTA BRAVES: WSB Radio (750) and WTBS-TV (Channel 17) are the anchor stations for the Braves' network. Ernie Johnson, Pete Van Wieren, John Sterling and Skip Caray provide the coverage.

CHICAGO CUBS: Harry Caray, Steve Stone and Dewayne Staats describe the action for WGN-TV (Channel 9), while Lou Boudreau, Vince Lloyd and Staats do it for WGN radio (720).

CINCINNATI REDS: Marty Brennaman, Joe Nuxhall and Steve Physioc are on WLTW-TV (Channel 5). Brennaman and Nuxhall team up on WLW radio (700).

HOUSTON ASTROS: Gene Elston and Milo Hamilton are the regulars on KTRH radio (740) and KTXH (Channel 20), with Larry Dierker pitching in for away TV games and radio for home games.

LOS ANGELES DODGERS: Vin Scully, Ross Porter and Jerry Doggett broadcast over KABC radio (790) and KTTV-TV (Channel 11). Spanish coverage is provided by Jaime Jarrin and Rene Cardenas on KTNQ radio (1020).

San Diego's Eric Show threw Pete Rose's Cobb-breaker.

MONTREAL EXPOS: Dave Van Horne and Duke Snider work the games for the English-speaking audience on CFCF radio (600) and the CBC-TV network. Jacques Doucet and Rodger Brulotte say it in French for radio CKAC (730), while Raymond Lebrun and Claude Raymond are the French play-by-play announcers for CBC-TV.

NEW YORK METS: Ralph Kiner, Tim McCarver and Steve Zabriskie handle television on WOR (Channel 9) and will be joined by Fran Healy on SportsChannel. Bob Murphy and Gary Thorne have radio duties for WHN (1050).

PHILADELPHIA PHILLIES: Harry Kalas, Andy Musser, Chris Wheeler and Richie Ashburn describe the action on WCAU radio (1210) and WTAF-TV (Channel 29).

PITTSBURGH PIRATES: Lanny Frattare, Jim Rooker and John Sanders line up for KDKA radio (1020) and also do the honors for KDKA-TV (Channel 2).

ST. LOUIS CARDINALS: Jack Buck, Mike Shannon and Ken Wilson are on KMOX radio (1120) and are joined by Jay Randolph on KSDK-TV (Channel 5).

SAN DIEGO PADRES: Jerry Coleman and Dave Campbell handle the play-by-play for KFMB radio (760) and KCST-TV (Channel 39).

SAN FRANCISCO GIANTS: Hank Greenwald is on radio station KNBR (680), while Gary Park and Greenwald work the television side for KTVU (Channel 2).

AMERICAN LEAGUE

BALTIMORE ORIOLES: Jon Miller and Tom Marr describe the action for radio station WFBR (1300), while Chuck Thompson and Brooks Robinson perform the chores for WMAR-TV (Channel 2). Mel Proctor, Rex Barney and John Lowenstein work the games for Home Team Sports cable network.

BOSTON RED SOX: Ken Coleman and Joe Castiglione broadcast over the Campbell Sports Network, including WRKO (680), while Ned Martin and Bob Montgomery handle television on WSBK-TV (Channel 38) and New England Sports Network cable.

CALIFORNIA ANGELS: Al Conin and Ron Fairly describe the action on KMPC radio (710). Telecasts will be carried by KTLA-TV (Channel 5), with Bob Starr and Joe Torre expected to man the mikes.

CHICAGO WHITE SOX: Don Drysdale and Del Crandall are the television crew for WFLD-TV (Channel 32) and SportsVision cable. Lorn Brown and an announcer to be named call the action on radio station WMAG (670).

CLEVELAND INDIANS: Herb Score and Steve LaMar will be behind the mike for WWWE (1100), the flagship station for a five-state radio network. Joe Tait anchors the telecasts for WUAB-TV (Channel 43).

DETROIT TIGERS: Ernie Harwell and Paul Carey broadcast on a radio network originating with WJR (760). George Kell and Al Kaline handle the chores for WDIV-TV (Channel 4).

KANSAS CITY ROYALS: Denny Trease, Denny Matthews and Fred White call the shots for WDAF-TV (Channel 4), while White and Matthews share radio time on a network headed by KMBZ (980) and WIBW (580).

MILWAUKEE BREWERS: Steve Shannon and Mike Hegan describe the action for WVTV-TV (Channel 18). Bob Uecker and Pat Hughes work the radio for WTMJ (620).

MINNESOTA TWINS: Harmon Killebrew and Bob Kurtz will be on KMSP-TV. Joe Angel and Herb Carneal call the plays for a radio network headed by WCCO (830).

NEW YORK YANKEES: Phil Rizzuto and Bill White, with an announcer to be named, will call it for WPIX (Channel 11). The voices were unconfirmed for SportsChannel Cable and a radio network originating with WABC (770).

OAKLAND A's: Bill King and Lon Simmons do the play-by-play on KFSO radio (560) and are joined by Ted Robinson on KPIX-TV (Channel 5).

SEATTLE MARINERS: Dave Niehaus and Rick Rizzs play it again for radio station KIRO (710) and KIRO-TV (Channel 7).

TORONTO BLUE JAYS: Tom Cheek and Jerry Howarth do the radio play-by-play on a network that originates with CJCL (1430). Don Chevrier, Tony Kubek and Fergie Olver are behind the mike for CTV Network. Olver, Kubek and Ken Singleton handle TSN Pay TV.

TEXAS RANGERS: Eric Nadel and Mark Holtz work the games for WBAP radio (820). KTVT-TV (Channel 11) will carry 50 road games with announcers to be named.

OFFICIAL 1986

EAST

	AT CHICAGO	AT MONTREAL	AT NEW YORK
Chicago		April 15,17 August 14*,15*,15*, 16*,17 Sept. 15*,16*	June 19*,20*,21,22 July 28*,29*,30* Sept. 17*,18
Montreal	April 24,25,26,27 June 30, July 1,2 Sept. 22,23		June 23*,24*,25 August 1*,2*,3 Sept. 8*,9*,10*
New York	June 27,28,29 August 4,5,6,7 Sept. 24,25	June 16*,17*,18* August 8*,9*,10 Sept. 30*, Oct. 1*,2*	
Philadelphia	June 16,17,18 August 8,9,10 Sept. 8,9,10	April 22,23 June 5*,6*,7*,8 Sept. 26*,27*,28	April 18*,19,20 June 9*,10*,11* Sept. 19*,20*,21
Pittsburgh	April 18,19,20 August 11,12,13 Sept. 19,20,21	June 19*,20*,21*,22 July 28*,29*,30* Sept. 17*,18	April 21*,22* June 13*,14,15,15 Oct. 3*,4,5
St. Louis	April 21,22,23 June 13, 14,15 Oct. 3,4,5	April 18,19,20 August 11*,12*,13* Sept. 19*,20*,21	April 14,16,17 August 14*,15*,16,17 Sept. 22*,23
Atlanta	May 30,31, June 1 August 19,20,21	May 14*,15 July 17*,18*,19*,20	May 12*,13* July 10*,11*,12,13
Cincinnati	May 26,27,28 August 22,23,24	May 12*,13 July 10*,11*,12,*13	May 9*,10,11 July 7*,8*,9
Houston	May 23,24,25 Sept. 1,2,3	May 2,3,4 July 7*,8*,9*	May 6*,7* July 3*,4,5*,6
Los Angeles	May 6,7,8 July 25,26,27	May 9,10,11 Sept. 1*,2*,3*	May 27*,28*,29* August 29*,30,31
San Diego	May 9,10,11 July 21,22,23	May 26*,27*,28* August 29*,30*,31	June 2*,3*,4* Sept. 5*,6,7
San Francisco	May 13,14 July 17,18,19,20	June 3*,4* Sept. 4*,5*,6*,7	May 30*,31*, June 1 Sept. 1,2*,3*

* NIGHT GAME
HEAVY BLACK FIGURES DENOTE SUNDAYS
NIGHT GAMES: ANY GAME STARTING AFTER 5:00 p.m.

NATIONAL LEAGUE SCHEDULE

EAST

	AT PHILADELPHIA	AT PITTSBURGH	AT ST. LOUIS
Chicago	June 23*,24*,25* August 1*,2,3 Sept. 29*,30*, Oct. 1*	April 11*,12,13 June 9*,10*,11* Sept. 12*,13*,14	April 8*,10 June 5*,6*,7,8 Sept. 26*,27,28
Montreal	May 5*,6*,7* June 13*,14*,15 Oct. 3*,4*,5	June 27*,28*,29 August 4*,5*,6*,7* Sept. 24*,25*	April 11*,12*,13 June 9*,10*,11* Sept. 12*,13*,14
New York	April 11*,12,13 August 11*,12*,13* Sept. 12*,13*,14	April 8*,10* June 5*,6*,7*,8 Sept. 26*, 27*,28	April 24*,25*,26,27 June 30*, July 1*,2* Sept. 15*,16*
Philadelphia		April 24*,25*,26,27 June 30*, July 1*,2 Sept. 22*, 23*	June 27*,28*,29 August 4*,5*,6*,7 Sept. 24*,25*
Pittsburgh	April 14*,15*,16* August 14,15*,16*,17 Sept. 15*,16*		June 23*,24*,25* August 8*,9*,10 Sept. 30*, Oct. 1*,2*
St. Louis	June 19*,20*,21*,22 July 28*,29*,30* Sept. 17*,18*	June 16*,17*,18* August 1*,2*,3 Sept. 8*,9*,10*	
Atlanta	May 2*,3,4 July 7*,8*,9	May 26,27*,28* August 22*,23*,24	May 23*,24*,25 August 25*,26*,27*
Cincinnati	May 14*,15* July 3*,4*,5*,6	May 23*,24*,25 August 25*,26*,27*	May 20*,21*,22 August 29*,30*,31
Houston	April 29*,30* July 24*,25*,26*,27	May 9*,10*,11 August 18*,19*,20*	May 26*,27*,28 August 22*,23*,24
Los Angeles	June 2*,3*,4* Sept. 5*,6*,7	May 30*,31*, June 1 July 22*,23*,24*	May 13*,14 July 17*,18*,19,20
San Diego	May 30*,31, June 1 Sept. 1*,2*,3*	May 13*,14* July 17*,18*,19,20	May 6*,7*,8 July 25*,26,27
San Francisco	May 27*,28*,29* August 29*,30*,31	May 6*,7*,8* July 25*,26*,27	May 9*,10*,11 July 21*,22*,23*

JULY 15 — ALL-STAR GAME AT HOUSTON

OFFICIAL 1986

WEST

	AT ATLANTA	AT CINCINNATI	AT HOUSTON
Chicago	May 20*,21*,22 August 29*,30,31	June 2*,3*,4* Sept. 5*,6*,7	May 16*,17*,18 August 25*,26*,27*
Montreal	April 8*,10* July 3*,4*,5,6	April 29*,30 July 24*,25*,26*,27	May 30*,31*, June 1 July 21*,22*,23
New York	April 29*,30*, May 1* July 25*,26*,27	May 2*,3,4 July 21*,22*,23*	May 14*,15* July 17*,18*,19*,20
Philadelphia	May 9*,10*,11 July 21*,22*,23*	April 7,9* July 17*,18*,19,20	May 12*,13* July 10*,11*,12,13
Pittsburgh	June 2*,3*,4* Sept. 5*,6,7	May 16*,17*,18 Sept. 1*,2*,3*	May 20*,21*,22 August 29*,30*,31
St. Louis	May 16*,17,18 Sept. 1*,2*,3*	May 30*,31, June 1 August 19*,20*,21*	June 2*,3*,4* Sept. 5*,6*,7
Atlanta		May 5*,6*,7*,8 June 20*,21*,22 Sept. 24*,25	April 11*,12*,13 July 28*,29*,30* Oct. 3*,4*,5
Cincinnati	April 15*,16* June 13*14,15,16* Sept. 30*, Oct. 1*,2*		April 24*,25*,26*,27 June 23*,24*,25* Sept. 8*,9
Houston	April 21*,22*,23* August 15*,16*,17 Sept. 26*,27,28	April 18*,19,20 June 17*,18*,19* Sept. 16*,17*,18	
Los Angeles	April 18*,19,20 June 17*,18*,19* Sept. 16*, 17*,18*	June 30*, July 1*,2* August 8*,9,10 Sept. 19*,20*,21	June 27*,28*,29 August 11*,12*,13*,14* Sept. 22*,23*
San Diego	June 27*,28*,29 August 11*,12*,13*,14* Sept. 22*,23*	April 22*,23 August 15*,16*,17,18 Oct. 3*,4,5	June 30*, July 1*,2 August 8*,9*,10 Sept. 19*,20*,21
San Francisco	June 30*, July 1*,2* August 8*,9*,10 Sept. 19*,20,21	June 27*,28*,29 August 11*,12*,13*,14* Sept. 22*,23*	April 8*,9*,10* June 12*,13*,14*,15 Sept. 24*,25

* NIGHT GAME
HEAVY BLACK FIGURES DENOTE SUNDAYS
NIGHT GAMES: ANY GAME STARTING AFTER 5:00 p.m.

NATIONAL LEAGUE SCHEDULE

WEST

	AT LOS ANGELES	AT SAN DIEGO	AT SAN FRANCISCO
Chicago	April 30*, May 1* July 10*,11*,12*,**13**	April 28*,29* July 3*,4*,5,**6**	May 2*,3,**4,4** July 8*,**9**
Montreal	May 20*,21*,22* August 22*,23*,**24**	May 16*,17*,**18** August 19*,20*,21	May 23*,24,**25** August 25,26*,27
New York	May 16*,17,**18** August 18*,19*,20*	May 23*,24*,**25** August 25*,26*,27*	May 20*,21,22 August 22*,23,**24**
Philadelphia	May 23*,24*,**25** August 25*,26*,27	May 20*,21*,22 August 22*,23*,**24**	May 16*,17,**18** August 19*,20,21
Pittsburgh	April 28*,29* July 3*,4*,5*,**6**	May 2*,3*,**4** July 7*,8*,9*	April 30, May 1 July 10,11*,12,**13**
St. Louis	May 2*,3*,**4** July 7*,8*,9*	April 30*, May 1 July 10,11*,12*,**13**	April 28,29* July 3*,4,5,**6**
Atlanta	April 24*,25*,26*,**27** June 23*,24*,25* Sept. 8*,9*	June 5*,6*,7*,**8** August 4*,5*,6* Sept. 10*,11*	June 10*,11 July 31*, August 1*,2,**3** Sept. 12*,13,**14**
Cincinnati	June 9*,10*,11* August 1*,2,**3** Sept. 12*,13,**14**	April 11*,12*,**13** July 28*,29*,30* Sept. 26*,27*,**28**	June 6*,7,**8,8** August 4,5*,6 Sept. 10,11
Houston	June 5*,6*,7,**8** August 4*,5*,6 Sept. 10*,11*	June 9*,10*,11 August 1*,2*,**3** Sept. 12*,13*,**14**	April 15,16 June 20*,21,**22,22** Sept. 30* Oct. 1,2
Los Angeles		April 14*,15*,16* June 13*,14*,**15** Sept. 29*,30*, Oct. 1*	April 21*,22*,23 August 15*,16,**17** Sept. 26*,27,**28**
San Diego	April 7,8*,9*,10* June 20*,21*,**22** Sept. 24*,25*		April 17,18*,19,**20** June 23,24*,25 Sept. 8*,9*
San Francisco	April 11*,12*,**13** July 28*,29*,30* Oct. 3*,4,**5**	April 25*,26*,**27** June 16*,17*,18*,19 Sept. 16*,17*	

JULY 15 — ALL-STAR GAME AT HOUSTON

OFFICIAL 1986 AMERICAN LEAGUE SCHEDULE

BOLD = SUNDAY ( ) = HOLIDAY * = NIGHT GAME TN = TWI-NIGHT DH **[2]** = DH TBA = TO BE ANNOUNCED

	AT SEATTLE	AT OAKLAND	AT CALIFORNIA	AT TEXAS	AT KANSAS CITY	AT MINNESOTA	AT CHICAGO
SEATTLE		April 24*,25*,26,**27** Aug. 11*,12,13	April 14,15*,16* Aug. 7*,8*,9*,**10**	June 6*,7TN,**8*** Sept. 9*,10*	June 9*,10*,11* Sept. 11*,12*,13*,**14**	April 11*,12,**13** July 28*,29*,30*	June 20*,21,**22** Sept. 29*,30* Oct. 1*
OAKLAND	April 18*,19*,**20** Aug. 4*,5*,6*		April 21*,22*,23* Aug. 15*,16*,**17**	June 19*,20*,21*,**22*** Sept. 29*,30* Oct. 1*	June 23*,24*,25*,26* Sept. 26*,27*,**28**	April 14*,15*,16 Aug. 1*,2*,**3**	June 5*,6*,7*,**8** Sept. 9*,10*,11*
CALIFORNIA	April 8*,9*,10* Aug. 1, 2*,**3**	April 11*,12,**13** July 28*,29*,30,31		July 23*,24*,25* Oct. 2*,3*,4*,**5**	June 20*,21*,**22** Sept. 29*,30* Oct. 1*	April 25*,26*,**27** Aug. 4*,5*,6	June 9*,10*,11 Sept. 12*,13*,**14**,15*
TEXAS	June 26*,27*,28*,**29** Sept. 22*,23*,24*	June 13*,14,**15** Sept. 15*,16,17	June 16*,17*,18* Sept. 26*,27,**28**		May 30*,31* June**1** Aug. 19*,20*,21*	June 9*,10*,11* Sept. 11*,12*,13,**14**	June 2*,3*,4* Aug. 28*,29*,30*,**31**
KANSAS CITY	June 30* July 1*,2* Sept. 19*,20*,**21**	June 16*,17,18 Oct. 3*,4,**5**	June 12*,13*,14,**15** Sept. 16*,17*,18*	May 19*,20*,21*,22* Sept. 5*,6*,**7***		June 27*,28*,**29** Sept. 22*,23*,24*,25	May 16*,17,**18** Aug. 25*,26*,27*
MINNESOTA	April 21*,22*,23 Aug. 14*,15*,16*,**17**	April 8*,9,10 Aug. 8*,9,**10[DH]**	April 17*,18*,19,**20** Aug. 11*,12*,13*	June 30* July 1*,2* Sept. 19*,20*,**21**	June 5*,6*,7*,**8** Sept. 8*,9*		June 23*,24*,25* Sept. 26*,27*,**28**
CHICAGO	June 12*,13*,14*,**15** Sept. 16*,17*,18*	June 27*,28,**29** Sept. 22*,23,24	June 30 July 1*,2* Sept. 19*,20,**21**	May (26*),27*.28* Aug. 22*,23*,**24***	May 23*,24*,**25** Sept. (1*),2*,3*,4*	June 17*,18*,19 Oct. 2*,3*,4*,**5**	

MILWAUKEE	May 12*,13*,14 July 25*,26*,**27**	May 7*,8 July 18*,19,**20(DH)**	May 9*,10,**11** July 21,22*,23*	April 25*,26*,**27** Aug. 12*,13*,14*	May (26*),27*,28* Aug. 29*,30*,**31**	May 23*,24*,**25** Sept. (1),2*,3*	April 7,9,10 Aug 15*,16***17**
DETROIT	May 30*,3-* June **1** Sept. (1),2*,3*	June 2*,3*,4 Sept. 5*,6,**7**	May 28*,29* Aug. 28*,29*,30*,**31**	May 5*,6*,7* July (4*),5*,**6***	May 12*,13* July 10*,11*,12,**13**	May 9*,10*,**11** July 7*,8*,9	April 14*,15*,16* Aug. 1*,2*,**3**
CLEVELAND	June 23*,24*,25 Sept. 26*,27*,**28**	June 30* July 1,2 Sept. 19*,20,**21**	June 27*,28*,**29** Sept 22*,23*,24*	April 29*,30* July 24*,25*,26*,**27***	May 14*,15* July 17*,18*,19*,**20**	June 20*,21*,**22** Sept. 29*,30* Oct. 1	May 2*,3*,**4** July 7*,8*,9
TORONTO	May 9*,10*,**11** July 21*,22*23	May 12*,13*,14 July 25*,26,**27**	May 7*,8* July 17*,18*,19,**20**	April 8*,9*,10* Aug. 8*,9*,**10***	April 11,12,**13** July 28*,29*,30*	May (26), 27*,28* Aug. 22*,23*,**24**	May 20*,21*,22* Sept. 5*,6,**7**
BALTIMORE	May 23*,24*,**25*** (26) Aug. 26*,27*	May 28,29 Aug. 28*,29*,30,**31**	May 30*,31* June **1** Sept. (1), 2*,3*	April 11*,12*,**13** July 28*,29*,30*	May 2*,3*,**4** July 7*,8*,9*	May 6*,7* July 3*,(4),5,**6**	April 29*,30* July 10*,11*,12*,**13**
NEW YORK	May 28*,29 Aug. 28*,29*,30***31***	May 30*,31 June **1** Sept. (1*),2*,3	June 2*,3*,4* Sept. 5*,6*,**7**	May 9*,10*,**11** July 7*,8*,9*	April 21*,22*,23* Aug. 15*,16,**17**	May 12*,13 July 10*,11*,12*,**13**	May 5*,6*,7* July (4*), 5,**6**
BOSTON	May 7*,8* July 17*,18*,19*,**20**	May 9*,10,**11** July 21*,22,23	May 12*,13*,14* July 25*,26*,**27**	May 23*,24*,**25** Aug. 25*,26*,27*	April 25*,26*,**27** Aug. 12*,13*,14*	May 30*,31*, June **1** Aug. 18*,19*,20*	April 11*,12*,**13** July 28*,29*,30*

ALL-STAR GAME AT THE ASTRODOME, IN HOUSTON, JULY 15

OFFICIAL 1986 AMERICAN LEAGUE SCHEDULE

BOLD = SUNDAY ( ) = HOLIDAY * = NIGHT GAME TN = TWI-NIGHT DH **[2]** = DH TBA = TO BE ANNOUNCED

	AT MILWAUKEE	AT DETROIT	AT CLEVELAND	AT TORONTO	AT BALTIMORE	AT NEW YORK	AT BOSTON
SEATTLE	May 5*,6 July 10*,11*,12*,**13***	May 20*,21*,22 Aug. 22*,23*,**24**	June 17*,18*,19* Oct. 3*,4,**5**	May 2*,3,**4** July 7*,8*,9*	June 3*,4*,5* Sept. 5*,6*,**7**	May 16*,17,**18** Aug. 19*,20,21*	April 29*,30* May 1* July (4*),5,**6**
OAKLAND	April 29*,30*, May 1 July (4*),5*,**6**	May 23*,24*,**25**,(26) Aug. 25*,26*	June 9*,10*,11* Sept. 12*,13,**14**	May 5*,6 July 10*,11*,12,**13**	May 16*,17*,**18** Aug. 19*,20*,21*	May 20*,21*,22* Aug. 22*,23*,**24**	May 2*,3,**4** July 7*,8*,9*
CALIFORNIA	May 2*,3,**4** July 7*,8*,9	May 16*,17,**18** Aug. 19*,20*,21*	June 6*,7,**8** Sept. 9*,10*,11*	April 29*,30* May 1* July (4*),5,**6**	May 19*,20*,21* Aug. 22*,23,**24**	May 23*,24,**25**,(26) Aug. 25*,26*	May 5*,6 July 10*,11*,12,**13**
TEXAS	April 14,16*,17 Aug. 1*,2*,**3**	May 14*,15* July 17*,18*,19*,**20**	May 12*,13* July 10*,11*,12,**13**	April 21*,22*,23 Aug. 15*,16,**17**	April 18*,19*,**20** Aug. 5*,6*,7*	May 2*,3,**4** July 21*,22*,23	May 16*,17,**18** Sept. (1*),2*,3*
KANSAS CITY	June 2*,3*,4 Aug. 22*,23*,**24**	April 29*,30* July 24*,25*,26*,**27**	May 5*,6*,7* July (4*),5,**6**	April 18*,19,**20** Aug. 5*,6*,7*	May 9*,10*,**11** July 21*,22*,23*	April 8,9*,10 Aug. 8*,9,**10**	April 14,16,17 Aug. 1*,2,**3**
MINNESOTA	May 16*,17,**18** Aug. 26*,27*,28	May 2*,3*,**4** July 21*,22*,23*	June 13*,14,**15** Sept. 15*,16*,17*	June 2*,3*,4* Aug. 29*,30,**31**	May 14*,15* July 17*,18*,19*,**20**	April 29*,30* May 1* July 25*,26,**27**	May 19*,20*,21* Sept. 5*,6,**7**
CHICAGO	April 22*,23* Aug. 8*,9*,**10**,11*	April 25*,26,**27** Aug. 12*,13*,14	May 9*,10,**11** July 21*,22*,23*	May 30*,31 June **1** Aug. 18*,19*,20	May 12*,13* July 24*,25*,26,**27**	May 14*,15* July 17*,18*,19,**20**	April 18*,19,**20** Aug. 4*,5*,6*

MILWAUKEE		June 27*,28,**29[DH]** Sept. 9*,10*,11*	May 30*,31 June **1** Aug. 18*,19*,20*	June 23*,24*,25 Oct. 3*,4,**5**	June 30* July 1*,2* Sept. 19*,20*,**21**	April 11*,12,**13** Aug. 4*,5*,6*,7*	June 12*,13*,14,**15** Sept. 16*,17*,18*
DETROIT	June 20*,21,**22** Sept. 30* Oct. 1*,2*		April 11,12,**13** July 28*,29*,30*,31*	June 12*,13*,14,**15** Sept. 16*,17*	July 16*,17*,18*,19* Oct. 3*,4 TBA,**5**	June 30* July 1*,2*,3* Sept. 26*,27,**28**	April 21,22*,23* Aug. 15*,16,**17**
CLEVELAND	May 20*,21*,22 Sept. 4*,5*,6*,**7**	April 18*,19,**20** Aug. 5*,6*,7*		May 16*,17,**18**,(19) Sept (1),2*,3*	April 7,9,10* Aug. 8*,9*,**10**	April 24*,25*,26,**27** Aug. 11*,12*,13*	June 2*,3*,4* Aug. 29*,30,**31**
TORONTO	June 16*,17*,18 Sept. 12*,13*,**14**,15*	June 6*,7*,**8** Sept. 22*,23*,24*,25*	May 23*,24,**25** Aug. 26*,27*,28*		April 25*,26*,**27** Aug. 11*,12*,13*	June 27*,28,**29** Sept. 29*,30* Oct. 1	June 30* July 1*,2*,3* Sept. 26*,27,**28**
BALTIMORE	June 9*,10*,11 Sept. 25*,26*,27*,**28**	June 24*,25*,26* Sept. 12*,13,**14**	April 21*,22*,23* Aug. 14*,15*,16,**17**	April 14,16,17 Aug. 1*,2,**3**,(4)		June 6*,7,**8** Sept. 15*,16*,17*	June 20*,21,**22** Sept. 29*,30* Oct. 1*
NEW YORK	April 18*,19,**20** July 28*,29*,30	June 9*,10*,11* Sept. 19*,20,**21**	April 15*,16*,17* Aug. 1*,2,**3**	June 19*,20*,21,**22** Sept. 9*,10*,11*	June 12*,13*,14,**15** Sept. 22*,23*,24*		June 23*,24*,25* Oct. 2*,3*,4,**5**
BOSTON	June 5*,6*,7*,**8** Sept. 23*,24*	April 7,9,10 Aug. 8*,9*,**10**,11*	May (26), 27*,28* Aug. 21*,22*,23,**24**	June 9*,10*,11* Sept. 19*,20,**21**	June 27*,28,**29** Sept. 8*,9*,10*,11*	June 16*,17*,18* Sept. 12*,13,**14**	

ALL-STAR GAME AT THE ASTRODOME, IN HOUSTON, JULY 15